Date Due

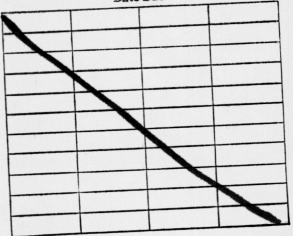

READINGS IN WORLD POLITICS

Readings in
WORLD POLITICS

Edited by
ROBERT A. GOLDWIN
with RALPH LERNER
and GERALD STOURZH

New York OXFORD UNIVERSITY PRESS 1959

Printed in the United States of America

PREFACE

The purpose of this volume of readings is threefold: to serve the college and university student as primary or supplementary course material, to offer the general reader an opportunity to acquaint himself systematically with the best thought on a wide range of the fundamental problems, and to function as the basic reading material for organized programs of adult education discussion groups.

Several unique features distinguish this book from other books of readings and affect the ways in which it can best be used. Its main characteristic is the plan of selection and editing. The articles are grouped in sections, each about 50 to 75 pages long, intended to be read as a unit. The selections have the continuity of a debate; opposing views are deliberately juxtaposed and the reader must judge the merits of each argument. The articles within each unit will be most instructive, therefore, if they are read in the order in which they appear. The sections are also best taken up in order, for the materials in later sections assume knowledge of the issues discussed in earlier sections.

This book has no index; although it contains a great deal of historical information, it is not a book for "looking up" isolated facts or events. It is a book of political argument. Although the readings present clear and forceful statements of a variety of positions—some quite partisan, others more detached and analytical—the collection as a whole is not meant to represent or support any particular viewpoint. Readers should not assume that any author in these pages is the spokesman of the editors. Nor is this volume intended to be comprehensive. The aim is rather to provoke thought on a limited number of highly significant problems and to provide a sound basis for further study.

These readings were originally prepared by members of the staff of the American Foundation for Political Education for use in discussion programs for the education of adults. During the years 1947–1958, the AFPE organized and conducted discussion groups in hundreds of communities, in cooperation with local educational institutions and civic agencies. Many of these programs continue, but in 1958 the AFPE ceased its practice of directly subsidizing the costs of local programs and has changed the nature of its activities. It now concentrates on the development of materials in different subject-matter fields and on the development of a variety of training programs. To conform to the changed focus of the work, the organization's name has been changed to the American Foundation for Continuing Education. The Foundation seeks to cooperate with persons and organizations interested in conducting discussion programs and welcomes requests for assistance or advice on leadership training or promotion. Inquiries may be addressed to the Executive Director, American Foundation for Continuing Education, 19 South La Salle Street, Chicago 3, Illinois.

THE EDITORS

Chicago, Illinois
April 1959

CONTENTS

THE AUTHORS

ALDOUS HUXLEY (1894–   ), British novelist and critic.

ALBERT EINSTEIN (1879–1955), German (later American) physicist and mathematician.

SIGMUND FREUD (1856–1939), Austrian psychiatrist and founder of psychoanalysis.

HERBERT BUTTERFIELD (1900–   ), Professor of Modern History, University of Cambridge.

PLATO (*ca.* 427–347 B.C.), Greek philosopher.

LEO TOLSTOY (1828–1910), Russian novelist, philosopher, and religious mystic.

EMERY REVES (1904–   ), publisher and author; born in Yugoslavia, resident of the United States since 1941.

BENITO MUSSOLINI (1883–1945), Italian dictator from 1922 until his death.

JOHN LOCKE (1632–1704), British philosopher.

HENRY DAVID THOREAU (1817–1862), American writer and philosopher.

JOHN STUART MILL (1806–1873), British philosopher and economist.

ALEXIS DE TOCQUEVILLE (1805–1859), French nobleman and political thinker. Foreign Minister of France in 1849; spent nine months in America in 1831–32. His *Democracy in America* was written as a result of this visit.

C. WRIGHT MILLS (1916–   ), Professor of Sociology, Columbia University; lecturer at the William A. White Institute of Psychiatry, New York City; author of *White Collar* and other works on social structure.

MULFORD Q. SIBLEY (1912–   ), Professor of Political Science, University of Minnesota; author of works on the political theory of pacifism.

THOMAS A. BAILEY (1902–   ), Professor of History, Stanford University; authority on American diplomatic history.

KARL MARX (1818–1883), German political philosopher and economist.

FRIEDRICH ENGELS (1820–1895), German economist and historian; collaborator with Marx.

VLADIMIR I. LENIN (1870–1924), Russian revolutionary leader and theorist; President of the Council of People's Commissars from 1917 until his death.

JOSEPH V. STALIN (1879–1953), ruler of the Soviet Union from 1928 until his death as Secretary of the Central Committee of the Communist Party of the Soviet Union.

NIKITA S. KHRUSHCHEV (1894–   ), First secretary of the Central Committee of the Communist Party of the Soviet Union since 1953, and Chairman of the Council of Ministers since 1958.

FEODOR DOSTOIEVSKY (1821–1881), Russian novelist.

FRIEDRICH SIEBURG (1893–   ), German publicist and essayist; author of *Gott in Frankreich*.

ERIC HOFFER (1902–   ), American longshoreman and writer.

ALBERT J. BEVERIDGE (1862–1929), American politician and Senator from Indiana, 1899–1911; author of biographies of Chief Justice John Marshall and Abraham Lincoln.

ERNEST RENAN (1823–1892), French historian, philosopher, and linguist.

ACHMED SUKARNO (1901–   ), President of the Republic of Indonesia.

WOODROW WILSON (1856–1924), 28th President of the United States.

CLYDE EAGLETON (1891–   ), Professor of International Law, New York University; legal expert, Department of State, 1943–1945.

EDWARD H. CARR (1892–   ), British historian and political scientist; member of the Foreign Office, 1916–1936.

MOHANDAS K. GANDHI (1870–1948), Indian political and religious leader; foremost figure in the fight for Indian independence.

THUCYDIDES (*ca.* 455–400 B.C.), Greek historian and general.

WILLIAM G. CARLETON (1903–   ), Professor of Social Science, University of Florida.

MARTIN WIGHT (1913–   ), British historian; now professor at Canberra (Australia) University College.

WALTER LIPPMANN (1889–   ), American columnist and political analyst; author of *The Public Philosophy* and other works.

DWIGHT D. EISENHOWER (1890–   ), 34th President of the United States.

VISCOUNT CHERWELL, FREDERICK A. LINDEMANN (1886–1957), British physicist; scientific advisor to Sir Winston Churchill, 1942–1945 and 1951–1953.

ROBERT M. HUTCHINS (1899–   ), American educator; president of the Fund for the Republic.

WALTER F. BERNS (1919–   ), American political scientist at Yale University.

CHARLES B. MARSHALL (1908–   ), Research Consultant, Washington Center of Foreign Policy Research, Johns Hopkins University; formerly member of the Policy Planning Staff, Department of State, 1950–1953.

HENRY L. STIMSON (1867–1950), United States Secretary of War, 1911–1913; Secretary of State, 1929–1930; Secretary of War, 1940–1945.

HARRY S. TRUMAN (1884–   ), 33rd President of the United States.

SIR WINSTON CHURCHILL (1874–   ), British statesman and historian; Prime Minister, 1940–1945 and 1951–1955.

WILLIAM D. LEAHY (1875–   ), Fleet Admiral of the United States Navy; Ambassador to France, 1940–1942.

ARTHUR H. COMPTON (1892–   ), Nobel Prize-winning atomic physicist; formerly Chancellor, Washington University (St. Louis).

HANSON W. BALDWIN (1903–   ), military editor of *The New York Times*.

GERTRUDE STEIN (1874–1946), American expatriate writer.

ABRAHAM LINCOLN (1809–1865), 16th President of the United States.

I

"A BETTER FUTURE FOR THE WORLD"

The Atlantic Charter

[August 14, 1941]

THE PRESIDENT of the United States of America and the Prime Minister, Mr. Churchill, representing his Majesty's Government in the United Kingdom, being met together, deem it right to make known certain common principles in the national policies of their respective countries on which they base their hopes for a better future for the world.

1. Their countries seek no aggrandizement, territorial or other.

2. They desire to see no territorial changes that do not accord with the freely expressed wishes of the people concerned.

3. They respect the right of all peoples to choose the form of government under which they will live; and they wish to see sovereign rights and self-government restored to those who have been forcibly deprived of them.

4. They will endeavor, with due respect for their existing obligations, to further the enjoyment by all States, great or small, victor or vanquished, of access, on equal terms, to the trade and to the raw materials of the world which are needed for their economic prosperity.

5. They desire to bring about the fullest collaboration between all nations in the economic field with the object of securing, for all, improved labor standards, economic advancement and social security.

6. After the final destruction of the Nazi tyranny, they hope to see established a peace which will afford to all nations the means of dwelling in safety within their own boundaries, and which will afford assurance that all men in all the lands may live out their lives in freedom from fear and want.

7. Such a peace should enable all men to traverse the high seas and oceans without hindrance.

8. They believe that all of the nations of the world, for realistic as well as spiritual reasons, must come to the abandonment of the use of force. Since no future peace can be maintained if land, sea or air armaments continue to be employed by nations which threaten, or may threaten, aggression outside of their frontiers, they believe, pending the establishment of a wider and permanent system of general security, that the disarmament of such nations is essential. They will likewise aid and encourage all other practicable measures which will lighten for peace-loving peoples the crushing burden of armaments.

Joint Declaration of Basic Principles*

[June 29, 1954]

As WE terminate our conversations on subjects of mutual and world interest, we again declare that:

1. In intimate comradeship, we will continue our united efforts to secure world peace based upon the principles of the Atlantic Charter, which we reaffirm.

2. We, together and individually, continue to hold out the hand of friendship to any and all nations, which by solemn pledge and confirming deeds show themselves desirous of participating in a just and fair peace.

3. We uphold the principle of self-government and will earnestly strive by every peaceful means to secure the independence of all countries whose peoples desire and are capable of sustaining an independent existence. We welcome the processes of development, where still needed, that lead toward that goal. As regards formerly sovereign states now in bondage, we will not be a party to any arrangement or treaty which would confirm or prolong their unwilling subordination. In the case of nations now divided against their will, we shall continue to seek to achieve unity through free elections supervised by the United Nations to insure they are conducted fairly.

4. We believe that the cause of world peace would be advanced by general and drastic reduction under effective safeguards of world armaments of all classes and kinds. It will be our persevering resolve to promote conditions in which the prodigious nuclear forces now in human hands can be used to enrich and not to destroy mankind.

5. We will continue our support of the United Nations and of existing international organizations that have been established in the spirit of the Charter for common protection and security. We urge

---

* British Prime Minister Sir Winston Churchill and Foreign Secretary Anthony Eden were in Washington June 25–29, 1954, for discussions with President Eisenhower and Secretary Dulles. This is the text of a joint statement issued by the President and the Prime Minister. Reprinted from the *Department of State Bulletin*, July 12, 1954.

the establishment and maintenance of such associations of appropriate nations as will best, in their respective regions, preserve the peace and independence of the peoples living there. When desired by the peoples of the affected countries we are ready to render appropriate and feasible assistance to such associations.

6. We shall, with our friends, develop and maintain the spiritual, economic and military strength necessary to pursue these purposes effectively. In pursuit of this purpose we will seek every means of promoting the fuller and freer interchange among us of goods and services which will benefit all participants.

(SIGNED) DWIGHT D. EISENHOWER

(SIGNED) WINSTON S. CHURCHILL

II

WHAT CAUSES WAR?

The Wish for War*

BY ALDOUS HUXLEY

[1937]

EVERY road towards a better state of society is blocked, sooner or later, by war, by threats of war, by preparations for war. That is the truth, the odious and unescapable truth. . . .

Let us very briefly consider the nature of war, the causes of war and the possible alternatives to war, the methods of curing the mania of militarism afflicting the world at the present time.[1]

NATURE OF WAR

(i) War is a purely human phenomenon. The lower animals fight duels in the heat of sexual excitement and kill for food and occasionally for sport. But the activities of a wolf eating a sheep or a cat playing with a mouse are no more war-like than the activities of butchers and fox-hunters. Similarly, fights between hungry dogs or rutting stags are like pot-house quarrels and have nothing in common with war, which is mass-murder organized in cold blood. Some social insects, it is true, go out to fight in armies; but their attacks are always directed against members of another species. Man is unique in organizing the mass murder of his own species.

(ii) Certain biologists, of whom Sir Arthur Keith is the most eminent, consider that war acts as "nature's pruning hook," ensuring the survival of the fittest among civilized individuals and nations. This is obviously nonsensical. War tends to eliminate the young and strong and to spare the unhealthy. Nor is there any reason for supposing that people with traditions of violence and a good technique of war-making are superior to other peoples. The most valuable human beings are not necessarily the most warlike. Nor as a matter of historical fact is it always the most warlike who survive.

---

* From Aldous Huxley, *Ends and Means.* Copyright 1937 by Aldous Huxley. Reprinted by arrangement with Harper & Brothers.

[1] Certain passages in this chapter are reprinted with little alteration from articles contributed by the author to "An Encyclopaedia of Pacifism" (London 1937).

We can sum up by saying that, so far as individuals are concerned, war selects dysgenically; so far as nations and peoples are concerned it selects purely at random, sometimes ensuring the domination and survival of the more warlike peoples, sometimes, on the contrary, ensuring their destruction and the survival of the unwarlike.

(iii) There exist at the present time certain primitive human societies, such as that of the Eskimos, in which war is unknown and even unthinkable. All civilized societies, however, are warlike. The question arises whether the correlation between war and civilization is necessary and unavoidable. The evidence of archaeology seems to point to the conclusion that war made its appearance at a particular moment in the history of early civilization. There is reason to suppose that the rise of war was correlated with an abrupt change in the mode of human consciousness. This change, as Dr. J. D. Unwin suggests,[2] may have been correlated with increased sexual continence on the part of the ruling classes of the warlike societies. The archaeological symptom of the change is the almost sudden appearance of royal palaces and elaborate funerary monuments. The rise of war appears to be connected with the rise of self-conscious leaders, preoccupied with the ideas of personal domination and personal survival after death. Even today when economic considerations are supposed to be supreme, ideas of "glory" and "immortal fame" still ferment in the minds of the dictators and generals, and play an important part in the causation of war.

(iv) The various civilizations of the world have adopted fundamentally different attitudes towards war. Compare the Chinese and Indian attitudes towards war with the European. Europeans have always worshipped the military hero and, since the rise of Christianity, the martyr. Not so the Chinese. The ideal human being, according to Confucian standards, is the just, reasonable, humane and cultivated man, living at peace in an ordered and harmonious society. Confucianism, to quote Max Weber, "prefers a wise prudence to mere physical courage and declares that an untimely sacrifice of life is unfitting for a wise man." Our European admiration for military heroism and martyrdom has tended to make men believe that a good death is more important than a good life and that a long course of folly and crime can be cancelled out by a single act of

---

[2] In "Sex and Culture" (Oxford 1934).

physical courage. The mysticism of Lao Tsu (or whoever was the author of the Tao Teh Ching) confirms and completes the rationalism of Confucius. The Tao is an eternal cosmic principle that is, at the same time, the inmost root of the individual's being. Those who would live in harmony with Tao must refrain from assertiveness, self-importance and aggressiveness, must cultivate humility and return good for evil.

Since the time of Confucius and Lao Tsu, Chinese ideals have been essentially pacifistic. European poets have glorified war; European theologians have found justification for religious persecution and nationalistic aggression. This has not been so in China. Chinese philosophers and Chinese poets have almost all been anti-militarists. The soldier was regarded as an inferior being, not to be put on the same level with the scholar or administrator. It is one of the tragedies of history that the Westernization of China should have meant the progressive militarization of a culture which, for nearly three thousand years, has consistently preached the pacifist ideal. Conscription was imposed on large numbers of Chinese in 1936, and the soldier is now held up for admiration. Comic, but significant, is the following quotation from the New York *Times* of June 17, 1937. "Sin Wan Pao, Shanghai's leading Chinese language newspaper, advised Adolf Hitler and Benito Mussolini to-day to follow the examples of General Yang Sen . . . war lord and commander of the Twentieth Army in Szechwan Province. The general has twenty-seven wives. 'Only 40 years old, General Yang has a child for every year of his life,' the newspaper said. 'General Yang has established complete military training for his offspring. It begins when a young Yang reaches the age of 7, with strict treatment by the time the child is 14. The family has an exclusive military camp. When visitors come, the Yang children hold a military reception and march past the guests in strict review order.'" One laughs; but the unfortunate truth is that General Yang and the forty little Yangs in their strict review order are grotesquely symptomatic of the new, worse, Western spirit of a China that has turned its back on the wisdom of Confucius and Lao Tsu and gone whoring after European militarism. Japanese aggression is bound to intensify this new militaristic spirit in China. Within a couple of generations, it is possible that China will be an aggressive imperialist power.

Indian pacifism finds its completest expression in the teaching of

Buddha. Buddhism, like Hinduism, teaches *ahimsa*, or harmlessness towards all living beings. It forbids even laymen to have anything to do with the manufacture and sale of arms, with the making of poisons and intoxicants, with soldiering or the slaughter of animals. Alone of all the great world religions, Buddhism made its way without persecution, censorship or inquisition. In all these respects its record is enormously superior to that of Christianity, which made its way among people wedded to militarism and which was able to justify the bloodthirsty tendencies of its adherents by an appeal to the savage Bronze-Age literature of the Old Testament. For Buddhists, anger is always and unconditionally disgraceful. For Christians, brought up to identify Jehovah with God, there is such a thing as "righteous indignation." Thanks to this possibility of indignation being righteous, Christians have always felt themselves justified in making war and committing the most hideous atrocities.

The fact that it should have been possible for the three principal civilizations of the world to adopt three distinct philosophic attitudes towards war is encouraging; for it proves that there is nothing "natural" about our present situation in relation to war. The existence of war and of our political and theological justifications of war is no more "natural" than were the sanguinary manifestations of sexual jealousy, so common in Europe up to the beginning of last century and now of such rare occurrence. To murder one's unfaithful wife, or the lover of one's sister or mother, was something that used to be "done." Being socially correct, it was regarded as inevitable, a manifestation of unchanging "human nature." Such murders are no longer fashionable among the best people, therefore no longer seem to us "natural." The malleability of human nature is such that there is no reason why, if we so desire and set to work in the right way, we should not rid ourselves of war as we have freed ourselves from the weary necessity of committing a *crime passionnel* every time a wife, mistress or female relative gets herself seduced. War is not a law of nature, nor even a law of human nature. It exists because men wish it to exist; and we know as a matter of historical fact, that the intensity of that wish has varied from absolute zero to a frenzied maximum. The wish for war in the contemporary world is widespread and of high intensity. But our wills are to some extent free; we can wish otherwise than we actually do. It is enormously difficult for us to change our wishes in this matter; but the enormously difficult is not the impossible. We must be grateful for even the smallest crumbs of comfort.

CAUSES OF WAR

War exists because people wish it to exist. They wish it to exist for a variety of reasons.

(i) Many people like war because they find their peace-time occupations either positively humiliating and frustrating, or just negatively boring. In their studies on suicide Durkheim and, more recently, Halbwachs have shown that the suicide-rate among non-combatants tends to fall during war-time to about two-thirds of its normal figure. This decline must be put down to the following causes: to the simplification of life during war-time (it is in complex and highly developed societies that the suicide rate is highest); to the intensification of nationalist sentiment to a point where most individuals are living in a state of chronic enthusiasm; to the fact that life during war-time takes on significance and purposefulness, so that even the most intrinsically boring job is ennobled as "war work"; to the artificial prosperity induced, at any rate for a time, by the expansion of war industries; to the increased sexual freedom which is always claimed by societies, all or some of whose members live under the menace of sudden death. Add to this the fact that life in war-time is (or at least was in previous wars) extremely interesting, at least during the first years of the war. Rumour runs riot, and the papers are crammed every morning with the most thrilling news. To the influence of the press must be attributed the fact that, whereas during the Franco-Prussian War the suicide rate declined only in the belligerent countries, during the World War a considerable decline was registered even in the neutral states. In 1870 about half the inhabitants of Europe were unable to read, and newspapers were few and expensive. By 1914 primary education had everywhere been compulsory for more than a generation and the addiction to newspaper reading had spread to all classes of the population. Thus, even neutrals were able to enjoy, vicariously and at second hand, the exciting experience of war.

Up to the end of the last war non-combatants, except in countries actually subject to invasion, were not in great physical danger. In any future war it is clear that they will be exposed to risks almost, if not quite, as great as those faced by the fighting men. This will certainly tend to diminish the enthusiasm of non-combatants for war. But if it turns out that the effects of air bombardment are less frightful than most experts at present believe they will be, this enthusiasm may not be extinguished altogether, at any rate during the first months of a war. During the last war, a fair proportion of the combatants actually enjoyed some phases at least of the fighting. The escape from the dull and often stultifying routines of peace-time life was welcomed, even though that escape was bought at a price of physical hardship and the risk of death and mutilation. It is possible that conditions in any future war will be so appalling that even the most naturally adventurous and combative human beings will soon come to hate and fear the process of fighting. But until the next war actually breaks out, nobody can have experience of the new conditions of fighting. Meanwhile, all the governments are actively engaged in making a subtle kind of propaganda that is directed against potential enemies but not against war. They warn their subjects that they will be bombarded from the air by fleets of enemy planes; they persuade or compel them to subject themselves to air-raid drills and other forms of military discipline; they proclaim the necessity of piling up enormous armaments for the purpose of counter-attack and retaliation and they actually build those armaments to the tune, in most European countries, of nearly or fully half the total national revenue. At the same time they do all in their power to belittle the danger from air raids. Millions of gas masks are made and distributed with assurances that they will provide complete protection. Those who make such assurances know quite well that they are false. Gas masks cannot be worn by infants, invalids or the old and give no protection whatsoever against vesicants and some of the poisonous smokes, which for this reason will be the chemicals chiefly used by the air navies of the world. Meanwhile warnings by impartial experts are either officially ignored or belittled. (The attitude of the government's spokesman at the British Medical Association meeting at Oxford in 1936 and that of the *Times* in 1937 towards the Cambridge scientists who warned the public against the probable effects of air bombardment are highly significant in this context.) The whole effort of all the governments is directed, I repeat, to making propaganda against enemies and in favour of war; against those who try to tell the truth about the nature and effects of the new armaments and in favour of manufacturing such armaments in ever increasing quantities. There are two reasons why such propaganda is as successful as it is. The first, as I have explained in this paragraph, must be sought in the fact that, up to the present, many non-combatants and some combatants have found war a welcome relief from the tedium of peace. The second reason will be set forth in the following paragraph, which deals with another aspect of the psychological causation of war.

(ii) A principal cause of war is nationalism, and nationalism is immensely popular because it is psychologically satisfying to individual nationalists. Every nationalism is an idolatrous religion, in which the god is the personified state, represented in many instances by a more or less deified king or dictator. Membership of the *ex-hypothesi* divine nation is thought of as imparting a kind of mystical pre-eminence. Thus, all "God's Englishmen" are superior to "the lesser breeds without the law" and every individual God's-Englishman is entitled to think himself superior to every member of the lesser breed, even the lordliest and wealthiest, even the most intelligent, the most highly gifted, the most saintly. Any man who believes strongly enough in the local nationalistic idolatry can find in his faith an antidote against even the most acute inferiority complex. Dictators feed the flames of national vanity and reap their reward in the gratitude of millions to whom the conviction that they are participants in the glory of the divine nation brings relief from the gnawing consciousness of poverty, social unimportance and personal insignificance.

Self-esteem has as its complement disparagement of others. Vanity and pride beget contempt and hatred. But contempt and hatred are exciting emotions—emotions from which people "get a kick." Devotees of one national idolatry enjoy getting the kick of hatred and contempt for devotees of other idolatries. They pay for that enjoyment by having to prepare for the wars which hatred and contempt render almost inevitable. Another point. In the normal course of events most men and women behave tolerably well. This means that they must frequently repress their anti-social impulses. They find a vicarious satisfaction for these impulses through films and stories about gangsters, pirates, swindlers, bad bold barons and the like. Now, the personified nation, as I have pointed out already, is divine in size, strength and mystical superiority, but sub-human in moral character. The ethics of international politics are precisely those of the gangster, the pirate, the swindler, the bad bold baron. The exemplary citizen can indulge in vicarious criminality, not only on the films, but also in the field of international relations. The divine nation of whom he is mystically a part bullies and cheats, blusters and threatens in a way which many people find profoundly satisfying to their sedulously repressed lower natures. Submissive to the wife, kind to the children, courteous to the neighbours, the soul of honesty in business, the good citizen feels a thrill of delight when his country "takes a strong line," "enhances its prestige," "scores a diplomatic victory," "increases its territory"—in other words when it bluffs, bullies, swindles and steals. The nation is a strange deity. It imposes difficult duties and demands the greatest sacrifices and, because it does this and because human beings have a hunger and thirst after righteousness, it is loved. But it is also loved because it panders to the lowest elements in human nature and because men and women like to have excuses to feel pride and hatred, because they long to taste even at second hand the joys of criminality.

* * *

CURE FOR WAR

(i) War, as we have seen, is tolerated, and by some even welcomed, because peace-time occupations seem boring, humiliating and pointless.

The application of the principle of self-government to industry and business should go far to deliver men and women in subordinate positions from the sense of helpless humiliation which is induced by the need of obeying the arbitrary orders of irresponsible superiors; and the fact of being one of a small co-operative group should do something to make the working life of its members seem more interesting. Heightened interest can also be obtained by suitably rearranging the individual's tasks. Fourier insisted long ago on the desirableness of variety in labour, and in recent years his suggestion has been acted upon, experimentally, in a number of factories in Germany, America, Russia and elsewhere. The result has been a diminution of boredom, and in many cases, an increase in the volume of production. Tasks may be varied slightly, as when a worker in a cigarette factory is shifted from the job of feeding tobacco into a machine to the job of packing and weighing. Or they may be varied radically and fundamentally, as when workers alternate between industrial and agricultural labour. In both cases the psychological effects seem to be good.

(ii) It was suggested that the war-time decline in the suicide rate was due, among other things, to the heightened significance and purposefulness of life during a national emergency. At such a time the end for which all are striving is clearly seen; duties are simple and explicit; the vagueness and uncertainty of peace-time ideals gives place to the sharp definition of the war-time ideal, which is: victory at all costs; the bewildering complexities of the peace-time social patterns are replaced by the beautifully simple pattern of a community fighting for its existence. Danger heightens the sense of social solidarity and quickens patriotic enthusiasm. Life takes on sense and meaning and is lived at a high pitch of emotional intensity.

The apparent pointlessness of modern life in time of peace and its lack of significance and purpose are due to the fact that, in the western world at least, the prevailing cosmology is what Mr. Gerald Heard has called the "mechanomorphic" cosmology of modern science. The universe is regarded as a great machine pointlessly grinding its way towards ultimate stagnation and death; men are tiny offshoots of the universal machine, running down to their own private death; physical life is the only real life; mind is a mere product of body; personal success and material well-being are the ultimate measures of value, the things for which a reasonable person should live. Introduced suddenly to this mechanomorphic cosmology, many of the Polynesian races have refused to go on multiplying their species and are in process of dying of a kind of psychological consumption. Europeans are of tougher fibre than the South Sea Islanders and besides they have had nearly three hundred years in which to become gradually acclimatized to the new cosmology. But even they have felt the effects of mechanomorphism. They move through life hollow with pointlessness, trying to fill the void within them by external stimuli—newspaper reading, day-dreaming at the films, radio music and chatter, the playing and above all the watching of games, "good times" of every sort. Meanwhile any doctrine that offers to restore point and purpose to life is eagerly welcomed. Hence the enormous success of the nationalistic and communistic idolatries which deny any meaning to the universe as a whole, but insist on the importance and significance of certain arbitrarily selected parts of the whole— the deified nation, the divine class.

Nationalism first became a religion in Germany, during the Napoleonic wars. Communism took its rise some fifty years later. Those who did not become devotees of the new idolatries either remained Christians, clinging to doctrines that became intellectually less and less acceptable with every advance of science, or else accepted mechanomorphism and became convinced of the pointlessness of life. The World War was a product of nationalism and was tolerated and even welcomed by the great masses of those who found life pointless. War brought only a passing relief to the victims of mechanomorphic philosophy. Disillusion, fatigue and cynicism succeeded the initial enthusiasm and when it was over, the sense of pointlessness became a yawning abyss that demanded to be filled with ever more and intenser distractions, even better "good times." But good times are not a meaning or a purpose; the void could never be filled by them. Consequently when the nationalists and communists appeared with their simple idolatries and their proclamation that, though life might mean nothing as a whole, it did at least possess a temporary and partial significance, there was a powerful reaction away from the cynicism of the post-war years. Millions of young people embraced the new idolatrous religions, found a meaning in life, a purpose for their existence and were ready, in consequence, to make sacrifices, accept hardships, display courage, fortitude, temperance and indeed all the virtues except the essential and primary ones, without which all the rest may serve merely as the means for doing evil more effectively. Love and awareness—these are the primary, essential virtues. But nationalism and communism are partial and exclusive idolatries that inculcate hatred, pride, hardness, and impose that intolerant dogmatism that cramps intelligence and narrows the field of interest and sympathetic awareness.

The "heads" of pointlessness has as its "tails" idolatrous nationalism and communism. Our world oscillates from a neurasthenia that welcomes war as a relief from boredom to a mania that results in war being made. The cure for both these fearful maladies is the same—the inculcation of a cosmology more nearly corresponding to reality than either mechanomorphism or the grotesque philosophies underlying the nationalistic and communistic idolatries.

An Exchange of Letters Between
Albert Einstein and Sigmund Freud

Why War?*

A. EINSTEIN TO S. FREUD

CAPUTH NEAR POTSDAM, 30th July, 1932

DEAR PROFESSOR FREUD:

The proposal of the League of Nations and its International Institute of Intellectual Cooperation at Paris that I should invite a person, to be chosen by myself, to a frank exchange of views on any problem that I might select affords me a very welcome opportunity of conferring with you upon a question which, as things now are, seems the most insistent of all the problems civilisation has to face. This is the problem: Is there any way of delivering mankind from the menace of war? It is common knowledge that, with the advance of modern science, this issue has come to mean a matter of life and death for civilisation as we know it; nevertheless, for all the zeal displayed, every attempt at its solution has ended in a lamentable breakdown.

I believe, moreover, that those whose duty it is to tackle the problem professionally and practically are growing only too aware of their impotence to deal with it, and have now a very lively desire to learn the views of men who, absorbed in the pursuit of science, can see world-problems in the perspective distance lends. As for me, the normal objective of my thought affords no insight into the dark places of human will and feeling. Thus, in the enquiry proposed, I can do little more than seek to clarify the question at issue and, clearing the ground of the more obvious solutions, enable you to bring the light of your far-reaching knowledge of man's instinctive life to bear upon the problem. There are certain psychological

---

* Reprinted by special permission of the estate of Professor Einstein and the Sigmund Freud Copyright, Ltd.

obstacles whose existence a layman in the mental sciences may dimly
surmise, but whose inter-relations and vagaries he is incompetent
to fathom; you, I am convinced, will be able to suggest educative
methods, lying more or less outside the scope of politics, which will
eliminate these obstacles.

As one immune from nationalist bias, I personally see a simple
way of dealing with the superficial (*i.e.* administrative) aspect of the
problem: the setting up, by international consent, of a legislative
and judicial body to settle every conflict arising between nations.
Each nation would undertake to abide by the orders issued by this
legislative body, to invoke its decision in every dispute, to accept
its judgments unreservedly and to carry out every measure the
tribunal deems necessary for the execution of its decrees. But here,
at the outset, I come up against a difficulty; a tribunal is a human
institution which, in proportion as the power at its disposal is inadequate to enforce its verdicts, is all the more prone to suffer these
to be deflected by extrajudicial pressure. This is a fact with which
we have to reckon; law and might inevitably go hand in hand,
and juridical decisions approach more nearly the ideal justice
demanded by the community (in whose name and interests these
verdicts are pronounced) in so far as the community has effective
power to compel respect of its juridical ideal. But at present we are
far from possessing any supranational organisation competent to
render verdicts of incontestable authority and enforce absolute submission to the execution of its verdicts. Thus I am led to my first
axiom: the quest of international security involves the unconditional
surrender by every nation, in a certain measure, of its liberty of
action, its sovereignty that is to say, and it is clear beyond all doubt
that no other road can lead to such security.

The ill-success, despite their obvious sincerity, of all the efforts
made during the last decade to reach this goal leaves us no room
to doubt that strong psychological factors are at work, which
paralyse these efforts. Some of these factors are not far to seek. The
craving for power which characterises the governing class in every
nation is hostile to any limitation of the national sovereignty. This
political powerhunger is wont to batten on the activities of another group, whose aspirations are on purely mercenary, economic
lines. I have specially in mind that small but determined group,
active in every nation, composed of individuals who, indifferent to

social considerations and restraints, regard warfare, the manufacture and sale of arms, simply as an occasion to advance their personal interests and enlarge their personal authority.

But recognition of this obvious fact is merely the first step towards an appreciation of the actual state of affairs. Another question follows hard upon it: How is it possible for this small clique to bend the will of the majority, who stand to lose and suffer by a state of war, to the service of their ambitions? (In speaking of the majority, I do not exclude soldiers of every rank who have chosen war as their profession, in the belief that they are serving to defend the highest interests of their race, and that attack is often the best method of defence.) An obvious answer to this question would seem to be that the minority, the ruling class at present, has the schools and press, usually the Church as well, under its thumb. This enables it to organise and sway the emotions of the masses, and make its tool of them.

Yet even this answer does not provide a complete solution. Another question arises from it: How is it these devices succeed so well in rousing men to such wild enthusiasm, even to sacrifice their lives? Only one answer is possible. Because man has within him a lust for hatred and destruction. In normal times this passion exists in a latent state, it emerges only in unusual circumstances; but it is a comparatively easy task to call it into play and raise it to the power of a collective psychosis. Here lies, perhaps, the crux of all the complex of factors we are considering, an enigma that only the expert in the lore of human instincts can resolve. And so we come to our last question. Is it possible to control man's mental evolution so as to make him proof against the psychosis of hate and destructiveness? Here I am thinking by no means only of the so-called uncultured masses. Experience proves that it is rather the so-called "Intelligentzia" that is most apt to yield to these disastrous collective suggestions, since the intellectual has no direct contact with life in the raw, but encounters it in its easiest, synthetic form—upon the printed page.

To conclude: I have so far been speaking only of wars between nations; what are known as international conflicts. But I am well aware that the aggressive instinct operates under other forms and in other circumstances. (I am thinking of civil wars, for instance, due in earlier days to religious zeal, but nowadays to social factors; or, again, the persecution of racial minorities.) But my insistence on what is the most typical, most cruel and extravagant form of conflict between man and man was deliberate, for here we have the best occasion of discovering ways and means to render all armed conflicts impossible.

I know that in your writings we may find answers, explicit and implied, to all the issues of this urgent and absorbing problem. But it would be of the greatest service to us all were you to present the problem of world peace in the light of your most recent discoveries, for such a presentation well might blaze the trail for new and fruitful modes of action.

Yours very sincerely,

A. EINSTEIN

S. FREUD TO A. EINSTEIN

VIENNA, September, 1932

DEAR PROFESSOR EINSTEIN:

When I learnt of your intention to invite me to a mutual exchange of views upon a subject which not only interested you personally, but seemed deserving, too, of public interest, I cordially assented. I expected you to choose a problem lying on the borderland of the knowable, as it stands to-day, a theme which each of us, physicist and psychologist, might approach from his own angle, to meet at last on common ground, though setting out from different premises. Thus the question which you put me—what is to be done to rid mankind of the war-menace?—took me by surprise. And, next, I was dumbfounded by the thought of my (of *our,* I almost wrote) incompetence; for this struck me as being a matter of practical politics, the statesman's proper study. But then I realised that you did not raise the question in your capacity of scientist or physicist, but as a lover of his fellow men. . . . And, next, I reminded myself that I was not being called on to formulate practical proposals, but rather, to explain how this question of preventing wars strikes a psychologist.

But here, too, you have stated the gist of the matter in your letter —and taken the wind out of my sails! Still, I will gladly follow in your wake and content myself with endorsing your conclusions, which, however, I propose to amplify to the best of my knowledge or surmise.

You begin with the relations between Might and Right, and this is assuredly the proper starting-point for our enquiry. But, for the term "might," I would substitute a tougher and more telling word —"violence." In right and violence we have to-day an obvious antinomy. It is easy to prove that one has evolved from the other and, when we go back to origins and examine primitive conditions, the solution of the problem follows easily enough. I must crave your indulgence if in what follows I speak of well-known, admitted facts as though they were new *data;* the context necessitates this method.

Conflicts of interest between man and man are resolved, in principle, by the recourse to violence. It is the same in the animal kingdom, from which man cannot claim exclusion; nevertheless, men are also prone to conflicts of opinion, touching, on occasion, the loftiest peaks of abstract thought, which seem to call for settlement by quite another method. This refinement is, however, a late development. To start with, brute force was the factor which, in small communities, decided points of ownership and the question which man's will was to prevail. Very soon physical force was implemented, then replaced, by the use of various adjuncts; he proved the victor whose weapon was the better, or handled the more skilfully. Now, for the first time, with the coming of weapons, superior brains began to oust brute force, but the object of the conflict remained the same: one party was to be constrained, by the injury done him or impairment of his strength, to retract a claim or a refusal. This end is most effectively gained when the opponent is definitively put out of action—in other words, is killed. This procedure has two advantages: the enemy cannot renew hostilities, and, secondly, his fate deters others from following his example. Moreover, the slaughter of a foe gratifies an instinctive craving—a point to which we shall revert hereafter. However, another consideration may be set off against this will to kill: the possibility of using an enemy for servile tasks if his spirit be broken and his life spared. Here violence finds an outlet not in slaughter, but in subjugation. Hence springs the practice of giving quarter; but the victor, having from now on to reckon with the craving for revenge that rankles in his victim, forfeits to some extent his personal security.

Thus, under primitive conditions, it is superior force—brute violence, or violence backed by arms—that lords it everywhere. We know that in the course of evolution this state of things was modified, a path was traced that led away from violence to law. But what was this path? Surely it issued from a single verity; that the superiority of one strong man can be overborne by an alliance of many weaklings. . . . Brute force is overcome by union, the allied might of scattered units makes good its right against the isolated giant. Thus we may define "right" (*i.e.* law) as the might of a community. Yet it, too, is nothing else than violence, quick to attack whatever individual stands in its path, and it employs the selfsame methods, follows like ends, with but one difference; it is the communal, not individual, violence that has its way. But, for the transition from crude violence to the reign of law, a certain psychological condition must first obtain. The union of the majority must be stable and enduring. If its sole reason for existence be the discomfiture of some overweening individual and, after his downfall, it be dissolved, it leads to nothing. Some other man, trusting to his superior power, will seek to reinstate the rule of violence and the cycle will repeat itself unendingly. Thus the union of the people must be permanent and well organised; it must enact rules to meet the risk of possible revolts; must set up machinery ensuring that its rules— the laws—are observed and that such acts of violence as the laws demand are duly carried out. This recognition of a community of interests engenders among the members of the group a sentiment of unity and fraternal solidarity which constitutes its real strength.

So far I have set out what seems to me the kernel of the matter: the suppression of brute force by the transfer of power to a larger combination, founded on the community of sentiments linking up its members. All the rest is mere tautology and glosses. Now the position is simple enough so long as the community consists of a number of equipollent individuals. The laws of such a group can determine to what extent the individual must forfeit his personal freedom, the right of using personal force as an instrument of violence, to ensure the safety of the group. But such a combination is only theoretically possible; in practice the situation is always complicated by the fact that, from the outset, the group includes elements of unequal power, men and women, elders and children, and very soon, as a result of war and conquest, victors and the vanquished— *i.e.,* masters and slaves—as well. From this time on the common law takes notice of these inequalities of power, laws are made by and for the rulers, giving the servile classes fewer rights. Thenceforward there exist within the state two factors making for legal instability, but legislative evolution, too: first, the attempts by members of the ruling class to set themselves above the law's restrictions and, secondly, the constant struggle of the ruled to extend their rights and see each gain embodied in the code, replacing legal disabilities by equal laws for all. The second of these tendencies will be particularly marked when there takes place a positive mutation of the balance of power within the community, the frequent outcome of certain historical conditions. In such cases the laws may gradually be adjusted to the changed conditions or (as more usually ensues) the ruling class is loath to reckon with the new developments, the result being insurrections and civil wars, a period when law is in abeyance and force once more the arbiter, followed by a new regime of law. There is another factor of constitutional change, which operates in a wholly pacific manner, viz., the cultural evolution of the mass of the community; this factor, however, is of a different order and can only be dealt with later.

Thus we see that, even within the group itself, the exercise of violence cannot be avoided when conflicting interests are at stake. But the common needs and habits of men who live in fellowship under the same sky favour a speedy issue of such conflicts and, this being so, the possibilities of peaceful solutions make steady progress. Yet the most casual glance at world-history will show an unending series of conflicts between one community and another or a group of others, between large and smaller units, between cities, countries, races, tribes and kingdoms, almost all of which were settled by the ordeal of war. Such wars end either in pillage or in conquest and its fruits, the downfall of the loser. No single all-embracing judgment can be passed on these wars of aggrandisement. Some, like the war between the Mongols and the Turks, have led to unmitigated misery; others, however, have furthered the transition from violence to law, since they brought larger units into being, within whose limits a recourse to violence was banned and a new regime determined all disputes. Thus, the Roman conquests brought that boon, the Roman Peace, to the Mediterranean lands. The French kings' lust for aggrandisement created a new France, flourishing in peace and unity. Paradoxical as it sounds, we must admit that warfare

well might serve to pave the way to that unbroken peace we so desire, for it is war that brings vast empires into being, within whose
frontiers all warfare is proscribed by a strong central power. In practice, however, this end is not attained, for as a rule the fruits of victory are but short-lived, the new-created unit falls asunder once
again, generally because there can be no true cohesion between the
parts that violence has welded. Hitherto, moreover, such conquests
have only led to aggregations which, for all their magnitude, had
limits, and disputes between these units could be resolved only by
recourse to arms. For humanity at large the sole result of all these
military enterprises was that, instead of frequent not to say incessant
little wars, they had now to face great wars which, for all they came
less often, were so much the more destructive.

. Regarding the world of today, the same conclusion holds good,
and you, too, have reached it, though by a shorter path. There is but
one sure way of ending war, and that is the establishment, by common consent, of a central control which shall have the last word in
every conflict of interest. For this, two things are needed: first, the
creation of such a supreme court of judicature; secondly, its investment with adequate executive force. Unless this second requirement
be fulfilled, the first is unavailing. Obviously the League of Nations,
acting as a Supreme Court, fulfils the first condition; it does not
fulfil the second. It has no force at its disposal and can only get it if
the members of the new body, its constituent nations, furnish it.
And, as things are, this is a forlorn hope. Still, we should be taking
a very short-sighted view of the League of Nations were we to
ignore the fact that here is an experiment the like of which has rarely
—never before, perhaps, on such a scale—been attempted in the
course of history. It is an attempt to acquire the authority (in other
words, coercive influence), which hitherto reposed exclusively on
the possession of power, by calling into play certain idealistic attitudes of mind. We have seen that there are two factors of cohesion
in a community; violent compulsion and ties of sentiment ("identi-
fications," in technical parlance) between the members of the group.
If one of these factors becomes inoperative, the other may still suffice
to hold the group together. Obviously such notions as these can only
be significant when they are the expression of a deeply-rooted sense
of unity, shared by all. . . . It is all too clear that the nationalistic
ideas, paramount today in every country, operate in quite a contrary

direction. Some there are who hold that the Bolshevist conceptions may make an end of war, but, as things are, that goal lies very far away and, perhaps, could only be attained after a spell of brutal internecine warfare. Thus it would seem that any effort to replace brute force by the might of an ideal is, under present conditions, doomed to fail. Our logic is at fault if we ignore the fact that right is founded on brute force and even today needs violence to maintain it.

I now can comment on another of your statements. You are amazed that it is so easy to infect men with the war-fever, and you surmise that man has in him an active instinct for hatred and destruction, amenable to such stimulations. I entirely agree with you. I believe in the existence of this instinct and have been recently at pains to study its manifestations. In this connection may I set out a fragment of that knowledge of the instincts, which we psychoanalysts, after so many tentative essays and gropings in the dark, have compassed? We assume that human instincts are of two kinds: those that conserve and unify, which we call "erotic" (in the meaning Plato gives to *Eros* in his *Symposium*), or else "sexual" (explicitly extending the popular connotation of "sex"); and, secondly, the instincts to destroy and kill, which we assimilate as the aggressive or destructive instincts. These are, as you perceive, the well known opposites, Love and Hate, transformed into theoretical entities; they are, perhaps, another aspect of those eternal polarities, attraction and repulsion, which fall within your province. But we must be chary of passing over-hastily to the notions of good and evil. Each of these instincts is every whit as indispensable as its opposite and all the phenomena of life derive from their activity, whether they work in concert or in opposition. It seems that an instinct of either category can operate but rarely in isolation; it is always blended ("alloyed," as we say) with a certain dosage of its opposite, which modifies its aim or even, in certain circumstances, is a prime condition of its attainment. Thus the instinct of self-preservation is certainly of an erotic nature, but to gain its ends this very instinct necessitates aggressive action. In the same way the love-instinct, which directed to a specific object, calls for an admixture of the acquisitive instinct if it is to enter into effective possession of that object. It is the difficulty of isolating the two kinds of instinct in their manifestations that has prevented us from recognising them.

If you will travel with me a little further on this road, you will
find that human affairs are complicated in yet another way. Only
exceptionally does an action follow on the stimulus of a single instinct. . . . As a rule several motives of similar composition concur
to bring about the act. . . . Thus, when a nation is summoned to
engage in war, a whole gamut of human motives may respond to
this appeal; high and low motives, some openly avowed, others
slurred over. The lust for aggression and destruction is certainly
included; the innumerable cruelties of history and man's daily life
confirm its prevalence and strength. The stimulation of these destructive impulses by appeals to idealism and the erotic instinct
naturally facilitates their release. Musing on the atrocities recorded
on history's page, we feel that the ideal motive has often served as a
camouflage for the lust of destruction; sometimes, as with the cruelties of the Inquisition, it seems that, while the ideal motives occupied the foreground of consciousness, they drew their strength from
the destructive instincts submerged in the unconscious. Both interpretations are feasible.

You are interested, I know, in the prevention of war, not in our
theories, and I keep this fact in mind. Yet I would like to dwell a
little longer on this destructive instinct, which is seldom given the
attention that its importance warrants. With the least of speculative
efforts we are led to conclude that this instinct functions in every
living being, striving to work its ruin and reduce life to its primal
state of inert matter. Indeed, it might well be called the "death-
instinct"; whereas the erotic instincts vouch for the struggle to live
on. The death instinct becomes an impulse to destruction when,
with the aid of certain organs, it directs its action outwards, against
external objects. The living being, that is to say, defends its own
existence by destroying foreign bodies. But, in one of its activities,
the death instinct is operative *within* the living being and we have
sought to trace back a number of normal and pathological phenomena to this *introversion* of the destructive instinct. We have even
committed the heresy of explaining the origin of human conscience
by some such "turning inward" of the aggressive impulse. Obviously,
when this internal tendency operates on too large a scale, it is no
trivial matter, rather a positively morbid state of things; whereas
the diversion of the destructive impulse towards the external world
must have beneficial effects. Here is, then, the biological justification

for all those vile, pernicious propensities which we now are combating. We can but own that they are really more akin to nature than this our stand against them, which, in fact, remains to be accounted for.

All this may give you the impression that our theories amount to a species of mythology and a gloomy one at that! But does not every natural science lead ultimately to this—a sort of mythology? Is it otherwise to-day with your physical science?

The upshot of these observations, as bearing on the subject in hand, is that there is no likelihood of our being able to suppress humanity's aggressive tendencies. In some happy corners of the earth, they say, where nature brings forth abundantly whatever man desires, there flourish races whose lives go gently by, unknowing of aggression or constraint. This I can hardly credit; I would like further details about these happy folk. The Bolshevists, too, aspire to do away with human aggressiveness by ensuring the satisfaction of material needs and enforcing equality between man and man. To me this hope seems vain. Meanwhile, they busily perfect their armaments, and their hatred of outsiders is not the least of the factors of cohesion amongst themselves. In any case, as you, too, have observed, complete suppression of man's aggressive tendencies is not in issue; what we may try is to divert it into a channel other than that of warfare.

From our "mythology" of the instincts we may easily deduce a formula for an indirect method of eliminating war. If the propensity for war be due to the destructive instinct, we have always its counter-agent, Eros, to our hand. All that produces ties of sentiment between man and man must serve us as war's antidote. These ties are of two kinds. First, such relations as those towards a beloved object, void though they be of sexual intent. The psychoanalyst need feel no compunction in mentioning "love" in this connection; religion uses the same language: Love thy neighbour as thyself. A pious injunction easy to enounce, but hard to carry out! The other bond of sentiment is by way of identification. All that brings out the significant resemblances between men calls into play this feeling of community, identification, whereon is founded, in large measure, the whole edifice of human society.

In your strictures on the abuse of authority I find another suggestion for an indirect attack on the war-impulse. That men are divided into leaders and the led is but another manifestation of their inborn and irremediable inequality. The second class constitutes the vast majority; they need a high command to make decisions for them, to which decisions they usually bow without demur. In this context we would point out that men should be at greater pains than heretofore to form a superior class of independent thinkers, unamenable to intimidation and fervent in the quest of truth, whose function it would be to guide the masses dependent on their lead. . . . The ideal conditions would obviously be found in a community where every man subordinated his instinctive life to the dictates of reason. Nothing less than this could bring about so thorough and so durable a union between men, even if this involved the severance of mutual ties of sentiment. But surely such a hope is utterly utopian, as things are. The other indirect methods of preventing war are certainly more feasible, but entail no quick results. They conjure up an ugly picture of mills that grind so slowly that, before the flour is ready, men are dead of hunger.

As you see, little good comes of consulting a theoretician, aloof from worldly contacts, on practical and urgent problems! Better it were to tackle each successive crisis with means that we have ready to our hands. However, I would like to deal with a question which, though it is not mooted in your letter, interests me greatly. Why do we, you and I and many another, protest so vehemently against war, instead of just accepting it as another of life's odious importunities? For it seems a natural thing enough, biologically sound and practically unavoidable. I trust you will not be shocked by my raising such a question. For the better conduct of an enquiry it may be well to don a mask of feigned aloofness. The answer to my query may run as follows: Because every man has a right over his own life and war destroys lives that were full of promise; it forces the individual into situations that shame his manhood, obliging him to murder fellow men, against his will; it ravages material amenities, the fruits of human toil, and much besides. Moreover wars, as now conducted, afford no scope for acts of heroism according to the old ideals and, given the high perfection of modern arms, war to-day would mean the sheer extermination of one of the combatants, if not of both. This is so true, so obvious, that we can but wonder why the conduct of war is not banned by general consent. Doubtless either of the points I have just made is open to debate. It may be asked if the community, in its turn, cannot claim a right over the individual lives of its members. Moreover, all forms of war cannot be indiscriminately condemned; so long as there are nations and empires, each prepared callously to exterminate its rival, all alike must be equipped for war. But we will not dwell on any of these problems; they lie outside the debate to which you have invited me. I pass on to another point, the basis, as it strikes me, of our common hatred of war. It is this: we cannot do otherwise than hate it. Pacifists we are, since our organic nature wills us thus to be. Hence it comes easy to us to find arguments that justify our standpoint.

This point, however, calls for elucidation. Here is the way in which I see it. The cultural development of mankind (some, I know, prefer to call it civilisation) has been in progress since immemorial antiquity. To this process we owe all that is best in our composition, but also much that makes for human suffering. Its origins and causes are obscure, its issue is uncertain, but some of its characteristics are easy to perceive. It well may lead to the extinction of mankind, for it impairs the sexual function in more than one respect, and even to-day the uncivilised races and the backward classes of all nations are multiplying more rapidly than the cultured elements. This process may, perhaps, be likened to the effects of domestication on certain animals—it clearly involves physical changes of structure —but the view that cultural development is an organic process of this order has not yet become generally familiar. The psychic changes which accompany this process of cultural change are striking, and not to be gainsaid. They consist in the progressive rejection of instinctive ends and a scaling down of instinctive reactions. Sensations which delighted our forefathers have become neutral or unbearable to us; and, if our ethical and aesthetic ideals have undergone a change, the causes of this are ultimately organic. On the psychological side two of the most important phenomena of culture are, firstly, a strengthening of the intellect, which tends to master our instinctive life, and, secondly, an introversion of the aggressive impulse, with all its consequent benefits and perils. Now war runs most emphatically counter to the psychic disposition imposed on us by the growth of culture; we are therefore bound to resent war, to find it utterly intolerable. With pacifists like us it is not merely an intellectual and affective repulsion, but a constitutional intolerance, an idiosyncrasy in its most drastic form. And it would seem that the aesthetic ignominies of warfare play almost as large a part in this repugnance as war's atrocities.

How long have we to wait before the rest of men turn pacifist? Impossible to say, and yet perhaps our hope that these two factors— man's cultural disposition and a well founded dread of the form that future wars will take—may serve to put an end to war in the near future, is not chimerical. But by what ways or by-ways this will come about we cannot guess. Meanwhile, we may rest on the assurance that whatever makes for cultural development is working also against war.

With kindest regards and, should this *exposé* prove a disappointment to you, my sincere regrets.

Yours,

SIGMUND FREUD

Tragic Conflict*

BY HERBERT BUTTERFIELD

[1949]

THERE is another aspect of human vicissitude which ought to be considered when we attempt to take stock of the whole spectacle of world-history; and that is the tragic element which so often appears in the wars and struggles of mankind, though the belligerents themselves are often too passionately engaged to recognise this element of tragedy, having eyes for nothing save the crimes of the enemy. The great conflicts that occur between vast bodies of human beings would obviously not have taken place if all men had been perfect saints or had been competing with one another in self-sacrifice. Yet—as in the great struggles between Protestant and Catholic in the sixteenth century—it has often happened that both of the parties carrying on the warfare have devoutly felt themselves to be in the right. It is even true that many of the inhuman conflicts of mankind would probably never have taken place if the situation had been one of completely righteous men confronted by undiluted and unmitigated crime. One can hardly fail to recognise the element of tragedy in many conflicts which take place between one half-right that is perhaps too wilful, and another half-right that is perhaps too proud. It is even possible that great wars should come about because idealists are too egotistical concerning their own plans of salvation for mankind, and because the righteous are stiff-necked. Here is a side of human history which makes it necessary to reflect further on the nature of human beings. . . .

Each of us is more or less restricted to a narrow vision, gravely conditioned by time, temperament and age, and by the platform on which we happen to be standing. The most friendly foreign offices, the most friendly historians belonging to different nationalities, find somewhere or other the place where they cannot enter into one another's points of view. The Marxists are right when they assume that a member of a certain social class, even if he is unselfish, is liable to be limited in his outlook by the fact that he sees things from the platform of that social class. We may think that we have a spacious vision, level and

* From *Christianity and History* by Herbert Butterfield, copyright 1950 by Charles Scribner's Sons. Reprinted by permission of the publisher.

equal as it takes in wide horizons; but in reality each of us looks upon the world from a special peep-hole of his own. Where actual interests complicate a question and a certain amount of wishful thinking may give a bias to our minds, it is doubtful whether it is possible for any of us to survey a problem comprehensively. And it is certain that we fail to realise our incompetence in an art that is of the greatest importance for human relations—the simple art of putting ourselves in the other person's place.

The situation is still further complicated by a certain human predicament which we are too seldom conscious of, and which I can only call the predicament of Hobbesian fear—Hobbesian because it was subjected to particular analysis by the seventeenth-century philosopher, Thomas Hobbes. If you imagine yourself locked in a room with another person with whom you have often been on the most bitterly hostile terms in the past, and suppose that each of you has a pistol, you may find yourself in a predicament in which both of you would like to throw the pistols out of the window, yet it defeats the intelligence to find a way of doing it. If you throw yours out the first you rob the other man of the only reason he had for getting rid of his own, and for anything you know he may break the bargain. If both of you swear to throw the pistols out together, you may feel that he may make the gesture of hurling his away, but in reality hold tight to it, while you, if you have done the honest thing, would then be at his mercy. You may even have an *arrière-pensée* that he may possibly be concealing a second pistol somewhere about his person. Both of you in fact may have an equal justification for suspecting one another, and both of you may be men who in all predicaments save this had appeared reasonably well-behaved and well-intentioned. You may both of you be utterly honest in your desire to be at peace and to put an end to the predicament, if only in order to enable you to get on with your business. If some great bully were to come into the room and try to take your pistols from you, then as likely as not you would both combine against him, you would find yourselves cherished allies, find yourselves for the time being as thick as thieves. Only, after you had eliminated this intruder, you would discover to your horrible surprise that you were back in the original predicament again.

In international affairs it is this situation of Hobbesian fear which, so far as I can see, has hitherto defeated all the endeavour of the human intellect. Not only may both sides feel utterly self-righteous, but where a great obstruction occurs—as over the question of toleration in the sixteenth century, and that of disarmament in the twentieth—both may feel utterly baffled and frustrated; and sometimes even allies fall to blaming one another, as on one occasion papers of all complexions in England, out of pure exasperation, blamed France for the failure of the Disarmament Conference. Though one side may have more justice than another in the particular occasion of a conflict, there is a sense in which war as such is in reality a judgment on all of us. The fundamental predicament would not exist if men in general were as righteous as the situation requires, and of course the fundamental predicament is itself so maddening and exasperating that men sometimes resort to desperate measures with an idea of cutting the Gordian knot.

The Scourge of War

BY ABRAHAM LINCOLN

[1865]

SECOND INAUGURAL ADDRESS (March 4, 1865)

* * *

On the occasion corresponding to this four years ago, all thoughts were anxiously directed to an impending civil war. All dreaded it —all sought to avert it. While the inaugural address was being delivered from this place, devoted altogether to *saving* the Union without war, insurgent agents were in the city seeking to *destroy* it without war—seeking to dissolve the Union, and divide effects, by negotiation. Both parties deprecated war; but one of them would *make* war rather than let the nation survive; and the other would *accept* war rather than let it perish. And the war came.

One eighth of the whole population were colored slaves, not distributed generally over the Union, but localized in the Southern part of it. These slaves constituted a peculiar and powerful interest. All knew that this interest was, somehow, the cause of the war. To strengthen, perpetuate, and extend this interest was the object for which the insurgents would rend the Union, even by war; while the government claimed no right to do more than to restrict the territorial enlargement of it. Neither party expected for the war, the magnitude, or the duration, which it has already attained. Neither anticipated that the *cause* of the conflict might cease with, or even before, the conflict itself should cease. Each looked for an easier triumph, and a result less fundamental and astounding. Both read the same Bible, and pray to the same God; and each invokes His aid against the other. It may seem strange that any men should dare to ask a just God's assistance in wringing their bread from the sweat of other men's faces; but let us judge not that we be not judged. The prayers of both could not be answered; that of neither has been answered fully. The Almighty has His own purposes. "Woe unto the world because of offences! for it must needs be that offences come; but woe to that man by whom the offence cometh!" If we shall suppose that American Slavery is one of those offences which, in the providence of God, must needs come, but which, having continued through His appointed time, He now wills to remove, and that He gives *to both North and South,* this terrible war, as the woe due to *those by whom the offence came,* shall we discern therein any departure from those divine attributes which the believers in a Living God always ascribe to Him? Fondly do we hope—fervently do we pray—that this mighty scourge of war may speedily pass away. Yet, if God wills that it continue, until all the wealth piled by the bond-man's two hundred and fifty years of unrequited toil shall be sunk, and until every drop of blood drawn with the lash, shall be paid by another drawn with the sword, as was said three thousand years ago, so still it must be said "the judgments of the Lord, are true and righteous altogether."

With malice toward none; with charity for all; with firmness in the right, as God gives us to see the right, let us strive on to finish the work we are in; to bind up the nation's wounds; to care for him who shall have borne the battle, and for his widow, and his orphan—to do all which may achieve and cherish a just and lasting peace, among ourselves, and with all nations.

Letter to Thurlow Weed

> Executive Mansion,
> Washington, March 15, 1865

Thurlow Weed, Esq.
My dear Sir.

Every one likes a compliment. Thank you for yours on . . . the recent Inaugural Address. I expect it to wear as well as—perhaps better than—anything I have produced; but I believe it is not immediately popular. Men are not flattered by being shown that there has been a difference of purpose between the Almighty and them. To deny it, however, in this case, is to deny that there is a God governing the world. It is a truth which I thought needed to be told; and as whatever of humiliation there is in it, falls most directly on myself, I thought others might afford for me to tell it.

> Yours truly,
> A. Lincoln

The Origin of War*

BY PLATO

[4th Century, B.C.]

'THE origin of a city," I said, "is, in my opinion, due to the fact that no one of us is self-sufficient, but each man is in need of many things. Or do you think there is any other cause for the founding of cities?"

"No," he said, "none."

"Then men, being in want of many things, gather into one settlement many partners and helpers; one taking to himself one man, and another another, to satisfy their diverse needs, and to this common settlement we give the name of city. Is not that so?"

"Certainly."

"And when they exchange with one another, giving or receiving as the case may be, does not each man think that such exchange is to his own good?"

"Certainly."

"Come, then," I said. "Let us in our argument construct the city from the beginning. Apparently it will be the outcome of our need?"

"Surely."

"But the first and greatest of our needs is the provision of food to support existence and life?"

"Yes, assuredly."

"The second the provision of a dwelling-place, and the third of clothing, and so on?"

"That is so."

"Come, then," I said, "how will our city be able to supply a sufficiency of all those things? Will it not be by having one man a farmer, another a builder, and a third a weaver? Shall we add a shoemaker, and perhaps another provider of bodily needs?"

"Certainly."

"Then the city of bare necessity will consist of four or five men?"

---

* From Plato's *Republic*, Book II, translated by A. D. Lindsay. Copyright 1950 by E. P. Dutton and Company, Inc. Reprinted by permission.

"Apparently."

"Well, then, should each of these men place his own work at the disposal of all in common? For example, should our one farmer provide corn for four and spend fourfold time and labour on the provision of corn, and then share it with the rest; or should he pay no attention to the others, and provide only a fourth part of the corn for himself in a fourth of the time, and spend the other three-fourths of his time in providing a house, clothes, and shoes? Should he not have the trouble of sharing with the others, but rather provide with his own hands what he wants for himself?"

Adeimantus answered: "The first alternative, Socrates, is perhaps the easier."

"Well, it is certainly not strange that it is. For as you were speaking, I myself was thinking that, in the first place, no two of us are by nature altogether alike. Our capacities differ. Some are fit for one work, some for another. Do you agree?"

"I do."

"Well, then, would better work be done on the principle of one man many trades, or of one man one trade?"

"One man one trade is better," he said.

"Yes, for I fancy that it is also evident that, in work, opportunities which we pass by are lost."

"That is evident."

"I fancy that things to be done will not wait the good time of the doer. Rather the doer must wait on the opportunity for action, and not leave the doing of it for his idle moments."

"He must."

"And so more tasks of each kind are accomplished, and the work is better and is done more easily when each man works at the one craft for which nature fits him, that being free from all other occupations he may wait on its opportunities."

"That is certainly the case."

"Then, Adeimantus, we need more citizens than four to provide the above-mentioned necessities. For the farmer, naturally, will not make his own plough if it is to be a good one, nor his mattock, nor any of the other farming tools. No more will the builder, who also needs many tools. And the same will hold of the weaver and the shoemaker, will it not?"

"True."

"Then carpenters and smiths and many other artisans of that kind will become members of our little city, and make it populous?"

"Certainly."

"Yet it would not be so very large if we added herdsmen and shepherds and others of that class, that the farmers may have oxen for ploughing, and both builders and farmers may have yoke animals for their carting, and that the weavers and shoemakers may have skins and wool."

"Nor so very small if so well provided."

"Again," I said, "it will be almost impossible to have our city so situated that it will need no imports."

"Yes, that will be impossible."

"Then it will need more men still to bring it what it needs from other cities?"

"It will."

"And if they are to get what they need from other people their agent must take with him something that those others want. If he goes empty-handed, he will return empty-handed, will he not?"

"I think so."

"Then the workers of our city must not only make enough for home consumption; they must also produce goods of the number and kind required by other people?"

"Yes, they must."

"Then our city will need more farmers, and more of all the other craftsmen?"

"Yes."

"And among the rest it will need more agents who are to import and export the different kinds of goods. These are merchants, are they not?"

"Yes."

"We shall need merchants, then?"

"Certainly."

"And if the commerce is over sea, we shall need a host of others who are experts in sea-trading."

"Yes, there will be many of them."

"Again, in the city itself how will men exchange the produce of their labors with one another? For this was the original reason of our establishing the principle of community and founding a city."

"Clearly," he said, "by selling and buying."

"This will give us a market-place, and money as a token for the sake of exchange."

"Certainly."

"Then if the farmer or any other craftsman brings his produce into the market-place, and meets there none who wish to exchange their goods with him, is he to sit idle in the market-place when he might be working?"

"Certainly not," said he. "There are men who have taken note of this, and devote themselves to this service. In well-governed cities they are usually those who are weakest in body, and incapable of any other work. They have to stay there in the market-place and exchange money for goods with those who want to sell, and goods for money with those who want to buy."

"Then," I said, "this necessity brings shopkeepers into our city. We give the name of shopkeepers, do we not, to those who serve buyers and sellers in their stations at the market-place, but the name of merchants to those who travel from city to city?"

"Certainly."

"Then are there not other agents also who have no mental gifts to make them at all worthy to share in the community, but who have bodily strength sufficient for hard labour? They sell the use of their strength, and the price they get for it being called hire, they are known, I fancy, as hired laborers?"

"Certainly."

"Then these hired laborers, too, serve to complete our city?"

"I think so."

"Then, Adeimantus, has our city now grown to its perfection?"

"Perhaps."

"Then, where in it shall we find justice and injustice? With which of the elements we have noticed did they make their entry?"

"I cannot see how they came in, Socrates," he said, "unless we find them somewhere in the mutual needs of these same persons."

"Well," I said, "perhaps you are right. But let us consider the matter and not draw back. And first, let us consider what will be the manner of life of men so equipped. Will they not spend their time in the production of corn and wine and clothing and shoes? And they will build themselves houses; in summer they will generally work without their coats and shoes, but in winter they will be well clothed and shod. For food they will make meal from their barley and flour from their wheat, and kneading and baking them they will heap their noble scones and loaves on reeds or fresh leaves, and lying on couches of bryony and myrtle boughs will feast with their children, drink wine after their repast, crown their heads with garlands, and sing hymns to the gods. So they will live with one another in happiness, not begetting children above their means, and guarding against the danger of poverty or war."

Here Glaucon interrupted and said: "Apparently you give your men dry bread to feast on."

"You are right," I said; "I forgot that they would have a relish with it. They will have salt and olives and cheese, and they will have boiled dishes with onions and such vegetables as one gets in the country. And I expect we must allow them a dessert of figs, and peas and beans, and they will roast myrtle berries and acorns at the fire, and drink their wine in moderation. Leading so peaceful and healthy a life they will naturally attain to a good old age, and at death leave their children to live as they have done."

"Why," said Glaucon, "if you had been founding a city of pigs, Socrates, this is just how you would have fattened them."

"Well, Glaucon, how must they live?"

"In an ordinary decent manner," he said. "If they are not to be miserable, I think they must have couches to lie on and tables to eat from, and the ordinary dishes and dessert of modern life."

"Very well," I said, "I understand. We are considering apparently, the making not of a city merely, but of a luxurious city. And perhaps there is no harm in doing so. From that kind, too, we shall soon learn, if we examine it, how justice and injustice arise in cities. I, for my part, think that the city I have described is the true one, what we may call the city of health. But if you wish, let us also inspect a city which is suffering from inflammation. There is no reason why we should not. Well, then, for some people the arrangements we have made will not be enough. The mode of living will not satisfy them. They shall have couches and tables and other furniture; rich dishes too, and fragrant oils and perfumes, and courtesans and sweetmeats, and many varieties of each. Then again we must make more than a bare provision for those necessities we mentioned at the first, houses and clothes and shoes. We must start painting and embroidery, and collect gold and ivory, and so on, must we not?"

"Yes," he said.

"Then we must make our city larger. For the healthy city will not now suffice. We need one swollen in size, and full of a multitude of things which necessity would not introduce into cities. There will be all kinds of hunters and there will be the imitators; one crowd of imitators in figure and color, and another of imitators in music; poets and their servants, rhapsodists, actors, dancers and theatrical agents; and makers of all kinds of articles, of those used for women's adornment, for example. Then, too, we shall need more servants; or do you think we can do without footmen, wet-nurses, dry-nurses, lady's maids, barbers, and cooks and confectioners, besides? Then we shall want swineherds too; we had none in our former city—there was no need—but we shall need them along with all the others for this city. And we shall need great quantities of all kinds of cattle if people are to eat them. Shall we not?"

"Surely."

"Then if we lead this kind of life we shall require doctors far more often than we should have done in the first city?"

"Certainly."

"Then I dare say even the land which was sufficient to support the first population will be now insufficient and too small?"

"Yes," he said.

"Then if we are to have enough for pasture and ploughland, we must take a slice from our neighbors' territory. And they will want to do the same to ours, if they also overpass the bounds of necessity and plunge into reckless pursuit of wealth?"

"Yes, that must happen, Socrates," he said.

"Then shall we go to war at that point, Glaucon, or what will happen?"

"We shall go to war," he said.

"And we need not say at present whether the effects of war are good or bad. Let us only notice that we have found the origin of war in those passions which are most responsible for all the evils that come upon cities and the men that dwell in them."

"Certainly."

The Idea of Cause*

BY LEO TOLSTOY

[1869]

Towards the end of the year 1811, there began to be greater activity
in levying troops and in concentrating the forces of Western Europe,
and in 1812 these forces—millions of men, reckoning those engaged
in the transport and feeding of the army—moved from the west
eastward, towards the frontiers of Russia, where, since 1811, the
Russian forces were being in like manner concentrated.

On the 12th of June the forces of Western Europe crossed the
frontier, and the war began, that is, an event took place opposed to
human reason and all human nature. Millions of men perpetrated
against one another so great a mass of crime—fraud, swindling, robbery, forgery, issue of counterfeit money, plunder, incendiarism, and
murder—that the annals of all the criminal courts of the world could
not muster such a sum of wickedness in whole centuries, though the
men who committed those deeds did not at that time look on them as
crimes.

What led to this extraordinary event? What were its causes? Historians, with simple-hearted conviction, tell us that the causes of this
event were the insult offered to the Duke of Oldenburg, the failure
to maintain the continental system, the ambition of Napoleon, the
firmness of Alexander, the mistakes of the diplomatists, and so on.

According to them, if only Metternich, Rumyantsev, or Talley-
rand had, in the interval between a levée and a court ball, really
taken pains and written a more judicious diplomatic note, or if only
Napoleon had written to Alexander, 'I consent to restore the duchy
to the Duke of Oldenburg,' there would have been no war.

We can readily understand that being the conception of the war
that presented itself to contemporaries. We can understand Napoleon's supposing the cause of the war to be the intrigues of England
(as he said, indeed, in St. Helena); we can understand how to the
members of the English House of Commons the cause of the war
seemed to be Napoleon's ambition; how to the Duke of Oldenburg

---

* Selections from the epilogue of *War and Peace*.

the war seemed due to the outrage done him; how to the trading
class the war seemed due to the continental system that was ruining
Europe; to the old soldiers and generals the chief reason for it
seemed their need of active service; to the regiments of the period,
the necessity of returning to the old traditions; while the diplomatists of the time set it down to the alliance of Russia with Austria in
1809 not having been with sufficient care concealed from Napoleon,
and the memorandum, No. 178, having been awkwardly worded.
We may well understand contemporaries believing in those causes,
and in a countless, endless number more, the multiplicity of which
is due to the infinite variety of men's points of view. But to us of a
later generation, contemplating in all its vastness the immensity of
the accomplished fact, and seeking to penetrate its simple and fearful significance, those explanations must appear insufficient. To us it
is inconceivable that millions of Christian men should have killed
and tortured each other, because Napoleon was ambitious, Alexander firm, English policy crafty, and the Duke of Oldenburg hardly
treated. We cannot grasp the connection between these circumstances and the bare fact of murder and violence, nor why the duke's
wrongs should induce thousands of men from the other side of Europe to pillage and murder the inhabitants of the Smolensk and
Moscow provinces and to be slaughtered by them.

For us of a later generation, who are not historians led away by
the process of research, and so can look at the facts with common-
sense unobscured, the causes of this war appear innumerable in
their multiplicity. The more deeply we search out the causes the
more of them we discover; and every cause, and even a whole class
of causes taken separately, strikes us as being equally true in itself,
and equally deceptive through its insignificance in comparison with
the immensity of the result, and its inability to produce (without all
the other causes that concurred with it) the effect that followed.
Such a cause, for instance, occurs to us as Napoleon's refusal to
withdraw his troops beyond the Vistula, and to restore the duchy
of Oldenburg; and then again we remember the readiness or the
reluctance of the first chance French corporal to serve on a second
campaign; for had he been unwilling to serve, and a second and a
third, and thousands of corporals and soldiers had shared that reluctance, Napoleon's army would have been short of so many men,
and the war could not have taken place.

If Napoleon had not taken offence at the request to withdraw beyond the Vistula, and had not commanded his troops to advance, there would have been no war. But if all the sergeants had been unwilling to serve on another campaign, there could have been no war either.

And the war would not have been had there been no intrigues on the part of England, no Duke of Oldenburg, no resentment on the part of Alexander; nor had there been no autocracy in Russia, no French Revolution and consequent dictatorship and empire, nor all that led to the French Revolution, and so on further back: without any one of those causes, nothing could have happened. And so all those causes—myriads of causes—coincided to bring about what happened. And consequently nothing was exclusively the cause of the war, and the war was bound to happen, simply because it was bound to happen. Millions of men, repudiating their common-sense and their human feelings, were bound to move from west to east, and to slaughter their fellows, just as some centuries before hordes of men had moved from east to west to slaughter their fellows.

The acts of Napoleon and Alexander, on whose words it seemed to depend whether this should be done or not, were as little voluntary as the act of each soldier, forced to march out by the drawing of a lot or by conscription. This could not be otherwise, for in order that the will of Napoleon and Alexander (on whom the whole decision appeared to rest) should be effective, a combination of innumerable circumstances was essential, without any one of which the effect could not have followed. It was essential that the millions of men in whose hands the real power lay—the soldiers who fired guns and transported provisions and cannons—should consent to carry out the will of those feeble and isolated persons, and that they should have been brought to this acquiescence by an infinite number of varied and complicated causes.

We are forced to fall back upon fatalism in history to explain irrational events (that is those of which we cannot comprehend the reason). The more we try to explain those events in history rationally, the more irrational and incomprehensible they seem to us. Every man lives for himself, making use of his free-will for attainment of his own objects, and feels in his whole being that he can do or not do any action. But as soon as he does anything, that act, committed at a certain moment in time, becomes irrevocable and is the property

of history, in which it has a significance, predestined and not subject
to free choice.

There are two aspects to the life of every man: the personal life,
which is free in proportion as its interests are abstract, and the elemental life of the swarm, in which a man must inevitably follow
the laws laid down for him.

Consciously a man lives on his own account in freedom of will,
but he serves as an unconscious instrument in bringing about the
historical ends of humanity. An act he has once committed is irrevocable, and that act of his, coinciding in time with millions of acts
of others, has an historical value. The higher a man's place in the
social scale, the more connections he has with others, and the more
power he has over them, the more conspicuous is the inevitability
and predestination of every act he commits. 'The hearts of kings are
in the hand of God.' The king is the slave of history.

History—that is the unconscious life of humanity in the swarm,
in the community—makes every minute of the life of kings its own,
as an instrument for attaining its ends.

Although in that year, 1812, Napoleon believed more than ever
that to shed or not to shed the blood of his peoples depended entirely on his will (as Alexander said in his last letter to him), yet
then, and more than at any time, he was in bondage to those laws
which forced him, while to himself he seemed to be acting freely, to
do what was bound to be his share in the common edifice of humanity, in history.

The people of the west moved to the east for men to kill one another. And by the law of the coincidence of causes, thousands of
petty causes backed one another up and coincided with that event to
bring about that movement and that war: resentment at the non-
observance of the continental system, and the Duke of Oldenburg,
and the massing of troops in Prussia—a measure undertaken, as
Napoleon supposed, with the object of securing armed peace—and
the French Emperor's love of war, to which he had grown accustomed, in conjunction with the inclinations of his people, who were
carried away by the grandiose scale of the preparations, and the expenditure on those preparations, and the necessity of recouping that
expenditure. Then there was the intoxicating effect of the honours
paid to the French Emperor in Dresden, and the negotiations too
of the diplomatists, who were supposed by contemporaries to be

guided by a genuine desire to secure peace, though they only in-flamed the self-love of both sides; and millions upon millions of other causes, chiming in with the fated event and coincident with it.

When the apple is ripe and falls—why does it fall? Is it because it is drawn by gravitation to the earth, because its stalk is withered, because it is dried by the sun, because it grows heavier, because the wind shakes it, or because the boy standing under the tree wants to eat it?

Not one of those is the cause. All that simply makes up the con-junction of conditions under which every living, organic, elemental event takes place. And the botanist who says that the apple has fallen because the cells are decomposing, and so on, will be just as right as the boy standing under the tree who says the apple has fallen be-cause he wanted to eat it and prayed for it to fall. The historian, who says that Napoleon went to Moscow because he wanted to, and was ruined because Alexander desired his ruin, will be just as right and as wrong as the man who says that the mountain of millions of tons, tottering and undermined, has been felled by the last stroke of the last workingman's pickaxe. In historical events great men—so called—are but the labels that serve to give a name to an event, and like labels, they have the least possible connection with the event itself.

Every action of theirs, that seems to them an act of their own free-will, is in an historical sense not free at all, but in bondage to the whole course of previous history, and predestined from all eternity.

• • •

HISTORY examines the manifestations of man's freewill in connection with the external world in time and in dependence on cause, that is, defines that freedom by the laws of reason; and so history is only a science in so far as that freedom is defined by those laws.

To history the recognition of the freewills of men as forces able to influence historical events, that is, not subject to laws, is the same as would be to astronomy the recognition of freewill in the movements of the heavenly bodies.

This recognition destroys the possibility of the existence of laws, that is, of any science whatever. If there is so much as one body mov-ing at its freewill, the laws of Kepler and of Newton are annulled, and every conception of the movement of the heavenly bodies is destroyed. If there is a single human action due to freewill, no historical law exists, and no conception of historical events can be formed. . . .

From the point of view from which the science of history now approaches its subject, by the method it now follows, seeking the causes of phenomena in the freewill of men, the expression of laws by science is impossible, since however we limit the freewill of men, so long as we recognize it as a force not subject to law, the existence of law becomes impossible.

By limiting this element of freewill to infinity, that is, regarding it as an infinitesimal minimum, we are convinced of the complete unattainability of causes, and then, instead of seeking causes, history sets before itself the task of seeking laws.

The seeking of those laws has been begun long ago, and the new lines of thought which history must adopt are being worked out simultaneously with the self-destruction towards which the old-fashioned history is going, forever dissecting and dissecting the causes of phenomena. . . .

The other sciences, too, have followed the same course, though under another form. When Newton formulated the law of gravitation, he did not say that the sun or the earth has the property of attraction. He said that all bodies—from the greatest to the smallest—have the property of attracting one another; that is, leaving on one side the question of the cause of the movements of bodies, he expressed the property common to all bodies, from the infinitely great to the infinitely small. The natural sciences do the same thing; leaving on one side the question of cause, they seek for laws. History, too, is entered on the same course. And if the subject of history is to be the study of the movements of peoples and of humanity, and not episodes from the lives of individual men, it too is bound to lay aside the idea of cause, and to seek the laws common to all the equal and inseparably interconnected, infinitesimal elements of freewill.

What Is War?*

BY EMERY REVES

[1945]

IT IS commonly taken for granted that we can never abolish war between nations, because war is in the nature of man. It is even more widely accepted that war has innumerable causes and that to try to abolish all of them would be a hopeless task.

We must refuse to accept such apparently true but basically deceptive statements, if we would avoid becoming the helpless victims of superstition. No one knows just what "human nature" is. Nor is this a relevant question. Assuming or even admitting that certain evils *are* part of "human nature," this does not mean that we should sit passively and refuse to investigate the conditions which cause the evils to become deadly and the possibility of avoiding their devastating effects.

Since man began to think about life and himself, it has been generally accepted that appendicitis and gallstones were in the nature of man. Indeed, they are. But after thousands of years, during which men died from these fatal evils of "human nature," some people had the courage to take a knife and cut open the diseased part to see what was happening. Appendicitis and gallstones continue to be "in the nature of man." But now man does not necessarily die from them.

Superficially, it looks as though wars have been waged for a great variety of reasons. The struggle for food and mere survival among primitive tribes, feuds between families and dynasties, quarrels between cities and provinces, religious fanaticism, rival commercial interests, antagonistic social ideals, the race for colonies, economic competition and many other forces have exploded in fatal and devastating wars.

Since time immemorial, among primitive people, families, clans and tribes have fought, enslaved and exterminated each other for food, shelter, women, pastures, hunting grounds. Each group had

* From Emery Reves: *The Anatomy of Peace*. Copyright 1945, 1946 by Emery Reves. Reprinted by arrangement with Harper & Brothers.

a "religion," a demon, a totem, a god, or several of each, whose divine and supreme will was interpreted by priests, medicine men and magicians, and who protected them from the dangers and depredations of other clans; inspired and incited them to war upon and to annihilate their neighbors. Life at that stage of society was no different from the life of fish in the deep and beasts in the jungle.

Later, at a higher level of civilization, we see larger settlements and city communities fighting and warring with each other. Nineveh, Babylon, Troy, Cnossos, Athens, Sparta, Rome, Carthage and many other similar rival settlements continuously battled, until all of them were finally destroyed.

Under the inspiration and leadership of dynamic personalities, powerful clans and races set out upon wars of conquest so that they might rule over new lands and subjects in safety and wealth. Tiglath Pileser, Nebuchadnezzar, Darius, Alexander, Attila, Genghis Khan and other conquerors in history waged large-scale wars to subdue the world as it was known to them.

For centuries after the fall of Rome, European society was rocked by endless clashes and battles among thousands of feudal barons.

After the consolidation of the three world religions originating in Judaism—Catholicism, Islamism and Protestantism—a long series of wars were fought by the followers of these expanding and conflicting faiths. Kings, princes and knights took part in crusades to defend and spread their own creeds, to destroy and exterminate the believers in the other creeds. The great wars fought by Constantine, Charles V, Suleiman, Philip II, Gustavus Adolphus and other mighty rulers of the Middle Ages were mostly attempts to unify the Western world under one religion.

Following the collapse of the feudal system, with the development of craftsmanship, trade and shipping, a middle class of modern bourgeois citizenry emerged and began to crystallize. The field of conflict again shifted, and wars were fought by great commercial centers, Venice, Florence, Augsburg, Hamburg, Amsterdam, Ghent, Danzig and other city units, which impressed their own citizens and hired mercenaries.

Then another series of wars were waged by absolute monarchs in the interest of their dynasties, to widen the domains of the great royal houses. The Hapsburg. Bourbon, Wittelsbach, Romanoff and

Stuart monarchies and dozens of minor dynasties led their subjects into battle to defend and extend their power and rule.

A different type of war was waged between smaller kingdoms and principalities to obtain supremacy within a particular system of monarchy, such as the wars between England and Scotland; Saxony, Bavaria and Prussia; Tuscany, Piedmont and Parma; Burgundy, Touraine and Normandy.

And finally, the creation of modern nation-states at the end of the eighteenth century has brought about a series of gigantic conflicts between whole conscripted nations, culminating in the first and second world wars.

Looking back over history, war appears a hundred-headed hydra. As soon as the peacemakers chop off one head, new ones immediately appear on the monster. Yet, if we analyze what seem to be the manifold causes of past wars, it is not difficult to observe a thread of continuity running through these strange historical phenomena.

Why did cities once wage wars against each other and why do municipalities no longer fight each other with weapons today? Why, at certain times, have great landowner barons warred with each other and why have they now ceased that practice? Why did the various churches plunge their adherents into armed warfare and why today are they able to worship side by side without shooting each other? Why did Scotland and England, Saxony and Prussia, Parma and Tuscany, at a certain period in their history, go to battle against each other and why have they ceased fighting today?

A careful study of human history reveals that the assumption that war is inherent in human nature—and therefore eternal—is shallow and faulty, that it is only a superficial impression. Far from being inexplicable or inevitable, we can invariably determine the situations that predispose to war, and the conditions which lead to war.

The real cause of all wars has always been the same. They have occurred with the mathematical regularity of a natural law at clearly determined moments as the result of clearly definable conditions.

If we try to detect the mechanism visibly in operation, the single cause ever-present at the outbreak of each and every conflict known to human history, if we attempt to reduce the seemingly innumerable causes of war to a common denominator, two clear and unmistakable observations emerge.

1. Wars between groups of men forming social units always take place when these units—tribes, dynasties, churches, cities, nations—exercise unrestricted sovereign power.

2. Wars between these social units cease the moment sovereign power is transferred from them to a larger or higher unit.

From these observations we can deduce a social law with the characteristics of an axiom that applies to and explains each and every war in the history of all time.

War takes place whenever and wherever non-integrated social units of equal sovereignty come into contact.

War between given social units of equal sovereignty is the permanent symptom of each successive phase of civilization. Wars always ceased when a higher unit established its own sovereignty, absorbing the sovereignties of the conflicting smaller social groups. After such transfers of sovereignty, a period of peace followed, which lasted only until the new social units came into contact. Then a new series of wars began.

The causes and reasons alleged by history to have brought about these conflicts are irrelevant, as they continued to exist long after the wars had ceased. Cities and provinces continue to compete with each other. Religious convictions are just as different today as they were during the religious wars.

The only thing that did change was the institutionalization of sovereignty, the transfer of sovereignty from one type of social unit to another and a higher one.

Just as there is one and only one cause for wars between men on this earth, so history shows that peace—not peace in an absolute and utopian sense, but concrete peace between given social groups warring with each other at given times—has always been established in one way and only in one way.

Peace between fighting groups of men was never possible and wars succeeded one another until some sovereignty, some sovereign source of law, some sovereign power was set up *over* and *above* the clashing social units, integrating the warring units into a higher sovereignty.

Once the mechanics and the fundamental causes of wars—of all wars—are realized, the futility and childishness of the passionate debates about armament and disarmament must be apparent to all.

If human society were organized so that relations between groups and units in contact were regulated by democratically controlled law and legal institutions, then modern science could go ahead, devise and produce the most devastating weapons, and there would be no war. But if we allow sovereign rights to reside in the separate units and groups without regulating their relations by law, then we can prohibit every weapon, even a penknife, and people will beat out each other's brains with clubs.

It is tragic to witness the utter blindness and ignorance of our governments and political leaders in regard to this all-important and vital problem of the world.

Voices are now being raised in the United States and in Great Britain demanding compulsory military service and the maintenance of extensive armaments in peacetime. The argument is that if in 1939 the United States and Great Britain had been armed, Germany and Japan would never have dared to start a war. The Western democracies must not be caught unprepared again. If conscription is introduced and America and England have large armed forces ready to fight at a moment's notice, no other power will dare attack them, and they will not be forced into war. That sounds logical. But what about France, the Soviet Union, Belgium, Czechoslovakia, Yugoslavia and the other countries which always had conscription and large standing armies? Did this save them from war?

After 1919, the peacemakers were obsessed by the idea that armaments lead to wars, that a *sine qua non* for world peace is the general limitation and reduction of armaments on sea, land and in the air. Disarmament completely dominated international thought for fifteen years after the signature of the Covenant. Tremendous amounts of propaganda were poured into the public ear by printed and spoken word, to the effect that "armament manufacturers" were the real culprits responsible for wars, that no nation should build battleships bigger than thirty-five thousand tons, that the caliber of guns should be reduced, submarine and gas warfare prohibited, military service shortened and so forth.

These views found the democratic victors receptive and persuaded them to disarm to a large extent. But naturally they were without effect on the vanquished who sought revenge and a revision of the *status quo* by force. The outbreak of the second World War proved conclusively the complete fallacy and uselessness of seeking peace between nations through disarmament.

Now our leaders are preaching the exact opposite. We are told today that only powerful armaments can maintain peace, that the democratic and so-called peace-loving nations must maintain omnipotent national navies, air forces and mechanized armies, that we must control strategic military bases spread around the globe, if we would prevent aggression and maintain peace.

This idea, the idea of maintaining peace by armaments, is just as complete a fallacy as the idea of maintaining peace through disarmament. Technical equipment, arms, have as much to do with peace as frogs with the weather. Conscription and large armies are just as incapable of maintaining peace as no conscription and disarmament.

The problem of peace is a social and political problem, not a technical one.

War is never the disease itself. War is a reaction to a disease of society, the symptom of disease. It is just like fever in the human body. We shall never be able to prevent all wars in advance, because it is impossible to foresee future differentiations of human society, exactly where divisions and splits of society will take place. In the twenty-fifth century perhaps the great conflict will be between the orange growers and the believers in Taoism. We do not know.

What we do know is that war is the result of contact between nonintegrated sovereign units, whether such units be families, tribes, villages, estates, cities, provinces, dynasties, religions, classes, nations, regions or continents.

We also know that today, the conflict is between the scattered units of nation-states. During the past hundred years, all major wars have been waged between nations. This division among men is the only condition which, in our age, can create—and undoubtedly will create—other wars.

The task therefore is to prevent wars between the nations—international wars.

Logical thinking and historical empiricism agree that there *is* a way to solve this problem and prevent wars between the nations once and for all. But with equal clarity they also reveal that there

is one way and one way alone to achieve this end: **The integration
of the scattered conflicting national sovereignties into one unified,
higher sovereignty,** capable of creating a legal order within which
all peoples may enjoy equal security, equal obligations and equal
rights under law.

'plato told' *

BY E. E. CUMMINGS

[1944]

plato told

him:he couldn't
believe it(jesus

told him;he
wouldn't believe
it)lao

tsze
certainly told
him,and general
(yes

mam)
sherman;
and even
(believe it
or

not)you
told him: i told
him;we told him
(he didn't believe it,no

sir)it took
a nipponized bit of
the old sixth

avenue
el;in the top of his head:to tell

him

* From *Poems 1923–1954*, Harcourt, Brace and Company. Copyright 1944 by E. E. Cummings. Reprinted by permission.

III

STATE AND INDIVIDUAL

The Declaration of Independence

[1776]

WHEN, in the course of human events, it becomes necessary for one people to dissolve the political bands which have connected them with another, and to assume, among the powers of the earth, the separate and equal station to which the laws of nature and of nature's God entitle them, a decent respect to the opinions of mankind requires that they should declare the causes which impel them to the separation.

We hold these truths to be self-evident, that all men are created equal; that they are endowed by their Creator with certain unalienable rights; that among these, are life, liberty, and the pursuit of happiness. That, to secure these rights, governments are instituted among men, deriving their just powers from the consent of the governed; that, whenever any form of government becomes destructive of these ends, it is the right of the people to alter or to abolish it, and to institute new government, laying its foundation on such principles, and organizing its powers in such form, as to them shall seem most likely to effect their safety and happiness. Prudence, indeed, will dictate that governments long established, should not be changed for light and transient causes; and, accordingly, all experience hath shown, that mankind are more disposed to suffer, while evils are sufferable, than to right themselves by abolishing the forms to which they are accustomed. But, when a long train of abuses and usurpations, pursuing invariably the same object, evinces a design to reduce them under absolute despotism, it is their right, it is their duty, to throw off such government, and to provide new guards for their future security. Such has been the patient sufferance of these colonies, and such is now the necessity which constrains them to alter their former systems of government. The history of the present king of Great Britain is a history of repeated injuries and usurpations, all having, in direct object, the establishment of an absolute tyranny over these States. To prove this, let facts be submitted to a candid world:

He has refused his assent to laws the most wholesome and necessary for the public good.

He has forbidden his Governors to pass laws of immediate and pressing importance, unless suspended in their operation till his assent should be obtained, and, when so suspended, he has utterly neglected to attend to them.

He has refused to pass other laws for the accommodation of large districts of people, unless those people would relinquish the right of representation in the legislature; a right inestimable to them, and formidable to tyrants only.

He has called together legislative bodies at places unusual, uncomfortable, and distant from the depository of their public records, for the sole purpose of fatiguing them into compliance with his measures.

He has dissolved representative houses repeatedly, for opposing, with manly firmness, his invasions on the rights of the people.

He has refused, for a long time after such dissolutions, to cause others to be elected; whereby the legislative powers, incapable of annihilation, have returned to the people at large for their exercise; the State remaining, in the meantime, exposed to all the danger of invasion from without, and convulsions within.

He has endeavored to prevent the population of these States; for that purpose, obstructing the laws for naturalization of foreigners; refusing to pass others to encourage their migration hither, and raising the conditions of new appropriations of lands.

He has obstructed the administration of justice, by refusing his assent to laws for establishing judiciary powers.

He has made judges dependent on his will alone, for the tenure of their offices, and the amount and payment of their salaries.

He has erected a multitude of new offices, and sent hither swarms of officers to harass our people, and eat out their substance.

He has kept among us, in times of peace, standing armies, without the consent of our legislature.

He has affected to render the military independent of, and superior to, the civil power.

He has combined, with others, to subject us to a jurisdiction foreign to our constitution, and unacknowledged by our laws; giving his assent to their acts of pretended legislation:

For quartering large bodies of armed troops among us:

For protecting them, by a mock trial, from punishment, for any murders which they should commit on the inhabitants of these States:

For cutting off our trade with all parts of the world:

For imposing taxes on us without our consent:

For depriving us, in many cases, of the benefits of trial by jury:

For transporting us beyond seas to be tried for pretended offences:

For abolishing the free system of English laws in a neighboring province, establishing therein an arbitrary government, and enlarging its boundaries, so as to render it at once an example and fit instrument for introducing the same absolute rule into these colonies:

For taking away our charters, abolishing our most valuable laws, and altering, fundamentally, the forms of our governments:

For suspending our own legislatures, and declaring themselves invested with power to legislate for us in all cases whatsoever.

He has abdicated government here, by declaring us out of his protection, and waging war against us.

He has plundered our seas, ravaged our coasts, burnt our towns, and destroyed the lives of our people.

He is, at this time, transporting large armies of foreign mercenaries to complete the works of death, desolation, and tyranny, already begun, with circumstances of cruelty and perfidy scarcely paralleled in the most barbarous ages, and totally unworthy the head of a civilized nation.

He has constrained our fellow-citizens, taken captive on the high seas, to bear arms against their country, to become the executioners of their friends and brethren, or to fall themselves by their hands.

He has excited domestic insurrections amongst us, and has endeavored to bring on the inhabitants of our frontiers, the merciless Indian savages, whose known rule of warfare is an undistinguished destruction, of all ages, sexes, and conditions.

In every stage of these oppressions, we have petitioned for redress, in the most humble terms; our repeated petitions have been answered only by repeated injury. A prince whose character is thus marked by every act which may define a tyrant, is unfit to be the ruler of a free people.

Nor have we been wanting in attention to our British brethren. We have warned them, from time to time, of attempts by their legislature to extend an unwarrantable jurisdiction over us. We have reminded them of the circumstances of our emigration and settlement here. We have appealed to their native justice and magnanimity, and we have conjured them, by the ties of our common kindred, to disavow these usurpations, which would inevitably interrupt our connections and correspondence. They, too, have been deaf to the voice of justice and consanguinity. We must, therefore, acquiesce in the necessity, which denounces our separation, and hold them, as we hold the rest of mankind, enemies in war, in peace, friends.

We, therefore, the representatives of the United States of America, in General Congress assembled, appealing to the Supreme Judge of the World for the rectitude of our intentions, do, in the name, and by authority of the good people of these colonies, solemnly publish and declare, That these United Colonies are, and of right ought to be, free and independent States; that they are absolved from all allegiance to the British crown, and that all political connection between them and the state of Great Britain, is, and ought to be, totally dissolved; and that, as free and independent states, they have full power to levy war, conclude peace, contract alliances, establish commerce, and to do all other acts and things which independent States may of right do. And, for the support of this declaration, with a firm reliance on the protection of Divine Providence, we mutually pledge to each other, our lives, our fortunes, and our sacred honor.

The foregoing declaration was, by order of Congress, engrossed, and signed by the following members:—

JOHN HANCOCK.

NEW HAMPSHIRE
Josiah Bartlett,
William Whipple,
Matthew Thornton.

RHODE ISLAND
Stephen Hopkins,
William Ellery.

MASSACHUSETTS BAY
Samuel Adams,
John Adams,
Robert Treat Paine,
Elbridge Gerry.

CONNECTICUT
Roger Sherman,
Samuel Huntington,
William Williams,
Oliver Wolcott.

NEW YORK
William Floyd,
Philip Livingston,
Francis Lewis,
Lewis Morris.

MARYLAND
Samuel Chase,
William Paca,
Thomas Stone,
Charles Carroll, of Carrollton

NEW JERSEY
Richard Stockton,
John Witherspoon,
Francis Hopkinson,
John Hart,
Abraham Clark.

VIRGINIA
George Wythe,
Richard Henry Lee,
Thomas Jefferson,
Benjamin Harrison,
Thomas Nelson, Jr.,
Francis Lightfoot Lee,
Carter Braxton.

PENNSYLVANIA
Robert Morris,
Benjamin Rush,
Benjamin Franklin,
John Morton,
George Clymer,
James Smith,
George Taylor,
James Wilson,
George Ross.

NORTH CAROLINA
William Hooper,
Joseph Hewes,
John Penn.

SOUTH CAROLINA
Edward Rutledge,
Thomas Heyward, Jr.,
Thomas Lynch, Jr.,
Arthur Middleton.

DELAWARE
Caesar Rodney,
George Read,
Thomas M'Kean.

GEORGIA
Button Gwinnett,
Lyman Hall,
George Walton.

Resolved, That copies of the Declaration be sent to the several assemblies, conventions, and committees, or councils of safety, and to the several commanding officers of the continental troops; that it be proclaimed in each of the United States, and at the head of the army.

Fascism*

BY BENITO MUSSOLINI

[1932]

. . . Many of the practical expressions of Fascism—such as party organisation, system of education, discipline—can only be understood when considered in relation to its general attitude toward life: a spiritual attitude. Fascism sees in the world not only those superficial, material aspects in which man appears as an individual, standing by himself, self-centred, subject to natural law which instinctively urges him toward a life of selfish momentary pleasure; it sees not only the individual but the nation and the country; individuals and generations bound together by a moral law, with common traditions and a mission which suppressing the instinct for life closed in a brief circle of pleasure, builds up a higher life, founded on duty, a life free from the limitations of time and space, in which the individual, by self-sacrifice, the renunciation of self-interest, by death itself, can achieve that purely spiritual existence in which his value as a man consists.

The conception is therefore a spiritual one, arising from the general reaction of the century against the flaccid materialistic positivism of the nineteenth century. Anti-positivistic but positive; neither sceptical nor agnostic; neither pessimistic nor supinely optimistic as are, generally speaking, the doctrines (all negative) which place the centre of life outside man; whereas, by the exercise of his free will, man can and must create his own world.

Fascism wants man to be active and to engage in action with all his energies; it wants him to be manfully aware of the difficulties besetting him and ready to face them. It conceives of life as a struggle in which it behooves a man to win for himself a really worthy place, first of all by fitting himself (physically, morally, intellectually) to become the implement required for winning it. As for the individual, so for the nation, and so for mankind. Hence the

* From the *Enciclopedia Italiana.* English translation reprinted from: Michael Oakeshott, *The Social and Political Doctrines of Contemporary Europe.* Reprinted by permission of Cambridge University Press.

high value of culture in all its forms (artistic, religious, scientific), and the outstanding importance of education. Hence also the essential value of work, by which man subjugates nature and creates the human world (economic, political, ethical, intellectual).

This positive conception of life is obviously an ethical one. It invests the whole field of reality as well as the human activities which master it. No action is exempt from moral judgment; no activity can be despoiled of the value which a moral purpose confers on all things. Therefore life, as conceived of by the Fascist, is serious, austere, religious; all its manifestations are poised in a world sustained by moral forces and subject to spiritual responsibilities. The Fascist disdains an "easy" life.

The Fascist conception of life is a religious one, in which man is viewed in his immanent relation to a higher law, endowed with an objective will transcending the individual and raising him to conscious membership of a spiritual society. Those who perceive nothing beyond opportunistic considerations in the religious policy of the Fascist régime fail to realise that Fascism is not only a system of government but also and above all a system of thought.

In the Fascist conception of history, man is man only by virtue of the spiritual process to which he contributes as a member of the family, the social group, the nation, and in function of history to which all nations bring their contribution. Hence the great value of tradition in records, in language, in customs, in the rules of social life. Outside history man is a nonentity. Fascism is therefore opposed to all individualistic abstractions based on eighteenth century materialism; and it is opposed to all Jacobinistic utopias and innovations. It does not believe in the possibility of "happiness" on earth as conceived by the economistic literature of the eighteenth century, and it therefore rejects the teleological notion that at some future time the human family will secure a final settlement of all its difficulties. This notion runs counter to experience which teaches that life is in continual flux and in process of evolution. In politics Fascism aims at realism; in practice it desires to deal only with those problems which are the spontaneous product of historic conditions and which find or suggest their own solutions. Only by entering into the process of reality and taking possession of the forces at work within it, can man act on man and on nature.

Anti-individualistic, the Fascist conception of life stresses the importance of the State and accepts the individual only in so far as his interests coincide with those of the State, which stands for the conscience and the universal will of man as a historic entity. It is opposed to classical liberalism which arose as a reaction to absolutism and exhausted its historical function when the State became the expression of the conscience and will of the people. Liberalism denied the State in the name of the individual; Fascism reasserts the rights of the State as expressing the real essence of the individual. And if liberty is to be the attribute of living men and not of abstract dummies invented by individualistic liberalism, then Fascism stands for liberty, and for the only liberty worth having, the liberty of the State and of the individual within the State. The Fascist conception of the State is all-embracing; outside of it no human or spiritual values can exist, much less have value. Thus understood, Fascism is totalitarian, and the Fascist State—a synthesis and a unit inclusive of all values—interprets, develops, and potentiates the whole life of a people.

No individuals or groups (political parties, cultural associations, economic unions, social classes) exist outside the State. Fascism is therefore opposed to Socialism to which unity within the State (which amalgamates classes into a single economic and ethical reality) is unknown, and which sees in history nothing but the class struggle. Fascism is likewise opposed to trade-unionism as a class weapon. But when brought within the orbit of the State, Fascism recognises the real needs which gave rise to socialism and trade-unionism, giving them due weight in the guild or corporative system in which divergent interests are coordinated and harmonised in the unity of the State.

Grouped according to their several interests, individuals form classes; they form trade-unions when organised according to their several economic activities; but first and foremost they form the State, which is no mere matter of numbers, the sum of the individuals forming the majority. Fascism is therefore opposed to that form of democracy which equates a nation to the majority, lowering it to the level of the largest number; but it is the purest form of democracy if the nation be considered—as it should be—from the point of view of quality rather than quantity, as an idea, the mightiest because the most ethical, the most coherent, the truest, expressing itself in a people as the conscience and will of the few, if not, indeed, of one, and tending to express itself in the conscience and the will of the mass, of the whole group ethnically moulded by natural and historical conditions into a nation, advancing, as one conscience and one will, along the self-same line of development and spiritual formation. Not a race, nor a geographically defined region, but a people, historically perpetuating itself; a multitude unified by an idea and imbued with the will to live, the will to power, self-awareness, personality.

In so far as it is embodied in a State, this higher personality becomes a nation. It is not the nation which generates the State; that is an antiquated naturalistic concept which afforded a basis for nineteenth century publicity in favor of national governments. Rather is it the State which creates the nation, conferring volition and therefore real life on a people made aware of their moral unity.

The right to national independence does not arise from any merely literary and idealistic form of self-awareness; still less from a more or less passive and unconscious *de facto* situation, but from an active, self-aware, political will expressing itself in action and ready to prove its rights. It arises, in short, from the existence, at least *in fieri,* of a State. Indeed, it is the State which, as the expression of a universal ethical will, creates the right to national independence.

A nation, as expressed in the State, is a living, ethical entity only in so far as it is progressive. Inactivity is death. Therefore the State is not only Authority which governs and confers legal form and spiritual value on individual wills, but it is also Power which makes its will felt and respected beyond its own frontiers, thus affording practical proof of the universal character of the decisions necessary to ensure its development. This implies organisation and expansion, potential if not actual. Thus the State equates itself to the will of man, whose development cannot be checked by obstacles and which, by achieving self-expression, demonstrates its own infinity.

The Fascist State, as a higher and more powerful expression of personality, is a force, but a spiritual one. It sums up all the manifestations of the moral and intellectual life of man. Its functions cannot therefore be limited to those of enforcing order and keeping the peace, as the liberal doctrine had it. It is no mere mechanical device for defining the sphere within which the individual may duly exercise his supposed rights. The Fascist State is an inwardly accepted standard and rule of conduct, a discipline of the whole person; it permeates the will no less than the intellect. It stands for a principle which becomes the central motive of man as a member of civilised society, sinking deep down into his personality; it dwells in the heart of the man of action and of the thinker, of the artist and of the man of science: soul of the soul.

Fascism, in short, is not only a law-giver and a founder of institutions, but an educator and a promoter of spiritual life. It aims at refashioning not only the forms of life but their content—man, his character, and his faith. To achieve this purpose it enforces discipline and uses authority, entering into the soul and ruling with undisputed sway. Therefore it has chosen as its emblem the Lictor's rods, the symbol of unity, strength, and justice.

The People Shall Be Judge*

BY JOHN LOCKE

[1690]

I

To UNDERSTAND political power right, and derive it from its original, we must consider what state all men are naturally in, and that is a state of perfect freedom to order their actions and dispose of their possessions and persons as they think fit, within the bounds of the law of nature, without asking leave or depending upon the will of any other man.

A state also of equality, wherein all the power and jurisdiction is reciprocal, no one having more than another; there being nothing more evident than that creatures of the same species and rank, promiscuously born to all the same advantages of nature and the use of the same faculties, should also be equal one amongst another without subordination or subjection. . . .

But though this be a state of liberty, yet it is not a state of licence; though man in that state have an uncontrollable liberty to dispose of his person or possessions, yet he has not liberty to destroy himself, or so much as any creature in his possession, but where some nobler use than its bare preservation calls for it. The state of nature has a law of nature to govern it which obliges every one; and reason, which is that law, teaches all mankind who will but consult it that, being all equal and independent, no one ought to harm another in his life, health, liberty, or possessions. . . . Every one, as he is bound to preserve himself and not to quit his station wilfully, so by the like reason, when his own preservation comes not in competition, ought he, as much as he can, to preserve the rest of mankind, and may not, unless it be to do justice to an offender, take away or impair the life, or what tends to the preservation of life: the liberty, health, limb, or goods of another.

And that all men may be restrained from invading others' rights and from doing hurt to one another, and the law of nature be observed which willeth the peace and preservation of all mankind, the execu-

* From *The Second Treatise of Civil Government.*

tion of the law of nature is, in that state, put into every man's hands, whereby everyone has a right to punish the transgressors of that law to such a degree as may hinder its violation; for the law of nature would, as all other laws that concern men in this world, be in vain, if there were nobody that in the state of nature had a power to execute that law and thereby preserve the innocent and restrain offenders. . . .

To this strange doctrine—viz., that in the state of nature every one has the executive power of the law of nature—I doubt not but it will be objected that it is unreasonable for men to be judges in their own cases, that self-love will make men partial to themselves and their friends, and, on the other side, that ill-nature, passion, and revenge will carry them too far in punishing others, and hence nothing but confusion and disorder will follow; and that therefore God hath certainly appointed government to restrain the partiality and violence of men. I easily grant that civil government is the proper remedy for the inconveniences of the state of nature, which must certainly be great where men may be judges in their own case; since it is easy to be imagined that he who was so unjust as to do his brother an injury will scarce be so just as to condemn himself for it; but I shall desire those who make this objection to remember that absolute monarchs are but men, and if government is to be the remedy of those evils which necessarily follow from men's being judges in their own cases, and the state of nature is therefore not to be endured, I desire to know what kind of government that is, and how much better it is than the state of nature, where one man commanding a multitude has the liberty to be judge in his own case, and may do to all his subjects whatever he pleases, without the least liberty to any one to question or control those who execute his pleasure, and in whatsoever he doth, whether led by reason, mistake, or passion, must be submitted to? Much better it is in the state of nature, wherein men are not bound to submit to the unjust will of another; and if he that judges, judges amiss in his own or any other case, he is answerable for it to the rest of mankind. . . .

The natural liberty of man is to be free from any superior power on earth, and not to be under the will or legislative authority of man, but to have only the law of nature for his rule. The liberty of man in society is to be under no other legislative power but that established by consent in the commonwealth; nor under the dominion of any will or restraint of any law, but what that legislative shall enact according to the trust put in it. Freedom then is not "a liberty for every one to do what he lists, to live as he pleases, and not to be tied by any laws"; but freedom of men under government is to have a standing rule to live by, common to every one of that society and made by the legislative power erected in it, a liberty to follow my own will in all things where the rule prescribes not, and not to be subject to the inconstant, uncertain, unknown, arbitrary will of another man; as freedom of nature is to be under no other restraint but the law of nature.

This freedom from absolute, arbitrary power is so necessary to and closely joined with a man's preservation that he cannot part with it but by what forfeits his preservation and life together; for a man not having power of his own life cannot by compact or his own consent enslave himself to any one, nor put himself under the absolute arbitrary power of another to take away his life when he pleases. Nobody can give more power than he has himself; and he that cannot take away his own life cannot give another power over it. . . .

II

If man in the state of nature be so free, as has been said, if he be absolute lord of his own person and possessions, equal to the greatest, and subject to nobody, why will he part with his freedom, why will he give up his empire and subject himself to the dominion and control of any other power? To which it is obvious to answer that though in the state of nature he hath such a right, yet the enjoyment of it is very uncertain and constantly exposed to the invasion of others; for all being kings as much as he, every man his equal, and the greater part no strict observers of equity and justice, the enjoyment of the property he has in this state is very unsafe, very unsecure. This makes him willing to quit a condition which, however free, is full of fears and continual dangers; and it is not without reason that he seeks out and is willing to join in society with others who are already united, or have a mind to unite, for the mutual preservation of their lives, liberties, and estates, which I call by the general name "property."

The great and <u>chief end</u>, therefore, of men's uniting into common-

wealths and putting themselves under government is the preservation of their property. To which in the state of nature there are many things wanting:

First, There wants an established, settled, known law, received and allowed by common consent to be the standard of right and wrong and the common measure to decide all controversies between them....

Secondly, In the state of nature there wants a known and indifferent judge with authority to determine all differences according to the established law....

Thirdly, in the state of nature, there often wants power to back and support the sentence when right, and to give it due execution....

Thus mankind, notwithstanding all the privileges of the state of nature, being but in an ill condition while they remain in it, are quickly driven into society. Hence it comes to pass that we seldom find any number of men live any time together in this state. The inconveniences that they are therein exposed to by the irregular and uncertain exercise of the power every man has of punishing the transgressions of others make them take sanctuary under the established laws of government and therein seek the preservation of their property. It is this makes them so willingly give up every one his single power of punishing, to be exercised by such alone as shall be appointed to it amongst them; and by such rules as the community, or those authorized by them to that purpose, shall agree on. And in this we have the original right of both the legislative and executive power, as well as of the governments and societies themselves....

But though men when they enter into society give up the equality, liberty, and executive power they had in the state of nature into the hands of the society, to be so far disposed of by the legislative as the good of the society shall require, yet it being only with an intention in every one the better to preserve himself, his liberty, and property—for no rational creature can be supposed to change his condition with an intention to be worse—the power of the society, or legislative constituted by them, can never be supposed to extend farther than the common good, but is obliged to secure every one's property by providing against those three defects above-mentioned that made the state of nature so unsafe and uneasy. And so whoever has the legislative or supreme power of any commonwealth is bound to govern by established standing laws, promulgated and known to the people, and not by extemporary decrees; by indifferent and upright judges who are to decide controversies by those laws; and to employ the force of the community at home only in the execution of such laws, or abroad to prevent or redress foreign injuries, and secure the community from inroads and invasion. And all this to be directed to no other end but the peace, safety, and public good of the people....

The great end of men's entering into society being the enjoyment of their properties in peace and safety, and the great instrument and means of that being the laws established in that society, the first and fundamental positive law of all commonwealths is the establishing of the legislative power; as the first and fundamental natural law which is to govern even the legislative itself is the preservation of the society and, as far as will consist with the public good, of every person in it.... Though the legislative ... be the supreme power in every commonwealth yet:

It is not, nor can possibly be, absolutely arbitrary over the lives and fortunes of the people; for it being but the joint power of every member of the society given up to that person or assembly which is legislator, it can be no more than those persons had in a state of nature before they entered into society and gave up to the community; for nobody can transfer to another more power than he has in himself, and nobody has an absolute arbitrary power over himself, or over any other, to destroy his own life, or take away the life or property of another. A man, as has been proved, cannot subject himself to the arbitrary power of another; and having in the state of nature no arbitrary power over the life, liberty, or possession of another, but only so much as the law of nature gave him for the preservation of himself and the rest of mankind, this is all he doth or can give up to the commonwealth, and by it to the legislative power, so that the legislative can have no more than this. Their power, in the utmost bounds of it, is limited to the public good of the society....

Government into whatsoever hands it is put, being, as I have before shown, entrusted with this condition, and for this end, that men might have and secure their properties, the prince, or senate, however it may have power to make laws for the regulating of property between the subjects one amongst another, yet can never have a power to take to themselves the whole or any part of the subject's property without their own consent; for this would be in effect to leave them no property at all. And to let us see that even absolute power, where it is necessary, is not arbitrary by being absolute, but is still limited by that reason and confined to those ends which required it in some cases to be absolute, we need look no farther than the common practice of martial discipline; for the preservation of the army, and in it of the whole commonwealth, requires an absolute obedience to the command of every superior officer, and it is justly death to disobey or dispute the most dangerous or unreasonable of them; but yet we see that neither the sergeant, that could command a soldier to march up to the mouth of a cannon or stand in a breach where he is almost sure to perish, can command that soldier to give him one penny of his money; nor the general, that can condemn him to death for deserting his post, or for not obeying the most desperate orders, can yet, with all his absolute power of life and death, dispose of one farthing of that soldier's estate or seize one jot of his goods, whom yet he can command anything, and hang for the least disobedience. Because such a blind obedience is necessary to that end for which the commander has his power, viz., the preservation of the rest; but the disposing of his goods has nothing to do with it.

It is true, governments cannot be supported without great charge, and it is fit every one who enjoys his share of the protection should pay out of his estate his proportion for the maintenance of it. But still it must be with his own consent—*i.e.*, the consent of the majority, giving it either by themselves or their representatives chosen by them. For if any one shall claim a power to lay and levy taxes on the people, by his own authority, and without such consent of the people, he thereby invades the fundamental law of property and subverts the end of government; for what property have I in that which another may by right take, when he pleases, to himself? . . .

III

Though in a constituted commonwealth, standing upon its own basis and acting according to its own nature, that is, acting for the preservation of the community, there can be but one supreme power which is the legislative, to which all the rest are and must be subordinate, yet, the legislative being only a fiduciary power to act for certain ends, there remains still in the people a supreme power to remove or alter the legislative when they find the legislative act contrary to the trust reposed in them; for all power given with trust for the attaining an end being limited by that end, whenever that end **is manifestly neglected or opposed, the trust must necessarily be** forfeited and the power devolve into the hands of those that gave it, who may place it anew where they shall think best for their safety and security. And thus the community perpetually retains a supreme power of saving themselves from the attempts and designs of any-body, even of their legislators, whenever they shall be so foolish or so wicked as to lay and carry on designs against the liberties and properties of the subject; for no man or society of men having a power to deliver up their preservation, or consequently the means of it, to the absolute will and arbitrary dominion of another, whenever any one shall go about to bring them into such a slavish condition, they will always have a right to preserve what they have not a power to part with, and to rid themselves of those who invade this fundamental, sacred, and unalterable law of self-preservation for which they entered into society, and thus the community may be said in this respect to be always the supreme power, but not as considered under any form of government, because this power of the people can never take place till the government be dissolved. . . .

In these and the like cases, when the government is dissolved, the people are at liberty to provide for themselves by erecting a new legislative, differing from the other by the change of persons or form, or both, as they shall find it most for their safety and good; for the society can never by the fault of another lose the native and original right it has to preserve itself, which can only be done by a settled legislative, and a fair and impartial execution of the laws made by it. But the state of mankind is not so miserable that they are not capable of using this remedy till it be too late to look for any. To tell people they may provide for themselves by erecting a new legislative, when by oppression, artifice, or being delivered over to a foreign power, their old one is gone, is only to tell them they may expect relief when it is too late and the evil is past cure. This is in effect no more than to bid them first be slaves, and then to take care of their liberty; and when their chains are on, tell them they may act like freemen. This, if barely so, is rather mockery than relief; and men can never be secure from tyranny if there be no means to escape it till they are perfectly under it; and therefore it is that they have not only a right to get out of it, but to prevent it. . . .

The reason why men enter into society is the preservation of their property; and the end why they choose and authorize a legislative is that there may be laws made and rules set as guards and fences to

the properties of all the members of the society, to limit the power
and moderate the dominion of every part and member of the society.
For since it can never be supposed to be the will of the society that
the legislative should have a power to destroy that which every one
designs to secure by entering into society, and for which the people
submitted themselves to legislators of their own making, whenever
the legislators endeavor to take away and destroy the property of the
people, or to reduce them to slavery under arbitrary power, they put
themselves into a state of war with the people, who are thereupon
absolved from any further obedience, and are left to the common
refuge which God hath provided for all men against force and violence. Whensoever, therefore, the legislative shall transgress this
fundamental rule of society, and either by ambition, fear, folly or
corruption, endeavour to grasp themselves, or put into the hands
of any other, an absolute power over the lives, liberties, and estates
of the people, by this breach of trust they forfeit the power the people
had put into their hands for quite contrary ends, and it devolves to
the people who have a right to resume their original liberty, and by
the establishment of a new legislative, such as they shall think fit,
provide for their own safety and security, which is the end for which
they are in society. What I have said here concerning the legislative
in general holds true also concerning the supreme executor, who
having a double trust put in him—both to have a part in the legislative
and the supreme execution of the law—acts against both when he
goes about to set up his own arbitrary will as the law of the society. . . .
What power they ought to have in the society who thus employ it
contrary to the trust that went along with it in its first institution is
easy to determine; and one cannot but see that he who has once
attempted any such thing as this cannot any longer be trusted. . . .

The end of government is the good of mankind. And which is best
for mankind? That the people should be always exposed to the
boundless will of tyranny, or that the rulers should be sometimes
liable to be opposed when they grow exorbitant in the use of their
power and employ it for the destruction and not the preservation of
the properties of their people?

Nor let any one say that mischief can arise from hence, as often as
it shall please a busy head or turbulent spirit to desire the alteration
of the government. It is true such men may stir whenever they please,
but it will be only to their own just ruin and perdition; for till the

mischief be grown general, and the ill designs of the rulers become visible, or their attempts sensible to the greater part, the people who are more disposed to suffer than right themselves by resistance are not apt to stir. The examples of particular injustice or oppression of here and there an unfortunate man, moves them not. But if they universally have a persuasion grounded upon manifest evidence that designs are carrying on against their liberties, and the general course and tendency of things cannot but give them strong suspicions of the evil intention of their governors, who is to be blamed for it? Who can help it if they, who might avoid it, bring themselves into this suspicion? Are the people to be blamed if they have the sense of rational creatures, and can think of things no otherwise than as they find and feel them? And is it not rather their fault who put things into such a posture that they would not have them thought to be as they are? I grant that the pride, ambition, and turbulency of private men have sometimes caused great disorders in commonwealths, and factions have been fatal to states and kingdoms. But whether the mischief hath oftener begun in the people's wantonness and a desire to cast off the lawful authority of their rulers, or in the rulers' insolence and endeavours to get and exercise an arbitrary power over their people—whether oppression or disobedience gave the first rise to the disorder, I leave it to impartial history to determine. . . .

Here, it is like, the common question will be made: "Who shall be judge whether the prince or legislative act contrary to their trust?" To this I reply: The people shall be judge; for who shall be judge whether his trustee or deputy acts well and according to the trust reposed in him but he who deputes him and must, by having deputed him, have still a power to discard him when he fails in his trust? If this be reasonable in particular cases of private men, why should it be otherwise in that of the greatest moment where the welfare of millions is concerned, and also where the evil, if not prevented, is greater and the redress very difficult, dear, and dangerous? . . .

If a controversy arise betwixt a prince and some of the people in a matter where the law is silent or doubtful, and the thing be of great consequence, I should think the proper umpire in such a case should be the body of the people; for in cases where the prince hath a trust reposed in him and is dispensed from the common ordinary rules of the law, there, if any men find themselves aggrieved and think the prince acts contrary to or beyond that trust, who so proper to judge as the body of the people—who, at first, lodged that trust in him—how far they meant it should extend? But if the prince, or whoever they be in the administration, decline that way of determination, the appeal then lies nowhere but to heaven; force between either persons who have no known superior on earth, or which permits no appeal to a judge on earth, being properly a state of war wherein the appeal lies only to heaven; and in that state the injured party must judge for himself when he will think fit to make use of that appeal and put himself upon it.

To conclude, the power that every individual gave the society when he entered into it can never revert to the individuals again as long as the society lasts, but will always remain in the community, because without this there can be no community, no commonwealth, which is contrary to the original agreement; so also when the society hath placed the legislative in any assembly of men, to continue in them and their successors with direction and authority for providing such successors, the legislative can never revert to the people whilst that government lasts, because having provided a legislative with power to continue for ever, they have given up their political power to the legislative and cannot resume it. But if they have set limits to the duration of their legislative and made this supreme power in any person or assembly only temporary, or else when by the mis-carriages of those in authority it is forfeited, upon the forfeiture, or at the determination of the time set, it reverts to the society, and the people have a right to act as supreme and continue the legislative in themselves, or erect a new form, or under the old form place it in new hands, as they think good.

Crito

BY PLATO

[4th Century, B.C.]

PERSONS OF THE DIALOGUE

SOCRATES   CRITO

SCENE:—*The Prison of Socrates*

Socrates. WHY have you come at this hour, Crito? it must be quite early?

Crito. Yes, certainly.

Soc. What is the exact time?

Cr. The dawn is breaking.

Soc. I wonder that the keeper of the prison would let you in.

Cr. He knows me, because I often come, Socrates; moreover, I have done him a kindness.

Soc. And are you only just arrived?

Cr. No, I came some time ago.

Soc. Then why did you sit and say nothing, instead of at once awakening me?

Cr. I should not have liked myself, Socrates, to be in such great trouble and unrest as you are—indeed I should not: I have been watching with amazement your peaceful slumbers; and for that reason I did not awake you, because I wished to minimize the pain. I have always thought you to be of a happy disposition; but never did I see anything like the easy, tranquil manner in which you bear this calamity.

Soc. Why, Crito, when a man has reached my age he ought not to be repining at the approach of death.

Cr. And yet other old men find themselves in similar misfortunes, and age does not prevent them from repining.

Soc. That is true. But you have not told me why you come at this early hour.

Cr. I come to bring you a message which is sad and painful; not, as I believe, to yourself, but to all of us who are your friends, and saddest of all to me.

Soc. What? Has the ship come from Delos, on the arrival of which I am to die?

Cr. No, the ship has not actually arrived, but she will probably be here to-day, as persons who have come from Sunium tell me that they left her there; and therefore to-morrow, Socrates, will be the last day of your life.

Soc. Very well, Crito; if such is the will of God, I am willing; but my belief is that there will be a delay of a day.

Cr. Why do you think so?

Soc. I will tell you. I am to die on the day after the arrival of the ship.

Cr. Yes; that is what the authorities say.

Soc. But I do not think that the ship will be here until to-morrow; this I infer from a vision which I had last night, or rather only just now, when you fortunately allowed me to sleep.

Cr. And what was the nature of the vision?

Soc. There appeared to me the likeness of a woman, fair and comely, clothed in bright raiment, who called to me and said: O Socrates,

'The third day hence to fertile Phthia shalt thou go[1].'

Cr. What a singular dream, Socrates!

Soc. There can be no doubt about the meaning, Crito, I think.

Cr. Yes; the meaning is only too clear. But, oh! my beloved Socrates, let me entreat you once more to take my advice and escape. For if you die I shall not only lose a friend who can never be replaced, but there is another evil: people who do not know you and me will believe that I might have saved you if I had been willing to give money, but that I did not care. Now, can there be a worse disgrace than this—that I should be thought to value money more than the life of a friend? For the many will not be persuaded that I wanted you to escape, and that you refused.

Soc. But why, my dear Crito, should we care about the opinion of the many? Good men, and they are the only persons who are worth considering, will think of these things truly as they occurred.

---

[1] Homer, *Iliad* ix. 363.

Cr. But you see, Socrates, that the opinion of the many must be regarded, for what is now happening shows that they can do the greatest evil to any one who has lost their good opinion.

Soc. I only wish it were so, Crito; and that the many could do the greatest evil; for then they would also be able to do the greatest good—and what a fine thing this would be! But in reality they can do neither; for they cannot make a man either wise or foolish; and whatever they do is the result of chance.

Cr. Well, I will not dispute with you; but please to tell me, Socrates, whether you are not acting out of regard to me and your other friends: are you not afraid that if you escape from prison we may get into trouble with the informers for having stolen you away, and lose either the whole or a great part of our property; or that even a worse evil may happen to us? Now, if you fear on our account, be at ease; for in order to save you, we ought surely to run this, or even a greater risk; be persuaded, then, and do as I say.

Soc. Yes, Crito, that is one fear which you mention, but by no means the only one.

Cr. Fear not—there are persons who are willing to get you out of prison at no great cost; and as for the informers, they are far from being exorbitant in their demands—a little money will satisfy them. My means, which are certainly ample, are at your service, and if you have a scruple about spending all mine, here are strangers who will give you the use of theirs; and one of them, Simmias the Theban, has brought a large sum of money for this very purpose; and Cebes and many others are prepared to spend their money in helping you to escape. I say, therefore, do not hesitate on our account, and do not say, as you did in the court, that you will have a difficulty in knowing what to do with yourself anywhere else. For men will love you in other places to which you may go, and not in Athens only; there are friends of mine in Thessaly, if you like to go to them, who will value and protect you, and no Thessalian will give you any trouble. Nor can I think that you are at all justified, Socrates, in betraying your own life when you might be saved; in acting thus you are playing into the hands of your enemies, who are hurrying on your destruction. And further I should say that you are deserting your own children; for you might bring them up and educate them; instead of which you go away and leave them, and they will have to take their chance; and if they do not meet with the usual fate of orphans, there will be small thanks to you. No man should bring children into the world who is unwilling to persevere to the end in their nurture and education. But you appear to be choosing the easier part, not the better and manlier, which would have been more becoming in one who professes to care for virtue in all his actions, like yourself. And indeed, I am ashamed not only of you, but of us who are your friends, when I reflect that the whole business will be attributed entirely to our want of courage. The trial need never have come on, or might have been managed differently; and this last act, or crowning folly, will seem to have occurred through our negligence and cowardice, who might have saved you, if we had been good for anything; and you might have saved yourself, for there was no difficulty at all. See now, Socrates, how sad and discreditable are the consequences, both to us and you. Make up your mind then, or rather have your mind already made up, for the time of deliberation is over, and there is only one thing to be done, which must be done this very night, and if we delay at all will be no longer practicable or possible; I beseech you therefore, Socrates, be persuaded by me, and do as I say.

Soc. Dear Crito, your zeal is invaluable, if a right one; but if wrong, the greater the zeal the greater the danger; and therefore we ought to consider whether I shall or shall not do as you say. For I am and always have been one of those natures who must be guided by reason, whatever the reason may be which upon reflection appears to me to be the best; and now that this chance has befallen me, I cannot repudiate my own words: the principles which I have hitherto honoured and revered I still honour, and unless we can at once find other and better principles, I am certain not to agree with you; no, not even if the power of the multitude could inflict many more imprisonments, confiscations, deaths, frightening us like children with hobgoblin terrors. What will be the fairest way of considering the question? Shall I return to your old argument about the opinions of men?—we were saying that some of them are to be regarded, and others not. Now were we right in maintaining this before I was condemned? And has the argument which was once good now proved to be talk for the sake of talking —mere childish nonsense? That is what I want to consider with your help, Crito:—whether, under my present circumstances, the argument appears to be in any way different or not; and is to be allowed by me or disallowed. That argument, which, as I believe, is maintained by many persons of authority, was to the effect, as I was saying, that the opinions of some men are to be regarded, and of other men not to be regarded. Now you, Crito, are not going to die to-morrow—at least, there is no human probability of this— and therefore you are disinterested and not liable to be deceived by the circumstances in which you are placed. Tell me then, whether I am right in saying that some opinions, and the opinions of some men only, are to be valued, and that other opinions, and the opinions of other men, are not to be valued. I ask you whether I was right in maintaining this?

Cr. Certainly.

Soc. The good are to be regarded, and not the bad?

Cr. Yes.

Soc. And the opinions of the wise are good, and the opinions of the unwise are evil?

Cr. Certainly.

Soc. And what was said about another matter? Is the pupil who devotes himself to the practice of gymnastics supposed to attend to the praise and blame and opinion of every man, or of one man only—his physician or trainer, whoever he may be?

Cr. Of one man only.

Soc. And he ought to fear the censure and welcome the praise of that one only, and not of the many?

Cr. Clearly so.

Soc. And he ought to act and train, and eat and drink in the way which seems good to his single master who has understanding, rather than according to the opinion of all other men put together?

Cr. True.

Soc. And if he disobeys and disregards the opinion and approval of the one, and regards the opinion of the many who have no understanding, will he not suffer evil?

Cr. Certainly he will.

Soc. And what will the evil be, whither tending and what affecting, in the disobedient person?

Cr. Clearly, affecting the body; that is what is destroyed by the evil.

Soc. Very good; and is not this true, Crito, of other things which we need not separately enumerate? In questions of just and unjust, fair and foul, good and evil, which are the subjects of our present consultation, ought we to follow the opinion of the many and to fear them; or the opinion of the one man who has understanding? ought we not to fear and reverence him more than all the rest of the world: and if we desert him shall we not destroy and injure that principle in us which may be assumed to be improved by justice and deteriorated by injustice;—there is such a principle?

Cr. Certainly there is, Socrates.

Soc. Take a parallel instance:—if, acting under the advice of those who have no understanding, we destroy that which is improved by health and is deteriorated by disease, would life be worth having? And that which has been destroyed is—the body?

Cr. Yes.

Soc. Could we live, having an evil and corrupted body?

Cr. Certainly not.

Soc. And will life be worth having, if that higher part of man be destroyed, which is improved by justice and depraved by injustice? Do we suppose that principle, whatever it may be in man, which has to do with justice and injustice, to be inferior to the body?

Cr. Certainly not.

Soc. More honourable than the body?

Cr. Far more.

Soc. Then, my friend, we must not regard what the many say of us: but what he, the one man who has understanding of just and unjust, will say, and what the truth will say. And therefore you begin in error when you advise that we should regard the opinion of the many about just and unjust, good and evil, honourable and dishonourable.—'Well,' some one will say, 'but the many can kill us.'

Cr. Yes, Socrates; that will clearly be the answer.

Soc. And it is true: but still I find with surprise that the old argument is unshaken as ever. And I should like to know whether I may say the same of another proposition—that not life, but a good life, is to be chiefly valued?

Cr. Yes, that also remains unshaken.

Soc. And a good life is equivalent to a just and honourable one—that holds also?

Cr. Yes, it does.

Soc. From these premises I proceed to argue the question whether I ought or ought not to try and escape without the consent of the Athenians: and if I am clearly right in escaping, then I will make the attempt; but if not, I will abstain. The other considerations which you mention, of money and loss of character and the duty of educating one's children, are, I fear, only the doctrines of the multitude, who would be as ready to restore people to life, if they were able, as they are to put them to death—and with as little reason. But now, since the argument has thus far prevailed, the only question which remains to be considered is, whether we shall do rightly either in escaping or in suffering others to aid in our escape and paying them in money and thanks, or whether in reality we shall not do rightly; and if the latter, then death or any other calamity which may ensue on my remaining here must not be allowed to enter into the calculation.

Cr. I think that you are right, Socrates; how then shall we proceed?

Soc. Let us consider the matter together, and do you either refute me if you can, and I will be convinced; or else cease, my dear friend, from repeating to me that I ought to escape against the wishes of the Athenians: for I highly value your attempts to persuade me to do so, but I may not be persuaded against my own better judgment. And now please to consider my first position, and try how you can best answer me.

Cr. I will.

Soc. Are we to say that we are never intentionally to do wrong, or that in one way we ought and in another we ought not to do wrong, or is doing wrong always evil and dishonourable, as I was just now saying, and as has been already acknowledged by us? Are all our former admissions which were made within a few days to be thrown away? And have we, at our age, been earnestly discoursing with one another all our life long only to discover that we are no better than children? Or, in spite of the opinion of the many, and in spite of consequences whether better or worse, shall we insist on the truth of what was then said, that injustice is always an evil and dishonour to him who acts unjustly? Shall we say so or not?

Cr. Yes.

Soc. Then we must do no wrong?

Cr. Certainly not.

Soc. Nor when injured injure in return, as the many imagine; for we must injure no one at all?

Cr. Clearly not.

Soc. Again, Crito, may we do evil?

Cr. Surely not, Socrates.

Soc. And what of doing evil in return for evil, which is the morality of the many—is that just or not?

Cr. Not just.

Soc. For doing evil to another is the same as injuring him?

Cr. Very true.

Soc. Then we ought not to retaliate or render evil for evil to any one, whatever evil we may have suffered from him. But I would have you consider, Crito, whether you really mean what you are saying. For this opinion has never been held, and never will be held, by any considerable number of persons; and those who are agreed and those who are not agreed upon this point have no common ground, and can only despise one another when they see how widely they differ. Tell me, then, whether you agree with and assent to my first principle, that neither injury nor retaliation nor warding off evil by evil is ever right. And shall that be the premiss of our argument? Or do you decline and dissent from this? For so I have ever thought, and continue to think; but, if you are of another opinion, let me hear what you have to say. If, however, you remain of the same mind as formerly, I will proceed to the next step.

Cr. You may proceed, for I have not changed my mind.

Soc. Then I will go on to the next point, which may be put in the form of a question:—Ought a man to do what he admits to be right, or ought he to betray the right?

Cr. He ought to do what he thinks right.

Soc. But if this is true, what is the application? In leaving the prison against the will of the Athenians, do I wrong any? or rather do I not wrong those whom I ought least to wrong? Do I not desert the principles which were acknowledged by us to be just—what do you say?

Cr. I cannot tell, Socrates; for I do not know.

Soc. Then consider the matter in this way:—Imagine that I am about to play truant (you may call the proceeding by any name which you like), and the laws and the government come and interrogate me: 'Tell us, Socrates,' they say; 'what are you about?

are you not going by an act of yours to overturn us—the laws, and
the whole state, as far as in you lies? Do you imagine that a state
can subsist and not be overthrown, in which the decisions of law
have no power, but are set aside and trampled upon by individuals?' What will be our answer, Crito, to these and the like words?
Any one, and especially a rhetorician, will have a good deal to say
on behalf of the law which requires a sentence to be carried out. He
will argue that this law should not be set aside; and shall we reply,
'Yes; but the state has injured us and given an unjust sentence.'
Suppose I say that?

  Cr. Very good, Socrates.

  Soc. 'And was that our agreement with you?' the law would answer; 'or were you to abide by the sentence of the state?' And if I
were to express my astonishment at their words, the law would
probably add: 'Answer, Socrates, instead of opening your eyes—
you are in the habit of asking and answering questions. Tell us,—
What complaint have you to make against us which justifies you in
attempting to destroy us and the state? In the first place did we
not bring you into existence? Your father married your mother by
our aid and begat you. Say whether you have any objection to urge
against those of us who regulate marriage?' None, I should reply.
'Or against those of us who after birth regulate the nurture and
education of children, in which you also were trained? Were not
the laws, which have the charge of education, right in commanding
your father to train you in music and gymnastic?' Right, I should
reply. 'Well then, since you were brought into the world and nurtured and educated by us, can you deny in the first place that you
are our child and slave, as your fathers were before you? And if
this is true you are not on equal terms with us; nor can you think
that you have a right to do to us what we are doing to you. Would
you have any right to strike or revile or do any other evil to your
father or your master, if you had one, because you have been struck
or reviled by him, or received some other evil at his hands?—you
would not say this? And because we think right to destroy you, do
you think that you have any right to destroy us in return, and your
country as far as in you lies? Will you, O professor of true virtue,
pretend that you are justified in this? Has a philosopher like you
failed to discover that our country is more to be valued and higher
and holier far than mother or father or any ancestor, and more to

be regarded in the eyes of the gods and of men of understanding? also to be soothed, and gently and reverently entreated when angry, even more than a father, and either to be persuaded, or if not persuaded, to be obeyed? And when we are punished by her, whether with imprisonment or stripes, the punishment is to be endured in silence; and if she leads us to wounds or death in battle, thither we follow as is right; neither may any one yield or retreat or leave his rank, but whether in battle or in a court of law, or in any other place, he must do what his city and his country order him; or he must change their view of what is just: and if he may do no violence to his father or mother, much less may he do violence to his country.' What answer shall we make to this, Crito? Do the laws speak truly, or do they not?

Cr. I think that they do.

Soc. Then the laws will say, 'Consider, Socrates, if we are speaking truly that in your present attempt you are going to do us an injury. For, having brought you into the world, and nurtured and educated you, and given you and every other citizen a share in every good which we had to give, we further proclaim to any Athenian by the liberty which we allow him, that if he does not like us when he has become of age and has seen the ways of the city, and made our acquaintance, he may go where he pleases and take his goods with him. None of us laws will forbid him or interfere with him. Any one who does not like us and the city, and who wants to emigrate to a colony or to any other city, may go where he likes, retaining his property. But he who has experience of the manner in which we order justice and administer the state, and still remains, has entered into an implied contract that he will do as we command him. And he who disobeys us is, as we maintain, thrice wrong; first, because in disobeying us he is disobeying his parents; secondly, because we are the authors of his education; thirdly, because he has made an agreement with us that he will duly obey our commands; and he neither obeys them nor convinces us that our commands are unjust; and we do not rudely impose them, but give him the alternative of obeying or convincing us;—that is what we offer, and he does neither.

'These are the sort of accusations to which, as we were saying, you, Socrates, will be exposed if you accomplish your intentions; you, above all other Athenians.' Suppose now I ask, why I rather

than anybody else? they will justly retort upon me that I above all
other men have acknowledged the agreement. 'There is clear proof,'
they will say, 'Socrates, that we and the city were not displeasing
to you. Of all Athenians you have been the most constant resident
in the city, which, as you never leave, you may be supposed to
love. For you never went out of the city either to see the games,
except once when you went to the Isthmus, or to any other place
unless when you were on military service; nor did you travel as
other men do. Nor had you any curiosity to know other states or
their laws: your affections did not go beyond us and our state; we
were your special favourites, and you acquiesced in our government
of you; and here in this city you begat your children, which is a
proof of your satisfaction. Moreover, you might in the course of the
trial, if you had liked, have fixed the penalty at banishment; the
state which refuses to let you go now would have let you go then.
But you pretended that you preferred death to exile, and that you
were not unwilling to die. And now you have forgotten these fine
sentiments, and pay no respect to us the laws, of whom you are the
destroyer; and are doing what only a miserable slave would do,
running away and turning your back upon the compacts and agreements which you made as a citizen. And first of all answer this very
question: Are we right in saying that you agreed to be governed
according to us in deed, and not in word only? Is that true or not?'
How shall we answer, Crito? Must we not assent?

Cr. We cannot help it, Socrates.

Soc. Then will they not say: 'You, Socrates, are breaking the
covenants and agreements which you made with us at your leisure, not in any haste or under any compulsion or deception, but
after you have had seventy years to think of them, during which
time you were at liberty to leave the city, if we were not to your
mind, or if our covenants appeared to you to be unfair. You had
your choice, and might have gone either to Lacedaemon or Crete,
both which states are often praised by you for their good government, or to some other Hellenic or foreign state. Whereas you,
above all other Athenians, seemed to be so fond of the state, or, in
other words, of us her laws (and who would care about a state
which has no laws?), that you never stirred out of her; the halt, the
blind, the maimed were not more stationary in her than you were.
And now you run away and forsake your agreements. Not so, Soc-

rates, if you will take our advice; do not make yourself ridiculous by escaping out of the city.

'For just consider, if you transgress and err in this sort of way, what good will you do either to yourself or to your friends? That your friends will be driven into exile and deprived of citizenship, or will lose their property, is tolerably certain; and you yourself, if you fly to one of the neighbouring cities, as, for example, Thebes or Megara, both of which are well governed, will come to them as an enemy, Socrates, and their government will be against you, and all patriotic citizens will cast an evil eye upon you as a subverter of the laws, and you will confirm in the minds of the judges the justice of their own condemnation of you. For he who is a corrupter of the laws is more than likely to be a corrupter of the young and foolish portion of mankind. Will you then flee from well-ordered cities and virtuous men? and is existence worth having on these terms? Or will you go to them without shame, and talk to them, Socrates? And what will you say to them? What you say here about virtue and justice and institutions and laws being the best things among men? Would that be decent of you? Surely not. But if you go away from well-governed states to Crito's friends in Thessaly, where there is great disorder and licence, they will be charmed to hear the tale of your escape from prison, set off with ludicrous particulars of the manner in which you were wrapped in a goatskin or some other disguise, and metamorphosed as the manner is of runaways; but will there be no one to remind you that in your old age you were not ashamed to violate the most sacred laws from a miserable desire of a little more life? Perhaps not, if you keep them in a good temper; but if they are out of temper you will hear many degrading things; you will live, but how?—as the flatterer of all men, and the servant of all men; and doing what?—eating and drinking in Thessaly, having gone abroad in order that you may get a dinner. And where will be your fine sentiments about justice and virtue? Say that you wish to live for the sake of your children—you want to bring them up and educate them—will you take them into Thessaly and deprive them of Athenian citizenship? Is this the benefit which you will confer upon them? Or are you under the impression that they will be better cared for and educated here if you are still alive, although absent from them; for your friends will take care of them? Do you fancy that if you are an inhabitant of

Thessaly they will take care of them, and if you are an inhabitant of the other world that they will not take care of them? Nay; but if they who call themselves friends are good for anything, they will— to be sure they will.

'Listen, then, Socrates, to us who have brought you up. Think not of life and children first, and of justice afterwards, but of justice first, that you may be justified before the princes of the world below. For neither will you nor any that belong to you be happier or holier or juster in this life, or happier in another, if you do as Crito bids. Now you depart in innocence, a sufferer and not a doer of evil; a victim, not of the laws but of men. But if you go forth, returning evil for evil, and injury for injury, breaking the covenants and agreements which you have made with us, and wronging those whom you ought least of all to wrong, that is to say, yourself, your friends, your country, and us, we shall be angry with you while you live, and our brethren, the laws in the world below, will receive you as an enemy; for they will know that you have done your best to destroy us. Listen, then, to us and not to Crito.'

This, dear Crito, is the voice which I seem to hear murmuring in my ears, like the sound of the flute in the ears of the mystic; that voice, I say, is humming in my ears, and prevents me from hearing any other. And I know that anything more which you may say will be vain. Yet speak, if you have anything to say.

Cr. I have nothing to say, Socrates.

Soc. Leave me then, Crito, to fulfil the will of God, and to follow whither he leads.

Civil Disobedience*

BY HENRY DAVID THOREAU

[1849]

I HEARTILY accept the motto—"That government is best which governs least"; and I should like to see it acted up to more rapidly and systematically. Carried out, it finally amounts to this, which also I believe—"That government is best which governs not at all"; and when men are prepared for it, that will be the kind of government which they will have. Government is at best but an expedient; but most governments are usually, and all governments are sometimes, inexpedient. . . .

This American government—what is it but a tradition, though a recent one, endeavoring to transmit itself unimpaired to posterity, but each instant losing some of its integrity? It has not the vitality and force of a single living man; for a single man can bend it to his will. It is a sort of wooden gun to the people themselves. But it is not the less necessary for this; for the people must have some complicated machinery or other, and hear its din, to satisfy that idea of government which they have. Governments show thus how successfully men can be imposed on, even impose on themselves, for their own advantage. It is excellent, we must all allow. Yet this government never of itself furthered any enterprise, but by the alacrity with which it got out of its way. *It* does not keep the country free. *It* does not settle the West. *It* does not educate. The character inherent in the American people has done all that has been accomplished; and it would have done somewhat more, if the government had not sometimes got in its way. For government is an expedient by which men would fain succeed in letting one another alone; and, as has been said, when it is most expedient, the governed are most let alone by it. . . .

But to speak practically and as a citizen, unlike those who call themselves no-government men, I ask for, not at once no government, but *at once* a better government. Let every man make known what

---

* From "Civil Disobedience," first published in *Aesthetic Papers*, 1849.

kind of government would command his respect, and that will be one step toward obtaining it.

After all, the practical reason why, when the power is once in the hands of the people, a majority are permitted, and for a long period continue, to rule is not because they are most likely to be in the right, nor because this seems fairest to the minority, but because they are physically the strongest. But a government in which the majority rule in all cases cannot be based on justice, even as far as men understand it. Can there not be a government in which majorities do not virtually decide right and wrong, but conscience?—in which majorities decide only those questions to which the rule of expediency is applicable? Must the citizen ever for a moment, or in the least degree, resign his conscience to the legislator? Why has every man a conscience, then? I think that we should be men first, and subjects afterward. It is not desirable to cultivate a respect for the law, so much as for the right. The only obligation which I have a right to assume is to do at any time what I think right. It is truly enough said, that a corporation has no conscience; but a corporation of conscientious men is a corporation *with* a conscience. Law never made men a whit more just; and, by means of their respect for it, even the well-disposed are daily made the agents of injustice. . . .

How does it become a man to behave toward this American government to-day? I answer, that he cannot without disgrace be associated with it. I cannot for an instant recognize that political organization as *my* government which is the *slave's* government also.

All men recognize the right of revolution; that is, the right to refuse allegiance to, and to resist, the government, when its tyranny or its inefficiency are great and unendurable. But almost all say that such is not the case now. But such was the case, they think, in the Revolution of '75. If one were to tell me that this was a bad government because it taxed certain foreign commodities brought to its ports, it is most probable that I should not make an ado about it, for I can do without them. All machines have their friction; and possibly this does enough good to counterbalance the evil. At any rate, it is a great evil to make a stir about it. But when the friction comes to have its machine, and oppression and robbery are organized, I say, let us not have such a machine any longer. In other words, when a sixth of the population of a nation which has undertaken to be the

refuge of liberty are slaves, ... I think that it is not too soon for honest
men to rebel and revolutionize. ...

Unjust laws exist: shall we be content to obey them, or shall we
endeavor to amend them, and obey them until we have succeeded,
or shall we transgress them at once? Men generally, under such a
government as this, think that they ought to wait until they have
persuaded the majority to alter them. They think that, if they should
resist, the remedy would be worse than the evil. But it is the fault
of the government itself that the remedy *is* worse than the evil. *It*
makes it worse. Why is it not more apt to anticipate and provide for
reform? Why does it not cherish its wise minority? Why does it
cry and resist before it is hurt? Why does it not encourage its citizens
to be on the alert to point out its faults, and *do* better than it would
have them? Why does it always crucify Christ, and excommunicate
Copernicus and Luther, and pronounce Washington and Franklin
rebels? ...

If the injustice is part of the necessary friction of the machine of
government, let it go, let it go: perchance it will wear smooth—
certainly the machine will wear out. If the injustice has a spring, or
a pulley, or a rope, or a crank, exclusively for itself, then perhaps you
may consider whether the remedy will not be worse than the evil;
but if it is of such a nature that it requires you to be the agent of
injustice to another, then, I say, break the law. Let your life be a
counter friction to stop the machine. What I have to do is to see, at
any rate, that I do not lend myself to the wrong which I condemn.

As for adopting the ways which the state has provided for remedy-
ing the evil, I know not of such ways. They take too much time, and
a man's life will be gone. I have other affairs to attend to. I came into
this world, not chiefly to make this a good place to live in, but to
live in it, be it good or bad. A man has not everything to do, but something; and because he cannot do *everything,* it is not necessary that
he should do *something* wrong. It is not my business to be petitioning
the Governor or the Legislature any more than it is theirs to petition
me; and if they should not hear my petition, what should I do then?
But in this case the state has provided no way: its very Constitution
is the evil. This may seem to be harsh and stubborn and unconcilia-
tory; but it is to treat with the utmost kindness and consideration the
only spirit that can appreciate or deserves it. So is all change for the
better, like birth and death, which convulse the body.

I do not hesitate to say, that those who call themselves Abolitionists should at once effectually withdraw their support, both in person and property, from the Government of Massachusetts and not wait till they constitute a majority of one, before they suffer the right to prevail through them. I think that it is enough if they have God on their side, without waiting for that other one. Moreover, any man more right than his neighbors constitutes a majority of one already.

I meet this American government, or its representative, the state government, directly, and face to face, once a year—no more—in the person of its tax-gatherer; this is the only mode in which a man situated as I am necessarily meets it; and it then says distinctly, Recognize me; and the simplest, most effectual, and, in the present posture of affairs, the indispensablest mode of treating with it on this head, of expressing your little satisfaction with and love for it, is to deny it then. . . . I know this well, that if one thousand, if one hundred, if ten men whom I could name—if ten *honest* men only—ay, if *one* HONEST man, in this State of Massachusetts, *ceasing to hold slaves,* were actually to withdraw from this copartnership, and be locked up in the county jail therefor, it would be the abolition of slavery in America. For it matters not how small the beginning may seem to be: what is once well done is done forever. . . .

Under a government which imprisons any unjustly, the true place for a just man is also a prison. The proper place to-day, the only place which Massachusetts has provided for her freer and less desponding spirits, is in her prisons, to be put out and locked out of the State by her own act, as they have already put themselves out by their principles. It is there that the fugitive slave . . . and the Indian come to plead the wrongs of his race should find them; on that separate, but more free and honorable ground, where the State places those who are not *with* her, but *against* her—the only house in a slave State in which a free man can abide with honor. If any think that their influence would be lost there, and their voices no longer afflict the ear of the State, that they would not be as an enemy within its walls, they do not know by how much truth is stronger than error, nor how much more eloquently and effectively he can combat injustice who has experienced a little in his own person. Cast your whole vote, not a strip of paper merely, but your whole influence. A minority is powerless while it conforms to the majority; it is not even a minority then; but it is irresistible when it clogs by its whole weight. If the alternative is to keep all just men in prison, or give up war and slavery, the State will not hesitate which to choose. If a thousand men were not to pay their tax-bills this year, that would not be a violent and bloody measure, as it would be to pay them, and enable the State to commit violence and shed innocent blood. This is, in fact, the definition of a peaceable revolution, if any such is possible. If the tax-gatherer, or any other public officer, asks me, as one has done, "But what shall I do?" my answer is, "If you really wish to do anything, resign your office." When the subject has refused allegiance, and the officer has resigned his office, then the revolution is accomplished. But even suppose blood should flow. Is there not a sort of blood shed when the conscience is wounded? Through this wound a man's real manhood and immortality flow out, and he bleeds to an everlasting death. I see this blood flowing now. . . .

When I converse with the freest of my neighbors, I perceive that, whatever they may say about the magnitude and seriousness of the question, and their regard for the public tranquillity, the long and the short of the matter is, that they cannot spare the protection of the existing government, and they dread the consequences to their property and families of disobedience to it. For my own part, I should not like to think that I ever rely on the protection of the State. But, if I deny the authority of the State when it presents its tax-bill, it will soon take and waste all my property, and so harass me and my children without end. This is hard. This makes it impossible for a man to live honestly, and at the same time comfortably, in outward respects. It will not be worth the while to accumulate property; that would be sure to go again. You must hire or squat somewhere, and raise but a small crop, and eat that soon. You must live within yourself, and depend upon yourself always tucked up and ready for a start, and not have many affairs. A man may grow rich in Turkey even, if he will be in all respects a good subject of the Turkish government. Confucius said: "If a state is governed by the principles of reason, poverty and misery are subjects of shame; if a state is not governed by the principles of reason, riches and honors are the subjects of shame." No: until I want the protection of Massachusetts to be extended to me in some distant Southern port, where my liberty is endangered, or until I am bent solely on building up an estate at home by peaceful enterprise, I can afford to refuse allegiance to Massachusetts, and her right to my property and life. It costs me less in every sense to incur the penalty of disobedience to the State than it would to obey. I should feel as if I were worth less in that case. . . .

I have paid no poll-tax for six years. I was put into a jail once on this account, for one night; and, as I stood considering the walls of solid stone, two or three feet thick, the door of wood and iron, a foot thick, and the iron grating which strained the light, I could not help being struck with the foolishness of that institution which treated me as if I were mere flesh and blood and bones, to be locked up. I wondered that it should have concluded at length that this was the best use it could put me to, and had never thought to avail itself of my services in some way. I saw that, if there was a wall of stone between me and my townsmen, there was a still more difficult one to climb or break through before they could get to be as free as I was. I did not for a moment feel confined, and the walls seemed a great waste of stone and mortar. I felt as if I alone of all my townsmen had paid my tax. They plainly did not know how to treat me, but behaved like persons who are underbred. In every threat and in every compliment there was a blunder; for they thought that my chief desire was to stand the other side of that stone wall. I could not but smile to see how industriously they locked the door on my meditations, which followed them out again without let or hindrance, and *they* were really all that was dangerous. As they could not reach me, they had resolved to punish my body; just as boys, if they cannot come at some person against whom they have a spite, will abuse his dog. I saw that the State was half-witted, that it was timid as a lone woman with her silver spoons, and that it did not know its friends from its foes, and I lost all my remaining respect for it, and pitied it.

Thus the State never intentionally confronts a man's sense, intellectual or moral, but only his body, his senses. It is not armed with superior wit or honesty, but with superior physical strength. I was not born to be forced. I will breathe after my own fashion. Let us see who is the strongest. What force has a multitude? They only can force me who obey a higher law than I. They force me to become like themselves. I do not hear of *men* being *forced* to live this way or that by masses of men. What sort of life were that to live? . . . If a plant cannot live according to its nature, it dies; and so a man. . . .

I have never declined paying the highway tax, because I am as desirous of being a good neighbor as I am of being a bad subject; and as for supporting schools, I am doing my part to educate my fellow-countrymen now. It is for no particular item in the tax-bill that I refuse to pay it. I simply wish to refuse allegiance to the State, to withdraw and stand aloof from it effectually. I do not care to trace the course of my dollar, if I could, till it buys a man or a musket to shoot with—the dollar is innocent—but I am concerned to trace the effects of my allegiance. In fact, I quietly declare war with the State, after my fashion, though I will still make what use and get what advantage of her I can, as is usual in such cases.

If others pay the tax which is demanded of me, from a sympathy with the State, they do but what they have already done in their own case, or rather they abet injustice to a greater extent than the State requires. If they pay the tax from a mistaken interest in me, to save my property, or prevent my going to jail, it is because they have not considered wisely how far they let their private feelings interfere with the public good.

This, then, is my position at present. But one cannot be too much on his guard in such a case, lest his action be biased by obstinacy or an undue regard for the opinions of men. Let him see that he does only what belongs to himself and to the hour.

I think sometimes, Why, this people mean well, they are only ignorant; they would do better if they knew how: why give your neighbors this pain to treat you as they are not inclined to? But I think again, This is no reason why I should do as they do, or permit others to suffer much greater pain of a different kind. Again, I sometimes say to myself, When many millions of men, without heat, without ill will, without personal feeling of any kind, demand of you a few shillings only, without the possibility, such is their constitution, of retracting or altering their present demand, and without the possibility, on your side, of appeal to any other millions, why expose yourself to this overwhelming brute force? You do not resist cold and hunger, the winds and the waves, thus obstinately; you quietly submit to a thousand similar necessities. You do not put your head into the fire. But just in proportion as I regard this as not wholly a brute force, but partly a human force, and consider that I have relations to those millions as to so many millions of men, and not of mere brute or inanimate things, I see that appeal is possible, first and instantaneously, from them to the Maker of them, and, secondly, from them to themselves. But if I put my head deliberately into the fire, there is no appeal to fire or to the Maker of fire, and I have only myself to blame. If I could convince myself that I have any right to be satisfied with men as they are, and to treat them accordingly, and not according, in some respects, to my requisitions and expectations of what they and I ought to be, then, like a good Mussulman and fatalist, I should endeavor to be satisfied with things as they are, and say it is the will of God. And, above all, there is this difference between resisting this and a purely brute or natural force, that I can resist this with some effect; but I cannot expect, like Orpheus, to change the nature of the rocks and trees and beasts.

I do not wish to quarrel with any man or nation. I do not wish to split hairs, to make fine distinctions, or set myself up as better than my neighbors. I seek rather, I may say, even an excuse for conforming to the laws of the land. I am but too ready to conform to them. Indeed, I have reason to suspect myself on this head; and each year, as the tax-gatherer comes round, I find myself disposed to review the acts and position of the general and State governments, and the spirit of the people, to discover a pretext for conformity.

> "We must affect our country as our parents,
> And if at any time we alienate
> Our love or industry from doing it honor,
> We must respect effects and teach the soul
> Matter of conscience and religion,
> And not desire of rule or benefit."

I believe that the State will soon be able to take all my work of this sort out of my hands, and then I shall be no better a patriot than my fellow-countrymen. Seen from a lower point of view, the Constitution, with all its faults, is very good; the law and the courts are very respectable; even this State and this American government are, in many respects, very admirable, and rare things, to be thankful for, such as a great many have described them; but seen from a point of view a little higher, they are what I have described them; seen from a higher still, and the highest, who shall say what they are, or that they are worth looking at or thinking of at all? ...

They who know of no purer sources of truth, who have traced up its stream no higher, stand, and wisely stand, by the Bible and the Constitution, and drink at it there with reverence and humility, but they who behold where it comes trickling into this lake or that pool, gird up their loins once more, and continue their pilgrimage toward its fountainhead.

No man with a genius for legislation has appeared in America. . . . If we were left solely to the wordy wit of legislators in Congress for our guidance, uncorrected by the seasonable experience and the effectual complaints of the people, America would not long retain her rank among the nations. For eighteen hundred years, though perchance, I have no right to say it, the New Testament has been written; yet where is the legislator who has wisdom and practical talent enough to avail himself of the light which it sheds on the science of legislation?

The authority of government, even such as I am willing to submit to—for I will cheerfully obey those who know and can do better than I, and in many things even those who neither know nor can do so well—is still an impure one: to be strictly just, it must have the sanction and consent of the governed. It can have no pure right over my person and property but what I concede to it. The progress from an absolute to a limited monarchy, from a limited monarchy to a democracy, is a progress toward a true respect for the individual. Even the Chinese philosopher was wise enough to regard the individual as the basis of the empire. Is a democracy, such as we know it, the last improvement possible in government? Is it not possible to take a step further towards recognizing and organizing the rights of man? There will never be a really free and enlightened State until the State comes to recognize the individual as a higher and independent power, from which all its own power and authority are derived, and treats him accordingly. I please myself with imagining a State at last which can afford to be just to all men, and to treat the individual with respect as a neighbor; which even would not think it inconsistent with its own repose if a few were to live aloof from it, not meddling with it, nor embraced by it, who fulfilled all the duties of neighbors and fellow-men. A State which bore this kind of fruit, and suffered it to drop off as fast as it ripened, would prepare the way for a still more perfect and glorious State, which also I have imagined, but not yet anywhere seen.

Extracts from the Proceedings of the

United Nations Commission on Human Rights*

[1947]

GENERAL ROMULO (PHILIPPINES): "History records the long and violent struggle that preceded the recognition of the rights of man, the centuried conflict between plebian and patrician, commoner and nobility, alien and citizen, subject and king, worker and capitalist, the individual and the State—in all conceivable situations where the factor of inherited or acquired wealth or power or position arrayed men or groups of men, one against the other, in relations of inevitable opposition.

"It is perhaps true to affirm that in the state of nature man is born free and equal, and it is certainly a comforting doctrine to proclaim that men are endowed with certain inalienable rights, among which are the right to life, liberty and the pursuit of happiness. Yet the experience of the human race, living in communities together or in separate nations and state, shows that history has played with man and with groups of men, much as a logician might play with theses and antitheses, in continual conflict with one another, in positions of unequal rights and privileges that have nothing to do with their God-given endowments.

"We have seen that men have been disinherited of rights regarded as inborn, or deprived of rights considered as inalienable. It is the glaring disparity between sound doctrine and unsound practice, be-

---

* Compiled by Anne Winslow for the Committee on Human Rights of the Commission to Study the Organization of Peace. Reproduced by permission of the American Association for the United Nations. The extracts quoted here have been selected from the various speeches made by each delegate during the session, rather than from any one speech made by him.

tween perfect ideal and imperfect fact which has served as the tocsin of revolution through the centuries. . . .

"The principle that man is endowed by nature with certain inherent and inalienable rights harks back to the ancient Greeks and Romans. The enthronement of this principle in the laws and constitutions of most modern States dates from a century and a half ago. What is new is the principle that these natural human rights need to be safeguarded by some authority more potent than the sovereignty of the State by an instrument of common consent more stable and efficacious than the law of nations as we know it today. It is to the task of fashioning such an instrument which shall lie outside and above the State that this Commission is dedicated. . . .

"We are here to prepare the way for a Bill of Rights that shall be for all races and conditions of men regardless of whether they are today in a position to enjoy each separate guarantee or any given benefit that may accrue therefrom. We hold that the postulation of fundamental human rights and freedoms is an act of conscience that has positive value in itself, apart from any practical and profitable use to which the specific rights and freedoms may be put by any given community at any given time. By postulating these rights and freedoms, we fix them permanently in the minds and hearts of men everywhere. On the one hand, we set certain inviolable limits to the possible encroachments of oppression and exploitation, despotism and tyranny. And on the other, we set the goals for the backward peoples to strive after. Education, economic progress, the advance of scientific knowledge, and the political consequences of all these different forces will do the rest. . . .

"We would favour a Bill of Rights sufficiently ample in its dispositions that it will cover the needs of men who are now free as well as of men who are still to be freed. . . .

"I wish to go on record on behalf of my Government that we hold to the familiar Jeffersonian maxim that governments derive their just powers from the consent of the governed, that the natural rights of men are anterior to the authority of the state, that the people are sovereign, and the state merely the instrument of their sovereign will. We hold that no state can exercise powers in excess of those prerogatives which the citizens have conferred upon it of their own free will and volition. It is the natural state of man to strive after perfection and the fullest development of personality and the principal function of the state is to safeguard the individual in his observance of this primordial law of being. . . ."

MR. RIBNIKAR (YUGOSLAVIA): "The first declarations of human rights that originated in the 18th Century, expressed the social and political ideal of young revolutionary bourgeoisie. The first of these principles with which the bourgeoisie started its historical fight was for individual liberty, and it is especially this principle that was fought for. It was quite natural, because in that time the young bourgeoisie had an acute necessity to push aside all the obstacles that were in her way, under a form of feudal privileges, and so forth. To achieve freedom of enterprise, it opposed liberalism to absolutism; to the privileges of the classes, it opposed free competition in the economic life. The fight for the liberation from the feudal chains was logically concentrated in the request for individual liberty. Later on, the individualist psychology was especially characteristic for the 19th Century. It had as a result, the creation and the spreading of the conception that was very often developed to an extreme. It was contrary to the nature itself of the human being. I am speaking now of the conception of certain animosity between the individual and the society.

"In societies there are divided classes. The ruling class has used this psychology of individualism as a tool in its fight against the aspirations of working classes, in spreading this ideology of individualism, with one purpose, to save its prerogatives. They have just put the poison of dislocation and of disruption among the different classes. . . .

"The new conditions of the economic, social and national life of our time have tended to develop the spirit of collectivity, and the conscience, and the solidarity of the popular masses. We are more and more aware that real individual liberty can be reached only in perfect harmony between the individual and the collectivity. It becomes quite obvious that this common interest is more important than the individual interest, and that a man can liberate himself only when the mass of a population is free.

"In our time the social principle comes first. It has one purpose, to create conditions necessary to the fulfilment of the interest of every individual. The social ideal is the ideal of the enormous majority of the world and it is in the identity of the interest of society and of the individual. Therefore, when we desire to speak today of the rights of man, of modern men, we must not think of the social ideal or of a political ideal of another age. This ideal belongs to the past, and if it remains in some countries, it is the ideal of one class only of a society. . . .

"To establish a modern declaration of human rights, we must look for the realities of the contemporary world and we must find, in these realities, the social principles that have validity for our age, ideals that, in the judgment of many sociologists, are now embodied in an age of transition, a revolutionary age. Our task would be perfectly illusory and our work perfectly incomplete if we would limit ourselves to reproduce, with some minor changes, the declarations of human rights that were created in other ages, that is, about two centuries ago. It would be, on our part, a gross error that history would never forgive. . . .

"The social picture of the contemporary world presents very different aspects. The social ideal, the political, the national ideals, are very different in the different countries, and from one social class to another.

"Before going on in our task, we must know, in a very definite way, what we would like to embody in the declaration that we are about to make. Should we consider only the rights that the ruling classes are defending, that is, the rights in countries where there exists an antagonism among the classes, or are we going to start with the rights that men have won in countries where a socialist regime exists, or are we going to note the aspirations of peoples that have not reached the stage of national independence?

"First of all, I think we must agree on this point. Should we make a declaration that will have a universal character for our time or should we limit this declaration to a certain extent only? In that case, it would have only very relative meaning. For my part, I think it is quite necessary for us to try to reach this universal character of declaration. In this case the declaration would not only be the logical proceeding and the logical development of rights of citizens and chosen in the constitution of one or another country, but it would contain the principles that are in agreement with the general aspirations of the popular masses of the entire world.

"If we set that goal, I think—and this is obvious by the nature of my declaration—that the rights of modern man, for the reason of diversity of the social structures and of political regimes in the world, can never be a formal obligation for all Member States. The form of this declaration that will be established cannot be an international convention, neither an annex to the Charter. It could only have the form of a resolution of the General Assembly of the United Nations. Only in this form and only if this declaration has a universal character, could this declaration have the importance of an historical document, and it would have a far-reaching moral significance that would correspond to the spirit of the Charter of the United Nations."

DR. MALIK (LEBANON): "I wish to say that the very phrase, 'human rights,' obviously refers to man, and by 'rights,' you can only mean that which belongs to the essence of man, namely, that which is not accidental, that which does not come and go with the passage of time and with the rise and fall of fads and styles and systems. It must be something belonging to man as such. We are, therefore, raising the fundamental question, what is man? And our differences will reflect faithfully the differences in our conceptions of men, namely, of ourselves. . . .

"The individual human being, you and I, today may not be in need of protection against the despotism of the individual. The day of individual dictators and tyrants may be passed. But if man is no longer in need of protection against the tyranny of kings and dictators, he is, Madam Chairman, desperately in need of protection against another kind of tyranny, in my opinion equally grievous.

"There has been rising in the last few decades a new tyranny, the tyranny of the masses, which seems to have an inevitable tendency of ultimately embodying itself in what I might call the tyranny of the state. If there is any danger to fundamental human rights today, it is certainly from that direction.

"The Charter speaks in the preamble of the worth and dignity of man, Madam Chairman. The states, governments, colonies, and non-self-governing territories—all these have other organs to plead their rights for them. They have other agencies to plead their rights. We here in this Commission represent and defend the individual man in his conscience and in his individual freedom, and there is no other body in the United Nations to do that. We must defend him against any tyranny, against the tyranny of the state and the tyranny of systems, because man has other loyalties than his loyalty to the state. He has his loyalty to his family, to his religion, to his profession; he has his loyalty to science and to truth. These loyalties are equally exacting as the loyalty to the state. And, in my opinion, the fight for freedom today consists primarily in asserting the rights of these intermediate institutions, between the individual and the state against the overwhelming claims of the state. Unless we succeed in embodying in our proposed Bill of Rights something of this fight, of the lonely human individual against the all-encompassing danger of the state, I am afraid we will have missed our greatest opportunity. . . .

"The real danger of the present age is that social claims are in danger of snuffing out any real personal liberty. It is not social security and responsibility that are not going to find advocates and therefore expression in our bill. It is rather the questions which relate to personal values and freedoms.

"May I express that what I ultimately mean is this. I am not setting an artificial antithesis between the individual and the State. I am asking this question. Which is for the sake of the other? Is the State for the sake of the human person or is the human person for the sake of the State? That, to me, is the ultimate question of the present day. I believe the State is for the sake of the person and therefore our Bill of Rights must express that for the sake of which everything else exists, including the State."

MR. DUKES (UNITED KINGDOM): "My Government wishes to emphasize our faith in the dignity and worth of the human person, as stated in the preamble of the Charter. We say, right here, that we attach the greatest importance to world-wide acceptance and practice of human rights and fundamental freedoms. Our society is founded on what might be called in one word 'tolerance.' We feel that tolerance is not only the essence of democracy but it is also the essence of civilization. We believe that, as a fundamental principle, every human person should be able to think, speak and worship as he pleases and be able to act in accordance with his beliefs, provided that the rights of others are equally recognized and provided the preservation of an ordered society is not endangered thereby. These freedoms of the individual can only be satisfactorily reconciled with these two provisos, through the existence of an independent judiciary and by the rule of law. . . .

"There is no such a thing as complete personal freedom. We must pay the price for the advantages that result from our calling upon the state to safeguard our liberties, both in the sense of personal freedoms and also in the direction of a minimum degree of economic security. . . . The state is not some mythical body. The state is composed of the people, all fully conscious of the freedom to change those governments if they do not comply with what may be regarded as the common will and the common obligation. . . . Therefore, we have got to try to produce a bill of rights which must carry with it, step by step as it proceeds along the road, the right and freedom of the individual to play his part in molding the society in which he lives and the right to change that society or to change its form of government if he disapproves of what is being done, which I regard as one of the highest freedoms. . . .

"The state exists and so does the individual. Higher civilization, as I conceive of it, can only be enjoyed by the impact of those two things one upon the other. And I am convinced that if we are to hold out any reasonable prospects of a developing civilization, we must provide for the minimum requirements of life, without which freedom becomes a meaningless thing—a very meaningless thing, unless we are going to develop along the roads for ensuring these minimums that we are seeking now to formulate and to recognize that the individual, as an individual, is in the majority of cases incapable of doing it without assistance from the state. . . ."

DR. CHANG (CHINA): "All the discussions so far have been on the word 'rights'—rights, rights, rights. And, of course, that is due to the fact that there have been so many wrongs, wrongs, wrongs. There are still wrongs, and they need to be righted. So, we will have to have rights. . . .

"I am not arguing against the rights, but I think the time has come for us to pay some attention to the word 'human.'

"From the middle of the nineteenth century, especially the famous year, I think, of 1859, the publication of a certain book that emphasized the struggle for existence in the *Origin of Species,* we have been proving ever since then down to the present day—that human beings are animals. . . . This recognition of man being not so far from animals is in all philosophies, but especially realized in the Chinese philosopher, Mencius. He recognized that very clearly, and then he gave a definition of civilization or human duty, which, I think, is very good. Realizing the difference between animal and man is very, very little, he said it is the duty of man to make that difference firm and to enlarge it.

"We should pay attention to that little bit of difference. It seems as though, ever since 1859, the whole idea has been to minimize that. That is all right—to say that, after all, we are animals. But, after all, there is that little bit of difference, and to make firm that difference and to enlarge that difference is the whole duty of human civilization and of human life, if human life is interpreted in the sense of being worthwhile, not simply to get food, clothing and other things."

MR. CASSIN (FRANCE): "The individual, the human being, is above all a social creature whose life and development and whose progress have been made possible only because he could lean upon his neighbors. And, by the same token, there is no social group, no state, not even this international community which could exist without the support of human beings with every characteristic nature gave to them. And we are forced since we live on this earth to try to solve in a practical way these two aspects of the problem.

"There is no doubt that the international community—not only of the mythical plan but even on the legal political level, which is now represented by the United Nations—that this international community now gives us possibilities which did not exist before.

"Should we give to the individual certain rights and state in our bill that these rights are unconditional? No. We know very well that, unfortunately, it is sometimes necessary, as in the case of crime, for society to take upon itself the right of eliminating criminals. . . . When the state is in danger, the nation is. When the reasons for the existence of society are threatened, we ourselves call upon human beings to sacrifice their lives for something even more sacred than life itself. Therefore, even the very right of life is not an unconditional right. But if a highly organized state should say that if there were too many children, 20,000 should be killed, our conscience would not admit it. Therefore, we can easily say that there are certain fundamental rights which all human consciences will support and which must be considered as the pillars of human society. . . ."

MR. LEBEAU (BELGIUM): ". . . the Industrial Revolution of the 19th century has brought about certain changes which the philosophers of the 18th century could not possibly foresee. The rhythm of production, for instance, has passed from, say one to a thousand or a hundred thousand, or in some cases, one million.

"The main difficulty which we have to conquer is not production in itself, but the distribution of production in order that each individual may have the benefit of this production. Distribution is modified and influenced by the fluctuation of prices and if the sale price of any commodity falls under the price of production, production itself comes down and, therefore, the individual finds himself without work, without the normal means of earning his livelihood. That, as I say, could not be foreseen by the philosophers of the 18th century and that is a point which we must deal with.

"I agree with the representative of Yugoslavia that we must state the rights of the individual to participate in the general economy without running the risk of being a victim of the various dangers which lie in this economy, that is, the dangers of unemployment and other dangers. And I do not agree with the representative of Yugoslavia when he says we should make, as a starting point of our Bill, the protection of the collectivity or of the mass. I think our starting point must be the human person, the human being. . . .

"The representative from Lebanon said and we also agree with that, that there are two main dangers which nowadays threaten human beings. The first is in our minds, the domination of the collectivity or of the mass of the state. I think we only have to look back in the last ten or fifteen years to see what terrible havoc can be wrought by such conceptions as that of the totalitarian state. I will not insist upon that point any more. It has been sufficiently stressed.

"The second danger is the overdevelopment of industrial life, the dangers of mass production, the dangers of very large cities, in which the human being finds himself completely crushed. I think we can see a striking example very close to where we are now of what becomes of the human being when he is crushed by houses which are too high, streets which are too many, telephones wires, I might say, which are too numerous, everything, finally, which would contribute to destroy him as a personality, as an individual. I think the main point is that we should in our Bill assert that we intend to protect the human being from those two dangers."

MRS. ROOSEVELT (UNITED STATES OF AMERICA): "It seems to me that . . . the rights of the individual are extremely important. It is not exactly that you set the individual apart from his society, but you recognize that within any society the individual must have rights that are guarded. . . .

"Many of us believe that an organized society in the form of a government, exists for the good of the individual; others believe that an organized society in the form of a government, exists for the benefit of a group. We may not have to decide that particular point, but I think we do have to make sure, in writing a bill of human rights, that we safeguard the fundamental freedoms of the individual. If you do not do that, in the long run, it seems to me that you run the risk of having certain conditions which we have just tried to prevent at great cost in human life, paramount in various groups."

MR. TEPLIAKOV (USSR): ". . . we are living as individuals in a community and a society, and we are working for the community and the society. The community has provided the material substance for our existence, first of all. . . .

"Equality of rights is recognized as equality, irrespective of nationality or race in all spheres of economic, state, cultural, social, and political life. Any direct or indirect restriction of the rights of citizens or conversely, any establishment of direct or indirect privileges for citizens, on account of their race or nationality, as well as any advocacy of racial or national exclusiveness or hatred or contempt, is, or must be, punishable by law."

MR. MORA (URUGUAY): ". . . Man today moves between two spheres, two sets of rules, one of which comes from national law and the other one comes from international law. I believe that we ought to complete this right of citizenship so that human beings might receive a certain degree of what we might almost call world citizenship. . . .

"The traditional bills of rights have a national character. It seems to me that in the twentieth century we must emphasize the international human rights, the international rights of man. . . .

"The classic doctrine says that only states are subject to international laws. We need now to declare that man is the most important element of any kind of law, national or international.

"I hope that in the future the United Nations will set up international tribunals of justice, or any kind of court of appeal for the individual, as for the states. But, for the moment, in the name of the Government of Uruguay, I want to make a proposition to enlarge the rights of citizenship, in order to establish the right of citizens to participate not only in their Government but also in the organization of the international community of states, that the right be granted to any man to have access to the United Nations."

IV

DEMOCRACY

That the Ideally Best Form of Government Is Representative Government*

BY JOHN STUART MILL

[1861]

It has long (perhaps throughout the entire duration of British free-dom) been a common saying, that if a good despot could be ensured, despotic monarchy would be the best form of government. I look upon this as a radical and most pernicious misconception of what good government is; which, until it can be got rid of, will fatally vitiate all our speculations on government.

The supposition is, that absolute power, in the hands of an eminent individual, would ensure a virtuous and intelligent performance of all the duties of government. Good laws would be established and enforced, bad laws would be reformed; the best men would be placed in all situations of trust; justice would be as well administered, the public burdens would be as light and as judiciously imposed, every branch of administration would be as purely and as intelligently con-ducted, as the circumstances of the country and its degree of intel-lectual and moral cultivation would admit. I am willing, for the sake of the argument, to concede all this; but I must point out how great the concession is; how much more is needed to produce even an approximation to these results than is conveyed in the simple expres-sion, a good despot. Their realization would in fact imply, not merely a good monarch, but an all-seeing one. . . . What should we then have? One man of superhuman mental activity managing the entire affairs of a mentally passive people. Their passivity is implied in the very idea of absolute power. The nation as a whole, and every indi-vidual composing it, are without any potential voice in their own destiny. They exercise no will in respect to their collective interests.

---

* Selections from Chapter III of *On Representative Government*.

All is decided for them by a will not their own, which it is legally a crime for them to disobey. What sort of human beings can be formed under such a regimen? . . . On matters of pure theory they might perhaps be allowed to speculate, so long as their speculations either did not approach politics, or had not the remotest connection with its practice. On practical affairs they could at most be only suffered to suggest; and even under the most moderate of despots, none but persons of already or reputed superiority could hope that their suggestions would be known to, much less regarded by, those who had the management of affairs. . . . But the public at large remains without information and without interest on all the greater matters of practice; or, if they have any knowledge of them, it is but a *dilettante* knowledge, like that which people have of the mechanical arts who have never handled a tool. Nor is it only in their intelligence that they suffer. Their moral capacities are equally stunted. Wherever the sphere of action of human beings is artificially circumscribed, their sentiments are narrowed and dwarfed in the same proportion. . . . Let a person have nothing to do for his country, and he will not care for it. It has been said of old, that in a despotism there is at most but one patriot, the despot himself; and the saying rests on a just appreciation of the effects of absolute subjection, even to a good and wise master. . . .

A good despotism means a government in which, so far as depends on the despot, there is no positive oppression by officers of state, but in which all the collective interests of the people are managed for them, all the thinking that has relation to collective interests done for them, and in which their minds are formed by, and consenting to, this abdication of their own energies. . . . With the exception, therefore, of a few studious men who take an intellectual interest in speculation for its own sake, the intelligence and sentiments of the whole people are given up to the material interests, and, when these are provided for, to the amusement and ornamentation, of private life. But to say this is to say, if the whole testimony of history is worth anything, that the era of national decline has arrived: that is, if the nation had ever attained anything to decline from. . . .

It is not much to be wondered at if impatient or disappointed reformers, groaning under the impediments opposed to the most salutary public improvements by the ignorance, the indifference, the intractableness, the perverse obstinacy of a people, and the corrupt combinations of selfish private interests armed with the powerful weapons afforded by free institutions, should at times sigh for a strong hand to bear down all these obstacles, and compel a recalcitrant people to be better governed. But (setting aside the fact, that for one despot who now and then reforms an abuse, there are ninety-nine who do nothing but create them) those who look in any such direction for the realization of their hopes leave out of the idea of good government its principal element, the improvement of the people themselves. One of the benefits of freedom is that under it the ruler cannot pass by the people's minds, and amend their affairs for them without amending them. If it were possible for the people to be well governed in spite of themselves, their good government would last no longer than the freedom of a people usually lasts who have been liberated by foreign arms without their own co-operation. It is true, a despot may educate the people; and to do so really, would be the best apology for his despotism. But any education which aims at making human beings other than machines, in the long run makes them claim to have the control of their own actions. . . .

* * *

There is no difficulty in showing that the ideally best form of government is that in which the sovereignty, or supreme controlling power in the last resort, is vested in the entire aggregate of the community; every citizen not only having a voice in the exercise of that ultimate sovereignty, but being, at least occasionally, called on to take an actual part in the government, by the personal discharge of some public function, local or general. . . .

The ideally best form of government, it is scarcely necessary to say, does not mean one which is practicable or eligible in all states of civilization, but the one which, in the circumstances in which it is practicable and eligible, is attended with the greatest amount of beneficial consequences, immediate and prospective. A completely popular government is the only polity which can make out any claim to this character. . . . *It is both more favorable to present good government, and promotes a better and higher form of national character, than any other polity whatsoever.*

Its superiority in reference to present well-being rests upon two principles, of as universal truth and applicability as any general propositions which can be laid down respecting human affairs. The first is, that the rights and interests of every or any person are only secure from being disregarded when the person interested is himself able, and habitually disposed, to stand up for them. The second is, that the general prosperity attains a greater height, and is more widely diffused, in proportion to the amount and variety of the personal energies enlisted in promoting it. . . .

The former proposition—that each is the only safe guardian of his own rights and interests—is one of those elementary maxims of prudence, which every person, capable of conducting his own affairs, implicitly acts upon, wherever he himself is interested. Many, indeed, have a great dislike to it as a political doctrine, and are fond of holding it up to obloquy, as a doctrine of universal selfishness. To which we may answer, that . . . in order to support the claim of all to participate in the sovereign power, we need not suppose that when power resides in an exclusive class, that class will knowingly and deliberately sacrifice the other classes to themselves: it suffces that, in the absence of its natural defenders, the interest of the excluded is always in danger of being overlooked; and, when looked at, is seen with very different eyes from those of the persons whom it directly concerns. . . .

It is an adherent condition of human affairs that no intention, however sincere, of protecting the interests of others can make it safe or salutary to tie up their own hands. Still more obviously true is it, that by their own hands only can any positive and durable improvement of their circumstances in life be worked out. Through the joint influence of these two principles, all free communities have both been more exempt from social injustice and crime, and have attained more brilliant prosperity, than any others, or than they themselves after they lost their freedom. Contrast the free states of the world, while their freedom lasted, with the contemporary subjects of monarchical or oligarchical despotism: the Greek cities with the Persian satrapies; the Italian republics and the free towns of Flanders and Germany, with the feudal monarchies of Europe; Switzerland, Holland, and England, with Austria or ante-revolutionary France. Their superior prosperity was too obvious ever to have been gainsaid: while their superiority in good government and social relations is proved by the prosperity, and is manifest besides in every page of history. If we compare, not one age with another, but the different governments which co-existed in the same age, no amount of disorder which exaggeration itself can pretend to have existed amidst the publicity of the free states can be compared for a moment with the contemptuous trampling upon the mass of the people which pervaded the whole life of the monarchical countries, or the disgusting individual tyranny which was of more than daily occurrence under the systems of plunder which they called fiscal arrangements, and in the secrecy of their frightful courts of justice.

It must be acknowledged that the benefits of freedom, so far as they have hitherto been enjoyed, were obtained by the extension of its privileges to a part only of the community; and that a government in which they are extended impartially to all is a desideratum still unrealized. But though every approach to this has an independent value, and in many cases more than an approach could not, in the existing state of general improvement, be made, the participation of all in these benefits is the ideally perfect conception of free government. In proportion as any, no matter who, are excluded from it, the interests of the excluded are left without the guarantee accorded to the rest, and they themselves have less scope and encouragement than they might otherwise have to that exertion of their energies for the good of themselves and of the community, to which the general prosperity is always proportioned.

Thus stands the case as regards present well-being; the good management of the affairs of the existing generation. If we now pass to the influence of the form of government upon character, we shall find the superiority of popular government over every other to be, if possible, still more decided and indisputable.

This question really depends upon a still more fundamental one, viz., which of two common types of character, for the general good of humanity, it is most desirable should predominate—the active, or the passive type; that which struggles against evils, or that which endures them; that which bends to circumstances, or that which endeavors to make circumstances bend to itself.

The commonplaces of moralists, and the general sympathies of mankind, are in favor of the passive type. Energetic characters may be admired, but the acquiescent and submissive are those which most men personally prefer. The passiveness of our neighbors increases our sense of security, and plays into the hands of our wilfulness. Passive characters, if we do not happen to need their ac-

tivity, seem an obstruction the less in our own path. A contented
character is not a dangerous rival. Yet nothing is more certain
than that improvement in human affairs is wholly the work of
the uncontented characters; and, moreover, that it is much easier
for an active mind to acquire the virtues of patience than for a
passive one to assume those of energy.

* * *

Very different is the state of the human faculties where a human
being feels himself under no other external restraint than the necessities of nature, or mandates of society which he has his share in
imposing, and which it is open to him, if he thinks them wrong,
publicly to dissent from, and exert himself actively to get altered.
No doubt, under a government partially popular, this freedom may
be exercised even by those who are not partakers in the full privileges of citizenship. But . . . the maximum of the invigorating
effect of freedom upon the character is only obtained when the
person acted on either is, or is looking forward to becoming, a
citizen as fully privileged as any other. What is still more important
than even this matter of feeling is the practical discipline which the
character obtains from the occasional demand made upon the citizens to exercise, for a time and in their turn, some social function.
It is not sufficiently considered how little there is in most men's
ordinary life to give any largeness either to their conceptions or
to their sentiments. Their work is a routine; not a labor of love,
but of self-interest in the most elementary form, the satisfaction of
daily wants; neither the thing done, nor the process of doing it,
introduces the mind to thoughts or feelings extending beyond individuals; if instructive books are within their reach, there is no
stimulus to read them; and in most cases the individual has no
access to any person of cultivation much superior to his own. Giving
him something to do for the public, supplies, in a measure, all these
deficiencies. If circumstances allow the amount of public duty assigned him to be considerable, it makes him an educated man. Notwithstanding the defects of the social system and moral ideas of
antiquity, the practice of the dicastery and the ecclesia raised the
intellectual standard of an average Athenian citizen far beyond
anything of which there is yet an example in any other mass of men,
ancient or modern. The proofs of this are apparent in every page of

our great historian of Greece; but we need scarcely look further than to the high quality of the addresses which their great orators deemed best calculated to act with effect on their understanding and will. A benefit of the same kind, though far less in degree, is produced on Englishmen of the lower middle class by their liability to be placed on juries and to serve parish offices; which, though it does not occur to so many, nor is so continuous, nor introduces them to so great a variety of elevated considerations, as to admit of comparison with the public education which every citizen of Athens obtained from her democratic institutions, must make them nevertheless very different beings, in range of ideas and development of faculties, from those who have done nothing in their lives but drive a quill, or sell goods over a counter. Still more salutary is the moral part of the instruction afforded by the participation of the private citizen, if even rarely, in public functions. He is called upon, while so engaged, to weigh interests not his own; to be guided, in case of conflicting claims, by another rule than his private partialities; to apply, at every turn, principles and maxims which have for their reason of existence the common good: and he usually finds associated with him in the same work minds more familiarized than his own with these ideas and operations, whose study it will be to supply reasons to his understanding, and stimulation to his feeling for the general interest. He is made to feel himself one of the public, and whatever is for their benefit to be for his benefit. Where this school of public spirit does not exist, scarcely any sense is entertained that private persons, in no eminent social situation, owe any duties to society, except to obey the laws and submit to the government. There is no unselfish sentiment of identification with the public. Every thought or feeling, either of interest or of duty, is absorbed in the individual and in the family. The man never thinks of any collective interest, of any objects to be pursued jointly with others, but only in competition with them, and in some measure at their expense. A neighbor, not being an ally or an associate, since he is never engaged in any common undertaking for joint benefit, is therefore only a rival. Thus even private morality suffers, while public is actually extinct. Were this the universal and only possible state of things, the utmost aspirations of the lawgiver or the moralist could only stretch to make the bulk of the community a flock of sheep innocently nibbling the grass side by side.

From these accumulated considerations it is evident that the only government which can fully satisfy all the exigencies of the social state is one in which the whole people participate; that any participation, even in the smallest public function, is useful; that the participation should everywhere be as great as the general degree of improvement of the community will allow; and that nothing less can be ultimately desirable than the admission of all to a share in the sovereign power of the state. But since all cannot, in a community exceeding a single small town, participate personally in any but some very minor portions of the public business, it follows that the ideal type of a perfect government must be representative.

Democracy: Tyranny or Freedom?*

BY ALEXIS DE TOCQUEVILLE

[1835]

I

WHEN THE opponents of democracy assert that a government of one man performs what it undertakes better than the government of a multitude, it appears to me that they are perfectly right. Supposing an equality of instruction on either side, the government of an individual is more consistent, more persevering, and more accurate than that of a multitude, and it is much better qualified judiciously to discriminate the characters of the men it employs. If any deny what I advance, they have certainly never seen a democratic government, or have formed their opinion upon very partial evidence. It is true that even when local circumstances and the disposition of the people allow democratic institutions to subsist, they never display a regular and methodical system of government. Democratic liberty is far from accomplishing all the projects it undertakes, with the skill of an adroit despotism. It frequently abandons them before they have borne their fruits, or risks them when the consequences may prove dangerous; but in the end it produces more than any absolute government, and if it does fewer things well, it does a greater number of things. Under its sway the transactions of the public administration are not nearly so important as what is done by private exertion. Democracy does not confer the most skilful kind of government upon the people, but it produces that which the most skilful governments are frequently unable to awaken, namely, an all-pervading and restless activity, a superabundant force, and an energy which is inseparable from it, and which may, under favorable circumstances, beget the most amazing benefits. These are the true advantages of democracy.

In the present age, when the destinies of Christendom seem to be

---

* From *Democracy in America,* translated by Henry Reeve.

in suspense, some hasten to assail democracy as its foe whilst it is yet in its early growth; and others are ready with their vows of adoration for this new deity which is springing forth from chaos: but both parties are very imperfectly acquainted with the object of their hatred or of their desires; they strike in the dark, and distribute their blows by mere chance.

We must first understand what the purport of society and the aim of government is held to be. If it be your intention to confer a certain elevation upon the human mind, and to teach it to regard the things of this world with generous feelings, to inspire men with a scorn of mere temporal advantage, to give birth to living convictions, and to keep alive the spirit of honorable devotedness; if you hold it to be a good thing to refine the habits, to embellish the manners, to cultivate the arts of a nation, and to promote the love of poetry, of beauty, and of renown; if you would constitute a people not unfitted to act with power upon all other nations, nor unprepared for those high enterprises which, whatever be the result of its efforts, will leave a name forever famous in time—if you believe such to be the principal object of society, you must avoid the government of democracy, which would be a very uncertain guide to the end you have in view.

But if you hold it to be expedient to divert the moral and intellectual activity of man to the production of comfort, and to the acquirement of the necessaries of life; if a clear understanding be more profitable to man than genius; if your object be not to stimulate the virtues of heroism, but to create habits of peace; if you had rather witness vices than crimes and are content to meet with fewer noble deeds, provided offences be diminished in the same proportion; if, instead of living in the midst of a brilliant state of society, you are contented to have prosperity around you; if, in short, you are of opinion that the principal object of a Government is not to confer the greatest possible share of power and of glory upon the body of the nation, but to ensure the greatest degree of enjoyment and the least degree of misery to each of the individuals who compose it—if such be your desires, you can have no surer means of satisfying them than by equalizing the conditions of men, and establishing democratic institutions.

But if the time be passed at which such a choice was possible, and if some superhuman power impel us toward one or the other of these two governments without consulting our wishes, let us at least endeavor to make the best of that which is allotted to us; and let us so inquire into its good and its evil propensities as to be able to foster the good and repress the evil to the utmost.

* * *

The very essence of democratic government consists in the absolute sovereignty of the majority; for there is nothing in democratic States which is capable of resisting it. . . . Several . . . circumstances concur in rendering the power of the majority in America not only preponderant, but irresistible. The moral authority of the majority is partly based upon the notion that there is more intelligence and more wisdom in a great number of men collected together than in a single individual, and that the quantity of legislators is more important than their quality. . . .

The French, under the old monarchy, held it for a maxim . . . that the King could do no wrong; and if he did do wrong, the blame was imputed to his advisers. This notion was highly favorable to habits of obedience, and it enabled the subject to complain of the law without ceasing to love and honor the lawgiver. The Americans entertain the same opinion with respect to the majority.

The moral power of the majority is founded upon yet another principle, which is, that the interests of the many are to be preferred to those of the few. . . . In the United States . . . all parties are willing to recognize the rights of the majority, because they all hope to turn those rights to their own advantage at some future time. The majority therefore in that country exercises a prodigious actual authority, and a moral influence which is scarcely less preponderant; no obstacles exist which can impede or so much as retard its progress, or which can induce it to heed the complaints of those whom it crushes upon its path. This state of things is fatal in itself and dangerous for the future.

* * *

I hold it to be an impious and an execrable maxim that, politically speaking, a people has a right to do whatsoever it pleases, and yet I assert that all authority originates in the will of the majority. Am I then, in contradiction with myself?

A general law—which bears the name of Justice—has been made and sanctioned, not only by a majority of this or that people, but by a majority of mankind. The rights of every people are consequently confined within the limits of what is just. A nation may be considered in the light of a jury which is empowered to represent society at large, and to apply the great and general law of justice. Ought such a jury, which represents society, to have more power than the society in which the laws it applies originate?

When I refuse to obey an unjust law, I do not contest the right which the majority has of commanding, but I simply appeal from the sovereignty of the people to the sovereignty of mankind. It has been asserted that a people can never entirely outstep the boundaries of justice and of reason in those affairs which are more peculiarly its own, and that consequently full power may fearlessly be given to the majority by which it is represented. But this language is that of a slave.

A majority taken collectively may be regarded as a being whose opinions, and most frequently whose interests, are opposed to those of another being, which is styled a minority. If it be admitted that a man, possessing absolute power, may misuse that power by wronging his adversaries, why should a majority not be liable to the same reproach? Men are not apt to change their characters by agglomeration; nor does their patience in the presence of obstacles increase with the consciousness of their strength. And for these reasons I can never willingly invest any number of my fellow-creatures with that unlimited authority which I should refuse to any one of them. . . .

I am of opinion that some one social power must always be made to predominate over the others; but I think that liberty is endangered when this power is checked by no obstacles which may retard its course, and force it to moderate its own vehemence.

Unlimited power is in itself a bad and dangerous thing; human beings are not competent to exercise it with discretion, and God alone can be omnipotent, because His wisdom and His justice are always equal to His power. But no power upon earth is so worthy of honor for itself, or of reverential obedience to the rights which it represents, that I would consent to admit its uncontrolled and all-predominant authority. When I see that the right and the means of absolute command are conferred on a people or upon a king, upon an aristocracy or a democracy, a monarchy or a republic, I recognize the germ of tyranny, and I journey onward to a land of more hopeful institutions.

In my opinion the main evil of the present democratic institutions of the United States does not arise, as is often asserted in Europe, from their weakness, but from their overpowering strength; and I am not so much alarmed at the excessive liberty which reigns in that country as at the very inadequate securities which exist against tyranny.

When an individual or a party is wronged in the United States, to whom can he apply for redress? If to public opinion, public opinion constitutes the majority; if to the legislature, it represents the majority, and implicitly obeys its injunctions; if to the executive power, it is appointed by the majority, and remains a passive tool in its hands; the public troops consist of the majority under arms; the jury is the majority invested with the right of hearing judicial cases; and in certain States even the judges are elected by the majority. However iniquitous or absurd the evil of which you complain may be, you must submit to it as well as you can.

If, on the other hand, a legislative power could be so constituted as to represent the majority without necessarily being the slave of its passions; an executive, so as to retain a certain degree of uncontrolled authority; and a judiciary, so as to remain independent of the two other powers; a government would be formed which would still be democratic without incurring any risk of tyrannical abuse.[1]

* * *

I know no country in which there is so little true independence of mind and freedom of discussion as in America. In any constitutional state in Europe every sort of religious and political theory may be advocated and propagated abroad; for there is no country in Europe so subdued by any single authority as not to contain citizens who are ready to protect the man who raises his voice in the cause of truth from the consequences of his hardihood. If he is unfortunate enough to live under an absolute government, the people is upon his side; if he inhabits a free country, he may find a shelter behind the authority of the throne, if he require one. The aristocratic part of society supports him in some countries, and the democracy in others. But in a nation where democratic institutions exist, organized like those of

---

[1] A distinction must be drawn between tyranny and arbitrary power. Tyranny may be exercised by means of the law, and in that case it is not arbitrary; arbitrary power may be exercised for the good of the community at large, in which case it is not tyrannical. Tyranny usually employs arbitrary means, but, if necessary, it can rule without them.

the United States, there is but one sole authority, one single element of strength and of success, with nothing beyond it.

In America the majority raises very formidable barriers to the liberty of opinion: within these barriers an author may write whatever he pleases, but he will repent it if he ever step beyond them. Not that he is exposed to the terrors of an auto-da-fé, but he is tormented by the slights and persecutions of daily obloquy. His political career is closed forever, since he has offended the only authority which is able to promote his success. Every sort of compensation, even that of celebrity, is refused to him. Before he published his opinions he imagined that he held them in common with many others; but no sooner has he declared them openly than he is loudly censured by his overbearing opponents, whilst those who think like him, without having the courage to speak, abandon him in silence. He yields at length, oppressed by the daily efforts he has been making, and he subsides into silence, as if he was tormented by remorse for having spoken the truth.

Fetters and headsmen were the coarse instruments which tyranny formerly employed; but the civilization of our age has refined the arts of despotism which seemed, however, to have been sufficiently perfected before. The excesses of monarchical power had devised a variety of physical means of oppression: the democratic republics of the present day have rendered it as entirely an affair of the mind as is that will which it is intended to coerce. Under the absolute sway of an individual despot the body was attacked in order to subdue the soul, and the soul escaped the blows which were directed against it and rose superior to the attempt; but such is not the course adopted by tyranny in democratic republics; there the body is left free, and the soul is enslaved. The sovereign can no longer say, "You shall think as I do on pain of death"; but he says, "You are free to think differently from me, and to retain your life, your property, and all that you possess; but if such be your determination, you are henceforth an alien among your people. You may retain your civil rights, but they will be useless to you, for you will never be chosen by your fellow-citizens if you solicit their suffrages, and they will affect to scorn you if you solicit their esteem. You will remain among men, but you will be deprived of the rights of mankind. Your fellow-creatures will shun you like an inpure being, and those who are most persuaded of your innocence will abandon you too, lest they should be shunned in their turn. Go in peace! I have given you your life, but it is an existence incomparably worse than death."

Monarchical institutions have thrown an odium upon despotism; let us beware lest democratic republics should restore oppression, and should render it less odious and less degrading in the eyes of the many, by making it still more onerous to the few.

*   *   *

The tendencies which I have just alluded to are as yet very slightly perceptible in political society, but they already begin to exercise an unfavorable influence upon the national character of the Americans. I am inclined to attribute the singular paucity of distinguished political characters to the ever-increasing activity of the despotism of the majority in the United States. When the American Revolution broke out they arose in great numbers, for public opinion then served, not to tyrannize over, but to direct the exertions of individuals. Those celebrated men took a full part in the general agitation of mind common at that period, and they attained a high degree of personal fame, which was reflected back upon the nation, but which was by no means borrowed from it.

In absolute governments the great nobles who are nearest to the throne flatter the passions of the sovereign, and voluntarily truckle to his caprices. But the mass of the nation does not degrade itself by servitude: it often submits from weakness, from habit, or from ignorance, and sometimes from loyalty. Some nations have been known to sacrifice their own desires to those of the sovereign with pleasure and with pride, thus exhibiting a sort of independence in the very act of submission. These peoples are miserable, but they are not degraded. There is a great difference between doing what one does not approve and feigning to approve what one does; the one is the necessary case of a weak person, the other befits the temper of a lackey.

In free countries, where everyone is more or less called upon to give his opinion in the affairs of state, in democratic republics, where public life is incessantly commingled with domestic affairs, where the sovereign authority is accessible on every side, and where its attention can almost always be attracted by vociferation, more persons are to be met with who gamble on its foibles and live at the cost of its passions than in absolute monarchies. Not because men are naturally worse in these States than elsewhere, but the temptation is stronger, and of easier access at the same time. The result is a far more extensive debasement of the characters of citizens.

Democractic republics extend the practice of currying favor with the many, and they introduce it into a greater number of classes at once: this is one of the most serious reproaches that can be addressed to them. In democratic States organized on the principles of the American republics, this is more especially the case, where the authority of the majority is so absolute and so irresistible that a man must give up his rights as a citizen, and almost abjure his quality as a human being, if he intends to stray from the track which it lays down.

In that immense crowd which throngs the avenues to power in the United States I found very few men who displayed any of that manly candor and that masculine independence of opinion which frequently distinguished the Americans in former times, and which constitutes the leading feature in distinguished characters, wheresoever they may be found. It seems, at first sight, as if all the minds of the Americans were formed upon one model, so accurately do they correspond in their manner of judging. A foreigner does, indeed, sometimes meet with Americans who dissent from these rigorous formularies; with men who deplore the defects of the laws, the mutability and the ignorance of democracy; who even go so far as to observe the evil tendencies which impair the national character, and to point out such remedies as it might be possible to apply; but no one is there to hear these things besides yourself, and you, to whom these secret reflections are confided, are a foreigner and a bird of passage. They are very ready to communicate truths which are useless to you, but they continue to hold a different language in public.

If ever these lines are read in America, I am well assured of two things: in the first place, that all who peruse them will raise their voices to condemn me; and in the second place, that very many of them will acquit me at the bottom of their conscience.

I have heard of patriotism in the United States, and it is a virtue which may be found among the people, but never among the leaders of the people. This may be explained by analogy; despotism debases the oppressed much more than the oppressor: in absolute monarchies the king has often great virtues, but the courtiers are invariably servile. It is true that the American courtiers do not say "Sire," or "Your

Majesty"—a distinction without a difference. They are forever talking of the natural intelligence of the populace they serve; they do not debate the question as to which of the virtues of their master is preeminently worthy of admiration, for they assure him that he possesses all the virtues under heaven without having acquired them, or without caring to acquire them; they do not give him their daughters and their wives to be raised at his pleasure to the rank of his concubines, but, by sacrificing their opinions, they prostitute themselves. Moralists and philosophers in America are not obliged to conceal their opinions under the veil of allegory; but, before they venture upon a harsh truth, they say, "We are aware that the people which we are addressing is too superior to all the weaknesses of human nature to lose the command of its temper for an instant; and we should not hold this language if we were not speaking to men whom their virtues and their intelligence render more worthy of freedom than all the rest of the world." It would have been impossible for the sycophants of Louis XIV to flatter more dexterously. For my part, I am persuaded that in all governments, whatever their nature may be, servility will cower to force, and adulation will cling to power. The only means of preventing men from degrading themselves is to invest no one with that unlimited authority which is the surest method of debasing them.

II

Some readers may perhaps be astonished that—firmly persuaded as I am that the democratic revolution which we are witnessing is an irresistible fact against which it would be neither desirable nor wise to struggle—I should often have had occasion to address language of such severity to those democratic communities which this revolution has brought into being. My answer is, simply, that it is because I am not an adversary of democracy that I have sought to speak of democracy in all sincerity.

Men will not accept truth at the hands of their enemies, and truth is seldom offered to them by their friends: for this reason I have spoken it. I was persuaded that many would take upon themselves to announce the new blessings which the principle of equality promises to mankind, but that few would dare to point out from afar the dangers with which it threatens them. To those perils therefore I have turned my chief attention, and believing that I had dis-

covered them clearly, I have not had the cowardice to leave them untold.

* * *

When the world was managed by a few rich and powerful individuals, these persons loved to entertain a lofty idea of the duties of man.
They were fond of professing that it is praiseworthy to forget one's
self, and that good should be done without hope of reward, as it is
by the Deity himself. Such were the standard opinions of that time in
morals. I doubt whether men were more virtuous in aristocratic ages
than in others; but they were incessantly talking of the beauties of
virtue, and its utility was only studied in secret. But since the imagination takes less lofty flights and everyman's thoughts are centered in
himself, moralists are alarmed by this idea of self-sacrifice, and they
no longer venture to present it to the human mind. They therefore
content themselves with inquiring whether the personal advantage of
each member of the community does not consist in working for the
good of all; and when they have hit upon some point on which
private interest and public interest meet and amalgamate, they are
eager to bring it into notice. Observations of this kind are gradually
multiplied; what was only a single remark becomes a general principle; and it is held as a truth that man serves himself in serving
his fellow-creatures, and that his private interest is to do good.

. . . In the United States hardly anybody talks of the beauty of
virtue; but they maintain that virtue is useful, and prove it every day.
The American moralists do not profess that men ought to sacrifice
themselves for their fellow-creatures because it is noble to make such
sacrifices; but they boldly aver that such sacrifices are as necessary
to him who imposes them upon himself as to him for whose sake
they are made. They have found out that in their country and their
age man is brought home to himself by an irresistible force; and
losing all hope of stopping that force, they turn all their thoughts to
the direction of it. They therefore do not deny that every man may
follow his own interest; but they endeavor to prove that it is the interest of every man to be virtuous. . . .

I might here pause, without attempting to pass a judgment on what
I have described. The extreme difficulty of the subject would be my
excuse, but I shall not avail myself of it; and I had rather that my
readers, clearly perceiving my object, should refuse to follow me

than that I should leave them in suspense. The principle of interest rightly understood is not a lofty one, but it is clear and sure. It does not aim at mighty objects, but it attains without excessive exertion all those at which it aims. As it lies within the reach of all capacities, everyone can without difficulty apprehend and retain it. By its admirable conformity to human weaknesses, it easily obtains great dominion; nor is that dominion precarious, since the principle checks one personal interest by another, and uses, to direct the passions, the very same instrument which excites them. The principle of interest rightly understood produces no great acts of self-sacrifice, but it suggests daily small acts of self-denial. By itself it cannot suffice to make a man virtuous, but it disciplines a number of citizens in habits of regularity, temperance, moderation, foresight, self-command; and, if it does not lead men straight to virtue by the will, it gradually draws them in that direction by their habits. If the principle of interest rightly understood were to sway the whole moral world, extraordinary virtues would doubtless be more rare; but I think that gross depravity would then also be less common. The principle of interest rightly understood perhaps prevents some men from rising far above the level of mankind; but a great number of other men, who were falling far below it, are caught and restrained by it. Observe some few individuals, they are lowered by it; survey mankind, it is raised. I am not afraid to say that the principle of interest rightly understood appears to me the best suited of all philosophical theories to the wants of the men of our time, and that I regard it as their chief remaining security against themselves. Towards it, therefore, the minds of the moralists of our age should turn; even should they judge it to be incomplete, it must nevertheless be adopted as necessary. . . .

* * *

In the ages of aristocracy which preceded our own, there were private persons of great power, and a social authority of extreme weakness. The outline of society itself was not easily discernible, and constantly confounded with the different powers by which the community was ruled. The principal efforts of the men of those times were required to strengthen, aggrandize, and secure the supreme power; and on the other hand, to circumscribe individual independence within narrower limits, and to subject private interests to the interests of the public. Other perils and other cares await the men of our age. Amongst the greater part of modern nations, the government, whatever may be its origin, its constitution, or its name, has become almost omnipotent, and private persons are falling, more and more, into the lowest stage of weakness and dependence. In olden society everything was different; unity and uniformity were nowhere to be met with. In modern society everything threatens to become so much alike, that the peculiar characteristics of each individual will soon be entirely lost in the general aspect of the world. Our forefathers were ever prone to make an improper use of the notion that private rights ought to be respected; and we are naturally prone on the other hand to exaggerate the idea that the interest of a private individual ought always to bend to the interest of the many. The political world is metamorphosed: new remedies must henceforth be sought for new disorders. To lay down extensive, but distinct and settled limits, to the action of the government; to confer certain rights on private persons, and to secure to them the undisputed enjoyment of those rights; to enable individual man to maintain whatever independence, strength, and original power he still possesses to raise him by the side of society at large, and uphold him in that position—these appear to me the main objects of legislators in the ages upon which we are now entering. It would seem as if the rulers of our time sought only to use men in order to make things great; I wish that they would try a little more to make great men; that they would set less value on the work, and more upon the workman; that they would never forget that a nation cannot long remain strong when every man belonging to it is individually weak, and that no form or combination of social polity has yet been devised, to make an energetic people out of a community of pusillanimous and enfeebled citizens.

* * *

The society of the modern world which I have sought to delineate, and which I seek to judge, has but just come into existence. Time has not yet shaped it into perfect form: the great revolution by which it has been created is not yet over: and amidst the occurrences of our time, it is almost impossible to discern what will pass away with the revolution itself, and what will survive its close. The world which is rising into existence is still half encumbered by the remains of the world which is waning into decay; and amidst the vast perplexity of human affairs, none can say how much of ancient institutions and former manners will remain, or how much will completely disappear. Although the revolution which is taking place in the social condition, the laws, the opinions, and the feelings of men, is still very far from being terminated, yet its results already admit of no comparison with anything that the world has ever before witnessed. I go back from age to age up to the remotest antiquity; but I find no parallel to what is occurring before my eyes: as the past has ceased to throw its light upon the future, the mind of man wanders in obscurity.

Nevertheless, in the midst of a prospect so wide, so novel and so confused, some of the more prominent characteristics may already be discerned and pointed out. The good things and the evils of life are more equally distributed in the world: great wealth tends to disappear, the number of small fortunes to increase; desires and gratifications are multiplied, but extraordinary prosperity and irremediable penury are alike unknown. The sentiment of ambition is universal, but the aim of ambition is seldom lofty. Each individual stands apart in solitary weakness; but society at large is active, provident, and powerful: the performances of private persons are insignificant, those of the State immense. There is little energy of character; but manners are mild, and laws humane. If there be few instances of exalted heroism or of virtues of the highest, brightest, and purest temper, men's habits are regular, violence is rare, and cruelty almost unknown. Human existence becomes longer, and property more secure: life is not adorned with brilliant trophies, but it is extremely easy and tranquil. Few pleasures are either very refined or very coarse; and highly polished manners are as uncommon as great brutality of tastes. Neither men of great learning, nor extremely ignorant communities, are to be met with; genius becomes more rare, information more diffused. The human mind is impelled by the small efforts of all mankind combined together, not by the strenuous activity of certain men. There is less perfection, but more abundance, in all the productions of the arts. The ties of race, of rank, and of country are relaxed; the great bond of humanity is strengthened. If I endeavor to find out the most general and the most prominent of all these different characteristics, I shall have occasion to perceive, that what is taking place in men's fortunes manifests itself under a thousand other forms. Almost all extremes are softened or blunted: all that was most prominent is superseded by some mean term, at once less lofty and less low, less brilliant and less obscure, than what before existed in the world.

When I survey this countless multitude of beings, shaped in each other's likeness, amidst whom nothing rises and nothing falls, the sight of such universal uniformity saddens and chills me, and I am tempted to regret that state of society which has ceased to be. When the world was full of men of great importance and extreme insignificance, of great wealth and extreme poverty, of great learning and extreme ignorance, I turned aside from the latter to fix my observation on the former alone, who gratified my sympathies. But I admit that this gratification arose from my own weakness: it is because I am unable to see at once all that is around me, that I am allowed thus to select and separate the objects of my predilection from among so many others. Such is not the case with that almighty and eternal Being whose gaze necessarily includes the whole of created things, and who surveys distinctly, though at once, mankind and man. We may naturally believe that it is not the singular prosperity of the few, but the greater well-being of all, which is most pleasing in the sight of the Creator and Preserver of men. What appears to me to be man's decline, is to His eye advancement; what afflicts me is acceptable to Him. A state of equality is perhaps less elevated, but it is more just; and its justice constitutes its greatness and its beauty. I would strive then to raise myself to this point of the divine contemplation, and thence to view and to judge the concerns of men.

... For myself, I am full of apprehensions and of hopes. I perceive mighty dangers which it is possible to ward off—mighty evils which may be avoided or alleviated; and I cling with a firmer hold to the belief, that for democratic nations to be virtuous and prosperous they require but to will it. I am aware that many of my contemporaries maintain that nations are never their own masters here below, and that they necessarily obey some insurmountable and unintelligent power, arising from anterior events, from their race, or from the soil and climate of their country. Such principles are false and cowardly; such principles can never produce aught but feeble men and pusillanimous nations. Providence has not created mankind entirely independent or entirely free. It is true that around every man a fatal circle is traced, beyond which he cannot pass; but within the wide verge of that circle he is powerful and free: as it is with man, so with communities. The nations of our time cannot prevent the conditions of men from becoming equal; but it depends upon themselves whether the principle of equality is to lead them to servitude or freedom, to knowledge or barbarism, to prosperity or to wretchedness.

The Mass Society*

BY C. WRIGHT MILLS

[1956]

IN THE standard image of power and decision, no force is held to be as important as The Great American Public. More than merely another check and balance, this public is thought to be the seat of all legitimate power. In official life as in popular folklore, it is held to be the very balance wheel of democratic power. In the end, all liberal theorists rest their notions of the power system upon the political role of this public; all official decisions, as well as private decisions of consequence, are justified as in the public's welfare; all formal proclamations are in its name.

Let us therefore consider the classic public of democratic theory in the generous spirit in which Rousseau once cried, "Opinion, Queen of the World, is not subject to the power of kings; they are themselves its first slaves."

The most important feature of the public of opinion, which the rise of the democratic middle class initiates, is the free ebb and flow of discussion. The possibilities of answering back, of organizing autonomous organs of public opinion, of realizing opinion in action, are held to be established by democratic institutions. The opinion that results from public discussion is understood to be a resolution that is then carried out by public action; it is, in one version, the "general will" of the people, which the legislative organ enacts into law, thus lending to it legal force. Congress, or Parliament, as an institution, crowns all the scattered publics; it is the archetype for each of the little circles of face-to-face citizens discussing their public business.

This eighteenth-century idea of the public of public opinion parallels the economic idea of the market of the free economy. Here is the market composed of freely competing entrepreneurs; there is the public composed of discussion circles of opinion peers. As price is the result of anonymous, equally weighted, bargaining individuals, so public

---

opinion is the result of each man's having thought things out for himself and contributing his voice to the great chorus. To be sure, some might have more influence on the state of opinion than others, but no one group monopolizes the discussion, or by itself determines the opinions that prevail.

Innumerable discussion circles are knit together by mobile people who carry opinions from one to another, and struggle for the power of larger command. The public is thus organized into associations and parties, each representing a set of viewpoints, each trying to acquire a place in the Congress, where the discussion continues. Out of the little circles of people talking with one another, the larger forces of social movements and political parties develop; and the discussion of opinion is the important phase in a total act by which public affairs are conducted.

The autonomy of these discussions is an important element in the idea of public opinion as a democratic legitimation. The opinions formed are actively realized within the prevailing institutions of power; all authoritative agents are made or broken by the prevailing opinions of these publics. And, in so far as the public is frustrated in realizing its demands, its members may go beyond criticism of specific policies; they may question the very legitimations of legal authority. That is one meaning of Jefferson's comment on the need for an occasional "revolution."

The public so conceived, is the loom of classic, eighteenth-century democracy; discussion is at once the threads and the shuttle tying the discussion circles together. It lies at the root of the conception of authority by discussion, and it is based upon the hope that truth and justice will somehow come out of society as a great apparatus of free discussion. The people are presented with problems. They discuss them. They decide on them. They formulate viewpoints. These viewpoints are organized, and they compete. One viewpoint "wins out." Then the people act out this view, or their representatives are instructed to act it out, and this they promptly do.

Such are the images of the public of classic democracy which are still used as the working justifications of power in American society. But now we must recognize this description as a set of images out of a fairy tale: they are not adequate even as an approximate model of how the American system of power works. The issues that now shape man's fate are neither raised nor decided by the public at large. The idea of the community of publics is not a description of fact, but an assertion of an ideal, an assertion of a legitimation masquerading—as legitimations are now apt to do—as fact. For now the public of public opinion is recognized by all those who have considered it carefully as something less than it once was.

These doubts are asserted positively in the statement that the classic community of publics is being transformed into a society of masses. This transformation, in fact, is one of the keys to the social and psychological meaning of modern life in America.

I. In the democratic society of publics it was assumed, with John Locke, that the individual conscience was the ultimate seat of judgment and hence the final court of appeal. But this principle was challenged—as E. H. Carr has put it—when Rousseau "for the first time thought in terms of the sovereignty of the whole people, and faced the issue of mass democracy."

II. In the democratic society of publics it was assumed that among the individuals who composed it there was a natural and peaceful harmony of interests. But this essentially conservative doctrine gave way to the Utilitarian doctrine that such a harmony of interests had first to be created by reform before it could work, and later to the Marxian doctrine of class struggle, which surely was then, and certainly is now, closer to reality than any assumed harmony of interests.

III. In the democratic society of publics it was assumed that before public action would be taken, there would be rational discussion between individuals which would determine the action, and that, accordingly, the public opinion that resulted would be the infallible voice of reason. But this has been challenged not only (1) by the assumed need for experts to decide delicate and intricate issues, but (2) by the discovery—as by Freud—of the irrationality of the man in the street, and (3) by the discovery—as by Marx—of the socially conditioned nature of what was once assumed to be autonomous reason.

IV. In the democratic society of publics it was assumed that after determining what is true and right and just, the public would act accordingly or see that its representatives did so. In the long run, public opinion will not only be right, but public opinion will prevail. This assumption has been upset by the great gap now existing between the underlying population and those who make decisions in its name, decisions of enormous consequence which the public often does not even know are being made until well after the fact.

Given these assumptions, it is not difficult to understand the articulate optimism of many nineteenth-century thinkers, for the theory of the public is, in many ways, a projection upon the community at large of the intellectual's ideal of the supremacy of intellect. The "evolution of the intellect," Comte asserted, "determines the main course of social evolution." If looking about them, nineteenth-century thinkers still saw irrationality and ignorance and apathy, all that was merely an intellectual lag, to which the spread of education would soon put an end.

How much the cogency of the classic view of the public rested upon a restriction of this public to the carefully educated is revealed by the fact that by 1859 even John Stuart Mill was writing of "the tyranny of the majority," and both Tocqueville and Burckhardt anticipated the view popularized in the recent past by such political moralists as Ortega y Gasset. In a word, the transformation of public into mass—and all that this implies—has been at once one of the major trends of modern societies and one of the major factors in the collapse of that liberal optimism which determined so much of the intellectual mood of the nineteenth century.

By the middle of that century: individualism had begun to be replaced by collective forms of economic and political life; harmony of interests by inharmonious struggle of classes and organized pressures; rational discussions undermined by expert decisions on complicated issues, by recognition of the interested bias of argument by vested position, and by the discovery of the effectiveness of irrational appeal to the citizen. Moreover, certain structural changes of modern society, which we shall presently consider, had begun to cut off the public from the power of active decision.

The transformation of public into mass is of particular concern to us, for it provides an important clue to the meaning of the power elite. If that elite is truly responsible to, or even exists in connection with, a community of publics, it carries a very different meaning than if such a public is being transformed into a society of masses.

The United States today is not altogether a mass society, and it has never been altogether a community of publics. These phrases are names for extreme types; they point to certain features of reality, but they are themselves constructions; social reality is always some sort of mixture of the two. Yet we cannot readily understand just how much of which is mixed into our situation if we do not first understand, in terms of explicit dimensions, the clear-cut and extreme types:

At least four dimensions must be attended to if we are to grasp the differences between public and mass.

I. There is first, the ratio of the givers of opinion to the receivers, which is the simplest way to state the social meaning of the formal media of mass communication. More than anything else, it is the shift in this ratio which is central to the problems of the public and of public opinion in latter-day phases of democracy. At one extreme on the scale of communication, two people talk personally with each other; at the opposite extreme, one spokesman talks impersonally through a network of communications to millions of listeners and viewers. In between these extremes there are assemblages and political rallies, parliamentary sessions, law-court debates, small discussion circles dominated by one man, open discussion circles with talk moving freely back and forth among fifty people, and so on.

II. The second dimension to which we must pay attention is the possibility of answering back an opinion without internal or external reprisals being taken. Technical conditions of the means of communication, in imposing a lower ratio of speakers to listeners, may obviate the possibility of freely answering back. Informal rules, resting upon conventional sanction and upon the informal structure of opinion leadership, may govern who can speak, when, and for how long. Such rules may or may not be in congruence with formal rules and with institutional sanctions which govern the process of communication. In the extreme case, we may conceive of an absolute monopoly of communication to pacified media groups whose members cannot answer back even "in private." At the opposite extreme, the conditions may allow and the rules may uphold the wide and symmetrical formation of opinion.

III. We must also consider the relation of the formation of opinion to its realization in social action, the ease with which opinion is effective in the shaping of decisions of powerful consequence. This opportunity for people to act out their opinions collectively is of course limited by their position in the structure of power. This structure may be such as to limit decisively this capacity, or it may allow or even invite such action. It may confine social action to local areas or it may enlarge the area of opportunity; it may make action intermittent or more or less continuous.

IV. There is, finally, the degree to which institutional authority, with its sanctions and controls, penetrates the public. Here the problem is the degree to which the public has genuine autonomy from instituted authority. At one extreme, no agent of formal authority moves among the autonomous public. At the opposite extreme, the public is terrorized into uniformity by the infiltration of informers and the universalization of suspicion. One thinks of the late Nazi street-and-block-system, the eighteenth-century Japanese kumi, the Soviet cell structure. In the extreme, the formal structure of power coincides, as it were, with the informal ebb and flow of influence by discussion, which is thus killed off.

By combining these several points, we can construct little models or diagrams of several types of societies. Since "the problem of public opinion" as we know it is set by the eclipse of the classic bourgeois public, we are here concerned with only two types: public and mass.

In a *public*, as we may understand the term, (1) virtually as many people express opinions as receive them. (2) Public communications are so organized that there is a chance immediately and effectively to answer back any opinion expressed in public. Opinion formed by such discussion (3) readily finds an outlet in effective action, even against—if necessary—the prevailing system of authority. And (4) authoritative institutions do not penetrate the public, which is thus more or less autonomous in its operations. When these conditions prevail, we have the working model of a community of publics, and this model fits closely the several assumptions of classic democratic theory.

At the opposite extreme, in a *mass*, (1) far fewer people express opinions than receive them; for the community of publics becomes an abstract collection of individuals who receive impressions from the mass media. (2) The communications that prevail are so organized that it is difficult or impossible for the individual to answer back immediately or with any effect. (3) The realization of opinion in action is controlled by authorities who organize and control the channels of such action. (4) The mass has no autonomy from institutions; on the contrary, agents of authorized institutions penetrate this mass, reducing any autonomy it may have in the formation of opinion by discussion.

The public and the mass may be most readily distinguished by their dominant modes of communication: in a community of publics, discussion is the ascendant means of communication, and the mass media, if they exist, simply enlarge and animate discussion, linking one *pri-*

mary public with the discussions of another. In a mass society, the dominant type of communication is the formal media, and the publics become mere *media markets:* all those exposed to the contents of given mass media.

From almost any angle of vision that we might assume, when we look upon the public, we realize that we have moved a considerable distance along the road to the mass society. At the end of that road there is totalitarianism, as in Nazi Germany or in Communist Russia. We are not yet at that end. In the United States today, media markets are not entirely ascendant over primary publics. But surely we can see that many aspects of the public life of our times are more the features of a mass society than of a community of publics.

What is happening might again be stated in terms of the historical parallel between the economic market and the public of public opinion. In brief, there is a movement from widely scattered little powers to concentrated powers and the attempt at monopoly control from powerful centers, which, being partially hidden, are centers of manipulation as well as of authority. The small shop serving the neighborhood is replaced by the anonymity of the national corporation: mass advertisement replaces the personal influence of opinion between merchant and customer. The political leader hooks up his speech to a national network and speaks, with appropriate personal touches, to a million people he never saw and never will see. Entire brackets of professions and industries are in the "opinion business," impersonally manipulating the public for hire.

In the primary public the competition of opinions goes on between people holding views in the service of their interests and their reasoning. But in the mass society of media markets, competition, if any, goes on between the manipulators with their mass media on the one hand, and the people receiving their propaganda on the other.

Under such conditions, it is not surprising that there should arise a conception of public opinion as a mere reaction—we cannot say "response"—to the content of the mass media. In this view, the public is merely the collectivity of individuals each rather passively exposed to the mass media and rather helplessly opened up to the suggestions and manipulations that flow from these media. The fact of manipulation from centralized points of control constitutes, as it were, an expropriation of the old multitude of little opinion producers and consumers operating in a free and balanced market.

In official circles, the very term itself, "the public"—as Walter Lippmann noted thirty years ago—has come to have a phantom meaning, which dramatically reveals its eclipse. From the standpoint of the deciding elite, some of those who clamor publicly can be identified as "Labor," others as "Business," still others as "Farmer." Those who can *not* readily be so identified make up "The Public." In this usage, the public is composed of the unidentified and the non-partisan in a world of defined and partisan interests. It is socially composed of well-educated salaried professionals, especially college professors; of non-unionized employees, especially white-collar people, along with self-employed professionals and small businessmen.

In this faint echo of the classic notion, the public consists of those remnants of the middle classes, old and new, whose interests are not explicitly defined, organized, or clamorous. In a curious adaptation, "the public" often becomes, in fact, "the unattached expert," who, although well informed, has never taken a clear-cut, public stand on controversial issues which are brought to a focus by organized interests. These are the "public" members of the board, the commission, the committee. What the public stands for, accordingly, is often a vagueness of policy (called open-mindedness), a lack of involvement in public affairs (known as reasonableness), and a professional disinterest (known as tolerance).

* * *

One of the most important of the structural transformations involved is the decline of the voluntary association as a genuine instrument of the public. As we have already seen, the executive ascendancy in economic, military, and political institutions has lowered the effective use of all those voluntary associations which operate between the state and the economy on the one hand, and the family and the individual in the primary group on the other. It is not only that institutions of power have become large-scale and inaccessibly centralized; they have at the same time become less political and more administrative, and it is within this great change of framework that the organized public has waned.

In terms of *scale,* the transformation of public into mass has been underpinned by the shift from a political public decisively restricted in size (by property and education, as well as by sex and age) to a greatly enlarged mass having only the qualifications of citizenship and age.

In terms of *organization,* the transformation has been underpinned by the shift from the individual and his primary community to the voluntary association and the mass party as the major units of organized power.

Voluntary associations have become larger to the extent that they have become effective; and to just that extent they have become inaccessible to the individual who would shape by discussion the policies of the organization to which he belongs. Accordingly, along with older institutions, these voluntary associations have lost their grip on the individual. As more people are drawn into the political arena, these associations become mass in scale; and as the power of the individual becomes more dependent upon such mass associations, they are less accessible to the individual's influence.

Mass democracy means the struggle of powerful and large-scale interest groups and associations, which stand between the big decisions that are made by state, corporation, army, and the will of the individual citizen as a member of the public. Since these middle-level associations are the citizen's major link with decision, his relation to them is of decisive importance. For it is only through them that he exercises such power as he may have.

The gap beween the members and the leaders of the mass association is becoming increasingly wider. As soon as a man gets to be a leader of an association large enough to count he readily becomes lost as an instrument of that association. He does so (1) in the interests of maintaining his leading position in, or rather over, his mass association, and he does so (2) because he comes to see himself not as a mere delegate, instructed or not, of the mass association he represents, but as a member of "an elite" composed of such men as himself. These facts, in turn, lead to (3) the big gap between the terms in which issues are debated and resolved among members of this elite, and the terms in which they are presented to the members of the various mass associations. For the decisions that are made must *take into account* those who are important—other elites—but they must be *sold* to the mass memberships.

The gap between speaker and listener, between power and public, leads less to any iron law of oligarchy than to the law of spokesmanship: as the pressure group expands, its leaders come to organize the opinions they "represent." So elections, as we have seen, become contests between two giant and unwieldly parties, neither of which the individual can truly feel that he influences, and neither of which is capable of winning psychologically impressive or politically decisive majorities. And, in all this, the parties are of the same general form as other mass associations. . . .

It is because they do not find available associations at once psychologically meaningful and historically effective that men often feel uneasy in their political and economic loyalties. The effective units of power are now the huge corporation, the inaccessible government, the grim military establishment. Between these, on the one hand, and the family and the small community on the other, we find no intermediate associations in which men feel secure and with which they feel powerful. There is little live political struggle. Instead, there is administration from above, and the political vacuum below. . . .

Public opinion exists when people who are not in the government of a country claim the right to express political opinions freely and publicly, and the right that these opinions should influence or determine the policies, personnel, and actions of their government. In this formal sense there has been and there is definite public opinion in the United States. And yet, with modern developments this formal right— when it does still exist as a right—does not mean what it once did.

* * *

The idea of a mass society suggests the idea of an elite of power. The idea of the public, in contrast, suggests the liberal tradition of a society without any power elite, or at any rate with shifting elites of no sovereign consequence. For, if a genuine public is sovereign, it needs no master; but the masses, in their full development, are sovereign only in some plebiscitarian moment of adulation to an elite as authoritative celebrity. The political structure of a democratic state requires the public; and, the democratic man, in his rhetoric, must assert that this public is the very seat of sovereignty.

But now, given all these forces that have enlarged and centralized the political order and made modern societies less political and more administrative; given the transformation of the old middle classes into something which perhaps should not even be called middle class; given all the mass communications that do not truly communicate; given all the metropolitan segregation that is not community; given the absence of voluntary associations that really connect the public at large with the centers of power—what is happening is the decline of a set of publics that is sovereign only in the most formal and rhetorical sense. Moreover, in many countries the remnants of such publics as remain are now being frightened out of existence. They lose their will for rationally considered decision and action because they do not possess the instruments for such decision and action; they lose their sense of political belonging because they do not belong; they lose their political will because they see no way to realize it.

The top of modern American society is increasingly unified, and often seems willfully co-ordinated: at the top there has emerged an elite of power. The middle levels are a drifting set of stalemated, balancing forces: the middle does not link the bottom with the top. The bottom of this society is politically fragmented, and even as a passive fact, increasingly powerless: at the bottom there is emerging a mass society.

Can Foreign Policy Be Democratic?*

BY MULFORD Q. SIBLEY

[1948]

DEMOCRACY AND PUBLIC POLICY

DEMOCRACY signifies that public policy shall be *made* by the community as a whole and not by any segment of the community and that policy shall be in the *interest* of the whole community rather than of any particular part. Both these elements are essential if we are to term a society or a policy "democratic." Thus, policy determined by the community but having as its substance arbitrary and special privileges for a class is not democratic. Policies determined by an individual or a class, although for the benefit of the entire community, are also undemocratic. Conceivably a despot or an aristocracy might govern *for* the people—many have claimed to do so—but that would not be a democracy.

In this discussion of foreign policy we are primarily concerned with democracy as method or means, since this would seem to be the crucial problem. In a sense, democracy is primarily a method; the democrat would argue that once a policy is molded by methods which are genuinely democratic, the substance of the decisions is more likely to be for the benefit of the whole community. What, then, in more specific terms, does democracy as means imply? It implies at least that:

(1) Leaders must be under the effective control of the community. There must be some mechanism or mechanisms whereby the community can select and depose those who are called upon to speak in its name. Those who assume the function of proposing alternative courses of action—the central function of leadership in democratic policy making—should be under such effective control of their con-

* From a symposium on Thomas A. Bailey's *The Man in the Street* in *American Perspective*, September 1948. Reprinted by permission of the Foundation for Foreign Affairs.

stituents that any suggested public policy could become definite and binding only after the community had given its free consent. In a democracy leaders suggest, advise, propose and advocate. It is the community which debates, selects, consents to and makes final a given course of action.

(2) Leaders should speak only truthfully. One of the most important points of distinction between democratic and non-democratic leadership is in their respective attitudes to the problem of the political lie. At one end of the scale stand the leaders who make it a conscious principle to utilize the political lie as a method of leadership; in the middle are those who deliberately use political lies only in situations which they define as "crises"; while at the other end are those leaders who steadfastly refuse to use the political lie, even in times which they may judge to be crises. Only the latter of the three classes, according to the framework of this discussion, could be called in any sense "democratic." They alone see that democracy is more than the achievement of a supposedly "democratic" goal: it is, above all, a method for making public decisions. Deception, even if used honestly for what the leader regards as the long-run welfare of society, in effect shifts the making of decisions from the community to the leader, and contradicts the central canon of democracy.

(3) All the relevant information available on a given issue must be before the public when it is called upon to make a decision, if the decision is to be intelligent and rational. One of the functions of true political leadership is to provide this information, withholding nothing of relevance and presenting it in such a form that it can serve as the basis for intelligent discussion. No leader, even though he be a high executive in government, has the moral right to withhold any *public* (as contrasted with purely private) information which comes into his possession and which has any relation to the subject under discussion.

(4) Decisions will be made only after thorough discussion, for only through discussion can a community will be discovered. A community will is not a mere aggregate of individual wills, uninformed and undisciplined by the social process which we call discussion; rather is it a new phenomenon which arises in the process of discussion.

(5) Factors which make for irrational decisions will be minimized. Such factors include lack of education, great disparities in in-

dividual incomes and any system of communications which does not adequately reflect or express all points of view. A democratic discussion must consist in deliberation on conflicting positions by citizens who are sufficiently freed from immediate concern for physical needs to make rational deliberation possible. If conflicting interpretations of public policy are not given widespread publicity, if some approaches to an issue of policy are excluded (through monopolistic controls of press and radio, for example), there will be little about which to deliberate. If, on the other hand, the community is adequately informed, but includes large numbers of over-fed and under-fed citizens, the rationality of the decision reached is also impaired.

APPLICATION OF PRINCIPLES TO FOREIGN POLICY

The specific application of these principles to the conduct of foreign policy suggests, as a minimum, that:

(1) No foreign commitment whatsoever could be made until, after thorough and public discussion under conditions required for a democratic decision, it is approved by a representative body. This principle would not exclude the representative body's delegating power to the executive, under specific limitations, to make agreements like those of the reciprocal trade program. It would, however, exclude any agreements not specifically authorized by Congress and any agreements not customarily submitted for senatorial approval—the so-called executive agreements.

(2) An executive making what purported to be secret commitments, of any kind and under any conditions, would on their discovery be subject to immediate impeachment. Likewise, a President who on the plea of "international crisis" disregards the conditions essential for a democratic decision, who uses deception for what *he* regards as the public good, should be removed forthwith from office.

(3) No executive would have the power to withhold information demanded by Congress or a congressional committee for any reason, except that the information was purely private in character. Even in this case, Congress or its committees should have the final right to decide whether the information was purely private or not. The present arrangement, whereby the President is held to have the power to withhold information whose release he deems contrary to the public interest, would be changed and Congress alone have the right of decision. It is absurd to speak of democratic processes so long as

one man has the power to decide whether publication of requested information is detrimental to the public welfare. If giving the information to a congressional body would in effect make it public immediately (as many argue), then it is better, from the democratic point of view, to undergo whatever risks might be involved than to rely on procedures which are the antithesis of democracy.

(4) All relevant information regarding progress in international negotiations should be made public immediately so that agreements can be formulated and molded in the full light of public debate. It is sometimes argued that such publicity might hamper negotiations and that democratic procedures are satisfied if the final agreement alone is submitted for public approbation or disapproval. But if the public has to wait until the final formulation of the proposal, collective wisdom, which democrats rightly value so highly elsewhere, would have no opportunity to develop and operate. Such procedure would be analogous to the formulation of ordinary statutes in secret and their approval or disapproval by public vote, the community not being consulted in their formulation. Democracy involves much more than a plebiscite; it implies continuous and public discussion of a principle from its embryonic form to its final statement, and the final statement might well differ widely from the initial proposal.

Objections and Comments

It may be objected that a line of argument of this kind smacks of purism, neglects the realities of political life and exalts an abstraction. Specific objections might take and have taken these forms:

(1) It is urged that political deception is permissible in time of crisis. The leader, it is said, being far-sighted and compelled to take into account a public opinion which is short-sighted, has to accept the short-run vision of the people and lead the community to disaster. Refusing to do so, he must resign his office or deliberately deceive the people into believing that he is leading where they wish to go, while in actuality taking them in the opposite direction. Thus Thomas A. Bailey in his recent book, *The Man in the Street*, admits that "Franklin Roosevelt repeatedly deceived the American people during the period before Pearl Harbor" (p. 11), and then goes on to justify those deceptions on the ground that the people were too short-sighted to see their own interests. Bailey frankly concedes, moreover, that Roosevelt's methods were undemocratic: "A President who cannot

entrust the people with the truth betrays a certain lack of faith in democracy" (p. 13).

To the advocate of democracy, this "certain lack of faith" is really a total absence of faith. If the people are not to be entrusted with their destiny in times of crisis, then *when* should they make decisions? According to those who uphold deception, it is to be used only in a crisis when there is not time to "educate" the community as to the true situation. But who determines when the crisis exists and when deception is necessary? The leader, of course. The final decision is his and not the community's. No theory could be a sharper thrust at the heart of democratic faith. Democracy, its defenders would reply, does not hold that it is the function of leaders to guarantee the safety of the nation at the expense of the truth.

This controversy turns on the question of values. Bailey argues in effect that Roosevelt's policy was the only one which would preserve the United States and that the only way he could get the policy adopted was by deception. To which the democrat would reply: "Admitting for the moment that Roosevelt's policy was the only one which would preserve the nation, there are greater values than the preservation of the nation. If the choice is actually between the absence of deception, with destruction of the nation on the one hand, and deception with preservation of the nation on the other, the democrat would choose the former. The existence of democracy is not bound up with the preservation of any given Nation State. Deception used in the supposed defense of the nation means in the long run the destruction of democracy." But the democrat would also question whether deception is ever necessary to preserve a nation which aspires to democracy: if it is, then that nation would seem well on the way to repudiation of the democratic faith.

(2) Another objection to a democratically controlled foreign policy would assert that the "masses" are not well-informed. Bailey calls them the "apathetic and ill-informed masses." No democrat would argue that the people are technically well-informed in foreign affairs, but he would contend that with communications adequate and relevant information available (today it is *not*, due to less than democratic attitudes in high places), leaders could present genuine alternatives and the community could make a competent final decision after hearing all the alternatives weighed. No democrat would argue that all the decisions made democratically will be "right" deci-

sions; but he will contend that in the long run they are more likely to be "right" than decisions made undemocratically, and that the risk is far less than that involved in discarding democratic methods on the plea of public necessity.

The community is certainly as competent to make final decisions of policy as Franklin Roosevelt was. Perhaps it would have been better for the cause of democracy had the United States remained out of the war (as Bailey implies it would have done had not Roosevelt "rightly" deceived it). The contrary proposition is at least not self-evident. Most persons now agree that the ignorant English mill-workers were right when they opposed British recognition of the southern Confederacy and that the British Cabinet, including the brilliant Gladstone, was wrong in advocating recognition. Likewise, contemporary and future events may show that the American people were right before their deception by Roosevelt and that Roosevelt was wrong in deceiving them into war, wrong in being less than honest with them from the election of 1940 through the many deceptions down to his death, wrong in making secret commitments at Yalta and deliberately denying that he had made them, wrong not only because of his methods but in the substance of his decisions.

(3) It might be argued that deception or withholding of relevant information is justified because all elements of a democratic society are not present. If communications *were* free, if all sides of a question *were* fairly presented through press and radio, if money *did not* shackle opinion, it will be argued, it might be right to insist on publication of all relevant information and on the evil of deception. But since no society is more than a semi-democracy, at best, for the leader to be perfectly truthful and to release all information would result only in the distortion of that information by press and radio. Rational decisions by the community would still not be possible.

This is a specious argument. Granted that no society is more than a semi-democracy at best, and that information would be twisted to serve the interests of special groups, still the publication of all relevant information would at least make more possible the intelligent discussion of alternative courses of action. There are likely to be a few minority organs of press and radio which would take issue with predominant interpretations. Moreover, if the bulk of the press and radio are opposed to the President, surely the latter through his prestige and prerogatives can combat what he might regard as distorted interpretations on at least equal terms.

(4) Finally, it may be urged that the nature of modern war makes democratic processes in foreign affairs increasingly impracticable. Bailey argues that in the "days of the atomic bomb" we may have to move "more rapidly" than a "lumbering public opinion" will allow, yielding a large part of our democratic control of foreign affairs.

There is some force to this argument. As war becomes total, as ostensible "democracies" invent and use the atomic bomb, democratic methods tend to be destroyed not only in formulating foreign policy, but in domestic as well. Hence we are told that we cannot permit democratic control: we must surrender it as gracefully as possible. The atomic bomb puts a premium on surprise attacks, making the congressional power to declare war even more of a mockery than it is today. Without secrecy and deception, modern war is impossible; therefore, delegate more authority to the President so that he can keep more information secret and decide more issues without reference to community consent. This would seem to be clearly implied in statements like those of Bailey. That is one solution. But it is not a democratic solution. The democrat, it seems to me, will take the same set of circumstances and infer that if modern war and democracy are incompatible, the solution is to refuse to use war as a method and to adopt other more effective realistic means to oppose tyranny. What possible logic is there in using methods to preserve democracy which by their very nature destroy the democratic process?

I do not think that at this point the democrat will be interested only in such long-run goals as the abolition of war by world organization. The problem is one of immediate strategy. Specifically, that national State which first renounces and abandons reliance on armaments and war as methods is the community most likely to preserve and extend democracy and to defeat tyranny, not merely specific tyrants. There is only one basic alternative to war as a technique, and that is the late Mr. Gandhi's method. Subconsciously, many seem to recognize this, as when the leaders of the western world paid lip-service to Gandhi's achievements at the time of the Mahatma's death. Actually, however, we have not been converted. We continue to construct the weapons of mass destruction whose effective use is incompatible with the democratic process, and to profess at the same time that we are using these means to preserve democracy. We cannot have it both ways at once. Until we choose clearly and definitely preparation for war and destruction of democracy, on the one hand, or elimination of war preparation and an adaptation of Mr. Gandhi's methods, on the other, the problem of democratic control of foreign policy will remain in its present ambiguous, confused and unsatisfactory state. Leaders will continue to deceive us, ostensibly to preserve us, and the basic right of the community to damn itself if it so chooses will be ignored.

The Dilemma of Democracy*

BY THOMAS A. BAILEY

[1948]

THE portion of my book which has been most vigorously attacked . . . states that Franklin D. Roosevelt, when confronted by an apathetic public and a critical foreign menace, felt compelled to deceive the people into an awareness of their peril. I then ask the rhetorical question, "Who shall say that posterity will not thank him for it?" . . .

I do not wish to condone lying in our public officials, and I regret that a situation should have developed which evidently convinced Roosevelt of the wisdom of telling white lies. But I am still not sure that I blame him for what he did.

The basic question is this: To what extent in a democracy, and particularly in time of crisis, can the leaders take the people into their confidence and defer to them?

I must at the outset endeavor to correct certain misconceptions which apparently are held by some of my critics. The first is that Roosevelt tricked the American people into war, despite their wishes to the contrary.

No one can deny that Roosevelt at times was less than candid in handling this problem, as well as in handling problems of a domestic nature. But it seems improbable that his liberties with the truth . . . had a decisive influence on the final outcome. The Gallup polls on the eve of Pearl Harbor showed that the American people, about eight out of ten, still wanted to stay out of war. The polls also showed that a strong majority wanted to aid Britain, even at the risk of hostilities. In short, we did not want war, but we wanted to do those things which would inevitably bring war. Several of my critics insist —and I thoroughly agree—that the President should not deliberately launch a major foreign policy in the face of strong public opposition. In the days before Pearl Harbor, Roosevelt adopted a program of aid

---

* Excerpts from Professor Bailey's reply to a critical symposium entitled "Can Foreign Policy Be Democratic?" *American Perspective*, October 1948. Reprinted by permission of the Foundation for Foreign Affairs.

at the risk of war, which the masses supported. And since war came, shall we say that the people did not go into it with their eyes in some degree open? . . .

Roosevelt was evidently worried about *minority* rather than *majority* opinion when he practiced deception. . . . The majority of the people were with him on all-aid-short-of-war; a strong minority was not. The minority numbered perhaps thirty-five percent of the people. If war were to come, how could the United States hope to defeat the Axis if the nation were riven by so substantial a minority, as it had been in the War of 1812? Roosevelt's appeals to the irrelevant issue of freedom of the seas and Attorney General Jackson's labored ruling in support of the destroyer deal were clearly attempts to quiet the vociferous minority. The critics of the President further overlook the fact that he *resisted* public pressure for a get-tough-with-Japan policy and for purposes of not provoking Japan prematurely lagged far behind public opinion in embargoing war supplies and freezing Japanese assets. I wonder if [they] would attack Roosevelt so severely if he had used deception to keep us out of war with Hitler.

The final misconception is the naive one that Roosevelt was the first president of the United States to deceive the electorate in order to accomplish purposes that he deemed desirable.

Again, I do not wish to defend lying, but I think we might just as well face the facts. Our social structure, including monogamy, would collapse if everybody told everybody else fully and frankly what he thought and what he knew. If deception is freely practiced in private life and private business, what shall we say about public and political life, in which an even lower standard often obtains? . . .

The historian may perhaps be permitted a backward glance at the record. Washington issued his Neutrality Proclamation in 1793 without seeking a mandate from the people—assuming that there was any machinery for securing a mandate. He acted in defiance of a vast body of opinion, which may have constituted a majority. Mr. Sibley would disapprove of all this. Washington communicated the unpopular Jay's treaty to the Senate without making it public, and the Senate tried earnestly but unsuccessfully to keep it a secret. Madison white-washed the administration's conduct of the War of 1812 in his famous message of 1815. Polk was less than truthful in his war message of 1846. McKinley in 1898 sent a war message to Congress knowing that Spain had capitulated. Wilson lied to a Senatorial committee about his knowledge of the secret treaties. Similar deceptions were practiced by other presidents, all of whom Mr. Sibley would have removed from office.

Certain presidents have also openly violated their oath to support the constitution. Jefferson, after much travail, accepted the Louisiana purchase knowing in his heart that he had no constitutional right to do so. Buchanan found no warrant in the constitution for preventing the Southern states from seceding, so the Union slowly dissolved before his eyes. Lincoln swore a solemn oath to uphold the constitution, and then in the interests of preserving the Union he proceeded to violate it in a wholesale fashion on the principle that the end justified the means. Yet Lincoln is widely praised and Buchanan is widely condemned.

. . . [Mr. Roosevelt] knew that the world was madly rearming, and when he called for increased military appropriations, he was branded a war monger. He knew that the dictators were running amok, and when he called for a quarantine, he was branded a sensationalist. He knew that if sore-beset Britain collapsed the torch of liberty would be extinguished in Europe, that the workers in the factories and naval yards of Europe would become Hitlerian slaves and that the liberties of the American people would be placed in grave jeopardy. He knew that if Hitler did not launch a direct frontal attack on us, he probably would undertake a flanking movement through Latin America, that we might be able to beat him off our shores at an awful cost, and that if we did not the lamp of liberty would go out in the world, perhaps for all time. Why not help England, while England was still afloat? And if we were finally drawn into the war, we would have bought time for preparation and, in addition, would have an indispensable European springboard.

. . . Statesmen in the position of Mr. Roosevelt have to weigh all possible alternatives, and this the President doubtless did. Mr. Sibley evidently thinks that we should have all been Gandhis, and that we should have wrapped our sheets around our shanks, while the wave of the future—whether Hitlerism or Stalinism—rolled over us. But Mr. Roosevelt happened to be the president of 130,000,000 people, whose forebears had won their freedom in the War for Independence. That was a long time ago, and the average citizen did not cherish his freedom as deeply or as vigilantly as he should have. How could

Mr. Roosevelt, with the thought of not only the living and the dead but of the millions of Americans yet unborn, fail to take active if on occasion disingenuous steps, despite the campaign of 1940, to protect the liberties of the American people, especially when the Gallup polls made it clear that a majority of those people were willing to face war in the interests of helping the democracies defend our liberties? . . .

As for Russia's having been able to win the war without our aid, I do not know. But we would have been taking an appalling chance. If we had won, all would have been well, temporarily. If we had lost, we presumably would have jeopardized not only our national existence but our liberties. Most Americans, as the Gallup polls showed, were not willing to take that chance. As for Stalin, many mistakes have been made, and perhaps things did not necessarily have to work out as they have. If war comes, we are infinitely better prepared to meet it now than we were in 1940. We may not sleep too well now, but do we not sleep better than we would if Hitler had won?

The brutal fact is that the world has changed and is changing. In the days of the horse and buggy, we could indulge in the luxury of indifference, ignorance, open discussion, and leisurely debate. But decisions now have to be made in the interests of national security much faster than the present cumbersome processes will permit. If we could assume that the oceans were still wide, that there were no atomic bombs, that there were no long range bombers and that there were no dictators seeking to impose their will on weaker peoples, the picture would be entirely different. Much of the discussion by my critics presupposes that we are living in an orderly world, that democratic processes obtain abroad, and that powerful foreign groups entertain only friendly thoughts toward us.

Let us imagine a situation which is by no means Jules Vernian. Suppose that information of unimpeachable veracity is placed in the hands of President Truman that the Soviets have poised a large fleet of long range, one-way bombers, laden with atomic bombs, and scheduled to knock out all our large cities and industrial centers, with a possible loss of some 30,000,000 lives. Take-off time is set for forty-eight hours hence. According to my critics, President Truman should summon Congress into special session, which would consume some ten days, lay all his evidence before it (which would automatically dry up such sources of information) and call for a full and free debate, with a probable filibuster thrown in by the Wallaceites.

Given such a situation, there would be no national capital in which Congress could convene. We might rise from the radioactive ruins of our civilization and beat off the invader, but the cost is too terrible to contemplate. Roosevelt in December 1941 knew that the Japanese were about to strike, but the war-declaring processes being what they are, and public opinion being sharply divided, he had to sit and wait for the blow to fall. Fortunately there were no atomic bombs then. In a future situation of similar gravity the first blow might well be the last.

In such a crisis I believe that the President would be derelict in his duty if he did not, as commander in chief of the army and navy, issue the orders to strike first. The responsibility for making this decision might well be shared with some kind of "inner cabinet," . . . so that we might know whom to blame. The Constitution does not forbid the chief executive to make war. It merely vests in Congress the power to declare war, and this might be done later if there still is a Congress and a place for it to meet. And if there is enough of Congress left to start impeachment proceedings against the President, assuming that any such desire exists, there will be time enough to lay bare the evidence on which action was taken.

This of course is not "pure" democracy. But in warfare we are inevitably pulled down to the level of our adversaries; in the recent conflict we trained thousands of men to fight dirty. In critical cold wars we are pulled down to the level of our adversaries, at least in some measures. Horse-and-buggy democracy is simply not geared to present day demands for speed of decision. Since these shackles exist, and since our leaders have to get things done in the interests of the people, circumventions inevitably develop. Deception is one. Presenting the people with accomplished facts, such as the occupation of Iceland in 1941, is another. Executive agreements, which we ideally deplore, and which I agree should be made public along with all treaties, have become increasingly numerous simply because the legislative process of ratification has become intolerably slow and uncertain. We should not deplore executive agreements nearly so much as the unwieldly machinery which forces them into existence.

To avoid all these uncandid subterfuges I urge in my book that we delegate more authority to the executive branch of the government. The British have long since done this, but we do not say that they have abandoned democracy. Yet Mr. Sibley argues that if we have to choose between giving up some of our democracy and giving up our national existence, we should give up the latter in the hope of retaining the former.

This view holds that we really have "pure" democracy, and more or less have had from the beginning. It assumes also that rather than impair that which we have never had we ought to let Stalinism engulf us, and then we will be sure to keep our democracy under the beneficent supervision of the Kremlin. But more than that, Mr. Sibley seems to hold that democracy of a "pure" type is an end in itself. I quite disagree. If we have to modify our democracy, even in the direction of socialism, in order to preserve a substantial residue of our liberties, I am in favor of doing so.

. . . The gist of my argument is that unless we are willing to face the fact that 19th century methods must be modified to accord with modern conditions, our conscientious and well meaning public servants will unfortunately be under increasing pressure to "do good by stealth." I have confidence that the mass of the people can make broad decisions with intelligence *if* all relevant information can be placed before them, *if* the issues can be fully discussed, *if* the problems are not too technical for the lay mind and *if* there is time for democratic judgments to jell. But I greatly fear that we are heading into a situation, if we are not there already, when in critical circumstances none of these four suppositions will be valid.

V

COMMUNISM

Selections from

Manifesto of the Communist Party

BY KARL MARX AND FRIEDRICH ENGELS

PREFACE

BY FRIEDRICH ENGELS

[1888]

* * *

THE *Manifesto* being our joint production, I consider myself bound to state that the fundamental proposition which forms its nucleus, belongs to Marx. That proposition is: That in every historical epoch, the prevailing mode of economic production and exchange, and the social organisation necessarily following from it, form the basis upon which is built up, and from which alone can be explained, the political and intellectual history of that epoch; that consequently the whole history of mankind (since the dissolution of primitive tribal society, holding land in common ownership) has been a history of class struggles, contests between exploiting and exploited, ruling and oppressed classes; that the history of these class struggles forms a series of evolutions in which, nowadays, a stage has been reached where the exploited and oppressed class—the proletariat—cannot attain its emancipation from the sway of the exploiting and ruling class—the bourgeoisie—without at the same time, and once and for all, emancipating society at large from all exploitation, oppression, class distinctions and class struggles.

This proposition, . . . in my opinion, is destined to do for history what Darwin's theory has done for biology. . . .

MANIFESTO OF THE COMMUNIST PARTY

[1848]

A spectre is haunting Europe—the spectre of Communism. All the powers of old Europe have entered into a holy alliance to exorcise this spectre: Pope and Czar, Metternich and Guizot, French Radicals and German police-spies.

Where is the party in opposition that has not been decried as communistic by its opponents in power? Where the Opposition that has not hurled back the branding reproach of Communism, against the more advanced opposition parties, as well as against its reactionary adversaries?

Two things result from this fact:

I. Communism is already acknowledged by all European powers to be itself a power.

II. It is high time that Communists should openly, in the face of the whole world, publish their views, their aims, their tendencies, and meet this nursery tale of the spectre of Communism with a manifesto of the party itself.

To this end, Communists of various nationalities have assembled in London, and sketched the following manifesto, to be published in the English, French, German, Italian, Flemish and Danish languages.

* * *

The history of all hitherto existing society is the history of class struggles.

Freeman and slave, patrician and plebeian, lord and serf, guildmaster and journeyman, in a word, oppressor and oppressed stood in constant opposition to one another, carried on an uninterrupted, now hidden, now open fight, a fight that each time ended, either in a revolutionary reconstitution of society at large, or in the common ruin of the contending classes.

In the earlier epochs of history, we find almost everywhere a complicated arrangement of society into various orders, a manifold gradation of social rank. In ancient Rome we have patricians, knights, plebeians, slaves; in the Middle Ages, feudal lords, vassals, guild-masters, journeymen, apprentices, serfs; in almost all of these classes, again, subordinate gradations.

The modern bourgeois society that has sprouted from the ruins of feudal society, has not done away with class antagonisms. It has but established new classes, new conditions of oppression, new forms of struggle in place of the old ones.

Our epoch, the epoch of the bourgeoisie, possesses, however, this distinctive feature: It has simplified the class antagonisms. Society as a whole is more and more splitting up into two great hostile camps, into two great classes directly facing each other—bourgeoisie and proletariat.[1]

Each step in the development of the bourgeoisie was accompanied by a corresponding political advance of that class. . . . The bourgeoisie has at last, since the establishment of modern industry and of the world market, conquered for itself, in the modern representative state, exclusive political sway. The executive of the modern state is but a committee for managing the common affairs of the whole bourgeoisie.

The bourgeoisie has played a most revolutionary rôle in history.

The bourgeoisie, wherever it has got the upper hand, has put an end to all feudal, patriarchal, idyllic relations. It has pitilessly torn asunder the motley feudal ties that bound man to his "natural superiors," and has left no other bond between man and man than naked self-interest, than callous "cash payment." It has drowned the most heavenly ecstasies of religious fervour, of chivalrous enthusiasm, of philistine sentimentalism, in the icy water of egotistical calculation. It has resolved personal worth into exchange value, and in place of the numberless indefeasible chartered freedoms, has set up that single, unconscionable freedom—Free Trade. In one word, for exploitation, veiled by religious and political illusions, it has substituted naked, shameless, direct, brutal exploitation.

The bourgeoisie has stripped of its halo every occupation hitherto honoured and looked up to with reverent awe. It has converted the physician, the lawyer, the priest, the poet, the man of science, into its paid wage-labourers.

The bourgeoisie has torn away from the family its sentimental veil, and has reduced the family relation to a mere money relation. . . .

The bourgeoisie cannot exist without constantly revolutionising the instruments of production, and thereby the relations of pro-

---

[1] By bourgeoisie is meant the class of modern capitalists, owners of the means of social production and employers of wage-labour; by proletariat, the class of modern wage-labourers who, having no means of production of their own, are reduced to selling their labour power in order to live. [Engels.]

duction, and with them the whole relations of society. Conservation of the old modes of production in unaltered form, was, on the contrary, the first condition of existence for all earlier industrial classes. Constant revolutionising of production, uninterrupted disturbance of all social conditions, everlasting uncertainty and agitation distinguish the bourgeois epoch from all earlier ones. All fixed, fast-frozen relations, with their train of ancient and venerable prejudices and opinions, are swept away, all new-formed ones become antiquated before they can ossify. All that is solid melts into air, all that is holy is profaned, and man is at last compelled to face with sober senses his real conditions of life and his relations with his kind.

The need of a constantly expanding market for its products chases the bourgeoisie over the whole surface of the globe. It must nestle everywhere, settle everywhere, establish connections everywhere.

The bourgeoisie has through its exploitation of the world market given a cosmopolitan character to production and consumption in every country. To the great chagrin of reactionaries, it has drawn from under the feet of industry the national ground on which it stood. All old-established national industries have been destroyed or are daily being destroyed. They are dislodged by new industries, whose introduction becomes a life and death question for all civilised nations, by industries that no longer work up indigenous raw material, but raw material drawn from the remotest zones; industries whose products are consumed, not only at home, but in every quarter of the globe. In place of the old wants, satisfied by the production of the country, we find new wants, requiring for their satisfaction the products of distant lands and climes. In place of the old local and national seclusion and self-sufficiency, we have intercourse in every direction, universal inter-dependence of nations. And as in material, so also in intellectual production. The intellectual creations of individual nations become common property. National one-sidedness and narrow-mindedness become more and more impossible, and from the numerous national and local literatures there arises a world literature.

The bourgeoisie, by the rapid improvement of all instruments of production, by the immensely facilitated means of communication, draws all nations, even the most barbarian, into civilisation. The cheap prices of its commodities are the heavy artillery with which it batters down all Chinese walls, with which it forces the bar-barians' intensely obstinate hatred of foreigners to capitulate. It compels all nations, on pain of extinction, to adopt the bourgeois mode of production; it compels them to introduce what it calls civilisation into their midst, *i.e.,* to become bourgeois themselves. In a word, it creates a world after its own image.

The bourgeoisie has subjected the country to the rule of the towns. It has created enormous cities, has greatly increased the urban population as compared with the rural, and has thus rescued a considerable part of the population from the idiocy of rural life. Just as it has made the country dependent on the towns, so it has made barbarian and semi-barbarian countries dependent on the civilised ones, nations of peasants on nations of bourgeois, the East on the West.

More and more the bourgeoisie keeps doing away with the scat-tered state of the population, of the means of production, and of property. It has agglomerated population, centralised means of production, and has concentrated property in a few hands. The necessary consequence of this was political centralisation. Inde-pendent, or but loosely connected provinces, with separate inter-ests, laws, governments and systems of taxation, became lumped together into one nation, with one government, one code of laws, one national class interest, one frontier and one customs tariff.

The bourgeoisie, during its rule of scarce one hundred years, has created more massive and more colossal productive forces than have all preceding generations together. Subjection of nature's forces to man, machinery, application of chemistry to industry and agricul-ture, steam-navigation, railways, electric telegraphs, clearing of whole continents for cultivation, canalisation of rivers, whole popu-lations conjured out of the ground—what earlier century had even a presentiment that such productive forces slumbered in the lap of social labour?

. . . Modern bourgeois society with its relations of production, of exchange and of property, a society that has conjured up such gigantic means of production and of exchange, is like the sorcerer who is no longer able to control the powers of the nether world whom he has called up by his spells. For many a decade past the his-tory of industry and commerce is but the history of the revolt of modern productive forces against modern conditions of production, against the property relations that are the conditions for the existence of the bourgeoisie and of its rule. It is enough to mention the commercial crises that by their periodical return put the existence of the entire bourgeois society on trial, each time more threateningly. In these crises a great part not only of the existing products, but also of the previously created productive forces, are periodically destroyed. In these crises there breaks out an epidemic that, in all earlier epochs, would have seemed an absurdity—the epidemic of over-production. Society suddenly finds itself put back into a state of momentary barbarism; it appears as if a famine, a universal war of devastation had cut off the supply of every means of subsistence; industry and commerce seem to be destroyed. And why? Because there is too much civilisation, too much means of subsistence, too much industry, too much commerce. The productive forces at the disposal of society no longer tend to further the development of the conditions of bourgeois property; on the contrary, they have become too powerful for these conditions, by which they are fettered, and no sooner do they overcome these fetters than they bring disorder into the whole of bourgeois society, endanger the existence of bourgeois property. The conditions of bourgeois society are too narrow to comprise the wealth created by them. And how does the bourgeoisie get over the crises? On the one hand by enforced destruction of a mass of productive forces; on the other, by the conquest of new markets, and by the more thorough exploitation of the old ones. That is to say, by paving the way for more extensive and more destructive crises, and by diminishing the means whereby crises are prevented. . . .

But not only has the bourgeoisie forged the weapons that bring death to itself; it has also called into existence the men who are to wield those weapons—the modern working class—the proletarians.

In proportion as the bourgeoisie, *i.e.*, capital, is developed, in the same proportion is the proletariat, the modern working class, developed—a class of labourers, who live only so long as they find work, and who find work only so long as their labour increases capital. These labourers, who must sell themselves piecemeal, are a commodity, like every other article of commerce, and are consequently exposed to all the vicissitudes of competition, to all the fluctuations of the market.

Owing to the extensive use of machinery and to division of labour, the work of the proletarians has lost all individual character, and, consequently, all charm for the workman. He becomes an appendage of the machine, and it is only the most simple, most monotonous, and most easily acquired knack, that is required of him. Hence, the cost of production of a workman is restricted, almost entirely, to the means of subsistence that he requires for his maintenance, and for the propagation of his race. But the price of a commodity, and therefore also of labour, is equal to its cost of production. In proportion, therefore, as the repulsiveness of the work increases, the wage decreases. Nay more, in proportion as the use of machinery and division of labour increases, in the same proportion the burden of toil also increases, whether by prolongation of the working hours, by increase of the work exacted in a given time, or by increased speed of the machinery, etc.

Modern industry has converted the little workshop of the patriarchal master into the great factory of the industrial capitalist. Masses of labourers, crowded into the factory, are organised like soldiers. As privates of the industrial army they are placed under the command of a perfect hierarchy of officers and sergeants. Not only are they slaves of the bourgeois class, and of the bourgeois state; they are daily and hourly enslaved by the machine, by the over-looker, and, above all, by the individual bourgeois manufacturer himself. The more openly this despotism proclaims gain to be its end and aim, the more petty, the more hateful and the more embittering it is. . . .

The lower strata of the middle class—the small tradespeople, shopkeepers, and retired tradesmen generally, the handicraftsmen and peasants—all these sink gradually into the proletariat, partly because their diminutive capital does not suffice for the scale on which modern industry is carried on, and is swamped in the competition with the large capitalists, partly because their specialised skill is rendered worthless by new methods of production. Thus the proletariat is recruited from all classes of the population. . . .

. . . With the development of industry the proletariat not only increases in number; it becomes concentrated in greater masses, its strength grows, and it feels that strength more. The various interests and conditions of life within the ranks of the proletariat are more and more equalised, in proportion as machinery obliterates all distinctions of labour and nearly everywhere reduces wages to the same low level. The growing competition among the bourgeois, and the resulting commercial crises, make the wages of the workers ever more fluctuating. The unceasing improvement of machinery, ever more rapidly developing, makes their livelihood more and more precarious; the collisions between individual workmen and individual bourgeois take more and more the character of collisions between two classes. Thereupon the workers begin to form combinations (trade unions) against the bourgeoisie; they club together in order to keep up the rate of wages; they found permanent associations in order to make provision beforehand for these occasional revolts. Here and there the contest breaks out into riots.

Now and then the workers are victorious, but only for a time. The real fruit of their battles lies, not in the immediate result, but in the ever expanding union of the workers. This union is furthered by the improved means of communication which are created by modern industry, and which place the workers of different localities in contact with one another. It was just this contact that was needed to centralise the numerous local struggles, all of the same character, into one national struggle between classes. But every class struggle is a political struggle. . . .

This organisation of the proletarians into a class, and consequently into a political party, is continually being upset again by the competition between the workers themselves. But it ever rises up again, stronger, firmer, mightier. It compels legislative recognition of particular interests of the workers, by taking advantage of the divisions among the bourgeoisie itself. Thus the ten-hour bill in England was carried.

Altogether collisions between the classes of the old society further the course of development of the proletariat in many ways. The bourgeoisie finds itself involved in a constant battle. At first with the aristocracy; later on, with those portions of the bourgeoisie itself whose interests have become antagonistic to the progress of industry; at all times with the bourgeoisie of foreign countries. In all these battles it sees itself compelled to appeal to the proletariat, to ask for its help, and thus, to drag it into the political arena. The bourgeoisie itself, therefore, supplies the proletariat with its own elements of political and general education, in other words, it

furnishes the proletariat with weapons for fighting the bourgeoisie. . . .

Of all the classes that stand face to face with the bourgeoisie
today, the proletariat alone is a really revolutionary class. The other
classes decay and finally disappear in the face of modern industry;
the proletariat is its special and essential product.

The lower middle class, the small manufacturer, the shopkeeper,
the artisan, the peasant, all these fight against the bourgeoisie, to
save from extinction their existence as fractions of the middle class.
They are therefore not revolutionary, but conservative. Nay more,
they are reactionary, for they try to roll back the wheel of history.
If by chance they are revolutionary, they are so only in view of their
impending transfer into the proletariat; they thus defend not their
present, but their future interests; they desert their own standpoint
to adopt that of the proletariat.

The "dangerous class," the social scum (*Lumpenproletariat*), that
passively rotting mass thrown off by the lowest layers of old society,
may, here and there, be swept into the movement by a proletarian
revolution; its conditions of life, however, prepare it far more for
the part of a bribed tool of reactionary intrigue.

The social conditions of the old society no longer exist for the
proletariat. The proletarian is without property; his relation to his
wife and children has no longer anything in common with
bourgeois family relations; modern industrial labour, modern
subjection to capital, the same in England as in France, in America
as in Germany, has stripped him of every trace of national
character. Law, morality, religion, are to him so many bourgeois
prejudices, behind which lurk in ambush just as many bourgeois
interests.

All the preceding classes that got the upper hand, sought to
fortify their already acquired status by subjecting society at large
to their conditions of appropriation. The proletarians cannot become masters of the productive forces of society, except by abolishing their own previous mode of appropriation, and thereby also
every other previous mode of appropriation. They have nothing of
their own to secure and to fortify; their mission is to destroy all
previous securities for, and insurances of, individual property.

All previous historical movements were movements of minorities.

or in the interest of minorities. The proletarian movement is the self-conscious, independent movement of the immense majority, in the interest of the immense majority. The proletariat, the lowest stratum of our present society, cannot stir, cannot raise itself up, without the whole superincumbent strata of official society being sprung into the air.

Though not in substance, yet in form, the struggle of the proletariat with the bourgeoisie is at first a national struggle. The proletariat of each country must, of course, first of all settle matters with its own bourgeoisie.

In depicting the most general phases of the development of the proletariat, we traced the more or less veiled civil war, raging within existing society, up to the point where that war breaks out into open revolution, and where the violent overthrow of the bourgeoisie lays the foundation for the sway of the proletariat.

Hitherto, every form of society has been based, as we have already seen, on the antagonism of oppressing and oppressed classes. But in order to oppress a class, certain conditions must be assured to it under which it can, at least, continue its slavish existence. The serf, in the period of serfdom, raised himself to membership in the commune, just as the petty bourgeois, under the yoke of feudal absolutism, managed to develop into a bourgeois. The modern labourer, on the contrary, instead of rising with the progress of industry, sinks deeper and deeper below the conditions of existence of his own class. He becomes a pauper, and pauperism develops more rapidly than population and wealth. And here it becomes evident, that the bourgeoisie is unfit any longer to be the ruling class in society, and to impose its conditions of existence upon society as an over-riding law. It it unfit to rule because it is incompetent to assure an existence to its slave within his slavery, because it cannot help letting him sink into such a state, that it has to feed him, instead of being fed by him. Society can no longer live under this bourgeoisie, in other words, its existence is no longer compatible with society.

The essential condition for the existence and sway of the bourgeois class, is the formation and augmentation of capital; the condition for capital is wage-labour. Wage-labour rests exclusively on competition between the labourers. The advance of industry, whose involuntary promoter is the bourgeoisie, replaces the isolation of the labourers, due to competition, by their revolutionary combination, due to association. The development of modern industry, therefore, cuts from under its feet the very foundation on which the bourgeoisie produces and appropriates products. What the bourgeoisie therefore produces, above all, are its own grave-diggers. Its fall and the victory of the proletariat are equally inevitable.

* * *

In what relation do the Communists stand to the proletarians as a whole?

The Communists do not form a separate party opposed to other working class parties.

They have no interests separate and apart from those of the proletariat as a whole. . . .

The Communists are distinguished from the other working class parties by this only: 1. In the national struggles of the proletarians of the different countries, they point out and bring to the front the common interests of the entire proletariat, independently of all nationality. 2. In the various stages of development which the struggle of the working class against the bourgeoisie has to pass through, they always and everywhere represent the interests of the movement as a whole. . . .

The immediate aim of the Communists is the same as that of all the other proletarian parties: Formation of the proletariat into a class, overthrow of bourgeois supremacy, conquest of political power by the proletariat.

The theoretical conclusions of the Communists are in no way based on ideas or principles that have been invented, or discovered, by this or that would-be universal reformer.

They merely express, in general terms, actual relations springing from an existing class struggle, from a historical movement going on under our very eyes. The abolition of existing property relations is not at all a distinctive feature of Communism.

All property relations in the past have continually been subject to historical change consequent upon the change in historical conditions.

The French Revolution, for example, abolished feudal property in favour of bourgeois property.

The distinguishing feature of Communism is not the abolition of property generally, but the abolition of bourgeois property. But

modern bourgeois private property is the final and most complete
expression of the system of producing and appropriating products
that is based on class antagonisms, on the exploitation of the many
by the few.

In this sense, the theory of the Communists may be summed up
in the single sentence: Abolition of private property.

We Communists have been reproached with the desire of abolishing the right of personally acquiring property as the fruit of a man's
own labour, which property is alleged to be the groundwork of all
personal freedom, activity and independence.

Hard-won, self-acquired, self-earned property! Do you mean the
property of the petty artisan and of the small peasant, a form of
property that preceded the bourgeois form? There is no need to
abolish that; the development of industry has to a great extent
already destroyed it, and is still destroying it daily.

Or do you mean modern bourgeois private property?

But does wage-labour create any property for the labourer? Not
a bit. It creates capital, *i.e.,* that kind of property which exploits
wage-labour, and which cannot increase except upon condition of
begetting a new supply of wage-labour for fresh exploitation. Property, in its present form, is based on the antagonism of capital and
wage-labour. Let us examine both sides of this antagonism.

To be a capitalist, is to have not only a purely personal, but a
social status in production. Capital is a collective product, and only
by the united action of many members, nay, in the last resort, only
by the united action of all members of society, can it be set in motion.

Capital is therefore not a personal, it is a social, power.

When, therefore, capital is converted into common property, into
the property of all members of society, personal property is not
thereby transformed into social property. It is only the social character of the property that is changed. It loses its class character.

Let us now take wage-labour.

The average price of wage-labour is the minimum wage, *i.e.,* that
quantum of the means of subsistence which is absolutely requisite to
keep the labourer in bare existence as a labourer. What, therefore,
the wage-labourer appropriates by means of his labour, merely suffices to prolong and reproduce a bare existence. We by no means
intend to abolish this personal appropriation of the products of
labour, an appropriation that is made for the maintenance and repro-

duction of human life, and that leaves no surplus wherewith to command the labour of others. All that we want to do away with is the miserable character of this appropriation, under which the labourer lives merely to increase capital, and is allowed to live only insofar as the interest of the ruling class requires it. . . .

You are horrified at our intending to do away with private property. But in your existing society, private property is already done away with for nine-tenths of the population; its existence for the few is solely due to its non-existence in the hands of those nine-tenths. You reproach us, therefore, with intending to do away with a form of property, the necessary condition for whose existence is the non-existence of any property for the immense majority of society.

In a word, you reproach us with intending to do away with your property. Precisely so; that is just what we intend.

From the moment when labour can no longer be converted into capital, money, or rent, into a social power capable of being monopolised, *i.e.*, from the moment when individual property can no longer be transformed into bourgeois property, into capital, from that moment, you say, individuality vanishes.

You must, therefore, confess that by "individual" you mean no other person than the bourgeois, than the middle class owner of property. This person must, indeed, be swept out of the way, and made impossible.

Communism deprives no man of the power to appropriate the products of society; all that it does is to deprive him of the power to subjugate the labour of others by means of such appropriation.

It has been objected, that upon the abolition of private property all work will cease, and universal laziness will overtake us.

According to this, bourgeois society ought long ago to have gone to the dogs through sheer idleness; for those of its members who work, acquire nothing, and those who acquire anything, do not work. The whole of this objection is but another expression of the tautology: There can no longer be any wage-labour when there is no longer any capital. . . .

But don't wrangle with us so long as you apply, to our intended abolition of bourgeois property, the standard of your bourgeois notions of freedom, culture, law, etc. Your very ideas are but the outgrowth of the conditions of your bourgeois production and bourgeois property, just as your jurisprudence is but the will of your class made into a law for all, a will whose essential character and direction are determined by the economic conditions of existence of your class.

The selfish misconception that induces you to transform into eternal laws of nature and of reason, the social forms springing from your present mode of production and form of property—historical relations that rise and disappear in the progress of production—this misconception you share with every ruling class that has preceded you. What you see clearly in the case of ancient property, what you admit in the case of feudal property, you are of course forbidden to admit in the case of your own bourgeois form of property. . . .

The Communists are further reproached with desiring to abolish countries and nationality.

The workingmen have no country. We cannot take from them what they have not got. Since the proletariat must first of all acquire political supremacy, must rise to be the leading class of the nation, must constitute itself *the* nation, it is, so far, itself national, though not in the bourgeois sense of the word.

National differences and antagonisms between peoples are vanishing gradually from day to day, owing to the development of the bourgeoisie, to freedom of commerce, to the world market, to uniformity in the mode of production and in the conditions of life corresponding thereto.

The supremacy of the proletariat will cause them to vanish still faster. United action, of the leading civilised countries at least, is one of the first conditions for the emancipation of the proletariat.

In proportion as the exploitation of one individual by another is put an end to, the exploitation of one nation by another will also be put an end to. In proportion as the antagonism between classes within the nation vanishes, the hostility of one nation to another will come to an end.

The charges against Communism made from a religious, a philosophical, and, generally, from an ideological standpoint, are not deserving of serious examination.

Does it require deep intuition to comprehend that man's ideas, views, and conceptions, in one word, man's consciousness, changes with every change in the conditions of his material existence, in his social relations and in his social life?

What else does the history of ideas prove, than that intellectual production changes its character in proportion as material production is changed? The ruling ideas of each age have ever been the ideas of its ruling class.

When people speak of ideas that revolutionise society, they do but express the fact that within the old society the elements of a new one have been created, and that the dissolution of the old ideas keeps even pace with the dissolution of the old conditions of existence.

When the ancient world was in its last throes, the ancient religions were overcome by Christianity. When Christian ideas succumbed in the 18th century to rationalist ideas, feudal society fought its death-battle with the then revolutionary bourgeoisie. The ideas of religious liberty and freedom of conscience, merely gave expression to the sway of free competition within the domain of knowledge.

"Undoubtedly," it will be said, "religion, moral, philosophical and juridical ideas have been modified in the course of historical development. But religion, morality, philosophy, political science, and law, constantly survived this change."

"There are, besides, eternal truths, such as Freedom, Justice, etc., that are common to all states of society. But Communism abolishes eternal truths, it abolishes all religion, and all morality, instead of constituting them on a new basis; it therefore acts in contradiction to all past historical experience."

What does this accusation reduce itself to? The history of all past society has consisted in the development of class antagonisms, antagonisms that assumed different forms at different epochs.

But whatever form they may have taken, one fact is common to all past ages, *viz.*, the exploitation of one part of society by the other. No wonder, then, that the social consciousness of past ages, despite all the multiplicity and variety it displays, moves within certain common forms, or general ideas, which cannot completely vanish except with the total disappearance of class antagonisms.

The Communist revolution is the most radical rupture with traditional property relations; no wonder that its development involves the most radical rupture with traditional ideas.

But let us have done with the bourgeois objections to Communism.

We have seen above, that the first step in the revolution by the working class, is to raise the proletariat to the position of ruling class, to establish democracy.

The proletariat will use its political supremacy to wrest, by degrees, all capital from the bourgeoisie, to centralise all instruments of production in the hands of the state, *i.e.*, of the proletariat organised as the ruling class; and to increase the total of productive forces as rapidly as possible.

Of course, in the beginning, this cannot be effected except by means of despotic inroads on the rights of property, and on the conditions of bourgeois production; by means of measures, therefore, which appear economically insufficient and untenable, but which, in the course of the movement, outstrip themselves, necessitate further inroads upon the old social order, and are unavoidable as a means of entirely revolutionising the mode of production.

These measures will of course be different in different countries.

Nevertheless in the most advanced countries, the following will be pretty generally applicable.

1. Abolition of property in land and application of all rents of land to public purposes.

2. A heavy progressive or graduated income tax.

3. Abolition of all right of inheritance.

4. Confiscation of the property of all emigrants and rebels.

5. Centralisation of credit in the hands of the state, by means of a national bank with state capital and an exclusive monopoly.

6. Centralisation of the means of communication and transport in the hands of the state.

7. Extension of factories and instruments of production owned by the state; the bringing into cultivation of waste lands, and the improvement of the soil generally in accordance with a common plan.

8. Equal obligation of all to work. Establishment of industrial armies, especially for agriculture.

9. Combination of agriculture with manufacturing industries; gradual abolition of the distinction between town and country, by a more equable distribution of the population over the country.

10. Free education for all children in public schools. Abolition of child factory labour in its present form. Combination of education with industrial production, etc.

When, in the course of development, class distinctions have disappeared, and all production has been concentrated in the hands of a vast association of the whole nation, the public power will lose its political character. Political power, properly so called, is merely the organised power of one class for oppressing another. If the proletariat during its contest with the bourgeoisie is compelled, by the force of circumstances, to organise itself as a class; if, by means of a revolution, it makes itself the ruling class, and, as such sweeps away by force the old conditions of production, then it will, along with these conditions, have swept away the conditions for the existence of class antagonisms, and of classes generally, and will thereby have abolished its own supremacy as a class.

In place of the old bourgeois society, with its classes and class antagonisms, we shall have an association, in which the free development of each is the condition for the free development of all.

* * *

In short, the Communists everywhere support every revolutionary movement against the existing social and political order of things.

In all these movements they bring to the front, as the leading question in each case, the property question, no matter what its degree of development at the time.

Finally, they labour everywhere for the union and agreement of the democratic parties of all countries.

The Communists disdain to conceal their views and aims. They openly declare that their ends can be attained only by the forcible overthrow of all existing social conditions. Let the ruling classes tremble at a Communist revolution. The proletarians have nothing to lose but their chains. They have a world to win.

Workingmen of all countries, unite!

Selections from

State and Revolution

BY V. I. LENIN

[1917]

THE STATE AS THE PRODUCT OF THE IRRECONCILABILITY OF CLASS ANTAGONISMS

WHAT is now happening to Marx's doctrine has, in the course of history, often happened to the doctrines of other revolutionary thinkers and leaders of oppressed classes struggling for emancipation. During the lifetime of great revolutionaries, the oppressing classes have visited relentless persecution on them and received their teaching with the most savage hostility, the most furious hatred, the most ruthless campaign of lies and slanders. After their death, attempts are made to turn them into harmless icons, canonise them, and surround their *names* with a certain halo for the "consolation" of the oppressed classes and with the object of duping them, while at the same time emasculating and vulgarising the *real essence* of their revolutionary theories and blunting their revolutionary edge. At the present time, the bourgeoisie and the opportunists within the labour movement are co-operating in this work of adulterating Marxism. They omit, obliterate, and distort the revolutionary side of its teaching, its revolutionary soul. They push to the foreground and extol what is, or seems, acceptable to the bourgeoisie. . . .

In such circumstances, the distortion of Marxism being so widespread, it is our first task to *resuscitate* the real teachings of Marx on the state. For this purpose it will be necessary to quote at length from the works of Marx and Engels themselves. . . .

Let us begin with the most popular of Engels' works, *The Origin of the Family, Private Property and the State.* . . .

Summarising his historical analysis Engels says:

The state is therefore by no means a power imposed on society from the outside; just as little is it "the reality of the moral idea," "the image and reality of reason," as Hegel asserted. Rather, it is a product of society at a certain stage of development; it is the admission that this society has become entangled in an insoluble contradiction with itself, that it is cleft into irreconcilable antagonisms which it is powerless to dispel. But in order that these antagonisms, classes with conflicting economic interests, may not consume themselves and society in sterile struggle, a power apparently standing above society becomes necessary, whose purpose is to moderate the conflict and keep it within the bounds of "order"; and this power arising out of society, but placing itself above it, and increasingly separating itself from it, is the state.

Here we have, expressed in all its clearness, the basic idea of Marxism on the question of the historical rôle and meaning of the state. The state is the product and the manifestation of the *irreconcilability* of class antagonisms. The state arises when, where, and to the extent that the class antagonisms *cannot* be objectively reconciled. And, conversely, the existence of the state proves that the class antagonisms *are* irreconcilable.

It is precisely on this most important and fundamental point that distortions of Marxism arise along two main lines.

On the one hand, the bourgeois, and particularly the petty-bourgeois, ideologists, compelled under the pressure of indisputable historical facts to admit that the state exists only where there are class antagonisms and the class struggle, "correct" Marx in such a way as to make it appear that the state is an organ for *reconciling* the classes. According to Marx, the state could neither arise nor maintain itself if a reconciliation of classes were possible. But with the petty-bourgeois and philistine professors and publicists, the state —and this frequently on the strength of benevolent references to Marx!—becomes a conciliator of the classes. According to Marx, the state is an organ of class *domination,* an organ of *oppression* of one class by another; its aim is the creation of "order" which legalises and perpetuates this oppression by moderating the collisions between the classes. But in the opinion of the petty-bourgeois politicians, order means reconciliation of the classes, and not oppression of one class by another; to moderate collisions does not mean, they say, to deprive the oppressed classes of certain definite means and methods of struggle for overthrowing the oppressors, but to practice reconciliation. . . .

. . . What is forgotten or glossed over is this: if the state is the product of the irreconcilable character of class antagonisms, if it is a force standing *above* society and "increasingly separating itself from it," then it is clear that the liberation of the oppressed class is impossible not only without a violent revolution, *but also without the destruction* of the apparatus of state power, which was created by the ruling class and in which this "separation" is embodied. . . .

The "Withering Away" of the State and Violent Revolution

Engels' words regarding the "withering away" of the state enjoy such popularity, they are so often quoted, and they show so clearly the essence of the usual adulteration by means of which Marxism is made to look like opportunism, that we must dwell on them in detail. Let us quote the whole passage from which they are taken.

The proletariat seizes state power, and then transforms the means of production into state property. But in doing this, it puts an end to itself as the proletariat, it puts an end to all class differences and class antagonisms, it puts an end also to the state as the state. Former society, moving in class antagonisms, had need of the state, that is, an organisation of the exploiting class at each period for the maintenance of its external conditions of production; therefore, in particular, for the forcible holding down of the exploited class in the conditions of oppression (slavery, bondage or serfdom, wage-labour) determined by the existing mode of production. The state was the official representative of society as a whole, its embodiment in a visible corporate body; but it was this only in so far as it was the state of that class which itself, in its epoch, represented society as a whole: in ancient times, the state of the slave-owning citizens; in the Middle Ages, of the feudal nobility; in our epoch, of the bourgeoisie. When ultimately it becomes really representative of society as a whole, it makes itself superfluous. As soon as there is no longer any class of society to be held in subjection; as soon as, along with class domination and the struggle for individual existence based on the former anarchy of production, the collisions and excesses arising from these have also been abolished, there is nothing more to be repressed, and a special repressive force, a state, is no longer necessary. The first act in which the state really comes forward as the representative of society as a whole—the seizure of the means of production in the name of society—is at the same time its last independent act as a state. The interference of a state power in social relations becomes superfluous in one sphere after another, and then becomes dormant of itself. Government over persons is replaced by the administration of things and the direction of the processes of production. The state is not "abolished," *it withers away.* . . .

. . . Engels at the very outset of his argument says that, in assuming state power, the proletariat by that very act "puts an end to the state as the state." . . . As a matter of fact, Engels speaks here of the destruction of the bourgeois state by the proletarian revolution, while the words about its withering away refer to the remains of *proletarian* statehood *after* the Socialist revolution. The bourgeois state does not "wither away," according to Engels, but is "put an end to" by the proletariat in the course of the revolution. What withers away after the revolution is the proletarian state or semi-state.

Secondly, the state is a "special repressive force." This splendid and extremely profound definition of Engels' is given by him here with complete lucidity. It follows from this that the "special repressive force" of the bourgeoisie for the suppression of the proletariat, of the millions of workers by a handful of the rich, must be replaced by a "special repressive force" of the proletariat for the suppression of the bourgeoisie (the dictatorship of the proletariat). It is just this that constitutes the destruction of "the state as the state." It is just this that constitutes the "act" of "the seizure of the means of production in the name of society." And it is obvious that such a substitution of one (proletarian) "special repressive force" for another (bourgeois) "special repressive force" can in no way take place in the form of a "withering away."

Thirdly, as to the "withering away" or, more expressively and colourfully, as to the state "becoming dormant," Engels refers quite clearly and definitely to the period *after* "the seizure of the means of production [by the state] in the name of society," that is, *after* the Socialist revolution. We all know that the political form of the "state" at that time is complete democracy. But it never enters the head of any of the opportunists who shamelessly distort Marx that when Engels speaks here of the state "withering away," or "becoming dormant," he speaks of *democracy*. At first sight this seems very strange. But it is "unintelligible" only to one who has not reflected on the fact that democracy is *also* a state and that, consequently, democracy will *also* disappear when the state disappears. The bourgeois state can be "put an end to" only by a revolution. Only the state in general, *i.e.*, most complete democracy, can "wither away." . . .

. . . In the same work of Engels, from which every one remembers his argument on the "withering away" of the state, there is also a disquisition on the significance of a violent revolution. The historical analysis of its rôle becomes, with Engels, a veritable panegyric on violent revolution. This, of course, "no one remembers"; to talk or even to think of the importance of this idea is not considered good form by contemporary Socialist parties, and in the daily propaganda and agitation among the masses it plays no part whatever. Yet it is indissolubly bound up with the "withering away" of the state in one harmonious whole.

Here is Engels' argument:

... That force, however, plays another rôle (other than that of a diabolical power) in history, a revolutionary rôle that, in the words of Marx, it is the midwife of every old society which is pregnant with the new; that it is the instrument with whose aid social movement forces its way through and shatters the dead, fossilised political forms—of this there is not a word in Herr Dühring. It is only with sighs and groans that he admits the possibility that force will perhaps be necessary for the overthrow of the economic system of exploitation—unfortunately! because all use of force, forsooth, demoralises the person who uses it. And this in spite of the immense moral and spiritual impetus which has resulted from every victorious revolution! ...

How can this panegyric on violent revolution . . . be combined with the theory of the "withering away" of the state to form one doctrine? . . .

We have already said above and shall show more fully later that the teaching of Marx and Engels regarding the inevitability of a violent revolution refers to the bourgeois state. It *cannot* be replaced by the proletarian state (the dictatorship of the proletariat) through "withering away," but, as a general rule, only through a violent revolution. . . . The necessity of systematically fostering among the masses *this* and just this point of view about violent revolution lies at the root of the *whole* of Marx's and Engels' teaching. . . .

The replacement of the bourgeois by the proletarian state is impossible without a violent revolution. The abolition of the proletarian state, *i.e.,* of all states, is only possible through "withering away."

* * *

The doctrine of the class struggle, as applied by Marx to the question of the state and of the Socialist revolution, leads inevitably to the recognition of the *political rule* of the proletariat, of its dictatorship, *i.e.,* of a power shared with none and relying directly upon the armed force of the masses. The overthrow of the bourgeoisie is realisable only by the transformation of the proletariat into the *ruling class*, able to crush the inevitable and desperate resistance of the bourgeoisie, and to organise, for the new economic order, *all* the toiling and exploited masses.

The proletariat needs state power, the centralised organisation of force, the organisation of violence, both for the purpose of crushing the resistance of the exploiters and for the purpose of *guiding* the great mass of the population—the peasantry, the petty-bourgeoisie, the semi-proletarians—in the work of organising Socialist economy.

By educating a workers' party, Marxism educates the vanguard of the proletariat, capable of assuming power and of *leading the whole people* to Socialism, of directing and organising the new order, of being the teacher, guide and leader of all the toiling and exploited in the task of building up their social life without the bourgeoisie and against the bourgeoisie. . . .

"The state, *i.e.,* the proletariat organised as the ruling class"—this theory of Marx's is indissolubly connected with all his teaching concerning the revolutionary rôle of the proletariat in history. The culmination of this rôle is proletarian dictatorship, the political rule of the proletariat.

But, if the proletariat needs the state, as a *special* form of organisation of violence *against* the capitalist class, the following question arises almost automatically: is it thinkable that such an organisation can be created without a preliminary break-up and destruction of the state machinery created for *its own* use by the bourgeoisie? The *Communist Manifesto* leads straight to this conclusion. . . .

* * *

The centralised state power peculiar to bourgeois society came into being in the period of the fall of absolutism. Two institutions are especially characteristic of this state machinery: bureaucracy and the standing army. . . .

The development, perfecting and strengthening of the bureaucratic and military apparatus has been going on through all the bourgeois revolutions of which Europe has seen so many since the fall of feudalism. It is particularly the petty bourgeoisie that is attracted to the side of the big bourgeoisie and to its allegiance, largely by means of this apparatus, which provides the upper strata of the peasantry, small artisans and tradesmen with a number of comparatively comfortable, quiet and respectable berths raising their holders *above* the people. . . .

But the longer the process of "re-apportioning" the bureaucratic apparatus among the various bourgeois and petty-bourgeois parties . . . goes on, the more clearly the oppressed classes, with the proletariat at their head, realise that they are irreconcilably hostile to the *whole* of bourgeois society. Hence the necessity for all bourgeois parties, even for the most democratic and "revolutionary-democratic" among them, to increase their repressive measures against the revolutionary proletariat, to strengthen the apparatus of repression, *i.e.*, the same state machinery. Such a course of events compels the revolution *"to concentrate all its forces of destruction"* against the state power, and to regard the problem as one, not of perfecting the machinery of the state, but of *breaking up and annihilating it.* . . .

The main point in the teaching of Marx is the class struggle. This has very often been said and written. But this is not true. . . . The theory of the class struggle was *not* created by Marx, but by the bourgeoisie *before* Marx and is, generally speaking, *acceptable* to the bourgeoisie. He who recognises *only* the class struggle is not yet a Marxist; he may be found not to have gone beyond the boundaries of bourgeois reasoning and politics. To limit Marxism to the teaching of the class struggle means to curtail Marxism—to distort it, to reduce it to something which is acceptable to the bourgeoisie. A Marxist is one who *extends* the acceptance of class struggle to the acceptance of the *dictatorship of the proletariat.* Herein lies the deepest difference between a Marxist and an ordinary petty or big bourgeois. On this touchstone it is necessary to test a *real* understanding and acceptance of Marxism. . . .

Opportunism *does not lead* the recognition of class struggle up to the main point, up to the period of *transition* from capitalism to Communism, up to the period of *overthrowing* and completely abolishing the bourgeoisie. In reality, this period inevitably becomes a period of unusually violent class struggles in their sharpest possible forms and, therefore, the state during this period inevitably must be a state that is democratic *in a new way* (for the proletariat and the poor in general) and dictatorial *in a new way* (against the bourgeoisie).

Further, the substance of the teachings of Marx about the state is assimilated only by one who understands that the dictatorship of a *single* class is necessary not only for any class society generally, not only for the *proletariat* which has overthrown the bourgeoisie, but for the entire *historic period* which separates capitalism from "classless society," from Communism. The forms of bourgeois states are exceedingly variegated, but their essence is the same: in one way or another, all these states are in the last analysis inevitably a *dictatorship of the bourgeoisie*. The transition from capitalism to Communism will certainly bring a great variety and abundance of political forms, but the essence will inevitably be only one: *the dictatorship of the proletariat*.

* * *

To decide once every few years which member of the ruling class is to repress and oppress the people through parliament—this is the real essence of bourgeois parliamentarism, not only in parliamentary-constitutional monarchies, but also in the most democratic republics. . . .

The venal and rotten parliamentarism of bourgeois society is replaced in the Commune by institutions in which freedom of opinion and discussion does not degenerate into deception, for the parliamentarians must themselves work, must themselves execute their own laws, must themselves verify their results in actual life, must themselves be directly responsible to their electorate. Representative institutions remain, but parliamentarism as a special system, as a division of labour between the legislative and the executive functions, as a privileged position for the deputies, *no longer exists*. Without representative institutions we cannot imagine democracy, not even proletarian democracy; but we can and *must* think of democracy without parliamentarism. . . .

In the current arguments about the state . . . it is constantly forgotten that the destruction of the state means also the destruction of democracy; that the withering away of the state also means the withering away of democracy.

At first sight such a statement seems exceedingly strange and incomprehensible; indeed, some one may even begin to fear lest we be expecting the advent of such an order of society in which the principle of the subordination of the minority to the majority will not be respected—for is not a democracy just the recognition of this principle?

No, democracy is *not* identical with the subordination of the minority to the majority. Democracy is a *state* recognising the subordination of the minority to the majority, *i.e.*, an organisation for the systematic use of *violence* by one class against the other, by one part of the population against another.

We set ourselves the ultimate aim of destroying the state, *i.e.*, every organised and systematic violence, every use of violence against man in general. We do not expect the advent of an order of society in which the principle of subordination of minority to majority will not be observed. But, striving for Socialism, we are convinced that it will develop into Communism; that, side by side with this, there will vanish all need for force, for the *subjection* of one man to another, and of one part of the population to another, since people will *grow accustomed* to observing the elementary conditions of social existence *without force and without subjection*.

In order to emphasise this element of habit, Engels speaks of a *new generation*, "reared under new and free social conditions," which "will be able to throw on the scrap heap all this state rubbish"—every kind of state, including even the democratic-republican state. . . .

* * *

The whole theory of Marx is an application of the theory of evolution—in its most consistent, complete, well considered and fruitful form—to modern capitalism. It was natural for Marx to raise the question of applying this theory both to the *coming* collapse of capitalism and to the *future* evolution of *future* Communism.

On the basis of what *data* can the future evolution of future Communism be considered?

On the basis of the fact that *it has its origin* in capitalism, that it develops historically from capitalism, that it is the result of the action of a social force to which capitalism *has given birth*. There is no shadow of an attempt on Marx's part to conjure up a Utopia, to make idle guesses about that which cannot be known. Marx treats the question of Communism in the same way as a naturalist would treat the question of the evolution of, say, a new biological species, if he knew that such and such was its origin, and such and such the direction in which it changed. . . .

The first fact that has been established with complete exactness by the whole theory of evolution, by science as a whole . . . is that, historically, there must undoubtedly be a special stage or epoch of *transition* from capitalism to Communism.

Transition from Capitalism to Communism

Between capitalist and Communist society lies the period of the revolutionary transformation of the former into the latter. To this also corresponds a political transition period, in which the state can be no other than *the revolutionary dictatorship of the proletariat.*

This conclusion Marx bases on an analysis of the rôle played by the proletariat in modern capitalist society, on the data concerning the evolution of this society, and on the irreconcilability of the opposing interests of the proletariat and the bourgeoisie.

Earlier the question was put thus: to attain its emancipation, the proletariat must overthrow the bourgeoisie, conquer political power and establish its own revolutionary dictatorship.

Now the question is put somewhat differently: the transition from capitalist society, developing towards Communism, towards a Communist society, is impossible without a "political transition period," and the state in this period can only be the revolutionary dictatorship of the proletariat.

What, then, is the relation of this dictatorship to democracy?

We have seen that the *Communist Manifesto* simply places side by side the two ideas: the "transformation of the proletariat into the ruling class" and the "establishment of democracy." On the basis of all that has been said above, one can define more exactly how democracy changes in the transition from capitalism to Communism.

In capitalist society, under the conditions most favourable to its development, we have more or less complete democracy in the democratic republic. But this democracy is always bound by the narrow framework of capitalist exploitation, and consequently always remains, in reality, a democracy for the minority, only for the possessing classes, only for the rich. Freedom in capitalist society always remains just about the same as it was in the ancient Greek republics: freedom for the slave-owners. The modern wage-slaves, owing to the conditions of capitalist exploitation, are so much crushed by want and poverty that "democracy is nothing to them," "politics is nothing to them"; that, in the ordinary peaceful course of events, the majority of the populaion is debarred from participating in social and political life. . . .

Marx splendidly grasped this *essence* of capitalist democracy, when, in analysing the experience of the Commune, he said that the oppressed were allowed, once every few years, to decide which particular representatives of the oppressing class should be in parliament to represent and repress them!

But from this capitalist democracy—inevitably narrow, subtly rejecting the poor, and therefore hypocritical and false to the core—progress does not march onward, simply, smoothly and directly, to "greater and greater democracy," as the liberal professors and petty-bourgeois opportunists would have us believe. No, progress marches onward, *i.e.,* towards Communism, through the dictatorship of the proletariat; it cannot do otherwise, for there is no one else and no other way to *break the resistance* of the capitalist exploiters.

But the dictatorship of the proletariat—*i.e.,* the organisation of the vanguard of the oppressed as the ruling class for the purpose of crushing the oppressors—cannot produce merely an expansion of democracy. *Together* with an immense expansion of democracy which *for the first time* becomes democracy for the poor, democracy for the people, and not democracy for the rich folk, the dictatorship of the proletariat produces a series of restrictions of liberty in the case of the oppressors, the exploiters, the capitalists. We must crush them in order to free humanity from wage-slavery; their resistance must be broken by force; it is clear that where there is suppression there is also violence, there is no liberty, no democracy. . . .

Only in Communist society, when the resistance of the capitalists has been completely broken, when the capitalists have disappeared, when there are no classes (*i.e.,* there is no difference between the members of society in their relation to the social means of production), *only then* "the state ceases to exist," and *"it becomes possible to speak of freedom."* Only then a really full democracy, a democracy without any exceptions, will be possible and will be realised. And only then will democracy itself begin to *wither away* due to the simple fact that, freed from capitalist slavery, from the untold horrors, savagery, absurdities and infamies of capitalist exploitation, people will gradually *become accustomed* to the observance of the elementary rules of social life that have been known for centuries and repeated for thousands of years in all school books; they will become accustomed to observing them without force, without compulsion, without subordination, without the *special apparatus* for compulsion which is called the state.

The expression "the state *withers away*," is very well chosen, for it indicates both the gradual and the elemental nature of the process. Only habit can, and undoubtedly will, have such an effect; for we see around us millions of times how readily people get accustomed to observe the necessary rules of life in common, if there is no exploitation, if there is nothing that causes indignation, that calls forth protest and revolt and has to be *suppressed*. . . .

Finally, only Communism renders the state absolutely unnecessary, for there is *no one* to be suppressed—"no one" in the sense of a *class*, in the sense of a systematic struggle with a definite section of the population. We are not Utopians, and we do not in the least deny the possibility and inevitability of excesses on the part of *individual* persons, nor the need to suppress *such* excesses. But, in the first place, no special machinery, no special apparatus of repression is needed for this; this will be done by the armed people itself, as simply and as readily as any crowd of civilised people, even in modern society, parts a pair of combatants or does not allow a woman to be outraged. And, secondly, we know that the fundamental social cause of excesses which consist in violating the rules of social life is the exploitation of the masses, their want and their poverty. With the removal of this chief cause, excesses will inevitably begin to *"wither away."* We do not know how quickly and in what succession, but we know that they will wither away. With their withering away, the state will also *wither away*.

Without going into Utopias, Marx defined more fully what can *now* be defined regarding this future, namely, the difference between the lower and higher phases (degrees, stages) of Communist society.

First Phase of Communist Society

. . . Marx undertakes a *concrete* analysis of the conditions of life of a society in which there is no capitalism, and says:

> What we are dealing with here [analysing the programme of the party] is not a Communist society which has *developed* on its own foundations, but, on the contrary, one which is just *emerging* from capitalist society, and which therefore in all respects—economic, moral and intellectual—still bears the birthmarks of the old society from whose womb it sprung.

And it is this Communist society—a society which has just come into the world out of the womb of capitalism, and which, in all respects, bears the stamp of the old society—that Marx terms the "first," or lower, phase of Communist society.

The means of production are no longer the private property of individuals. The means of production belong to the whole of society. Every member of society, performing a certain part of socially-necessary work, receives a certificate from society to the effect that he has done such and such a quantity of work. According to this certificate, he receives from the public warehouses, where articles of consumption are stored, a corresponding quantity of products. Deducting that proportion of labour which goes to the public fund, every worker, therefore, receives from society as much as he has given it.

"Equality" seems to reign supreme. . . .

"Equal right," says Marx, we indeed have here; but it is *still* a "bourgeois right," which, like every right, *presupposes inequality*. Every right is an application of the *same* measure to *different* people who, in fact, are not the same and are not equal to one another; this is why "equal right" is really a violation of equality, and an injustice. In effect, every man having done as much social labour as every other, receives an equal share of the social products (with the above-mentioned deductions).

But different people are not alike: one is strong, another is weak; one is married, the other is not; one has more children, another has less, and so on.

. . . With equal labour—Marx concludes—and therefore an equal share in the social consumption fund, one man in fact receives more than the other, one is richer than the other, and so forth. In order to avoid all these defects, rights, instead of being equal, must be unequal.

The first phase of Communism, therefore, still cannot produce justice and equality; differences, and unjust differences, in wealth will still exist, but the *exploitation* of man by man will have become impossible, because it will be impossible to seize as private property the *means of production,* the factories, machines, land, and so on. . . .

And so, in the first phase of Communist society (generally called Socialism) "bourgeois right" is *not* abolished in its entirety, but only in part, only in proportion to the economic transformation so far attained, *i.e.,* only in respect of the means of production. "Bourgeois right" recognises them as the private property of separate individuals. Socialism converts them into common property. *To that extent,* and to that extent alone, does "bourgeois right" disappear.

However, it continues to exist as far as its other part is concerned; it remains in the capacity of regulator (determining factor) distributing the products and allotting labour among the members of society. "He who does not work, shall not eat"—this Socialist principle is *already* realised; "for an equal quantity of labour, an equal quantity of products"—this Socialist principle is also *already* realised. However, this is not yet Communism, and this does not abolish "bourgeois right," which gives to unequal individuals, in return for an unequal (in reality unequal) amount of work, an equal quantity of products.

This is a "defect," says Marx, but it is unavoidable during the first phase of Communism; for, if we are not to fall into Utopianism, we cannot imagine that, having overthrown capitalism, people will at once learn to work for society *without any standards of right*; indeed, the abolition of capitalism *does not immediately lay* the economic foundations for *such* a change.

And there is no other standard yet than that of "bourgeois right." To this extent, therefore, a form of state is still necessary, which, while maintaining public ownership of the means of production, would preserve the equality of labour and equality in the distribution of products.

The state is withering away in so far as there are no longer any capitalists, any classes, and, consequently, no *class* can be suppressed.

But the state has not yet altogether withered away, since there still remains the protection of "bourgeois right" which sanctifies actual inequality. For the complete extinction of the state, complete Communism is necessary.

Higher Phase of Communist Society

Marx continues:

In a higher phase of Communist society, when the enslaving subordination of individuals in the division of labour has disappeared, and with it also the antagonism between mental and physical labour; when labour has become not only a means of living, but itself the first necessity of life; when, along with the all-round development of individuals, the productive forces too have grown, and all the springs of social wealth are flowing more freely—it is only at that stage that it will be possible to pass completely beyond the narrow horizon of bourgeois rights, and for society to inscribe on its banners: from each according to his ability; to each according to his needs!

Only now can we appreciate the full correctness of Engels' remarks in which he mercilessly ridiculed all the absurdity of combining the words "freedom" and "state." While the state exists there is no freedom. When there is freedom, there will be no state.

The economic basis for the complete withering away of the state is that high stage of development of Communism when the antagonism between mental and physical labour disappears, that is to say, when one of the principal sources of modern *social* inequality disappears—a source, moreover, which it is impossible to remove immediately by the mere conversion of the means of production into public property, by the mere expropriation of the capitalists. . . .

The state will be able to wither away completely when society has realised the rule: "From each according to his ability; to each according to his needs," *i.e.,* when people have become accustomed to observe the fundamental rules of social life, and their labour is so productive, that they voluntarily work *according to their ability.* "The narrow horizon of bourgeois rights," which compels one to calculate, with the hard-heartedness of a Shylock, whether he has not worked half an hour more than another, whether he is not getting less pay than another—this narrow horizon will then be left behind. There will then be no need for any exact calculation by society of the quantity of products to be distributed to each of its members; each will take freely "according to his needs." . . .

Until the "higher" phase of Communism arrives, the Socialists demand the *strictest* control, *by society and by the state,* of the quantity of labour and the quantity of consumption; only this control must *start* with the expropriation of the capitalists, with the control of the workers over the capitalists, and must be carried out, not by a state of bureaucrats, but by a state of *armed workers.* . . .

Democracy is of great importance for the working class in its struggle for freedom against the capitalists. But democracy is by no means a limit one may not overstep; it is only one of the stages in the course of development from feudalism to capitalism, and from capitalism to Communism.

Democracy means equality. The great significance of the struggle of the proletariat for equality, and the significance of equality as a slogan, are apparent, if we correctly interpret it as meaning the abolition of *classes.* But democracy means only *formal* equality. Immediately after the attainment of equality for all members of society *in respect of* the ownership of the means of production, that is, of equality of labour and equality of wages, there will inevitably arise before humanity the question of going further from formal equality to real equality, *i.e.,* to realising the rule, "From each according to his ability; to each according to his needs." By what stages, by means of what practical measures humanity will proceed to this higher aim—this we do not and cannot know. But it is important to realise how infinitely mendacious is the usual bourgeois presentation of Socialism as something lifeless, petrified, fixed once for all, whereas in reality, it is *only* with Socialism that there will commence a rapid, genuine, real mass advance, in which first the *majority* and then the whole of the population will take part—an advance in all domains of social and individual life.

Democracy is a form of the state—one of its varieties. Consequently, like every state, it consists in organised, systematic application of force against human beings. This on the one hand. On the other hand, however, it signifies the formal recognition of the equality of all citizens, the equal right of all to determine the structure and administration of the state. This, in turn, is connected with the fact that, at a certain stage in the development of democracy, it first rallies the proletariat as a revolutionary class against capitalism, and gives it an opportunity to crush, to smash to bits, to wipe off the face of the earth the bourgeois state machinery—even its republican variety: the standing army, the police, and bureaucracy; then it substitutes for all this a *more* democratic, but still a state machinery in the shape of armed masses of workers, which becomes transformed into universal participation of the people in the militia.

Here "quantity turns into quality": *such* a degree of democracy is bound up with the abandonment of the framework of bourgeois society, and the beginning of its Socialist reconstruction. If *every one* really takes part in the administration of the state, capitalism cannot retain its hold. In its turn, capitalism, as it develops, itself creates *prerequisites* for "every one" *to be able* really to take part in the administration of the state. Among such prerequisites are: universal literacy, already realised in most of the advanced capitalist countries, then the "training and disciplining" of millions of workers by the huge, complex, and socialised apparatus of the post-office, the railways, the big factories, large-scale commerce, banking, etc., etc.

With such *economic* prerequisites it is perfectly possible, immediately, within twenty-four hours after the overthrow of the capitalists and bureaucrats, to replace them, in the control of production and distribution, in the business of *control* of labour and products, by the armed workers, by the whole people in arms. (The question of control and accounting must not be confused with the question of the scientifically educated staff of engineers, agronomists and so on. These gentlemen work today, obeying the capitalists; they will work even better tomorrow, obeying the armed workers.)

Accounting and control—these are the *chief* things necessary for the organising and correct functioning of the *first phase* of Communist society. *All* citizens are here transformed into hired employees of the state, which is made up of the armed workers. *All* citizens become employees and workers of *one* national state "syndicate." All that is required is that they should work equally, should regularly do their share of work, and should receive equal pay. The accounting and control necessary for this have been *simplified* by capitalism to the utmost, till they have become the extraordinarily simple operations of watching, recording and issuing receipts, within the reach of anybody who can read and write and knows the first four operations of arithmetic.[1]

When the *majority* of the people begin everywhere to keep such accounts and maintain such control over the capitalists (now converted into employees) and over the intellectual gentry, who still retain capitalist habits, this control will really become universal, general, national; and there will be no way of getting away from it, there will be "nowhere to go."

The whole of society will have become one office and one factory, with equal work and equal pay.

But this "factory" discipline, which the proletariat will extend to the whole of society after the defeat of the capitalists and the overthrow of the exploiters, is by no means our ideal, or our final aim. It is but a *foothold* necessary for the radical cleansing of society of all the hideousness and foulness of capitalist exploitation, *in order to advance further.*

From the moment when all members of society, or even only the overwhelming majority, have learned how to govern the state *them-*

---

[1] When most of the functions of the state are reduced to this accounting and control by the workers themselves, then it ceases to be a "political state," and the "public functions will lose their political character and be transformed into simple administrative functions." . . .

selves, have taken this business into their own hands, have "established" control over the insignificant minority of capitalists, over the gentry with capitalist leanings, and the workers thoroughly demoralised by capitalism—from this moment the need for any government begins to disappear. The more complete the democracy, the nearer the moment when it begins to be unnecessary. The more democratic the "state" consisting of armed workers, which is "no longer a state in the proper sense of the word," the more rapidly does *every* state begin to wither away.

For when *all* have learned to manage, and independently are actually managing by themselves social production, keeping accounts, controlling the idlers, the gentlefolk, the swindlers and similar "guardians of capitalist traditions," then the escape from this national accounting and control will inevitably become so increasingly difficult, such a rare exception, and will probably be accompanied by such swift and severe punishment (for the armed workers are men of practical life, not sentimental intellectuals, and they will scarcely allow any one to trifle with them), that very soon the *necessity* of observing the simple, fundamental rules of every-day social life in common will have become a *habit.*

The door will then be wide open for the transition from the first phase of Communist society to its higher phase, and along with it to the complete withering away of the state.

Capitalist Encirclement and Socialist Encirclement*

BY JOSEPH STALIN

[1939]

[ONE] of the defects of our propagandist and ideological work is the absence of full clarity among our comrades on certain theoretical questions of vital practical importance. . . .

It is sometimes asked: "We have abolished the exploiting classes; there are no longer any hostile classes in the country; there is nobody to suppress; hence there is no more need for the state; it must die away.—Why then do we not help our Socialist state to die away? Why do we not strive to put an end to it? Is it not time to throw out all this rubbish of a state?"

Or further: "The exploiting classes have already been abolished in our country: Socialism has been built in the main; we are advancing towards Communism. Now, the Marxist doctrine of the state says that there is to be no state under Communism.—Why then do we not help our Socialist state to die away? Is it not time we relegated the state to the museum of antiquities?"

These questions show that those who ask them have conscientiously memorized certain propositions contained in the doctrine of Marx and Engels about the state. But they also show that these comrades have failed to understand the essential meaning of this doctrine; that they have failed to realize in what historical conditions the various propositions of this doctrine were elaborated; and, what is more, that they do not understand present-day international conditions, have overlooked the capitalist encirclement and the dangers it entails for the Socialist country. These questions not only betray an underestimation of the capitalist encirclement, but also an underestimation of the rôle and significance of the bourgeois states and their organs, which send spies, assassins and wreckers into our country and are waiting for a favorable opportunity to

*An excerpt from Stalin's Report on the Work of the Central Committee to the 18th Congress of the Communist Party of the Soviet Union, March 10, 1939.

attack it by armed force. They likewise betray an underestimation of the rôle and significance of our Socialist state and of its military, punitive and intelligence organs, which are essential for the defense of the Socialist land from foreign attack. . . .

What could have given rise to this underestimation?

It arose owing to the fact that certain of the general propositions in the Marxist doctrine of the state were incompletely worked out and inadequate. It received currency owing to our unpardonably heedless attitude to matters pertaining to the theory of the state, in spite of the fact that we have twenty years of practical experience in matters of state which provide rich material for theoretical generalizations, and in spite of the fact that, given the desire, we have every opportunity of successfully filling this gap in theory. We have forgotten Lenin's highly important injunction about the theoretical duties of Russian Marxists, that it is their mission to further develop the Marxist theory. Here is what Lenin said in this connection:

"We do not regard Marxist theory as something completed and inviolable: on the contrary, we are convinced that it has only laid the corner-stone of the science which Socialists *must* further advance in all directions if they wish to keep pace with life. We think that an *independent* elaboration of the Marxist theory is especially essential for Russian Socialists, for this theory provides only general *guiding* principles, which, *in particular,* are applied in England differently from France, in France differently from Germany, and in Germany differently from Russia." (Lenin, *Collected Works,* Russian edition, Vol. II, p. 492.)

Consider, for example, the classical formulation of the theory of the development of the Socialist state given by Engels:

"As soon as there is no longer any class of society to be held in subjection; as soon as, along with class domination and the struggle for individual existence based on the former anarchy of production, the collisions and excesses arising from these have also been abolished, there is nothing more to be repressed which would make a special repressive force, a state, necessary. The first act in which the state really comes forward as the representative of society as a whole—the taking possession of the means of production in the name of society—is at the same time its last independent act as a state. The interference of the state power in social relations becomes superfluous in one sphere after another, and then ceases of itself. The government of persons is replaced by the administration of things and the direction of the process of production. The state is not 'abolished,' *it withers away.*" (*Herr Eugen Dühring's Revolution in Science* [*Anti-Dühring*], p. 308–09).

Is this proposition of Engels' correct?

Yes, it is correct, but only on one of two conditions: (1) *if* we study the Socialist state only from the angle of the internal development of the country, abstracting ourselves in advance from the international factor, isolating, for the convenience of investigation, the country and the state from the international situation; or (2) *if* we assume that Socialism is already victorious in all countries, or in the majority of countries, that a Socialist encirclement exists instead of a capitalist encirclement, that there is no more danger of foreign attack, and that there is no more need to strengthen the army and the state.

Well, but what if Socialism has been victorious only in one country, taken singly, and if, in view of this, it is quite impossible to abstract oneself from international conditions—what then? Engels' formula does not furnish an answer to this question. As a matter of fact, Engels did not set himself this question, and therefore could not have given an answer to it. Engels proceeds from the assumption that Socialism has already been victorious in all countries, or in a majority of countries, more or less simultaneously. Consequently, Engels is not here investigating any specific Socialist state of any particular country, but the development of the Socialist state in general, on the assumption that Socialism has been victorious in the majority of countries, that a Socialist encirclement exists that Socialism is victorious in a majority of countries, what changes must the proletarian, Socialist state undergo?" Only this general and abstract character of the problem can explain why in his investigation of the question of the Socialist state Engels completely abstracted himself from such a factor as international conditions, the international situation.

But it follows from this that Engels' general formula about the destiny of the Socialist state in general cannot be extended to the partial and specific case of the victory of Socialism in one country only, a country which is surrounded by a capitalist world, is subject to the menace of foreign military attack, cannot therefore abstract itself from the international situation, and must have at its disposal a well-trained army, well-organized punitive organs, and a strong intelligence service—consequently, must have its own state, strong enough to defend the conquests of Socialism from foreign attack.

We have no right to expect of the classical Marxist writers, separated as they were from our day by a period of forty-five or fifty-five years, that they should have foreseen each and every zigzag of history in the distant future in every separate country. It would be ridiculous to expect that the classical Marxist writers should have elaborated for our benefit ready-made solutions for each and every theoretical problem that might arise in any particular country fifty or one hundred years afterwards, so that we, the descendants of the classical Marxist writers, might calmly doze at the fireside and munch ready-made solutions. (*General laughter.*) But we can and should expect of the Marxists-Leninists of our day that they do not confine themselves to learning by rote a few general tenets of Marxism; that they delve deeply into the essence of Marxism; that they learn to take account of the experience gained in the twenty years of existence of the Socialist state in our country; that, lastly, they learn, with the use of this experience and with knowledge of the essence of Marxism, to apply the various general theses of Marxism concretely, to lend them greater precision and improve them. Lenin wrote his famous book, *The State and Revolution,* in August 1917, that is, a few months before the October Revolution and the establishment of the Soviet state. Lenin considered it the main task of this book to defend Marx's and Engels' doctrine of the state from the distortions and vulgarizations of the opportunists. Lenin was preparing to write a second volume of *The State and Revolution,* in which he intended to sum up the principal lessons of the experience of the Russian revolutions of 1905 and 1917. There can be no doubt that Lenin intended in the second volume of his book to elaborate and develop the theory of the state on the basis of the experience gained during the existence of Soviet power in our country. Death, however, prevented him from carrying this task into execution. But what Lenin did not manage to do should be done by his disciples. (*Loud applause.*)

The state arose because society split up into antagonistic classes; it arose in order to keep in restraint the exploited majority in the interests of the exploiting minority. The instruments of state authority have been mainly concentrated in the army, the punitive organs, the espionage service, the prisons. Two basic functions characterize the activity of the state: at home (the main function), to keep in restraint the exploited majority; abroad (not the main function), to extend the territory of its class, the ruling class, at the expense of the territory of other states, or to defend the territory of its own state from attack by other states. Such was the case in slave society and under feudalism. Such is the case under capitalism.

In order to overthrow capitalism it was not only necessary to remove the bourgeoisie from power, it was not only necessary to expropriate the capitalists, but also to smash entirely the bourgeois state machine and its old army, its bureaucratic officialdom and its police force, and to substitute for it a new, proletarian form of state, a new, Socialist state. And that, as we know, is exactly what the Bolsheviks did. But it does not follow that the new proletarian state may not preserve certain functions of the old state, changed to suit the requirements of the proletarian state. Still less does it follow that the forms of our Socialist state must remain unchanged, that all the original functions of our state must be fully preserved in the future. As a matter of fact, the forms of our state are changing and will continue to change in line with the development of our country and with the changes in the international situation.

Lenin was absolutely right when he said:

"The forms of bourgeois states are extremely varied, but in essence they are all the same: in one way or another, in the final analysis, all these states are inevitably the *dictatorship of the bourgeoisie*. The transition from capitalism to Communism will certainly create a great variety and abundance of political forms, but in essence there will inevitably be only one: *the dictatorship of the proletariat*." (Lenin, *Selected Works*, Vol. VII, p. 34.)

Since the October Revolution, our Socialist state has passed through two main phases in its development.

The first phase was the period from the October Revolution to the elimination of the exploiting classes. The principal task in that period was to suppress the resistance of the overthrown classes, to organize the defense of the country against the attack of the interventionists, to restore industry and agriculture, and to prepare the conditions for the elimination of the capitalist elements. Accordingly, in this period our state performed two main functions. The first function was to suppress the overthrown classes inside the country. In this respect our state bore a superficial resemblance to previous states whose functions had also been to suppress recalcitrants, with the fundamental difference, however, that our state suppressed the exploiting minority in the interests of the laboring majority, while previous states had suppressed the exploited majority in the interests of the exploiting minority. The second function was to defend the country from foreign attack. In this respect it likewise bore a superficial resemblance to previous states, which also undertook the armed defense of their countries, with the fundamental difference, however, that our state defended from foreign attack the gains of the laboring majority, while previous states in such cases defended the wealth and privileges of the exploiting minority. Our state had yet a third function: this was the work of economic organization and cultural education performed by our state bodies with the purpose of developing the infant shoots of the new, Socialist economic system and re-educating the people in the spirit of Socialism. But this new function did not attain to any considerable development in that period.

The second phase was the period from the elimination of the capitalist elements in town and country to the complete victory of the Socialist economic system and the adoption of the new Constitution. The principal task in this period was to establish the Socialist economic system all over the country and to eliminate the last remnants of the capitalist elements, to bring about a cultural revolution, and to form a thoroughly modern army for the defense of the country. And the functions of our Socialist state changed accordingly. The function of military suppression inside the country ceased, died away; for exploitation had been abolished, there were no more exploiters left, and so there was no one to suppress. In place of this function of suppression the state acquired the function of protecting Socialist property from thieves and pilferers of the people's property. The function of defending the country from foreign attack fully remained; consequently, the Red Army and the Navy also fully remained, as did the punitive organs and the intelligence service, which are indispensable for the detection and punishment of the spies, assassins and wreckers sent into our country by foreign espionage services. The function of economic organization and cultural education by the state organs also remained, and was developed to the full. Now the main task of our state inside the country is the work of peaceful economic organization and cultural education. As for our army, punitive organs, and intelligence service, their edge is no longer turned to the inside of the country but to the outside, against external enemies.

As you see, we now have an entirely new, Socialist state, without precedent in history and differing considerably in form and functions from the Socialist state of the first phase.

But development cannot stop there. We are going ahead, towards Communism. Will our state remain in the period of Communism also?

Yes, it will, unless the capitalist encirclement is liquidated, and unless the danger of foreign military attack has disappeared. Naturally of course, the forms of our state will again change in conformity with the change in the situation at home and abroad.

No, it will not remain and will atrophy if the capitalist encirclement is liquidated and a Socialist encirclement takes its place.

That is how the question stands with regard to the Socialist state.

The International Position
of the Soviet Union*

BY NIKITA S. KHRUSHCHEV

[1956]

THE emergence of socialism from within the bounds of a single country and its transformation into a world system is the main feature of our era. Capitalism has proved powerless to prevent this process of world-historic significance. The simultaneous existence of two opposite world economic systems, the capitalist and the socialist, developing according to different laws and in opposite directions, has become an indisputable fact.

Socialist economy is developing towards the ever-increasing satisfaction of the material and cultural requirements of all members of society, the continuous expansion and improvement of production on the basis of higher techniques, and closer co-operation and mutual assistance between the socialist countries.

The trend of capitalist economy is that of the ever-increasing enrichment of the monopolies, the further intensification of exploitation and cuts in the living standards of millions of working people, particularly in the colonial and dependent countries, of increased militarization of the economy, the exacerbation of the competitive struggle among the capitalist countries, and the maturing of new economic crises and upheavals.

1. The Steady Economic Advance in the U.S.S.R. and the People's Democracies

The socialist countries' development is distinguished by their complete independence, both political and economic. At the same time, the further strengthening of the economic ties and the extension of co-operation between them is a highly important result of the period under review. The socialist countries have established commercial rela-

---

* Selections from the first part of the *Report of the Central Committee of the Communist Party of the Soviet Union to the 20th Party Congress*. This address was delivered on February 14, 1956. Published by Foreign Languages Publishing House, Moscow, 1956.

tions based on equality and mutual benefit. They are exchanging technical experience, giving each other all-round assistance, and efficiently co-ordinating their national-economic plans.

Close economic co-operation provides exceptional opportunities for the best possible utilization of productive and raw material resources and successfully combines the interests of each country with those of the socialist camp as a whole. The development of specialization and co-operation is of great importance here. Today it is no longer necessary for each socialist country to develop all branches of heavy industry, as had to be done by the Soviet Union, which for a long time was the only socialist country, and existed in a capitalist encirclement. Now that there is a powerful community of socialist countries whose defence potential and security are based on the industrial might of the entire socialist camp, each European People's Democracy can specialize in developing those industries and producing those goods for which it has the most favourable natural and economic conditions. This at the same time creates the prerequisites for releasing considerable resources to develop agriculture and the light industries, and on this basis to satisfy increasingly the material and cultural requirements of the peoples. . . .

2. The Economic Situation in the Capitalist Countries and the Further Aggravation of the Contradictions of Capitalism

. . . The capitalist world economy is developing extremely unevenly and has become still more unstable.

In the post-war decade old capitalist countries such as Britain and France increased their industrial output, but this growth is proceeding slowly and contradictorily. Of the defeated countries, Western Germany and Italy regained their pre-war level of production only in 1949–50, while Japan's industrial output is on the 1944 level. Since the war, the United States, the chief capitalist country, has experienced three substantial cut-backs in production; a serious economic crisis began in 1948 but was subsequently stopped by an intensified arms drive arising from the war in Korea.

Instability in industrial production is supplemented by financial instability in most capitalist countries, by the issue of an immense amount of paper money and the depreciation of currency. To this should be added the agrarian crisis in a number of countries, and also the stagnation in world trade that has been observed in recent years on the capitalist market.

The general crisis of capitalism continues to deepen. Capitalism's insoluble contradiction—the contradiction between the modern productive forces and capitalist relations of production—has become still more acute. The rapid development of present-day technology does not remove this contradiction but only emphasizes it.

It should be said that the idea that the general crisis of capitalism means complete stagnation, a halt in production and technical progress, has always been alien to Marxism-Leninism. Lenin pointed out that capitalism's general tendency to decay did not preclude technical progress or an upswing in production in one period or another. "It would be a mistake to believe," he wrote, "that this tendency to decay precludes the rapid growth of capitalism. It does not. In the epoch of imperialism, certain branches of industry, certain strata of the bourgeoisie and certain countries betray, to a greater or lesser degree, now one and now another of these tendencies." (*Works,* Vol. 22, p. 286.) Therefore we must study the capitalist economy attentively and not over-simplify Lenin's thesis on the decay of imperialism but study the best that capitalist science and technology have to offer, in order to use the achievements of world technological progress in the interests of socialism. . . .

Based on the present business activity, talk about "prosperity" has again begun in some Western circles. They are attempting to prove that the Marxist theory of crises has "become antiquated." Bourgeois economists are silent about the fact that only a temporary coincidence of circumstances favourable to capitalism prevented the crisis phenomena from developing into a deep economic crisis. Even today, during a revival of business activity, underlying crisis symptoms are evident. Production capacities are by no means being used to the full. Commodity stocks and consumer credit have reached dangerous proportions in the United States.

The situation is aggravated by the fact that huge stocks of farm produce which cannot find a market have accumulated in a number of capitalist countries. Governments, particularly the United States Government, are trying to cut crop areas and reduce harvests by every means. All this is being done at a time when in vast areas of South-East Asia and Africa millions of people are hungry, and when even in the metropolitan countries considerable sections of the population are seriously undernourished. Increasing production, a certain technological progress, and intensification of labour coupled with a home market which, far from expanding, is becoming relatively narrower, inevitably give rise to new economic crises and upheavals in the capitalist countries.

The capitalists and the learned defenders of their interests are circulating the "theory" that uninterrupted expansion of arms manufacture brings salvation from economic crisis. The representatives of Marxist-Leninist science have more than once pointed out that this is a hollow illusion. The arms race does not cure the disease, it drives it deeper. And the more extensive the militarization of the economy, the graver will be its consequences for capitalism.

The representatives of the capitalist groups repose special hopes in government regulation of the economy. Monopoly capital is establishing direct control over government agencies, sending its representatives to work in them and making the government "regulate" the country's economy in the interests of the monopolies. The government agencies try to sustain business activity, placing orders worth billions of dollars with the corporations, giving them special privileges and subsidies, controlling wages and the prices of many commodities, buying up surpluses, and financing exports. However, the state's intervention in economic activity does not eliminate the fundamental defects of the capitalist system. The state is powerless to do away with the objective laws of capitalist economy, which lead to anarchy of production and economic crises. Crises are inherent in the very nature of capitalism, they are inevitable.

The prospects of capitalist economy are in many ways determined by the situation in the capitalist world market. Here substantial changes have taken place during recent years. The United States of America is losing the monopoly position it held during the first postwar years. . . .

The situation in the capitalist world market has become especially aggravated since the re-appearance in it of Western Germany and Japan. They, like Britain and France, have practically regained their pre-war positions in the world market. Today a further increase in each country's exports is possible only as a result of fierce struggle against competitors. Britain does not like the growing activity of Western Germany and Japan, and Western Germany and Japan are dissatisfied because Britain keeps them out of its markets. All these contries have more than sufficient reason to be dissatisfied with the United States, which has disorganized the world market by carrying on unilateral trade, fencing off its market from foreign imports, prohibiting trade with the East, dumping agricultural produce, and resorting to other measures which seriously affect other countries. The economic struggle between the capitalist countries is gaining momentum.

As before, the main conflict is that between the United States and Great Britain. Anglo-American antagonism embraces a wide range of questions. Under the "Atlantic co-operation" slogan the trans-Atlantic competitors are taking possession of the principal strategic and economic positions of the British Empire, they are working to obtain a grip on the imperial lines of communication, break up the system of preferential tariffs, and get control of the sterling area. It is not surprising therefore that in Britain, and in France too, there is growing desire to put an end to the situation in which "Atlantic co-operation" is of advantage only to one partner.

The revival of Western Germany's economic power is especially aggravating the situation in the world market. The experience of two world wars shows that in their struggle for markets the German monopolies will stop at nothing. As a result the situation in Western Europe is also becoming acute, for the emergence of a rapidly developing German competitor bodes no good for France or Britain, if, moreover, it is pushed further along the path of militarization. Within Western Germany too the situation is becoming acute, since the resurgence of the trusts and monopolies enhances the danger of a revival of the forces which once brought fascism to power.

The problem of markets is becoming all the more acute, because the capitalist world market is steadily shrinking as a result of the formation of the new and growing socialist world market. Besides, the underdeveloped countries, on casting off the colonial yoke, begin to develop their own industry, which inevitably leads to a further narrowing of markets for industrial products. All this means that the struggle for markets and spheres of influence will become still sharper within the imperialist camp.

The steady sharpening of social contradictions is also a feature of the present situation in the capitalist countries.

Despite the fact that the capitalist governments have resorted to particularly harsh anti-labour legislation, to government "regulation" of labour conflicts, and to restriction of the rights of trade unions, the strike struggle has assumed much wider scope during the post-war years than it did before the war. . . .

What conclusions should be drawn from the analysis of the situation in the capitalist countries?

The situation in the capitalist world is marked by intensifying profound contradictions. The contradiction between the social character of production and private capitalist appropriation, between the expansion of production and the diminishing effective demand, which leads to economic crises, is becoming greater. The contradictions between the capitalist states are growing and their struggle for markets and spheres of influence is becoming increasingly acute. Social contradictions are deepening, and the struggle of the working class and the broad masses for their vital rights and interests is becoming more vigorous. Thus, capitalism is steadily moving towards new economic and social upheavals.

3. The Imperialist Policy of Lining up Aggressive Blocs and Fanning the "Cold War." The Struggle of the Peoples for Relaxation of International Tension

Comrades, between the Nineteenth and Twentieth Congresses of the Communist Party of the Soviet Union, very important changes have taken place in international relations.

Soon after the Second World War ended, the influence of reactionary and militarist groups began to be increasingly evident in the policy of the United States of America, Britain and France. Their desire to enforce their will on other countries by economic and political pressure, threats and military provocation prevailed. This became known as the "positions of strength" policy. It reflects the aspiration of the most aggressive sections of present-day imperialism to win world supremacy, to suppress the working class and the democratic and national-liberation movements; it reflects their plans for military adventures against the socialist camp.

The international atmosphere was poisoned by war hysteria. The arms race began to assume more and more monstrous dimensions. Many big U.S. military bases designed for use against the U.S.S.R. and the People's Democracies were built in countries thousands of miles from the borders of the United States. "Cold war" was begun against the socialist camp. International distrust was artificially kindled, and nations set against one another. A bloody war was launched in Korea; the war in Indo-China dragged on for years.

The inspirers of the "cold war" began to establish military blocs, and many countries found themselves, against the will of their peoples, involved in restricted aggressive alignments—the North Atlantic bloc, Western European Union, SEATO (military bloc for South-East Asia) and the Baghdad pact.

The organizers of military blocs allege that they have united for defence, for protection against the "communist threat." But that is sheer hypocrisy. We know from history that when planning a re-division of the world, the imperialist powers have always lined up military blocs. Today the "anti-communism" slogan is again being used as a smokescreen to cover up the claims of one power for world domination. The new thing here is that the United States wants, by means of all kinds of blocs and pacts, to secure a dominant position in the capitalist world for itself, and to reduce all its partners in the blocs to the status of obedient executors of its will.

The inspirers of the "positions of strength" policy assert that this policy makes another war impossible, because it ensures a "balance of power" in the world arena. This view is widespread among Western statesmen and it is therefore all the more important to thoroughly expose its real meaning.

Can peace be promoted by an arms race? It would seem that it is simply absurd to pose such a question. Yet the adherents of the "positions of strength" policy offer the arms race as their main recipe for the preservation of peace! It is perfectly obvious that when nations compete to increase their military might, the danger of war becomes greater, not lesser.

The arms race, the "positions of strength" policy, the lining up of aggressive blocs and the "cold war"—all this could not but aggravate the international situation, and it did. This has been one trend of world events during the period under review.

But other processes have also taken place in the international arena during these years, processes showing that in the world today monopolist circles are by no means controlling everything.

The steady consolidation of the forces of socialism, democracy and peace, and of the forces of the national-liberation movement is of decisive significance. The international position of the Soviet Union, the People's Republic of China, and the other socialist countries has been further strengthened during this period, and their prestige and international ties have grown immeasurably. The international camp of socialism is exerting ever-growing influence on the course of international events. (*Applause.*)

The forces of peace have been considerably augmented by the emergence in the world arena of a group of peace-loving European and Asian states which have proclaimed non-participation in blocs as a principle of their foreign policy. The leading political circles of these states rightly hold that to participate in restricted military imperialist alignments would merely increase the danger of their countries being involved in military gambles by the aggressive forces and draw them into the maelstrom of the arms drive.

As a result, a vast Zone of Peace including peace-loving states, both socialist and non-socialist, of Europe and Asia, has emerged in the world. This zone includes vast areas inhabited by nearly 1,500 million people, that is, the majority of the population of our planet. . . .

Not a few of the misfortunes harassing the world today are due to the fact that in many countries the working class has been split for many years and its different groups do not present a united front, which only plays into the hands of the reactionary forces. Yet, today, in our opinion, the prospect of changing this situation is opening up. Life has put on the agenda many questions which not only demand rapprochement and co-operation between all workers' parties but also create real possibilities for this co-operation. The most important of these questions is that of preventing a new war. If the working class comes out as a united organized force and acts with firm resolution, there will be no war.

All this places an historic responsibility upon all leaders of the labour movement. The interests of the struggle for peace make it imperative to find points of contact and on these grounds to lay the foundations for co-operation, sweeping aside mutual recriminations. Here co-operation with those circles of the socialist movement whose views on the forms of transition to socialism differ from ours is also possible and essential. Among them are not a few people who are honestly mistaken on this question, but this is no obstacle to co-operation. Today many Social-Democrats stand for active struggle against the war danger and militarism, for rapprochement with the socialist countries, for unity of the labour movement. We sincerely greet these Social-Democrats and are willing to do everything necessary to join our efforts in the struggle for the noble cause of upholding peace and the interests of the working people. (*Applause.*)

All international developments in recent years show that big popular forces have risen to fight for the preservation of peace. The ruling imperialist circles cannot but reckon with this factor. Their more farsighted representatives are beginning to admit that the "positions of strength" policy could not put pressure on the countries against which it was directed and that it has failed. At the same time this policy weighs heavily on the masses in the capitalist world and has increased their dissatisfaction. The overwhelming majority of mankind rejects the "positions of strength" policy as a policy of gambles directed against the people and enhancing the war danger.

Under the impact of these incontestable facts, symptoms of a certain sobering up are appearing among influential Western circles. More and more people among these circles are realizing what a dangerous gamble war against the socialist countries may prove for the destinies of capitalism. Undoubtedly, the working class and the labouring masses of the capitalist countries, should their rulers dare to precipitate such a war, would draw decisive conclusions regarding the system which periodically plunges the nations into the bloodbath of war. (*Prolonged applause.*) Nor is it fortuitous that prominent leaders of bourgeois countries frankly admit with increasing frequency that "there will be no victor" in a war in which atomic weapons are used. These leaders still do not venture to state that capitalism will find its grave in another world war, should it unleash it, but they are already compelled openly to admit that the socialist camp is invincible. (*Stormy applause.*)

The position of the imperialist forces is growing weaker not only because their aggressive policy is rejected by the peoples of their countries, but because in the last ten years imperialism has sustained defeat in the East as well, where the centuries-old mainstays of colonialism are crumbling and the peoples themselves are with increasing boldness beginning to decide their own destinies.

* * *

6. Some Fundamental Questions of Present-Day International Development

Comrades, I should like to dwell on some fundamental questions concerning present-day international development, which determine not only the present course of events, but also the prospects for the future.

These questions are the peaceful co-existence of the two systems, the possibility of preventing wars in the present era, and the forms of transition to socialism in different countries.

Let us examine these questions in brief.

The peaceful co-existence of the two systems. The Leninist principle of peaceful co-existence of states with different social systems has always been and remains the general line of our country's foreign policy.

It has been alleged that the Soviet Union advances the principle of peaceful co-existence merely out of tactical considerations, considerations of expediency. Yet it is common knowledge that we have always, from the very first years of Soviet power, stood with equal firmness for peaceful co-existence. Hence, it is not a tactical move, but a fundamental principle of Soviet foreign policy.

This means that if there is indeed a threat to the peaceful co-existence of countries with differing social and political systems, it by no means comes from the Soviet Union or the rest of the socialist camp. Is there a single reason why a socialist state should want to unleash aggressive war? Do we have classes and groups that are interested in war as a means of enrichment? We do not. We abolished them long ago. Or, perhaps, we do not have enough territory or natural wealth, perhaps we lack sources of raw materials or markets for our goods? No, we have sufficient of all those and to spare. Why then should we want war? We do not want it, as a matter of principle we renounce any policy that might lead to millions of people being plunged into war for the sake of the selfish interests of a handful of multi-millionaires. Do those who shout about the "aggressive intentions" of the U.S.S.R. know all this? Of course they do. Why then do they keep up the old monotonous refrain about some imaginary "communist aggression"? Only to stir up mud, to conceal their plans for world domination, a "crusade" against peace, democracy, and socialism.

To this day the enemies of peace allege that the Soviet Union is out to overthrow capitalism in other countries by "exporting" revolution. It goes without saying that among us Communists there are no supporters of capitalism. But this does not mean that we have interfered or plan to interfere in the internal affairs of countries where capitalism still exists. Romain Rolland was right when he said that "freedom is not brought in from abroad in baggage trains like Bourbons." (*Animation.*) It is ridiculous to think that revolutions are made to order.

We often hear representatives of bourgeois countries reasoning thus: "The Soviet leaders claim that they are for peaceful co-existence between the two systems. At the same time they declare that they are fighting for communism, and say that communism is bound to win in all countries. Now if the Soviet Union is fighting for communism, how can there be any peaceful co-existence with it?" This view is the result of bourgeois propaganda. The ideologists of the bourgeoisie distort the facts and deliberately confuse questions of ideological struggle with questions of relations between states in order to make the Communists of the Soviet Union look like advocates of aggression.

When we say that the socialist system will win in the competition between the two systems—the capitalist and the socialist—this by no means signifies that its victory will be achieved through armed interference by the socialist countries in the internal affairs of the capitalist countries. Our certainty of the victory of communism is based on the fact that the socialist mode of production possesses decisive advantages over the capitalist mode of production. Precisely because of this, the ideas of Marxism-Leninism are more and more capturing the minds of the broad masses of the working people in the capitalist countries, just as they have captured the minds of millions of men and women in our country and the People's Democracies. (*Prolonged applause.*) We believe that all working men in the world, once they have become convinced of the advantages communism brings, will sooner or later take the road of struggle for the construction of socialist society. (*Prolonged applause.*) Building communism in our country, we are resolutely against war. We have always held and continue to hold that the establishment of a new social system in one or another country is the internal affair of the peoples of the countries concerned. This is our attitude, based on the great Marxist-Leninist teaching. . . .

The possibility of preventing war in the present era. Millions of people all over the world are asking whether another war is really inevitable, whether mankind which has already experienced two devastating world wars must still go through a third one? Marxists must answer this question taking into consideration the epoch-making changes of the last decades.

There is, of course, a Marxist-Leninist precept that wars are inevitable as long as imperialism exists. This precept was evolved at a time when 1) imperialism was an all-embracing world system, and 2) the social and political forces which did not want war were weak, poorly organized, and hence unable to compel the imperialists to renounce war.

People usually take only one aspect of the question and examine only the economic basis of wars under imperialism. This is not enough. War is not only an economic phenomenon. Whether there is to be a war or not depends in large measure on the correlation of class, political forces, the degree of organization and the awareness and resolve of the people. Moreover, in certain conditions the struggle waged by progressive social and political forces may play a decisive role. Hitherto the state of affairs was such that the forces that did not want war and opposed it were poorly organized and lacked the means to check the schemes of the war-makers. Thus it was before the First World War, when the main force opposed to the threat of war—the world proletariat—was disorganized by the treachery of the leaders of the Second International. Thus it was on the eve of the Second World War, when the Soviet Union was the only country that pursued an active peace policy, when the other Great Powers to all intents and purposes encouraged the aggressors, and the Right-wing Social-Democratic leaders had split the labour movement in the capitalist countries.

In that period this precept was absolutely correct. At the present time, however, the situation has changed radically. Now there is a world camp of socialism, which has become a mighty force. In this camp the peace forces find not only the moral, but also the material means to prevent aggression. Moreover, there is a large group of other countries with a population running into many hundreds of millions which are actively working to avert war. The labour movement in the capitalist countries has today become a tremendous force. The movement of peace supporters has sprung up and developed into a powerful factor.

In these circumstances certainly the Leninist precept that so long as imperialism exists, the economic basis giving rise to wars will also be preserved remains in force. That is why we must display the greatest vigilance. As long as capitalism survives in the world, the reactionary forces representing the interests of the capitalist monopolies will continue their drive towards military gambles and aggression, and may try to unleash war. But war is not fatalistically inevitable. Today there are mighty social and political forces possessing formidable means to prevent the imperialists from unleashing war, and if they actually try to start it, to give a smashing rebuff to the aggressors and frustrate their adventurist plans. To be able to do this all anti-war forces must be vigilant and prepared, they must act as a united front and never relax their efforts in the battle for peace. The more actively the peoples defend peace, the greater the guarantees that there will be no new war. (*Stormy, prolonged applause.*)

Forms of transition to socialism in different countries. In connection with the radical changes in the world arena new prospects are also opening up in respect to the transition of countries and nations to socialism.

As far back as the eve of the Great October Socialist Revolution Lenin wrote: "All nations will arrive at socialism—this is inevitable, but not all will do so in exactly the same way, each will contribute something of its own in one or another form of democracy, one or another variety of the dictatorship of the proletariat, one or another rate at which socialist transformations will be effected in the various aspects of social life. There is nothing more primitive from the viewpoint of theory or more ridiculous from that of practice than to paint, 'in the name of historical materialism,' *this* aspect of the future in a monotonous grey. . . ." (*Works,* Vol. 23, p. 58.)

Historical experience has fully confirmed Lenin's brilliant precept. Alongside the Soviet form of reconstructing society on socialist lines, we now have the form of People's Democracy.

In Poland, Bulgaria, Czechoslovakia, Albania, and the other European People's Democracies, this form sprang up and is being utilized in conformity with the concrete historical, social and economic conditions, and peculiarities of each of these countries. It has been thoroughly tried and tested in the course of ten years and has fully proved its worth.

Much that is unique in socialist construction is being contributed by the Chinese People's Republic, whose economy prior to the victory of the revolution was exceedingly backward, semi-feudal and semi-colonial in character. Having taken over the decisive commanding positions, the people's democratic state is using them in the social revolution to implement a policy of peaceful reorganization of private industry and trade and their gradual transformation into a component of socialist economy.

The leadership of the great cause of socialist reconstruction by the Communist Party of China and the Communist and Workers' Parties of the other People's Democracies, exercised in keeping with the peculiarities and specific features of each country, is creative Marxism in action.

In the Federative People's Republic of Yugoslavia, where state power belongs to the working people, and society is based on public ownership of the means of production, specific concrete forms of economic management and organization of the state apparatus are arising in the process of socialist construction.

It is probable that more forms of transition to socialism will appear. Moreover, the implementation of these forms need not be associated with civil war under all circumstances. Our enemies like to depict us Leninists as advocates of violence always and everywhere. True, we recognize the need for the revolutionary transformation of capitalist society into socialist society. It is this that distinguishes the revolutionary Marxists from the reformists, the opportunists. There is no doubt that in a number of capitalist countries the violent overthrow of the dictatorship of the bourgeoisie and the sharp aggravation of class struggle connected with this are inevitable. But the forms of social revolution vary. It is not true that we regard violence and civil war as the only way to remake society.

It will be recalled that in the conditions that arose in April 1917 Lenin granted the possibility that the Russian Revolution might develop peacefully, and that in the spring of 1918, after the victory of the October Revolution, Lenin drew up his famous plan for peaceful socialist construction. It is not our fault that the Russian and international bourgeoisie organized counter-revolution, intervention, and civil war against the young Soviet state and forced the workers and peasants to take up arms. It did not come to civil war in the European People's Democracies, where the historical situation was different.

Leninism teaches us that the ruling classes will not surrender their power voluntarily. And the greater or lesser degree of intensity which the struggle may assume, the use or the non-use of violence in the transition to socialism depends on the resistance of the exploiters, on whether the exploiting class itself resorts to violence, rather than on the proletariat.

In this connection the question arises of whether it is possible to go over to socialism by using parliamentary means. No such course was open to the Russian Bolsheviks, who were the first to effect this transition. Lenin showed us another road, that of the establishment of a republic of Soviets, the only correct road in those historical conditions. Following that course we achieved a victory of history-making significance.

Since then, however, the historical situation has undergone radical changes which make possible a new approach to the question. The forces of socialism and democracy have grown immeasurably throughout the world, and capitalism has become much weaker. The mighty camp of socialism with its population of over 900 million is growing and gaining in strength. Its gigantic internal forces, its decisive advantages over capitalism, are being increasingly revealed from day to day. Socialism has a great power of attraction for the workers, peasants, and intellectuals of all countries. The ideas of socialism are indeed coming to dominate the minds of all toiling humanity.

At the same time the present situation offers the working class in a number of capitalist countries a real opportunity to unite the overwhelming majority of the people under its leadership and to secure the transfer of the basic means of production into the hands of the people. The Right-wing bourgeois parties and their governments are suffering bankruptcy with increasing frequency. In these circumstances the working class, by rallying around itself the toiling peasantry, the intelligentsia, all patriotic forces, and resolutely repulsing the opportunist elements who are incapable of giving up the policy of compromise with the capitalists and landlords, is in a position to defeat the reactionary forces opposed to the popular interest, to capture a stable majority in parliament, and transform the latter from an organ of bourgeois democracy into a genuine instrument of the people's will. (*Applause.*) In such an event this institution, traditional in many highly developed capitalist countries, may become an organ of genuine democracy, democracy for the working people.

The winning of a stable parliamentary majority backed by a mass revolutionary movement of the proletariat and of all the working people could create for the working class of a number of capitalist and former colonial countries the conditions needed to secure fundamental social changes.

In the countries where capitalism is still strong and has a huge military and police apparatus at its disposal, the reactionary forces will of course inevitably offer serious resistance. There the transition to socialism will be attended by a sharp class, revolutionary struggle.

Whatever the form of transition to socialism, the decisive and indispensable factor is the political leadership of the working class headed by its vanguard. Without this there can be no transition to socialism.

It must be strongly emphasized that the more favourable conditions for the victory of socialism created in other countries are due to the fact that socialism has won in the Soviet Union and is winning in the People's Democracies. Its victory in our country would have been impossible had Lenin and the Bolshevik Party not upheld revolutionary Marxism in battle against the reformists, who broke with Marxism and took the path of opportunism.

Such are the considerations which the Central Committee of the Party finds necessary to set out in regard to the forms of transition to socialism in present-day conditions.

* * *

What are the tasks confronting the Party in the sphere of foreign policy? They are:

1. To pursue steadfastly the Leninist policy of peaceful co-existence between different states irrespective of their social systems. To work vigorously for the cause of peace and the security of the peoples, for the establishment of confidence between states, with a view to transforming the relaxation of international tension achieved to date into a stable peace.

2. To strengthen in every way our fraternal relations with the People's Republic of China, Poland, Czechoslovakia, Bulgaria, Hungary, Rumania, Albania, the German Democratic Republic, the Korean People's Democratic Republic, the Democratic Republic of Viet-Nam, and the Mongolian People's Republic, bearing in mind that the greater the unity and might of the socialist countries the more secure is the cause of peace. (*Prolonged applause.*)

To strengthen in every way friendship and co-operation with the fraternal peoples of the Federative People's Republic of Yugoslavia. (*Applause*).

3. To consolidate untiringly the bonds of friendship and co-operation with the Republic of India, Burma, Indonesia, Afghanistan, Egypt, Syria, and other countries which stand for peace; to support countries which refuse to be involved in military blocs; to co-operate with all forces seeking to preserve peace. (*Prolonged applause.*)

To develop and strengthen friendly relations with Finland, Austria, and other neutral countries. (*Applause.*)

4. To pursue a vigorous policy of further improving relations with the United States of America, Britain, France, Western Germany, Japan, Italy, Turkey, Iran, Pakistan, and other countries with a view to strengthening mutual confidence, extending trade, and expanding contacts and co-operation in the sphere of culture and science. (*Prolonged applause.*)

5. To follow vigilantly the intrigues of circles that do not want a relaxation of international tension; to expose in good time the subversive activities of the enemies of peace and the peoples' security; to take all measures necessary to further strengthen the defence potential of our socialist state; to maintain our defences at the level required by present-day military science, and to ensure the security of our socialist country. (*Stormy, prolonged applause*).

VI
DOMINATION

The Grand Inquisitor*

BY FEODOR DOSTOIEVSKY

[1880]

"Even this must have a preface—that is, a literary preface," laughed Ivan, "and I am a poor hand at making one. You see, my action takes place in the sixteenth century, and at that time, as you probably learnt at school, it was customary in poetry to bring down heavenly powers on earth. Not to speak of Dante, in France, clerks, as well as the monks in the monasteries, used to give regular performances in which the Madonna, the saints, the angels, Christ, and God Himself were brought on the stage. In those days it was done in all simplicity. In Victor Hugo's 'Notre Dame de Paris' an edifying and gratuitous spectacle was provided for the people in the Hotel de Ville of Paris in the reign of Louis XI. in honor of the birth of the dauphin. It was called *Le bon jugement de la très sainte et gracieuse Vierge Marie,* and she appears herself on the stage and pronounces her *bon jugement.* Similar plays, chiefly from the Old Testament, were occasionally performed in Moscow too, up to the times of Peter the Great. But besides plays there were all sorts of legends and ballads scattered about the world, in which the saints and angels and all the powers of Heaven took part when required. In our monasteries the monks busied themselves in translating, copying, and even composing such poems—and even under the Tatars. There is, for instance, one such poem (of course, from the Greek), 'The Wanderings of Our Lady through Hell,' with descriptions as bold as Dante's. Our Lady visits Hell, and the Archangel Michael leads her through the torments. She sees the sinners and their punishment. There she sees among others one noteworthy set of sinners in a burning lake; some of them sink to the bottom of the lake so that they can't swim out, and 'these God forgets'—an expression of extraordinary depth and force. And so Our Lady, shocked and weeping, falls before the throne of God and begs for mercy for all in Hell—for all she has seen there, indiscriminately. Her conversation with God is immensely

* From Book V, Chapter v, of *The Brothers Karamazov.* Reprinted by courtesy of The Modern Library.

interesting. She beseeches Him, she will not desist, and when God points to the hands and feet of her Son, nailed to the Cross, and asks, 'How can I forgive His tormentors?' she bids all the saints, all the martyrs, all the angels and archangels to fall down with her and pray for mercy on all without distinction. It ends by her winning from God a respite of suffering every year from Good Friday till Trinity day, and the sinners at once raise a cry of thankfulness from Hell, chanting. 'Thou art just, O Lord, in this judgment.' Well, my poem would have been of that kind if it had appeared at that time. He comes on the scene in my poem, but He says nothing, only appears and passes on. Fifteen centuries have passed since He promised to come in His glory, fifteen centuries since His prophet wrote, 'Behold, I come quickly'; 'Of that day and that hour knoweth no man, neither the Son, but the Father,' as He Himself predicted on earth. But humanity awaits him with the same faith and with the same love. Oh, with greater faith, for it is fifteen centuries since man has ceased to see signs from Heaven.

> *No signs from Heaven come to-day*
> *To add to what the heart doth say.*

There was nothing left but faith in what the heart doth say. It is true there were many miracles in those days. There were saints who performed miraculous cures; some holy people, according to their biographies, were visited by the Queen of Heaven herself. But the devil did not slumber, and doubts were already arising among men of the truth of these miracles. And just then there appeared in the north of Germany a terrible new heresy. 'A huge star like to a torch' (that is, to a church) 'fell on the sources of the waters and they became bitter.' These heretics began blasphemously denying miracles. But those who remained faithful were all the more ardent in their faith. The tears of humanity rose up to Him as before, awaited His coming, loved Him, hoped for Him, yearned to suffer and die for Him as before. And so many ages mankind had prayed with faith and fervor, 'O Lord our God, hasten Thy coming,' so many ages called upon Him, that in His infinite mercy He deigned to come down to His servants. Before that day He had come down, He had visited some holy men, martyrs and hermits, as is written in their 'Lives.' Among us, Tyutchev, with absolute faith in the truth of his words, bore witness that

> *Bearing the Cross, in slavish dress*
> *Weary and worn, the Heavenly King*
> *Our mother, Russia, came to bless,*
> *And through our land went wandering.*

And that certainly was so, I assure you.

"And behold, He deigned to appear for a moment to the people, to the tortured, suffering people, sunk in iniquity, but loving Him like children. My story is laid in Spain, in Seville, in the most terrible time of the Inquisition, when fires were lighted every day to the glory of God, and 'in the splendid *auto da fé* the wicked heretics were burnt.' Oh, of course, this was not the coming in which He will appear according to His promise at the end of time in all His heavenly glory, and which will be sudden 'as lightning flashing from east to west.' No, He visited His children only for a moment, and there where the flames were crackling round the heretics. In His infinite mercy He came once more among men in that human shape in which He walked among men for three years fifteen centuries ago. He came down to the 'hot pavement' of the southern town in which on the day before almost a hundred heretics had, *ad majorem gloriam Dei,* been burnt by the cardinal, the Grand Inquisitor, in a magnificent *auto da fé,* in the presence of the king, the court, the knights, the cardinals, the most charming ladies of the court, and the whole population of Seville.

"He came softly, unobserved, and yet, strange to say, every one recognized Him. That might be one of the best passages in the poem. I mean, why they recognized Him. The people are irresistibly drawn to Him, they surround Him, they flock about Him, follow Him. He moves silently in their midst with a gentle smile of infinite compassion. The sun of love burns in His heart, light and power shine from His eyes, and their radiance, shed on the people, stirs their hearts with responsive love. He holds out His hands to them, blesses them, and a healing virtue comes from contact with Him, even with His garments. An old man in the crowd, blind from childhood, cries out, 'O Lord, heal me and I shall see Thee!' and, as it were, scales fall from his eyes and the blind man sees Him. The crowd weeps and kisses the earth under His feet. Children throw flowers before Him, sing, and cry hosannah. 'It is He—it is He!' all repeat. 'It must be He, it can be no one but Him!' He stops at the steps of the Seville cathedral at the moment when the weeping mourners are bringing in a little open white coffin. In it lies a child of seven, the only daughter of a prominent citizen. The dead child lies hidden in flowers. 'He will raise your child,' the crowd shouts to the weeping mother. The priest, coming to meet the coffin, looks perplexed, and frowns, but the mother of the dead child throws herself at His feet with a wail. 'If it is Thou, raise my child!' she cries, holding out her hands to Him. The procession halts, the coffin is laid on the steps at His feet. He looks with compassion, and His lips once more softly pronounce, 'Maiden, arise!' and the maiden arises. The little girl sits up in the coffin and looks round, smiling with wide-open wondering eyes, holding a bunch of white roses they had put in her hand.

"There are cries, sobs, confusion among the people, and at that moment the cardinal himself, the Grand Inquisitor, passes by the cathedral. He is an old man, almost ninety, tall and erect, with a withered face and sunken eyes, in which there is still a gleam of light. He is not dressed in his gorgeous cardinal's robes, as he was the day before, when he was burning the enemies of the Roman Church—at that moment he was wearing his coarse, old, monk's cassock. At a distance behind him come his gloomy assistants and slaves and the 'holy guard.' He stops at the sight of the crowd and watches it from a distance. He sees everything; he sees them set the coffin down at His feet, sees the child rise up, and his face darkens. He knits his thick grey brows and his eyes gleam with a sinister fire. He holds out his finger and bids the guards take Him. And such is his power, so completely are the people cowed into submission and trembling obedience to him, that the crowd immediately make way for the guards, and in the midst of deathlike silence they lay hands on Him and lead Him away. The crowd instantly bows down to the earth, like one man, before the old inquisitor. He blesses the people in silence and passes on. The guards lead their prisoner to the close, gloomy vaulted prison in the ancient palace of the Holy Inquisition and shut Him in it. The day passes and is followed by the dark, burning 'breathless' night of Seville. The air is 'fragrant with laurel and lemon.' In the pitch darkness the iron door of the prison is suddenly opened and the Grand Inquisitor himself comes in with a light in his hand. He is alone; the door is closed at once behind him. He stands in the doorway and for a minute or two gazes into His face. At last he goes up slowly, sets the light on the table and speaks.

" 'Is it Thou? Thou?' but receiving no answer, he adds at once, 'Don't answer, be silent. What canst Thou say, indeed? I know too well what Thou wouldst say. And Thou hast no right to add anything to what Thou hadst said of old. Why, then, are Thou come to hinder us? For Thou hast come to hinder us, and Thou knowest that. But dost Thou know what will be to-morrow? I know not who Thou art and care not to know whether it is Thou or only a semblance of Him, but to-morrow I shall condemn Thee and burn Thee at the stake as the worst of heretics. And the very people who have to-day kissed Thy feet, to-morrow at the faintest sign from me will rush to heap up the embers of Thy fire. Knowest Thou that? Yes, maybe Thou knowest it,' he added with thoughtful penetration, never for a moment taking his eyes off the Prisoner."

"I don't quite understand, Ivan. What does it mean?" Alyosha, who had been listening in silence, said with a smile. "Is it simply a wild fantasy, or a mistake on the part of the old man—some impossible *qui pro quo?*"

"Take it as the last," said Ivan, laughing, "if you are so corrupted by modern realism and can't stand anything fantastic. If you like it to be a case of mistaken identity, let it be so. It is true," he went on, laughing, "the old man was ninety, and he might well be crazy over his set idea. He might have been struck by the appearance of the Prisoner. It might, in fact, be simply his ravings, the delusion of an old man of ninety, over-excited by the *auto da fé* of a hundred heretics the day before. But does it matter to us after all whether it was a mistake of identity or a wild fantasy? All that matters is that the old man should speak out, should speak openly of what he has thought in silence for ninety years."

"And the Prisoner too is silent? Does He look at him and not say a word?"

"That's inevitable in any case," Ivan laughed again. "The old man has told Him He hasn't the right to add anything to what He has said of old. One may say it is the most fundamental feature of Roman Catholicism, in my opinion at least. 'All has been given by Thee to the Pope,' they say, 'and all, therefore, is still in the Pope's hands, and there is no need for Thee to come now at all. Thou must not meddle for the time, at least.' That's how they speak and write too—the Jesuits, at any rate. I have read it myself in the works of their theologians. 'Hast Thou the right to reveal to us one of the mysteries of that world from which Thou hast come?' my old man asks Him, and answers the question for Him. 'No, Thou hast not; that Thou mayest not add to what has been said of old, and mayest not take from men the freedom which Thou didst exalt when Thou wast on earth. Whatsoever Thou revealest anew will encroach on men's freedom of faith; for it will be manifest as a miracle, and the freedom of their faith was dearer to Thee than anything in those days fifteen hundred years ago. Didst Thou not often say then, "I will make you free"? But now Thou hast seen these "free" men,' the old man adds suddenly, with a pensive smile. 'Yes, we've paid dearly for it,' he goes on, looking sternly at Him, 'but at last we have completed that work in Thy name. For fifteen centuries we have been wrestling with Thy freedom, but now it is ended and over for good. Dost Thou not believe that it's over for good? Thou lookest meekly at me and deignest not even to be wroth with me. But let me tell Thee that now, to-day, people are more persuaded than ever that they have perfect freedom, yet they have brought their freedom to us and laid it humbly at our feet. But that has been our doing. Was this what Thou didst? Was this Thy freedom?' "

"I don't understand again," Alyosha broke in. "Is he ironical, is he jesting?"

"Not a bit of it! He claims it as a merit for himself and his Church that at last they have vanquished freedom and have done so to make men happy. 'For now' (he is speaking of the Inquisition, of course) 'for the first time it has become possible to think of the happiness of men. Man was created a rebel; and how can rebels be happy? Thou wast warned,' he says to Him. 'Thou hast had no lack of admonitions and warnings, but Thou didst not listen to those warnings; Thou didst reject the only way by which men might be made happy. But, fortunately, departing Thou didst hand on the work to us. Thou hast promised, Thou hast established by Thy word, Thou has given to us the right to bind and to unbind, and now, of course, Thou canst not think of taking it away. Why, then, hast Thou come to hinder us?' "

"And what's the meaning of 'no lack of admonitions and warnings'?" asked Alyosha.

"Why, that's the chief part of what the old man must say."

" 'The wise and dread Spirit, the spirit of self-destruction and non-existence,' the old man goes on, 'the great spirit talked with Thee in the wilderness, and we are told in the books that he "tempted" Thee. Is that so? And could anything truer be said than what he revealed to Thee in three questions and what Thou didst reject, and what in the books is called "the temptation"? And yet if there has ever been on earth a real stupendous miracle, it took place on that day, on the day of the three temptations. The statement of those three questions was itself the miracle. If it were possible to imagine simply for the sake of argument that those three questions of the dread spirit had perished utterly from the books, and that we had to restore them and to invent them anew, and to do so had gathered together all the wise men of the earth—rulers, chief priests, learned men, philosophers, poets—and had set them the task to invent three questions, such as would not only fit the occasion, but express in three words, three human phrases, the whole future history of the world and of humanity—dost Thou believe that all the wisdom of the earth united could have invented anything in depth and force equal to the three questions which were actually put to Thee then by the wise and mighty spirit in the wilderness? From those questions alone, from the miracle of their statement, we can see that we have here to do not with the fleeting human intelligence, but with the absolute and eternal. For in those three questions the whole subsequent history of mankind is, as it were, brought together into one whole, and foretold, and in them are united all the unsolved historical contradictions of human nature. At the time it could not be so clear, since the future was unknown; but now that fifteen hundred years have passed, we see that everything in those three questions was so justly divined and foretold, and has been so truly fulfilled, that nothing can be added to them or taken from them.

" 'Judge Thyself who was right—Thou or he who questioned Thee then? Remember the first question; its meaning, in other words, was this: "Thou wouldst go into the world, and art going with empty hands, with some promise of freedom which men in their simplicity and their natural unruliness cannot even understand, which they fear and dread—for nothing has ever been more insupportable for a man and a human society than freedom. But seest Thou these stones in this parched and barren wilderness? Turn them into bread, and mankind will run after Thee like a flock

of sheep, grateful and obedient, though for ever trembling, lest
Thou withdraw Thy hand and deny them Thy bread." But Thou
wouldst not deprive man of freedom and didst reject the offer,
thinking, what is that freedom worth, if obedience is bought with
bread? Thou didst reply that man lives not by bread alone. But dost
Thou know that for the sake of that earthly bread the spirit of the
earth will rise up against Thee and will strive with Thee and
overcome Thee, and all will follow him, crying, "Who can compare
with this beast? He has given us fire from heaven!" Dost Thou
know that the ages will pass, and humanity will proclaim by the
lips of their sages that there is no crime, and therefore no sin; there
is only hunger? "Feed men, and then ask of them virtue!" that's
what they'll write on the banner, which they will raise against Thee,
and with which they will destroy Thy temple. Where Thy temple
stood will rise a new building; the terrible tower of Babel will be
built again, and though, like the one of old, it will not be finished,
yet Thou mightest have prevented that new tower and have cut
short the sufferings of men for a thousand years; for they will come
back to us after a thousand years of agony with their tower. They
will seek us again, hidden underground in the catacombs, for we
shall be again persecuted and tortured. They will find us and cry
to us, "Feed us, for those who have promised us fire from heaven
haven't given it!" And then we shall finish building their tower,
for he finishes the building who feeds them. And we alone shall
feed them in Thy name, declaring falsely that it is in Thy name.
Oh, never, never can they feed themselves without us! No science
will give them bread so long as they remain free. In the end they
will lay their freedom at our feet, and say to us, "Make us your
slaves, but feed us." They will understand themselves, at last, that
freedom and bread enough for all are inconceivable together, for
never, never will they be able to share between them! They will be
convinced, too, that they can never be free, for they are weak,
vicious, worthless and rebellious. Thou didst promise them the bread
of Heaven, but, I repeat again, can it compare with earthly bread
in the eyes of the weak, ever sinful and ignoble race of man? And
if for the sake of the bread of Heaven thousands and tens of thousands shall follow Thee, what is to become of the millions and tens
of thousands of millions of creatures who will not have the strength
to forego the earthly bread for the sake of the heavenly? Or dost
Thou care only for the tens of thousands of the great and strong,

while the millions, numerous as the sands of the sea, who are weak but love Thee, must exist only for the sake of the great and strong? No, we care for the weak too. They are sinful and rebellious, but in the end they too will become obedient. They will marvel at us and look on us as gods, because we are ready to endure the freedom which they have found so dreadful and to rule over them—so awful it will seem to them to be free. But we shall tell them that we are Thy servants and rule them in Thy name. We shall deceive them again, for we will not let Thee come to us again. That deception will be our suffering, for we shall be forced to lie.

" 'This is the significance of the first question in the wilderness, and this is what Thou hast rejected for the sake of that freedom which Thou hast exalted above everything. Yet in this question lies hid the great secret of this world. Choosing "bread," Thou wouldst have satisfied the universal and everlasting craving of humanity—to find some one to worship. So long as man remains free he strives for nothing so incessantly and so painfully as to find some one to worship. But man seeks to worship what is established beyond dispute, so that all men would agree at once to worship it. For these pitiful creatures are concerned not only to find what one or the other can worship, but to find something that all would believe in and worship; what is essential is that all may be *together* in it. This craving for *community* of worship is the chief misery of every man individually and of all humanity from the beginning of time. For the sake of common worship they've slain each other with the sword. They have set up gods and challenged one another, "Put away your gods and come and worship ours, or we will kill you and your gods!" And so it will be to the end of the world, even when gods disappear from the earth; they will fall down before idols just the same. Thou didst know, Thou couldst not but have known, this fundamental secret of human nature, but Thou didst reject the one infallible banner which was offered Thee to make all men bow down to Thee alone—the banner of earthly bread; and Thou hast rejected it for the sake of freedom and the bread of Heaven. Behold what Thou didst further. And all again in the name of freedom! I tell Thee that man is tormented by no greater anxiety than to find some one quickly to whom he can hand over that gift of freedom with which the ill-fated creature is born. But only one who can appease their conscience can take over their freedom. In bread there was offered Thee an invincible banner; give bread, and man will worship Thee, for nothing is more certain than bread. But if some one else gains possession of his conscience—oh! then he will cast away Thy bread and follow after him who has ensnared his conscience. In that Thou wast right. For the secret of man's being is not only to live but to have something to live for. Without a stable conception of the object of life, man would not consent to go on living, and would rather destroy himself than remain on earth, though he had bread in abundance. That is true. But what happened? Instead of taking men's freedom from them, Thou didst make it greater than ever! Didst Thou forget that man prefers peace, and even death, to freedom of choice in the knowledge of good and evil? Nothing is more seductive for man than his freedom of conscience, but nothing is a greater cause of suffering. And behold, instead of giving a firm foundation for setting the conscience of man at rest for ever, Thou didst choose all that is exceptional, vague and enigmatic; Thou didst choose what was utterly beyond the strength of men, acting as though Thou didst not love them at all—Thou who didst come to give Thy life for them! Instead of taking possession of men's freedom, Thou didst increase it, and burdened the spiritual kingdom of mankind with its sufferings for ever. Thou didst desire man's free love, that he should follow Thee freely, enticed and taken captive by Thee. In place of the rigid ancient law, man must hereafter with free heart decide for himself what is good and what is evil, having only Thy image before him as his guide. But didst Thou not know he would at last reject even Thy image and Thy truth, if he is weighed down with the fearful burden of free choice? They will cry aloud at last that the truth is not in Thee, for they could not have been left in greater confusion and suffering than Thou hast caused, laying upon them so many cares and unanswerable problems.

" 'So that, in truth, Thou didst Thyself lay the foundation for the destruction of Thy kingdom, and no one is more to blame for it. Yet what was offered Thee? There are three powers, three powers alone, able to conquer and to hold captive for ever the conscience of these impotent rebels for their happiness—those forces are miracle, mystery and authority. Thou hast rejected all three and hast set the example for doing so. When the wise and dread spirit set Thee on the pinnacle of the temple and said to Thee, "If Thou wouldst know whether Thou art the Son of God then cast Thyself down, for it is written: the angels shall hold him up lest he fall and bruise himself, and Thou shalt know then whether Thou art the Son of God and shalt prove then how great is Thy faith in Thy Father." But Thou didst refuse and wouldst not cast Thyself down. Oh! of course, Thou didst proudly and well, like God; but the weak, unruly race of men, are they gods? Oh, Thou didst know then that in taking one step, in making one movement to cast Thyself down, Thou wouldst be tempting God and have lost all Thy faith in Him, and wouldst have been dashed to pieces against that earth which Thou didst come to save. And the wise spirit that tempted Thee would have rejoiced. But I ask again, are there many like Thee? And couldst Thou believe for one moment that men, too, could face such a temptation? Is the nature of men such, that they can reject miracle, and at the great moments of their life, the moments of their deepest, most agonizing spiritual difficulties, cling only to the free verdict of the heart? Oh, Thou didst know that Thy deed would be recorded in books, would be handed down to remote times and the utmost ends of the earth, and Thou didst hope that man, following Thee, would cling to God and not ask for a miracle. But Thou didst not know that when man rejects miracle he rejects God too; for man seeks not so much God as the miraculous. And as man cannot bear to be without the miraculous, he will create new miracles of his own for himself, and will worship deeds of sorcery and witchcraft, though he might be a hundred times over a rebel, heretic and infidel. Thou didst not come down from the Cross when they shouted to Thee, mocking and reviling Thee, "Come down from the cross and we will believe that Thou art He." Thou didst not come down, for again Thou wouldst not enslave man by a miracle, and didst crave faith given freely, not based on miracle. Thou didst crave for free love and not the base raptures of the slave before the might that has overawed him for ever. But Thou didst think too highly of men therein, for they are slaves, of course, though rebellious by nature. Look round and judge; fifteen centuries have passed, look upon them. Whom hast Thou raised up to Thyself? I swear, man is weaker and baser by nature than Thou hast believed him! Can he, can he do what Thou didst? By showing him so much respect, Thou didst, as it were, cease to feel for him, for Thou didst ask far too much from him— Thou who hast loved him more than Thyself! Respecting him less,

Thou wouldst have asked less of him. That would have been more like love, for his burden would have been lighter. He is weak and vile. What though he is everywhere now rebelling against our power, and proud of his rebellion? It is the pride of a child and a schoolboy. They are little children rioting and barring out the teacher at school. But their childish delight will end; it will cost them dear. They will cast down temples and drench the earth with blood. But they will see at last, the foolish children, that, though they are rebels, they are impotent rebels, unable to keep up their own rebellion. Bathed in their foolish tears, they will recognize at last that He who created them rebels must have meant to mock at them. They will say this in despair, and their utterance will be a blasphemy which will make them more unhappy still, for man's nature cannot bear blasphemy, and in the end always avenges it on itself. And so unrest, confusion and unhappiness—that is the present lot of man after Thou didst bear so much for their freedom! Thy great prophet tells in vision and in image, that he saw all those who took part in the first resurrection and that there were of each tribe twelve thousand. But if there were so many of them, they must have been not men but gods. They had borne Thy cross, they had endured scores of years in the barren, hungry wilderness, living upon locusts and roots—and Thou mayest indeed point with pride at those children of freedom, of free love, of free and splendid sacrifice for Thy name. But remember that they were only some thousands; and what of the rest? And how are the other weak ones to blame, because they could not endure what the strong have endured? How is the weak soul to blame that it is unable to receive such terrible gifts? Canst Thou have simply come to the elect and for the elect? But if so, it is a mystery and we cannot understand it. And if it is a mystery, we too have a right to preach a mystery, and to teach them that it's not the free judgment of their hearts, not love that matters, but a mystery which they must follow blindly, even against their conscience. So we have done. We have corrected Thy work and have founded it upon *miracle, mystery* and *authority*. And men rejoiced that they were again led like sheep, and that the terrible gift that had brought them such suffering, was, at last, lifted from their hearts. Were we right teaching them this? Speak! Did we not love mankind, so meekly acknowledging their feebleness, lovingly lightening their burden, and permitting their weak nature even sin with our sanction? Why hast Thou come now to hinder us? And why dost Thou look silently and searchingly at me with Thy mild eyes? Be angry. I don't want Thy love, for I love Thee not. And what use is it for me to hide anything from Thee? Don't I know to Whom I am speaking? All that I can say is known to Thee already. And is it for me to conceal from Thee our mystery? Perhaps it is Thy will to hear it from my lips. Listen, then. We are not working with Thee, but with *him*—that is our mystery. It's long —eight centuries—since we have been on *his* side and not on Thine. Just eight centuries ago, we took from him what Thou didst reject with scorn, that last gift he offered Thee, showing Thee all the kingdoms of the earth. We took from him Rome and the sword of Cæsar, and proclaimed ourselves sole rulers of the earth, though hitherto we have not been able to complete our work. But whose fault is that? Oh, the work is only beginning, but it has begun. It has long to await completion and the earth has yet much to suffer, but we shall triumph and shall be Cæsars, and then we shall plan the universal happiness of man. But Thou mightest have taken even then the sword of Cæsar. Why didst Thou reject that last gift? Hadst Thou accepted that last counsel of the mighty spirit, Thou wouldst have accomplished all that man seeks on earth—that is, some one to worship, some one to keep his conscience, and some means of uniting all in one unanimous and harmonious ant-heap, for the craving for universal unity is the third and last anguish of men. Mankind as a whole has always striven to organize a universal state. There have been many great nations with great histories, but the more highly they were developed the more unhappy they were, for they felt more acutely than other people the craving for world-wide union. The great conquerors, Timours and Ghenghis-Khans, whirled like hurricanes over the face of the earth striving to subdue its people, and they too were but the unconscious expression of the same craving for universal unity. Hadst Thou taken the world and Cæsar's purple, Thou wouldst have founded the universal state and have given universal peace. For who can rule men if not he who holds their conscience and their bread in his hands. We have taken the sword of Cæsar, and in taking it, of course, have rejected Thee and followed *him*. Oh, ages are yet to come of the confusion of free thought, of their science and cannibalism. For having begun to build their tower of Babel without us, they will end, of course, with cannibalism. But then the beast will crawl to us and lick our feet and spatter them with tears of blood. And we shall sit upon the beast and raise the cup, and on it will be written, "Mystery." But then, and only then, the reign of peace and happiness will come for men. Thou art proud of Thine elect, but Thou hast only the elect, while we give rest to all. And besides, how many of those elect, those mighty ones who could become elect, have grown weary waiting for Thee, and have transferred and will transfer the powers of their spirit and the warmth of their heart to the other camp, and end by raising their *free* banner against Thee. Thou didst Thyself lift up that banner. But with us all will be happy and will no more rebel nor destroy one another as under Thy freedom. Oh, we shall persuade them that they will only become free when they renounce their freedom to us and submit to us. And shall we be right or shall we be lying? They will be convinced that we are right, for they will remember the horrors of slavery and confusion to which Thy freedom brought them. Freedom, free thought and science, will lead them into such straits and will bring them face to face with such marvels and insoluble mysteries, that some of them, the fierce and rebellious, will destroy themselves, others, rebellious but weak, will destroy one another, while the rest, weak and unhappy, will crawl fawning to our feet and whine to us: "Yes, you were right, you alone possess His mystery, and we come back to you, save us from ourselves!"

" 'Receiving bread from us, they will see clearly that we take the bread made by their hands from them, to give it to them, without any miracle. They will see that we do not change the stones to bread, but in truth they will be more thankful for taking it from our hands than for the bread itself! For they will remember only too well that in old days, without our help, even the bread they made turned to stones in their hands, while since they have come back to us, the very stones have turned to bread in their hands. Too, too well they know the value of complete submission! And until men know that, they will be unhappy. Who is most to blame for their not knowing it, speak? Who scattered the flock and sent it astray on unknown paths? But the flock will come together again and will submit once more, and then it will be once for all. Then we shall give them the quiet humble happiness of weak creatures such as they are by nature. Oh, we shall persuade them at last not to be proud, for Thou didst lift them up and thereby taught them to be proud. We shall show them that they are weak, that they are only pitiful children, but that childlike happiness is the sweetest of all. They will become timid and will look to us and huddle close to us in fear, as chicks to the hen. They will marvel at us and will be awestricken before us, and will be proud at our being so powerful and clever, that we have been able to subdue such a turbulent flock of thousands of millions. They will tremble impotently before our wrath, their minds will grow fearful, they will be quick to shed tears like women and children, but they will be just as ready at a sign from us to pass to laughter and rejoicing, to happy mirth and childish song. Yes, we shall set them to work, but in their leisure hours we shall make their life like a child's game, with children's songs and innocent dance. Oh, we shall allow them even sin, they are weak and helpless, and they will love us like children because we allow them to sin. We shall tell them that every sin will be expiated, if it is done with our permission, that we allow them to sin because we love them, and the punishment for these sins we take upon ourselves. And we shall take it upon ourselves, and they will adore us as their saviors who have taken on themselves their sins before God. And they will have no secrets from us. We shall allow or forbid them to live with their wives and mistresses, to have or not to have children—according to whether they have been obedient or disobedient—and they will submit to us gladly and cheerfully. The most painful secrets of their conscience, all, all they will bring to us, and we shall have an answer for all. And they will be glad to believe our answer, for it will save them from the great anxiety and terrible agony they endure at present in making a free decision for themselves. And all will be happy, all the millions of creatures except the hundred thousand who rule over them. For only we, we who guard the mystery, shall be unhappy. There will be thousands of millions of happy babes, and a hundred thousand sufferers who have taken upon themselves the curse of the knowledge of good and evil. Peacefully they will die, peacefully they will expire in Thy name, and beyond the grave they will find nothing but death. But we shall keep the secret, and for their happiness we shall allure them with the reward of heaven and eternity. Though if there were anything in the other world, it certainly would not be for such as they. It is prophesied that Thou wilt come again in victory, Thou wilt come with Thy chosen, the proud and strong, but we will say that they have only saved themselves, but we have saved all. We are told that the harlot who sits upon the beast, and holds in her hands the *mystery*, shall be put to shame, that the weak will rise up again, and will rend her royal purple and will strip naked her loathsome body. But then I will stand up and point out to Thee the thousand millions of happy children who have known no sin. And we who have taken their sins upon us for their happiness will stand up before Thee and say: "Judge us if Thou canst and darest." Know that I fear Thee not. Know that I too have been in the wilderness, I too have lived on roots and locusts, I too prized the freedom with which Thou hast blessed men, and I too was striving to stand among Thy elect, among the strong and powerful, thirsting "to make up the number." But I awakened and would not serve madness. I turned back and joined the ranks of those *who have corrected Thy work*. I left the proud and went back to the humble, for the happiness of the humble. What I say to Thee will come to pass, and our dominion will be built up. I repeat, to-morrow Thou shalt see that obedient flock who at a sign from me will hasten to heap up the hot cinders about the pile on which I shall burn Thee for coming to hinder us. For if any one has ever deserved our fires, it is Thou. To-morrow I shall burn Thee. Dixi.' "

Ivan stopped. He was carried away as he talked and spoke with excitement; when he had finished, he suddenly smiled.

Alyosha had listened in silence; towards the end he was greatly moved and seemed several times on the point of interrupting, but restrained himself. Now his words came with a rush.

"But . . . that's absurd!" he cried, flushing. "Your poem is in praise of Jesus, not in blame of Him—as you meant it to be. And who will believe you about freedom? Is that the way to understand it? That's not the idea of it in the Orthodox Church . . . That's Rome, and not even the whole of Rome, it's false—those are the worst of the Catholics, the Inquisitors, the Jesuits! . . . And there could not be such a fantastic creature as your Inquisitor. What are these sins of mankind they take on themselves? Who are these keepers of the mystery who have taken some curse upon themselves for the happiness of mankind? When have they been seen? We know the Jesuits, they are spoken ill of, but surely they are not what you describe? They are not that at all, not at all. . . . They are simply the Romish army for the earthly sovereignty of the world in the future, with the Pontiff of Rome for Emperor . . . that's their ideal, but there's no sort of mystery or lofty melancholy about it. . . . It's simple lust of power, of filthy earthly gain, of domination—something like a universal serfdom with them as masters—that's all they stand for. They don't even believe in God perhaps. Your suffering inquisitor is a mere fantasy."

"Stay, stay," laughed Ivan, "how hot you are! A fantasy you say, let it be so! Of course it's a fantasy. But allow me to say: do you really think that the Roman Catholic movement of the last centuries is actually nothing but the lust of power, of filthy earthly gain? Is that Father Païssy's teaching?"

"No, no, on the contrary, Father Païssy did once say something rather the same as you . . . but of course it's not the same, not a bit the same," Alyosha hastily corrected himself.

"A precious admission, in spite of your 'not a bit the same.' I ask you why your Jesuits and Inquisitors have united simply for vile material gain? Why can there not be among them one martyr oppressed by great sorrow and loving humanity? You see, only suppose that there was one such man among all those who desire nothing but filthy material gain—if there's only one like my old inquisitor, who had himself eaten roots in the desert and made frenzied efforts to subdue his flesh to make himself free and perfect. But yet all his life he loved humanity, and suddenly his eyes were opened, and he saw that it is no great moral blessedness to attain perfection and freedom, if at the same time one gains the conviction that millions of God's creatures have been created as a mockery, that they will never be capable of using their freedom, that these poor rebels can never turn into giants to complete the tower, that it was not for such geese that the great idealist dreamt his dream of harmony. Seeing all that he turned back and joined—the clever people. Surely that could have happened?"

"Joined whom, what clever people?" cried Alyosha, completely carried away. "They have no such great cleverness and no mysteries and secrets. . . . Perhaps nothing but Atheism, that's all their secret. Your inquisitor does not believe in God, that's his secret!"

"What if it is so! At last you have guessed it. It's perfectly true that that's the whole secret, but isn't that suffering, at least for a man like that, who has wasted his whole life in the desert and yet could not shake off his incurable love of humanity? In his old age he reached the clear conviction that nothing but the advice of the great dread spirit could build up any tolerable sort of life for the feeble, unruly, 'incomplete, empirical creatures created in jest.' And so, convinced of this, he sees that he must follow the council of the wise spirit, the dread spirit of death and destruction, and therefore accept lying and deception, and lead men consciously to death and destruction, and yet deceive them all the way so that they may not notice where they are being led, that the poor blind creatures may at least on the way think themselves happy. And note, the deception is in the name of Him in Whose ideal the old man had so fervently believed all his life long. Is not that tragic? And if only one such stood at the head of the whole army 'filled with the lust of power only for the sake of filthy gain'—would not one such be enough to make a tragedy? More than that, one such standing at the head is enough to create the actual leading idea of the Roman Church with all its armies and Jesuits, its highest idea. I tell you frankly that I firmly believe that there has always been such a man among those who stood at the head of the movement. Who knows, there may have been some such even among the Roman Popes. Who knows, perhaps the spirit of that accursed old man who loves mankind so obstinately in his own way, is to be found even now in a whole multitude of such old men, existing not by chance but by agreement, as a secret league formed long ago for the guarding of the mystery, to guard it from the weak and the unhappy, so as to make them happy. No doubt it is so, and so it must be indeed. I fancy that even among the Masons there's something of the same mystery at the bottom, and that that's why the Catholics so detest the Masons as their rivals breaking up the unity of the idea, while it is so essential that there should be one flock and one shepherd. . . . But from the way I defend my idea I might be an author impatient of your criticism. Enough of it."

"You are perhaps a Mason yourself!" broke suddenly from Al-yosha. "You don't believe in God," he added, speaking this time very sorrowfully. He fancied besides that his brother was looking at him ironically. "How does your poem end?" he asked, suddenly looking down. "Or was it the end?"

"I meant to end it like this. When the Inquisitor ceased speaking he waited some time for his Prisoner to answer him. His silence weighed down upon him. He saw that the Prisoner had listened intently all the time, looking gently in his face and evidently not wishing to reply. The old man longed for Him to say something, however bitter and terrible. But He suddenly approached the old man in silence and softly kissed him on his bloodless aged lips. That was all his answer. The old man shuddered. His lips moved. He went to the door, opened it, and said to Him: 'Go, and come no more. . . . come not at all, never, never!' And he let Him out into the dark alleys of the town. The Prisoner went away."

"And the old man?"

"The kiss glows in his heart, but the old man adheres to his idea."

* * *

Our Tyrants:

*The Self-Enslavement of Modern Civilization**

BY FRIEDRICH SIEBURG

[1954]

THE prison door opens, light streams in, and a harsh voice says: "You are free. You can go!"

"Free?" exclaims the prisoner. "What do you mean, free? Where am I to go?"

"You are released, the door is open, and you can go where you like."

A wave of happiness floods through the prisoner's frame, but it is mingled with bewilderment. He has forgotten what it means to be able to make up his mind for himself. Even freedom has to be learned. He hesitates.

"Get out of here," his liberator says impatiently. "See that you disappear as quickly as possible."

The prisoner stands in the open air, blinking in the bright light and looking around helplessly at a world that seems threatening and demands decisions from him. Cheer up, poor man, your old tyrants have gone and can torment you no longer. But newer ones have been provided. You have only to go out into the world to see for yourself. You will soon meet people who will tell you. Those who believed that with the fall of the bloodstained tyrants a day was dawning in which man would be able to act in accordance with his own laws did not know that even the most damnable institution can never be totally uprooted. The stones of demolished prisons are built into the dwellings of the new generation, and their evil life lives on. Even bondage can become a habit, to which our weaker selves secretly look back with regret.

* From the *Atlantic Monthly,* March 1957. Reprinted by permission of Rowohlt Verlag GMBH from *Die Lust am Untergang* by Friedrich Sieburg. Copyright 1954. Translated by Eric Mosbacher.

It is a wonderful thing no longer to have to live in the world of camps and patient holding of your eating utensils. It is a deliverance that everyone should be able to speak his mind and be able to protest against injustice. But the old habit of falling in in ranks and carefully keeping one's mouth shut goes echoing on inside us. There are no more booted tyrants to be frightened of. They have gone, the devil has taken them. But the devil himself remains, for he is no loyal helper; he rejoices that we can never again be completely free, because the technique of oppression has become a part of progress.

It has been demonstrated that the overcoming of the problems of the modern age is inconsistent with an unrestricted measure of freedom. He who wishes to bring order into the world dare not place unlimited reliance on reason and good will. It is impossible to do without compulsion—not the compulsion that lies behind the law in the freest society, but the compulsion that does not trust the individual's goodness. Even the Western world has become deeply pessimistic, and in the long run that is inconsistent with the democratic organization of society. It is possible that man may be good, but we had better not put it to the test.

Totalitarianism so thoroughly eliminated the frontier between public and private life that it has not yet been possible to re-erect it. Authority once set itself up as an idol which tolerated no personal area, no retreat, into which the ruled could creep. But now it is the ruled, because they have no knowledge of their rights and at bottom have ceased to be very inquisitive about them, who show no inclination to re-enter the area that has become free. The old yoke was evil and deadly, and was felt to be so, but of the new yoke nobody is really aware. The state picked up and is now busying itself with what we dropped from our weakened hands. Where man retreats, the state steps in.

Now the state is by no means the same as the government; we should not be living in the Federal Republic if we did not know that. It is possible to have an efficient administration which is not the state. But who would deny that the administration shows an uncanny tendency to play the state and to treat the individual with severity? What should be an instrument tends readily to regard itself as the embodiment of a principle, and as soon as this occurs it starts striving for power and encroaching on our private sphere. In Germany the administration has always tended to let itself be identified with the state and to profit from the idolization of the state to which we so readily tend. Since 1914 so many new tasks in the economic and social field have accrued to the state that it has been forced to change its essential nature to be able to perform them. Thus it has become second nature for it to want to think and act for the individual. The day before yesterday it was the necessities of war, yesterday it was the harsh demands of economic and social planning, today it is the turn of "civilization" and the "formation of public opinion," and tomorrow our private life will again be the object of official solicitude and effort.

Though the shock given us by Nazism may provide us with no sufficient philosophical justification for regarding the state as an absolute evil or as a permanent danger to the individual, a certain mistrust of it is still appropriate. Whatever form authority may assume— and in our country at the present time its aspect is thoroughly genial— the economic, social, military, and propaganda tasks which devolve upon it throughout the world actually compel it to transform its influence into power. The state acts continually under an impulse which brings it into ever closer contact with the individual and positively forces it to encroach upon the private field. Whatever the impulse may be, even if it be a belief in liberty, in the hands of the ruling authorities it is bound always to assume the form of power.

True, authority is a human creation, but creator and created have broken irretrievably apart, and at best the relations between them have assumed the form of conflict. For the time being the conflict is confined to the material burdens imposed on us from above. Who is there who wishes to defend what is the center of his life? Who is even conscious that it is threatened? Bit by bit we are abandoning what used to constitute the sovereignty of Western man. The private sphere, which was once surrounded by a certain sanctity, is dwindling. Man evacuates one field after another, and the state cannot be expected not to move into the empty space which we are unable to fill.

Democracy does not protect man from the juggernaut of power when he is too apathetic to exercise democracy. Without bloodshed and without glory, bureaucracy mounts the throne and presses its subjects hard. Controlled economies, concealed military dictatorships, and scarcely concealed military dictatorships are the levers by which the free personality is lifted off its hinges. Where I fail, the state is at hand, for it is clear that no area of human activity can be left to chance. Values for which past generations fell in battle evaporate in the routine of the cold war. If I do not know what to do with my spare time, I call in the state. If I am incapable of looking after the produce of my field, or educating my children, the authorities are immediately at hand to act in the public interest.

Thus our tyrants are involuntary tyrants of our own creation. Our subjection to mass rule is not in the least inconsistent with this. For the masses are a tyrannical fiction. The human beings of whom the masses allegedly consist play only a small part in them. Never was there a more hypocritical instrument for the disarmament and diminution of the free personality than this concept of the "masses." The word originates from the romantic vocabulary of the class struggle, and has long since lost its old meaning. That makes it all the more serviceable in the modern struggle of competing interests. It is a terrible weapon in the hands of the groups and entities which today contend for the reality of power. These struggles, of which we poor devils are impotent spectators, whether they be the new struggles for power of parties or points of view, or of associations representing special interests, trade unions, employers, or professions, are not only conducted between states and continents, but cut across nations. Invariably they are imperfectly concealed by the dilapidated curtain of parliamentarianism.

The more selfishly and inhumanly this struggle for power is conducted, the more necessary it is to keep referring to the masses, for whose interests each group claims to stand. Hand in hand with this goes an artful wooing of the masses, from which nowadays no country in the world is exempt. Whether sympathy for the masses is prompted by a genuine interest in the lot of mankind or whether it is only an excuse, obeisance to the masses must be made. The securing of justice for the masses, which should be a worthy object of public concern, turns into a form of idolatry, the cult of a tyrant who has completely forgotten that he is dealing with living human beings. It is a form of demagoguery without which nowadays no one dares make a public utterance.

Mass needs are called into being out of which much money is earned and power acquired. But in reality, perhaps, these needs have no real existence. The precipitous driving down of the level of taste, the unrestricted competition in offering more and more banal illusions and more and more stupid entertainments with less and less intellectual content, take place as an apparent service to the "broad masses," about whose impulses the boldest theories are put forward. The more prominently mass needs are pushed into the foreground, the harder it becomes to discern the struggles for power of the contending groups.

Demagoguery and propaganda have become tyrants of whose insatiability we did not dream when the devil fetched the men with the boots. Since then the world has become more moral, because it is at any rate aware of morality again, but it is still perceptibly in bondage. Perhaps this can never completely disappear so long as the two halves of the divided world maintain their fearful fighting trim. For, since world politics have been sharply separated into black and white to the exclusion of all intervening shades, any action, any utterance, commits one to a position which must not be a disloyal position.

Thus a new form of tyranny has been created which lies like frost over the multiplicity of life and extinguishes its colors, and, on top of the political loyalty which men naturally grant it as members of the Free World, imposes a general, total adherence to the correct line. Every aspect of life is thus subjected to the compulsion of a political choice. An American who rejected Soviet imperialism but praised Russian methods of plant cultivation could be suspected of "un-American activities." A Soviet citizen who opposed the Atlantic Pact but praised American dentistry would—if such an event is thinkable—attract the attention of the police.

This is the state of mind of the Wars of Religion, which led the faith to victory but was deadening to the soul. So we hear Montaigne sighing in desperation: "May we not say of a thief that he has a handsome leg?" No, old Montaigne, you may not, because if you do your tyrants will say that you are on the thieves' side. In a trice even the best of men can find himself committed to something he does not want. If he is wrong, propaganda is there to show him the light; and finally there are the police to put him on the right track. Whatever our future may be, whether it be an Arcadian dream of a smooth-working, parliamentary democracy or a nightmare of totalitarian darkness, the future belongs to the police state.

It will certainly be a police state whose functionaries will have the phrase "rights of the masses" continually on their lips. The gentle Rousseau, anticipating the terrorist rule of the single-party state, spoke of "the good people"; today the latter have turned into the "masses." It is no longer possible to say aloud that the rights of the masses do not exist, that the term "masses" does not stand for anything real, and that not the slightest sanctity should be attributed to it. A man who proclaimed such a thing today would exceed in temerity all those who once contested the legitimacy principle; he would actually send a deeper shudder through his audience than any atheist who ever denied the existence of God in the open market place. The fashion with which the whole modern world prostrates itself before the concept of the masses has hardly any counterpart in the history of mankind, because in the past the powers before which men bent the knee had a reality which was a matter of everyday experience, while the rise of the idea of the masses goes hand in hand with peoples' delivery gagged and bound to needs invented for them.

We think we have broken the oppressive influence of economic power, proclaimed the dignity of labor, the sanctity of leisure, and the "majesty" of the consumer. In reality, however, mankind, in so far as it takes part in civilization, is floundering in the net of a tyranny of the market, before which the powers of the state itself are beginning to bend the knee. He who has anything to put over—whether it be a commodity, or a habit leading to the consumption of commodities, or a fashion or trend calculated to create a demand—appeals to the principle of man's right to unrestricted access to all that civilization has to offer. It is a matter of indifference whether what is offered is a commodity or an idea, because in any event we shall be offered whatever will lead to an increase in the consumption of goods.

The romantic times in which one could hold individuals or groups responsible for these compulsions have gone. Never again will the critically minded have such easy targets at their disposal as in the period of opposition to good old capitalism, the representatives of which earned money by convincing people of their need for refrigerators. Those were the days! Then the sharpshooting critic of society at least knew on whom to set his sights. But the tyranny of the market of the present day and the wicked cunning of the old-fashioned capitalist are in different categories. Man is now digging his own grave; the evil is the individual's participation in what he takes to be civilization. All ideas of progress and improvement in living center around buying the things which are dreamt about by those who believe themselves to be on the ladder of progress.

What ranks as the civilization to which everyone has a right is the possession of certain objects and gadgets, access to certain forms of stimulus and entertainment, use of all the goods, commodities, and amenities characteristic of modern life. Tremendous industries and elaborate organizations exist to satisfy needs that they have themselves created—needs for materials, pictures, scents, new luxuries, drugs, and games; in short, all the things which are recommended to the individual as desirable on the ground that the masses want them. In relation to these needs no man is free, unless he feels capable of living the life of an outcast.

Our rump Germany is just as much involved in this servitude as all other countries. Indeed, the responsibility of our leading intellectual circles for this state of affairs is particularly great, because they have demonstrated no power of resistance to the myth of the masses. On the contrary, they cooperated with positively suicidal zeal in the lie about civilization based on alleged mass needs, and assiduously branded as heresy any attempt to protect the individual against the oppression of artificial cultural needs.

Thus the century-old struggle to liberate man so that he might enjoy an unrestricted share in the fruits of civilization has led to a new condition of servitude, and imposed on him a new kind of tyrant which he is unable to recognize as such. It is impossible for him to discern the trap into which he has fallen by reason of the continuous expansion of the possibilities of pleasure. It is even more difficult to preach him sermons about moderating his consumer drive, because only a saint would be capable of setting voluntary limits to the consumer in himself.

Man's liberty is indivisible, and therefore no one can prevent him from becoming a slave of civilization. His liberty to spoil the existence of himself and others by noise, restlessness, slogans, and substitute pleasures leads him straight into annihilating dependence on the banalities, the mass-produced goods, the stereotyped behavior, which he takes to be infallible signs of progress. Who, after all, would not wish to take part in a progress which would seem to be pointing the way upward for humanity? You only have to walk once down a metropolitan street with your eyes open, or to look through the advertisements in a newspaper, to see that what is offered far exceeds the individual's power of resistance. The abundance displayed presents itself as the bright counterpole of the stark desolation and devastation that was our lot only a few years ago.

In these circumstances how can a man be expected to distinguish

between increasing his consumption and increasing his human stat-
ure? How can one suggest to him the dreadful truth that he is continually declining, that his inner being is shrinking, and that with
every new refinement in his way of living he is sinking deeper into
the condition of a new barbarism, the chaotic crudity of which cannot be conjured away by any pharmaceutical product, or increase in
speed, or improvement in the means of communication? It would
certainly be idle to try to dissuade one's fellow from the use of
narcotics or television sets, but perhaps it may still be worth while to
call on him not to let himself be the slave of a civilization of which
he is called the master.

Once upon a time savages were identifiable by their terror of blun-
derbusses and belief in the power of the medicine man. Today the
place of these things has been taken by number of tubes, the cubic
capacity of cylinders, and the effectiveness of sleep-inducing drugs; in
other words, things intended to drive away fear at the passage of time
and the certainty of death. Doctors and engineers are there to bam-
boozle the mortal about his lot and banish from sight the abyss of the
fleeting nature of life. With that the counterpole of philosophy has
been reached. The object of civilization is to help people bury their
heads in the sand. We have entered upon a new barbarism, the clock
of which points glitteringly to high noon.

The True Believer*

BY ERIC HOFFER

[1951]

ALL MASS movements generate in their adherents a readiness to die and a proclivity for united action; all of them, irrespective of the doctrine they preach and the program they project, breed fanaticism, enthusiasm, fervent hope, hatred and intolerance; all of them are capable of releasing a powerful flow of activity in certain departments of life; all of them demand blind faith and singlehearted allegiance.

All movements, however different in doctrine and aspiration, draw their early adherents from the same types of humanity; they all appeal to the same types of mind.

Though there are obvious differences between the fanatical Christian, the fanatical Mohammedan, the fanatical nationalist, the fanatical Communist and the fanatical Nazi, it is yet true that the fanaticism which animates them may be viewed and treated as one. The same is true of the force which drives them on to expansion and world dominion. There is a certain uniformity in all types of dedication, of faith, of pursuit of power, of unity and of self-sacrifice. There are vast differences in the contents of holy causes and doctrines, but a certain uniformity in the factors which make them effective. . . .

It is necessary for most of us these days to have some insight into the motives and responses of the true believer. For though ours is a godless age, it is the very opposite of irreligious. The true believer is everywhere on the march, and both by converting and antagonizing he is shaping the world in his own image. And whether we are to line up with him or against him, it is well that we should know all we can concerning his nature and potentialities.

* * *

There is in us a tendency to locate the shaping forces of our existence outside ourselves. Success and failure are unavoidably related in our minds with the state of things around us. Hence it is that people with a sense of fulfillment think it a good world and would like to con-

---

* Selections from Eric Hoffer, *The True Believer. Thoughts on the Nature of Mass Movements.* Copyright by Eric Hoffer. Published by Harper & Brothers. Reprinted by permission.

serve it as it is, while the frustrated favor radical change. The tendency to look for all causes outside ourselves persists even when it is clear that our state of being is the product of personal qualities such as ability, character, appearance, health and so on. "If anything ail a man," says Thoreau, "so that he does not perform his functions, if he have a pain in his bowels even . . . he forthwith sets about reforming—the world."

It is understandable that those who fail should incline to blame the world for their failure. The remarkable thing is that the successful, too, however much they pride themselves on their foresight, fortitude, thrift and other "sterling qualities," are at bottom convinced that their success is the result of a fortuitous combination of circumstances. The self-confidence of even the consistently successful is never absolute. They are never sure that they know all the ingredients which go into the making of their success. The outside world seems to them a precariously balanced mechanism, and so long as it ticks in their favor they are afraid to tinker with it. Thus the resistance to change and the ardent desire for it spring from the same conviction, and the one can be as vehement as the other.

Discontent by itself does not invariably create a desire for change. Other factors have to be present before discontent turns into disaffection. One of these is a sense of power.

Those who are awed by their surroundings do not think of change, no matter how miserable their condition. When our mode of life is so precarious as to make it patent that we cannot control the circumstances of our existence, we tend to stick to the proven and the familiar. We counteract a deep feeling of insecurity by making of our existence a fixed routine. We hereby acquire the illusion that we have tamed the unpredictable. Fisherfolk, nomads and farmers who have to contend with the willful elements, the creative worker who depends on inspiration, the savage awed by his surroundings—they all fear change. They face the world as they would an all-powerful jury. The abjectly poor, too, stand in awe of the world around them and are not hospitable to change. It is a dangerous life we live when hunger and cold are at our heels. There is thus a conservatism of the destitute as profound as the conservatism of the privileged, and the former is as much a factor in the perpetuation of a social order as the latter.

The men who rush into undertakings of vast change usually feel they are in possession of some irresistible power. The generation that made the French Revolution had an extravagant conception of the omnipotence of man's reason and the boundless range of his intelligence. Never, says de Tocqueville, had humanity been prouder of itself nor had it ever so much faith in its own omnipotence. And joined with this exaggerated self-confidence was a universal thirst for change which came unbidden to every mind. Lenin and the Bolsheviks who plunged recklessly into the chaos of the creation of a new world had blind faith in the omnipotence of Marxist doctrine. The Nazis had nothing as potent as that doctrine, but they had faith in an infallible leader and also faith in a new technique. For it is doubtful whether National Socialism would have made such rapid progress if it had not been for the electrifying conviction that the new techniques of blitzkrieg and propaganda made Germany irresistible.

Even the sober desire for progress is sustained by faith—faith in the intrinsic goodness of human nature and in the omnipotence of science. It is a defiant and blasphemous faith, not unlike that held by the men who set out to build "a city and a tower, whose top may reach unto heaven" and who believed that "nothing will be restrained from them, which they have imagined to do."

Offhand one would expect that the mere possession of power would automatically result in a cocky attitude toward the world and a receptivity to change. But it is not always so. The powerful can be as timid as the weak. What seems to count more than possession of instruments of power is faith in the future. Where power is not joined with faith in the future, it is used mainly to ward off the new and preserve the status quo. On the other hand, extravagant hope, even when not backed by actual power, is likely to generate a most reckless daring. For the hopeful can draw strength from the most ridiculous sources of power—a slogan, a word, a button. No faith is potent unless it is also faith in the future; unless it has a millennial component. So, too, an effective doctrine: as well as being a source of power, it must also claim to be a key to the book of the future.

Those who would transform a nation or the world cannot do so by breeding and captaining discontent or by demonstrating the reasonableness and desirability of the intended changes or by coercing people into a new way of life. They must know how to kindle and fan an extravagant hope. It matters not whether it be hope of a heavenly kingdom, of heaven on earth, of plunder and untold riches, of fabulous achievement or world dominion. If the Communists win Europe and

a large part of the world, it will not be because they know how to stir
up discontent or how to infect people with hatred, but because they
know how to preach hope.

Thus the differences between the conservative and the radical seem
to spring mainly from their attitude toward the future. Fear of the
future causes us to lean against and cling to the present, while faith in
the future renders us receptive to change. Both the rich and the poor,
the strong and the weak, they who have achieved much or little can
be afraid of the future. When the present seems so perfect that the most
we can expect is its even continuation in the future, change can only
mean deterioration. Hence men of outstanding achievement and those
who live full, happy lives usually set their faces against drastic innovation. The conservatism of invalids and people past middle age stems,
too, from fear of the future. They are on the lookout for signs of decay,
and feel that any change is more likely to be for the worse than for the
better. The abjectly poor also are without faith in the future. The future seems to them a booby trap buried on the road ahead. One must
step gingerly. To change things is to ask for trouble.

As for the hopeful: it does not seem to make any difference who it
is that is seized with a wild hope—whether it be an enthusiastic intellectual, a land-hungry farmer, a get-rich-quick speculator, a sober merchant or industrialist, a plain workingman or a noble lord—they all
proceed recklessly with the present, wreck it if necessary, and create
a new world. There can thus be revolutions by the privileged as well
as by the underprivileged. The movement of enclosure in sixteenth and
seventeenth century England was a revolution by the rich. The woolen
industry rose to high prosperity, and grazing became more profitable
than cropping. The landowners drove off their tenants, enclosed the
commons and wrought profound changes in the social and economic
texture of the country. "The lords and nobles were upsetting the social
order, breaking down ancient law and custom, sometimes by means
of violence, often by pressure and intimidation." Another English
revolution by the rich occurred at the end of the eighteenth and the
beginning of the nineteenth century. It was the Industrial Revolution.
The breathtaking potentialities of mechanization set the minds of
manufacturers and merchants on fire. They began a revolution "as
extreme and radical as ever inflamed the minds of sectarians," and in
a relatively short time these respectable, Godfearing citizens changed
the face of England beyond recognition. . . .

For men to plunge headlong into an undertaking of vast change, they must be intensely discontented yet not destitute, and they must have the feeling that by the possession of some potent doctrine, infallible leader or some new technique they have access to a source of irresistible power. They must also have an extravagant conception of the prospects and potentialities of the future. Finally, they must be wholly ignorant of the difficulties involved in their vast undertaking. Experience is a handicap. The men who started the French Revolution were wholly without political experience. The same is true of the Bolsheviks, Nazis and the revolutionaries in Asia. The experienced man of affairs is a latecomer. He enters the movement when it is already a going concern. It is perhaps the Englishman's political experience that keeps him shy of mass movements. . . .

There is a fundamental difference between the appeal of a mass movement and the appeal of a practical organization. The practical organization offers opportunities for self-advancement, and its appeal is mainly to self-interest. On the other hand, a mass movement, particularly in its active, revivalist phase, appeals not to those intent on bolstering and advancing a cherished self, but to those who crave to be rid of an unwanted self. A mass movement attracts and holds a following not because it can satisfy the desire for self-advancement, but because it can satisfy the passion for self-renunciation.

People who see their lives as irremediably spoiled cannot find a worth-while purpose in self-advancement. The prospect of an individual career cannot stir them to a mighty effort, nor can it evoke in them faith and a single-minded dedication. They look on self-interest as on something tainted and evil, something unclean and unlucky. Anything undertaken under the auspices of the self seems to them foredoomed. Nothing that has its roots and reasons in the self can be good and noble. Their innermost craving is for a new life—a rebirth—or, failing this, a chance to acquire new elements of pride, confidence, hope, a sense of purpose and worth by an identification with a holy cause. An active mass movement offers them opportunities for both. If they join the movement as full converts they are reborn to a new life in its close-knit collective body, or if attracted as sympathizers they find elements of pride, confidence and purpose by identifying themselves with the efforts, achievements and prospects of the movement.

To the frustrated a mass movement offers substitutes either for the whole self or for the elements which make life bearable and which they cannot evoke out of their individual resources. . . .

The nature of the complete substitute offered by conversion is discussed in the chapters on self-sacrifice and united action in Part III. Here we shall deal with the partial substitutes.

Faith in a holy cause is to a considerable extent a substitute for the lost faith in ourselves.

The less justified a man is in claiming excellence for his own self, the more ready is he to claim all excellence for his nation, his religion, his race or his holy cause.

A man is likely to mind his own business when it is worth minding. When it is not, he takes his mind off his own meaningless affairs by minding other people's business.

This minding of other people's business expresses itself in gossip, snooping and meddling, and also in feverish interest in communal, national and racial affairs. In running away from ourselves we either fall on our neighbor's shoulder or fly at his throat.

The burning conviction that we have a holy duty toward others is often a way of attaching our drowning selves to a passing raft. What looks like giving a hand is often a holding on for dear life. Take away our holy duties and you leave our lives puny and meaningless. There is no doubt that in exchanging a self-centered for a selfless life we gain enormously in self-esteem. The vanity of the selfless, even those who practice utmost humility, is boundless.

One of the most potent attractions of a mass movement is its offering of a substitute for individual hope. This attraction is particularly effective in a society imbued with the idea of progress. For in the conception of progress, "tomorrow" looms large, and the frustration resulting from having nothing to look forward to is the more poignant. Hermann Rauschning says of pre-Hitlerian Germany that "The feeling of having come to the end of all things was one of the worst troubles we endured after that lost war." In a modern society people can live without hope only when kept dazed and out of breath by incessant hustling. The despair brought by unemployment comes not only from the threat of destitution, but from the sudden view of a vast nothingness ahead. The unemployed are more likely to follow the peddlers of hope than the handers-out of relief.

Mass movements are usually accused of doping their followers with hope of the future while cheating them of the enjoyment of the present. Yet to the frustrated the present is irremediably spoiled. Comforts and pleasures cannot make it whole. No real content or comfort can ever arise in their minds but from hope.

When our individual interests and prospects do not seem worth living for, we are in desperate need of something apart from us to live for. All forms of dedication, devotion, loyalty and self-surrender are in essence a desperate clinging to something which might give worth and meaning to our futile, spoiled lives. Hence the embracing of a substitute will necessarily be passionate and extreme. We can have qualified confidence in ourselves, but the faith we have in our nation, religion, race or holy cause has to be extravagant and uncompromising. A substitute embraced in moderation cannot supplant and efface the self we want to forget. We cannot be sure that we have something worth living for unless we are ready to die for it. This readiness to die is evidence to ourselves and others that what we had to take as a substitute for an irrevocably missed or spoiled first choice is indeed the best there ever was.

*   *   *

Freedom aggravates at least as much as it alleviates frustration. Freedom of choice places the whole blame of failure on the shoulders of the individual. And as freedom encourages a multiplicity of attempts, it unavoidably multiplies failure and frustration. Freedom alleviates frustration by making available the palliatives of action, movement, change and protest.

Unless a man has the talents to make something of himself, freedom is an irksome burden. Of what avail is freedom to choose if the self be ineffectual? We join a mass movement to escape individual responsibility, or, in the words of the ardent young Nazi, "to be free from freedom." It was not sheer hypocrisy when the rank-and-file Nazis declared themselves not guilty of all the enormities they had committed. They considered themselves cheated and maligned when made to shoulder responsibility for obeying orders. Had they not joined the Nazi movement in order to be free from responsibility?

It would seem then that the most fertile ground for the propagation of a mass movement is a society with considerable freedom but lacking the palliatives of frustration. It was precisely because the peasants of eighteenth century France, unlike the peasants of Germany and Austria, were no longer serfs and already owned land that they were receptive to the appeal of the French Revolution. Nor perhaps would there have been a Bolshevik revolution if the Russian peasant had not been free for a generation or more and had had a taste of the private ownership of land.

Even the mass movements which rise in the name of freedom against an oppressive order do not realize individual liberty once they start rolling. So long as a movement is engaged in a desperate struggle with the prevailing order or must defend itself against enemies within or without, its chief preoccupation will be with unity and self-sacrifice, which require the surrender of the individual's will, judgment and advantage. According to Robespierre, the revolutionary government was "the despotism of liberty against tyranny."

The important point is that in forgetting or postponing individual liberty, the active mass movement does not run counter to the inclinations of a zealous following. Fanatics, says Renan, fear liberty more than they fear persecution. It is true that the adherents of a rising movement have a strong sense of liberation even though they live and breathe in an atmosphere of strict adherence to tenets and commands. This sense of liberation comes from having escaped the burdens, fears and hopelessness of an untenable individual existence. It is this escape which they feel as a deliverance and redemption. The experience of vast change, too, conveys a sense of freedom, even though the changes are executed in a frame of strict discipline. It is only when the movement has passed its active stage and solidified into a pattern of stable institutions that individual liberty has a chance to emerge. The shorter the active phase, the more will it seem that the movement itself, rather than its termination, made possible the emergence of individual freedom. This impression will be the more pronounced the more tyrannical the dispensation which the mass movement overthrew and supplanted.

Those who see their lives as spoiled and wasted crave equality and fraternity more than they do freedom. If they clamor for freedom, it is but freedom to establish equality and uniformity. The passion for equality is partly a passion for anonymity: to be one thread of the many which make up a tunic; one thread not distinguishable from the others. No one can then point us out, measure us against others and expose our inferiority.

They who clamor loudest for freedom are often the ones least likely to be happy in a free society. The frustrated, oppressed by their shortcomings, blame their failure on existing restraints. Actually their innermost desire is for an end to the "free for all." They want to eliminate free competition and the ruthless testing to which the individual is continually subjected in a free society.

Where freedom is real, equality is the passion of the masses. Where equality is real, freedom is the passion of a small minority.

Equality without freedom creates a more stable social pattern than freedom without equality.

* * *

Policy Regarding the Philippines*

BY SENATOR ALBERT J. BEVERIDGE

[1900]

Mr. BEVERIDGE. I ask for the reading of the joint resolution introduced by me on Thursday last.

The PRESIDENT pro tempore. The Chair lays before the Senate the joint resolution introduced by the Senator from Indiana, which was laid on the table subject to his call. The joint resolution will be read.

The Secretary read the joint resolution (S. R. 53) defining the policy of the United States relative to the Philippine Islands, as follows:

Be it resolved by the Senate and House of Representatives of the United States of America in Congress assembled, That the Philippine Islands are territory belonging to the United States; that it is the intention of the United States to retain them as such and to establish and maintain such governmental control throughout the archipelago as the situation may demand.

Mr. BEVERIDGE. Mr. President, I address the Senate at this time because Senators and Members of the House on both sides have asked that I give to Congress and the country my observations in the Philippines and the far East, and the conclusions which those observations compel; and because of hurtful resolutions introduced and utterances made in the Senate, every word of which will cost and is costing the lives of American soldiers.

Mr. President, the times call for candor. The Philippines are ours forever, "territory belonging to the United States," as the Constitution calls them. And just beyond the Philippines are China's illimitable markets. We will not retreat from either. We will not repudiate our duty in the archipelago. We will not abandon our opportunity in the Orient. We will not renounce our part in the mission of our race, trustee, under God, of the civilization of the world. And we will move forward to our work, not howling out regrets like slaves whipped to their burdens, but with gratitude for a task worthy of our

---

* Adapted from the *Congressional Record*, January 9, 1900.

strength, and thanksgiving to Almighty God that He has marked us as
His chosen people, henceforth to lead in the regeneration of the world.

This island empire is the last land left in all the oceans. If it should
prove a mistake to abandon it, the blunder once made would be ir-
retrievable. If it proves a mistake to hold it, the error can be corrected
when we will. Every other progressive nation stands ready to relieve
us.

But to hold it will be no mistake. Our largest trade henceforth must
be with Asia. The Pacific is our ocean. More and more Europe will
manufacture the most it needs, secure from its colonies the most it
consumes. Where shall we turn for consumers of our surplus? Geography answers the question. China is our natural customer. She is
nearer to us than to England, Germany, or Russia, the commercial
powers of the present and the future. They have moved nearer to
China by securing permanent bases on her borders. The Philippines
gives us a base at the door of all the East.

Lines of navigation from our ports to the Orient and Australia; from
the Isthmian Canal to Asia; from all Oriental ports to Australia, con-
verge at and separate from the Philippines. They are a self-supporting,
dividend-paying fleet, permanently anchored at a spot selected by the
strategy of Providence, commanding the Pacific. And the Pacific is the
ocean of the commerce of the future. Most future wars will be conflicts for commerce. The power that rules the Pacific, therefore, is the
power that rules the world. And, with the Philippines, that power is
and will forever be the American Republic.

China's trade is the mightiest commercial fact in our future. Her
foreign commerce was $285,738,300 in 1897, of which we, her neighbor,
had less than 9 per cent, of which only a little more than half was
merchandise sold to China by us. We ought to have 50 per cent, and
we will. And China's foreign commerce is only beginning. Her resources, her possibilities, her wants, all are undeveloped. She has only
340 miles of railway. I have seen trains loaded with natives and all the
activities of modern life already appearing along the line. But she
needs, and in fifty years will have, 20,000 miles of railway.

Who can estimate her commerce, then? That statesman commits a
crime against American trade—against the American grower of cot-
ton and wheat and tobacco, the American manufacturer of machinery
and clothing—who fails to put America where she may command that
trade. Germany's Chinese trade is increasing like magic. She has estab-

lished ship lines and secured a tangible foothold on China's very soil. Russia's Chinese trade is growing beyond belief. She is spending the revenues of the Empire to finish her railroad into Pekin itself, and she is in physical possession of the imperial province of Manchuria. Japan's Chinese trade is multiplying in volume and value. She is bending her energy to her merchant marine, and is located along China's very coast; but Manila is nearer China than Yokohama is. The Philippines command the commercial situation of the entire East. Can America best trade with China from San Francisco or New York? From San Francisco, of course. But if San Francisco were closer to China than New York is to Pittsburgh, what then? And Manila is nearer Hong-kong than Habana is to Washington. And yet American statesmen plan to surrender this commercial throne of the Orient where Providence and our soldiers' lives have placed us. When history comes to write the story of that suggested treason to American supremacy and therefore to the spread of American civilization, let her in mercy write that those who so proposed were merely blind and nothing more.

But if they did not command China, India, the Orient, the whole Pacific for purposes of offense, defense, and trade, the Philippines are so valuable in themselves that we should hold them. I have cruised more than 2,000 miles through the archipelago, every moment a surprise at its loveliness and wealth. I have ridden hundreds of miles on the islands, every foot of the way a revelation of vegetable and mineral riches.

No land in America surpasses in fertility the plains and valleys of Luzon. Rice and coffee, sugar and cocoanuts, hemp and tobacco, and many products of the temperate as well as the tropic zone grow in various sections of the archipelago. I have seen hundreds of bushels of Indian corn lying in a road fringed with banana trees. The forests of Negros, Mindanao, Mindora, Paluan, and parts of Luzon are invaluable and intact. The wood of the Philippines can supply the furniture of the world for a century to come. At Cebu the best informed man in the island told me that 40 miles of Cebu's mountain chain are practically mountains of coal. Pablo Majia, one of the most reliable men on the islands, confirmed the statement. Some declare that the coal is only lignite; but ship captains who have used it told me that it is better steamer fuel than the best coal of Japan.

I have a nugget of pure gold picked up in its present form on the banks of a Philippine creek. I have gold dust washed out by crude processes of careless natives from the sands of a Philippine stream. Both indicate great deposits at the source from which they come. In one of the islands great deposits of copper exist untouched. The mineral wealth of this empire of the ocean will one day surprise the world. I base this statement partly on personal observation, but chiefly on the testimony of foreign merchants in the Philippines, who have practically investigated the subject, and upon the unanimous opinion of natives and priests. And the mineral wealth is but a small fraction of the agricultural wealth of these islands.

And the wood, hemp, copra, and other products of the Philippines supply what we need and can not ourselves produce. And the markets they will themselves afford will be immense. Spain's export and import trade, with the islands undeveloped, was $11,534,731 annually. Our trade with the islands developed will be $125,000,000 annually, for who believes that we can not do ten times as well as Spain? Consider their imperial dimensions. Luzon is larger and richer than New York, Pennsylvania, Illinois, or Ohio. Mindanao is larger and richer than all New England, exclusive of Maine. Manila, as a port of call and exchange, will, in the time of men now living, far surpass Liverpool. Behold the exhaustless markets they command. It is as if a half dozen of our States were set down between Oceania and the Orient, and those States themselves undeveloped and unspoiled of their primitive wealth and resources.

Nothing is so natural as trade with one's neighbors. The Philippines make us the nearest neighbors of all the East. Nothing is more natural than to trade with those you know. This is the philosophy of all advertising. The Philippines bring us permanently face to face with the most sought-for customers of the world. National prestige, national propinquity, these and commercial activity are the elements of commercial success. The Philippines give the first; the character of the American people supply the last. It is a providential conjunction of all the elements of trade, of duty, and of power. If we are willing to go to war rather than let England have a few feet of frozen Alaska, which affords no market and commands none, what should we not do rather than let England, Germany, Russia, or Japan have all the Philippines? And no man on the spot can fail to see that this would be their fate if we retired.

The climate is the best tropic climate in the world. This is the belief of those who have lived in many tropic countries, with scores of whom

I have talked on this point. My own experience with tropical conditions has not been exhaustive; yet, speaking from that experience, I testify that the climate of Iloilo, Sulu, Cebu, and even of Manila, greatly surpasses that of Hongkong. And yet on the bare and burning rock of Hongkong our constructing race has builded one of the noblest cities of all the world, and made the harbor it commands the focus of the commerce of the East. And the glory of that achievement illumines with a rarer splendor than that of Waterloo the flag that floats above it, for from Hongkong's heights civilization is irradiating all the Orient. If this be imperialism, its final end will be the empire of the Son of Man. . . .

Here, then, Senators, is the situation. Two years ago there was no land in all the world which we could occupy for any purpose. Our commerce was daily turning toward the Orient, and geography and trade developments made necessary our commercial empire over the Pacific. And in that ocean we had no commercial, naval, or military base. Today we have one of the three great ocean possessions of the globe, located at the most commanding commercial, naval, and military points in the eastern seas, within hail of India, shoulder to shoulder with China, richer in its own resources than any equal body of land on the entire globe, and peopled by a race which civilization demands shall be improved. Shall we abandon it? That man little knows the common people of the Republic, little understands the instincts of our race, who thinks we will not hold it fast and hold it forever, administering just government by simplest methods. We may trick up devices to shift our burden and lessen our opportunity; they will avail us nothing but delay. We may tangle conditions by applying academic arrangements of self-government to a crude situation; their failure will drive us to our duty in the end.

* * *

But, Senators, it would be better to abandon this combined garden and Gibraltar of the Pacific, and count our blood and treasure already spent a profitable loss, than to apply any academic arrangement of self-government to these children. They are not capable of self-government. How could they be? They are not of a self-governing race. They are Orientals, Malays, instructed by Spaniards in the latter's worst estate.

They know nothing of practical government except as they have witnessed the weak, corrupt, cruel, and capricious rule of Spain. What magic will anyone employ to dissolve in their minds and characters those impressions of governors and governed which three centuries of misrule has created? What alchemy will change the oriental quality of their blood and set the self-governing currents of the American pouring through their Malay veins? How shall they, in the twinkling of an eye, be exalted to the heights of self-governing peoples which required a thousand years for us to reach, Anglo-Saxon though we are?

Let men beware how they employ the term "self-government." It is a sacred term. It is the watchword at the door of the inner temple of liberty, for liberty does not always mean self-government. Self-government is a method of liberty—the highest, simplest, best—and it is acquired only after centuries of study and struggle and experiment and instruction and all the elements of the progress of man. Self-government is no base and common thing, to be bestowed on the merely audacious. It is the degree which crowns the graduate of liberty, not the name of liberty's infant class, who have not yet mastered the alphabet of freedom. Savage blood, oriental blood, Malay blood, Spanish example—are these the elements of self-government?

We must act on the situation as it exists, not as we would wish it. I have talked with hundreds of these people, getting their views as to the practical workings of self-government. The great majority simply do not understand any participation in any government whatever. The most enlightened among them declare that self-government will succeed because the employers of labor will compel their employees to vote as their employer wills and that this will insure intelligent voting. I was assured that we could depend upon good men always being in office because the officials who constitute the government will nominate their successors, choose those among the people who will do the voting, and determine how and where elections will be held.

The most ardent advocate of self-government that I met was anxious that I should know that such a government would be tranquil because, as he said, if anyone criticised it, the government would shoot the offender. A few of them have a sort of verbal understanding of the democratic theory, but the above are the examples of the ideas of the practical workings of self-government entertained by the aristocracy, the rich planters and traders, and heavy employers of labor, the men who would run the government.

Example for decades will be necessary to instruct them in American

ideas and methods of administration. Example, example; always example—this alone will teach them. As a race, their general ability is not
excellent. Educators, both men and women, to whom I have talked in
Cebu and Luzon, were unanimous in the opinion that in all solid and
useful education they are, as a people, dull and stupid. In showy things,
like carving and painting or embroidery or music, they have apparent
aptitude, but even this is superficial and never thorough. They have
facility of speech, too.

The three best educators on the island at different times made to
me the same comparison, that the common people in their stupidity
are like their caribou bulls. They are not even good agriculturists.
Their waste of cane is inexcusable. Their destruction of hemp fiber is
childish. They are incurably indolent. They have no continuity or
thoroughness of industry. They will quit work without notice and
amuse themselves until the money they have earned is spent. They are
like children playing at men's work.

No one need fear their competition with our labor. No reward could
beguile, no force compel, these children of indolence to leave their
trifling lives for the fierce and fervid industry of high-wrought America. The very reverse is the fact. One great problem is the necessary
labor to develop these islands—to build the roads, open the mines, clear
the wilderness, drain the swamps, dredge the harbors. The natives will
not supply it. A lingering prejudice against the Chinese may prevent
us from letting them supply it. Ultimately, when the real truth of the
climate and human conditions is known, it is barely possible that our
labor will go there. Even now young men with the right moral fiber
and a little capital can make fortunes there as planters. . . .

Mr. President, self-government and internal development have
been the dominant notes of our first century; administration and the
development of other lands will be the dominant notes of our second
century. And administration is as high and holy a function as self-
government, just as the care of a trust estate is as sacred an obligation
as the management of our own concerns. Cain was the first to violate
the divine law of human society which makes of us our brother's
keeper. And administration of good government is the first lesson in
self-government, that exalted estate toward which all civilization tends.

Administration of good government is not denial of liberty. For
what is liberty? It is not savagery. It is not the exercise of individual
will. It is not dictatorship. It involves government, but not necessarily

self-government. It means law. First of all, it is a common rule of action, applying equally to all within its limits. Liberty means protection of property and life without price, free speech without intimidation, justice without purchase or delay, government without favor or favorites. What will best give all this to the people of the Philippines—American administration, developing them gradually toward self-government, or self-government by a people before they know what self-government means?

The Declaration of Independence does not forbid us to do our part in the regeneration of the world. If it did, the Declaration would be wrong, just as the Articles of Confederation, drafted by the very same men who signed the Declaration, was found to be wrong. The Declaration has no application to the present situation. It was written by self-governing men for self-governing men.

It was written by men who, for a century and a half, had been experimenting in self-government on this continent, and whose ancestors for hundreds of years before had been gradually developing toward that high and holy estate. The Declaration applies only to people capable of self-government. How dare any man prostitute this expression of the very elect of self-governing peoples to a race of Malay children of barbarism, schooled in Spanish methods and ideas? And you, who say the Declaration applies to all men, how dare you deny its application to the American Indian? And if you deny it to the Indian at home, how dare you grant it to the Malay abroad?

The Declaration does not contemplate that all government must have the consent of the governed. It announces that man's "inalienable rights are life, liberty, and the pursuit of happiness; that to secure these rights governments are established among men deriving their just powers from the consent of the governed; that when any form of government becomes destructive of those rights, it is the right of the people to alter or abolish it." "Life, liberty, and the pursuit of happiness" are the important things; "consent of the governed" is one of the means to those ends.

If "any form of government becomes destructive of those ends, it is the right of the people to alter or abolish it," says the Declaration. "Any form" includes all forms. Thus the Declaration itself recognizes other forms of government than those resting on the consent of the governed. The word "consent" itself recognizes other forms, for "consent" means the understanding of the thing to which the "consent" is given;

and there are people in the world who do not understand any form of government. And the sense in which "consent" is used in the Declaration is broader than mere understanding; for "consent" in the Declaration means participation in the government "consented" to. And yet these people who are not capable of "consenting" to any form of government must be governed.

And so the Declaration contemplates all forms of government which secure the fundamental rights of life, liberty, and the pursuit of happiness. Self-government, when that will best secure these ends, as in the case of people capable of self-government; other appropriate forms when people are not capable of self-government. And so the authors of the Declaration themselves governed the Indian without his consent; the inhabitants of Louisiana without their consent; and ever since the sons of the makers of the Declaration have been governing not by theory, but by practice, after the fashion of our governing race, now by one form, now by another, but always for the purpose of securing the great eternal ends of life, liberty, and the pursuit of happiness, not in the savage, but in the civilized meaning of those terms—life according to orderly methods of civilized society; liberty regulated by law; pursuit of happiness limited by the pursuit of happiness by every other man.

If this is not the meaning of the Declaration, our Government itself denies the Declaration every time it receives the representative of any but a republican form of government, such as that of the Sultan, the Czar, or other absolute autocrats, whose governments, according to the opposition's interpretation of the Declaration, are spurious governments, because the people governed have not "consented" to them.

Senators in opposition are estopped from denying our constitutional power to govern the Philippines as circumstances may demand, for such power is admitted in the case of Florida, Louisiana, Alaska. How, then, is it denied in the Philippines? Is there a geographical interpretation to the Constitution? Do degrees of longitude fix constitutional limitations? Does a thousand miles of ocean diminish constitutional power more than a thousand miles of land?

The ocean does not separate us from the field of our duty and endeavor—it joins us, an established highway needing no repair, and landing us at any point desired. The seas do not separate the Philippine Islands from us or from each other. The seas are highways through the archipelago, which would cost hundreds of millions of dollars to construct if they were land instead of water. Land may separate men from their desire, the ocean never. Russia has been centuries in crossing Siberian wastes; the Puritans crossed the Atlantic in brief and flying weeks.

If the Boers must have traveled by land, they would never have reached the Transvaal; but they sailed on liberty's ocean; they walked on civilization's untaxed highway, the welcoming sea. Our ships habitually sailed round the cape and anchored in California's harbors before a single trail had lined the desert with the whitening bones of those who made it. No! No! The ocean unites us; steam unites us; electricity unites us; all the elements of nature unite us to the region where duty and interest call us. There is in the ocean no constitutional argument against the march of the flag, for the oceans, too, are ours. With more extended coast lines than any nation of history; with a commerce vaster than any other people ever dreamed of, and that commerce as yet only in its beginnings; with naval traditions equaling those of England or of Greece, and the work of our Navy only just begun; with the air of the ocean in our nostrils and the blood of a sailor ancestry in our veins; with the shores of all the continents calling us, the Great Republic before I die will be the acknowledged lord of the world's high seas. And over them the Republic will hold dominion, by virtue of the strength God has given it, for the peace of the world and the betterment of man.

No; the oceans are not limitations of the power which the Constitution expressly gives Congress to govern all territory the nation may acquire. The Constitution declares that "Congress shall have power to dispose of and make all needful rules and regulations respecting the territory belonging to the United States." Not the Northwest Territory only; not Louisiana or Florida only; not territory on this continent only, but any territory anywhere belonging to the nation. The founders of the nation were not provincial. Theirs was the geography of the world. They were soldiers as well as landsmen, and they knew that where our ships should go our flag might follow. They had the logic of progress, and they knew that the Republic they were planting must, in obedience to the laws of our expanding race, necessarily develop into the greater Republic which the world beholds today, and into the still mightier Republic which the world will finally acknowledge as the arbiter, under God, of the destinies of mankind. And so our fathers wrote into the Constitution these words of growth, of expansion, of empire, if you will, unlimited by geography or climate or by anything but the vitality and possibilities of the American people: "Congress shall have power to dispose of and make all needful rules and regulations respecting the territory belonging to the United States."

The power to govern all territory the nation may acquire would have been in Congress if the language affirming that power had not been written in the Constitution. For not all powers of the National Government are expressed. Its principal powers are implied. The written Constitution is but the index of the living Constitution. Had this not been true, the Constitution would have failed. For the people in any event would have developed and progressed. And if the Constitution had not had the capacity for growth corresponding with the growth of the nation, the Constitution would and should have been abandoned as the Articles of Confederation were abandoned. For the Constitution is not immortal in itself, is not useful even in itself. The Constitution is immortal and even useful only as it serves the orderly development of the nation. The nation alone is immortal. The nation alone is sacred. The Army is its servant. The Navy is its servant. The President is its servant. The Senate is its servant. Our laws are its methods. Our Constitution is its instrument.

This is the golden rule of constitutional interpretation: The Constitution was made for the people, not the people for the Constitution....

Mr. President, this question is deeper than any question of party politics; deeper than any question of the isolated policy of our country even; deeper even than any question of constitutional power. It is elemental. It is racial. God has not been preparing the English-speaking and Teutonic peoples for a thousand years for nothing but vain and idle self-contemplation and self-admiration. No! He has made us the master organizers of the world to establish system where chaos reigns. He has given us the spirit of progress to overwhelm the forces of reaction throughout the earth. He has made us adepts in government that we may administer government among savage and senile peoples. Were it not for such a force as this the world would relapse into barbarism and night. And of all our race He has marked the American people as His chosen nation to finally lead in the regeneration of the world. This is the divine mission of America, and it holds for us all the profit, all the glory, all the happiness possible to man. We are trustees of the world's progress, guardians of its righteous peace. The judgment of the Master is upon us: "Ye have been faithful over a few things; I will make you ruler over many things."

What shall history say of us? Shall it say that we renounced that holy trust, left the savage to his base condition, the wilderness to the reign of waste, deserted duty, abandoned glory, forgot our sordid profit even, because we feared our strength and read the charter of our powers with the doubter's eye and the quibbler's mind? Shall it say that, called by events to captain and command the proudest, ablest, purest race of history in history's noblest work, we declined that great commission? Our fathers would not have had it so. No! They founded no paralytic government, incapable of the simplest acts of administration. They planted no sluggard people, passive while the world's work calls them. They established no reactionary nation. They unfurled no retreating flag.

That flag has never paused in its onward march. Who dares halt it now—now, when history's largest events are carrying it forward; now, when we are at last one people, strong enough for any task, great enough for any glory destiny can bestow? How comes it that our first century closes with the process of consolidating the American people into a unit just accomplished, and quick upon the stroke of that great hour presses upon us our world opportunity, world duty, and world glory, which none but a people welded into an indivisible nation can achieve or perform?

Blind indeed is he who sees not the hand of God in events so vast, so harmonious, so benign. Reactionary indeed is the mind that perceives not that this vital people is the strongest of the saving forces of the world; that our place, therefore, is at the head of the constructing and redeeming nations of the earth; and that to stand aside while events march on is a surrender of our interests, a betrayal of our duty as blind as it is base. Craven indeed is the heart that fears to perform a work so golden and so noble; that dares not win a glory so immortal.

Do you tell me that it will cost us money? When did Americans ever measure duty by financial standards? Do you tell me of the tremendous toil required to overcome the vast difficulties of our task? What mighty work for the world, for humanity, even for ourselves, has ever been done with ease? Even our bread must we eat by the sweat of our faces. Why are we charged with power such as no people ever knew, if we are not to use it in a work such as no people ever wrought? Who will dispute the divine meaning of the fable of the talents?

Do you remind me of the precious blood that must be shed, the lives that must be given, the broken hearts of loved ones for their slain? And this is indeed a heavier price than all combined. And yet as a nation every historic duty we have done, every achievement we have accomplished, has been by the sacrifice of our noblest sons. Every holy memory that glorifies the flag is of those heroes who have died that its onward march might not be stayed. It is the nation's dearest lives yielded for the flag that makes it dear to us; it is the nation's most precious blood poured out for it that makes it precious to us. That flag is woven of heroism and grief, of the bravery of men and women's tears, of righteousness and battle, of sacrifice and anguish, of triumph and of glory. It is these which make our flag a holy thing. Who would tear from that sacred banner the glorious legends of a single battle where it has waved on land or sea? What son of a soldier of the flag whose father fell beneath it on any field would surrender that proud record for the heraldry of a king? In the cause of civilization, in the service of the Republic anywhere on earth, Americans consider wounds the noblest decorations man can win, and count the giving of their lives a glad and precious duty.

Pray God that spirit never fails. Pray God the time may never come when Mammon and the love of ease shall so debase our blood that we will fear to shed it for the flag and its imperial destiny. Pray God the time may never come when American heroism is but a legend like the story of the Cid, American faith in our mission and our might a dream dissolved, and the glory of our mighty race departed.

And that time will never come. We will renew our youth at the fountain of new and glorious deeds. We will exalt our reverence for the flag by carrying it to a noble future as well as by remembering its ineffable past. Its immortality will not pass, because everywhere and always we will acknowledge and discharge the solemn responsibilities our sacred flag, in its deepest meaning, puts upon us. And so, Senators, with reverent hearts, where dwells the fear of God, the American people move forward to the future of their hope and the doing of His work.

Mr. President and Senators, adopt the resolution offered, that peace may quickly come and that we may begin our saving, regenerating, and uplifting work. Adopt it, and this bloodshed will cease when these deluded children of our islands learn that this is the final word of the representatives of the American people in Congress assembled. Reject it, and the world, history, and the American people will know where to forever fix the awful responsibility for the consequences that will surely follow such failure to do our manifest duty. How dare we delay when our soldiers' blood is flowing? (*Applause in the galleries.*)

The PRESIDENT pro tempore. Applause is not permitted in the United States Senate. . . .

VII

SELF-DETERMINATION

What Is a Nation?*

BY ERNEST RENAN

[1882]

I PROPOSE to analyse with you an idea, simple in appearance, but capable of the most dangerous misunderstanding. The forms of human society are of the most varied types. Great conglomerations of people, as in the case of China, of Egypt, of ancient Babylon; the tribe, as in the case of the Hebrews and the Arabs; the city, as in the case of Athens and Sparta; unions of different countries, in the fashion of the Empire of Achaemenes, the Roman Empire, or the Carlovingian Empire; communities of no country, held together by the bond of religion, like the Israelites or the Parsees; nations like France, England, and the majority of modern European autonomies; confederations, as in the case of Switzerland and America; relationships similar to those which race and, in a greater degree, language establish between the different branches of the Teutonic family, the different branches of the Slavs;—these are modes of grouping which all exist, or at least have existed, and which cannot be confounded, the one with the other, without the most serious inconvenience. At the time of the French Revolution there was a belief that the institutions of small independent towns, such as Sparta and Rome, could be applied to our great nations of thirty or forty millions of souls. In our own day a still graver error is committed: the race is confounded with the nation, and to racial, or rather to linguistic groups, is attributed a sovereignty analogous to that of really existent peoples. Let us attempt to arrive at some precision in these difficult questions, where the least confusion in the sense of words, at the beginning of the discussion, may produce in the end the most fatal errors. What we are about to undertake is a delicate task; it is almost vivisection. We are to deal with living men, as, under ordinary circumstances, the dead alone are treated. In doing so we shall use coolness, and the most absolute impartiality.

Since the end of the Roman Empire, or rather since the disruption of the Empire of Charlemagne, Western Europe appears to us divided

---

* Reprinted from Ernest Renan, *The Poetry of the Celtic Races, and Other Studies.*

into nations, of which some, at certain epochs, have sought to exercise a supremacy over others, without any lasting success. What Charles V, Louis XIV, and Napoleon I were unable to do in the past, is hardly likely to be achieved by any one in the future. The establishment of a new Roman Empire, or a new Carlovingian Empire, has become an impossibility. Europe is too deeply divided for an attempt at universal dominion not to provoke, and that quickly, a coalition which would force the ambitious nation to retire within its natural bounds. A species of equilibrium has long been in existence. France, England, Germany, and Russia will still be, in centuries to come, and in spite of the vicissitudes they will have gone through, historic individualities, essential pieces of a chess-board, the squares of which vary unceasingly in importance and greatness, but are never altogether confused.

Nations, understood in this way, are a new feature in history. Antiquity knew them not; Egypt, China, ancient Chaldea, were to no extent nations. There were flocks led by a son of the Sun, or a son of Heaven. There were no Egyptian citizens, as there are no Chinese citizens. Classical antiquity had republics, and municipal kingdoms, confederations of neighbouring republics, and empires; it scarcely had the nation, in the sense in which we understand it. Athens, Sparta, Sidon, and Tyre were little centres of admirable patriotism; but they were cities with a comparatively restricted territory. Gaul, Spain, and Italy, before their absorption in the Roman Empire, were clusters of peoples, often in league with one another, but unpossessed of central institutions or dynasties. Nor were even the Assyrian Empire, the Persian Empire, or that of Alexander, nations. There were never Assyrian patriots; the Persian Empire was one vast feudality. Not a single nation traces its origin to the colossal enterprise of Alexander, which was nevertheless so pregnant with consequences for the general history of civilisation.

The Roman Empire was much nearer to being a nation. In return for the immense boon of the cessation of wars, the Roman dominion, at first so painful, was very quickly loved. It was a great association, synonymous with order, peace, and civilisation. In the later days of the Empire there was among the greater minds, among enlightened bishops, and among the lettered, a genuine feeling for "the Roman Peace," as opposed to the menacing chaos of barbarism. But an Empire twelve times greater in extent than the France of the present day could not form a state in the modern acceptance of the term. The severance of East and West was inevitable. The attempts at a Gaulish Empire in the third century were unsuccessful. It was the Teutonic invasion that introduced into the world the principle which, later, served as a basis to the existence of nationalities.

What, in fact, were those Teutonic peoples doing, from their great invasions of the fifth century to the last Norman conquests in the tenth? They changed the essential character of races only slightly; but they imposed dynasties and a military aristocracy upon more or less considerable portions of the former Empire of the West, which took the name of their invaders. Thence arose a France, a Burgundy, a Lombardy—later still, a Normandy. . . .

What, then, is the characteristic feature of these different states? It consists in the fusion of the populations which compose them. In the countries that we have just enumerated, there is nothing analogous to what you will find in Turkey, where the Turk, the Slav, the Greek, the Armenian, the Arab, the Syrian, and the Kurd are as distinct now as on the day of their conquest. Two essential circumstances contributed to bring this result to pass. First of all is the fact, that the Teutonic tribes adopted Christianity as soon as they had had relations of some little duration with the Greek and Latin peoples. When conqueror and conquered are of the same religion, or rather when the conqueror adopts the religion of the conquered, the Turkish system, the absolute distinction of men according to their respective faiths, can no longer be possible. The second circumstance was the conquerors' forgetfulness of their own language. . . .

Forgetfulness, and I shall even say historical error, form an essential factor in the creation of a nation; and thus it is that the progress of historical studies may often be dangerous to the nationality. Historical research, in fact, brings back to light the deeds of violence that have taken place at the commencement of all political formations, even of those the consequences of which have been most beneficial. Unity is ever achieved by brutality. The union of Northern and Southern France was the result of an extermination, and of a reign of terror that lasted for nearly a hundred years. . . .

The modern nation is then the historical result of a series of events, converging in the same direction. Sometimes unity has been achieved by a dynasty, as in the case of France; sometimes by the direct will of the provinces, as in the case of Holland, Switzerland, and Belgium; sometimes by a general feeling slowly vanquishing the caprices of feudality, as in the case of Italy and Germany. But a profound *raison d'etre* has always governed these formations. The principles in such cases come to light in the most unexpected ways. In our own times we have seen Italy united by her defeats, and Turkey destroyed by her victories. Every defeat advanced the cause of Italy, every victory was a loss to Turkey; for Italy is a nation, Turkey, outside Asia Minor, is not. It is the glory of France to have proclaimed by the French Revolution that a nation exists by itself. We ought not to complain because we find ourselves imitated. Ours is the principle of nations. But what then is a nation? Why is Holland a nation, while Hanover or the Grand Duchy of Parma is not? How does France persist in being a nation, when the principle which created her has disappeared? How is Switzerland, with three languages, two religions, and three or four races, a nation, while Tuscany, for example, which is homogeneous, is not? Why is Austria a state and not a nation? In what respect does the principle of nationality differ from the principle of races? . . .

In the opinion of certain political theorists a nation is, before all else, a dynasty representing an ancient conquest, a conquest first accepted and then forgotten by the mass of the people. According to the theorists of whom I speak, the grouping of provinces effected by a dynasty, by its wars, by its marriages, or by its treaties, comes to an end with the dynasty which has formed it. It is very true that the majority of modern nations owe their existence to a family of feudal origin, which contracted a marriage with the soil, and was in some measure a nucleus of centralisation. There was nothing natural or necessary about the boundaries of France in 1789. . . . The union of England, Ireland, and Scotland was in like manner a dynastic act. The reason for Italy delaying so long in becoming a nation was that no one of her numerous reigning houses, before the present century, made itself the centre of unity. . . .

But is such a law as this absolute? Certainly not. Switzerland and the United States, conglomerations formed by successive additions, have no dynastic base. I shall not discuss the question with regard to France. It would be necessary to have the secret of the future. Let us only say that the great royal house of France had been so highly national, that, on the morrow of its fall, the nation was able to stand without its support. And then the eighteenth century had changed everything. Man had returned, after centuries of abasement, to the old spirit, to self-respect, to the idea of his rights. The words "country" and "citizen" had resumed their significance. Thus it was that the boldest operation ever attempted in history was accomplished—an operation which might be compared to what in physiology would be the gift of life and its first identity, to a body from which head and heart had been removed.

It must then be admitted that a nation can exist without a dynastic principle; and even that nations formed by dynasties can separate themselves from them without, for that reason, ceasing to exist. The old principle, which held account of no right but that of princes, can no longer be maintained; above the dynastic right there is the national right. On what foundation shall we build up this national right, by what sign shall we know it, from what tangible fact shall we derive it?

(I) From race, say several with assurance. Artificial divisions resulting from feudality, royal marriages, or diplomatic congresses, are unstable. What does remain firm and fixed is the race of populations. That it is which constitutes right and legitimacy. The Teutonic family, for example, according to this theory, has the right of reclaiming such of its members as are beyond the pale of Teutonism—even when these members do not seek reunion. The right of Teutonism over such a province is greater than the right of the inhabitants of the province over themselves. Thus is created a kind of primordial right, analogous to that of the divine right of kings; for the principle of nations is substituted that of anthropology. This is a very grave error, which, if it became dominant, would cause the ruin of European civilisation. So far as the national principle is just and legitimate, so far is the primordial right of races narrow, and full of danger for true progress.

It may be admitted that, in the tribe and the city of antiquity, the fact of race had an importance of the highest order. But the ancient tribe and city were only extensions of the family. In Sparta and in Athens all the citizens were more or less closely related. It was the same in the Beni-Israel, it is so to this day among the Arab tribes. From Athens, from Sparta, from the Israelite tribe, let us now turn to the Roman Empire. The situation is altogether different. Founded by violence, then maintained by self-interest, this great agglomeration of towns, and altogether diverse provinces, dealt a blow of the gravest kind to the idea of race. Christianity, with its universal and absolute character, tended still more efficiently in the same direction. It entered into a close alliance with the Roman Empire, and the effect of those two incomparable agents of unity was to banish anthropological reason for centuries from the government of human affairs.

The barbarian invasion was, despite appearances, a step further in the same direction. There was nothing racial in the division of barbaric kingdoms; they were governed by the force or the caprice of the invaders. The race of the populations that they subjugated was, for them, a matter of the greatest indifference. Charlemagne achieved again, in his own way, what Rome had achieved already: a single empire composed of the most diverse races. . . .

Racial considerations have then been for nothing in the constitution of modern nations. France is Celtic, Iberian, Teutonic. Germany is Teutonic, Celtic, and Slavonic. Italy is the country where anthropology is most confused. Gauls, Etruscans Pelasgians, and Greeks, to say nothing of many other elements, are crossed in an undecipherable medley. The British Isles, as a whole, exhibit a mixture of Celtic and Teutonic blood, the relative proportions of which it is singularly difficult to define.

The truth is that there is no pure race; and that making politics depend upon anthropological analysis, is allowing it to be borne upon a chimaera. The most noble countries, England, France, Italy, are those where blood is most mingled. Is Germany an exception to this rule? Is she purely Teutonic? What an illusion is this! The whole of the South was once Gaulish. The whole of the East beyond the Elbe is Slavonic. And what, in point of fact, are the parts alleged to be really pure? . . .

The study of race is of capital importance to the student who occupies himself with the history of mankind. It has no application in politics. The instinctive consciousness which presided over the construction of the map of Europe took no account of race; and the greatest European nations are nations of essentially mixed blood.

Racial facts then, important as they are in the beginning, have a constant tendency to lose their importance. Human history is essentially different from zoology. . . . You may be sure that if science is charged with the duty of furnishing the elements of diplomacy, it will be, in many cases, found to be in the gravest error. It has better work to do; let us simply demand of it the truth.

(II) What we have been saying about race must also be said of language. Language invites re-union; it does not force it. The United States and England, Spanish America and Spain, speak the same languages, and do not form single nations. On the contrary, Switzerland, which owes her stability to the fact that she was founded by the assent of her several parts, counts three or four languages. In man there is something superior to language—will. The will of Switzerland to be united, in spite of the variety of her languages, is a much more important fact than a similarity of language, often obtained by persecution.

It is an honourable fact for France, that she has never sought to procure unity of speech by measures of coercion. Can we not have the same feelings and thoughts, and love the same things in different languages? . . . Languages are historical formations, which give but little indication of the blood of those who speak them; and, in any case, cannot enchain human liberty, when there is a question of determining the family with which we unite ourselves for life and death.

The exclusive consideration of language has, like the unduly great attention given to race, its dangers and its drawbacks. When we thus exaggerate it, we imprison ourselves in a limited culture, held as being national; we are hemmed in, cooped up. We quit the great atmosphere that we breathe in the vast field of humanity, to shut ourselves up in conventicles of compatriots. Nothing can be worse for the mind, nothing more hurtful to civilisation. Do not let us abandon this fundamental principle, that man is a reasonable and moral being before being allotted to such and such a language, before being a member of such and such a race, an adherent of such and such a culture. . . .

(III) Nor can religion offer a sufficient basis for the establishment of a modern nationality. In the beginning religion was essential to the very existence of the social group. The social group was an extension of the family. Religious rites were family rites. The Athenian religion was the cult of Athens itself, of its mythical founders, of its laws and customs. It implied no dogmatic theology. This religion was in every sense of the term a State religion. If any one refused to practise it, he was no longer an Athenian. . . . To refuse to participate in such a worship was like a refusal of military service in our modern societies. It was a declaration that one was not an Athenian. From another point of view, it is clear that such a religion had no force for any one who was not an Athenian; and thus no proselytism was exercised to compel aliens to accept it. . . .

In our own days the position is perfectly clear. No longer are there masses of people professing a uniform belief. Every one believes and practises after his own fashion, what he can, as he pleases. The state-religion is a thing of the past. One can be a Frenchman, an Englishman, or a German; and at the same time be a Catholic, a Protestant, or a Jew, or else be of no creed at all. Religion has become a matter for the individual; it affects the individual's conscience alone. The division of nations into Catholic and Protestant no longer exists. Religion, which fifty-two years ago was so considerable an element in the formation of Belgium, retains all its importance in the spiritual jurisdiction of each man; but it has almost completely disappeared from the considerations that trace the limits of peoples.

(IV) Community of interests is assuredly a powerful bond between men. But nevertheless can interests suffice to make a nation? I do not believe it. Community of interests makes commercial treaties. There is a sentimental side to nationality; it is at once body and soul; a *Zollverein** is not a fatherland.

(V) Geography, or what we may call natural frontiers, certainly plays a considerable part in the division of nations. Geography is one of the essential factors of history. Rivers have carried races forward; mountains have checked them. The former have favoured, the latter limited, historic movements. Can it be said, however, that, as certain persons believe, the boundaries of a nation are inscribed upon the map; and that this nation has a right to judge what is necessary, to round off certain contours, to reach some mountain or river, to which a species of *a priori* faculty of limitation is ascribed? I know of no doctrine more arbitrary, or more disastrous. By it all violence is justified. First, let us ask, do mountains or rivers constitute these so-called natural frontiers? It is incontestable that mountains separate; but, on the other hand, rivers unite. And then all mountains cannot cut off states. Which are those that separate, and those that do not separate? . . . No, it is no more the land than the race that makes a nation. The land provides the *substratum,* the field of battle and work; man provides the soul. Man is everything in the formation of that sacred thing which we call a people. Nothing of a material nature suffices for it. A nation is a spiritual principle, the result of profound historical complications, a spiritual family, not a group determined by the configuration of the soil. We have now seen what does not suffice for the creation of such a spiritual principle: race, language, interests, religious affinity, geography, military necessities. What more, then, is necessary?

A nation is a living soul, a spiritual principle. Two things, which in

---

* Editor's Note: *Zollverein* is a German word for customs union.

truth are but one, constitute this soul, this spiritual principle. One is
in the past, the other in the present. One is the common possession of a
rich heritage of memories; the other is the actual consent, the desire to
live together, the will to preserve worthily the undivided inheritance
which has been handed down. Man does not improvise. The nation,
like the individual, is the outcome of a long past of efforts, and sacrifices, and devotion. Ancestor-worship is therefore all the more legitimate; for our ancestors have made us what we are. A heroic past, great
men, glory—I mean glory of the genuine kind—these form the social
capital, upon which a national idea may be founded. To have common
glories in the past, a common will in the present; to have done great
things together, to will to do the like again—such are the essential conditions for the making of a people. We love in proportion to the sacrifices we have consented to make, to the sufferings we have endured.
We love the house that we have built, and will hand down to our descendants. The Spartan hymn, "We are what you were; we shall be
what you are," is in its simplicity the national anthem of every land.

In the past an inheritance of glory and regrets to be shared, in the
future a like ideal to be realised; to have suffered, and rejoiced, and
hoped together; all these things are worth more than custom-houses
in common, and frontiers in accordance with strategical ideas; all these
can be understood in spite of diversities of race and language. I said
just now, "to have suffered together," for indeed suffering in common
is a greater bond of union than joy. As regards national memories,
mournings are worth more than triumphs; for they impose duties, they
demand common effort.

A nation is then a great solidarity, constituted by the sentiment of
the sacrifices that its citizens have made, and of those that they feel
prepared to make once more. It implies a past; but it is summed up in
the present by a tangible fact—consent, the clearly expressed desire to
live a common life. A nation's existence is—if you will pardon the
metaphor—a daily plebiscite, as the individual's existence is a perpetual
affirmation of life. I know very well that this is less metaphysical than
divine right, less brutal than pseudo-historic right. In the order of ideas
that I submit to you, a nation has no more right than a king to say to
a province, "Thou art mine; I take thee unto myself." For us, a province means its inhabitants; and if any one has a right to be consulted
in such an affair, it is the inhabitants. A nation never favours its true
interests when it annexes or retains a country, regardless of the latter's

wishes. The will of nations is then the only legitimate criterion; and to it we must always return.

We have banished from politics metaphysical and theological abstractions. What still remains? There remains man, his desires and his needs. Dismemberment, you will tell me, and, in the long run, natural decay, are the consequences of a system that puts those old organisms at the mercy of wills that are often little enlightened. It is clear that, in such a matter, no principle ought to be pushed to excess. Truths of this order are only applicable when taken as a whole, and in a very general way. Human wills change, but is there here on earth anything changeless? The nations are not something eternal. They have had their beginnings, they shall have their end. A European confederation will probably take their place. But such is not the law of the age in which we live. At the present hour, the existence of nations is good, even necessary. Their existence is the guarantee of liberty, which would be lost if the world had but one law and one master.

By their diverse and often antagonistic faculties, the nations take part in the common work of civilisation; each brings a note to that great chorus of humanity, which in sum is the highest ideal reality to which we attain. Isolated, their parts are feeble. I often tell myself that an individual who should have the faults regarded by nations as good qualities, who should feed himself with vain glory, who should be in the same way jealous, egoistical, and quarrelsome, who should be able to bear nothing without drawing the sword, would be the most unsupportable of men. . . .

But to resume: man is neither enslaved by his race, nor by his language, nor by his religion, nor by the course of rivers, nor by the direction of mountain ranges. A great aggregation of men, sane of mind, and warm of heart, creates a moral consciousness, which is called a nation. So far as this moral consciousness proves its strength, through the sacrifices exacted by the individual's abdication for the good of the community, it is legitimate and has a right to exist. If doubts arise concerning frontiers, consult the populations in dispute. They have a very good right to have a voice in the matter.

Address to the Congress of the United States*

BY PRESIDENT ACHMED SUKARNO OF INDONESIA

[May 17, 1956]

MR. SPEAKER,

I deem it a great honour and privilege to be able to address this honourable Congress, and I express my gratitude to you, for this opportunity.

Standing here before you, Mr. Speaker, and before all the other honourable members of this Congress, my thoughts go to the homes and hearts of the multitudes of the American people from all strata of your society, for whom you act as elected representatives. May I, therefore, convey to you and through you to the people of America, the most sincere greetings of the Indonesian people and their thanks for your past generous assistance, with the hope that this visit to the United States of America will foster closer relations between our two nations.

In our contemporary world, the impact of America is felt more and more. The influence of the American with his outlook, his ideas, his technical and scientific advances, reaches to almost every corner of Asia and Africa, whilst in America itself, Asia, the Asian and his personality, his ideals, the fruits of his labour, are gradually becoming a living reality. Americans and Indonesians are no longer strangers to each other. We know each other from the films, the beams of the radio reach into our very homes, and the magazines and daily press provoke us to think of each other. These cultural exchanges, coupled with the products of your industries and the fruits of our soil, have kept us always much closer together than the thousands of sea miles which separate our two countries.

I have come to the United States, as I said yesterday, to see your country with my own eyes and to observe the achievements of the great American nation. I have come here to confirm or to modify the impressions of your country which I have collected from a distance

---

* From a press release of the Embassy of Indonesia.

over many years. But above all, I have come here to learn something from America—from America not merely as a place, not merely as a nation, but America as a state of mind, America as the centre of an idea.

It was this very America which was in fact the first product of nationalism, of anti-colonialism and of the principle of independence. It is this America which, as the hothouse of American technology, surpassed the development of older sister-nations and became a great power—nay, one of the most powerful nations in the world today. Present-day America as a world phenomenon, with all its impact on the peoples of the earth, was the child of a marriage between the revolutionary America of Washington, Jefferson and Lincoln, and the technological America imbued with the prodigious technical spirit of Edison and Ford.

The shot that was fired at Lexington on the nineteenth of April 1775 was heard around the world. It echoes still in the hearts of all who have recently won their independence, and it echoes still in the hearts of peoples who still struggle against their colonial bonds.

Over half the world the burning words which fired the American War of Independence have been closely studied as a source of inspiration and a plan of action. Yes, this period is the period of Asian and African resurgence.

If we could see the passage of history as yesterday I saw your country from the windows of an aeroplane, we could have no doubt that the world is passing through the period of Asian and African nationalism.

I hesitate at using that word "nationalism," for I know that in many countries and in many nations nationalism is an out-of-date political doctrine. Please remember, Mr. Speaker, that for us of Asia and Africa nationalism is a young and progressive creed. We do not equate nationalism with chauvinism, and we do not interpret nationalism as meaning the superiority of our peoples over others. No! For us, nationalism means the rebuilding of our nations; it means the effort to provide equal esteem for our peoples; it means the determination to take the future into our own hands. For us, nationalism is the love of country and the determination to improve it which, not so very long ago, illumined the actions of the founders of your nation. Nationalism may be an out-of-date doctrine for many in this world; for us of Asia and Africa, it is the mainspring of our efforts. Understand that, and you have the key to much of post-war history. Fail to understand it,

and no amount of thinking, no torrent of words, and no Niagara of
dollars will produce anything but bitterness and disillusionment.

We who are living in Asia and Africa during this period of Asian
and African nationalism, and particularly those of us who have been
called upon to guide the destiny of nations, we ask that the rest of the
world should show understanding and sympathy. After all, for what
do we struggle? Not for fame; not for conquests; not for territorial aggrandisement; not for domination over other peoples. Our efforts and
the sacrifices we have made have been for the release of our people
from a colonial tyranny lasting for generations and centuries. It has
been a struggle—it is still a struggle—for the simple human demands
which the rest of the world has long taken for granted.

We ask you to understand our national struggle, and we ask you
to sympathize with it. We ask you to understand and sympathize with
the fact that our national struggle is still incomplete. How can it be
complete when millions of our people in Asia and Africa are still under colonial domination, are still not free? How can the national struggle in Indonesia be complete when part of our own country and part
of our own nation are still unfree?

I recall with the very greatest pleasure that shortly after the first
Asian-African Conference last year, this Congress unanimously approved a resolution reaffirming America's traditional anti-colonial attitude. That Conference in Bandung, in which the leaders of twenty-
nine States took part, and which represented far more than half the
population of the world, was a clear indication of history's direction.
Practically all shades of the political spectrum were represented there,
and almost all were but recently emancipated from colonialism. They
were united by many things, but chiefly by their abhorrence of colonialism. They produced a Declaration which explicitly stated their
continuing opposition to colonialism in all its forms. This Congress,
noting that Conference and its Declaration, then unanimously re-
stated, for all the world to know, its own long-standing opposition to
colonialism. By that action, this Congress demonstrated its sympathy
with our efforts. In the scales of history, your weight was placed re-
soundingly onto the side of the future.

It is now almost eleven years since, on the 17th of August 1945, the
Indonesian people proclaimed themselves independent. Note! I said
the Indonesian people. Not those of Java alone, nor Sumatra alone, nor
Celebes alone, but all of them, from the north of Sumatra to the

southernmost corner of West New Guinea, which we call Irian Barat.

That Declaration of Independence covered every part of what was once called the Netherlands East Indies, which constituted the vast colonial empire in Asia of a small European country. We had no quarrel with the Dutch as a people; we had no quarrel with the Government of the Netherlands as a Government. Our quarrel, and the quarrel of our forefathers, was with colonialism; we had a quarrel with the colonial attitudes of some Dutch people; we had a quarrel with the colonial attitudes and actions of the Netherlands Government.

Four and a half years of fighting and negotiation followed. Four and a half years in which our colonially-impoverished country, suffering already from the torments of Japanese occupation, suffered more from the attempts forcibly to re-impose the colonialism we had rejected. Finally, due in no small part to the efforts of the United Nations and its bodies in which America was prominent, the Netherlands made formal recognition of complete and unconditional sovereignty to Indonesia.

But our struggle was not yet at an end. One part of our country, one section of our brothers, were not free—and even today are not free. The territory of Irian Barat, West New Guinea, is still a colonial outpost on Indonesian soil. Our Declaration of Independence had covered all of the Netherlands East Indies. The agreements by which Holland recognized that independence and that sovereignty had made reference to the whole territory of the Netherlands East Indies. But—part of our land, a part of the territories covered by those agreements, is still a colonial cancer in the body politic of our Motherland.

We are told that the people of West Irian are not our brothers, and that they come from different racial stock and that therefore West Irian is not Indonesian. Where, again: where is the country whose citizens are ethnically pure? In fact, for many hundreds of years past, West Irian has been recognized as being part of the Indonesian archipelago. Before colonial days, West Irian was part of the Indonesian national state of Modjopahit, one of the glories of the Hindu-Javanese civilization. West Irian was part of the Dutch Empire in Asia, and was administered and recognized without question as being a unit of the Netherlands East Indies. In all ways, and by ties of common colonial experience, West Irian has been, and still is, an essential part of Indonesia.

We are told that the people of West Irian are not ready for a change from their colonial status, and that they need the continued guidance of the West to train them for the transition to liberty.

We know this "guidance"! We have had experience of this "training"! It left us, after three hundred and fifty years, with an illiteracy rate of 94 percent. It left us without sufficient doctors to treat even those who are sick unto death. It left us with a typically colonial economic and social structure.

I tell you this in all solemnity. In the eleven years of our independence, the Indonesian nation has made more human progress, and has been the scene of greater human happiness, than in all the tens of generations of colonialism that went before. Our people are free, and in freedom they have found their soul—just as the people of West Irian will do when they too are free. They can do what we have done. The figures are available. The lists of schools built, of recurrent epidemics abated, of diets improved, of infant mortality decreased. Forgive me, if I seem to boast. I do not intend to boast. I wish to give you a factual account. Let me cite just one item in the field of education. Illiteracy before the war was 94 percent; today it is 40 percent. That is what the ending of colonialism has meant. That is what the ending of colonialism will mean in West Irian.

The return of West Irian is for us the remaining part of our national political aspiration. It is the final installment on the colonial debt. We see our brothers still in chains, who joined with us in proclaiming our common independence, and so our own freedom is not yet complete. The salt of liberty cannot have its full savour for us until all of Indonesia is again united under the freedom which is the birthright of all men.

Permit me to remind you, Sir, of one of America's greatest sons, who said that this nation could not exist half slave and half free. That father of the American tradition was not speaking then of colonial slavery, but his words apply in all their moving strength to this case.

Mr. Speaker, although somewhat belatedly, we of Indonesia are now in the stage of national turmoil through which you passed before us some one hundred and fifty years ago. We are anti-colonialists, for the sweat of our labor has been extorted by other nations, leaving us poverty-stricken with the sorrow of our hearts. We are nationalists, for it is our right to win back the worthy place in the family of nations torn from our forefathers three and a half centuries ago. In all of this, we do not claim to have discovered novel principles. No, but like your forefathers, we regard our findings as universal values, as the common property of all mankind.

Present-day Indonesia has so much in common with the growth of the United States of America in the past. You are now reaping the fruits of your pioneering struggle, while we are still busy sowing the seeds from which our future national life will spring. You achieved your material and cultural prosperity based upon the principles of the democracy which is one of your proudest boasts today. Democracy is part of our principles too, part of our Pantja Sila, an instrument to build national prosperity and stability. But we Indonesians are well aware that, however noble the aim, practical democracy is not always easily attainable.

Last year we twice faced the test of the free and secret ballot, one of the fundamentals of political democracy. The conduct of these elections, one for the House of Representatives and the other for the Constituent Assembly, showed that Indonesia is capable, as the international press reported, of taking the first steps along the road to democracy. Although the elections are not compulsory, about 80 percent of the electors, numbering some 35 million souls and scattered over thousands of miles in thousands of islands in our great archipelago, came to the polls and fulfilled their duties as responsible citizens. As a result of these elections, it has been possible to form a coalition government between the largest political parties. The P. N. I. (Nationalist Party), the Masjumi and the Nahdatul Ulama (both Moslem parties), with the support of some of the smaller parties, have formed a coalition cabinet. I trust that this coalition, with more than ample support from Parliament, will be stable enough to maintain itself throughout the entire four years of its mandate, so that the national process of growth will not be interrupted by intermittent changes of government.

Although these first elections have been successfully accomplished, I shall be modest, Mr. Speaker, in my claims for the establishment of democracy. For who has absolute democracy? We have our feet on the road to democracy, and we have made a good start. But we will not deceive ourselves with the false illusion that we have traversed the full extent of the road to democracy, if indeed any end there be. The secret ballot, the free press, the freedom of belief, the voting in parliaments—these are all merely expressions of democracy. Freedom of expression has a guardian in a certain measure of prosperity, the achievement of freedom from want. For us, then, democratic principles are not simply an aim, the expression of desires inherent in human nature, they are also a means of providing our people with a reasonable standard of living. The freedom of expression and the freedom from want are indivisibles, two inter-dependent souls in one body. As with all other freedoms, freedom of expression is no absolute; its indiscriminate and unrestrained exercise could hamper the harmonious growth of other freedoms, could hamper the harmonious growth from want, and thus sow the seed for the destruction of the fundamentals of human freedom itself.

Your nation began your struggle for liberty, equality, fraternity and prosperity at a period in history when there was no great gap between the standards of nations. There was no great gap between haves and have-nots, there were no nations of abject poverty and extreme wealth, there were no nations of super technical development and utter technical backwardness, there was not so great a gap between the fortunates possessing full-fledged democracy and the sufferers living under complete tyranny. The contrasts today are great. The contrast between the joy of life cherished by some nations, and the burden of suffering imposed upon more than one half of the human race has outstripped all proportions. Such conditions do not stimulate normal growth towards emancipation, especially when the less-privileged are subjected to the competition of the privileged and the powerful in their daily human activities. But if the development of the newly independent countries in the direction of their prosperity be regarded as indispensable for the preservation of civilized man, there certainly will be no need for regrets over the world's wealth and the almost unlimited resources for the further development of man's technological civilization.

Mr. Speaker, the impact of your revolution has not always been of the same kind upon all countries of the globe. We in Indonesia attach great importance to the freedom of expression, to be preserved even in the Herculean task of firmly founding our national economy. Other revolutions have aimed immediately upon building heavy industry as the basis for freedom from want in the future, if necessary even at the sacrifice of some aspects of freedom of expression for the time being. These are rival conceptions, and they constitute a challenge to Indonesia which she must answer in translating ideals into practice.

The development of Indonesia in particular and of certain other countries of Asia in general will be the test-case of the success or failure of the modern world's application of democratic principles. The solvency of less technically developed countries, the solution of the social and economic problems of newly independent peoples at a pace which can keep up with their consciousness of their own worth as equal members of the human family—these are all questions to measure the success of our democracy. In Indonesia, apart from the wealth of nature, our main capital is the sweat and tears of our population, the sacrifices even to the death of those who have gone before. It has been, and it still is, an investment of voluntary human cooperation and sacrifice, which is needed for the development of our country. There is no imposition upon the people to save part of their meagre income as a means of accumulating badly-needed national capital, neither would we introduce forced labour for national undertakings, nor the expropriation of existing big companies which are run mainly on the basis of profit motives.

Moreover, the present situation in the world is, as I have already mentioned, such that even we the economically weak nations have to compete in order to grow, compete with the forces of powerful and experienced nations, in order to survive the drives and thrusts of the current of elimination. Democracy, when all is said and done, is the introduction of equal opportunity in human activities amongst the indigenous people themselves, and, next to that, some degree of opportunity for foreign competitors to ensure the best performance. This sometimes leads towards the presence of an anachronism in which colonial vestiges become strengthened at the expense of national growth. Taking all this into consideration, the question arises: will democracy succeed in Indonesia? Will democracy really bring prosperity and happiness in Indonesia? What is the reason for Indonesia's firm belief in the democratic process and progress? These are questions, Mr. Speaker, which have long occupied the minds of many Indonesian leaders. These problems I think also raise doubts—or hopes —among the statesmen and politicians of a number of western countries about the ability of the Indonesian people to outlive the shock of national responsibility in this turbulent world.

Have no doubts about that, Mr. Speaker.

Immediately we had proclaimed our Independence in August 1945, we attached as preamble to our Constitution the Pantja Sila, the five guiding principles of our national life. Perhaps you know already what our Pantja Sila is. It gives us the five principles of our State. These are:

1. Belief in God
2. Nationalism
3. Humanity
4. *Democracy*
5. Social Justice.

These five principles are the combined reflection of Indonesia's natural climate and the personality of its inhabitants. They were also partly formulated by President Eisenhower in his speech before the American Society of Newspaper Editors on the 21st of April last, when he spoke of certain principles:

1. "they believe deeply in the right of self-government";
2. "they believe deeply in the dignity of man";
3. "they aspire to improve the welfare of the individual as a basis of organized society."

Again: Have no doubts about democracy in Indonesia, Mr. Speaker. Even in the most difficult years immediately after the recognition of sovereignty, we were able to guard the unity of our country through another democratic concept, expressed in the motto of the State "Bhinneka Tunggal Ika"—Unity in Diversity. Voluntary loyalty to the Indonesian Motherland as a whole has been settled in our country without compulsion, without the process of civil war, despite subversive actions by people who don't want to see us free, despite provocation at home and abroad.

Having survived the early most critical years of our national existence, more attention can be paid to upbuilding and rehabilitation, and especially to the investment of human skill. Just before I left Indonesia, we inaugurated a campaign for village community development, and parliament is soon to discuss the first national Five Year Plan, with a total allocation of eleven billion rupiahs, or one billion dollars.

However important they may be, our own national efforts on their own will not suffice to achieve steady progress towards viability for our country against the impact of economic or political competition from overseas. It is in this field that we ask your understanding and your cooperation for our mutual benefit. America is known the world over for generosity; if I am not mistaken the American tax payer has

already spent more than 50 billion dollars in foreign aid. But that aid
has brought variable results. An example of good results is the re-
covery of Western Europe after World War II; other results are
still prospective in other parts of the world, whereas elsewhere American aid is regarded as of doubtful benefit for national progress.

Indonesia is indeed grateful for the technical assistance she has received to date from America, and in acknowledging my gratitude I
want to express myself with the frankness of a friend. Am I allowed
to be frank, Mr. Speaker? For the furtherance of their function as defenders of freedom, America and Indonesia need to realize how to
obtain lasting results, and these depend upon the specific conditions
of Asian countries and the development of the national aspirations
of the Asian people, which, indeed, America cannot be expected immediately to know, or to understand. The approach to the question
of foreign aid should be based upon different principles in different
countries. Without adequate knowledge of those countries, and even
if your motives in granting aid were solely the stability of this region,
the results could be adverse, and the flow of even billions of dollars
could lead only to strained relations. Certainly military aid is no substitute for Asian stability. It will only serve to make countries accepting it more dependent upon America, and their worth as genuine
partners in the universal struggle for liberty, peace and prosperity will
consequently decline. The main aim should be for the people of Asia,
like the Western nations, to become economically stable but also
politically stable, and thus be able to defend their freedom against all
assaults. Political stability comes only with the stability of the political
heart. And this heart of ours is now still an unsatisfied heart. The
Asian people must soon be brought to the stage of development where
they are capable of cherishing their hard-won freedom.

This two-sided struggle is a longer and a harder struggle, but until
it is won, the process of emancipation of our people will not be complete. The Republic of Indonesia is a democracy which has leaned
heavily upon the experience of the West, and particularly of your great
Union for its national ideals. We know that is not enough. To the
famished man, democracy can never be more than a slogan. What can
a vote mean to a woman worn out by toil, whose children fret and ail
with the fever of malaria? Democracy is not merely government by
the people; democracy is also government for the people. . . .

The Fourteen Points*

BY WOODROW WILSON

[1918]

I

Open covenants of peace, openly arrived at, after which there shall be no private international understandings of any kind but diplomacy shall proceed always frankly and in the public view.

II

Absolute freedom of navigation upon the seas, outside territorial waters, alike in peace and in war, except as the seas may be closed in whole or in part by international action for the enforcement of international covenants.

III

The removal, so far as possible, of all economic barriers and the establishment of an equality of trade conditions among all the nations consenting to the peace and associating themselves for its maintenance.

IV

Adequate guarantees given and taken that national armaments will be reduced to the lowest point consistent with domestic safety.

V

A free, open-minded, and absolutely impartial adjustment of all colonial claims, based upon a strict observance of the principle that in determining all such questions of sovereignty the interests of the populations concerned must have equal weight with the equitable claims of the government whose title is to be determined.

VI

The evacuation of all Russian territory and such a settlement of all questions affecting Russia as will secure the best and freest co-

---

* The Fourteen Points were presented in a speech by President Wilson before a joint session of Congress, January 8, 1918.

operation of the other nations of the world in obtaining for her an unhampered and unembarrassed opportunity for the independent determination of her own political development and national policy and assure her of a sincere welcome into the society of free nations under institutions of her own choosing; and, more than a welcome, assistance also of every kind that she may need and may herself desire. The treatment accorded Russia by her sister nations in the months to come will be the acid test of their good will, of their comprehension of her needs as distinguished from their own interests, and of their intelligent and unselfish sympathy.

VII

Belgium, the whole world will agree, must be evacuated and restored, without any attempt to limit the sovereignty which she enjoys in common with all other free nations. No other single act will serve to restore confidence among the nations in the laws which they have themselves set and determined for the government of their relations with one another. Without this healing act the whole structure and validity of international law is forever impaired.

VIII

All French territory should be freed and the invaded portions restored, and the wrong done to France by Prussia in 1871 in the matter of Alsace-Lorraine, which has unsettled the peace of the world for nearly fifty years, should be righted, in order that peace may once more be made secure in the interest of all.

IX

A readjustment of the frontiers of Italy should be effected along clearly recognizable lines of nationality.

X

The peoples of Austria-Hungary, whose place among the nations we wish to see safeguarded and assured, should be accorded the freest opportunity of autonomous development.

XI

Rumania, Serbia, and Montenegro should be evacuated; occupied territories restored; Serbia accorded free and secure access to the sea;

and the relations of the several Balkan states to one another determined by friendly counsel along historically established lines of allegiance and nationality; and international guarantees of the political and economic independence and territorial integrity of the several Balkan states should be entered into.

XII

The Turkish portions of the present Ottoman Empire should be assured a secure sovereignty, but the other nationalities which are now under Turkish rule should be assured an undoubted security of life and an absolutely unmolested opportunity of autonomous development, and the Dardanelles should be permanently opened as a free passage to the ships and commerce of all nations under international guarantees.

XIII

An independent Polish state should be erected which should include the territories inhabited by indisputably Polish populations, which should be assured a free and secure access to the sea, and whose political and economic independence and territorial integrity should be guaranteed by international covenant.

XIV

A general association of nations must be found under specific covenants for the purpose of affording mutual guarantees of political independence and territorial integrity to great and small states alike.

Excesses of
Self-determination*

BY CLYDE EAGLETON

[1953]

IT IS SAD to see a noble word abused, as is the fate—among other good words—of the term "self-determination." Perhaps it has always been abused, in the sense that nationalism tends to run to extremes, but it is being torn to pieces in the United Nations today. The concept which lies behind the term is one which appeals to all human beings. It reaches back to the "consent of the governed" in the American Declaration of Independence; to the "divine right of the people" in the French Revolution; to the democratic nationalism of Mazzini. Woodrow Wilson, in the Fourteen Points and in speeches, made it a basic principle of freedom: "peoples and provinces are not to be bartered about from sovereignty to sovereignty" ... "every territorial settlement ... must be made in the interest and for the benefit of the populations concerned." Such words found lodgings in every human heart; they became the foundation of thought and desire for millions of people. There were actual examples in the peace settlement of 1919 at which they could look; and there was a "wild rush" of nationalism after World War I, which soon became lost in other things.

There is today another wild rush, and in it the United Nations is inevitably entangled. The term "self-determination" was crowded into Article 1 of the Charter without relevance and without explanation; and upon that basis delegates are today making fantastic claims. Their irresponsibility alienates Americans who have sympathized with the struggles of many peoples for independence; they are typical of wild claims being made in other fields, such as Human Rights—so irresponsible as to arouse the fears of the American Bar Association, for example, and to induce the Senate to consider the Bricker amendment to the Constitution, which in reaction swings disastrously far toward the other extreme. The speeches go far beyond anything hitherto

* Reprinted by special permission from *Foreign Affairs*, July 1953. Copyright by Council on Foreign Relations, New York.

thought of in connection with self-determination; it is not merely
independence which the speakers demand, but perfect satisfaction for
all human desires. Furthermore, they would limit the claims to self-
determination to colonial peoples only; and thus self-determination
is made the basis of combination against the colonial Powers and
against the "domination of the white race."

Even so, most Americans—and probably most whites, with some
shame for past misdeeds or realization of present needs of Asian and
African peoples—have some sympathy with the feeling which inspires
this attitude. The trouble is that the movement thus far has no standards, no common sense, indeed, no clear objectives. It seems chiefly an
urge, born of a resentment which is natural enough, to "get at" the
colonial Powers. But these Powers feel that they have much reason to
feel pride in achievement. They can justly claim that they have contributed greatly to the advancement of the peoples who now denounce
them; indeed, it is that very advancement which has made colonial
peoples realize that they could have more, and has given them such
ability to stand alone as they may now have. These Western Powers
do not believe that they have held back the process of self-determination unduly. After all, they have freed at least half a billion people to
manage their own affairs within the last decade.

There is no gain to anyone in pressing every possible cleavage in the
community of nations, nor in reducing the strength of the free world
by breaking it up into helplessly weak units. The fears and desires of
smaller states and of non-self-governing peoples deserve consideration,
and valid needs should be met; but the community of nations to which
the apostles of fragmentation appeal also has rights and needs.

The concept of self-determination is not a simple one, and it has
always defied definition. It is a two-edged concept which can disinte-
grate as well as unify; consider the Austro-Hungarian Empire. There
has never been a judge to pass upon its claims; indeed, there has never
been a law by which judgment could be issued. The textbooks of international law do not recognize any legal right of self-determination,
nor do they know any standards for determining which groups are
entitled to independence; on the contrary, international law holds that
a state which intervenes to aid a rebellious group to break away from
another state is itself committing an illegal act. Furthermore, if and
when a group has factually established itself, other states have no obligation to recognize it as a legal power, a sovereign state. The emphasis

has been upon the word "self"; the group itself must fight through to what it wanted. Secession or revolution could not be recognized as a legal right. There was no community law, or judge, or machinery, to uphold a claim of self-determination.

Today, the community of nations is organized—a fact which profoundly modifies all concepts of "self." The United Nations exists, and appeals are in fact being made to it. It should have criteria and methods by which to measure and satisfy the hunger of peoples to control their own political destinies; but the Charter of the United Nations does not empower it to handle such claims. The United Nations has no authority in the matter, in a legal or constitutional sense; it is not authorized to issue a ukase freeing a people from a state and setting up a group as independent; it cannot establish rules or criteria for self-determination which are legally binding on anyone. On the contrary, the famous Article 2, Paragraph 7,* reaffirming the rule of international law mentioned above, forbids the United Nations to intervene in the domestic affairs of any Member; and surely, providing self-government or independence to a part of a state would be interfering in the domestic affairs of that state.

It is apparent, however, that the United Nations can build up tremendous pressures in support of its recommendations—pressure strong enough, for example, to tear Indonesia away from the Netherlands and give to it the independence which it sought, in the face of the indubitably correct legal argument of the Dutch that all this was contrary to the Charter. The combination of political forces which led to independence in this case, while it was denied in other cases, is worthy of more study than it has received, for it was clearly a political decision and set a grave precedent. (To say this, be it noted, is not to comment on the rightfulness of the Indonesian claim; there was no way of determining whether it was rightful or not.) Not only in this case, but in many others, United Nations organs have ridden roughshod over the domestic-questions clause of the Charter. In practice, granted a proper majority, that obstacle may now be regarded as removed; an organ of the United Nations can do whatever it has the votes to do. One may rejoice in achievement, or grieve (as the writer is inclined to do) at the disregard for law thus shown; but, legal or not, the United Nations has shown that it can be a powerful force for the satisfaction of claims for self-determination.

* Editor's Note: See Appendix, p. 223.

One more point should be noted here: if the decision on such a claim is made by the United Nations, it is no longer correct to speak of *self*-determination; and this changes the whole nature of the inquiry. A group, a people, may as heretofore set up its claim and seek to justify it in one way or another; but if the group employs force, as has been necessary in the past, it may be charged with having committed a threat to or breach of the peace. It is no answer (though it should be a legal answer) to say that Article 2, Paragraph 7, forbids the United Nations to interfere in a civil war. If that Article can be overridden to help the claimant group, it can be overridden to help the colonial Power. This consequence of appealing to the United Nations—either not seen or not acknowledged in speeches made before it—is, indeed, a gain; it is a gain, that is, if the United Nations can find fair and responsible principles and procedures for answering claims of self-determination, rather than having them settled by local wars which may result in world war.

II

Who are these "peoples" or "nations" that are entitled to self-determination by the United Nations? The General Assembly, it must be recalled, instructed the Human Rights Commission to insert into the proposed Covenant on Human Rights the exact words: "All peoples shall have the right of self-determination." * This, incidentally, was a Soviet initiative, though the Soviet resolution itself was not adopted. The Commission, after some uncertainty, added the words "and nations" but it did not identify either of these units which have the right. No answer, indeed, can be found in the literature of self-

---

* Editor's Note: This resolution was adopted by the General Assembly on February 5, 1952, by a vote of 36 to 11 with 12 abstentions. The breakdown of the vote was as follows:

In favor: Afghanistan, Bolivia, Burma, Byelorussian Soviet Socialist Republic, Chile, Cuba, Czechoslovakia, Dominican Republic, Ecuador, Egypt, El Salvador, Ethiopia, Greece, Guatemala, Haiti, India, Indonesia, Iran, Iraq, Lebanon, Liberia, Mexico, Nicaragua, Pakistan, Panama, Paraguay, Peru, Philippines, Poland, Saudi Arabia, Syria, Thailand, Ukrainian Soviet Socialist Republic, Union of Soviet Socialist Republics, Yemen, Yugoslavia.

Against: Australia, Belgium, Brazil, Canada, Denmark, France, Luxemburg, Netherlands, New Zealand, United Kingdom, United States.

Abstaining: Argentina, China, Colombia, Costa Rica, Honduras, Iceland, Israel, Norway, Sweden, Turkey, Uruguay, Venezuela.

It may be recalled that the Universal Declaration of Human Rights, adopted by the United Nations General Assembly in 1948, does not contain the right to self-determination. See Appendix, pp. 252–56.

determination, though this would seem to be a necessary starting point. Doubtless, the real test is the desire of a group to live together under their own chosen political system. But how is this desire to be measured or ascertained? Should the United Nations listen to the loudest voices? How can it know that they truly represent the wishes of the people? Should the U.N., in its political wisdom, say yes, Indonesia has the genuine desire for independence but no, the Republic of the South Moluccas does not have it?* Should the U.N. hold a plebiscite to determine the wishes of the people? This costs money and effort: how can the U.N. make the preliminary decision that the effort is worth while? And, granted the plebiscite, should the will of the majority prevail? And if a desire is ascertained, shall it be granted solely because there is a desire?

Such questions have not burdened the United Nations orators. Occasionally, a definition is attempted, but no agreement has ever been reached. The representative of Egypt asserted that the definition would be found in international law, but I have never been able to find it there. The delegate of India spoke of "large compact national groups"; Jugoslavia thought that the people should have territory and be related "ethnically, culturally, historically or otherwise." Others insisted that the group must be widely separated from the parent state by distance. The delegates apparently took the view expressed by the Polish delegate who said that "the search for definitions was unnecessary as self-determination should be proclaimed for all."

Indeed, the arguments advanced and the action taken would seem to give to each individual human being a right to be an independent country. It is the purpose of the Covenant on Human Rights to state the rights of individuals, rights which the world organization is to protect; among them is now the right of self-determination. The argument was advanced during the debates that each individual should have the right to uphold the group of his choice in its struggle for independence; the Jugoslav delegate felt that "exercise of the right of peoples to self-determination could [not] be assured unless every individual was entitled to exercise it." A United States amendment to say "in accordance with constitutional processes" was voted down. This would seem to establish a legal right to engage in revolution; it would leave us in the same anarchy as before, except that the individual could

---

* Editor's Note: The South Moluccas are a group of islands which were part of the Netherlands' Indies and subsequently a part of Indonesia.

legally fight not only against the parent state but against other individuals on behalf of the group which he supports. It cannot be assumed that all "peoples" want the same thing.

But if there is no definition of "people" or "nation" to guide us, there is a very definite and significant limitation set. If one thinks back to earlier uses of the term, one finds that "self-determination" applied only to nationalistic minority groups, such as Czechoslovakia or Poland. Wilson and his colleagues—among whom were some wise experts and some wise statesmen—were thinking in terms of European minorities, and not of colonies. They thought of colonies as, for the most part, unable to stand alone in the strenuous conditions of modern civilization and therefore in need of a period of tutelage before being considered for independence. But the original Soviet resolution, in the United Nations, differentiated between Non-Self-Governing Territories which were to be assisted toward "national self-determination," and national minorities which should have only the right to use their native tongues and cultures. It was explained in connection with the resolution which supplanted this one that some delegations were afraid to include the word "peoples" because minorities might thus be encouraged to ask for self-determination. Though the clause finally adopted and incorporated into the Covenant on Human Rights says "all peoples and all nations," the states which voted for it, as the debates clearly show, were thinking only in terms of colonies. The colonial Powers opposed this discrimination and argued for universal application of the principle. They were defeated, and the rest of the article concerning self-determination stipulates no more than that all states should promote self-determination for Non-Self-Governing Territories. This was adopted in the Human Rights Commission by a vote of 13 for (including the United States) and four against, with one abstention.

Thus self-determination is to be applied only to colonies, and is identified with anti-colonialism—a sad comedown for a great principle once thought applicable to all mankind. If it is a fundamental human right, as its inclusion in the Covenant would indicate, why limit it to colonies? One can sympathize with colonial peoples who are oppressed; one can understand the resentment of others now independent, who support those not yet self-governing or even make claims on their behalf. But colonial peoples are not the only ones who have suffered mistreatment or injustice; why should there not also be sympathy with equally oppressed groups in the Soviet Union, or in the United States, if they can be found? One can argue that the U.N. cannot do everything at once, and that it should deal first with colonial claims; but it might be difficult to show that these claims are more urgent than those of groups within metropolitan areas.

In sum, we have this limitation: only "colonial" peoples are to be allowed to base claims on the Charter term "self-determination." But we still do not know what a people or a nation is; indeed, we do not know what a colony is.

III

What do the delegates themselves mean when they claim self-determination? What aims, what objectives, have they in mind? In the past, the popular assumption has been that what was sought was national independence—though it is to be doubted whether Wilson and his associates went so far in 1919. They were thinking rather of autonomy and protection for national minorities; the independence of several states resulted probably from the circumstances of disintegration at the time rather than from their conscious aim or effort.

More broadly, self-determination has been defined as the right of a people to determine their own political destiny: this might mean incorporation into a state, or some measure of autonomy within a state, or a somewhat larger degree of freedom in a federation, or commonwealth, or union; or it might mean complete independence. But today, if we may judge by U.N. debates, the claim leaps far beyond this. What is sought is not merely independence; this is rather a minimum. The delegate of Pakistan interpreted self-determination to mean that weak peoples ought not to be dominated by strong peoples. To Jugoslavia it meant protection against threats to independence emanating from other states. Even the United States asserted that the doctrine applied

not only to peoples which have not yet attained their independence but also to politically independent States which needed protection from external pressure, threats, the use of force, and subversive activities. . . .

That would be quite a job for the United Nations! Thus self-determination becomes collective security; but the claims reached much further, to include rights adumbrated in the Commission on Human Rights in the economic and social field—rights which go so far that the United States has now announced that it will not accept the Covenant of Human Rights. The delegate of Chile demanded full economic sovereignty; self-determination in his view

should enable any State in a condition of economic subordination to recover full sovereignty, by acquiring complete control over its own natural resources, even if this meant expulsion or nationalization of certain undertakings.

Subsequent discussion revealed well-grounded fears that this meant a right to confiscate all foreign investments or, at any rate, to compensate for them at the pleasure of the state in which they happened to be found.

With such aims, self-determination loses all meaning, for it is extended to cover everything. Anything a "people" or a "nation" (provided it is a colony), whether already independent or not, may desire it is entitled to have. It would include the right to the protection of collective security, and full protection for all nationalistic economic actions. No law would be allowed to stand in the way of what a group desired—or what an individual desired. The United Nations, which is asked to furnish these guarantees, would thus become the midwife of all groups desiring to be politically born. Its purpose would no longer be to uphold peace and justice, but to assure to each "people" or "nation" anything it wanted, regardless of what other "peoples," having the same right, might want. And who would pay for all this? The very Powers against whom this nationalistic movement is directed, the only ones who have the economic, political or military strength to establish such guarantees.

This does not appear to be a practical approach to a solution. Let us assume that the feeling for self-determination is a worthy one; and let us assume that appeals should be addressed to the United Nations. Both assumptions are, I think, sound. What then? The problem is a new one in history, for never before has the organized community of nations been called upon to decide—upon principle rather than by force —when a group is entitled to independence or to self-government or to economic sovereignty, or whatever that group means by self-determination. Some scattered precedents may be found: in the League of Nations Mandates system; in provisions by which a territory becomes a state in the United States; in methods by which a people have been advanced to membership in a federation, commonwealth or union, as tried by the Netherlands, England or France. And some vague principles are to be found in the Charter of the United Nations as regards Non-Self-Governing Territories or Trust Territories. . . .

From the viewpoint of a group claiming self-determination, the most important factor would seem to be a common desire; without this, there is no foundation. At this point the problem of the United Nations would be procedural—how is it to ascertain and measure that desire? Perhaps it would have enough information before it to decide; perhaps it would need to send out a commission of inquiry; after that, a plebiscite might be needed. Presumably, a territorial basis for the group would be essential. Assuming all this—desire, unity and territorial basis—is this enough to justify the United Nations in saying that independence—or whatever is called for in the name of self-determination—should be granted? The assertion is often made that this is enough, and that what may happen thereafter does not matter: the group wants independence so badly that it does not care whether it will be swallowed up immediately by an aggressive neighbor, or what vicissitudes of an economic or political character it might be called upon to endure. The mere fact that it wants independence and is willing to take the risks involved is said to be enough.

But of course the United Nations must take other matters into consideration. Its primary responsibility is the welfare of the whole community which it represents. Independence for an ambitious group may be dangerous for the community of nations. The new state may be weak or quarrelsome, and bring upon itself the attack of a covetous or injured or aggressive neighbor; the United Nations nevertheless would then be called upon to defend it. The group seeking independence may be located at a strategic point which the community cannot afford to have weakly held; it may control a strategic waterway of wide importance; it may have within its area natural resources which it is incapable of developing but which the community needs. Does the mere fact that resources vital to the whole community happen to be located within an area to which a group wants exclusive title require the community to surrender control over it?

Other factors must also be considered, including those which affect the happiness of the claimant group itself. Is it able to maintain itself, in an economic sense? If not, the people themselves suffer, and the United Nations may have to support it financially. Should the United Nations make the ability of the new state to protect certain human rights a condition for providing it with self-government or independence? It will be recalled that such conditions were set with regard to

European minorities; they would appear to be desirable for a colonial people, who might be misled by false prophets. Some guarantee of democratic procedure seems necessary also, otherwise self-determination would have betrayed itself. And finally—a matter of much importance to the community of nations—there should be some assurance of the ability and willingness of the new group to meet its responsibilities as a member of that community. Will it be disposed to respect the rights of others, or will it selfishly claim "full economic or political sovereignty" for itself, regardless of the needs of the community?

These are not academic questions. Already Libya, created by the United Nations without consideration of such questions, is in economic difficulties. Italian Somaliland has been promised its independence in ten years' time; this is better, for it will during that time be taught something of governing itself; but there is no assurance that it will have learned its lesson or be able to pass an examination. Indonesia is struggling with both economic and political problems, some of them of its own making.

The duty of the United Nations to guard the welfare of the whole community appears to be in direct conflict with its supposed obligation to produce more and more infant states and turn them loose upon the streets. Three-fourths of its members now are weak states, in the sense that they are unable to contribute to its support in any effective military or economic way; each of them, however, has a vote. Having little responsibility for what results, they are tempted to vote through half-thought-out enterprises, the consequences of which must be faced by the few members strong enough to face them. These members cannot be expected to welcome greater responsibilities forced upon them by the additional votes of other weak states. The United Nations as an organization could be brought to collapse by such disproportionate burdening.

IV

Self-determination, in other words, has reached the age of responsibility. It cannot be allowed to any group for the sole reason that the group chooses to claim it. The United Nations must inquire whether there is enough homogeneity or unity or common desire to hold the new state together; whether it has economic resources and political capacity; how far it can defend itself against attack. And the United Nations must provide some criteria for its own judgment, so that it may act fairly and consistently; it should provide methods of training and testing, to be sure that the new state, when established, will not be a burden on the community, and bring unhappiness to those within it. How far the United Nations should demand democratic forms of government is a difficult question, not only because of the various meanings now attached to the word, but also because there is no assurance that man will not find another form of government more pleasing to him. It does seem clear, however, that self-determination implies a decision based upon the will of the people in the group and that, therefore, some means should be provided by which the people can express their will.

Other difficulties stand in the way of finding criteria for judgment. In view of the current tendencies in the United Nations to take law lightly, one can hardly believe that rules of law could be laid down for the satisfaction of claims based on self-determination—though decision by law might be much more satisfactory to the claimant. The decisions made by the U.N. will doubtless be political ones; and the only hope for just and reasonable solutions must therefore depend upon the attitude of member states. That hope must remain slight indeed, if their delegates continue to make the extravagant, impractical and irresponsible claims which have so far characterized the debates—claims which do not at all consider the needs of the community of nations, or even the welfare of the peoples concerned.

Another great difficulty is to be found in the striking historical fact— commented upon by Lloyd George and others in connection with the 1919 settlement—that when a group has maintained a claim for self-determination and struggled under that banner to independent national existence, it immediately abandons the principle for which it struggled and seeks to ingurgitate any accessible claimant to the same right. This autophagous tendency can be illustrated from Napoleon, from Prussia, from Poland; Hitler called upon the principle to justify the unification of all Germans; the Soviet Union employs it today for propaganda against the West. It can also be illustrated, unfortunately, from the recent actions of Asian states with whose claims to independence Americans have had deep sympathy. India marched her armed forces into Hyderabad even while the Security Council was hearing the plea of the latter for protection, and in the face of the legal right of the princely states (under the India Independence Act of 1947) to remain independent if they wished; she rejected arbitration which had been promised under the Stand Still Agreement, promised a plebiscite which was never held, and drove out Hyderabadi from their offices, property and jobs. Hyderabad is now the center of Communism in India. The pressure is being applied also in Kashmir, where the opposition of Pakistan makes the absorption slower; and she is reaching out now for Portuguese and French territories. This is inconsistent behavior for an outstanding champion of self-determination and anti-imperialism.

In the case of Indonesia the inconsistency is both hers and that of the United Nations. The agreement establishing Indonesia as an independent state provided for a federation with autonomous parts, but Indonesia almost at once converted herself into a unitary republic. The group calling itself the Republic of the South Moluccas, deprived thus of its autonomy, claimed self-determination; but Indonesia, forgetting her recent reliance upon that principle, denied the claim by force and is also reaching out for New Guinea.* In the United Nations, the Security Council, which had turned a deaf ear to Hyderabad, labored diligently, in the face of international law and Article 2, Paragraph 7, of the Charter, to achieve "self-determination" for Indonesia. Why one, but not the other? Of course an easy answer will be given to that question: Indonesia was a "colony," whereas others were not. Only colonies can claim self-determination and the support of the United Nations. But the others, too, are human beings. It is most confusing to find the United States, which gave independence to the Philippines and self-government to Puerto Rico, scorning Hyderabad, supporting Indonesia, and on the fence as to Tunisia. Now, on the edge of Central Asia, a new group calling itself Pakhtunistan lays claim to a third of the territory of Pakistan; others will come along.

It is sad that anti-colonial resentment should have so distorted a noble principle; and it is also understandable. But we can plead with those who feel this resentment to consider the consequences of their extreme demands; and we can plead with all states to vote in the United Nations with regard to some consistent principles, rather than in accord with the political opportunism of the moment. Perhaps the term "self-determination" should be dropped, now that the United Nations is called upon to do the determining, and we should think in terms of such separate problems as self-government, independence, col-

---

* Editor's Note: Indonesia refers to the part of New Guinea it claims as West Irian.

lective security, economic security and human rights—all in the framework of the safety and welfare of the world community. Peoples who, in the future, call upon the United Nations to give them control over their own destinies, invoking the right of self-determination, must be answered in terms of principles on which they can educate themselves in the hope that, when they have proven themselves, the United Nations will support them. Surely it is time for the United Nations, and for its member states both large and small, to take a deep breath and examine the premises on which they are acting in these important matters.

A Few Words on Non-intervention*

BY JOHN STUART MILL

[1859]

THERE is a country in Europe, equal to the greatest in extent of dominion, far exceeding any other in wealth, and in the power that wealth bestows, the declared principle of whose foreign policy is, to let other nations alone. No country apprehends or affects to apprehend from it any aggressive designs. Power, from of old, is wont to encroach upon the weak, and to quarrel for ascendancy with those who are as strong as itself. Not so this nation. It will hold its own, it will not submit to encroachment, but if other nations do not meddle with it, it will not meddle with them. Any attempt it makes to exert influence over them, even by persuasion, is rather in the service of others, than of itself: to mediate in the quarrels which break out between foreign States, to arrest obstinate civil wars, to reconcile belligerents, to intercede for mild treatment of the vanquished, or finally, to procure the abandonment of some national crime and scandal to humanity, such as the slave-trade. Not only does this nation desire no benefit to itself at the expense of others, it desires none in which all others do not as freely participate. It makes no treaties stipulating for separate commercial advantages. If the aggressions of barbarians force it to a successful war, and its victorious arms put it in a position to command liberty of trade, whatever it demands for itself it demands for all mankind. The cost of the war is its own; the fruits it shares in fraternal equality with the whole human race. Its own ports and commerce are free as the air and the sky: all its neighbours have full liberty to resort to it, paying either no duties, or, if any, generally a mere equivalent for what is paid by its own citizens; nor does it concern itself though they, on their part, keep all to themselves, and persist in the most jealous and narrow-minded exclusion of its merchants and goods.

A nation adopting this policy is a novelty in the world; so much so,

---

* From John Stuart Mill, *Dissertations and Discussions*, Vol. III.

it would appear, that many are unable to believe it when they see it. By one of the practical paradoxes which often meet us in human affairs, it is this nation which finds itself, in respect of its foreign policy, held up to obloquy as the type of egoism and selfishness; as a nation which thinks of nothing but of out-witting and out-generalling its neighbours. An enemy, or a self-fancied rival who had been distanced in the race, might be conceived to give vent to such an accusation in a moment of ill-temper. But that it should be accepted by lookers-on, and should pass into a popular doctrine, is enough to surprise even those who have best sounded the depths of human prejudice. Such, however, is the estimate of the foreign policy of England most widely current on the Continent. Let us not flatter ourselves that it is merely the dishonest pretence of enemies, or of those who have their own purposes to serve by exciting odium against us, a class including all the Protectionist writers, and the mouthpieces of all the despots and of the Papacy. The more blameless and laudable our policy might be, the more certainly we might count on its being misrepresented and railed at by these worthies. Unfortunately the belief is not confined to those whom they can influence, but is held with all the tenacity of a prejudice, by innumerable persons free from interested bias. So strong a hold has it on their minds, that when an Englishman attempts to remove it, all their habitual politeness does not enable them to disguise their utter unbelief in his disclaimer. They are firmly persuaded that no word is said, nor act done, by English statesmen in reference to foreign affairs, which has not for its motive principle some peculiarly English interest. Any profession of the contrary appears to them too ludicrously transparent an attempt to impose upon them. Those most friendly to us think they make a great concession in admitting that the fault may possibly be less with the English people, than with the English Government and aristocracy. We do not even receive credit from them for following our own interest with a straightforward recognition of honesty as the best policy. They believe that we have always other objects than those we avow; and the most far-fetched and unplausible suggestion of a selfish purpose appears to them better entitled to credence than anything so utterly incredible as our disinterestedness. Thus, to give one instance among many, when we taxed ourselves twenty millions (a prodigious sum in their estimation) to get rid of negro slavery, and, for the same object, perilled, as everybody thought, destroyed as many thought, the very existence of our West Indian colonies, it was, and still is, believed, that our fine professions were but to delude the world, and that by this self-sacrificing behaviour we were endeavouring to gain some hidden object, which could neither be conceived nor described, in the way of pulling down other nations. The fox who had lost his tail had an intelligible interest in persuading his neighbours to rid themselves of theirs: but we, it is thought by *our* neighbours, cut off our own magnificent brush, the largest and finest of all, in hopes of reaping some inexplicable advantage from inducing others to do the same.

It is foolish attempting to despise all this—persuading ourselves that it is not our fault, and that those who disbelieve *us* would not believe though one should rise from the dead. Nations, like individuals, ought to suspect some fault in themselves when they find they are generally worse thought of than they think they deserve; and they may well know that they are somehow in fault when almost everybody but themselves thinks them crafty and hypocritical. It is not solely because England has been more successful than other nations in gaining what they are all aiming at, that they think she must be following after it with a more ceaseless and a more undivided chase. This indeed is a powerful predisposing cause, inclining and preparing them for the belief. It is a natural supposition that those who win the prize have striven for it; that superior success must be the fruit of more unremitting endeavour; and where there is an obvious abstinence from the ordinary arts employed for distancing competitors, and they are distanced nevertheless, people are fond of believing that the means employed must have been arts still more subtle and profound. This preconception makes them look out in all quarters for indications to prop up the selfish explanation of our conduct. If our ordinary course of action does not favour this interpretation, they watch for exceptions to our ordinary course, and regard these as the real index to the purposes within. They moreover accept literally all the habitual expressions by which we represent ourselves as worse than we are; expressions often heard from English statesmen, next to never from those of any other country—partly because Englishmen, beyond all the rest of the human race, are so shy of professing virtues that they will even profess vices instead; and partly because almost all English statesmen, while careless to a degree which no foreigner can credit, respecting the impression they produce on foreigners, commit the obtuse blunder of supposing that low objects are the only ones to which the minds of their non-aristocratic fellow-countrymen are amenable, and that it is always expedient, if not necessary, to place those objects in the foremost rank. . . .

We are now in one of those critical moments, which do not occur once in a generation, when the whole turn of European events, and the course of European history for a long time to come, may depend on the conduct and on the estimation of England. At such a moment, it is difficult to say whether by their sins of speech or of action our statesmen are most effectually playing into the hands of our enemies, and giving most colour of justice to injurious misconception of our character and policy as a people.

To take the sins of speech first: What is the sort of language held in every oration which, during the present European crisis, any English minister, or almost any considerable public man, addresses to parliament or to his constituents? The eternal repetition of this shabby *refrein*—"We did not interfere, because no English interest was involved"; "We ought not to interfere where no English interest is concerned." England is thus exhibited as a country whose most distinguished men are not ashamed to profess, as politicians, a rule of action which no one, not utterly base, could endure to be accused of as the maxim by which he guides his private life; not to move a finger for others unless he sees his private advantage in it.

There is much to be said for the doctrine that a nation should be willing to assist its neighbours in throwing off oppression and gaining free institutions. Much also may be said by those who maintain that one nation is incompetent to judge and act for another, and that each should be left to help itself, and seek advantage or submit to disadvantage as it can and will. But of all attitudes which a nation can take up on the subject of intervention, the meanest and worst is to profess that it interferes only when it can serve its own objects by it. Every other nation is entitled to say, "It seems, then, that non-interference is not a matter of principle with you. When you abstain from interference, it is not because you think it wrong. You have no objection to interfere, only it must not be for the sake of those you interfere with; they must not suppose that you have any regard for their good. The good of others is not one of the things you care for; but you are willing to meddle, if by meddling you can gain anything for yourselves." Such is the obvious interpretation of the language used.

There is scarcely any necessity to say, writing to Englishmen, that this is not what our rulers and politicians really mean. Their language is not a correct exponent of their thoughts. They mean a part only of what they seem to say. They do mean to disclaim interference for the sake of doing good to foreign nations. They are quite sincere and in earnest in repudiating this. But the other half of what their words express, a willingness to meddle if by doing so they can promote any interest of England, they do not mean. The thought they have in their minds, is not the interest of England, but her security. What they would say, is, that they are ready to act when England's safety is threatened, or any of her interests hostilely or unfairly endangered. This is no more than what all nations, sufficiently powerful for their own protection, do, and no one questions their right to do. It is the common right of self-defence. But if we mean this, why, in Heaven's name, do we take every possible opportunity of saying, instead of this, something exceedingly different? Not self-defence, but aggrandizement, is the sense which foreign listeners put upon our words. Not simply to protect what we have, and that merely against unfair arts, not against fair rivalry; but to add to it more and more without limit, is the purpose for which foreigners think we claim the liberty of intermeddling with them and their affairs. If our actions make it impossible for the most prejudiced observer to believe that we aim at or would accept any sort of mercantile monopolies, this has no effect on their minds but to make them think that we have chosen a more cunning way to the same end....

Of all countries which are sufficiently powerful to be capable of being dangerous to their neighbours, we are perhaps the only one whom mere scruples of conscience would suffice to deter from it. We are the only people among whom, by no class whatever of society, is the interest or glory of the nation considered to be any sufficient excuse for an unjust act; the only one which regards with jealousy and suspicion, and a proneness to hostile criticism, precisely those acts of its Government which in other countries are sure to be hailed with applause, those by which territory has been acquired, or political influence extended. Being in reality better than other nations, in at least the negative part of international morality, let us cease, by the language we use, to give ourselves out as worse.

But if we ought to be careful of our language, a thousand times more obligatory is it upon us to be careful of our deeds, and not suffer ourselves to be betrayed by any of our leading men into a line of conduct on some isolated point, utterly opposed to our habitual principles of action—conduct such that if it were a fair specimen of us, it would verify the calumnies of our worst enemies, and justify them in representing not only that we have no regard for the good of other nations, but that we actually think their good and our own incompatible, and will go all lengths to prevent others from realizing even an advantage in which we ourselves are to share. This pernicious, and, one can scarcely help calling it, almost insane blunder, we seem to be committing on the subject of the Suez Canal.

It is the universal belief in France that English influence at Constantinople, strenuously exerted to defeat this project, is the real and only invincible obstacle to its being carried into effect. And unhappily the public declarations of our present Prime Minister not only bear out this persuasion, but warrant the assertion that we oppose the work because, in the opinion of our Government, it would be injurious to the interest of England. If such be the course we are pursuing, and such the motive of it, and if nations have duties, even negative ones, towards the weal of the human race, it is hard to say whether the folly or the immorality of our conduct is the most painfully conspicuous.

Here is a project, the practicability of which is indeed a matter in dispute, but of which no one has attempted to deny that, supposing it realized, it would give a facility to commerce, and consequently a stimulus to production, and encouragement to intercourse, and therefore to civilization, which would entitle it to a high rank among the great industrial improvements of modern times. The contriving of new means of abridging labour and economizing outlay in the operations of industry, is the object to which the larger half of all the inventive ingenuity of mankind is at present given up; and this scheme, if realized, will save, on one of the great highways of the world's traffic, the circumnavigation of a continent. An easy access of commerce is the main source of that material civilization, which, in the more backward regions of the earth, is the necessary condition and indispensable machinery of the moral; and this scheme reduces practically by one half, the distance, commercially speaking, between the self-improving nations of the world and the most important and valuable of the unimproving. The Atlantic Telegraph is esteemed an enterprise of worldwide importance because it abridges the transit of mercantile intelligence merely. What the Suez Canal would shorten is the transport of the goods themselves, and this to such an extent as probably to augment it manifold.

Let us suppose, then—for in the present day the hypothesis is too un-English to be spoken of as anything more than a supposition—let us suppose that the English nation saw in this great benefit to the civilized and uncivilized world a danger or damage to some peculiar interest of England. Suppose, for example, that it feared, by shortening the road, to facilitate the access of foreign navies to its Oriental possessions. The supposition imputes no ordinary degree of cowardice and imbecility to the national mind; otherwise it could not but reflect that the same thing which would facilitate the arrival of an enemy, would facilitate also that of succour; that we have had French fleets in the Eastern seas before now, and have fought naval battles with them there, nearly a century ago; that if we ever became unable to defend India against them, we should assuredly have them there without the aid of any canal; and that our power of resisting an enemy does not depend upon putting a little more or less of obstacle in the way of his coming, but upon the amount of force which we are able to oppose to him when come.

Let us assume, however, that the success of the project would do more harm to England in some separate capacity, than the good which, as the chief commercial nation, she would reap from the great increase of commercial intercourse. Let us grant this: and I now ask, what then? Is there any morality, Christian or secular, which bears out a nation in keeping all the rest of mankind out of some great advantage, because the consequences of their obtaining it may be to itself, in some imaginable contingency, a cause of inconvenience? Is a nation at liberty to adopt as a practical maxim, that what is good for the human race is bad for itself, and to withstand it accordingly? What is this but to declare that its interest and that of mankind are incompatible— that, thus far at least, it is the enemy of the human race? And what ground has it of complaint if, in return, the human race determine to be *its* enemies? So wicked a principle, avowed and acted on by a nation, would entitle the rest of the world to unite in a league against it, and never to make peace until they had, if not reduced it to insignificance, at least sufficiently broken its power to disable it from ever again placing its own self-interest before the general prosperity of mankind.

There is no such base feeling in the British people. They are accustomed to see their advantage in forwarding, not in keeping back, the growth in wealth and civilization of the world. The opposition to the Suez Canal has never been a national opposition. With their usual indifference to foreign affairs, the public in general have not a thought about it, but have left it, as (unless when particularly excited) they leave all the management of their foreign policy, to those who, from causes and reasons connected only with internal politics, happen for the time to be in office. Whatever has been done in the name of England in the Suez affair has been the act of individuals; mainly, it is probable, of one individual; scarcely any of his countrymen either prompting or sharing his purpose, and most of those who have paid any attention to the subject (unfortunately a very small number) being, to all appearance, opposed to him.

But (it is said) the scheme cannot be executed. If so, why concern ourselves about it? If the project can come to nothing, why profess gratuitous immorality and incur gratuitous odium to prevent it from being tried? Whether it will succeed or fail is a consideration totally irrelevant; except thus far, that if it is sure to fail, there is in our resistance to it the same immorality, and an additional amount of folly; since, on that supposition, we are parading to the world a belief that our interest is inconsistent with its good, while if the failure of the project would really be any benefit to us, we are certain of obtaining that benefit by merely holding our peace. . . .

There seems to be no little need that the whole doctrine of non-interference with foreign nations should be reconsidered, if it can be said to have as yet been considered as a really moral question at all. We have heard something lately about being willing to go to war for an idea. To go to war for an idea, if the war is aggressive, not defensive, is as criminal as to go to war for territory or revenue; for it is as little justifiable to force our ideas on other people, as to compel them to submit to our will in any other respect. But there assuredly are cases in which it is allowable to go to war, without having been ourselves attacked, or threatened with attack; and it is very important that nations should make up their minds in time, as to what these cases are. There are few questions which more require to be taken in hand by ethical and political philosophers, with a view to establish some rule or criterion whereby the justifiableness of intervening in the affairs of other countries, and (what is sometimes fully as questionable) the justifiableness of refraining from intervention, may be brought to a definite and rational test. Whoever attempts this, will be led to recognize more than one fundamental distinction, not yet by any means familiar to the public mind, and in general quite lost sight of by those who write in strains of indignant morality on the subject. There is a great difference (for example) between the case in which the nations concerned are of the same, or something like the same, degree of civilization, and that in which one of the parties to the situation is of a high, and the other of a very low, grade of social improvement. To suppose that the same international customs, and the same rules of international morality, can obtain between one civilized nation and another, and between civilized nations and barbarians, is a grave error, and one which no statesman can fall into, however it may be with those who, from a safe and unresponsible position, criticise statesmen.

Among many reasons why the same rules cannot be applicable to situations so different, the two following are among the most important. In the first place, the rules of ordinary international morality imply reciprocity. But barbarians will not reciprocate. They cannot be depended on for observing any rules. Their minds are not capable of so great an effort, nor their will sufficiently under the influence of distant motives. In the next place nations which are still barbarous have not got beyond the period during which it is likely to be for their benefit that they should be conquered and held in subjection by foreigners. Independence and nationality, so essential to the due growth and development of a people further advanced in improvement, are generally impediments to theirs. The sacred duties which civilized nations owe to the independence and nationality of each other, are not binding towards those to whom nationality and independence are either a certain evil, or at best a questionable good. The Romans were not the most cleanhanded of conquerors, yet would it have been better for Gaul and Spain, Numidia and Dacia, never to have formed part of the Roman Empire? To characterize any conduct whatever towards a barbarous people as a violation of the law of nations, only shows that he who so speaks has never considered the subject. A violation of great principles of morality it may easily be; but barbarians have no rights as a *nation,* except a right to such treatment as may, at the earliest possible period, fit them for becoming one. The only moral laws for the relation between a civilized and a barbarous government, are the universal rules of morality between man and man.

The criticisms, therefore, which are so often made upon the conduct of the French in Algeria, or of the English in India, proceed, it would seem, mostly on a wrong principle. The true standard by which to judge their proceedings never having been laid down, they escape such comment and censure as might really have an improving effect, while they are tried by a standard which can have no influence on those practically engaged in such transactions, knowing as they do that it cannot, and if it could, ought not to be observed, because no human being would be the better, and many much the worse, for its observance. A civilized government cannot help having barbarous neighbours: when it has, it cannot always content itself with a defensive position, one of mere resistance to aggression. After a longer or shorter interval of forbearance, it either finds itself obliged to conquer them, or to assert so much authority over them, and so break their spirit, that they gradually sink into a state of dependence upon itself: and when that time arrives, they are indeed no longer formidable to it, but it has had so much to do with setting up and pulling down their governments, and they have grown so accustomed to lean on it, that it has become morally responsible for all evil it allows them to do. This is the history of the relations of the British Government with the native States of India. . . .

But among civilized peoples, members of an equal community of nations, like Christian Europe, the question assumes another aspect, and must be decided on totally different principles. It would be an affront to the reader to discuss the immorality of wars of conquest, or of conquest even as the consequence of lawful war; the annexation of any civilized people to the dominion of another, unless by their own spontaneous election. Up to this point, there is no difference of opinion among honest people; nor on the wickedness of commencing an aggressive war for any interest of our own, except when necessary to avert from ourselves an obviously impending wrong. The disputed question is that of interfering in the regulation of another country's internal concerns; the question whether a nation is justified in taking part, on either side, in the civil wars or party contests of another; and chiefly, whether it may justifiably aid the people of another country in struggling for liberty; or may impose on a country any particular government or institutions, either as being best for the country itself, or as necessary for the security of its neighbours.

Of these cases, that of a people in arms for liberty is the only one of any nicety, or which, theoretically at least, is likely to present conflicting moral considerations. The other cases which have been mentioned hardly admit of discussion. Assistance to the government of a country in keeping down the people, unhappily by far the most frequent case of foreign intervention, no one writing in a free country needs take the trouble of stigmatizing. A government which needs foreign support to enforce obedience from its own citizens, is one which ought not to exist; and the assistance given to it by foreigners is hardly ever anything but the sympathy of one despotism with another. A case requiring consideration is that of a protracted civil war, in which the contending parties are so equally balanced that there is no probability of a speedy issue; or if there is, the victorious side cannot hope to keep down the vanquished but by severities repugnant to humanity, and injurious to the permanent welfare of the country. In this exceptional case it seems now to be an admitted doctrine, that the neighbouring nations, or one powerful neighbour with the acquiescence of the rest, are warranted in demanding that the contest shall cease, and a reconciliation take place on equitable terms of compromise. Intervention of this description has been repeatedly practised during the present generation, with such general approval, that its legitimacy may be considered to have passed into a maxim of what is called international law. The interference of the European Powers between Greece and Turkey, and between Turkey and Egypt, were cases in point. That between Holland and Belgium was still more so. The intervention of England in Portugal, a few years ago, which is probably less remembered than the others, because it took effect without the employment of actual force, belongs to the same category. At the time, this interposition had the appearance of a bad and dishonest backing of the government against the people, being so timed as to hit the exact moment when the popular party had obtained a marked advantage, and seemed on the eve of overthrowing the government, or reducing it to terms. But if ever a political act which looked ill in the commencement could be justified by the event, this was; for, as the fact turned out, instead of giving ascendancy to a party, it proved a really healing measure; and the chiefs of the so-called rebellion were, within a few years, the honoured and successful ministers of the throne against which they had so lately fought.

With respect to the question, whether one country is justified in helping the people of another in a struggle against their government for free institutions, the answer will be different, according as the yoke which the people are attempting to throw off is that of a purely native government, or of foreigners; considering as one of foreigners, every government which maintains itself by foreign support. When the contest is only with native rulers, and with such native strength as those rulers can enlist in their defense, the answer I should give to the question of the legitimacy of intervention is, as a general rule, No. The reason is, that there can seldom be anything approaching to assurance that intervention, even if successful, would be for the good of the people themselves. The only test possessing any real value, of a people's having become fit for popular institutions, is that they, or a sufficient portion of them to prevail in the contest, are willing to brave labour and danger for their liberation. I know all that may be said. I know it may be urged that the virtues of freemen cannot be learnt in the school of slavery, and that if a people are not fit for freedom, to have any chance of becoming so they must first be free. And this would be conclusive, if the intervention recommended would really give them freedom. But the evil is, that if they have not sufficient love of liberty to be able to wrest it from merely domestic oppressors, the liberty which is bestowed on them by other hands than their own, will have nothing real, nothing permanent.

No people ever was and remained free, but because it was determined to be so; because neither its rulers nor any other party in the nation could compel it to be otherwise. If a people—especially one whose freedom has not yet become prescriptive—does not value it sufficiently to fight for it, and maintain it against any force which can be mustered *within* the country, even by those who have the command of the public revenue, it is only a question in how few years or months that people will be enslaved. Either the government which it has given to itself, or some military leader or knot of conspirators who contrive to subvert the government, will speedily put an end to all popular institutions: unless indeed it suits their convenience better to leave them standing, and be content with reducing them to mere forms; for, unless the spirit of liberty is strong in a people, those who have the executive in their hands easily work any institutions to the purposes of despotism. There is no sure guarantee against this deplorable issue, even in a country which has achieved its own freedom; as may be seen in the present day by striking examples both in the Old and New Worlds: but when freedom has been achieved *for* them, they have little prospect indeed of escaping this fate. When a people has had the misfortune to be ruled by a government under which the feelings and the virtues needful for maintaining freedom could not develop themselves, it is during an arduous struggle to become free by their own efforts that these feelings and virtues have the best chance of springing up. Men become attached to that which they have long fought for and made sacrifices for; they learn to appreciate that on which their thoughts have been much engaged; and a contest in which many have been called on to devote themselves for their country, is a school in which they learn to value their country's interest above their own.

It can seldom, therefore—I will not go so far as to say never—be either judicious or right, in a country which has a free government, to assist, otherwise than by the moral support of its opinion, the endeavours of another to extort the same blessing from its native rulers. We must except, of course, any case in which such assistance is a measure of legitimate self-defence. If (a contingency by no means unlikely to occur) this country, on account of its freedom, which is a standing reproach to despotism everywhere, and an encouragement to throw it off, should find itself menaced with attack by a coalition of Continental despots, it ought to consider the popular party in every nation of the Continent as its natural ally: the Liberals should be to it, what the Protestants of Europe were to the Government of Queen Elizabeth. So, again, when a nation, in her own defence, has gone to war with a despot, and has had the rare good fortune not only to succeed in her resistance, but to hold the conditions of peace in her own hands, she is entitled to say that she will make no treaty, unless with some other ruler than the one whose existence as such may be a perpetual menace to her safety and freedom. These exceptions do but set in a clearer light the reasons of the rule; because they do not depend on any failure of those reasons, but on considerations paramount to them, and coming under a different principle.

But the case of a people struggling against a foreign yoke, or against a native tyranny upheld by foreign arms, illustrates the reasons for non-intervention in an opposite way; for in this case the reasons themselves do not exist. A people the most attached to freedom, the most capable of defending and of making a good use of free institutions, may be unable to contend successfully for them against the military strength of another nation much more powerful. To assist a people thus kept down, is not to disturb the balance of forces on which the permanent maintenance of freedom in a country depends, but to redress that balance when it is already unfairly and violently disturbed.

The doctrine of non-intervention, to be a legitimate principle of morality, must be accepted by all governments. The despots must consent to be bound by it as well as the free States. Unless they do, the profession of it by free countries comes but to this miserable issue, that the wrong side may help the wrong, but the right must not help the right. Intervention to enforce non-intervention is always rightful, always moral, if not always prudent. Though it be a mistake to *give* freedom to a people who do not value the boon, it cannot but be right to insist that if they do value it, they shall not be hindered from the pursuit of it by foreign coercion.

It might not have been right for England (even apart from the question of prudence) to have taken part with Hungary in its noble struggle against Austria; although the Austrian Government in Hungary was in some sense a foreign yoke. But when, the Hungarians having shown themselves likely to prevail in this struggle, the Russian despot interposed, and joining his force to that of Austria, delivered back the Hungarians, bound hand and foot, to their exasperated oppressors, it would have been an honourable and virtuous act on the part of England to have declared that this should not be, and that if Russia gave assistance to the wrong side, England would aid the right. It might not have been consistent with the regard which every nation is bound to pay to its own safety, for England to have taken up this position single-handed. But England and France together could have done it; and if they had, the Russian armed intervention would never have taken place, or would have been disastrous to Russia alone: while all that those Powers gained by not doing it, was that they had to fight Russia five years afterwards, under more difficult circumstances, and without Hungary for an ally. The first nation which, being powerful enough to make its voice effectual, has the spirit and courage to say that not a gun shall be fired in Europe by the soldiers of one Power against the revolted subjects of another, will be the idol of the friends of freedom throughout Europe. That declaration alone will ensure the almost immediate emancipation of every people which desires liberty sufficiently to be capable of maintaining it: and the nation which gives the word will soon find itself at the head of an alliance of free peoples, so strong as to defy the efforts of any number of confederated despots to bring it down. The prize is too glorious not to be snatched sooner or later by some free country; and the time may not be distant when England, if she does not take this heroic part because of its heroism, will be compelled to take it from consideration for her own safety.

VIII

POWER POLITICS AND IDEOLOGY

Morality + power are 2 necessary ingredients of politics.

The Nature of Politics*

BY EDWARD H. CARR

[1940]

MAN has always lived in groups. The smallest kind of human group, the family, has clearly been necessary for the maintenance of the species. But so far as is known, men have always from the most primitive times formed semi-permanent groups larger than the single family; and one of the functions of such a group has been to regulate relations between its members. Politics deals with the behaviour of men in such organised permanent or semi-permanent groups. All attempts to deduce the nature of society from the supposed behaviour of man in isolation are purely theoretical, since there is no reason to assume that such a man ever existed. Aristotle laid the foundation of all sound thinking about politics when he declared that man was by nature a political animal.

Man in society reacts to his fellow men in two opposite ways. Sometimes he displays egoism, or the will to assert himself at the expense of others. At other times he displays sociability, or the desire to co-operate with others, to enter into reciprocal relations of goodwill and friendship with them, and even to subordinate himself to them. In every society, these two qualities can be seen at work. No society can exist unless a substantial proportion of its members exhibits in some degree the desire for co-operation and mutual goodwill. But in every society some sanction is required to produce the measure of solidarity requisite for its maintenance; and this sanction is applied by a controlling group or individual acting in the name of the society. Membership of most societies is voluntary, and the only ultimate sanction which can be applied is expulsion. But the peculiarity of political society, which in the modern world takes the form of the state, is that membership is compulsory. The state, like other societies, must be based on some sense of common interests and obligations among its members. But coercion is regularly exercised by a governing group to enforce loyalty and obedience; and

* From *The Twenty Years' Crisis,* copyright 1939, 1940 by Macmillan and Co., Ltd., London. Reprinted by permission.

this coercion inevitably means that the governors control the governed and "exploit" them for their own purposes.

The dual character of political society is therefore strongly marked. Professor Laski tells us that "every state is built upon the consciences of men."[1] On the other hand, anthropology, as well as much recent history, teaches that "war seems to be the main agency in producing the state;"[2] and Professor Laski himself, in another passage, declares that "our civilisation is held together by fear rather than by good-will."[3] There is no contradiction between these apparently opposite views. When Tom Paine, in the *Rights of Man,* tries to confront Burke with the dilemma that "governments arise either *out* of the people or *over* the people," the answer is that they do both. Coercion and conscience, enmity and good-will, self-assertion and self-subordination, are present in every political society. The state is built up out of these two conflicting aspects of human nature. Utopia and reality, the ideal and the institution, morality and power, are from the outset inextricably blended in it. In the making of the United States, as a modern American writer has said, "Hamilton stood for strength, wealth and power, Jefferson for the American dream;" and both the power and the dream were necessary ingredients.[4]

If this be correct, we can draw one important conclusion. The utopian who dreams that it is possible to eliminate self-assertion from politics and to base a political system on morality alone is just as wide of the mark as the realist who believes that altruism is an illusion and that all political action is based on self-seeking. These errors have both left their mark on popular terminology. The phrase "power politics" is often used in an invidious sense, as if the element of power or self-assertion in politics were something abnormal and susceptible of elimination from a healthy political life. Conversely, there is a disposition, even among some writers who are not strictly speaking realists, to treat politics as the science of power and self-assertion and exclude from it by definition actions inspired by the moral consciousness. Professor Catlin describes the *homo politicus* as one who "seeks to bring into conformity with his own will the

---

[1] *A Defence of Liberty against Tyrants (Vindiciae contra Tyrannos),* ed. Laski, Introd. p. 55.
[2] Linton, *The Study of Man,* p. 240.
[3] Laski, *A Grammar of Politics,* p. 20.
[4] J. Truslow Adams, *The Epic of America,* p. 112.

wills of others, so that he may the better attain his own ends." [5]
Such terminological implications are misleading. Politics cannot be
divorced from power. But the *homo politicus* who pursues nothing
but power is as unreal a myth as the *homo economicus* who pursues
nothing but gain. Political action must be based on a co-ordination
of morality and power.

This truth is of practical as well as theoretical importance. It is
as fatal in politics to ignore power as it is to ignore morality. The
fate of China in the nineteenth century is an illustration of what
happens to a country which is content to believe in the moral
superiority of its own civilisation and to despise the ways of power.
The Liberal Government of Great Britain nearly came to grief in
the spring of 1914 because it sought to pursue an Irish policy based
on moral authority unsupported (or rather, directly opposed) by
effective military power. In Germany, the Frankfort Assembly of
1848 is the classic example of the impotence of ideas divorced
from power; and the Weimar Republic broke down because many
of the policies it pursued—in fact, nearly all of them except its
opposition to the communists—were unsupported, or actively opposed, by effective military power. The utopian, who believes that
democracy is not based on force, refuses to look these unwelcome
facts in the face.

On the other hand, the realist, who believes that, if you look
after the power, the moral authority will look after itself, is equally
in error. The most recent form of this doctrine is embodied in the
much-quoted phrase: "The function of force is to give moral ideas
time to take root." Internationally, this argument was used in 1919
by those who, unable to defend the Versailles Treaty on moral
grounds, maintained that this initial act of power would pave the
way for subsequent moral appeasement. Experience has done little
to confirm this comfortable belief. The same fallacy is implicit in
the now commonly held view that the aim of our policy should be
"to rebuild the League of Nations, to make it capable of holding a
political aggressor in restraint by armed power, and thereafter
to labour faithfully for the mitigation of just and real grievances."[6]
Once the enemy has been crushed or the "aggressor" restrained

---

[5] Catlin, *The Science and Method of Politics*, p. 309.
[6] Winston Churchill, *Arms and the Covenant*, p. 368.

by force, the "thereafter" fails to arrive. The illusion that priority can be given to power and that morality will follow, is just as dangerous as the illusion that priority can be given to moral authority and that power will follow.

Before proceeding, however, to consider the respective roles of power and morality in politics, we must take some note of the views of those who, though far from being realists, identify politics with power and believe that moral concepts must be altogether excluded from its scope. There is, according to this view, an essential antinomy between politics and morality; and the moral man as such will therefore have nothing to do with politics. This thesis has many attractions, and reappears at different periods of history and in different contexts. It takes at least three forms.

(i) Its simplest form is the doctrine of non-resistance. The moral man recognises the existence of political power as an evil, but regards the use of power to resist power as a still greater evil. This is the basis of such doctrines of non-resistance as those of Jesus or of Gandhi, or of modern pacifism. It amounts, in brief, to a boycott of politics.

(ii) The second form of the antithesis between politics and morality is anarchism. The state, as the principal organ of political power, is "the most flagrant, most cynical and most complete negation of humanity."[7] The anarchist will use power to overthrow the state. This revolutionary power is, however, not thought of as political power, but as the spontaneous revolt of the outraged individual conscience. It does not seek to create a new political society to take the place of the old one, but a moral society from which power, and consequently politics, are completely eliminated. "The principles of the Sermon on the Mount," an English divine recently remarked, would mean "sudden death to civilised society."[8] The anarchist sets out to destroy "civilised society" in the name of the Sermon on the Mount.

(iii) A third school of thought starts from the same premise of the essential antithesis between morality and politics, but arrives at a totally different conclusion. The injunction of Jesus to "render unto Caesar the things that are Caesar's, and unto God the things

---

[7] Bakunin, Œuvres, i. p. 150.
[8] The Dean of St. Paul's, quoted in a leading article in The Times, August 2, 1937.

that are God's," implies the coexistence of two separate spheres: the political and the moral. But the moral man is under an obligation to assist—or at any rate not to obstruct—the politician in the discharge of his non-moral functions. "Let every soul be subject to the higher powers. The powers that be are ordained of God." We thus recognise politics as necessary but non-moral. This tradition, which remained dormant throughout the Middle Ages, when the ecclesiastical and the secular authority was theoretically one, was revived by Luther in order to effect his compromise between reformed church and state. Luther "turned on the peasants of his day in holy horror when they attempted to transmute the 'spiritual' kingdom into an 'earthly' one by suggesting that the principles of the gospel had social significance."[9] The division of functions between Caesar and God is implicit in the very conception of an "established" church. But the tradition has been more persistent and more effective in Lutheran Germany than anywhere else. "We do not consult Jesus," wrote a German liberal nineteenth-century pastor, "when we are concerned with things which belong to the domain of the construction of the state and political economy,"[10] and Bernhardi declared that "Christian morality is personal and social, and in its nature cannot be political."[11] The same attitude is inherent in the modern theology of Karl Barth, which insists that political and social evils are the necessary product of man's sinful nature and that human effort to eradicate them is therefore futile; and the doctrine that Christian morality has nothing to do with politics is vigorously upheld by the Nazi régime. This view is basically different from that of the realist who makes morality a function of politics. But in the field of politics it tends to become indistinguishable from realism.

The theory of the divorce between the spheres of politics and morality is superficially attractive, if only because it evades the insoluble problem of finding a moral justification for the use of force. But it is not ultimately satisfying. Both non-resistance and anarchism are counsels of despair, which appear to find widespread acceptance only where men feel hopeless of achieving anything by political action; and the attempt to keep God and Caesar

---

[9] R. Niebuhr, *Moral Man and Immoral Society*, p. 77.
[10] Quoted in W. F. Bruck, *Social and Economic History of Germany*, p. 65.
[11] Bernhardi, *Germany and the Next War* (Engl. transl.), p. 29.

in watertight compartments runs too much athwart the deep-seated desire of the human mind to reduce its view of the world to some kind of moral order. We are not in the long run satisfied to believe that what is politically good is morally bad; and since we can neither moralise power nor expel power from politics, we are faced with a dilemma which cannot be completely resolved. The planes of utopia and of reality never coincide. The ideal cannot be institutionalised, nor the institution idealised. "Politics," writes Dr. Niebuhr, "will, to the end of history, be an area where conscience and power meet, where the ethical and coercive factors of human life will interpenetrate and work out their tentative and uneasy compromises."[12] The compromises, like solutions of other human problems, will remain uneasy and tentative. But it is an essential part of any compromise that both factors shall be taken into account.

*   *   *

[12] R. Niebuhr, *Moral Man and Immoral Society*, p. 4.

The Principle of
Non-violence[*]

BY M. K. GANDHI

I [1]

I DO BELIEVE that, where there is only a choice between cowardice and violence, I would advise violence. Thus when my eldest son asked me what he should have done, had he been present when I was almost fatally assaulted in 1908, whether he should have run away and seen me killed or whether he should have used his physical force which he could and wanted to use, and defended me, I told him that it was his duty to defend me even by using violence. Hence it was that I took part in the Boer War, the so-called Zulu Rebellion and the late War. Hence also do I advocate training in arms for those who believe in the method of violence. I would rather have India resort to arms in order to defend her honour than that she would, in a cowardly manner, become or remain a helpless witness to her own dishonour.

But I believe that non-violence is infinitely superior to violence, forgiveness is more manly than punishment. Forgiveness adorns a soldier. But abstinence is forgiveness only when there is the power to punish; it is meaningless when it pretends to proceed from a helpless creature. A mouse hardly forgives a cat when it allows itself to be torn to pieces by her. . . . But I do not believe India to be helpless. I do not believe myself to be a helpless creature. Only I want to use India's and my strength for a better purpose.

Let me not be misunderstood. Strength does not come from physical capacity. It comes from an indomitable will. An average Zulu is any way more than a match for an average Englishman in bodily capacity. But he flees from an English boy, because he fears the boy's revolver or those who will use it for him. He fears death and is nerveless in spite of his burly figure. We in India may in a moment realize that one hun-

---

[*] Selections from articles by M. K. Gandhi, collected in M. K. Gandhi, *Non-Violence in Peace and War*, 2 vols., Navajivan Publishing House, Ahmedabad. Reprinted by permission of the Navajivan Trust.

[1] "The Doctrine of the Sword," *Young India*, August 11, 1920.

dred thousand Englishmen need not frighten three hundred million human beings. A definite forgiveness would, therefore, mean a definite recognition of our strength. With enlightened forgiveness must come a mighty wave of strength in us, which would make it impossible for a Dyer and a Frank Johnson to heap affront on India's devoted head. It matters little to me that for the moment I do not drive my point home. We feel too downtrodden not to be angry and revengeful. But I must not refrain from saying that India can gain more by waiving the right of punishment. We have better work to do, a better mission to deliver to the world.

I am not a visionary. I claim to be a practical idealist. The religion of non-violence is not meant merely for the *rishis* [2] and saints. It is meant for the common people as well. Non-violence is the law of our species as violence is the law of the brute. The spirit lies dormant in the brute, and he knows no law but that of physical might. The dignity of man requires obedience to a higher law—to the strength of the spirit.

I have therefore ventured to place before India the ancient law of self-sacrifice. For *satyagraha* [3] and its offshoots, non-cooperation and civil resistance, are nothing but new names for the law of suffering. The *rishis,* who discovered the law of non-violence in the midst of violence, were greater geniuses than Newton. They were themselves greater warriors than Wellington. Having themselves known the use of arms, they realized their uselessness, and taught a weary world that its salvation lay not through violence but through non-violence.

Non-violence in its dynamic condition means conscious suffering. It does not mean meek submission to the will of the evil-doer, but it means putting of one's whole soul against the will of the tyrant. Working under this law of our being, it is possible for a single individual to defy the whole might of an unjust empire to save his honour, his religion, his soul, and lay the foundation for that empire's fall or its regeneration.

And so I am not pleading for India to practise non-violence because she is weak. I want her to practise non-violence being conscious of her strength and power. No training in arms is required for realization of her strength. We seem to need it, because we seem to think that we are but a lump of flesh. I want India to recognize that she has a soul that

---

[2] Editor's Note: *Rishis* are sages of Hindu mythology with superhuman powers.
[3] Editor's Note: *Satyagraha* means literally soul-force; used for civil disobedience, non-violent resistance.

cannot perish and that can rise triumphant above every physical weakness and defy the physical combination of a whole world. . . .

If India takes up the doctrine of the sword, she may gain momentary victory. Then India will cease to be the pride of my heart. I am wedded to India because I owe my all to her. I believe absolutely that she has a mission for the world. She is not to copy Europe blindly. India's acceptance of the doctrine of the sword will be the hour of my trial. I hope I shall not be found wanting. My religion has no geographical limits. If I have a living faith in it, it will transcend my love for India herself. My life is dedicated to the service of India through the religion of non-violence which I believe to be the root of Hinduism.

II [4]

Rev. B. De Light has written in a French journal called *Evolution* a long open letter to me. He has favoured me with a translation of it. The open letter strongly criticises my participation in the Boer War and then the Great War of 1914, and invites me to explain my conduct in the light of *Ahimsa*.[5] Other friends too have put the same question. I have attempted to give the explanation more than once in these columns.

There is no defence for my conduct weighed only in the scales of *Ahimsa*. I draw no distinction between those who wield the weapons of destruction and those who do Red Cross work. Both participate in war and advance its cause. Both are guilty of the crime of war. But even after introspection during all these years, I feel that, in the circumstances in which I found myself, I was bound to adopt the course I did both during the Boer War and the Great European War and for that matter the so-called Zulu "Rebellion" of Natal in 1906.

Life is governed by a multitude of forces. It would be smooth sailing, if one could determine the course of one's actions only by one general principle whose application at a given moment was too obvious to need even a moment's reflection. But I cannot recall a single act which could be so easily determined.

Being a confirmed war resister I have never given myself training in the use of destructive weapons in spite of opportunities to take such training. It was perhaps thus that I escaped direct destruction of human life. But so long as I lived under a system of government based

[4] "My Attitude Towards War," *Young India*, Sept. 13, 1928.
[5] Editor's Note: *Ahimsa* means non-violence.

on force and voluntarily partook of the many facilities and privileges it created for me, I was bound to help that Government to the extent of my ability when it was engaged in a war, unless I non-cooperated with that Government and renounced to the utmost of my capacity the privileges it offered me.

Let me take an illustration. I am a member of an institution which holds a few acres of land whose crops are in imminent peril from monkeys. I believe in the sacredness of all life, and hence I regard it as a breach of *Ahimsa* to inflict any injury on the monkeys. But I do not hesitate to instigate and direct an attack on the monkeys in order to save the crops. I would like to avoid this evil. I can avoid it by leaving or breaking up the institution. I do not do so because I do not expect to be able to find a society where there will be no agriculture and therefore no destruction of some life. In fear and trembling, in humility and penance, I therefore participate in the injury inflicted on the monkeys, hoping some day to find a way out.

Even so did I participate in the three acts of war. I could not, it would be madness for me to, sever my connection with the society to which I belong. And on those three occasions I had no thought of non-cooperating with the British Government. My position regarding that Government is totally different today, and hence I should not voluntarily participate in its war, and I should risk imprisonment and even the gallows, if I was forced to take up arms or otherwise take part in its military operations.

But that still does not solve the riddle. If there was a national Government, whilst I should not take any direct part in any war, I can conceive occasions when it would be my duty to vote for the military training of those who wish to take it. For I know that all its members do not believe in non-violence to the extent I do. It is not possible to make a person or a society non-violent by compulsion.

Non-violence works in a most mysterious manner. Often a man's actions defy analysis in terms of non-violence; equally often his actions may wear the appearance of violence when he is absolutely non-violent in the highest sense of the term and is subsequently found so to be. All I can then claim for my conduct is that it was, in the instances cited, actuated in the interests of non-violence. There was no thought of sordid national or other interest. I do not believe in the promotion of national or any other interest at the sacrifice of some other interest.

I may not carry my argument any further. Language at best is but a poor vehicle for expressing one's thoughts in full. For me non-violence is not a mere philosophical principle. It is the rule and the breath of my life. I know I fail often, sometimes consciously, more often unconsciously. It is a matter not of the intellect but of the heart. True guidance comes by constant waiting upon God, by utmost humility, self-abnegation, by being ever ready to sacrifice one's self. Its practice requires fearlessness and courage of the highest order. I am painfully aware of my failings.

But the Light within me is steady and clear. There is no escape for any of us save through Truth and non-violence. I know that war is wrong, is an unmitigated evil. I know too that it has got to go. I firmly believe that freedom won through bloodshed or fraud is no freedom. Would that all the acts alleged against me were found to be wholly indefensible rather than that by any act of mine non-violence was held to be compromised or that I was ever thought to be in favour of violence or untruth in any shape or form. Not violence, not untruth, but non-violence, Truth is the law of our being.

III [6]

. . .A human being, however debased or fallen he may be, has in him the capacity of rising to the greatest height ever attained by any human being irrespective of race or colour. Therefore, even whilst I may go with my countrymen a long way in satisfying their need for preparation for war, I should do so in the fullest hope of weaning them from war and of their seeing one day its utter futility. Let it be remembered that the largest experiment known to history in mass non-violence is being tried by me even as I seem to be lending myself for the purpose of war. For want of skill the experiment may fail. But the war-resister in Europe should strain every nerve to understand and appreciate the phenomenon going on before him in India of the same man trying the bold experiment in non-violence whilst hobnobbing with those who would prepare for war.

It is part of the plan of non-violence that I should share the feelings of my countrymen if I would ever expect to bring them to non-violence. The striking fact is that India including the educated politician is *nolens volens* driven to the belief that non-violence

---

[6] "A Complex Problem," *Young India,* May 9, 1929.

alone will free the masses from the thraldom of centuries. It is true that all have not followed out the logical consequences of non-violence. Who can? In spite of my boast that I know the truth of non-violence and try my best to practise it, I fail often to follow out the logical conclusions of the doctrine. The working of nature's processes in the human breast is mysterious and baffles interpretation.

This I know that, if India comes to her own demonstrably through non-violent means, India will never want to carry a vast army, an equally grand navy, and a grander air force. If her self-consciousness rises to the height necessary to give her a non-violent victory in her fight for freedom, the world values will have changed and most of the paraphernalia of war would be found to be useless. Such an India may be a mere daydream, a childish folly. But such, in my opinion, is undoubtedly the implication of an India becoming free through non-violence.

When that freedom comes, if it ever does, it will have come through a gentlemanly understanding with Great Britain. But then it will not be an imperialistic haughty Britain manoeuvring for world supremacy, but a Britain humbly trying to serve the common end of humanity. India will no longer then be helplessly driven into Britain's wars of exploitation, but hers will be the voice of a powerful nation seeking to keep under restraint all the violent forces of the world.

Whether all these fanciful ideas are ever realized or not, my own life line is cast. I can no longer, in any conceivable circumstance, take part in Britain's wars. And I have already said in these pages that, if India attains (what will be to me so-called) freedom by violent means, she will cease to be a country of my pride; that time will be a time for me of civil death. There can, therefore, never be any question of my participation, direct or indirect, in any war of exploitation by India.

But I have already pointed out in these pages that fellow war-resisters in the West are participants in war even in peace time inasmuch as they pay for the preparations that are being made for it and otherwise sustain governments whose main occupation is such preparation. Again, all activity for stopping war must prove fruitless so long as the causes of war are not understood and radically dealt with. Is not the prime cause of modern wars the inhuman race for exploitation of the so-called weaker races of the earth?

IV [7]

Non-violence is at the root of every one of my activities and therefore also of the three public activities on which I am just now visibly concentrating all my energy. These are untouchability, khadi, and village regeneration in general. Hindu Muslim unity is my fourth love. But so far as any visible manifestation is concerned, I have owned defeat on that score. Let the public, however, not assume therefrom that I am inactive. If not during my lifetime, I know that after my death both Hindus and Mussalmans will bear witness that I had never ceased to yearn after communal peace.

Non-violence to be a creed has to be all-pervasive. I cannot be non-violent about one activity of mine and violent about others. That would be a policy, not a life-force. That being so, I cannot be indifferent about the war that Italy is now waging against Abyssinia. But I have resisted most pressing invitations to express my opinion and give a lead to the country. Self-suppression is often necessary in the interest of Truth and Non-violence. If India had as a nation imbibed the creed of non-violence, corporate or national, I should have had no hesitation in giving a lead. But, in spite of a certain hold I have on the millions of this country, I know the very grave and glaring limitations of that hold. India has an unbroken tradition of non-violence from times immemorial. But at no time in her ancient history, as far as I know it, has it had complete non-violence in action pervading the whole land. Nevertheless, it is my unshakable belief that her destiny is to deliver the message of non-violence to mankind. It may take ages to come to fruition. But so far as I can judge, no other country will precede her in the fulfilment of that mission.

Be that as it may, it is seasonable to contemplate the implications of that matchless force. Three concrete questions were, the other day, incidentally asked by friends:

1. What could ill-armed Abyssinia do against well-armed Italy, if she were non-violent?

2. What could England, the greatest and the most powerful member of the League, do against determined Italy, if she (England) were non-violent in your sense of the term?

3. What could India do, if she suddenly became non-violent in your sense of the term?

[7] "The Greatest Force," *Harijan*, October 12, 1935.

Before I answer the questions let me lay down five simple axioms of non-violence as I know it:

(a) Non-violence implies as complete self-purification as is humanly possible.

(b) Man for man the strength of non-violence is in exact proportion to the ability, not the will, of the non-violent person to inflict violence.

(c) Non-violence is without exception superior to violence, i.e., the power at the disposal of a non-violent person is always greater than he would have if he was violent.

(d) There is no such thing as defeat in non-violence. The end of violence is surest defeat.

(e) The ultimate end of non-violence is surest victory—if such a term may be used of non-violence. In reality, where there is no sense of defeat, there is no sense of victory.

The foregoing questions may be answered in the light of these axioms.

1. If Abyssinia were non-violent, she would have no arms, would want none. She would make no appeal to the League or any other power for armed intervention. She would never give any cause for complaint. And Italy would find nothing to conquer if Abyssinians would not offer armed resistance, nor would they give co-operation willing or forced. Italian occupation in that case would mean that of the land without its people. That, however, is not Italy's exact object. She seeks submission of the people of that beautiful land.

2. If Englishmen were as a nation to become non-violent at heart, they would shed imperialism, they would give up the use of arms. The moral force generated by such an act of renunciation would stagger Italy into willing surrender of her designs. England would then be a living embodiment of the axioms I have laid down. The effect of such conversion would mean the greatest miracle of all ages. And yet if non-violence is not an idle dream, some such thing has some day to come to pass somewhere. I live in that faith.

3. The last question may be answered thus. As I have said, India as a nation is not non-violent in the full sense of the term. Neither has she any capacity for offering violence—not because she has no arms. Physical possession of arms is the least necessity of the brave. Her non-violence is that of the weak; she betrays her weakness in many of her daily acts. She appears before the world today as a

decaying nation. I mean here not in the mere political sense but essentially in the non-violent, moral sense. She lacks the ability to offer physical resistance. She has no consciousness of strength. She is conscious only of her weakness. If she were otherwise, there would be no communal problems, nor political. If she were non-violent in the consciousness of her strength, Englishmen would lose their role of distrustful conquerors. We may talk politically as we like and often legitimately blame the English rulers. But if we, as Indians, could but for a moment visualize ourselves as a strong people disdaining to strike, we should cease to fear Englishmen, whether as soldiers, traders or administrators, and they to distrust us. Therefore, if we became truly non-violent, we should carry Englishmen with us in all we might do. In other words, we being millions would be the greatest moral force in the world, and Italy would listen to our friendly word.

The reader has, I hope, by now perceived that my argument is but a feeble and clumsy attempt to prove my axioms which to be such must be self-proved.

Till my eyes of geometrical understanding had been opened, my brain was swimming as I read and re-read the twelve axioms of Euclid. After the opening of my eyes geometry seemed to be the easiest science to learn. Much more so is the case with non-violence. It is a matter of faith and experience, not of argument, beyond a point. So long as the world refuses to believe, she must await a miracle, i.e., an ocular demonstration of non-violence on a mass scale. They say this is against human nature—non-violence is only for the individual. If so, where is the difference in kind between man and beast?

V [8]

. . . I have often said that, if one takes care of the means, the end will take care of itself. Non-violence is the means; the end for every nation is complete independence. There will be an international league only when all the nations, big or small, composing it are fully independent. The nature of that independence will correspond to the extent of non-violence assimilated by the nations concerned. One thing is certain. In a society based on non-violence, the

---

[8] "Working of Non-Violence," *Harijan*, February 11, 1939.

smallest nation will feel as tall as the tallest. The idea of superiority
and inferiority will be wholly obliterated. . . .

VI [9]

Q. Wherever in the world today one casts one's eye, there is
nothing but violence and power politics to be seen. And this obtains
even in democratic countries like England and America. Have you
pondered as to what your *ahimsa* can do under such circumstances?

A. It is true that power politics exist everywhere; but you are
very much mistaken if you imagine that true democracy obtains
either in America or England. The voice of the people may be said
to be God's voice, the voice of the *Panchayat*.[10] But how can there
be the voice of God where the people themselves are the exploiters
as England and America are? They live on the coloured races by
exploiting them. If the voice of the people is the voice of God, they
will be above party. His scales will ever be evenly weighted with
truth and non-violence. This statement embraces my reply. My *ahimsa*
is neither maimed nor weak. It is all-powerful. Where there is *ahimsa,*
there is Truth and Truth is God. How He manifests Himself, I
cannot say. All I know is that He is all-pervading and where He
is, all is well. There is, therefore, one law for all. Wherever in the
world Truth and Non-violence reign supreme, there is peace and
bliss. That these exist nowhere shows that they are hidden from man
for the time being. But they cannot disappear for ever. That faith
must sustain the faithful.

VII [11]

I would love to attempt an answer to a question which has been
addressed to me from more than one quarter of the globe. It is:

How can you account for the growing violence among your people on the part of political parties for the furtherance of political
ends? Is this the result of the thirty years of non-violent practice for
ending British rule? Does your message of non-violence still hold
good for the world? I have condensed the sentiments of my correspondents in my own language.

---

[9] "What Can Ahimsa Do?," *Harijan*, September 29, 1946.

[10] Editor's Note: *Panchayat* means a village council of five members.

[11] "Non-Violence." The above is from Gandhi's written message for the prayer
gathering on June 15, 1947. *Harijan*, June 29, 1947.

In answer I must confess my bankruptcy, not that of non-violence. I have already said that the non-violence that was offered during the past thirty years was that of the weak. Whether it is a good enough answer or not is for others to judge. It must be further admitted that such non-violence can have no play in the altered circumstances. India has no experience of the non-violence of the strong. It serves no purpose for me to continue to repeat that the non-violence of the strong is the strongest force in the world. The truth requires constant and extensive demonstration. This I am endeavouring to do to the best of my ability. What if the best of my ability is very little? May I not be living in a fool's paradise? Why should I ask people to follow me in the fruitless search? These are pertinent questions. My answer is quite simple. I ask nobody to follow me. Everyone should follow his or her own inner voice. If he or she has no ears to listen to it, he or she should do the best he or she can. In no case should he or she imitate others sheeplike.

One more question has been and is being asked. If you are sure that India is going the wrong way, why do you associate with the wrongdoers? Why do you not plough your own lonely furrow and have faith that if you are right, your erstwhile friends and followers will seek you out? I regard this as a very fair question. I must not attempt to argue against it. All I can say is that my faith is as strong as ever. It is quite possible that my technique is faulty. There are old and tried precedents to guide one in such a complexity. Only, no one should act mechanically. Hence I can say to all my counsellors that they should have patience with me and even share my belief that there is no hope for the aching world except through the narrow and straight path of non-violence. Millions like me may fail to prove the truth in their own lives, that would be their failure, never of the eternal law.

The Melian Conference*

BY THUCYDIDES

[5th Century B.C.]

THE next summer** Alcibiades sailed with twenty ships to Argos and seized the suspected persons still left of the Lacedæmonian faction to the number of three hundred, whom the Athenians forthwith lodged in the neighbouring islands of their empire. The Athenians also made an expedition against the isle of Melos with thirty ships of their own, six Chian, and two Lesbian vessels, sixteen hundred heavy infantry, three hundred archers, and twenty mounted archers from Athens, and about fifteen hundred heavy infantry from the allies and the islanders. The Melians are a colony of Lacedæmon that would not submit to the Athenians like the other islanders, and at first remained neutral and took no part in the struggle, but afterwards upon the Athenians using violence and plundering their territory, assumed an attitude of open hostility. Cleomedes, son of Lycomedes, and Tisias, son of Tisimachus, the generals, encamping in their territory with the above armament, before doing any harm to their land, sent envoys to negotiate. These the Melians did not bring before the people, but bade them state the object of their mission to the magistrates and the few; upon which the Athenian envoys spoke as follows:—

Athenians.—"Since the negotiations are not to go on before the people, in order that we may not be able to speak straight on without interruption, and deceive the ears of the multitude by seductive arguments which would pass without refutation (for we know that this is the meaning of our being brought before the few), what if you who sit there were to pursue a method more cautious still! Make no set speech yourselves, but take us up at whatever you do not like, and settle that before going any farther. And first tell us if this proposition of ours suits you."

The Melian commissioners answered:—

Melians.—"To the fairness of quietly instructing each other as you

---

* From *The Peloponnesian War,* the Crawley translation. Reprinted by courtesy of the Modern Library.
** This was the sixteenth year[416 B.C.] of the war between Athens and Lacedæmon (Sparta).

propose there is nothing to object; but your military preparations are too far advanced to agree with what you say, as we see you are come to be judges in your own cause, and that all we can reasonably expect from this negotiation is war, if we prove to have right on our side and refuse to submit, and in the contrary case, slavery."

Athenians.—"If you have met to reason about presentiments of the future, or for anything else than to consult for the safety of your state upon the facts that you see before you, we will give over; otherwise we will go on."

Melians.—"It is natural and excusable for men in our position to turn more ways than one both in thought and utterance. However, the question in this conference is, as you say, the safety of our country; and the discussion, if you please, can proceed in the way which you propose."

Athenians.—"For ourselves, we shall not trouble you with specious pretences—either of how we have a right to our empire because we overthrew the Mede, or are now attacking you because of wrong that you have done us—and make a long speech which would not be believed; and in return we hope that you, instead of thinking to influence us by saying that you did not join the Lacedæmonians, although their colonists, or that you have done us no wrong, will aim at what is feasible, holding in view the real sentiments of us both; since you know as well as we do that right, as the world goes, is only in question between equals in power, while the strong do what they can and the weak suffer what they must."

Melians.—"As we think, at any rate, it is expedient—we speak as we are obliged, since you enjoin us to let right alone and talk only of interest—that you should not destroy what is our common protection, the privilege of being allowed in danger to invoke what is fair and right, and even to profit by arguments not strictly valid if they can be got to pass current. And you are as much interested in this as any, as your fall would be a signal for the heaviest vengeance and an example for the world to meditate upon."

Athenians.—"The end of our empire, if end it should, does not frighten us: a rival empire like Lacedæmon, even if Lacedæmon was our real antagonist, is not so terrible to the vanquished as subjects who by themselves attack and overpower their rulers. This, however, is a risk that we are content to take. We will now proceed to show you that we are come here in the interest of our empire, and that we shall say what we are now going to say, for the preservation of your country; as we would fain exercise that empire over you without trouble, and see you preserved for the good of us both."

Melians.—"And how, pray, could it turn out as good for us to serve as for you to rule?"

Athenians.—"Because you would have the advantage of submitting before suffering the worst, and we should gain by not destroying you."

Melians.—"So that you would not consent to our being neutral, friends instead of enemies, but allies of neither side."

Athenians.—"No; for your hostility cannot so much hurt us as your friendship will be an argument to our subjects of our weakness, and your enmity of our power."

Melians.—"Is that your subjects' idea of equity, to put those who have nothing to do with you in the same category with peoples that are most of them your own colonists, and some conquered rebels?"

Athenians.—"As far as right goes they think one has as much of it as the other, and that if any maintain their independence it is because they are strong, and that if we do not molest them it is because we are afraid; so that besides extending our empire we should gain in security by your subjection; the fact that you are islanders and weaker than others rendering it all the more important that you should not succeed in baffling the masters of the sea."

Melians.—"But do you consider that there is no security in the policy which we indicate? For here again if you debar us from talking about justice and invite us to obey your interest, we also must explain ours, and try to persuade you, if the two happen to coincide. How can you avoid making enemies of all existing neutrals who shall look at our case and conclude from it that one day or another you will attack them? And what is this but to make greater the enemies that you have already, and to force others to become so who would otherwise have never thought of it?"

Athenians.—"Why, the fact is that continentals generally give us but little alarm; the liberty which they enjoy will long prevent their taking precautions against us; it is rather islanders like yourselves, outside our empire, and subjects smarting under the yoke, who would be the most likely to take a rash step and lead themselves and us into obvious danger."

Melians.—"Well then, if you risk so much to retain your empire, and your subjects to get rid of it, it were surely great baseness and cowardice in us who are still free not to try everything that can be tried, before submitting to your yoke."

Athenians.—"Not if you are well advised, the contest not being an equal one, with honour as the prize and shame as the penalty, but a question of self-preservation and of not resisting those who are far stronger than you are."

Melians.—"But we know that the fortune of war is sometimes more impartial than the disproportion of numbers might lead one to suppose; to submit is to give ourselves over to despair, while action still preserves for us a hope that we may stand erect."

Athenians.—"Hope, danger's comforter, may be indulged in by those who have abundant resources, if not without loss at all events without ruin; but its nature is to be extravagant, and those who go so far as to put their all upon the venture see it in its true colours only when they are ruined; but so long as the discovery would enable them to guard against it, it is never found wanting. Let not this be the case with you, who are weak and hang on a single turn of the scale; nor be like the vulgar, who, abandoning such security as human means may still afford, when visible hopes fail them in extremity, turn to invisible, to prophecies and oracles, and other such inventions that delude men with hopes to their destruction."

Melians.—"You may be sure that we are as well aware as you of the difficulty of contending against your power and fortune, unless the terms be equal. But we trust that the gods may grant us fortune as good as yours, since we are just men fighting against unjust, and that what we want in power will be made up by the alliance of the Lacedæmonians, who are bound, if only for very shame, to come to the aid of their kindred. Our confidence, therefore, after all is not so utterly irrational."

Athenians.—"When you speak of the favour of the gods, we may as fairly hope for that as yourselves; neither our pretensions nor our conduct being in any way contrary to what men believe of the gods, or practise among themselves. Of the gods we believe, and of men we know, that by a necessary law of their nature they rule wherever they can. And it is not as if we were the first to make this law, or to act upon it when made: we found it existing before us, and shall leave it to exist for ever after us; all we do is to make use of it, knowing that you and everybody else, having the same power as we have, would do the same as we do. Thus, as far as the gods are concerned, we have no fear and no reason to fear that we shall be at a disadvantage. But when we come to your notion about the Lacedæmonians, which leads you to believe that shame will make them help you, here we bless your simplicity but do not envy your folly. The Lacedæmonians, when their own interests or their country's laws are in question, are the worthiest men alive; of their conduct towards others much might be said, but no clearer idea of it could be given than by shortly saying that of all the men we know they are most conspicuous in considering what is agreeable honourable, and what is expedient just. Such a way of thinking does not promise much for the safety which you now unreasonably count upon."

Melians.—"But it is for this very reason that we now trust to their respect for expediency to prevent them from betraying the Melians, their colonists, and thereby losing the confidence of their friends in Hellas and helping their enemies."

Athenians.—"Then you do not adopt the view that expediency goes with security, while justice and honour cannot be followed without danger; and danger the Lacedæmonians generally court as little as possible."

Melians.—"But we believe that they would be more likely to face even danger for our sake, and with more confidence than for others, as our nearness to Peloponnese makes it easier for them to act, and our common blood insures our fidelity."

Athenians.—"Yes, but what an intending ally trusts to, is not the goodwill of those who ask his aid, but a decided superiority of power for action; and the Lacedæmonians look to this even more than others. At least, such is their distrust of their home resources that it is only with numerous allies that they attack a neighbour; now is it likely that while we are masters of the sea they will cross over to an island?"

Melians.—"But they would have others to send. The Cretan sea is a wide one, and it is more difficult for those who command it to intercept others, than for those who wish to elude them to do so safely. And should the Lacedæmonians miscarry in this, they would fall upon your land, and upon those left of your allies whom Brasidas did not reach; and instead of places which are not yours, you will have to fight for your own country and your own confederacy."

Athenians.—"Some diversion of the kind you speak of you may one day experience, only to learn, as others have done, that the Athenians never once yet withdrew from a siege for fear of any. But we are struck by the fact, that after saying you would consult for the safety of your country, in all this discussion you have mentioned nothing which men might trust in and think to be saved by. Your strongest arguments depend upon hope and the future, and your actual resources are too scanty, as compared with those arrayed against you, for you to come out victorious. You will therefore show great blindness of judgment, unless, after allowing us to retire, you can find some counsel more prudent than this. You will surely not be caught by that idea of disgrace, which in dangers that are disgraceful, and at the same time too plain to be mistaken, proves so fatal to mankind; since in too many cases the very men that have their eyes perfectly open to what they are rushing into, let the thing called disgrace, by the mere influence of a seductive name, lead them on to a point at which they become so enslaved by the phrase as in fact to fall wilfully into hopeless disaster, and incur disgrace more disgraceful as the companion of error, than when it comes as the result of misfortune. This, if you are well advised, you will guard against; and you will not think it dishonourable to submit to the greatest city in Hellas, when it makes you the moderate offer of becoming its tributary ally, without ceasing to enjoy the country that belongs to you; nor when you have the choice given you between war and security, will you be so blinded as to choose the worse. And it is certain that those who do not yield to their equals, who keep terms with their superiors, and are moderate towards their inferiors, on the whole succeed best. Think over the matter, therefore, after our withdrawal, and reflect once and again that it is for your country that you are consulting, that you have not more than one, and that upon this one deliberation depends its prosperity or ruin."

The Athenians now withdrew from the conference; and the Melians, left to themselves, came to a decision corresponding with what they had maintained in the discussion, and answered, "Our resolution, Athenians, is the same as it was at first. We will not in a moment deprive of freedom a city that has been inhabited these seven hundred years; but we put our trust in the fortune by which the gods have preserved it until now, and in the help of men, that is, of the Lacedæmonians; and so we will try and save ourselves. Meanwhile we invite you to allow us to be friends to you and foes to neither party, and to retire from our country after making such a treaty as shall seem fit to us both."

Such was the answer of the Melians. The Athenians now departing from the conference said, "Well, you alone, as it seems to us, judging from these resolutions, regard what is future as more certain than what is before your eyes, and what is out of sight, in your eagerness, as already coming to pass; and as you have staked most on, and trusted most in, the Lacedæmonians, your fortune, and your hopes, so will you be most completely deceived."

The Athenian envoys now returned to the army; and the Melians showing no signs of yielding, the generals at once betook themselves to hostilities, and drew a line of circumvallation round the Melians, dividing the work among the different states. Subsequently the Athenians returned with most of their army, leaving behind them a certain number of their own citizens and of the allies to keep guard by land and sea. The force thus left stayed on and besieged the place.

. . . Meanwhile the Melians attacked by night and took the part of the Athenian lines over against the market, and killed some of the men, and brought in corn and all else that they could find useful to them, and so returned and kept quiet, while the Athenians took measures to keep better guard in future.

Summer was now over. The next winter the Lacedæmonians intended to invade the Argive territory, but arriving at the frontier found the sacrifices for crossing unfavourable, and went back again. This intention of theirs gave the Argives suspicions of certain of their fellow-citizens, some of whom they arrested; others, however, escaped them. About the same time the Melians again took another part of the Athenian lines which were but feebly garrisoned. Reinforcements afterwards arriving from Athens in consequence, under the command of Philocrates, son of Demeas, the siege was now pressed vigorously; and some treachery taking place inside, the Melians surrendered at discretion to the Athenians, who put to death all the grown men whom they took, and sold the women and children for slaves, and subsequently sent out five hundred colonists and inhabited the place themselves.

Ideology or Balance
of Power?*

BY WILLIAM G. CARLETON

[1947]

IF YOU are a teacher of a college class in international relations, as I
have been for the past decade, the moment will inevitably come that
you half dread and half eagerly welcome: one day some student will
rise and ask the sixty-four dollar question. "Professor," he will say,
"are we Americans wary of Russia because we fear Communism or
because we fear that Russia will upset the balance of power? Which
is more important—that thing we call 'ideology' or the balance of
power?" That question raises the fundamental philosophic issue of our
time—the issue which goes to the very heart of international relations.

What is the chief element in formulating the foreign policy of a
nation? Is it ideology or is it balance of power? Is it both? If both,
which weighs the more?

Did Sparta and Athens fight the Peloponnesian War because of
the conflict of their social and political systems or because each feared
the collective power of the other? Was Whig Britain at war with
Bourbon France because of the rivalry of different institutions or because of the clash of competitive imperialisms? Did Burke's Britain
fight Revolutionary France because of Tory fear of the Jacobins or
because Britain feared for the balance of power? Did the United States
go to war with Germany in 1917 and again in 1941 because of a conflict of cultures or a conflict of power?

What is this thing called "ideology"? There are, of course, ideologies and ideologies, and the term needs clarification.

Nations differ from each other in cultural and institutional patterns. But institutions inside nations are forever undergoing changes.
These changes bring on institutional conflict within nations. Some
fear these changes while others favor them. Very often the institu-

---

* From *Yale Review,* Summer 1947. Copyright, 1947, by Yale University Press.
Reprinted by permission.

tional conflict taking place inside one nation is at the same time also taking place inside other nations. In other words, the struggle for institutional change often cuts across national boundaries.

In one age, the emphasis is on one aspect of cultural or institutional change; in another age, the emphasis is on another aspect. In the sixteenth century and the early seventeenth century, the chief institutional conflict inside countries involved religion. In some countries the Protestants won, and in other countries the Catholics won. But inside Protestant countries, there were Catholic minorities, and inside Catholic countries, there were Protestant minorities. Later, the chief institutional conflict was over constitutional and representative government. In some countries constitutional government won, and in other countries absolute monarchy held its own; but in countries where constitutional government won, there were still those who clung to the divinity of kings, and in countries where absolutism won, there were minority groups which favored constitutional and representative government. Still later, the chief institutional conflict was over political democracy. However, in countries where democracy triumphed, there were minority groups which opposed it, and in countries where democracy made little headway, there were minority groups which championed it. Today, in this middle of the twentieth century, the chief institutional conflict centers around the ownership of productive property. The struggle is one of capitalism versus some form of collectivism. Inside almost every country this struggle is taking place in one way or another. In some countries collectivism is farther advanced than in others. Those in one country who favor collectivism find themselves in sympathy with those in other countries who favor it. Those in one country who oppose collectivism find themselves in sympathy with those in other countries who oppose it.

The decisive institutional conflict of any age has come to be known as the "ideological" conflict. While, in general, that conflict was in the seventeenth century waged over religion, in the eighteenth century over constitutional and representative government, and in the nineteenth century over political democracy, in the present century it is being waged over Socialism.

That the institutional or ideological conflict is waged inside many nations at the same time, that the new institution struggling to be born is farther advanced in some countries than in others, that this conflict cuts across national lines and leaves people and groups within the various countries with ideological sympathies for similar groups in other countries—all of this enormously complicates international relations. International wars often take on the appearance of deep-seated ideological conflict involving not only national interests but future institutional and cultural development. Men who belong to minority groups are often torn between two loyalties—loyalty to ideology and loyalty to nation. Such men may be damned as "Trojan horses" and "fifth columnists" if they follow their ideological impulse; they may be damned as disloyal to their ideology if they follow their national impulse.

What if a situation arises in international politics in which ideology and national interest do not coincide? In that case, which is put first by those who conduct the nation's foreign policy—ideology or national interest?

As we look back on the past, it seems that, when the hour of decision struck, the national urge was generally stronger than the ideological. During the Thirty Years' War, in an age when the chief ideological conflict was religious, Catholic France went to the aid of Sweden and the German Protestants in their conflict with Catholic Austria. To Cardinal Richelieu and other French leaders of the day it was more important for France to check Austria, for the Bourbons to humble the Hapsburgs, than for Catholics to stand together against Protestants. In the late seventeenth century and in the eighteenth century, it usually seemed more important to the absolute monarchs of Vienna and Berlin to check the French nation than that Hapsburgs, Hohenzollerns, and Bourbons should stand together in ideological alliance to maintain absolutism against the slowly rising tide of constitutionalism. Britain fought Bourbon France, Revolutionary France, and Napoleonic France, for while the ideologies shifted and changed, the national rivalry and imperialist conflict did not. In more recent times, Tsarist Russia has been allied with republican France, democratic Britain with oligarchic Japan, democratic America and democratic Britain with Communist Russia, and Communist Russia with Nazi Germany. National interests make strange bedfellows—in the face of a threat to the balance of power, nations will make alliances with the ideological devil.

Where, in general, the dominant ideology within the nation and the national interest do coincide, in what direction have the ideological minorities usually gone? In a crisis, what have these minorities done

—have they followed their ideologies or their national patriotisms? In the past, the tug of national loyalty has generally won out over ideological persuasion. British Catholics rallied to Elizabeth in her fight with Catholic Spain. Charles James Fox's Whigs rallied to Pitt in the national fight against Napoleon. And in the two global wars of this century the Socialists did what they boasted they would never do —in the main, they rallied to the national standards. A Coriolanus and an Alcibiades, a Vallandigham, and a Petigru, a Quisling and an Einstein, a Laval and a Thomas Mann are relatively rare in history. (This is, I know, an incongruous list of saints and sinners, but they have this one thing in common: in one way or another, all sacrificed homeland for ideology.) And should all our hopes of peace collapse and the future see a third world war involving the Soviet Union against the United States, it is still a safe prediction that Eleanor Roosevelt and Colonel Robert McCormick, Max Lerner and Hamilton Fish, Philip Murray and John Bricker, Henry Wallace and Lawrence Dennis would be fighting side by side in the name of national interest and national survival.

However, it would be a mistake to come to the conclusion that because ideology has not played the leading part in historic international relations it has played no part at all. It has played its part, an important part. Where national interests and dominant ideology within the nation coincide, a national war can be made to appear an ideological one, morale can be strengthened, and enthusiasm intensified. If a nation possesses considerable ideological unity it will be in a stronger position to win a war; if a nation's enemies are ideologically divided those enemies will be more susceptible to fifth-column tactics. When a country is rising to challenge the old balance of power, nations thus threatened will make alliances more easily and earlier if they have similar institutions and cultures; alliances will be more difficult and will come later (perhaps too late!) if the nations thus threatened have dissimilar institutions and cultures.

Just as national interests and balance-of-power considerations seem to have been the most important causes of war, so also they seem to have been most affected by war. The results of international wars seem to have been more significant in their national and balance-of-power aspect than in their ideological aspect. The Grand Alliance against Napoleonic France checked France and saved the European balance of power but did not succeed in arresting the spread of revolutionary ideas. The Grand Alliance won the war nationally but in the end lost it ideologically. However, when nations outside of France became more and more influenced by French Revolutionary ideas, those ideas took on the appearance of being their own—they were assimilated into their own national cultures. Again, at the close of the First World War, it appeared that middle-class democracy would triumph in the world, but now we can see that instead, the First World War marked virtually the end of the advance of middle-class democracy in any large areas of the world. However, the First World War did parry the German threat to the balance of power; it did temporarily satisfy the national interests of the victors; the war was won nationally even though it was lost ideologically. Again, the victory of the United Nations in the Second World War saved the world from a second German threat to the balance of power—that much is certain. Perhaps it will also have hastened Socialism, but, in any event, the ideological results are not so clear as the national ones.

It seems, then, that the influence of great wars on the cultural and institutional trends of the time is exaggerated. These trends arise out of conditions and forces operating within the nations. Wars affect them. Wars may accelerate these trends or slow them up. Wars hardly create them.

The Marxists would claim that what appears to be the national interest has in fact been primarily the interest of the dominant class in control of the state and that class interest has governed the foreign policy of national states and involved national states in wars for class ends. The great national wars, according to Marxist doctrine, have been wars in the interests of the dominant economic classes in the warring nations—conflicts of rival imperialisms. Where, in the past, ideology has seemed to split the dominant class, such ideological conflict, according to the Marxists, has been superficial or at least secondary to that class's economic interest. When a threat has appeared to the economic interest of the dominant class, these secondary ideological ranks have been closed in the class interest masquerading in the name of the nation. Of course, say the Marxists, the Catholic landlords and business men of Elizabeth's day rallied to the fight against Catholic Spain because their profits were involved. Of course, the Marxists say again, the Charles James Fox Whigs, enamored though they were of many of the principles of the French Revolution, rallied to the war against Revolutionary France because their dividends from the British East

India Company and from many another chartered company were at stake. (They fail to recall that the peace party in Britain led by Fox did not actually "rally" to the war until France under Napoleon had threatened to control the Channel and invade Britain.)

To be sure, the great conflict *is* ideological, say the Marxists—an ideological conflict between the exploiting capitalists and the exploited workers—and when this ideological conflict comes to the fore and cuts across national states, then the conflict between nations will be seen to be a sham and a swindle, the ideological factor will become stronger than the national factor in international relations, national wars will be converted into civil wars, and the erstwhile dominant economic class, now embattled, will find it more and more difficult to cloak its class interests in the garment of nationalism.

It may be that the Marxists are correct as to the future. It may be that the ideological will supersede the national as the number one factor in international relations. It may be that now the great institutional conflict within nations has come to be directly economic (and not indirectly so, as in the case of many of the ideological conflicts of the past) and the fundamental issue easier for all to see, that more and more will men respond to the class and ideological appeal rather than the national appeal. And if men more and more are learning to think as the Marxists do (the post-war elections in Britain and especially in Continental Europe indicate that they are) then it is quite possible that our century will see international relations conducted in fact and in name more along ideological than national lines. Indeed, the Second World War was in many ways a series of civil wars, with Socialists and Communists in Axis countries praying for an Allied victory and fascists in Allied countries supporting collaboration with the Axis. Ideological minorities were co-operating with the national enemy on a scale never equalled in the days when Protestantism or constitutional government or political democracy was the pivot of ideological conflict—though perhaps some of this co-operation should be credited to the increase and improvement in the means of communication. And today, Henry Wallace speaking to Britain in a way hostile to the views of a majority of his own countrymen or Winston Churchill speaking to America in a way hostile to the views of millions of Left-wing Britons is another example of how in our time ideology cuts across national boundaries.

At present, the United States and the Soviet Union face each other as the predominant powers of the earth. Each is viewing world politics in a different light from the other.

Our policy-makers are thinking more in the old terms of nationalism, self-determination, and the balance of power. Soviet influence on Leftist parties the world over is looked upon largely as old-fashioned aggression and imperialism. There is widespread fear that Russia as Russia will upset the balance of power in Europe and Asia. Poland and Rumania and Bulgaria and Yugoslavia and China are appealed to by our government on the basis of national self-determination. (National self-determination, once a liberal rallying cry, has become also a conservative shibboleth.)

The Soviet leaders, on the other hand, are thinking more and more in terms of ideological conflict, class warfare, social politics. To Soviet policy-makers the contest in the world today is not so much one between the United States and Russia as it is between world fascism and world Communism. And those in other countries who follow the Soviet lead take much the same view. Communists and extreme Leftists the world over are giving their allegiance not so much to nations as to ideology. Russia is merely the instrument to be used in spreading ideology. Moscow influences Communist parties in all countries, and Communist parties everywhere influence Moscow. There is common indoctrination, consultation, co-operation. It is a two-way street, though the pre-eminence of Russia in the movement makes the outgoing counsel from Moscow weightier than the incoming counsel.

If a third world war should come—a war between the United States and the Soviet Union—for millions of Leftists the world over that war would be viewed almost exclusively as an ideological one. In countries where the extreme Left is in control, national policy would be made less on the balance-of-power idea and more on ideological considerations. In the United States, where Marxist ideas have scarcely penetrated at all, the war would be viewed in the old nationalistic terms. It would be a war to protect our shores from invasion, to uphold the balance of power, to save the world from Russian domination. As has already been said, in a final showdown nearly all of us would stand together. Our Communist fifth column would be smothered by the avalanche of nationalistic sentiment. American psychological warfare abroad would naturally reflect our own view of the situation, and we should probably err on the side of making too much appeal to nationalistic sentiments, which in large areas of the world would be effective only in Rightist circles. Our own failure to take into account the enormous strides the ideological point of view has made among the masses of people in Europe and Asia in recent decades, and particularly since the Second World War, might betray us into making very serious mistakes in the conduct of that war.

Should the Communists eventually win control in important countries outside Russia—in China, in Germany, in France, in Italy—it is quite possible that ideology would triumph over nationalism and a new international state emerge. After all, the nations themselves were built not so much on contract as on class and functional foundations. The feudal states of western Europe were put together into national states by the rising bourgeoisie joining hands across the boundaries of feudal provinces and communes. Just as the national state (which sometimes cut across nationality) was made by the bourgeoisie, so a new international state may be made by the co-operation of Leftist parties joining hands across national boundaries. If an international state should come about in this way, then, of course, the old balance of power as played by national states will be relegated to the historical limbo. The Communists still confidently expect that Communism will lead to such an international state.

Of course, the Communists may be wrong about this. Nationalistic forces may be stronger than Communist intentions. When the Communists come into actual power in a country they inherit the national paraphernalia—the nation's history, culture, aspirations—and concessions have to be made to them. The Russian Communists have made many concessions to nationalism. The Chinese Communists have often pursued a course independent of Moscow, and if they should gain actual power in all China they might have to follow an even more independent course. Thorez, Communist leader in France, says over and again: "Different countries, different methods." And the moderate Socialists, even more than the extreme Socialists or Communists, have, of course, made many more concessions to nationalism and have proclaimed this as a virtue. Moreover, if the United States should use the moderate Left (Socialists) to check the extreme Left (Communists), such a policy might help to prevent a third world war and also help to halt a trend towards a Communist world state with the Soviet Union as its nucleus. Then, too, it is even possible, as Edward Hallett Carr has suggested, that in a state where everybody's work and wages and social security are dependent upon government, where the mass of people will seem to have as direct a stake in the national government as at one time only the bourgeoisie enjoyed, the mass of people may feel even more keenly their tie to the national government, and Socialist states might end by being as nationalistic or even more nationalistic than bourgeoisie states. If this should turn out to be the case (although the Marxist analysis that private ownership of the productive processes and private profits are the basis of imperialism and international conflict may prove to be sounder) then Socialism, like the Commercial Revolution and the Protestant Reformation and the French Revolution and the early stages of the Industrial Revolution before it, will have ended by intensifying nationalism, in spite of the aims and intentions of many of its disciples. And then, should Socialism spread and thus turn out nationalistic, the old historic pattern of the national balance of power would continue the dominant role in international relations, even though Socialist and Communist states remained nominal members of an international organization like the United Nations.

Of one thing, I think, we can be sure: even the creation of an international Communist state would not end the conflict over power. Within the international state would be different social and economic groups with different interests. They would fight for control, just as groups and classes within national states now fight for control. The international state would end the national balance-of-power conflict, but it would not end the ideological conflict inside it. The ideological conflict of the future will be different, but it will continue in some form. Even if the Marxists should achieve one-half of their ideal, the international state, they would not succeed in achieving the other half —the abolition of all its internal group differences. Within the international state would be geographical sections, cultural diversities, a wide gamut of different industries and economic enterprises, and various social classes: commissars, managers, engineers, technicians, skilled workers, unskilled workers, farmers, and so forth. These various factors and groups would generate conflict over government policies and there would arise struggles for power which even Communist purges could not keep down. These struggles would cut across the old national boundaries.

In short, evidence is already strong that the Marxists may be able to make the ideological conflict rather than the national conflict the pivot of mid-twentieth-century international politics. As a result of this ideological conflict the more extreme Marxists—the Communists—may even be able to establish an international Communist state, but this is far less certain either because they may not win the ultimate international conflict even after succeeding in making the issue an ideological issue, or because the forces of nationalism may be too strong for the Communists once they inherit the various national governments. But even should the Communists win and establish an international Communist state, it is almost certain that new social and economic groups would arise to continue the struggle for power within the international state, peacefully perhaps, but a struggle none the less. If so, then national conflict over the balance of power would disappear, but ideological conflict within the international state would persist.

Should there be a third world war and should the United States, using the old shibboleths of nationalism, win the war, it is doubtful even then if political nationalism and the balance of power would continue as they have done in the past. We are perhaps too close to events of the last thirty years to be able to see just how far the old foundations of nationalism have already been eroded away. In the fifteenth century, participants in the wars of Louis XI and in the Wars of the Roses were too close to those events to realize that feudal power was being overthrown before their very eyes and a strong national power built. So probably with us today. The historians of the twenty-second century, more clear-eyed than we, may look back and see that the great international wars of the twentieth century were in fact dissolving nationalism and building internationalism.

For nationalism today is truly beset from all directions. Among the dissolving agents are: the cumulative impact of technology and science resulting in the continued drastic elimination of distance and space, the atomic bomb, the release of atomic energy, and the overwhelming necessity of having to extend international functionalism to control what in the future will probably be the world's most important source of industrial production; the palpable absurdities of fascist nationalism and the revulsion from fascist nationalism even in countries which experienced it; the realistic education given millions of men who participated in the great wars of the twentieth century in areas remote from their homelands; the glaring fact that real national power in the international power conflict is today possessed by only two nations, leaving all other nations as mere outsiders with no important power;

the growth of international cartels; the Socialist appeal to the brotherhood of man; the Communist insistence on international action and the actual co-operation of Communist parties from country to country; the Socialist outlook of many of the "nationalistic" leaders of the colonial countries in revolt against imperialism; the body of practical experience in international co-operation gained through the League of Nations and the United Nations. The Communists would put the world together through something like a Communist International; a majority of the people of Britain and the United States would prefer to see the world put together by the slow functional growth of an organization which originated in contract—the United Nations. (Inside the United Nations, too, there would, of course, be power politics, but as international functionalism grew it would come to be less and less power politics based on nationalism and more and more power politics based on ideology, that is, group and class conflicts cutting across the old national lines.) And there are those, like James Burnham and the oversimplifiers and distorters of Arnold Toynbee, who are so impatient with the slower and wiser methods of bringing an international state that they would have America attempt to build a "universal empire" to end "a time of troubles." Whatever method of putting the world together will ultimately prevail is still anybody's guess, but that the world in our time is in painful process of being put together is more than a guess—it is a hypothesis based upon a growing accumulation of evidence.

Thus anyone called upon to answer the crucial question in international relations today would be, I think, on safe ground in saying that, from the rise of national states and up to about now, the chief element in international relations has been nationalism and the national balance of power. But he should warn the questioner not to be misled by this historic fact or by the superficial aspects of the present diplomatic duel between the United States and the Soviet Union, especially as that duel is generally interpreted in the United States. Because this middle of the twentieth century may be witnessing the epoch-making shift in the foundation of international politics from the nationalistic balance of power to ideology, evidence of which we shall ignore at our peril.

A Case Study:
The Great Powers in 1939*

BY MARTIN WIGHT

[1952]

Western Powers. "It is true that the present arrangement of the world has some of the characteristics of a hegemony of the Anglo-Saxon and French nations. It is also true that the establishment of their great empires and spheres of interest in the extra-European world was largely brought about by aggressions which, on the whole, few people now seek to defend morally. However, we have now embarked on the endeavour to turn the former anarchy of international relations into a reign of law and order and a reasonable measure of justice, such as has already been achieved on the whole in the national life of the more advanced countries of the world today. The League of Nations provides a basis for approximating towards a higher concept of civilization and an unprecedented degree of world co-operation."

Axis Powers. "Is it difficult for you to understand that for us the League of Nations is simply part of the Versailles Treaty? that it is an expression of the predominance you achieved at the end of the World War? We suspected from the outset that the League was to be only a coalition of the rich nations against the proletarian nations. And our suspicion has been confirmed by the consistent neglect of that part of the League Covenant which provides for revision of treaties, and the employment of those parts that are concerned with the maintenance of the established order, as in the attempt to strangle Italy by sanctions."

Western Powers. "It is true that the League is part of the Versailles Settlement. But we believe that the Versailles Settlement is far from being unjust. You yourselves pay lip-service to the principle of national self-determination. The Versailles Settlement has reorganized Europe on that principle with a much higher degree of honesty, reasonableness, disinterestedness, and success than might have been expected, and

* From "The Balance of Power" by Martin Wight in *Survey of International Affairs 1939-1946. The World in March 1939.* Ed. by Arnold Toynbee and Frank T. Ashton-Gwatkin. Issued under the auspices of the Royal Institute of International Affairs, Oxford University Press, 1952. Reprinted by permission.

certainly in a manner never before attempted by any general European treaty."

Axis Powers. "A treaty brutally dictated to the defeated Powers; which severed or excluded more than 10 million Germans from their fatherland; which partitioned Hungary so that a third of the Hungarian nation passed under alien rule. A treaty which ignored or violated the promises made to Italy during the war. A treaty, anyway, which is obsolete. Have you sufficiently recognized the fact that two of us were your allies in the war, but have long ago ceased to accept the authority of the Versailles Settlement? Twenty years have passed since 1919, and you seek, by appealing to age-yellowed archives, to arrest the outward march, the dynamic growth of the young and virile nations. What solution have you to offer to these practical and imperative problems— the desire for reunion of 80 million Germans and their demand for the return of their stolen colonies, the need for expansion of Italy and Japan with their soaring birth-rates and their inadequate resources?"

Soviet Union. "Neither the Western Powers nor yourselves have the answer to that question, nor the solutions for those problems. They are economic problems which cannot be solved within the limits of the system of production which you all alike exist to maintain. The most important thing about the First World War was not that it produced a new division of the world between the imperialist Powers, for that division (as your argument itself shows) was inherently unstable, and is now being challenged by the Fascist states for the sake of a new division of the world that would not be less unstable. Such is the predatory nature, such is the inner contradiction of imperialism. But during the First World War the imperialist crust was broken at its weakest point by the international revolutionary working-class movement, and there was established in Russia the first proletarian state. From then on there were two camps in the world, a capitalist camp originally led by Britain and America and a socialist camp led by the Soviet Union. If the rise of Fascism has since seemed to confuse this alinement, it is only the supreme example of the conflicts and antagonisms that are generated by capitalism in extreme decay. Fascism is the open terrorist dictatorship established against the rising revolt of the working class by the most aggressive, chauvinist, and reactionary elements of finance-capitalism; and it is at the same time the highest expression of the preparation for a new imperialist war to redivide the spoils of the world. Thus it is that the hopes of all progressive mankind are fixed on the Soviet Union, where Socialism holds power, and the economic system which produces this anarchy of possessors and pursuers has over one-sixth of the earth been for ever transcended."

Axis Powers. "We who have had practical experience of the revolutions, disturbances, and bloody uprisings produced by Bolshevism in our own countries, and who have successfully undertaken the duty of stamping it out, know best how to answer the pretensions of international Marxism. Whatever its philosophical claims, Bolshevism breeds anarchy. Soviet Russia is the exponent of an international political system which promotes world unrest with the declared aim of world revolution. For the natural and living solidarity of the nation and of the state, Marxism tries to substitute an international solidarity of the proletariat, and pursues that end by disseminating strife, bloodshed, and violence. For spiritual and cultural values, for heroism and leadership, for the creative work of great men and gifted races, it offers the negative and inhuman doctrine of historical materialism, by which men would be only the by-products of economic forces. Thus Marxism is a solvent of all the beliefs and ties we hold most sacred, of our whole human order in state and society. Far from being a higher stage of social development, Communism is the starting-point, the most primitive form of existence: it means a retrogression in every aspect of culture and the subversion of our faith, our morals, and our whole conception of civilization. We who understand this are the bulwark of European discipline and civilization against the enemy of mankind, and by taking upon ourselves the struggle against Bolshevism we are undertaking a truly European mission, which sooner or later the Western Powers will be compelled to recognize."

Western Powers. "We must say that your talk of the menace of Bolshevism and your crusade against it seem to us to be disingenuous. We were ready to believe in the danger of Communism until your immoderate insistence on it (together with your other activities) made us begin to think that we might be faced by more immediate dangers. We suspect that the Anti-Comintern Pact may be a good piece of propaganda, serving to conceal your designs against us. From our point of view the similarities between yourselves and Russia are not less striking than the contrasts. You and she are all alike totalitarian states, copying one another's methods and profiting from one another's existence in a dialectic of interdependent hostility. You are all equally far from democracy as we understand it and value it; and this indeed underlies the lack of confidence we have generally felt about the possibility of successful co-operation with Russia. But, however that may be, we do not think it useful to enter into argument about the ideological inter-pretation of our international tensions. Our approach is empirical, and we have been hoping to build a law-abiding society in which we could all make our contribution to the common good of mankind according to our several lights. That is why our immediate controversy is with you, the Axis Powers. We are ready to admit considerable truth in what you have said about your economic problems, and latterly in particular we have gone far to meet you. We are ready to discuss the revision of treaties and the redistribution of the resources of the globe—or at least, the question of your easier access to them. But it is impossible to start discussions unless you honestly accept the prin-ciple of negotiation and repudiate the principle of force. So long as we live in expectation of acts of aggression and *faits accomplis* from you there can be no confidence between us, and it is impossible for the normal machinery of diplomatic intercourse to be effective. It is our view that the system of international law and order which we now possess, based on the Versailles Settlement and inadequate in many respects as it is, is as precious as it is fragile, and that to respect it and seek its gradual modification is a much surer road towards justice than are acts of violence which endanger our common interests and destroy the foundations of orderliness upon which alone justice can be built."

Axis Powers. "But it has been our experience that we have never ob-tained what we believe to be justice by the normal machinery of diplo-matic intercourse, as you call it, by conferences, in a word by waiting for you. We have obtained it by the process of being strong enough to take it for ourselves. (Sometimes you have then called conferences to pronounce a verbal condemnation of our act, which has satisfied you without bothering us; of recent years, however, as we have grown stronger, you have shown greater readiness to excuse and condone our acts—a development that we welcome.) And we believe that this pro-cedure, of relying upon our own strength to defend our interests, is as a matter of fact far more normal than what you call 'the normal machinery of diplomatic intercourse.' Indeed we have the feeling that throughout this argument we are talking about *facts,* about the forces that govern history and make the real stuff of politics, while you are talking about *theories,* about legal abstractions and moral utopias. We are realists, and perhaps we understand the nature of international relations more clearly than you do. Man's existence is subject to the law of eternal struggle; men, by a natural law, always rule where they are stronger. We have not made this law, nor are we the first to act on it; we see it existing, and you yourselves have supplied the precedent. You cannot expect to arrest the process of history at the point at which you happen to be on top; at least you cannot expect less favoured nations to share your hope. It is plain to us that liberal democracy is exhausted and decadent, and that all the vital movements of the present century are anti-liberal. We believe that the process by which you—English, French, and Americans alike—built your empires at the expense of the Spanish world-empire or of the Habsburg Monarchy in Europe is likely to be repeated in the present century in favour of new and dynamic Powers like ourselves. The only question that remains is whether you are ready to co-operate with the onward march of history, in which case we shall be ready to give consideration to your legitimate interests, or whether, by a selfish and useless obstruction, you will bring about a head-on collision between us which we should be glad to avoid."

Soviet Union. "When you identify 'the process of history' with the sterile struggles of imperialism, it becomes necessary once again to assert a secure and scientific interpretation of that process. It is true that the hegemony of the Western Powers is not the culmination of history: it represents only the highest stage capable of being reached by the bourgeois order. The disruption of that order is historically inevitable, because it breaks on its own contradictions and because out of those very contradictions the forces of the future grow in strength. But Fascism, aggressive socially as well as internationally, and seeking to reduce the working class, above all in Russia, once again to slavery, follows a policy which can divert the path to the ultimate world socialist organization through an epoch of immense destruction and human suffering. That is why the Soviet Union, which came into existence in the struggle of the working class against the First World War, and whose earliest action was the famous decree calling for immediate peace without annexations and without indemnities, has consistently fought to avert the menace of a new imperialist war. That is why, in these last years, the Soviet Union has entered the League of Nations and put itself at the head of those elements within imperialism which are against immediate war, and thus carries on its historic role in actively leading the struggle for peace of the peoples of all countries."

Western Powers. "Though we naturally do not agree with the terms in which you state your case, we acknowledge some degree of force in what you say. Indeed we confess that, in certain moods, the Marxist analysis of recent history has seemed cogent to us, and made us wish to believe that what divides us from you is a disagreement about means rather than an incompatibility of ends. But more important for our immediate purpose, we are happy to recognize that you, like us, are anxious above all for peace. This leads us to hope that, if the Axis Powers insist on pursuing their objectives by other than peaceful means, it may be possible to co-operate with you in the preservation of our common security. For we must make one thing clear to the Axis Powers without more ado: that if their final appeal is to force, we shall meet them with force. It is true that, since 1914, aversion to war as a means of policy has become one of our accepted principles; and so great indeed is our reluctance to consider it that sometimes optimism may have swayed our judgment, and encouraged us to speak as if we did not think war possible. If this be an illusion (and that will be shown by what you, the Axis Powers, decide to do) it may be creditable to our hearts rather than our heads, but we cannot think it dishonourable. Nevertheless, do not be mistaken. In the last analysis you will find us defending our interests and fulfilling our obligations as stubbornly as yourselves. We feel it necessary to say this so that you may make no mistake about it."

Axis Powers. "We are glad to have an admission from your own mouths of your Marxist foible. We have always thought that the decadence of liberal democracy was in nothing more clearly shown than in its inherent drift towards Communism. As for your declarations of contingent defiance, they are the common form of diplomacy, and we shall know what value to give them. We have noted that as our power has increased your resolution appears to have faltered; and it has been natural for us to entertain the idea that you may after all be prepared to acquiesce in the establishment of a more just order in the world."

Western Powers. "You are making another mistake, more far-reaching than the first, if you assume that our readiness in recent years to go to such lengths to seek an accommodation with you has been altogether inspired by material weakness. It is at this point, thanks to the frankness with which you have been speaking, that our fundamental differences are laid bare. You spoke just now as if the forces which you claim to represent are the only 'facts' in history; but we believe that morality and the conscience of mankind are equally facts that must be taken into account. We believe that civilization consists, not in the mere assertion of vitality, impulse, and will, but in their control; not in the exhibition and accumulation of force, but in disciplining it to serve settled habits of persuasion and law, and so reducing as far as possible the need for its use. Thus our dealings with you in these two decades have been grounded upon the premiss that another war would be an immeasurable disaster for all of us, and that the test of civilization is its ability to avert such a catastrophe."

Soviet Union. "The point at which you say 'your fundamental differences are laid bare' appears, in an objective view, to be the point at which your fundamental similarities to the Fascist states are revealed. Your sentiments are formally irreproachable; it is when they are compared with your practice that their value becomes apparent. Your readiness to seek an accommodation with the Fascist Powers, your efforts to avoid another war, have been entirely at the expense of other states, not of your own interests. Your policy of non-intervention has sacrificed to the aggressors successively China, Abyssinia, Spain, Austria, and now Czechoslovakia. The Soviet Union has reason to know this, since it alone has striven to enforce the policy of collective security on which you congratulate yourselves. During the Italo-Ethiopian War it was only the Soviet Union who took a firm and honest stand against imperialist aggression; since then only the Soviet Union has striven to obtain collective action against German aggressions. You have abandoned the policy of collective security for a policy of non-intervention, whereby you seek only to defend yourselves, and make no discrimination between the aggressors and their victims. It is not for the Soviet Union to moralize upon this, for the policy of non-intervention simply shows that in practice bourgeois politicians acknowledge no human morality at all. It is only necessary to point out that such a policy of cynical self-interest, while it is all that can be expected from bourgeois states, is based upon a fundamental miscalculation and will inevitably accelerate the imperialist war which it pretends to avert."

Axis Powers. "We have no concern with this quarrel between the supporters of the Geneva institution, except that it confirms our belief in the Geneva institution's futility. But we decisively repudiate the assumption which underlies the arguments of the Western Powers, that they are still as ever the guardians and interpreters of civilization.

This conscious assumption of effortless superiority is all the more offensive in that it has become obsolete and hypocritical. You who remind us of the sanctity of international obligations broke your assurances to Germany after the Armistice of 1918. You who exhort us to settle international problems by peaceful discussion have solved no decisive international problem in that way through the League of Nations, and the greatest of you has refused to join the League. You who condemn our struggle for living space (a struggle which in the European field has been successfully carried on without resort to arms) possess vast empty territories, with illimitable fertility and mineral resources, and a density of population that is inconsiderable compared with ours. You who attribute all the unrest in the world to us ignore your own continuing record of violence, bloodshed, and oppression in Ireland, Egypt, Palestine, Syria, India, and Latin America."

Western Powers. "It is the weakness of open diplomacy, which we invented and you have perverted, that it reduces diplomatic intercourse to a competition of simultaneous gramophone programmes in unrelated languages. We have honestly sought to give weight to your views and to meet your reasonable demands, but our divided conscience about the lengths to which we have gone is likely in the long run to be forgotten and overlaid by anger at the realization that you have made no attempt to meet us."

Soviet Union. "You are wrong: open diplomacy was inaugurated not by Wilson but by the Soviet Government, with the publication of the imperialist secret treaties immediately after the October Revolution. But the forms of diplomacy are less important than the forces of politics, and understanding is to be inferred from facts rather than from arguments. Why have the Western Powers abandoned their professions of collective security and adopted a policy of non-intervention? Because in the last resort all capitalist states, whether aggressive or non-aggressive, have a common fear of the working-class movement throughout the world, and a common hostility to the U.S.S.R. From the first establishment of Mussolini in Italy and of Hitler in Germany the governments of the Western states have consistently courted Fascism, for the governments of the Western states represent the same social forces which in Italy and Germany brought Fascism into being. Thus the first diplomatic repercussion of the Nazi Revolution in Germany was the project for a Four-Power Pact of Italy,

Germany, France, and England, which by excluding the Soviet Union was implicitly directed against her. Since then the Western policy of non-intervention has in fact been a policy of conniving at and encouraging aggression. Behind the readiness of the Western Powers to sacrifice small and weak states to the greed of the Fascist Powers lies the hope of directing the Fascist Powers against the U.S.S.R. The policy of the Four-Power Pact and the policy of non-intervention together culminated in the Munich Conference, when the four European capitalist Powers met together, to arrange the partition of Czechoslovakia and again deliberately excluded the Soviet Union. The lesson of these facts is inescapable. The Soviet Union is well able to draw the lesson and to defend its own interests, which are the interests of humanity at large, by every means that the current diplomatic and political situation may offer."

This was the state of the argument between the Great Powers on 15 March 1939. At that time the balance of power appeared extremely fluid owing to the imbecility of Western policy, the arbitrariness and caprice of German, the inscrutability of Russian. Great Power relationships fell into an equilateral triangle; and it was possible for different observers to convince themselves that destiny would be fulfilled by the alliance of the Western Powers with Russia to encircle Germany, or of Russia with Germany to overbalance the Western Powers, or of the Western Powers with the Fascist Powers against the interests of Russia. Each of these combinations had its historical precedents. . . . Each of these combinations had its arguments from interest. . . .

This fluid threefold arrangement of power not only made it uncertain on what alinements the coming war would be fought. It also showed, though few saw it at the time, that those alinements would be temporary and precarious. The victors in the war, whoever they were, would be only an incongruous *ad hoc* combination of Powers. If the Axis were to defeat the Western Powers with the co-operation or the benevolent neutrality of Russia, the Axis and Russia would not be likely thereafter to set up an international organization for the harmonious future ordering of the world. Alternatively if Germany with the tacit encouragement of the Western Powers were to conquer Russia, the turn of the Western Powers would follow. Even if the Axis Powers by their unaided strength were to defeat successively both the Western Powers and Russia, partitioning the world between themselves, it would soon become clear that the Axis was a fortuitous coalition for predatory purposes, and Germany and Japan would probably proceed to a further struggle for ultimate mastery. And if the Western Powers in alliance with Russia were to defeat the Axis, the future co-operation of such ill-assorted and suspicious partners could only be assumed by those who ignored the gulf between the Byzantino-Marxist ideology of the Soviet Union and the liberalism of the West.

The Rivalry of Nations*

BY WALTER LIPPMANN

[1948]

IF we study the history of American foreign relations during the past forty years, we must be struck by an extraordinary paradox. During this period the United States has emerged from its long isolation. It has become one of the leading powers of the world. Not once but twice during this period the American people have had to face the awful issues of war and peace. Can it be said that during this momentous period we have ever succeeded in forming and agreeing on a foreign policy which foresaw correctly and enabled us to deal successfully with the actual course of events? The record is, I think, clear. We have won both wars. But on the crucial issues our diplomacy has thus far always miscarried. It has been unable to prevent war. It has been unable to avoid war. It has not prepared us for war. It has not been able to settle the wars when they have been fought and won.

At no critical phase in this epoch has the actual outcome conformed with our declarations and our expectations. Never has the country been able to achieve any of the principal objectives to which again and again it has been so solemnly and fervently committed.

Thus from 1914 to 1917 the country believed and hoped that it could avoid participation in the First World War. Yet it was compelled to participate. And when it did participate, it was unprepared because it had believed that it would not have to participate. During that war the country hoped and believed that by a victory it would achieve a lasting and democratic peace. The victory was attained. But the peace which had been promised was not achieved. After the First World War the country again believed that if there were another war, it would be able to remain out of it. Again it did not prepare for war. Once again it was unable to remain out of the war when it came.

* From *The Atlantic Monthly*, February 1948. Copyright 1948 by The Atlantic Monthly Co. Reprinted by permission.

During the Second World War the country again believed that with victory over the Germans there would begin an era in which all the victorious powers would agree and be harmonious and become unanimous on the terms and conditions of a just and durable peace. We have had the victory. But we have not been able to attain that peace.

Now, after two victorious world wars we find ourselves discussing the possibility of a third world war. And so we must ask ourselves whether we have become entangled in a degenerating cycle of wars that breed more wars, each more savage and more inconclusive than the last. It is a grim question. We must, however, face it; and I believe that we must answer it by saying that if our present estimates and calculations are no more correct than those on which we acted before, during, and immediately after the First and Second World Wars, then we shall be surprised and disappointed again. Once more we shall not know how to prevent war, or how to prepare for it correctly, or how, assuming we win it, to make peace after it. And if a second world war leads to the third—because we cannot make a settlement of the war we have just won—what ground is there to suppose that we could settle a third world war so that it did not lead to a fourth?

Is it not true that in the twentieth century we have witnessed on the one hand the rise of the United States to pre-eminence among the nations, to a position of great leadership and immense responsibility in shaping the destiny of mankind? And on the other hand, is it not also true that the course of events during the American rise to pre-eminence is strewn with the debris and wreckage of high and hopeful declarations of policy: with Wilson's neutrality, Wilson's Fourteen Points, and the Covenant of the League of Nations; with the Washington treaties of disarmament and the Kellogg pact to outlaw war; with the Dawes Plan, the Young Plan, and the Hoover Moratorium to reconstruct the world after the First World War; with the Stimson doctrine to prevent aggression; with the Neutrality Act before the Second World War; with the quarantine speech of Franklin Roosevelt, and the Four Freedoms, and Hull's Seventeen Points, and the Atlantic Charter, and the Yalta Declaration, and the Truman Doctrine?

When we reflect on this series of declarations and the disappointments which followed them all, we must be struck by the contrast between our capacity as a people to develop national power, and our ability to use it and to manage it successfully. And is it not plain that our failures lie in the field of policy—that is to say, in deciding correctly when, where, how, and to what ends we shall exert the enormous power and influence which we are able to generate?

It cannot be argued that the miscarriages of American diplomacy during the past forty years are due to the weakness of the American nation. Among the powers of the world the United States is the least vulnerable to invasion, to blockade, or, with existing weapons, to decisive assault. The United States has the material resources and it has the productive capacity to develop enormous offensive power in time of war. In time of peace it produces a great export surplus —a surplus above and beyond a high standard of life at home— which renders it economically invulnerable in the outer world. Two great wars have proved the valor of American troops, the fortitude of the American people, and the military competence of American military commanders. Our institutions and our traditions are respected. And on the whole our participation in world affairs is welcomed by the great masses of mankind as promising liberty, justice, peace, and plenty.

We must seek the cause of our diplomatic failures, therefore, in our own minds. We must look for the cause of trouble not in material circumstances but in our own habits of thought when we are dealing with foreign affairs and with the formation of American policy. In the period from Woodrow Wilson to Harry S. Truman our foreign policy has miscarried so regularly because there has been interposed within our own minds, between the outer world and ourselves, a collection of stereotyped prejudices and sacred cows and wishful conceptions, which misrepresent the nature of things, which falsify our judgments of events, and which inhibit the formation of workable policies by which our available means can be devoted efficiently to realizable ends.

We have brought along with us from our age of innocence, from the nineteenth century when we were isolated and when we were sheltered from the rivalries of states and empires, an ideological picture of the world, a philosophical framework of preconceptions. We think this picture of the world is real and noble. In fact it is imaginary and false. And because our philosophy of the nature of international life is imaginary and false our efforts to play an effective part in world affairs are frustrated.

What then is it in our philosophy which, instead of guiding us, misguides us continually? I think that the question can be answered. The point, as I have already indicated, where our declarations of policy have regularly miscarried is in avoiding war, in preparing for war, and in settling wars. We must ask ourselves whether there is here some common factor of error which confuses all of us on the issues of war and peace. I think there is. I think the error is a refusal to recognize, to admit, to take as the premise of our thinking, the fact that rivalry and strife and conflict among states, communities, and factions are the normal condition of mankind. The popular American philosophy of international life refuses to recognize this fact. It denies that in the world as it is, the struggle for existence is fundamental and in the nature of things. This, I believe, is the philosophical error which prevents us from forming an effective foreign policy.

In the American ideology the struggle for existence, and the rivalry of nations for advantages, are held to be wrong, abnormal, and transitory. Our foreign policy throughout this period has been dominated by the belief that the struggle does not exist, or that it can be avoided, or that it can be abolished. Because of this belief our aim has not been to regulate and to moderate and to compose the conflicts and the issues, to check and to balance the contending forces. Our aim has been either to abstain from the struggle, or to abolish the struggle immediately, or to conduct crusades against those nations that most actively continue the struggle.

Yet in the world as it actually is, the struggle is not abnormal, and it is perpetually renewed. Twice during this period we have sought to abstain from the struggle by declaring our neutrality. We have not been able to stay out of it. Twice we have conducted victorious crusades against the chief troublemaker, believing what was soon disproved by events: that if he could be eliminated, we would then have eliminated all troublemakers. Twice we have sought, by forming universal societies like the League of Nations and the United Nations, to abolish the struggle. They have not abolished the struggle.

Our refusal to recognize the struggle for existence as the normal state of mankind in international affairs has resulted in the repeated miscarriage of American policies. Our efforts to deal with events, as if they conformed or could be made to conform with our ideological picture of what they ought to be, has been rather like using a map of Utopia to find your way around New York City.

The American refusal to recognize the struggle for existence has in this century crystallized in three recognizable patterns of conduct: in a neutrality which assumes that the struggle can be ignored and avoided; in crusades that assume that by defeating the chief troublemaker the struggle for existence will end; in the sponsorship of a universal society which assumes that the struggle can be abolished.

Since 1914 American relations with the outer world have oscillated among these three patterns of conduct. The great debates within this country have turned upon them. But the experience of these forty years show conclusively, I think, that if we insist on treating the conflict of states, communities, and factions as abnormal, as exceptional, as transitory, we are unable to form an efficient foreign policy. Our American ideology, which we have brought over from a time when we did not have to play a responsible part among the powers of the earth, distorts our judgment when we deal with the problems of power. It distorts our judgment when we have to calculate how a balance can be struck between our aims and our power to realize them.

In practical judgments—and diplomacy, when the stakes are life and death, calls for very practical judgments—the criteria are always relative. There is no such thing as absolute power. Whatever the wealth, the power, and the prestige of a nation may be, its means are always limited. The problem of the maker of policy is to select objectives that are limited—not the best that could be desired but the best that can be realized without committing the whole power and the whole wealth and the very existence of the nation.

But if we examine the issues of foreign policy as they are presented to our people, we find an overwhelming disposition to regard the choices before us not as relative but as absolute. We are disposed to think that the issue is either this or that, either all or nothing, either isolationism or globalism, either total peace or total war, either one world or no world, either disarmament or absolute weapons, either pious resolutions or atomic bombs, either disarmament or military supremacy, either nonintervention or a crusade, either democracy or tyranny, either the abolition of war or a preventive war, either appeasement or unconditional surrender, either non-resistance or a strategy of annihilation.

There is no place in this ideological pattern of the world for the adoption of limited ends or limited means, for the use of checks and balances among contending forces, for the demarcation of spheres of influence and of power and of interest, for accommodation and compromise and adjustment, for the stabilization of the status quo, for the restoration of an equilibrium. Yet this is the field of diplomacy. These are the substance and the matter of an efficient diplomacy.

Our ideologists, however, regard the use of power to achieve and maintain an equilibrium of power as "power politics." And they regard the recognition of spheres of influence as "appeasement." Yet in the absence of a world state, and except in a world dominated by one supreme power, there must be an equilibrium among several powers and a recognition of their spheres of influence. A diplomacy for the world as it is, which is not to expend itself in verbal declarations on the one hand, and on crusades of annihilation on the other, must deal with the balance of power and the determination of spheres of influence.

But under the spell of our ideological picture of the world, we exclude from our minds the very subject matter of diplomacy itself. We would exclude it, we would outlaw it, and we would excommunicate those who discuss it. We insist on treating the rivalry of nations as something that could not exist among right-thinking men. We do not regulate the rivalries because we hold that the rivalries ought not to exist. And so we are left with our three patterns of policy: to ignore the rivalries by proclaiming our neutrality, or to deny the rivalry and to believe it will disappear if the nations are members of a universal society, or to conduct crusades of annihilation against the lions who do not wish to lie down with the lambs.

How does what I have been saying bear upon the subject which preoccupies us all so anxiously and so profoundly—upon our relations with the Soviet Union, with which we are now engaged in a world-wide diplomatic conflict?

The beginning of wisdom on the Russian question is, I believe, to recognize the historic fact that the division between eastern and western Europe, the rivalry between Russia and the nations of the West, did not begin with Marx, Lenin, and Stalin, nor would it end if the Soviet regime were overthrown or defeated. The cultural and ideological division of Europe is as old as the division of Christendom between Rome and Byzantium. The imperial rivalry with Russia in the Baltic, in eastern and central Europe, in the Danube valley, in the Balkans, in the Middle East, and in the Far East did not begin with the Communists and will not end with Communism. It was one of the great fields of diplomacy under the Czars as it is under the Communists. Rivalry with Russia is a new problem for the United States. But the British Foreign Office has been preoccupied with it for a hundred and fifty years. We had better make up our minds that we shall now be preoccupied with it for a very long time to come.

That being the case, we must give up the notion that the choice is between one world, in which the Russians are our partners, and two worlds, in which we must annihilate the Russians or they must annihilate us. I do not believe that we must either marry the Russians or must fight them, that we must have either a perfect peace or a total war. I believe that the best policy is to recognize that the rivalry will remain, and not to expect it to disappear, and not to think it could be abolished by the United Nations, and not to think it could be abolished by a victorious war; and having recognized that the rivalry is a permanent fact, to use our whole power and influence to regulate it, to keep it within bounds, to establish spheres of influence which limit the rivalry, and a balance of power in the world which checks it.

I do not believe that we can settle the Russian problem once and for all. I do believe we have enough power and influence, if we use them efficiently, to bring about a settlement with Russia in this generation. But it will have to be a settlement which aims not at unanimity, not at ideological harmony, not at the abolition of all our differences and disagreements, but at a truce in the cold war, a *modus vivendi* during which the nations can recover from World War II, at treaties which end in the withdrawal of the armies of occupation in Europe, and the restoration of Europe to the Europeans.

This will not be easy to achieve. It will require the pressure of power—which will offend those among us who do not like power politics. It will require political and economic compromises—which will offend those who regard all compromise as appeasement. But if a truce, and a *modus vivendi,* and a treaty are hard to achieve by power and by compromise, it is certain that without power on the one hand, and compromise on the other, nothing can be achieved.

If we will not or cannot use the classic procedure of diplomacy—which is always a combination of power and compromise—then the best we can look forward to is an era of disintegration in the civilized world, followed perhaps by a war which, once it began, would be savage, universal, and indecisive.

That must not happen. And it need not happen if only our people will abjure their illusions about the nature of the world in which they have so recently become a leading power, and will permit and assist those who must form our policy, to go forward on the assumption that our aim is not to marry the Russians and then to live with them happily ever after, nor to fight them and let the whole world be devastated. Our aim is to transact our necessary business with the Russians, at arm's length, coolly, shrewdly, without fear and without extravagant hope, and with as much justice as may be possible where there is as yet no agreement on first principles and where the rivals do not live in the same moral order.

IX

INTERNATIONAL ORGANIZATION
AND WORLD GOVERNMENT

A League for Permanent Peace*

BY WOODROW WILSON

[1917]

I HAVE sought this opportunity to address you because I thought that I owed it to you, as the council associated with me in the final determination of our international obligations, to disclose to you without reserve the thought and purpose that have been taking form in my mind in regard to the duty of our Government in the days to come when it will be necessary to lay afresh and upon a new plan the foundations of peace among nations.

It is inconceivable that the people of the United States should play no part in that great enterprise. To take part in such a service will be the opportunity for which they have sought to prepare themselves by the very principles and purposes of their polity and the approved practices of their Government ever since the days when they set up a new nation in the high and honorable hope that it might in all that it was and did show mankind the way to liberty. They cannot in honor withhold the service to which they are now about to be challenged. They do not wish to withhold it. But they owe it to themselves and to the other nations of the world to state the conditions under which they will feel free to render it.

That service is nothing less than this, to add their authority and their power to the authority and force of other nations to guarantee peace and justice throughout the world. Such a settlement cannot now be long postponed. It is right that before it comes this Government should frankly formulate the conditions upon which it would feel justified in asking our people to approve its formal and solemn adherence to a league for peace. I am here to attempt to state those conditions.

The present war must first be ended; but we owe it to candor and to a just regard for the opinion of mankind to say that, so far as our participation in guarantees of future peace is concerned, it makes a

* Address delivered to the Senate, Jan. 22, 1917. From *Messages and Papers of the Presidents*, Vol. XVII. Published by Bureau of National Literature, Inc.

great deal of difference in what way and upon what terms it is ended. The treaties and agreements which bring it to an end must embody terms which will create a peace that is worth guaranteeing and preserving, a peace that will win the approval of mankind, not merely a peace that will serve the several interests and immediate aims of the nations engaged. We shall have no voice in determining what those terms shall be, but we shall, I feel sure, have a voice in determining whether they shall be made lasting or not by the guarantees of a universal covenant; and our judgment upon what is fundamental and essential as a condition precedent to permanency should be spoken now, not afterwards when it may be too late.

No covenant or co-operative peace that does not include the peoples of the New World can suffice to keep the future safe against war; and yet there is only one sort of peace that the peoples of America could join in guaranteeing. The elements of that peace must be elements that engage the confidence and satisfy the principles of the American governments, elements consistent with their political faith and with the practical convictions which the peoples of America have once for all embraced and undertaken to defend.

I do not mean to say that any American government would throw any obstacle in the way of any terms of peace the governments now at war might agree upon, or seek to upset them when made, whatever they might be. I only take it for granted that mere terms of peace between the belligerents will not satisfy even the belligerents themselves. Mere agreements may not make peace secure. It will be absolutely necessary that a force be created as a guarantor of the permanency of the settlement so much greater than the force of any nation now engaged or any alliance hitherto formed or projected that no nation, no probable combination of nations could face or withstand it. If the peace presently to be made is to endure, it must be a peace made secure by the organized major force of mankind.

The terms of the immediate peace agreed upon will determine whether it is a peace for which such a guarantee can be secured. The question upon which the whole future peace and policy of the world depends is this: Is the present war a struggle for a just and secure peace, or only for a new balance of power? If it be only a struggle for a new balance of power, who will guarantee, who can guarantee, the stable equilibrium of the new arrangement? Only a tranquil Europe can be a stable Europe. There must be, not a balance of power, but a community of power; not organized rivalries, but an organized common peace.

. . . Only a peace between equals can last. Only a peace the very principle of which is equality and a common participation in a common benefit. The right state of mind, the right feeling between nations, is as necessary for a lasting peace as is the just settlement of vexed questions of territory or of racial and national allegiance.

The equality of nations upon which peace must be founded if it is to last must be an equality of rights; the guarantees exchanged must neither recognize nor imply a difference between big nations and small, between those that are powerful and those that are weak. Right must be based upon the common strength, not upon the individual strength, of the nations upon whose concert peace will depend. Equality of territory or of resources there of course cannot be; nor any other sort of equality not gained in the ordinary peaceful and legitimate development of the peoples themselves. But no one asks or expects anything more than an equality of rights. Mankind is looking now for freedom of life, not for equipoises of power.

And there is a deeper thing involved than even equality of right among organized nations. No peace can last, or ought to last, which does not recognize and accept the principle that governments derive all their just powers from the consent of the governed, and that no right anywhere exists to hand peoples about from sovereignty to sovereignty as if they were property. I take it for granted, for instance, if I may venture upon a single example, that statesmen everywhere are agreed that there should be a united, independent, and autonomous Poland, and that henceforth inviolable security of life, of worship, and of industrial and social development should be guaranteed to all peoples who have lived hitherto under the power of governments devoted to a faith and purpose hostile to their own.

I speak of this, not because of any desire to exalt an abstract political principle which has always been held very dear by those who have sought to build up liberty in America, but for the same reason that I have spoken of the other conditions of peace which seem to me clearly indispensable—because I wish frankly to uncover realities. Any peace which does not recognize and accept this principle will inevitably be upset. It will not rest upon the affections or the convictions of mankind. The ferment of spirit of whole populations will fight subtly and constantly against it, and all the world will sympathize. The world can be at peace only if its life is stable, and there can be no stability where the will is in rebellion, where there is not tranquility of spirit and a sense of justice, of freedom, and of right.

. . . Difficult and delicate as these questions are, they must be faced with the utmost candor and decided in a spirit of real accommodation if peace is to come with healing in its wings, and come to stay. Peace cannot be had without concession and sacrifice. There can be no sense of safety and equality among the nations if great preponderating armaments are henceforth to continue here and there to be built up and maintained. The statesmen of the world must plan for peace and nations must adjust and accommodate their policy to it as they have planned for war and made ready for pitiless contest and rivalry. The question of armaments, whether on land or sea, is the most immediately and intensely practical question connected with the future fortunes of nations of mankind. . . .

In holding out the expectation that the people and Government of the United States will join the other civilized nations of the world in guaranteeing the permanence of peace upon such terms as I have named I speak with the greater boldness and confidence because it is clear to every man who can think that there is in this promise no breach in either our traditions or our policy as a nation, but a fulfillment, rather, of all that we have professed or striven for.

I am proposing, as it were, that the nations should with one accord adopt the doctrine of President Monroe as the doctrine of the world: that no nation should seek to extend its polity over any other nation or people, but that every people should be left free to determine its own polity, its own way of development, unhindered, unthreatened, unafraid, the little along with the great and powerful.

I am proposing that all nations henceforth avoid entangling alliances which would draw them into competitions of power, catch them in a net of intrigue and selfish rivalry, and disturb their own affairs with influences intruded from without. There is no entangling alliance in a concert of power. When all unite to act in the same sense and with the same purpose all act in the common interest and are free to live their own lives under a common protection.

I am proposing government by the consent of the governed; that freedom of the seas which in international conference after conference representatives of the United States have urged with the eloquence of those who are the convinced disciples of liberty; and that moderation of armaments which makes of armies and navies a power for order merely, not an instrument of aggression or of selfish violence.

These are American principles, American policies. We could stand for no others. And they are also the principles and policies of forward-looking men and women everywhere, of every modern nation, of every enlightened community. They are the principles of mankind and must prevail.

The United Nations and the Middle Eastern Crisis

BY DWIGHT D. EISENHOWER

I. ADDRESS TO THE NATION, OCTOBER 31, 1956.*

My fellow Americans:

Tonight I report to you as your President.

We all realize that the full and free debate of a political campaign surrounds us. But the events and issues I wish to place before you this evening have no connection whatsoever with matters of partisanship. They are concerns of every American—his present and his future.

I wish, therefore, to give you a report of essential facts so that you—whether belonging to either one of our two great parties, or to neither—may give thoughtful and informed consideration to this swiftly changing world scene.

The changes of which I speak have come in two areas of the world—Eastern Europe and the Mideast. . . .

The Middle East . . . was, as we all know, an area long subject to colonial rule. This rule ended after World War II when all countries there won full independence.

Out of the Palestinian mandated territory was born the new State of Israel.

These historic changes could not, however, instantly banish animosities born of the ages. Israel and her Arab neighbors soon found themselves at war with one another. And the Arab nations showed continuing anger toward their former rulers, notably France and Great Britain.

The United States, through all the years since the close of World War II, has labored tirelessly to bring peace and stability to this area.

We have considered it a basic matter of United States policy to support the new State of Israel and, at the same time, to strengthen our bonds both with Israel and with the Arab countries. But, unfortunately, through all these years, passion in the area threatened to

* From *The New York Times*, November 1, 1956.

prevail over peaceful purpose, and, in one form or another, there has been almost continuous fighting.

This situation recently was aggravated by Egyptian policy including rearmament with Communist weapons. We felt this to be a misguided policy on the part of the Government of Egypt. The State of Israel, at the same time, felt increasing anxiety for its safety. And Great Britain and France feared more and more that Egyptian policies threatened their life line of the Suez Canal.

These matters came to a crisis on July 26 of this year when the Egyptian Government seized the Universal Suez Canal Company. For ninety years, ever since the inauguration of the canal, that company has operated the canal—largely under British and French technical supervision.

Now, there were some among our allies who urged an immediate reaction to this event by use of force. We insistently urged otherwise, and our wish prevailed, through a long succession of conferences and negotiations, for weeks—even months—with participation by the United Nations.

And there, in the United Nations, only a short while ago, on the basis of agreed principles, it seemed that an acceptable accord was within our reach.

But the direct relations of Egypt with both Israel and France kept worsening to a point at which first Israel, then France—and Great Britain also—determined that, in their judgment, there could be no protection of their vital interests without resort to force.

Upon this decision events followed swiftly.

On Sunday, the Israeli Government ordered total mobilization.

On Monday, their armed forces penetrated deeply into Egypt and to the vicinity of the Suez Canal—nearly 100 miles away.

And on Tuesday the British and French Governments delivered a twelve-hour ultimatum to Israel and Egypt, now followed up by armed attack against Egypt.

The United States was not consulted in any way about any phase of these actions. Nor were we informed of them in advance.

As it is the manifest right of any of these nations to take such decisions and actions, it is likewise our right if our judgment so dictates, to dissent.

We believe these actions to have been taken in error, for we do not accept the use of force as a wise or proper instrument for the settlement of international disputes.

To say this, in this particular instance, is in no way to minimize our friendship with these nations, nor our determination to maintain those friendships.

And we are fully aware of the grave anxieties of Israel, of Britain and France. We know that they have been subjected to grave and repeated provocations.

The present fact nonetheless seems clear. This action taken can scarcely be reconciled with the principles and purposes of the United Nations to which we have all subscribed. And beyond this we are forced to doubt that resort to force and war will for long serve the permanent interests of the attacking nations.

Now we must look to the future. . . .

It is—and it will remain—the dedicated purpose of your Government to do all in its power to localize the fighting and to end the conflict.

We took our first measure in this action yesterday. We went to the United Nations with a request that the forces of Israel return to their own line and that hostilities in the area be brought to a close.

This proposal was not adopted because it was vetoed by Great Britain and by France.

It is our hope and intent that this matter will be brought before the United Nations General Assembly. There, with no veto operating, the opinion of the world can be brought to bear in our quest for a just end to this tormenting problem.

In the past the United Nations has proved able to find a way to end bloodshed. We believe it can and that it will do so again.

My fellow citizens, as I review the march of world events in recent years I am ever more deeply convinced that the United Nations represents the soundest hope for peace in the world. For this very reason I believe that the processes of the United Nations need further to be developed and strengthened.

I speak particularly of increasing its ability to secure justice under international law.

In all the recent troubles in the Middle East there have, indeed, been injustices suffered by all nations involved. But I do not believe that another instrument of injustice—war—is a remedy for these wrongs.

There can be no peace without law. And there can be no law if we work to invoke one code of international conduct for those who oppose, and another for our friends.

The society of nations has been slow in developing means to apply this truth. But the passionate longing for peace on the part of all peoples of the earth compels us to speed our search for new and more effective instruments of justice.

The peace we seek and need means much more than mere absence of war. It means the acceptance of law and the fostering of justice in all the world.

To our principles guiding us in this quest we must stand fast. In so doing, we can honor the hopes of all men for a world in which peace will truly and justly reign.

I thank you, and goodnight.

2. ADDRESS TO THE NATION, FEBRUARY 20, 1957.*

I come to you again to talk about the situation in the Middle East. The future of the United Nations and peace in the Middle East may be at stake.

In the 4 months since I talked to you about the crisis in that area, the United Nations has made considerable progress in resolving some of the difficult problems. We are now, however, faced with a fateful moment as the result of the failure of Israel to withdraw its forces behind the armistice lines, as contemplated by the United Nations resolutions on this subject. . . .

When I talked to you last October, I pointed out that the United States fully realized that military action against Egypt resulted from grave and repeated provocations. But I said also that the use of military force to solve international disputes could not be reconciled with the principles and purposes of the United Nations. I added that our country could not believe that resort to force and war would for long serve the permanent interests of the attacking nations, which were Britain, France, and Israel.

So I pledged that the United States would seek through the United Nations to end the conflict. We would strive to bring about a recall of the forces of invasion and then make a renewed and earnest effort through that organization to secure justice, under international law, for all the parties concerned.

Since that time much has been achieved and many of the dangers implicit in the situation have been avoided. The Governments of Britain and France have withdrawn their forces from Egypt. Thereby

* From *The Department of State Bulletin*, March 11, 1957.

they showed respect for the opinions of mankind as expressed almost unanimously by the 80 nation members of the United Nations General Assembly.

I want to pay tribute to the wisdom of this action of our friends and allies. They made an immense contribution to world order. Also they put the other nations of the world under a heavy obligation to see to it that these two nations do not suffer by reason of their compliance with the United Nations resolutions. . . .

We are approaching a fateful moment when either we must recognize that the United Nations is unable to restore peace in this area or the United Nations must renew with increased vigor its efforts to bring about Israeli withdrawal.

Repeated, but, so far, unsuccessful, efforts have been made to bring about a voluntary withdrawal by Israel. These efforts have been made both by the United Nations and by the United States and other member states.

Equally serious efforts have been made to bring about conditions designed to assure that, if Israel will withdraw in response to the repeated requests of the United Nations, there will then be achieved a greater security and tranquillity for that nation. This means that the United Nations would assert a determination to see that in the Middle East there will be a greater degree of justice and compliance with international law than was the case prior to the events of last October-November.

A United Nations Emergency Force, with Egypt's consent, entered that nation's territory in order to help maintain the cease-fire which the United Nations called for on November 2. . . .

Israel seeks something more. It insists on firm guaranties as a condition to withdrawing its forces of invasion.

This raises a basic question of principle. Should a nation which attacks and occupies foreign territory in the face of United Nations disapproval be allowed to impose conditions on its own withdrawal?

If we agree that armed attack can properly achieve the purposes of the assailant, then I fear we will have turned back the clock of international order. We will, in effect, have countenanced the use of force as a means of settling international differences and through this gaining national advantages.

I do not, myself, see how this could be reconciled with the Charter of the United Nations. The basic pledge of all the members of the United Nations is that they will settle their international disputes by peaceful means and will not use force against the territorial integrity of another state.

If the United Nations once admits that international disputes can be settled by using force, then we will have destroyed the very foundation of the organization and our best hope of establishing a world order. That would be a disaster for us all.

I would, I feel, be untrue to the standards of the high office to which you have chosen me if I were to lend the influence of the United States to the proposition that a nation which invades another should be permitted to exact conditions for withdrawal.

Of course, we and all the members of the United Nations ought to support justice and conformity with international law. The first article of the Charter states the purpose of the United Nations to be "the suppression of acts of aggression or other breaches of the peace, and to bring about by peaceful means, and in conformity with . . . justice and international law, adjustment or settlement of international disputes." But it is to be observed that conformity with justice and international law are to be brought about "by peaceful means."

We cannot consider that the armed invasion and occupation of another country are "peaceful means" or proper means to achieve justice and conformity with international law.

We do, however, believe that upon the suppression of the present act of aggression and breach of the peace there should be a greater effort by the United Nations and its members to secure justice and conformity with international law. Peace and justice are two sides of the same coin.

Perhaps the world community has been at fault in not having paid enough attention to this basic truth. The United States, for its part, will vigorously seek solutions of the problems of the area in accordance with justice and international law. And we shall in this great effort seek the association of other like-minded nations which realize, as we do, that peace and justice are in the long run inseparable.

But the United Nations faces immediately the problem of what to do next. If it does nothing, if it accepts the ignoring of its repeated resolutions calling for the withdrawal of invading forces, then it will have admitted failure. That failure would be a blow to the authority and influence of the United Nations in the world and to the hopes which humanity placed in the United Nations as the means of achieving peace with justice.

I do not believe that Israel's default should be ignored because the United Nations has not been able effectively to carry out its resolutions condemning the Soviet Union for its armed suppression of the people of Hungary. Perhaps this is a case where the proverb applies that two wrongs do not make a right.

No one deplores more than I the fact that the Soviet Union ignores the resolutions of the United Nations. Also no nation is more vigorous than is the United States in seeking to exert moral pressure against the Soviet Union, which by reason of its size and power, and by reason of its veto in the Security Council, is relatively impervious to other types of sanction.

The United States and other free nations are making clear by every means at their command the evil of Soviet conduct in Hungary. It would indeed be a sad day if the United States ever felt that it had to subject Israel to the same type of moral pressure as is being applied to the Soviet Union.

There can, of course, be no equating of a nation like Israel with that of the Soviet Union. The people of Israel, like those of the United States, are imbued with a religious faith and a sense of moral values. We are entitled to expect, and do expect, from such peoples of the free world a contribution to world order which unhappily we cannot expect from a nation controlled by atheistic despots.

It has been suggested that United Nations actions against Israel should not be pressed because Egypt has in the past violated the Armistice Agreement and international law. It is true that both Egypt and Israel, prior to last October, engaged in reprisals in violation of the Armistice Agreements. Egypt ignored the United Nations in exercising belligerent rights in relation to Israeli shipping in the Suez Canal and in the Gulf of Aqaba. However, such violations constitute no justification for the armed invasion of Egypt by Israel which the United Nations is now seeking to undo.

Failure to withdraw would be harmful to the long-term good of Israel. It would, in addition to its injury to the United Nations, jeopardize the prospects of the peaceful solution of the problems of the Mid-East. This could bring incalculable ills to our friends and indeed to our nation itself. . . .

The United Nations must not fail. I believe that—in the interests of peace—the United Nations has no choice but to exert pressure upon Israel to comply with the withdrawal resolutions. Of course, we still hope that the Government of Israel will see that its best immediate and long-term interests lie in compliance with the United Nations and in placing its trust in the resolutions of the United Nations and in the declaration of the United States with reference to the future.

Egypt, by accepting the six principles adopted by the Security Council last October in relation to the Suez Canal, bound itself to free and open transit through the canal without discrimination and to the principle that the operation of the canal should be insulated from the politics of any country.

We should not assume that, if Israel withdraws, Egypt will prevent Israeli shipping from using the Suez Canal or the Gulf of Aqaba. If, unhappily, Egypt does hereafter violate the Armistice Agreement or other international obligations, then this should be dealt with firmly by the society of nations.

The present moment is a grave one, but we are hopeful that reason and right will prevail. Since the events of last October-November, solid progress has been made, in conformity with the Charter of the United Nations. . . .

What I have spoken about tonight is only one step in a long process calling for patience and diligence, but at this moment it is the critical issue on which future progress depends.

It is an issue which can be solved if only we will apply the principles of the United Nations.

That is why, my fellow Americans, I know that you want the United States to continue to use its maximum influence to sustain those principles as the world's best hope for peace.

The United Nations and the Middle Eastern Crisis*

BY VISCOUNT CHERWELL

[April 10, 1957]

The point I propose to consider is the part played, I may say the harm done, by the United Nations in the Middle East in recent years. As the noble Earl said, the root of our difficulties goes right back to the Balfour Declaration. At the time it was made it did not seem unreasonable. Allied arms had liberated the whole of Arabia, a region nearly as big as Western Europe without Russia, inhabited by only a few million people. In the circumstances, it did not seem unfair to establish a Mandate over Palestine, an area no larger than Wales, and to promise that the Jews, who had helped us honourably all through the war, should be allowed to make a national home there.

Perhaps we should have seen that this Mandate would ultimately become the State of Palestine, under Jewish rule. Perhaps we should have realized that it would be very hard to reconcile the Arabs to such a development. But at the time, and for years thereafter, these prospects seemed remote—until Hitler's persecution of the Jews raised the pressure of would-be Jewish immigrants to an intolerable level. It is easy to be wise after the event. Rightly or wrongly, Israel is now a fact, which can be obliterated only by exterminating the Jews. And as my noble friend Lord Dundee said, I can scarcely imagine that any Member of your Lordships' House would wish to sponsor such a programme.

As has been said, particularly by the noble Lord, Lord Ashbourne, it was only in the 'thirties that what happened in this part of the world began to matter very much to the West. The reason is the economic importance of the oil deposits on the eastern coast of Arabia. By the expenditure of vast amounts of capital, and the untiring efforts of English and American engineers, it has been possible to raise this

---

* From *House of Lords Weekly Hansard*, No. 320. An address to the British House of Lords.

oil to the surface and make it available to the world; and much of
Europe's and British civilization is built up on the assumption that
we can count upon plentiful and regular supplies.

I must say (though this perhaps will not fall into line with what
some others think) that I have often been rather surprised at the way
the local sheikhs are conceded complete control and ownership of the
oil pumped up from the depths, merely because their forbears and a
few camels have been roaming about on the surface for some centuries.
If a mountain of uranium 235 were discovered in New Guinea, I
wonder whether we should feel bound to let the local pigmies decide
what should be done about it. Anyhow, the point is rather academic,
for nobody has raised it; and civilized countries of the West have been
prepared to pay the local rulers huge sums so long as they did not
interfere with our getting the vital liquid fuels. Other inhabitants of
Arabia have been paid large amounts of money for graciously allowing
the oil to be exported, at no cost to themselves, by pipelines running
through their countries; and, of course, Egypt has gained enormous
sums from the tolls paid by tankers transporting this oil to the Mediterranean through the Suez Canal, which was built in the main by
European enterprise and capital.

It may be that we should have foreseen the danger of allowing our
economy to depend so much on these oil imports. Perhaps we ought to
have realized that within a generation of the Balfour Declaration it
would have become fashionable, indeed habitual, to break contracts
and to tear up treaties. But I do not think anybody could have imagined that an international body, the so-called United Nations, would be
set up by our joint efforts, which would allow, not to say encourage, little insignificant so-called nations to fly in the face of all their treaties
and agreements, and to hold the whole of Europe to ransom. The
harm that can be done by allowing organs such as the Assembly of this
body to extend their activities far beyond the limitations imposed by
the Charter is shown most clearly precisely by what has happened in
the Middle East.

I do not propose to examine all the various steps that have led to
this unfortunate result: the pressure that was put upon us in August to
endeavour to come to an agreement with the Egyptians, after they had
confiscated the Canal, so as not to compromise the position of the
United Nations; the way action was inhibited for months by threats
as to what the United Nations might or might not do if we did inter-

vene; the violent outcry when we did finally send troops to try to re-store order—and as I personally hoped, to re-establish our rights on the Canal; the collection of 2,000 or 3,000 heterogeneous troops to form a so-called United Nations force to maintain law and so on. All these complicated issues have been dealt with—and very much better than I could deal with them—by other noble Lords. Like the noble Lord, Lord Killearn, all I will say is that I wish we had sent troops in much earlier and forced Nasser to respect the treaties and contracts which he was treating with such contempt. For without respect for contracts and treaties, modern civilisation cannot survive.

Some people, of course, say that that would have been very improper. But under Article 51 of the Charter we are told that nothing should impair a nation's inherent right of self-defence if an armed attack occurs against it. Surely to repudiate unilaterally a solemn treaty on which the life of a country depends, and to enforce such a breach with armed police, is just as much an act of aggression as to send armed forces across the frontier. To claim the power to cut a nation's lifeline is just as bad as to claim the right to occupy its fortresses. Other-wise, any nation might claim and assert the right to blockade, say, the Thames Estuary or the entrance to the Baltic. It is as though your neighbour, through whose land your electricity mains run, suddenly insisted that he would put in a main switch with which to turn the current on or off as he desired. Any nation has the right to resist such an act of aggression by force, if the other party refuses to accept reason-able arrangements which would safeguard the position. But all these considerations have been brushed aside. Throughout the Assembly, one-third of whose members belong to the Afro-Asian *bloc,* has been playing politics, with no pretence of being impartial or of seeking justice. The noble Earl, Lord Gosford, said we want justice. We shall not find it there.

Perhaps the greatest outrage in the Middle East is the way the Israelis have been treated in comparison with the Egyptians. . . .

During all these years we heard none of the highfalutin talk which has nauseated so many of us during the last few months about the sanctity of the United Nations Charter and the importance of all countries rallying round to enforce it. Egypt continued to defy the Security Council without any action being taken. After all, it was only Jews who were being hurt. But when, finally, the Israelis, finding that the Egyptians, who were openly proclaiming their intentions of liquidating them, decided last autumn to make a move to defend themselves before it was too late, and reoccupied the Gaza Strip and moved into the Sinai peninsula, there was a most terrific outcry. They were labelled as aggressors, and the whole paraphernalia of the United Nations was mobilised against them.

The Egyptian claim that they were in a state of war with Israel was forgotten. The Israelis were vilified in the Press, and every conceivable form of pressure was brought to bear to force them to retire, not merely beyond their real legal frontier but right out of the Gaza Strip, to which the Egyptians had no claim whatsoever, except that they had occupied it in the war they unleashed against Israel in 1948 and which, according to their story, still persists. Only Egyptians, apparently, are allowed to break the conditions of the truce. Israelis must fulfill them to the last iota. I can understand a strong anti-Semite taking this line, but it is amazing to find so many honourable people adopting it without any explanation.

Similar arguments, of course, apply to the Gulf of Aqaba. Egypt's refusal to allow Israeli ships to proceed to the only port they have on the Red Sea is alleged to be justified because, it is said a state of war exists between the two countries. But when the Israelis advance along the coast and dismantle the Egyptian batteries, we are told that they are behaving scandalously and that they must instantly retreat. I must say that, to me, a unilateral "state of war," in which one country is allowed to take belligerent action, while the other country is forbidden to reply, is a very strange new conception.

Now why have so many decent people combined to force the Israelis to stick to the letter of the truce and to withdraw their troops, whilst the Egyptians are allowed to break it right, left and centre? Rude people, of course, say that it is because the Egyptians are closely linked with the so-called Governments of the oil-rich countries in Arabia. I am sure that in many cases, at any rate, this is not the deliberate conscious reason. Rather, I think that many of them take this course because it is recommended by the Assembly of the United Nations. If this is really so, and not merely a rationalisation of anti-Semitism, it is surely conclusive proof of the absurdity of allowing this organ of the United Nations, which according to the Charter is merely a platform on which the various members can air their views, to seize control and initiate action. I believe that . . . it would be laughable, if it were not so serious, to see the way they send the Secretary-General scurrying about the world, endeavouring to placate Oriental despots and dictators with oil-rich friends, and trying, usually unsuccessfully, to persuade them to fulfil their clear obligations; to see him charged with raising an army and directing its movements; to see the Foreign Secretaries of major Powers hanging on his words and begging him to insert favourable phrases in his reports.

As I have said before, the fact that the leaders of some of the greatest nations in the world have put their consciences in pawn to this weird body is one of the greatest dangers of our present situation. For anybody who imagines that he will get moral guidance, or even unbiased advice, from the Assembly, cannot have studied the antics of many of its members during recent months. Clearly, international organisations can do useful work in matters in which all nations' interests agree—for instance, in fixing up world-wide postal arrangements, in tracing criminals, in preventing drug smuggling and countering the white slave traffic. Incidentally, I deliberately specify "white slaves" in the technical sense, so as not to offend the susceptibilities of a certain King who appears to be held in such high esteem in many influential quarters.

Unhappily, it is becoming increasingly clear that the world cannot rely upon the effectiveness of the United Nations if vital interests of various major countries conflict. It is easy to state in comfortable phrases what is required to maintain peace which the people, if not the Governments, of the world all desire. All that is needed is some impartial supermen to agree upon a just solution and to impose it on the nations concerned. While this is easy to say, it is impossible to do. What is a just solution? It is not merely a matter of interpreting an existing body of laws, for usually no such code exists for the really important conflicts upon which a nation's very life may depend. How is a just solution to be defined? Is it just that a nation should be free to block established air routes by suddenly refusing landing rights on its territory; or to close a canal which has been built by foreign initiative, with foreign capital, on which free navigation in peace and war has been guaranteed by a treaty? Was it just to allow scores of thousands of Jews, many of whom risked being murdered in their countries of origin, to settle in a small corner of Arabia, the whole of which we had liberated from the Turks; or had the previous inhabitants, who had been ruled for centuries by the Pashas from Constantinople, an absolute right to prohibit this Jewish immigration?

I mention these questions merely to illustrate how difficult it is to lay down broad general principles of natural justice which any tribunal can be adjured to maintain when interests of nations clash. Almost always we are faced with the choice of evils.

Probably the best we can do at present is to insist on adherence to the pledged word or the sanctity of contracts. But even this has its troubles, for in the modern world words change their meaning very quickly. Fifty years ago a franc was something very different from what it means to-day. But supposing we could solve these difficult questions of principle, where are we to find the impartial supermen who are to form our tribunal? The United Nations Assembly is, of course, the very opposite of an impartial tribunal. The representatives of the various nations are selected, not for their unbiased judicial attitude, or even for their knowledge of International Law, but for their ability to put their country's case forward effectively. They are told by the home Government how to vote, often as the result of bargains made in the corridors, quite irrespective of the merits or justice of the case. There is no pretence of a proper collection of evidence; nor, of course, is there any definite rule according to which they act. Naturally, any glib politician—at any rate one from a foreign country—who is allowed to make untested, unchecked assertions the basis of his argument can make sententious speeches which appear to show that his Government's actions, however self-interested, accord with the precepts of the Sermon on the Mount or any other set of ethical principles.

The system by which every nation or pseudo-nation has an equal vote, no matter what its form of government, stage of civilisation, population, or what part it is able to take in enforcing a judgment, is, of course, perfectly ludicrous. Any petty dictator can cancel out the vote of the democratically-elected president of a great world Power. The most civilised countries on the planet are equated to tiny States many of whose inhabitants are fetichists who cannot even read or write. Nations containing 5 per cent. of the world's inhabitants can get a majority in the Assembly. With 10 per cent., a two-thirds majority could be achieved.

It has been suggested that this trouble could be overcome by weighting the votes of the various nations according to their populations. This would be, if possible, even more absurd, for the most populous countries are composed, as it happens, of individuals most of whom have the smallest knowledge or comprehension of international affairs. Not one Chinese or Indian in a thousand has probably ever heard of the Suez or the Panama Canals or understands what a satellite country is. Yet, if we could weigh it by population, India's population, nearly one-seventh of humanity, would cast its vote through Mr. Nehru, and China's population, nearly one-quarter of the total, would cast its vote through Mr. Chou en Lai. These two men, though they may have managed to achieve domination for the time being in their countries, have no right to claim nearly two-fifths of the weight of the whole world for their personal views. Even if, by hook or by crook, they have succeeded in getting hold of the reins of government, it does not make them wiser or more impartial in international affairs than the next man.

Even if all the people on the planet could have a plebiscite, it would be worth very little. We have seen what the peoples' courts are like in China, Germany and elsewhere. And, as I have said, the ordinary Indian peasant, or Indonesian in New Guinea, or Pigmy in the Congo has no more comprehension of international affairs than a three-year-old child. In any event, the idea of holding a plebiscite among the 2,500 million inhabitants of the earth to decide the justice of the claims of one side or the other in a dispute, say, about Okinawa or Cyprus or what proportion of the Suez Canal tolls should be paid to Egypt is too fantastic to consider. Clearly, there is no hope of finding an acceptable body of jurors or judges capable of giving a just verdict, quite apart from the impossibility of defining what is "just."

I will not enlarge upon the fact that, even if just solutions could be found, they could not be imposed upon all nations alike, without which they would be of little use. As I explained at some length last December, moral, economic or armed force cannot be exerted by the Assembly save in special cases. Moral force has little weight, whatever people may say. . . . Nor, I trust, is it true, as has been said, that we withdrew our forces from Egypt because of moral pressure. Immoral pressure if you like—in fact Party pressure—may have played some part. But the real cause, I believe, was economic pressure, especially the economic pressure exerted against us by America who seems to have been led up the garden path by the siren voices of the Assembly of the United Nations. Unfortunately, economic pressure can usually be applied only to highly civilised nations, notably Great Britain. It would be quite useless against many others, especially if they were backed by

Russia. And a mechanism which allows decisions to be enforced only against selected members is clearly unacceptable.

There remains armed force, the celebrated United Nations police force to which some people pin their faith. This, of course, is mere day-dreaming. A police force capable of imposing decisions on all alike would have to be more powerful than the armed services of Russia or America, or even both combined. I need not labour the point of how absurd that is. But, even if it were feasible, I can scarcely believe that anyone in his senses would desire to entrust the government of the world to a body whose decisions were reached in the weird, and in some cases scarcely reputable, ways I have described. Considered une-motionally, therefore, I fear that to tie the policy, when major Powers disagree, to some international body is to follow a mere *ignis fatuus*.

As I have said, Middle East affairs have been bedevilled by the inter-ference of the Assembly of the United Nations. Somehow, many peo-ple in this country and leading personalities in America seem to think that they will not go to Heaven unless they accept its decisions. Even if they are not under a legal obligation to do so—and they are not—they seem to believe that these decisions have some valid moral force. Thanks to the cooperation of America and Russia, we were forced last autumn to refrain from insisting on our rights. But, when America and Russia do not agree, as in the case of Hungary, the United Nations can do nothing.

In the old days, Egypt would not have ventured, in breach of all treaties and agreements, to confiscate British and French property and to throw the world's shipping into disarray. Now they know that they will find sufficient support in the United Nations to prevent any action from being taken. Even the Yemen, whose tribesmen have been quar-relling and fighting with those in the Aden Protectorate for genera-tions, has discovered that it can find many anti-English votes at the United Nations and is trying to put the blame on England. Every-where these wretched little pseudo-nations, banking on the irre-sponsible antics of the United Nations Assembly, are seizing the opportunity to make trouble. Instead of being an agent for peace, it is the world's great trouble-maker. Many other nations all over the world have looked on at the difficulties created for us and France by this disastrous body with a certain amount of *Schadenfreude*. But it is a risky line to take. To paraphrase a well-known saying, I suppose "an honest nation is one that stays bought." Hitherto, honesty in this sense has prevailed amongst many client States. But disenchantment lurks round the corner. *Volte faces* have happened before when attractive counter offers were made. If the Assembly, for instance, ordered the United States out of Formosa or even Panama, I am sure that the determination of the American Government to make her policy conform to the United Nations Charter would be subjected to an agonising reappraisal.

To sum up, no international organisation can preserve world peace when vital interests of the great Powers conflict. There are no general agreed principles according to which just solutions can be found. There is no hope of finding acceptable impartial judges; and, even if there were, there is no chance of enforcing verdicts on all alike, by moral, economic or armed pressure. This has been amply proved in recent years in the Middle East. I can only hope, therefore, that the major Powers will soon realise it and will disentangle their policies from the irresponsible and, to put it mildly, often inelegant interventions of the Assembly of the United Nations.

World Government Now*

BY ROBERT M. HUTCHINS

[1947]

WE have a mystical notion that all the issues that perplex us are going to be settled by improvements in transportation. They will give us one world. A colleague of mine has asked, one world, but whose? We may also inquire, one world, but how long? And one world, but what kind? One world which brings in closer contact the sparks of greed and ambition is sure to be in constant explosion. One world under one tyrant, or one association of tyrants, would be worse than many. In many worlds there is at least the chance of escape from one to the other.

But let us suppose that by one world we mean one good world. Will we stop to ask what one good world involves? It involves, unless we propose to kill them all, such people as the Russians. The proposal to kill them all seems to be gaining in popularity. If we are going to do that we had better do it at once. Now we have a monopoly of the atomic bomb.

There are two propositions about the atomic bomb that are worth remembering. There is no secret. There is no defense. Since there is no secret, other nations will have the bomb almost any day. Since there is no defense, we cannot use the bomb after our monopoly ends to kill other people without being killed ourselves.

In a war in which both sides have atomic bombs the cities of both sides will be destroyed. Since one to ten atomic bombs can reduce any city in the world to ashes, superiority in atomic bombs will not give material advantage to the side possessing it. Superiority in land, sea, and air forces will mean little. The atomic bomb is a weapon directed against civilians. The economy which supports the military can be wiped out before the military can get started. As General Groves said in Chicago a few weeks ago, "I do not see how it will

* From Robert M. Hutchins, "The Constitutional Foundations for World Order," *Foundations for World Order.* Copyright 1947 by Social Science Foundation, University of Denver. Reprinted by permission of Social Science Foundation.

be possible to supply large armies in the field." When two nations have the atomic bomb, it will be impossible for either of them to win a war. The day of force as the determining factor in world affairs ends with the end of our monopoly of the atomic bomb.

Yet just as the day of force is waning, the official American attitude is to rely on it more than ever. In the greatest moral crisis in history we do not say, "Let us be good." We say, "Let us be powerful—and then we can compel other people to be good." Instead of saying, "Let us use our knowledge and our resources for the benefit of all mankind," we say, "Let us use our knowledge to make more terrifying weapons of destruction; and let us use our resources to usher in the American Century, in which we shall dominate the world." Instead of saying, "Let us feed the starving because all men are brothers," we say, "Let us feed the starving, if we feed them at all, so that they will not vote the Communist ticket." Instead of saying, "Let us have moral education in the United States," we say, "Let us have military training."

Three weeks ago the Chairman of the Federal Reserve Board said that we had spent twenty-five billions on military forces in the first two post-war fiscal years, compared with sixteen billion spent on foreign aid in that period.

Yet even before the atomic bomb it is possible that General Montgomery was right in saying, as he did the other day, that it is not weapons or large armies that win victories, but the character, that is, the education, of the people. A tremendous military establishment can be, and usually is, a Frankenstein; and all history confirms the doctrine that those who rely upon the sword shall perish by it. Power corrupts. A false sense of superiority leads to a false sense of security. Behind an impressive facade the building falls into ruins. The building can be no better than the character of the people who inhabit it.

Force is absolutely amoral, and therefore has no role, except in support of law, in a world that has any title to be called good. Force is almost certain to be immoral. The essence of fascism is pushing other people around; you frighten them into doing what you want them to do. A country composed of people who want to push other people around is a fascist country; a government which pursues a fascist policy will eventually produce a lot of fascist citizens. It will produce a population of immoral individuals who regard other

ROBERT M. HUTCHINS 413

individuals as means to their ends and who will seek the power to make other individuals serve their ends. Such a country cannot long remain strong; such a population cannot be happy. If the official American attitude is to rely upon force, it follows that the power and the happiness of America have already passed their zenith.

And, if the official policy of America is to rely upon force, it follows that the security of America cannot be guaranteed by force after the day of force is over. The day of force can last only a moment longer. There are only two possibilities: to use the bomb at once, or to create a situation in which nobody can ever use it.

Of these two possibilities, we hear more and more about the first and less and less about the second. The first possibility is a preventive war on Russia. If we seriously entertain this possibility, we ought first to make our apologies to the Nazis we hanged at Nuremberg.

If we are concerned to create a situation in which the bomb will not be used, we must recognize that international agreements for the control of atomic energy will simply mean that the next war will end with atomic bombs instead of beginning with them. The minute war breaks out, every nation that knows how will start making atomic bombs.

The *New York Times,* in its editorial on the second anniversary of the bomb, says that the ultimate protection against it can only be the abolition of war itself. The *Times* suggests that the final success of efforts to abolish war can be realized only in an ultimate world government.

I do not understand the use of the word "ultimate" in this connection. We have now arrived at the ultimate stage in history. We cannot do something intermediate now and ultimately do something ultimate. What is ultimately required of us is required of us now. If what is ultimately required of us is the abolition of war through a world government, then we had better set about trying to get war abolished through world government now.

Any proposal for a world atomic authority is a proposal for world government. Such an authority must have a monopoly of atomic bombs, which means that every nation would be at its mercy, and it must have the right to enter, inspect, and destroy atomic installations anywhere in the world. No nation could call itself sovereign in any usual sense under such conditions.

The major premise of all discussions looking toward agreements for the control of atomic energy has been that the nations retain their sovereignty. Hence, these discussions have not succeeded and cannot succeed. Either we have world federal government and real atomic control, or we have no agreements, or agreements that are meaningless, and eventually atomic war.

It will be said, of course, that if nations will not collaborate in an alliance or debating society or propaganda forum like the United Nations, they cannot be expected to come together or to stay together in a world state. The American states could not or would not collaborate under the Articles of Confederation before 1787, but they did come together, and, with the exception of one period, they stayed together under the Constitution.

It may be admitted that there were ties which united them which do not unite the nations today. Moreover, they were remote from the rest of the world. Both their enemies and their friends were too preoccupied to bother them. They had the safety valve of a new country and the western lands. On the other hand, we should not forget that many differences deeply divided the American states, so much so that, three months before the Constitutional Convention, Madison wrote that he "trembled for the issue."

Mr. Hooker has lately shown in the magazine *Common Cause* how serious the divisions among the states in the Confederation were. Virginia had twelve times as many people as Delaware. Georgia claimed a hundred times as many square miles as Rhode Island. There were so many Germans in Pennsylvania that Franklin feared they might make German the language of the state. It was impossible to get along in some sections of New York without knowing Dutch. The trip from Boston to New York, which now takes less than an hour, took four days to a week along the finest road, or longer than it takes now to go around the world.

Gouverneur Morris thought that a federal tax was impossible because of the extent of the country; and one member of the Convention asked, "How can it be supposed that this vast country, including the western territory, will, one hundred and fifty years hence, remain one nation?"

When Washington took charge of the armies surrounding Boston, he wrote that the New Englanders were an exceedingly dirty and nasty people. On the other hand, Ephraim Paine of Vermont complained that the southern members of Congress regarded themselves as a superior order of animals. Tariffs were levied by New York, Pennsylvania, and Maryland on the goods of other states; and New Jersey taxed the New York lighthouse on Sandy Hook. New York, New Hampshire, and Massachusetts quarreled about Vermont, and Pennsylvanians battled Virginians on the Upper Ohio. It is no wonder that when the Constitution was completed by the Convention, the principal attack upon it was that it was utopian, a visionary project, an indigestible panacea.

And it barely was accepted. In the conventions in the critical states it just squeaked through. In Massachusetts it carried by twenty-nine votes; in Virginia by ten; and in New York by only three.

What we are talking about is the relation between world community and world law. Reinhold Niebuhr, whom I greatly admire, takes the view that we cannot discuss world government because we have no world community to support it. The discussion of world government, he thinks, may even retard the development of world community and hence retard world government.

It is true that one good world presupposes a world community. In one good world every man is our neighbor, because every man is our fellow-citizen. The commands of the political community supplement the demands of charity. Three or four years ago the Council of the American Federation of Labor, in response to the suggestion that China was our ally, voted to reaffirm its support of the Chinese Exclusion Act. Mr. William Green took the occasion to announce that "A Chinaman is still a Chinaman." If this is so, the one good world at which Mr. Green doubtless aims is still far off.

Our traditional attitude toward the rest of the world has been expressed in the old question, "Should foreigners be abolished, or should we save some to sell things to?" We have been dedicated to a policy of high tariffs and no immigration. Twenty years ago we regarded national relief of the unemployed as revolutionary socialism. Our system of social security is only twelve years old. We are not yet committed to give national aid to the education of under-privileged American children. And yet, in one good world, we should be called on to support, to educate, to buy from, and to receive as fellow citizens, men of every race, creed, and color, at every economic level, and at every stage of ignorance or enlightenment.

One good world requires more than the sacrifice of ancient prejudices. It requires the formulation and adoption of common principles and common ideals. It requires that this be done on a world-wide basis. A world organization cannot be held together simply by fear. Not transportation but communication lies at the foundation of any durable community. By communication I do not refer to the means of communication, but to a common understanding of what is communicated. The extraordinary development of the telegraph, the telephone, the radio, the motion picture, and airmail in our time has done as much as any single factor to disrupt international relations and exacerbate wounded feelings throughout the world. A vice-president of the General Electric Company has lately commented on the benefits to civilization from television. He said that, since the principal market for television sets was taverns, what this triumph of technology had meant to society was more booze, less fresh air, and the same old ball-game. It would have been very fortunate if almost every speech made by representatives of great powers in the last two years . . . could have been heard or read only by their own people, and a very small fraction of them. Confucius remarked that men cannot work together unless they have common principles. Common principles are essential to communication.

Here it will not do to say that common principles cannot be found. They must be found. And they can be found in the common humanity of all mankind. By patience, tolerance, and good will we can come to understand other human beings, because they are human beings like ourselves. The most salutary reflection about the Russians in which we can indulge is to imagine how we would feel about the United States if we were Russians. And it would do the Russians no harm to consider how Mr. Vishinky's speeches would affect them if they were Americans. By patience, tolerance, and good will we can come to understand one another; understanding is essential to communication. Communication is the basis of community. Transportation hastens consolidation; there can be no doubt about that. In the last century it has hastened consolidation of the most unstable and disagreeable kind, consolidation by conquest. One good world presupposes that the moral, intellectual, and spiritual foundations of the community have been laid. Otherwise the improvement of transportation must simply mean more frequent and terrible wars leading to the despotism of that power which discovers how best to apply the latest inventions to the destruction of its neighbors.

But I am afraid that Mr. Niebuhr exaggerates the state of perfection which world community must achieve before world government can be considered. Before the atomic bomb we could take world government or leave it. We could rely on the long process of evolution to bring world community and world government hand in hand. Any such program today means another war, and another war means the end of civilization. The slogan of our faith today must be, world government is necessary, and therefore possible.

Furthermore, those who oppose discussion of world government on the ground that a world community must precede a world government seem to me to overlook the interaction between the two. This is what the Greeks had in mind when they said that law was an educational force and that the city educates the man. The Constitution of the United States has educated the people of this country to believe in and support the Constitution of the United States. We are so used to thinking of law as repressive and constitutions as the embodiment of pre-existing agreement that we neglect the tremendous force which any constitution and any system of law exerts in behalf of its own acceptance and perpetuation. Anybody who has studied the relation between the political institutions of a state and its educational system, for example, must agree with Aristotle that politics is the architectonic science. One of the reasons Aristotle gives for this conclusion is that politics determines what is studied in the state.

The way to promote world community is to have world government. But since we cannot establish a world government here tonight the next best thing we can do to promote world community is to talk about world government. World discussion of world government, far from disrupting the world, may have some chance of uniting it; for the consideration of what is necessary to unite the world, the discussion of a common problem of overwhelming importance, should lead to a growing sense of community among all peoples.

An important reason for talking about world government is that nobody knows what it is. Should a world government aim at limited measures designed to maintain what is called security, or is security itself dependent on the pursuit of broader purposes? Should a world state be federal or unitary, or should it, perhaps, contain the best features of each? What should be the relation of the world government to the citizens of extant states? What taxing powers shall the world state have, and what order of military forces, if any? This list of questions can be prolonged indefinitely, and there are countless possible answers to each of them. Yet people go around saying world government is wonderful or world government is impossible. It may be that many forms of world government would be something less than wonderful; and it may be that some form of world government is possible. The only way to find out whether any form of world government is possible and practicable in our time is to work at it and talk about it.

Such discussion cannot legitimately be interpreted as an attack upon the United Nations. We must support the United Nations; it is all we have. We support it, not because it can guarantee peace, but because it is a highly tentative first step toward world government and world law. To say that the discussion of world government is a criticism of the United Nations is like saying that to talk about buying an automobile is an attack on the baby-carriage industry. The notion that if only we don't say anything about it the United Nations will in some way, while nobody is looking, turn gradually into an effective world government is surely naive. Constitution framing is a highly technical problem. The organization of sentiment for a new constitution is a matter of time, thought, and effort. And when the task must be carried forward on a global scale we must realize that no matter how soon we start we may be too late.

Mr. Molotov defends the United Nations and proposes as a remedy for the ills of the world what he calls the peaceful competition of states and social systems. This is certainly better, if it may be taken at face value, than the stirring calls issued by our statesmen for the largest army, navy, and air force in the world. But Mr. Molotov overlooks or suppresses the fact that between states and social systems there cannot in the long run be peaceful competition unless peace is enforced by law. The history of our own country from the Gold Rush to the Chicago newspaper wars shows that competition between individuals can be made peaceful only with some difficulty, and then only within a framework of law. The competition of sovereign states is competing anarchy. It is peaceful only so long as all nations want it to be. When one nation thinks that its competitive position would be improved if it stopped being peaceful, it will engage in warlike, instead of peaceful, competition, and there is no way for other nations to stop this process except to abandon peaceful competition, too. The United Nations is composed of independent, sovereign states. Their competition must be anarchical. Therefore, in the long run it cannot be peaceful.

Every alteration in the constitution of the United Nations looking toward making it a world government is to the good. But any important limitation on the powers of sovereign states means that the whole theory of the United Nations is changed. To allege that anybody who insists on the basic theory of the United Nations is in some way an enemy of world peace is unfair. This applies, for example, to criticism on constitutional grounds of the use of the veto. Such criticism assumes that the United Nations is a world government and assails Russia on the ground that it does not recognize this obvious fact. Actually, the United Nations was not designed to put an end to the competing anarchy of sovereign states, but to perpetuate it.

Does anybody imagine that the United States would consent to any modification of the veto which would endanger our present majority position? Suppose that we were in a minority in the United Nations. Would we part with the veto, which would be the only weapon with which we could protect ourselves against the majority? Does anybody imagine that we would consent to effective inspection by an international body of atomic installations in this country? The United Nations is and is by its charter declared to be an association of independent, sovereign states. How can we complain if one of the members insists on asserting its independent sovereignty?

Tinkering with the United Nations will not help us, if we agree with the *New York Times* that our only hope is in the ultimate abolition of war through an ultimate world government. An entirely different constitutional foundation is required. A new set of commitments must be made. Commitments to an alliance can be transformed into allegiance to a government only by a change of heart which is embodied in a fundamental constitutional reform.

The most futile of all the things we can do is to speculate about the intentions of the Politburo. Even if we were sure at some given moment that we knew what these gentlemen were planning, we could not be positive that they would adhere to these plans for more than a few minutes. What we should be thinking about is what

America should stand for, regardless of what other nations may have in mind. If that policy fails, we shall at least have the satisfaction of knowing that we have done the best we could and that the catastrophe cannot be laid at our door. The policies we have been following—peace by intimidation and peace by purchase—do not seem to be succeeding very well; and, if the catastrophe comes, we shall be unable to evade a large share of the responsibility for it.

The policy of peace by intimidation, otherwise known as "getting tough with Russia," has produced Mr. Vishinsky, who proclaims a policy of peace by vilification, which is the *reductio ad absurdum* of peace by intimidation. Peace by vilification is that version of peace by intimidation which can be adopted by powerful and remote nations who do not yet have the atomic bomb, but who, since they are powerful and remote, can respond to attempts to intimidate them by showing in as rude and noisy a fashion as possible that two can play at that game. The policy of peace by purchase may succeed temporarily in those portions of the world which are purchasable. In those areas it will last as long as the purchase price is being paid or as long as no other bidder will offer more or until the nations bought come to value their independence more than food, clothing, and houses. But we have really made no attempt to buy peace. We have been attempting to buy allies for the next war. Yet we cannot contemplate another war. Another war will mean the end of civilization. We have reached the point where we cannot have war and civilization, too.

If peace through intimidation and peace through purchase are failing and in the nature of things are bound to fail, we might try peace through justice. Justice means giving every man his due; it means not doing to others what you are unwilling to have them do to you. Justice is suggested to us by a well-known American document which states that all men are created equal. Justice is the cement which holds a political organization together.

If we will grant that what we want is peace, and that justice is the only way to peace, then we may begin dimly to perceive both the outlines of a policy for the present and the constitutional foundations of a future world order. We are required to abandon a policy of power and purchase and pursue a policy of justice at home and abroad.

In order to pursue this policy we have to make certain moral and intellectual commitments, commitments that threaten to take us, in fact, into the realm of metaphysics. We have to admit that men are different from the other animals and that their moral, rational, and spiritual qualities are the qualities that make them men. These characteristics prevent us from dealing with men as we are free to deal with other animals. Human dignity forbids us to apply force to men, except by law. It forbids us to regard other men as means to our ends, for every man is an end in himself. The prospects of a human community result from our common humanity.

To give every man his due, therefore, is to treat every man as a man, black or white, British or Russian, rich or poor, ignorant or educated. And we may remember, as John Stuart Mill pointed out long ago, that we cannot expect the slave to show the virtues of the free man unless we first make him free. To say that certain men cannot be treated as men means simply that they have never had a chance to be men, and they must be given that chance.

To give every man his due is to give him the Rights of Man. This means that he must be free from want as long as he is willing to work. It means that he must be free from the fear of tyranny, oppression, and exploitation. It means that his claims to life, liberty, and the dignity of the human person are inalienable. It means that the necessities of life must be the common property of the human race, and that the management of the necessities of life by individual owners is a trusteeship which such owners hold subject always to the common good. It means that a world government must be a democracy, because only democracy gives every man his due.

It will be said that a world government which is founded on justice goes further than world government has to go and that we should limit ourselves to those objects as to which there can be no debate, the principal one of which is security. It will be said that nobody wants war and that all that a world government should do is to try to prevent war. This it can do by securing a monopoly of arms. Why talk about justice, the rights of man, and the law of nature when all we want is peace?

The answer is that men will fight until they get their rights. The minimum structural requirements of world government are plain enough. A world government, so as to preserve the cultural values that now exist in the states and regions of the world. It must be a government which acts directly on the individual, wherever he may be; for otherwise it is merely a league of sovereign, and hence ultimately warlike states. But these are minimum structural requirements. There are minimum moral and spiritual requirements, too; and these may be summed up in the single word justice. The advancement of man in spiritual excellence and physical welfare is the common goal of mankind. Universal peace is the prerequisite for the pursuit of that goal. Justice in turn is the prerequisite of peace. Peace and justice stand or fall together. Men will fight until they get their rights.

These are hard sayings; for if we are going to promote justice throughout the world we shall have to rely largely on the power of example. We shall have to start doing justice at home, and shall have to sacrifice many ancient prejudices that are very dear to us. And if we are to have a world government based on justice, we, as the most prosperous and powerful nation of the earth, shall have to give up many economic and political advantages. We shall have to give up also the notion that there are some people in the world who are sub-human and not qualified to participate in any government that will hold sway over us. If we are going to have peace we must pay for it; and the price of peace is justice. If it will cost us a good deal to have world government, it will cost us far more to have war.

We are in no present danger from Russia. We have the atomic bomb. We have the industrial power. We are in no present danger from communism. The people of this country could be made communistic only by conquest, and probably not then. At present we are our own worst enemy. The present danger to us lies in our own hysteria and inertia. Our hysteria means that we will not face the facts of life, and our inertia means that we will not do anything about them. We hysterically build up tremendous military preparations, oblivious to the fact that while we have a monopoly of the atomic bomb we do not need these preparations, and when other nations have the bomb these preparations will do us no good. These preparations are, in fact, a danger to us for they can be used to convince other nations that we are out to dominate the world. Because of our inertia we will not recognize that our first obligation is to make our own system work until it must command the admiration and imitation of the world. We will not see that the atomic bomb puts all further talk of force out of the question and that the hope of civilization is in world government. The Pax Romana existed before the atomic bomb. The atomic bomb makes a Pax Americana a romantic dream. The attempt to get a Pax Americana will give us not one Rome, but two Carthages.

The task of this generation is to establish peace. Gibbon in a celebrated chapter seeks to relieve the fears of Europe by assuring his contemporaries that there can never be another barbarian conqueror. The reason is simple. War is now so far advanced and requires the knowledge of so many arts and sciences that only highly educated men can hope to wage war successfully. The inference is that if men are highly educated they will not be so stupid or so vulgar as to wage war. But the last war was the most barbarous in history precisely because so much knowledge was at the disposal of those who waged it; and the atomic bomb is the final refutation of Gibbon's comforting theory. It can be little consolation to the Japanese who died at Hiroshima and Nagasaki that they were killed by Ph.D.'s.

The crisis of our time may be summed up in the proposition that our knowledge now exceeds our capacity to use it for good. The solution is not to reduce our knowledge, or to halt the progress of science, but to make our moral stamina equal to it. We have now reached the point where the bad character, or even the momentary carelessness, of the human race may lead to its extermination by the tremendous discoveries which the human intellect has achieved. The problem of preserving our civilization is a moral problem. Our difficulty is not to get more knowledge or more goods, but to do the right thing with them when we get them. Today we are confident that every scientific question will in time be answered. We know that every material deficiency of mankind can with good will be supplied. The problem is obtaining the good will. This is a moral problem.

The task of our generation is to establish peace. We cannot establish it by power or by purchase. We can establish it only by justice which begins at home and extends throughout the world. If you ask, what good will it do for us to be just if other nations are unjust, I reply as Plato did 2500 years ago, that the unjust man and the unjust state bear within themselves the seeds of their own destruction; and as General Montgomery did the other day that the character of a people is its best defense. Character implies moral and intellectual conviction. We must know, understand, and believe in what we are defending. What we are defending is not the American Way of Life, by which we usually seem to mean All the Comforts of Home. We are defending the cause of suffering humanity everywhere. This is justice, which is the foundation of any constitutional order and the basis of one good world.

The Case Against World Government*

BY WALTER F. BERNS

[1955]

As fear is the principle of despotic government, its end is tranquility; but this tranquility cannot be called a peace: no, it is only the silence of those towns which the enemy is ready to invade.

—Montesquieu, *The Spirit of the Laws*

FOR SEVERAL years now we have heard it asserted that the dropping of the atomic bomb made world government a moral necessity. Those who are appalled at the destructive power of the new bombs, and this means everyone, are told by men of the first rank in science, education and the humanities that the only alternative to universal destruction is world government. No less a man than Albert Einstein was one of the first to support the cause, and it was educator Robert M. Hutchins who wrote with compelling passion that we had "arrived at the ultimate stage in history" and that the common principles needed to unite all men under one government had to be found.

The common principles, however, have not been found, or manufactured; instead, we have built a bomb infinitely more destructive than the one dropped on Hiroshima, and our sensibilities are assailed with reports of still other weapons dreadful almost beyond imagination. In such a situation, the task of uniting all men of good will in a one-world-or-none crusade would seem to present only minor difficulties of a technical sort, difficulties easily overcome in our day of technological achievement and mass communication. Surely in the 300 years since the Enlightenment man had acquired the skills to solve this, albeit his most desperate, problem. Surely, and especially in America, the most enlightened nation of all, the call for world government would be heard and the response would be overwhelming.

Nothing of the sort has happened. Instead, those who still have the courage and will to plead for men to "acquiesce in their own survival," as a leader in the world government movement once put it,

---

* Copyright 1955 by the American Foundation for Political Education.

are villified as muddle-headed idealists or disloyal scoundrels, even traitors. These unfair tactics have been used principally by persons devoted to the cause of isolation, and they have won the day. For the advocates of world government there is the small comfort in knowing that battles are not necessarily won by those whose cause is just—our situation might not be so desperate if they were—and that accusations are not an answer to any argument.

Our purpose here is to examine the argument for world government free from the passion that has marked most of the public debate on both sides, and to do so without discrediting world government by imputing disloyalty to those who are devoted to it. Having said only this, however, we are certain to have angered those defenders of world government who imply or assert that a dispassionate examination of the world government proposal is impossible, immoral even, because war *must* be abolished, the common principles to unite all peoples *must* be found and therefore *will* be found, because the alternative is universal destruction. Anyone who hangs back in doubt, who stops short of the conclusion of this quivering syllogism, is a morally obtuse "logician"—a monster of some sort, or a fool. What a time for dispassion, when the alternative to passionate commitment is annihilation! To plead for a calm examination of the argument under these circumstances is to be oblivious of the naked facts of our situation, one of which is that "modern man is obsolete," which means that he is incapable of analyzing his situation with his traditional (that is, obsolete) methods. The conclusion? National sovereignty must be relinquished in the name of survival. It is to this conclusion that the isolationists shriek "treason!" And it is this hostile tone of the debate that makes it advisable to argue it out on another level. That and the need to face our problems as they should be faced.

II

To the extent to which the argument over the world government issue has not been vituperative, it has proceeded on the political level; that is to say, the disputants have addressed their arguments to the question: How can we get world government? This very question, however, assumes agreement on a more fundamental and, we shall insist, more debatable question: Is world government desirable at all? Even in the face of universal destruction is world government a desirable alternative? Instead of fixing our vision on some mirage compounded out of our delusions, we must see the proposal in its entirety, and as such it divides itself naturally into these two parts, or better, presents two aspects for consideration: as a political problem and as a fundamental problem.

A political problem is a practical problem, a problem demanding action here and now, to be solved within the situation as it exists today and as it is likely to exist in the foreseeable future. Those persons whose duty it is to make political decisions are not permitted to count on extremely improbable changes for the better, because decisions must be based on the factual situation as it exists today. The situation today and in the foreseeable future finds the world divided into two hostile camps each led by a colossus armed with the means of utterly destroying the other. If atomic war were to break out, we must also count on the destruction of civilization. The political problem is how to deal with this situation. What can we do, now? The fundamental problem, on the other hand, would disregard the limits set by the present situation and concern itself with world government as an ultimate objective, as the object of our most optimistic hopes.

The political problem can be disposed of quickly. The Soviet Union does not trust the West; the West does not trust the Soviet Union. Neither would ever submit to a world government controlled by the other. Neither would ever submit to a world government controlled by someone else, if such a thing were possible, without the right to nullify decisions taken by this someone else. The example of the veto in the Security Council allows us to be as certain of this as we have to be. But the right to nullify decisions taken in important matters is incompatible with government (Andrew Jackson threatened to hang John C. Calhoun when he advocated nullification, and the point at issue was merely a tariff). To mention only the well-known Communist argument: the non-Communist world is controlled by Capitalists, and Capitalism and Communism are incompatible. Not only is there no common ground between the two, hence no agreement regarding fundamentals, but the Communist world is pledged to hasten the inevitable destruction of the non-Communist governments. But subjection to a common power such as a world government requires trust, and trust is impossible from the Soviet point of view. He would be a foolish Westerner who, in the face of Communist doctrine and all that has happened, would trust the Soviet Union—especially when we are told that atom bombs may be carried in attaché cases.

The usual objection to this analysis, an analysis that leads any reasonable man to the conclusion that we must arm ourselves to the teeth instead of putting our hopes in world government, is that the required agreement on fundamentals does exist: almost everyone agrees with the principle that there must be no atomic war. Furthermore, the argument runs, atomic war remains a possibility (and possibilities become actualities sooner or later) as long as hostile states refuse to give up their sovereignty to a world state. Whatever the disagreements separating the USSR and the West, they are insignificant beside this massive agreement that there must be no atomic war. The threat of the bomb compels the agreement and the agreement is the required foundation for world government. The conclusion? "The argument for world government is simple and irrefutable."

It is indeed simple, but it is refuted by one look at the political situation. There is no agreement. There is no agreement and we will not get one by repeating endlessly that there must be one. Even if all our leaders were to plead for world government, we could not get the consent of the Soviet Union; Communists are unmoved by our pleas and arguments and cajolery, because, among other reasons, they *know* that no ruling class ever abdicates. They distrust everything we do and say. And as long as the Politburo is controlled by Communists, and we must presume this means indefinitely, there is no hope for a change in this fundamental idea. One gets nowhere by calling Stalin "Uncle Joe." But this is not all.

Those who persist in agitating for world government in the light of these facts must explain how they intend to get the assent of the Soviet Union. There are two possible paths to assent: persuasion or force. They must get the assent of the Soviet Union either by persuasion, but this is impossible, or force, which means, in the present state of mind and armaments, by atomic war. The propaganda for world government is so far from reducing the danger of atomic war that it actually increases it, since the propaganda must appear to the Soviet government as a shrewdly camouflaged attempt to subject their country and the people's democracies, as they call them, to Western control.

Let us quickly do our bit to avert this danger by assuring the Soviet leaders that the devotees of world government are not shrewd. They are naive. Their argument is too simple; it is abstract; it is based on abstractions from all the relevant elements in the political situation.

Even if everyone in the West believed in the necessity of world government, the political situation would be determined by the existence of a powerful Communist Russia rigidly controlled by a Politburo which is impervious to our way of arguing and which, on the basis of everything we know, cannot be trusted. To say, as Hutchins does, that "men will fight until they get their rights," is to lose sight of the fact that men have fought to get more than their rights, and this overlooks the fact that men sometimes have peculiar notions of what their rights are. Less than any generation in the Christian era can we deny that there are madmen with political power who are willing to commit any crime at any cost, even a cost involving the lives of millions of people, in the name of an unjust cause, which they, in their madness, call their rights.

One does not appeal to a sense of justice in these men. One does not attend cultural congresses with them with any justifiable hope of finding the common principle needed to form the basis of the non-Communist world state. "How many divisions does the Pope have?" Stalin asked. Well, will his successor not also ask, how many divisions do the World Federalists have?

These are the "simple and irrefutable" facts controlling the answer to the political question. We cannot persuade the Soviets to join a world government; we cannot force them to join by any method short of atomic war; there can be no world government without them.

III

The political question of how we can get world government is one thing. The fundamental problem is to consider whether the world state is a desirable goal in itself, and here we launch out on our own since one does not find the disputants discussing this. In fact, the opponents as well as the devotees of world government *assume* that a world state would be desirable if possible; and while the opponents scoff at the practical prospect of world government now, the devotees heroically draw up their liberal-democratic world constitutions and debate how many representatives Afghanistan should have in the world parliament. (Whether Afghanistan's consent to the dispensation is sought, to say nothing of obtained, is not known.)

But the existence on paper of a liberal-democratic constitution does not guarantee the existence of a liberal-democratic regime in fact—our knowledge of the disparity between the Soviet constitution and the Soviet regime proves that. However exasperating it is to have to think about such complicated things, we cannot avoid the question of whether the world state is likely to be liberal-democratic or something else, especially since we can get one kind of one world any time we are willing to submit to the control of the Soviet Union. Let us imagine a world government in existence, which would include the Communist and non-Communist worlds, built on the foundation of a universally shared principle: there must be no atomic war. What sort of government will this be?

There will be a parliament, we are told, based on proportional representation, and we shall dismiss the nasty possibility that, like New Jersey, Delaware and Maryland in 1787, some small but stupidly proud nations would insist on equal representation. No, the fundamental agreement to avoid atomic war will be so compelling that agreement on a minor matter like representation will be achieved swiftly and amicably.

But being assembled to avoid war and the use of the bomb, one of the first matters to be dealt with will be the necessity to guard against the gravest danger, namely, the bomb. True, all the existing bombs, or at least all that are *supposed* to exist, will have been turned over to the World State to be guarded, somehow, someplace (Rome, Mecca, Moscow or Hollywood?) by a mixed force composed largely of political janissaries; but everyone will agree that this is not enough and that it is also necessary to guard against the future production of the bomb.

Although this aspect is generally skipped over in the world government blueprints, it can be shown and will be shown that to prevent the production of the bomb will require the creation of an enormous secret police force, an international FBI at best and an international MVD or Gestapo at worst, with the power to inspect everywhere at all times—and without a warrant. Of course there will be wire-tapping, and on a vast scale. The man with the most experience for the job of directing this bureaucracy, Lavrenti P. Beria, is no longer available, it having been discovered that he was a bourgeois deviationist all along, but his methods and experience will be of incalculable assistance to the new bureau and will be placed at its disposal. Furthermore, anyone familiar with the damage wrought on the bureaucracy in the United States by Congressional investigations will recognize that there can be nothing comparable to this in the world state;

satire on possible world gov.

and for that matter, our own Congress is reluctant to urge its right to investigate our own Central Intelligence Agency. Eventually, of course, the World Parliament will become the equivalent of the impotent Supreme Soviet; the real power will be in the hands of the secret police or in the army that is charged with maintaining the peace, and Parliament will perforce acknowledge the authority of whoever has custody of the bombs. No representative assembly will be allowed to stand in the way of swift intervention in a future Korea; there can be no debating and no filibustering.

The purpose of the secret police will be to prevent the manufacture of the bomb and to ferret out potential manufacturers of the bomb, that is, anyone against whom there is the *slightest* suspicion. There can be no doubt that this will require eternal vigilance and rigorous methods. The goal, after all, is *no atomic war,* and whatever is conducive to the attainment of that end is a legitimate policy, an essential policy, a *moral* policy, however harsh and seemingly inhuman it may appear to those who have no appreciation of the difficulties of the task or of the catastrophic consequences of the failure to perform it. Whatever is conducive to the avoidance of atomic war will be morally legitimate—even if it violates the first of the Ten Commandments, to say nothing of lesser rules of human conduct. Fear of the bomb is the principle from which all moral rules will be deduced, and the bomb will remain a terrible possibility as long as people do not trust one another. To prevent someone from manufacturing the bomb, supervision by the secret police must be pervasive and foolproof. We cannot afford to trust the Communists and they will not trust us, so the world government will have to exercise the strictest of supervisions. In short, world government based on the fear of the atomic bomb will be world despotism.

Now, even if we conceded for a moment that this description of the world state is imaginary, we contend that it is possible. The central question is, how *probable* is world despotism. It is especially probable if universal destruction is regarded as a greater evil than universal despotism, for this means that those who advocate world government will accept despotism in order to avoid destruction. One is permitted to wonder whether that simple insight to which civilization is indebted—that there are greater evils than death and that there are some things for which men will give their lives—whether this simple insight did not survive the process of obsolescence that is said to have overtaken modern man. Is it not dangerous to regard death as the greatest evil, even the death of practically everyone? For if we truly believe death is the worst thing that could befall us, we must then concede that universal despotism is preferable to universal death, indeed, that it is a blessed alternative. It is a goal we are compelled to seek. The conclusion is clear: if our fear of destruction is so great that we are willing to suffer loss of everything we cherish in order to continue to exist, the question of what kind of one world it would be loses its relevance for us—a universal despotism even on the pattern of the Soviet Union becomes a blessing.

We are investigating the assertion that the agreement to avoid atomic war is all the agreement needed to form a world government. A world state built on this foundation is indeed possible, but a world state as the salvation from physical destruction *and nothing more* appeals to us as a lesser evil than universal destruction; it appeals to us as a terrible necessity. Not only are we asked to believe that universal despotism is preferable to universal destruction, but we are asked to work for universal despotism. But no reasonable man can work with any enthusiasm for universal despotism; in fact, no reasonable man would concede that world government is a necessity, precisely because he would not concede that destruction is the worst of all evils. That is, world government is a necessity only for those persons who look upon destruction as the greatest evil. Doubtless there are among world government enthusiasts some persons who do believe this, but we have a right to demand that they say so.

Although they have never considered the possibility of universal despotism, many advocates of the world state concede that agreement based on fear alone is not enough, that there must be positive goals. They speak of justice, a new freedom, and assemblies based on proportional representation; admirable goals. We are assured that in the world state men will get their rights. But are we not entitled to some proof of this assertion? Must we accept these assurances on faith?

These people have only assumed that world government would not be world despotism, they have not convinced us, primarily because they have not considered it necessary to investigate the possibility of despotism. Their serious arguments have not been carried beyond the limits of a political discussion. This is not far enough, nor is it as far as our knowledge permits us to go.

A world government like any other government could be despotic or, let us assume for the moment, non-despotic. Which is more probable? It could be non-despotic, and hence a desirable way to avoid universal destruction, if the people comprising it were united not by fear but by mutual trust. Without this trust there can be no freedom. In the United States, for example, for over a century—if one excepts the Civil War period when Lincoln closed down newspapers and had the Copperheads thrown into Army jails by the thousands—there was not only freedom of movement but of speech and opinion as well. Americans became accustomed to regarding this freedom as part of the natural order of things under liberal-democratic government; they trusted their fellow countrymen not to engage in espionage or other activities that were fundamentally contrary to the American way of life. As a matter of fact, almost everyone was so busy taking advantage of the unprecedented opportunity of making money, that there was no need for the government to be alarmed by, or even to suspect the presence of, what later came to be known as un-American activities. No one was suspected of being un-American because all alike were pursuing the same goal.

With the first World War, however, this widespread trust was to some extent replaced by fear, and the government responded with the Espionage Act of 1917, and in the next few years thousands of people somewhat new to these shores, that is, people who were to some extent strangers, were put in jail because they were not trusted. Two were put to death. In dangerous times strangers, people who are suspected of being not like us, or who are suspected of holding alien ideas, are not trusted; and when we are gradually apprised of the alarming information that not only are these alien ideas held by men who appear to be typical Americans, like Alger Hiss, but that these ideas are consciously hostile to the United States, the range of freedom is restricted of necessity. There can be no freedom for these men and their ideas, or even men who are suspected of holding their ideas. To a considerable extent the political atmosphere once so free becomes charged with suspicion, with well-known results.

There is, then, a relation between trust and freedom. We can say that there is a lack of freedom to the extent to which there is a lack of mutual trust. Though we may deplore the necessity of distrusting and deplore a suspicion that knows no limit, our situation is so fraught with danger today that to trust without limit is to be foolhardy.

Whether a world government could be non-despotic would seem to depend, then, on the possibility of replacing the acknowledged distrust which now exists in the world by mutual trust. The character of the world state would be determined by our ability to trust one another, and this means to trust strangers, aliens, people who are unlike us in what appears to be fundamental respects.

To achieve world government we must either create the universal trust without which there can be no freedom or impose a supervision that is complete, a police state. To create the trust we must understand the conditions under which trust is possible. In the interests of brevity let us say that there can be mutual trust when men pursue the same positive goals. The goal suggested by some World Federalists, no atomic war, is not a positive goal; it does not engender mutual trust, and any government based on this goal would be despotic. World government could be non-despotic if men were united regarding the positive goals. What are the chances of getting agreement on the positive goals?

A positive goal may be described briefly as the purpose for which one lives. For men to be united in this fundamental respect they would have to agree as to what this purpose is, or, we may say, they would have to agree regarding the right way of life. At present there is considerable disagreement on this point. Some people, for example, worship graven images, others regard the worship of graven images as an abomination; some people regard certain animals as sacred, others regard them as unclean, and still others look upon them as food; some people achieve salvation by dying in battle, others by turning the other cheek; some believe in private enterprise, others in Socialism, and still others in a classless society. The list could be extended almost indefinitely, but the point is that these are not minor differences regarding matters of no consequence; they are fundamental disagreements concerning the most important things, the things for which men give up their lives. Most people simply do not believe that death is the greatest of evils. If they were of no consequence, we might expect the Jews and the Arabs to recognize that even the *threat* of war is ruinous to them both, to form a united "Israbia," and to live and prosper in a state of everlasting peace. But the tragic fact is that not even the prospect of a war of annihilation is powerful enough to dispel the distrust.

A modern scientist might argue that the Jews and Moslems are both naive and that the faiths they profess and for which they are only too willing to give their lives are, both of them, naive anachronisms in the modern scientific world. He might argue that it is silly for them to distrust each other because of these ancient beliefs, that the point at issue is of no consequence. Without passing judgment on the spiritual life of either the Jews or the Moslems, could they not reply with considerable justification that to them the life of this scientist appears singularly devoid of any spiritual content? Could they not with good reason look with contempt and dismay on the achievements of this science: television and the atomic bomb? Could they not with reason prefer their spiritual beliefs even at the risk of war to the belief in science and a life spent vapidly staring at a television screen?

We urge this scientist to reflect on some recent history: the very political regime which claims to be based squarely on a *science* of history, which regards all religion as the "opiate of the masses," which did not hesitate systematically to eradicate all opposition to the collective farm program at the price of millions of lives, this regime with all its power and ruthlessness finally capitulated before the demand by its peoples that they be permitted to worship God without interference from the police. We conclude from this example, as well as other reflections, that while the life of science may satisfy the spiritual cravings of those few persons who delve into the secrets of history or the secrets of the atom, for the great mass of mankind this belief in science is an inadequate substitute for a spiritual life.

A World Federalist would probably argue that the trouble in the Middle East lies not in the religious diversity or the unbelief in science, but in the anachronistic political institutions. What is needed, according to this version, is a federal constitution to which all Jews and Arabs can repair. This, of course, is the nostrum the World Federalist prescribes for the anarchistic world as a whole: the rule of law.

The Arab would probably reply: Jewish law administered by Jews or Arabian law administered by Arabs? And the Jew, who after all has lived under someone else's law for many centuries, most recently under Nazi law, knows from terrible experience that the rule of law is an empty phrase until the substance of that law is defined and someone is appointed to administer it. To argue that nations must live under the rule of law is to say no more than that nations should unite under a world government, and how this can be achieved without world-wide despotism is the problem we are investigating, not the solution to the problem.

We can make this point more clearly by raising the question: Why do men obey law? Men either obey law freely or because their obedience is coerced in some manner. Men obey law freely when they believe the law is a good law, the just or moral law; because they are taught to believe that it is right to obey law. But the law which the Arab believes it is right to obey is different from the law which the Jew believes it is right to obey. And the Communist believes it is right to obey Communist law, but this is not the law Americans will obey unless their obedience is coerced. But coercion is incompatible with trust.

A non-despotic world government in which men trust one another, or world law freely obeyed, would require free agreement on the positive goals to be pursued by that government or by that law. This in turn would require either a universal *faith* in the rightness of the goal or a universal *knowledge* of the rightness of the goal. On the basis of the historical evidence alone, we are prevented from believing that a universal faith is possible. Anyone who believes differently can prove his case by converting either the Moslems to Judaism or the Jews to Islam, or both to Christianity, or, for that matter, Khrushchev and Bulganin to World Federalism.

It is conceivable that the Jews and Arabs could reach an agreement which would permit them to live in peace side by side, but it is inconceivable that they could subscribe to the common faith needed to live under one government—so long as the faiths they now profess are not corrupted.

The final chance for world government to be non-despotic rests on the possibility of achieving universal and free agreement regarding positive goals through *knowledge* of the rightness of these goals. To be hopeful of this possibility requires us to believe, first, that knowledge of the right life is accessible to human reason alone, without the support of faith, and second, that this knowledge is within the reach of practically everyone. There have been men who have argued that knowledge of the right life is accessible to unassisted human reason, but how many sane men have ever argued that this knowledge is within the reach of everyone? Under these circumstances, no one, least of all a devotee of world government, can protest if we bring the argument to a close at this point. In the course of this argument we have investigated the various conditions under which world government could be non-despotic, and now that we have exhausted the possibilities without success, we must conclude that a non-despotic world government cannot be achieved through human effort.

IV

We have argued that the envisaged world government is a mirage; that far from being a government of limited powers ruled through a world parliament, it would be a vast bureaucracy, highly centralized and controlled by men who had no choice, and in all likelihood no inclination, but to be despots. This is readily demonstrated if the only basis of such a government is fear of the atomic bomb. But a world government based on positive principles would be equally despotic because of the impossibility of getting all men to give their consent freely to these principles. Since consent is essential and since there is no principle to which all men now give their free consent, since in fact the principles by which men now live conflict with one another, a new principle will have to be found and consent to it will have to be coerced. We have seen this done. We have seen principles manufactured and marketed in glittering packages bearing the imprimatur of government officials; we have seen them advertised by the multitude of subtle and sordid devices at the disposal of a government; we have seen them endorsed by alleged scientists in journals reputedly scientific; we have seen them acclaimed in mass torchlight processions; and we have been struck dumb with awe and shame by the fervid demonstrations of devotion to the squalid human embodiment of the new principles. Far from being a moral necessity, a world government would be something like Nazi Germany, where the common principle that had to be found was manufactured and promulgated to the public under the trade mark of the Master Race. This is the case against world government.

Finally, by way of concluding the case, it should be pointed out that we might have reached the same conclusion if, instead of asking whether a world state could be non-despotic, we had begun at the other end and had investigated the question of how a good society is achieved, that is, a society in which and through which men can become what they should be. Proceeding in this fashion, it is not impossible to show that such a society must be considerably smaller in area than a world state and must possess qualities alien to a world state. Its citizens, to mention only one condition, must freely accept the guidance of rational rulers.

But the fact that a world government would necessarily be a despotism is not sufficient reason to despair. Despite the predictions of disaster awaiting a world divided into sovereign states, that disaster has not yet taken place and there is no necessity of its taking place. True, we must rub the One-World mist from our eyes and pay our taxes; we must learn to distinguish between reasonable arguments and unreasonable arguments and between fact and fancy; we must learn to keep our mouths shut on more occasions; we must maintain a posture that is powerful but not aggressive, which means to acquire a patience that we have lacked in the past; and most of all we must learn that the highest claim to political leadership is wisdom, not availability, not bellicosity, not a winning smile (Lincoln was ugly), not even honesty, and certainly not generosity with the public domain.

There is no necessity of an atomic war; the example of poison gas is sufficient to show that. There is even good reason to hope that there will not be such a war, since for the first time in history all the powers that alone can make total war do not need that war and do not desire that war. Now that the West has to a great extent redressed the balance of power by rearmament, there exists the possibility of a *modus vivendi,* an agreement to live and let live. Such an agreement, brought about by top-level conferences, would commit each side only to respect the vital interests, the security interests, of the other side—and to nothing more. This is not all that World Federalists would like, and it is less than some of our professional patriots insist we have. But such an understanding may be all we can get, and it could work for the foreseeable future—the maximum one has a right to expect of any settlement by mortal beings.

X

MEANS AND ENDS IN WORLD POLITICS

The Nature
of Foreign Policy*

BY CHARLES B. MARSHALL

[1952]

I SHALL define the foreign policy of the United States as the courses of action undertaken by authority of the United States in pursuit of national objectives beyond the span of jurisdiction of the United States.

That is a lot of big words. Let me put the idea another way. Our foreign policy unfolds in the things done by the U.S. Government to influence forces and situations abroad. The meaning of the phrase "things done" should not be construed too narrowly. In this field, utterance is a form of action, and pronouncements may be deeds, especially when they convey meaning about intended or possible actions rather than merely expressing abstractions and moralizations.

My definition of foreign policy may sound strange. Let me justify it. Foreign policy may be viewed as something distilled into chapters of a book or as a process involving a lot of daily hard work by many people. I am discussing it in the second sense—in the way that one might talk of a painting as the resultant in a process of putting paint on canvas, rather than as an ultimate effect hanging statically in a museum.

The two elements in my definition to be stressed are these: Foreign policy is generated in actions. The things acted upon in foreign policy are things lying beyond the direct control of this country. Those two things are simple and obvious. Yet they are often overlooked. The overlooking of them leads to a lot of misunderstanding.

A year or so ago I spoke in a midwestern city. In the question period a lady in the audience asked me to lay out briefly the course of policy for the next 10 years. I declined, saying I could not foresee events that far ahead. The lady reduced to 5 years the span of the prophecy she sought. I disavowed clairvoyance even in that more

---

* From *The Department of State Bulletin*, March 17, 1952.

modest degree. She became impatient. She said surely I could tell something about the future—something to be counted on—something to be taken for granted by a policy planner such as I in the laying of plans.

I said there was indeed a sure element in the future: it was trouble; it was bound to occur; its timing, its points of arrival, and its guises were unpredictable; but that trouble would come was as safe a proposition as I could imagine. My lady questioner became more impatient. She asked: If foreign policy was not a design to keep trouble away, then why have one—since one obviously could find trouble without the expense, effort and time required for attending to foreign policy?

I said that the test for a nation as for an individual was not its success in abolishing trouble but its success in keeping trouble manageable—in generating the moral strength to face it and the capacity for handling it. She spurned that answer. The lady said that if the Department of State was full of individuals like me, who took trouble for granted, that it was no wonder that the United States found itself in so much of it all the time.

A few weeks ago I had a different—yet in some ways similar—experience.

I took part in a round-table. Another participant appeared to hold me personally to blame for the shortcomings of what he described as a foreign policy of expediency.

My question as to whether he preferred a foreign policy of inexpediency did nothing to stem the tide of his scorn.

He said a foreign policy must consist of principles discovered in natural law and not susceptible of being compromised or tampered with and that the only way to conduct a successful foreign policy was to set these principles up as absolute standards of conduct and then persevere in them without regard to the limitations of circumstance.

The limitations of circumstance as a factor in foreign policy, he assured me, were figments of the craven mind that wants to avoid trouble instead of seeing national life as the opportunity of service to the eternal principles of right.

I did not fare very well in either of those arguments. In both cases the other participants were thinking about foreign policy only in terms of objectives.

I was thinking of foreign policy as relating to means and ends and to the gap between them.

Ends are concepts. Means are facts. Making foreign policy consists of meshing concepts and facts in the field of action.

Suppose money grew on trees. Suppose power were for the asking. Suppose time could be expanded and contracted by a machine as in the story by H. G. Wells. Suppose Aladdin's lamp, the seven-league boots, and the other fairy-tale formulae for complete efficacy were to come true and be made monopolistically available to Americans. We would have then a situation in which we could do anything we wanted. We could then equate our policy with our goals.

In the world of fact, however, making foreign policy is not like that at all. It is not like cheer-leading. It is like quarterbacking. The real work comes not in deciding where you want to go—that is the easiest part of it—but in figuring out how to get there.

One could no more describe a nation's foreign policy in terms solely of objectives than one could write a man's biography in terms of his New Year's resolutions.

Foreign policy consists of what a nation does in the world—not what it yearns for or aspires to. The sphere of doing, as distinguished from the sphere of desire and aspiration, is governed by limits. Adam Smith pointed out that economic behavior derives from imbalance between means and ends and the circumstance that ends therefore tend to conflict. The same is true in foreign policy.

Let me illustrate that in terms of present problems.

To begin, let me identify the fundamental purpose enlightening our conduct as that of preserving a world situation and enabling our constitutional values to survive.

That we must keep in mind when speaking of national interest as the basis of our foreign policy. To me the phrase "national interest" does not mean a set of aims arrived at without regard to values. I cannot think of our foreign policy except in relation to the character of the Nation and its political institutions.

That has a bearing on the choice of means in the conduct of foreign policy. An accountable government cannot lead a double life. It is foreclosed from using such means as would destroy the very values it would save.

The main purpose enlightening our foreign policy holds true in all stages of our national life. It will continue as long as our country continues in the tradition we know. It is objectified in different ways as the world situation changes.

The world situation concerning us in the recent past and the present has been characterized by five main elements.

The first is the result of complex historic changes, notably two World Wars. A falling away in power among several nations once of primary greatness has occurred. This leaves two states of first magnitude, each with a great geographic span and great resources of power. One of these is our country.

The second relates to the situation of the other main element in this bipolar world of power, the Soviet Union. It is in the grip of tyrannous rulers. They achieved power by conspiracy. They have never dared risk their hold on power by resort to any procedure of consent. They have remained conspirators after becoming governors. They require tension and conflict within and at the periphery so as to hold onto power. They use in the service of this aim a political doctrine emphasizing the patterns of violence—class conflict, subversion, and so on.

As the third element, I cite the climate of intimidation and fear in much of the world resulting from the circumstance that the Soviet Union has great military forces either under direct control or amenable to its purposes and that these forces are deployed along a huge span bearing on northern and central Europe, the Mediterranean area, the Middle East, southeast Asia, and Japan.

Fourth, the dislocation of economic patterns and the exhaustion and demoralization of peoples in consequence of invasion, occupation, and oppression in World War II have created situations affording special opportunities for Soviet communism working within other countries as a conspiratorial force in the service of the Soviet rulers.

Fifth, the weakening of old restraints in Africa, the Middle East, and east Asia and the impulse to wayward use of freedom among peoples unaccustomed to the usages of responsibility and preoccupied with redressing old grievances, real or fancied, have created opportunities for the Soviet Union, alert as it is to the quest of advantage in the troubles of others.

In these circumstances our endeavor has been along four general lines.

First, we have sought to develop stronger situations in the areas where the choices made by the peoples and governments in the great confrontation coincide with ours. We have done this so as to relieve the sense of anxiety—and with it the intimidatory power of the Kremlin—among the nations disposed to go along with us. In this category I put our alliances, military and economic assistance to our allies, and our efforts to return our former enemies to full relationships with other nations.

Second, we have sought to insure that the areas where the crisis of politics is sharpest—the areas of contest, such as southeast Asia, the Middle East, and the Arab areas—shall not be lost.

Third, we have sought to exercise leadership in working toward the ideas of responsibility and peaceful adjustment in contradistinction to the Soviet pattern of turmoil and conflict. This aim enlightens our attitude of trying to combine responsibility with new found freedom among the Middle Eastern and the southeast Asian countries. It reflects itself in our support of the United Nations pattern, in our confrontation of aggression in Korea, and in our attempts to bring about a system of arms limitation that will not reward faithless performance.

Fourth, we have sought to steer away from the tragedy of another world war.

I am referring here not to objectives divided into neat categories distinct from each other but to concurrent phases of a process. That sounds very bureaucratic, but I do not know how better to convey the idea that in reality these things do not have such nice separateness as they seem to have when one talks or writes about them. These interrelated aims tend in part to support each other, and in part they also tend to contradict each other.

For example, at a certain point the pace of generating military strength may run counter to the requirements for a sound economic basis among our allies.

In another instance, the effort at countering aggression might be carried to lengths that bear against the aim to avoid a general war.

In still another, the impulse to deal sympathetically with the aspirations of a people new to freedom and not adjusted to its obligations may run counter to the economic necessities of another country which is allied with us or to the strategic necessities of our allies and ourselves.

Again, trying to help with the military needs of one area may require the diversion of arms and supplies from others who also need them.

Such are the dilemmas that arise when our power is not sufficient for doing all the things we want to do.

What requires judgment and timing in the highest degree, along with the fortitude that can defer hopes without surrendering them, is the job of threading a course through such contradictions as these and striving as best one can to find choices of action consistent with all of the aims concurrently.

That is the job of making the best of situations in the knowledge that such is the only way of making them better. The job consists mainly of the rationing of power among aims. There—not in the formulation of aims but in the rationing of power among aims—is where a foreign policy really takes form.

In my definition at the outset I said that the decisions were made under authority of the United States. That authority exists in the grant of the executive power to the President and in the grant of legislative power to the Congress. I shall wave aside the constitutional question and the political question of the paramountcy of authority in these matters.

The agencies and departments of the Government concerned in foreign policy serve as staff advisors to the President and, under his direction, to the Congress in the making of the fundamental decisions.

A staff function of this character carries duties but no prerogatives. The President and the Congress are entitled to seek counsel where they wish within the Government or outside it.

The same holds true within the Department of State. In making up his mind as to what advice to give the President, the Secretary is certainly entitled to seek counsel where he wishes.

I am one of several members of a staff which is only one among many elements within the Department of State producing advice for the Secretary of State. I am setting forth here not the conclusive word but only my own views, developed not in theory, but by observations.

As I see it, the job of making the decisions which generate foreign policy calls for two ranges of perception.

The first of these is the sense of the situation being dealt with. By that I mean knowledge of the background and of the local factors.

The second is a sense of perspective. By that I mean a grasp of the relation and proportions between the instant problem and all other problems arising in other places and foreseeable in other ranges of time and competing with the instant problem in the apportionment of power.

These two ranges of perception are not mutually exclusive things. A situation can exist only in an environment. An environment entails a relation to other things. Moreover, a perspective can be taken only from a point in space or a moment in time—and a point in space and moment in time mean a situation. The differences between these two senses are differences in emphasis.

As I see it, the planning function in foreign policy relates to a particular sense of responsibility for the perspectives. The usefulness of planning is as an essential ingredient in the process of bringing problems to decision. The job of keeping clear on proportions and relations is indispensable in this business. Only systematic and continuous forethought can insure that a problem will be viewed in all its implications before a decision is made and action launched. Without it, decision and action would all too likely be quixotically impulsive, and the resources of capability would all too likely be overdrawn and the policy itself rendered insolvent.

I do not suggest that this special attention to perspectives originated only when the Policy Planning Staff was established in 1947. No doubt the Jeffersons, the John Quincy Adamses, and the Sewards had recourse to forethought in making up their minds.

In recent years, however, the concerns of the United States have become unprecedentedly various and their scope unprecedentedly vast. That circumstance accounts for the usefulness of having within the Department a staff with a frame of reference as wide as that of the Secretary, the Under Secretary, and the Deputy Under Secretary for Political Affairs.

It is exacting business. Our problems reflect upon and from each other like the facets of a crystal. An alteration in any facet shifts the light that shines from and through all the rest. The proportions and interrelation of our problems undergo unceasing change.

I take note of a fallacy that planning contains the remedy for all vexations and points the way around every dilemma. The idea that all our problems can be solved through the employment of total planning is persistently put forth. Since some planning is good, more would be better, and the most possible best of all—thus runs the reasoning. Imagine trying to salt a stew according to that scheme of logic.

The limit of utility in planning inheres in this. At any moment it is possible to draw one's perspectives on the future in the light of the data at hand, but it is not possible to draw a perspective on what one's perspective will be at some later stage in time.

Wisdom cannot be stockpiled. Brains are not susceptible of being carried around in a brief case. There is no sound way of pre-empting judgment.

It is not possible to tell better today how to handle a problem arising 6 months hence than it will be when the time comes. It may be—it is—possible and necessary to keep proportions intact and up to date so as to have them ready for the moment of decision—but the judgment of the moment itself cannot be foreclosed.

I take note also of the notion that planning is a self-inductive process and that planners should stay remote from the arena of responsibility and plan and plan and plan in communion with other planners who plan and plan and plan. Quite the contrary, the important thing is for the planner to keep the roots of his thinking in the exigencies of real problems.

I recall the story of the shingler who became so fascinated with his work on a foggy day that he shingled five feet beyond the eaves. That is what would happen if planning were carried on as a self-contained activity complete within its own system of logic.

The idea that planning can make everything tidy, answer all problems before they happen, foresee all eventualities, and prepare in advance the pat answer for every exigency is first cousin to the idea that power can be just as great as you want to make it. Power is the capacity to achieve intended results. It is always limited. Not all the elements bearing on a nation's destiny can ever be brought completely within the nation's control. Machiavelli pondered this in *The Prince.* He concluded that a .500 batting average on the field of destiny was about as much as might be hoped for. The figure strikes me as too high, but many persons expect much more than the Florentine did. I refer not to their personal expectations. Most people are not dismayed by having to manage their financial problems along month to month. People go on driving cars year after year without ever permanently solving their parking problems.

Yet some of my friends, and many persons in this country, some of whom write editorials or sit in seats of authority, persist in believing the desirable and achievable situation for the State to be one of perfect efficacy in its world relations. When perfect efficacy is not obtained, these people feel dismay and sense betrayal.

I recall a story told in Mexico. A man heavy in need and great in faith wrote a letter asking for 100 pesos. He addressed it to God and mailed it. The postmaster had no idea how to handle the letter. He opened it, seeking a clue. He was touched by the man's story of need. He passed the hat among the postal employees. Thus 75 pesos were raised. These were placed in an envelope to await the return of the importuning man. A few days later he was back, inquiring for mail. He was given the envelope, opened it, counted the money, and glowered. Then he went to the counter and scribbled out another letter. It read: "Dear God: I am still 25 pesos short. Please make up the difference. But don't send it through the local post office. I think it is full of thieves."

The expectation of perfect efficacy in the conduct of foreign affairs reflects itself in the "whodunit" approach to world problems.

I am concerned here, however, not so much with the tendency to ascribe to personal villainies all the difficulties of national existence as with the question of the proper proportions in which to view the problems.

This is consequential. As an accountable Government, our Government must stay within the limits permitted by public opinion. To the degree that unrealistic notions about what is feasible are factors in public opinion, unnecessary limits are imposed on the scope of action in foreign affairs, and rigidities harmful to our true interests result. This is borne constantly upon the mind of anyone having responsibilities in the making of foreign policy.

Several things occur to me as sources of the expectation of complete efficacy.

One of them is the consciousness of an extraordinarily successful past. The diplomatic course in the evolution from a colonial beachhead to a power of highest magnitude was one of matchless performance. Just as a man may lose his perspectives in calling up his departed youth, it is all too easy for us to lose a sense of proportion about our national problems by harking back to what we did when horizons were open and distance and the balance of power afforded us a shield.

Another influence I might call faith in engineering. That stems from our natural pride in the physical development of our country. Popular tradition treasures the idea that in the realm of creation all things are possible to those who will them. The margins available to us have made this almost true so far as the development of our own country is concerned.

Some of the popular ideas derived from science reflect this same material optimism. I think these are due not so much to the leaders of science themselves as to the popular interpreters of scientific achievement. From them we get the notion that cumulative knowledge can solve anything and that every problem is by definition solvable. Whatever may be the validity of this notion in the material relations which are the field of science, an error comes in trying to apply it as a universal.

Another contributing circumstance is that so much of foreign policy now stems from legislation. Legislation is law, law is to be obeyed, and an objective expressed in law is bound to be achieved. So goes the notion.

This idea bears particularly on congressional expectations in relation to foreign aid. The Congress has written into foreign aid legislation as conditions upon recipients many purposes whose consummation is devoutly to be wished. Some of these are such that they could be realized only in considerable spans of time and under governments with great margins of political power derived from energized and purposeful public support. The lack of such conditions in Europe is the heart of the difficulty. I find incredible the idea that phrases enacted by one's country's legislature can *ipso facto* solve problems, the solution of which requires redressing the factors of political power in another country.

This topic came up the other day in a conversation with a friend of mine who serves very ably in the House of Representatives. He was perturbed at the lag among European nations in realizing some of the domestic and international reforms prescribed by the Congress in the foreign aid legislation. I commented along the same line as I have spoken here. He agreed with me. Then he added that the

Congress would have to write the conditions tighter next time. Thus runs the endless faith in the compulsiveness of law.

Besides faith in making laws, let me mention faith in advertising. Where a perfume is marketed not only for its odor but also as a guarantee of domestic bliss, where automobiles are sold as means to capture the esteem of neighbors as well as means of transport, and where life insurance is offered not only as protection but also as a help for insomnia, it is natural to demand of foreign policy not only that it should handle the problems at hand but also that it should lead to a transfiguration of history.

This idea and all its implications are fit to be spurned. I shudder whenever I hear anyone refer to "selling" our foreign policy. Let me say for my Planning Staff colleagues and for myself that we regard foreign policy not as a commodity but as a responsibility, the American public not as our customers but as our masters, and ourselves not as salesmen but as stewards.

I spoke along these lines recently to a very able group of business men visiting the State Department, Sloan Foundation Fellows from the Massachusetts Institute of Technology. One of them commented that by disclosing its foreign policy too much in terms of moral purposes rather than in terms of actual problems to be handled within practical limits of capability, the Government itself encouraged the tendency that I was decrying. That was a good point. I was reminded of the story that at the Battle of New Orleans, General Jackson, seeing that the targets were being missed, ordered his artillerymen to elevate the guns a little lower. That counsel applies here.

As one other influence, a very important one, giving rise to the expectation of perfect performance, I shall cite the confusion of force and power. By force I mean first the capacity to transmit energy and so to expend it as to do vital harm to a foe, and second, the deterrent, compulsive effect exerted by the existence of this capacity. The capacity for force is only one of many elements in a nation's power reservoir. The others pertain to its economic strength, the internal integrity of its political position, the degree of confidence and good will which it commands abroad, and many other factors.

A nation's intentions and its power interact on each other. What we seek is in part determined by what we can do. What we can do is determined in part by what we are after. Furthermore, our own

aims and power acting as functions of each other are in an inter-
active relation with adversary intentions and capabilities, which also
relate to each other as interdependent variables.

Foreign affairs are a complex business. Gross errors result in the
attempt to treat them on the basis of the misleading notion that all
the problems of power can be reduced to the nice simplicity of
calculations of force.

Wars occur when nations seek to impose their wills by effecting
drastic changes in the ratios of power through radical action in the
factors of force. The force factors are susceptible of precision in
military planning. The elements are concrete. The speeds of ships,
their capabilities for carrying men and cargo, the distances, the fuel
requirements of planes and tanks, and the fire power of divisions,
and so on are known factors. The military planning process, insofar
as it relates to the ponderables of real or hypothetical campaigns,
turns out tidy and complete results. I do not mean that battles and
campaigns are fought according to preconceived schedules. I mean
only that insofar as advance planning is employed in the military
field, the quotients are precise, the columns are even, and the conclusions concrete.

Furthermore, within the time and space limits of a campaign, the
problem of force can be brought to an absolute solution. It really is
possible to achieve the surrender of all of an enemy's forces or to
eliminate armed resistance in a particular place for a particular time.
I speak here in no sense of professional disdain for military methods.
I have served more of my life as a staff officer in the Army than in
the line of foreign policy. I recognize the utility and necessity of
military methods of thinking for military purposes. I am aware also
of their limitations for other purposes.

It is easy for the unwary to jump to a fallacious conclusion that
if all human affairs were laid out with the precision of military
plans, then all problems could be brought to as complete solution as
can the problem of force in the conduct of a victorious military
campaign.

This is the sort of thing one gets to when one tries to find the
solution of all of the Nation's problems in the world, instead of
taking the historically realistic view that the job is one of managing
the problems, not of getting rid of them.

It is only a few steps from the notion of solution to the notion of employing force as a solvent. This is an easy fallacy for those souls anxious for history to be tidy and all conclusions certain. The exercise of force, however, is only an incident. The problems of power are endless. Wars only occur. Politics endures.

Some of my colleagues who bore with me as I tried out these comments thought I discounted too heavily the qualitative importance of objectives in foreign policy and reflected too somber an outlook.

Let me make the proportions clear. I do not disparage the importance of objectives. Only in the light of ultimate purposes can one know how to proceed problem by problem in this field. Moreover, I do not believe that good is forever beyond reach, but I am sure that the way to it is difficult and long.

The young Gladstone was advised by his mentor that politics was an unsatisfactory business and that he would have to learn to accept imperfect results. That advice has wisdom for the conduct of a foreign policy. The never ending dilemmas inherent in measuring what we would like to do against what we can do impose great moral burdens. These are beyond the capacity of some individuals to bear. Sometimes they become intolerable for whole societies.

The rebellion against that burden sometimes takes the form of an abdication of will, and relief is sought in a passive fatalism about the problems of national existence. Again the rebellion may take the form of resorting to the counsel of violence as the solvent for the difficulties and restraints which life imposes. In either form, the rejection is a rejection of life itself, for life imposes on nations, as on men, the obligation to strive without despair even though the way may be long and the burdens heavy.

To recognize this is in itself a source of strength.

As Keats tells us,

To bear all naked truths; And to envisage circumstance, all calm; That is the top of sovereignty.

The Decision to Drop the Atomic Bomb

I. SOCIAL AND POLITICAL IMPLICATIONS OF ATOMIC ENERGY.*

The only reason to treat nuclear power differently from all the other developments in the field of physics is the possibility of its use as a means of political pressure in peace and sudden destruction in war. All present plans for the organization of research, scientific and industrial development, and publication in the field of nucleonics are conditioned by the political and military climate in which one expects those plans to be carried out. Therefore, in making suggestions for the postwar organization of nucleonics, a discussion of political problems cannot be avoided. The scientists on this Project do not presume to speak authoritatively on problems of national and international policy. However, we found ourselves, by the force of events, during the last five years, in the position of a small group of citizens cognizant of a grave danger for the safety of this country as well as for the future of all the other nations, of which the rest of mankind is unaware. We therefore feel it our duty to urge that the political problems, arising from the mastering of nuclear power, be recognized in all their gravity, and that appropriate steps be taken for their study and the preparation of necessary decisions.

* * *

One possible way to introduce nuclear weapons to the world—which may particularly appeal to those who consider nuclear bombs primarily as a secret weapon developed to help win the present war—is to use them without warning on appropriately selected objects in Japan.

Although important tactical results undoubtedly can be achieved by a sudden introduction of nuclear weapons, we nevertheless think that

* A report prepared by a committee of three physicists (Drs. James Franck, chairman, D. Hughes, and L. Szilard), three chemists (Drs. T. Hogness, G. Seaborg, and E. Rabinowitch), and one biologist (Dr. J. J. Nickson), transmitted to Secretary of War Henry L. Stimson on June 11, 1945. *Bulletin of the Atomic Scientists,* May 1, 1946. Reprinted by permission.

the question of the use of the very first available atomic bombs in the Japanese war should be weighed very carefully, not only by military authorities, but by the highest political leadership of this country.

Russia, and even allied countries which bear less mistrust of our ways and intentions, as well as neutral countries may be deeply shocked by this step. It may be very difficult to persuade the world that a nation which was capable of secretly preparing and suddenly releasing a new weapon, as indiscriminate as the rocket bomb and a thousand times more destructive, is to be trusted in its proclaimed desire of having such weapons abolished by international agreement. We have large accumulations of poison gas, but do not use them, and recent polls have shown that public opinion in this country would disapprove of such a use even if it would accelerate the winning of the Far Eastern war. It is true that some irrational element in mass psychology makes gas poisoning more revolting than blasting by explosives, even though gas warfare is in no way more "inhuman" than the war of bombs and bullets. Nevertheless, it is not at all certain that American public opinion, if it could be enlightened as to the effect of atomic explosives, would approve of our own country being the first to introduce such an indiscriminate method of wholesale destruction of civilian life.

Thus, from the "optimistic" point of view—looking forward to an international agreement on the prevention of nuclear warfare—the military advantages and the saving of American lives achieved by the sudden use of atomic bombs against Japan may be outweighed by the ensuing loss of confidence and by a wave of horror and repulsion sweeping over the rest of the world and perhaps even dividing public opinion at home.

From this point of view, a demonstration of the new weapon might best be made, before the eyes of representatives of all the United Nations, on the desert or a barren island. The best possible atmosphere for the achievement of an international agreement could be achieved if America could say to the world, "You see what sort of a weapon we had but did not use. We are ready to renounce its use in the future if other nations join us in this renunciation and agree to the establishment of an efficient international control."

After such a demonstration the weapon might perhaps be used against Japan if the sanction of the United Nations (and of public opinion at home) were obtained, perhaps after a preliminary ulti-

matum to Japan to surrender or at least to evacuate certain regions as
an alternative to their total destruction. This may sound fantastic, but
in nuclear weapons we have something entirely new in order of magnitude of destructive power, and if we want to capitalize fully on the
advantage their possession gives us, we must use new and imagi-
native methods.

* * *

It must be stressed that if one takes the pessimistic point of view
and discounts the possibility of an effective international control over
nuclear weapons at the present time, then the advisability of an early
use of nuclear bombs against Japan becomes even more doubtful—
quite independently of any humanitarian considerations. If an international agreement is not concluded immediately after the first demonstration, this will mean a flying start toward an unlimited armaments
race. If this race is inevitable, we have every reason to delay its beginning as long as possible in order to increase our head start still further.

* * *

The benefit to the nation, and the saving of American lives in the
future, achieved by renouncing an early demonstration of nuclear
bombs and letting the other nations come into the race only reluctantly, on the basis of guesswork and without definite knowledge that
the "thing does work," may far outweigh the advantages to be gained
by the immediate use of the first and comparatively inefficient bombs
in the war against Japan. On the other hand, it may be argued that
without an early demonstration it may prove difficult to obtain adequate support for further intensive development of nucleonics in this
country and that thus the time gained by the postponement of an open
armaments race will not be properly used. Furthermore one may suggest that other nations are now, or will soon be, not entirely unaware
of our present achievements, and that consequently the postponement
of a demonstration may serve no useful purpose as far as the avoidance
of an armaments race is concerned, and may only create additional mistrust, thus worsening rather than improving the chances of an ultimate
accord on the international control of nuclear explosives.

Thus, if the prospects of an agreement will be considered poor in the
immediate future, the pros and cons of an early revelation of our possession of nuclear weapons to the world—not only by their actual use
against Japan, but also by a pre-arranged demonstration—must be

carefully weighed by the supreme political and military leadership of the country, and the decision should not be left to the considerations of military tactics alone.

One may point out that scientists themselves have initiated the development of this "secret weapon" and it is therefore strange that they should be reluctant to try it out on the enemy as soon as it is available. The answer to this question was given above—the compelling reason for creating this weapon with such speed was our fear that Germany had the technical skill necessary to develop such a weapon, and that the German government had no moral restraints regarding its use.

Another argument which could be quoted in favor of using atomic bombs as soon as they are available is that so much taxpayers' money has been invested in these Projects that the Congress and the American public will demand a return for their money. The attitude of American public opinion, mentioned earlier, in the matter of the use of poison gas against Japan, shows that one can expect the American public to understand that it is sometimes desirable to keep a weapon in readiness for use only in extreme emergency; and as soon as the potentialities of nuclear weapons are revealed to the American people, one can be sure that they will support all attempts to make the use of such weapons impossible. . . .

2. HENRY L. STIMSON, THE DECISION TO USE THE ATOMIC BOMB.*

The policy adopted and steadily pursued by President Roosevelt and his advisers was a simple one. It was to spare no effort in securing the earliest possible successful development of an atomic weapon. The reasons for this policy were equally simple. The original experimental achievement of atomic fission had occurred in Germany in 1938, and it was known that the Germans had continued their experiments. In 1941 and 1942 they were believed to be ahead of us, and it was vital that they should not be the first to bring atomic weapons into the field of battle. Furthermore, if we should be the first to develop the weapon, we should have a great new instrument for shortening the war and minimizing destruction. At no time, from 1941 to 1945, did I ever hear it suggested by the President, or by any other responsible member of the government, that atomic energy should not be used in the war.

---

* From *Harper's Magazine*. February 1947. Reprinted by permission.

All of us of course understood the terrible responsibility involved in our attempt to unlock the doors to such a devastating weapon; President Roosevelt particularly spoke to me many times of his own awareness of the catastrophic potentialities of our work. But we were at war, and the work must be done. I therefore emphasize that it was our common objective, throughout the war, to be the first to produce an atomic weapon and use it. The possible atomic weapon was considered to be a new and tremendously powerful explosive, as legitimate as any other of the deadly explosive weapons of modern war. The entire purpose was the production of a military weapon; on no other ground could the wartime expenditure of so much time and money have been justified. The exact circumstances in which that weapon might be used were unknown to any of us until the middle of 1945, and when that time came, as we shall presently see, the military use of atomic energy was connected with larger questions of national policy.

* * *

On March 15, 1945 I had my last talk with President Roosevelt. My diary record of this conversation gives a fairly clear picture of the state of our thinking at that time. I have removed the name of the distinguished public servant who was fearful lest the Manhattan (atomic) project be "a lemon"; it was an opinion common among those not fully informed.

The President . . . had suggested that I come over to lunch today. . . . First I took up with him a memorandum which he sent to me from _____ who had been alarmed at the rumors of extravagance in the Manhattan project. _____ suggested that it might become disastrous and he suggested that we get a body of "outside" scientists to pass upon the project because rumors are going around that Vannevar Bush and Jim Conant have sold the President a lemon on the subject and ought to be checked up on. It was rather a jittery and nervous memorandum and rather silly, and I was prepared for it and I gave the President a list of the scientists who were actually engaged on it to show the very high standing of them and it comprised four Nobel Prize men, and also how practically every physicist of standing was engaged with us in the project. Then I outlined to him the future of it and when it was likely to come off and told him how important it was to get ready. I went over with him the two schools of thought that exist in respect to the future control after the war of this project, in case it is successful, one of them being the secret close-in attempted control of the project by those who control it now, and the other being the international control based upon freedom both of science and of access. I told him that those things must be settled before the first projectile is used and that he must be ready with a statement to come out to the people on it just as soon as that is done. He agreed to that. . . .

This conversation covered the three aspects of the question which were then uppermost in our minds. First, it was always necessary to suppress a lingering doubt that any such titanic undertaking could be successful. Second, we must consider the implications of success in terms of its long-range postwar effect. Third, we must face the problem that would be presented at the time of our first use of the weapon, for with that first use there must be some public statement.

I did not see Franklin Roosevelt again. The next time I went to the White House to discuss atomic energy was April 25, 1945, and I went to explain the nature of the problem to a man whose only previous knowledge of our activities was that of a Senator who had loyally accepted our assurance that the matter must be kept a secret from him. Now he was President and Commander-in-Chief, and the final responsibility in this as in so many other matters must be his. President Truman accepted this responsibility with the same fine spirit that Senator Truman had shown before in accepting our refusal to inform him.

I discussed with him the whole history of the project. We had with us General Groves, who explained in detail the progress which had been made and the probable future course of the work. I also discussed with President Truman the broader aspects of the subject, and the memorandum which I used in this discussion is again a fair sample of the state of our thinking at the time.

MEMORANDUM DISCUSSED WITH
PRESIDENT TRUMAN APRIL 25, 1945

"1. Within four months we shall in all probability have completed the most terrible weapon ever known in human history, one bomb of which could destroy a whole city.

"2. Although we have shared its development with the U. K., physically the U. S. is at present in the position of controlling the resources with which to construct and use it and no other nation could reach this position for some years.

"3. Nevertheless it is practically certain that we could not remain in this position indefinitely.

"a. Various segments of its discovery and production are widely known among many scientists in many countries, although few scientists are now acquainted with the whole process which we have developed.

"b. Although its construction under present methods requires great scientific and industrial effort and raw materials, which are temporarily mainly within the possession and knowledge of U. S. and U. K., it is extremely probable that much easier and cheaper methods of production will be discovered by scientists in the future, together with the use of materials of much wider distribution. As a result, it is extremely probable that the future will make it possible for atomic bombs to be constructed by smaller nations or even groups, or at least by a larger nation in a much shorter time.

"4. As a result, it is indicated that the future may see a time when such a weapon may be constructed in secret and used suddenly and effectively with devastating power by a wilful nation or group against an unsuspecting nation or group of much greater size and material power. With its aid even a very powerful unsuspecting nation might be conquered within a very few days by a very much smaller one. . . .

"5. The world in its present state of moral advancement compared with its technical development would be eventually at the mercy of such a weapon. In other words, modern civilization might be completely destroyed.

"6. To approach any world peace organization of any pattern now likely to be considered, without an appreciation by the leaders of our country of the power of this new weapon, would seem to be unrealistic. No system of control heretofore considered would be adequate to control this menace. Both inside any particular country and between the nations of the world, the control of this weapon will undoubtedly be a matter of the greatest difficulty and would involve such thoroughgoing rights of inspection and internal controls as we have never heretofore contemplated.

"7. Furthermore, in the light of our present position with reference to this weapon, the question of sharing it with other nations and, if so shared, upon what terms, becomes a primary question of our foreign relations. Also our leadership in the war and in the development of this weapon has placed a certain moral responsibility upon us which we cannot shirk without very serious responsibility for any disaster to civilization which it would further.

"8. On the other hand, if the problem of the proper use of this weapon can be solved, we would have the opportunity to bring the world into a pattern in which the peace of the world and our civilization can be saved.

"9. As stated in General Groves' report, steps are under way looking towards the establishment of a select committee of particular qualifications for recommending action to the executive and legislative branches of our government when secrecy is no longer in full effect. The committee would also recommend the actions to be taken by the War Department prior to that time in anticipation of the postwar problems. All recommendations would of course be first submitted to the President."

The next step in our preparations was the appointment of the committee referred to in paragraph (9) above. This committee, which was known as the Interim Committee, was charged with the function of advising the President on the various questions raised by our apparently imminent success in developing an atomic weapon. I was its chairman, but the principal labor of guiding its extended deliberations fell to George L. Harrison, who acted as chairman in my absence. It will be useful to consider the work of the committeee in some detail. Its members were the following, in addition to Mr. Harrison and myself:

James F. Byrnes (then a private citizen) as personal representative of the President.

Ralph A. Bard, Under Secretary of the Navy.

William L. Clayton, Assistant Secretary of State.

Dr. Vannevar Bush, Director, Office of Scientific Research and Development, and president of the Carnegie Institution of Washington.

Dr. Karl T. Compton, Chief of the Office of Field Service in the Office of Scientific Research and Development, and president of the Massachusetts Institute of Technology.

Dr. James B. Conant, Chairman of the National Defense Research Committee, and president of Harvard University.

The discussions of the committee ranged over the whole field of atomic energy, in its political, military, and scientific aspects. That part of its work which particularly concerns us here relates to its recommendations for the use of atomic energy against Japan, but it should be borne in mind that these recommendations were not made in a vacuum. The committee's work included the drafting of the statements which were published immediately after the first bombs were dropped, the drafting of a bill for the domestic control of atomic energy, and recommendations looking toward the international control of atomic energy. The Interim Committee was assisted in its work by a Scientific Panel whose members were the following: Dr. A. H. Compton, Dr. Enrico Fermi, Dr. E. O. Lawrence, and Dr. J. R. Oppenheimer. All four were nuclear physicists of the first rank; all four had held positions of great importance in the atomic project from its inception. At a meeting with the Interim Committee and the Scientific Panel on May 31, 1945 I urged all those present to feel free to express themselves on any phase of the subject, scientific or political. Both General Marshall and I at this meeting expressed the view that atomic energy could not be considered simply in terms of military weapons but must also be considered in terms of a new relationship of man to the universe.

On June 1, after its discussions with the Scientific Panel, the Interim Committee unanimously adopted the following recommendations:

(1) The bomb should be used against Japan as soon as possible.

(2) It should be used on a dual target—that is, a military installation or war plant surrounded by or adjacent to houses and other buildings most susceptible to damage, and

(3) It should be used without prior warning [of the nature of the weapon]. One member of the committee, Mr. Bard, later changed his view and dissented from recommendation (3).

In reaching these conclusions the Interim Committee carefully considered such alternatives as a detailed advance warning or a demonstration in some uninhabited area. Both of these suggestions were discarded as impractical. They were not regarded as likely to be effective in compelling a surrender of Japan, and both of them involved serious risks. Even the New Mexico test would not give final proof that any given bomb was certain to explode when dropped from an airplane. Quite apart from the generally unfamiliar nature of atomic explosives, there was the whole problem of exploding a bomb at a predetermined height in the air by a complicated mechanism which could not be tested in the static test of New Mexico. Nothing would have been more damaging to our effort to obtain surrender than a warning or a demonstration followed by a dud—and this was a real possibility. Furthermore, we had no bombs to waste. It was vital that a sufficient effect be quickly obtained with the few we had.

The Interim Committee and the Scientific Panel also served as a channel through which suggestions from other scientists working on the atomic project were forwarded to me and to the President. Among the suggestions thus forwarded was one memorandum which questioned using the bomb at all against the enemy.* On June 16, 1945, after consideration of that memorandum, the Scientific Panel made a report, from which I quote the following paragraphs:

> The opinions of our scientific colleagues on the initial use of these weapons are not unanimous: they range from the proposal of a purely technical demonstration to that of the military application best designed to induce surrender. Those who advocate a purely technical demonstration would wish to outlaw the use of atomic weapons, and have feared that if we use the weapons now our position in future negotiations will be prejudiced. Others emphasize the opportunity of saving American lives by immediate military use, and believe that such use will improve the international prospects, in that they are more concerned with the prevention of war than with the elimination of this special weapon. We find ourselves closer to these latter views; *we can propose no technical demonstration likely to bring an end to the war; we see no acceptable alternative to direct military use.* [Italics mine.]

> With regard to these general aspects of the use of atomic energy, it is clear that we, as scientific men, have no proprietary rights. It is true that we are among the few citizens who have had occasion to give thoughtful consideration to these problems during the past few years. We have, however, no claim to special competence in solving the political, social, and military problems which are presented by the advent of atomic power.

The foregoing discussion presents the reasoning of the Interim Committee and its advisers. I have discussed the work of these gentlemen at length in order to make it clear that we sought the best advice that we could find. The committee's function was, of course, entirely advisory. The ultimate responsibility for the recommendation to the President rested upon me, and I have no desire to veil it. . . . I felt that to extract a genuine surrender from the Emperor and his military advisers, they must be administered a tremendous shock which would carry convincing proof of our power to destroy the Empire. Such an effective shock would save many times the number of lives, both American and Japanese, that it would cost.

The facts upon which my reasoning was based and steps taken to carry it out now follow.

The principal political, social, and military objective of the United States in the summer of 1945 was the prompt and complete surrender of Japan. Only the complete destruction of her military power could open the way to lasting peace.

* Editor's Note: For this document, see above, pp. 176-79.

Japan, in July 1945, had been seriously weakened by our increasingly violent attacks. It was known to us that she had gone so far as to make tentative proposals to the Soviet government, hoping to use the Russians as mediators in a negotiated peace. These vague proposals contemplated the retention by Japan of important conquered areas and were therefore not considered seriously. There was as yet no indication of any weakening in the Japanese determination to fight rather than accept unconditional surrender. If she should persist in her fight to the end, she had still a great military force.

* * *

As we understood it in July, there was a very strong possibility that the Japanese government might determine upon resistance to the end, in all the areas of the Far East under its control. In such an event the Allies would be faced with the enormous task of destroying an armed force of five million men and five thousand suicide aircraft, belonging to a race which had already amply demonstrated its ability to fight literally to the death.

The strategic plans of our armed forces for the defeat of Japan, as they stood in July, had been prepared without reliance upon the atomic bomb, which had not yet been tested in New Mexico. We were planning an intensified sea and air blockade, and greatly intensified strategic air bombing, through the summer and early fall, to be followed on November 1 by an invasion of the southern island of Kyushu. This would be followed in turn by an invasion of the main island of Honshu in the spring of 1946. The total U. S. military and naval force involved in this grand design was of the order of 5,000,000 men; if all those indirectly concerned are included, it was larger still.

We estimated that if we should be forced to carry this plan to its conclusion, the major fighting would not end until the latter part of 1946, at the earliest. I was informed that such operations might be expected to cost over a million casualties, to American forces alone. Additional large losses might be expected among our allies, and, of course, if our campaign were successful and if we could judge by previous experience, enemy casualties would be much larger than our own.

It was already clear in July that even before the invasion we should be able to inflict enormously severe damage on the Japanese homeland by the combined application of "conventional" sea and air power. The critical question was whether this kind of action would induce surrender. It therefore became necessary to consider very carefully the probable state of mind of the enemy, and to assess with accuracy the line of conduct which might end his will to resist.

With these considerations in mind, I wrote a memorandum for the President, on July 2, which I believe fairly represents the thinking of the American government as it finally took shape in action. . . .

"July 2, 1945.

"Memorandum for the President.

"PROPOSED PROGRAM FOR JAPAN

"1. The plans of operation up to and including the first landing have been authorized and the preparations for the operation are now actually going on. This situation was accepted by all members of your conference on Monday, June 18.

"2. There is reason to believe that the operation for the occupation of Japan following the landing may be a very long, costly, and arduous struggle on our part. The terrain, much of which I have visited several times, has left the impression on my memory of being one which would be susceptible to a last ditch defense such as has been made on Iwo Jima and Okinawa and which of course is very much larger than either of those two areas. According to my recollection it will be much more unfavorable with regard to tank maneuvering than either the Philippines or Germany.

"3. If we once land on one of the main islands and begin a forceful occupation of Japan, we shall probably have cast the die of last ditch resistance. The Japanese are highly patriotic and certainly susceptible to calls for fanatical resistance to repel an invasion. Once started in actual invasion, we shall in my opinion have to go through with an even more bitter finish fight than in Germany. We shall incur the losses incident to such a war and we shall have to leave the Japanese islands even more thoroughly destroyed than was the case with Germany. This would be due both to the difference in the Japanese and German personal character and the differences in the size and character of the terrain through which the operations will take place.

"4. A question then comes: Is there any alternative to such a forceful occupation of Japan which will secure for us the equivalent of an unconditional surrender of her forces and a permanent destruction of her power again to strike an aggressive blow at the 'peace of the

Pacific'? I am inclined to think that there is enough such chance to make it well worthwhile our giving them a warning of what is to come and a definite opportunity to capitulate. As above suggested, it should be tried before the actual forceful occupation of the homeland islands is begun and furthermore the warning should be given in ample time to permit a national reaction to set in.

"We have the following enormously favorable factors on our side—factors much weightier than those we had against Germany:

"Japan has no allies.

"Her navy is nearly destroyed and she is vulnerable to a surface and underwater blockade which can deprive her of sufficient food and supplies for her population.

"She is terribly vulnerable to our concentrated air attack upon her crowded cities, industrial and food resources.

"She has against her not only the Anglo-American forces but the rising forces of China and the ominous threat of Russia.

"We have inexhaustible and untouched industrial resources to bring to bear against her diminishing potential.

"We have great moral superiority through being the victim of her first sneak attack.

"The problem is to translate these advantages into prompt and economical achievement of our objectives. I believe Japan *is* susceptible to reason in such a crisis to a much greater extent than is indicated by our current press and other current comment. Japan is not a nation composed wholly of mad fanatics of an entirely different mentality from ours. On the contrary, she has within the past century shown herself to possess extremely intelligent people, capable in an unprecedentedly short time of adopting not only the complicated technique of Occidental civilization but to a substantial extent their culture and their political and social ideas. Her advance in all these respects during the short period of sixty or seventy years has been one of the most astounding feats of national progress in history—a leap from the isolated feudalism of centuries into the position of one of the six or seven great powers of the world. She has not only built up powerful armies and navies. She has maintained an honest and effective national finance and respected position in many of the sciences in which we pride ourselves. Prior to the forcible seizure of power over her government by the fanatical military group in 1931, she had for ten years lived a reasonably responsible and respectable international life.

"My own opinion is in her favor on the two points involved in this question:

"a. I think the Japanese nation has the mental intelligence and versatile capacity in such a crisis to recognize the folly of a fight to the finish and to accept the proffer of what will amount to an unconditional surrender; and

"b. I think she has within her population enough liberal leaders (although now submerged by the terrorists) to be depended upon for her reconstruction as a responsible member of the family of nations. I think she is better in this last respect than Germany was. Her liberals yielded only at the point of the pistol and, so far as I am aware, their liberal attitude has not been personally subverted in the way which was so general in Germany.

"On the other hand, I think that the attempt to exterminate her armies and her population by gunfire or other means will tend to produce a fusion of race solidity and antipathy which has no analogy in the case of Germany. We have a national interest in creating, if possible, a condition wherein the Japanese nation may live as a peaceful and useful member of the future Pacific community.

"5. It is therefore my conclusion that a carefully timed warning be given to Japan by the chief representatives of the United States, Great Britain, China, and, if then a belligerent, Russia by calling upon Japan to surrender and permit the occupation of her country in order to insure its complete demilitarization for the sake of the future peace.

"This warning should contain the following elements:

"The varied and overwhelming character of the force we are about to bring to bear on the islands.

"The inevitability and completeness of the destruction which the full application of this force will entail.

"The determination of the Allies to destroy permanently all authority and influence of those who have deceived and misled the country into embarking on world conquest.

"The determination of the Allies to limit Japanese sovereignty to her main islands and to render them powerless to mount and support another war.

"The disavowal of any attempt to extirpate the Japanese as a race or to destroy them as a nation.

"A statement of our readiness, once her economy is purged of its militaristic influence, to permit the Japanese to maintain such industries, particularly of a light consumer character, as offer no threat of aggression against their neighbors, but which can produce a sustaining economy, and provide a reasonable standard of living. The statement should indicate our willingness, for this purpose, to give Japan trade access to external raw materials, but no longer any control over the sources of supply outside her main islands. It should also indicate our willingness, in accordance with our now established foreign trade policy, in due course to enter into mutually advantageous trade relations with her.

"The withdrawal from their country as soon as the above objectives of the Allies are accomplished, and as soon as there has been established a peacefully inclined government, of a character representative of the masses of the Japanese people. I personally think that if in saying this we should add that we do not exclude a constitutional monarchy under her present dynasty, it would substantially add to the chances of acceptance.

"6. Success of course will depend on the potency of the warning which we give her. She has an extremely sensitive national pride and, as we are now seeing every day, when actually locked with the enemy will fight to the very death. For that reason the warning must be tendered before the actual invasion has occurred and while the impending destruction, though clear beyond peradventure, has not yet reduced her to fanatical despair. If Russia is a part of the threat, the Russian attack, if actual, must not have progressed too far. Our own bombing should be confined to military objectives as far as possible."

It is important to emphasize the double character of the suggested warning. It was designed to promise destruction if Japan resisted, and hope, if she surrendered.

It will be noted that the atomic bomb is not mentioned in this memorandum. On grounds of secrecy the bomb was never mentioned except when absolutely necessary, and furthermore, it had not yet been tested. It was of course well forward in our minds, as the memorandum was written and discussed, that the bomb would be the best possible sanction if our warning were rejected.

The adoption of the policy outlined in the memorandum of July 2 was a decision of high politics; once it was accepted by the President, the position of the atomic bomb in our planning became quite clear. I find that I stated in my diary, as early as June 19, that "the last chance warning ... must be given before an actual landing of the ground forces in Japan, and fortunately the plans provide for enough time to bring in the sanctions to our warning in the shape of heavy ordinary bombing attack and an attack of S-1." S-1 was a code name for the atomic bomb.

There was much discussion in Washington about the timing of the warning to Japan. The controlling factor in the end was the date already set for the Potsdam meeting of the Big Three. It was President Truman's decision that such a warning should be solemnly issued by the U.S. and the U.K. from this meeting, with the concurrence of the head of the Chinese government, so that it would be plain that *all* of Japan's principal enemies were in entire unity. This was done, in the Potsdam ultimatum of July 26, which very closely followed the above memorandum of July 2, with the exception that it made no mention of the Japanese Emperor.

On July 28 the Premier of Japan, Suzuki, rejected the Potsdam ultimatum by announcing that it was "unworthy of public notice." *

* Editor's Note: In a letter to Mr. Stimson, dated February 12, 1947, Joseph C. Grew, former ambassador to Japan and under secretary of state, wrote:

[The main point at issue is whether, if in May, 1945,] "the President had made a public categorical statement that surrender would not mean the elimination of the present dynasty if the Japanese people desired its retention, the surrender of Japan could have been hastened.

"That question can probably never be definitely answered but a good deal of evidence is available to shed light on it. From statements made by a number of the moderate former Japanese leaders to responsible Americans after the American occupation, it is quite clear that the civilian advisers to the Emperor were working toward surrender long before the Potsdam Proclamation, even indeed before my talk with the President on May 28, for they knew then that Japan was a defeated nation. The stumbling block that they had to overcome was the complete dominance of the Japanese Army over the Government, and even when the moderates finally succeeded in getting a decision by the controlling element of the Government to accept the Potsdam terms, efforts were made by the unreconciled elements in the Japanese Army to bring about nullification of that decision. The Emperor needed all the support he could get, and in the light of available evidence I myself and others felt and still feel that if such a categorical statement about the dynasty had been issued in May, 1945, the surrender-minded elements in the Government might well have been afforded by such a statement a valid reason and the necessary strength to come to an early clear-cut decision.

"If surrender could have been brought about in May, 1945, or even in June or July, before the entrance of Soviet Russia into the war and the use of the atomic bomb, the world would have been the gainer.

"The action of Prime Minister Suzuki in rejecting the Potsdam ultimatum by announcing on July 28, 1945, that it was 'unworthy of public notice' was a most unfortunate if not an utterly stupid step. Suzuki, who was severely wounded and very nearly assassinated as a moderate by the military extremists in 1936, I believe from the evidence which has reached me was surrender-minded even before May, 1945, if only it were made clear that surrender would not involve the downfall

In the face of this rejection we could only proceed to demonstrate that the ultimatum had meant exactly what it said when it stated that if the Japanese continued the war, "the full application of our military power, backed by our resolve, will mean the inevitable and complete destruction of the Japanese armed forces and just as inevitably the utter devastation of the Japanese homeland."

For such a purpose the atomic bomb was an eminently suitable weapon. The New Mexico test occurred while we were at Potsdam, on July 16. It was immediately clear that the power of the bomb measured up to our highest estimates. We had developed a weapon of such a revolutionary character that its use against the enemy might well be expected to produce exactly the kind of shock on the Japanese ruling oligarchy which we desired, strengthening the position of those who wished peace, and weakening that of the military party.

Because of the importance of the atomic mission against Japan, the detailed plans were brought to me by the military staff for approval. With President Truman's warm support I struck off the list of suggested targets the city of Kyoto. Although it was a target of considerable military importance, it had been the ancient capital of Japan and was a shrine of Japanese art and culture. We determined that it should be spared. I approved four other targets including the cities of Hiroshima and Nagasaki.

Hiroshima was bombed on August 6, and Nagasaki on August 9.

---

of the dynasty. That point was clearly *implied* in Article 12 of the Potsdam Proclamation that 'The occupying forces of the Allies shall be withdrawn from Japan as soon as . . . there has been established in accordance with the freely expressed will of the Japanese people a peacefully inclined and responsible government.' This however was not, at least from the Japanese point of view, a categorical undertaking regarding the dynasty, nor did it comply with your [Henry L. Stimson's] suggestion that it would substantially add to the chances of acceptance if the ultimatum should contain a statement that we would not exclude a constitutional monarchy under the present dynasty. Suzuki's reply was typical of oriental methods in retaining his supposed bargaining position until he knew precisely what the Potsdam Proclamation meant in that respect. The Asiatic concern over the loss of assumed bargaining power that might arise from exhibiting what might be interpreted as a sign of weakness is always uppermost in Japanese mental processes. He can seldom be made to realize that the time for compromise has passed if it ever existed. This explains but certainly does not excuse Suzuki's reply, and the result of his reply was to release the atom bomb to fulfill its appointed purpose. Yet I and a good many others will always feel that had the President issued as far back as May, 1945, the recommended categorical statement that the Japanese dynasty would be retained if the Japanese people freely desired its retention, the atom bomb might never have had to be used at all. . . ." From Joseph C. Grew, *Turbulent Era, A Diplomatic Record of Forty Years*, Vol. II. Houghton Mifflin Company, 1952. Reprinted by permission.

These two cities were active working parts of the Japanese war effort. One was an army center; the other was naval and industrial. Hiroshima was the headquarters of the Japanese Army defending southern Japan and was a major military storage and assembly point. Nagasaki was a major seaport and it contained several large industrial plants of great wartime importance. We believe that our attacks had struck cities which must certainly be important to the Japanese military leaders, both Army and Navy, and we waited for a result. We waited one day.

Many accounts have been written about the Japanese surrender. After a prolonged Japanese cabinet session in which the deadlock was broken by the Emperor himself, the offer to surrender was made on August 10. It was based on the Potsdam terms, with a reservation concerning the sovereignty of the Emperor. While the Allied reply made no promises other than those already given, it implicitly recognized the Emperor's position by prescribing that his power must be subject to the orders of the Allied Supreme Commander. These terms were accepted on August 14 by the Japanese, and the instrument of surrender was formally signed on September 2, in Tokyo Bay. Our great objective was thus achieved, and all the evidence I have seen indicates that the controlling factor in the final Japanese decision to accept our terms of surrender was the atomic bomb.

The two atomic bombs which we had dropped were the only ones we had ready, and our rate of production at the time was very small. Had the war continued until the projected invasion on November 1, additional fire raids of B-29's would have been more destructive of life and property than the very limited number of atomic raids which we could have executed in the same period. But the atomic bomb was more than a weapon of terrible destruction; it was a psychological weapon. In March 1945 our Air Force had launched its first great incendiary raid on the Tokyo area. In this raid more damage was done and more casualties were inflicted than was the case at Hiroshima. Hundreds of bombers took part and hundreds of tons of incendiaries were dropped. Similar successive raids burned out a great part of the urban area of Japan, but the Japanese fought on. On August 6 one B-29 dropped a single atomic bomb on Hiroshima. Three days later a second bomb was dropped on Nagasaki and the war was over. So far as the Japanese could know, our ability to execute atomic attacks, if necessary by many planes at a time, was unlimited.

As Dr. Karl Compton has said, "it was not one atomic bomb, or two, which brought surrender; it was the experience of what an atomic bomb will actually do to a community, *plus the dread of many more,* that was effective."

The bomb thus served exactly the purpose we intended. The peace party was able to take the path of surrender, and the whole weight of the Emperor's prestige was exerted in favor of peace. When the Emperor ordered surrender, and the small but dangerous group of fanatics who opposed him were brought under control, the Japanese became so subdued that the great undertaking of occupation and disarmament was completed with unprecedented ease.

In the foregoing pages I have tried to give an accurate account of my own personal observations of the circumstances which led up to the use of the atomic bomb and the reasons which underlay our use of it. To me they have always seemed compelling and clear, and I cannot see how any person vested with such responsibilities as mine could have taken any other course or given any other advice to his chiefs.

Two great nations were approaching contact in a fight to a finish which would begin on November 1, 1945. Our enemy, Japan, commanded forces of somewhat over 5,000,000 armed men. Men of these armies had already inflicted upon us, in our breakthrough of the outer perimeter of their defenses, over 300,000 battle casualties. Enemy armies still unbeaten had the strength to cost us a million more. *As long as the Japanese government refused to surrender,* we should be forced to take and hold the ground, and smash the Japanese ground armies, by close-in fighting of the same desperate and costly kind that we had faced in the Pacific islands for nearly four years.

In the light of the formidable problem which thus confronted us, I felt that every possible step should be taken to compel a surrender of the homelands, and a withdrawal of all Japanese troops from the Asiatic mainland and from other positions, before we had commenced an invasion. We held two cards to assist us in such an effort. One was the traditional veneration in which the Japanese Emperor was held by his subjects and the power which was thus vested in him over his loyal troops. It was for this reason that I suggested in my memorandum of July 2 that his dynasty should be continued. The second card was the use of the atomic bomb in the manner best calculated to persuade that Emperor and the counselors about him to submit to our demand for what was essentially unconditional surrender, placing his immense power over his people and his troops subject to our orders.

In order to end the war in the shortest possible time and to avoid the enormous losses of human life which otherwise confronted us, I felt that we must use the Emperor as our instrument to command and compel his people to cease fighting and subject themselves to our authority through him, and that to accomplish this we must give him and his controlling advisers a compelling reason to accede to our demands. This reason furthermore must be of such a nature that his people could understand his decision. The bomb seemed to me to furnish a unique instrument for that purpose.

My chief purpose was to end the war in victory with the least possible cost in the lives of the men in the armies which I had helped to raise. In the light of the alternatives which, on a fair estimate, were open to us I believe that no man, in our position and subject to our responsibilities, holding in his hands a weapon of such possibilities for accomplishing this purpose and saving those lives, could have failed to use it and afterwards looked his countrymen in the face.

As I read over what I have written, I am aware that much of it, in this year of peace, may have a harsh and unfeeling sound. It would perhaps be possible to say the same things and say them more gently. But I do not think it would be wise. As I look back over the five years of my service as Secretary of War, I see too many stern and heartrending decisions to be willing to pretend that war is anything else than what it is. The face of war is the face of death; death is an inevitable part of every order that a wartime leader gives. The decision to use the atomic bomb was a decision that brought death to over a hundred thousand Japanese. No explanation can change that fact and I do not wish to gloss it over. But this deliberate, premeditated destruction was our least abhorrent choice. The destruction of Hiroshima and Nagasaki put an end to the Japanese war. It stopped the fire raids, and the strangling blockade; it ended the ghastly specter of a clash of great land armies.

In this last great action of the Second World War we were given final proof that war is death. War in the twentieth century has grown steadily more barbarous, more destructive, more debased in all its aspects. Now, with the release of atomic energy, man's ability to destroy himself is very nearly complete. The bombs dropped on Hiroshima and Nagasaki ended a war. They also made it wholly clear that we must never have another war. This is the lesson men and leaders everywhere must learn, and I believe that when they learn it they will find a way to lasting peace. There is no other choice.

3. HARRY S. TRUMAN, SELECTIONS FROM HIS MEMOIRS.*

The historic message of the first explosion of an atomic bomb was flashed to me in a message from Secretary of War Stimson on the morning of July 16. The most secret and the most daring enterprise of the war had succeeded. We were now in possession of a weapon that would not only revolutionize war but could alter the course of history and civilization. This news reached me at Potsdam the day after I had arrived for the conference of the Big Three. . . .

Acting Secretary of State Grew had spoken to me in late May about issuing a proclamation that would urge the Japanese to surrender but would assure them that we would permit the Emperor to remain as head of the state. Grew backed this with arguments taken from his ten years' experience as our Ambassador in Japan, and I told him that I had already given thought to this matter myself and that it seemed to me a sound idea. . . .

On June 18 Grew reported that the proposal had met with the approval of his Cabinet colleagues and of the Joint Chiefs. The military leaders also discussed the subject with me when they reported the same day. Grew, however, favored issuing the proclamation at once, to coincide with the closing of the campaign on Okinawa, while the service chiefs were of the opinion that we should wait until we were ready to follow a Japanese refusal with the actual assault of our invasion forces.

It was my decision then that the proclamation to Japan should be issued from the forthcoming conference at Potsdam. This, I believed, would clearly demonstrate to Japan and to the world that the Allies were united in their purpose. By that time, also, we might know more about two matters of significance for our future effort: the participation of the Soviet Union and the atomic bomb. We knew that the bomb would receive its first test in mid-July. If the test of the bomb was successful, I wanted to afford Japan a clear chance to end the fighting before we made use of this newly gained power. If the test should fail, then it would be even more important to us to bring about a surrender before we had to make a physical conquest of

---

* From Harry S. Truman, *Memoirs*, Vol. I: *Year of Decisions*. Doubleday & Co., 1955. Copyright by Time, Inc. Reprinted by permission.

Japan. General Marshall told me that it might cost half a million American lives to force the enemy's surrender on his home grounds.

But the test was now successful. The entire development of the atomic bomb had been dictated by military considerations. The idea of the atomic bomb had been suggested to President Roosevelt by the famous and brilliant Dr. Albert Einstein, and its development turned out to be a vast undertaking. It was the achievement of the combined efforts of science, industry, labor, and the military, and it had no parallel in history. The men in charge and their staffs worked under extremely high pressure, and the whole enormous task required the services of more than one hundred thousand men and immense quantities of material. It required over two and a half years and necessitated the expenditure of two and a half billions of dollars. . . .

My own knowledge of these developments had come about only after I became President, when Secretary Stimson had given me the full story. He had told me at that time that the project was nearing completion and that a bomb could be expected within another four months. It was at his suggestion, too, that I had then set up a committee of top men and had asked them to study with great care the implications the new weapon might have for us. . . .

The final decision of where and when to use the atomic bomb was up to me. Let there be no mistake about it. I regarded the bomb as a military weapon and never had any doubt that it should be used. The top military advisers to the President recommended its use, and when I talked to Churchill he unhesitatingly told me that he favored the use of the atomic bomb if it might aid to end the war.

In deciding to use this bomb I wanted to make sure that it would be used as a weapon of war in the manner prescribed by the laws of war. That meant that I wanted it dropped on a military target. I had told Stimson that the bomb should be dropped as nearly as possibly upon a war production center of prime military importance.

Stimson's staff had prepared a list of cities in Japan that might serve as targets. Kyoto, though favored by General Arnold as a center of military activity, was eliminated when Secretary Stimson pointed out that it was a cultural and religious shrine of the Japanese.

Four cities were finally recommended as targets: Hiroshima, Kokura, Nigata, and Nagasaki. They were listed in that order as targets for the first attack. The order of selection was in accordance with the military importance of these cities, but allowance would be given for weather conditions at the time of the bombing. Before the selected targets were approved as proper for military purposes, I personally went over them in detail with Stimson, Marshall, and Arnold, and we discussed the matter of timing and the final choice of the first target. . . .

My statements on the atomic bomb, which had been released in Washington by Stimson, read in part as follows:

". . . But the greatest marvel is not the size of the enterprise, its secrecy, nor its cost, but the achievement of scientific brains in putting together infinitely complex pieces of knowledge held by many men in different fields of science into a workable plan. And hardly less marvelous has been the capacity of industry to design, and of labor to operate, the machines and methods to do things never done before, so that the brain child of many minds came forth in physical shape and performed as it was supposed to do. Both science and industry worked under the direction of the United States Army, which achieved a unique success in managing so diverse a problem in the advancement of knowledge in an amazingly short time. It is doubtful if such another combination could be got together in the world. What has been done is the greatest achievement of organized science in history. It was done under high pressure and without failure.

"We are now prepared to obliterate more rapidly and completely every productive enterprise the Japanese have above ground in any city. We shall destroy their docks, their factories, and their communications. Let there be no mistake; we shall completely destroy Japan's power to make war.

"It was to spare the Japanese people from utter destruction that the ultimatum of July 26 was issued at Potsdam. Their leaders promptly rejected that ultimatum. If they do not now accept our terms, they may expect a rain of ruin from the air, the like of which has never been seen on this earth. Behind this air attack will follow sea and land forces in such numbers and power as they have not yet seen and with the fighting skill of which they are already well aware.

". . . The fact that we can release atomic energy ushers in a new era in man's understanding of nature's forces. Atomic energy may in the future supplement the power that now comes from coal, oil, and falling water, but at present it cannot be produced on a basis to compete with them commercially. Before that comes there must be a long period of intensive research.

"It has never been the habit of the scientists of this country or the policy of this Government to withhold from the world scientific knowledge. Normally, therefore, everything about the work with atomic energy would be made public.

"But under present circumstances it is not intended to divulge the technical processes of production or all the military applications, pending further examination of possible methods of protecting us and the rest of the world from the danger of sudden destruction.

"I shall recommend that the Congress of the United States consider promptly the establishment of an appropriate commission to control the production and use of atomic power within the United States.

"I shall give further consideration and make further recommendations to the Congress as to how atomic power can become a powerful and forceful influence towards the maintenance of world peace."

4. WINSTON S. CHURCHILL, SELECTIONS FROM HIS MEMOIRS.*

On July 17 world-shaking news had arrived. In the afternoon Stimson called at my abode and laid before me a sheet of paper on which was written, "Babies satisfactorily born." By his manner I saw something extraordinary had happened. "It means," he said, "that the experiment in the New Mexican desert has come off. The atomic bomb is a reality." Although we had followed this dire quest with every scrap of information imparted to us, we had not been told beforehand, or at any rate I did not know, the date of the decisive trial. No responsible scientist would predict what would happen when the first full-scale atomic explosion was tried. Were these bombs useless or were they annihilating? Now we know. The "babies" had been "satisfactorily born." No one could yet measure the immediate military consequences of the discovery, and no one has yet measured anything else about it.

Next morning a plane arrived with a full description of this tremendous event in the human story. Stimson brought me the report. I tell the tale as I recall it. The bomb, or its equivalent, had been detonated at the top of a pylon 100 feet high. Everyone had been cleared away for ten miles round, and the scientists and their staffs crouched

---

* From Winston S. Churchill, *Triumph and Tragedy,* Houghton Mifflin, 1953. Reprinted by permission.

behind massive concrete shields and shelters at about that distance. The blast had been terrific. An enormous column of flame and smoke shot up to the fringe of the atmosphere of our poor earth. Devastation inside a one-mile circle was absolute. Here then was a speedy end to the Second World War, and perhaps to much else besides.

The President invited me to confer with him forthwith. He had with him General Marshall and Admiral Leahy. Up to this moment we had shaped our ideas towards an assault upon the homeland of Japan by terrific air bombing and by the invasion of very large armies. We had contemplated the desperate resistance of the Japanese fighting to the death with Samurai devotion, not only in pitched battles, but in every cave and dug-out. I had in my mind the spectacle of Okinawa island, where many thousands of Japanese, rather than surrender, had drawn up in line and destroyed themselves by hand-grenades after their leaders had solemnly performed the rite of *hara-kiri*. To quell the Japanese resistance man by man and conquer the country yard by yard might well require the loss of a million American lives and half that number of British—or more if we could get them there: for we were resolved to share the agony. Now all this nightmare picture had vanished. In its place was the vision—fair and bright indeed it seemed—of the end of the whole war in one or two violent shocks. I thought immediately myself of how the Japanese people, whose courage I had always admired, might find in the apparition of this almost supernatural weapon an excuse which would save their honour and release them from their obligation of being killed to the last fighting man.

Moreover, we should not need the Russians. The end of the Japanese war no longer depended upon the pouring in of their armies for the final and perhaps protracted slaughter. We had no need to ask favours of them. A few days later I minuted to Mr. Eden: "It is quite clear that the United States do not at the present time desire Russian participation in the war against Japan." The array of European problems could therefore be faced on their merits and according to the broad principles of the United Nations. We seemed suddenly to have become possessed of a merciful abridgment of the slaughter in the East and of a far happier prospect in Europe. I have no doubt that these thoughts were present in the minds of my American friends. At any rate, there never was a moment's discussion as to whether the atomic bomb should be used or not. To avert a vast, indefinite butchery, to bring the war to an end, to give peace to the world, to lay healing hands upon its tortured peoples by a manifestation of overwhelming power at the cost of a few explosions, seemed, after all our toils and perils, a miracle of deliverance.

British consent in principle to the use of the weapon had been given on July 4, before the test had taken place. The final decision now lay in the main with President Truman, who had the weapon; but I never doubted what it would be, nor have I ever doubted since that he was right. The historic fact remains, and must be judged in the after-time, that the decision whether or not to use the atomic bomb to compel the surrender of Japan was never even an issue. There was unanimous, automatic, unquestioned agreement around our table; nor did I ever hear the slightest suggestion that we should do otherwise.

5. FLEET ADMIRAL WILLIAM D. LEAHY, SELECTIONS FROM HIS MEMOIRS.*

Both sides were prepared throughout the war that had just ended to unloose deadly gases, but not even the fanatical followers of Hitler and Hirohito, who committed so many other unspeakable atrocities, dared use poison gas—for fear of retaliation.

To me, the atomic bomb belongs in exactly the same category.

I have admitted frankly in the preceding chapter that I misjudged the terrible efficiency of this entirely new concept of an explosive. In the fall of 1944 I held conferences with Professor Bush, Lord Cherwell, the British expert on atomic energy, and Major General Groves. They had convinced President Roosevelt and Prime Minister Churchill of the potential effectiveness of atomic energy for military purposes. As a result, vast sums of money were appropriated to push the development with all possible speed.

In the spring of 1945 President Truman directed Mr. Byrnes to make a special study of the status and prospects of the new atomic explosive on which two billion dollars already had been spent. Byrnes came to my home on the evening of June 4 to discuss his findings. He was more favorably impressed than I had been up to that time with the prospects of success in the final development and use of this new weapon.

---

*From *I Was There*. McGraw-Hill Book Company, Inc. Copyright 1950 by William D. Leahy. Reprinted by permission.

Once it had been tested, President Truman faced the decision as to whether to use it. He did not like the idea, but was persuaded that it would shorten the war against Japan and save American lives. It is my opinion that the use of this barbarous weapon at Hiroshima and Nagasaki was of no material assistance in our war against Japan. The Japanese were already defeated and ready to surrender because of the effective sea blockade and the successful bombing with conventional weapons.

It was my reaction that the scientists and others wanted to make this test because of the vast sums that had been spent on the project. Truman knew that, and so did the other people involved. However, the Chief Executive made a decision to use the bomb on two cities in Japan. We had only produced two bombs at that time. We did not know which cities would be the targets, but the President specified that the bombs should be used against military facilities.

I realized that my original error in discounting the effectiveness of the atomic bomb was based on long experience with explosives in the Navy. I had specialized in gunnery and at one time headed the Navy Department's Bureau of Ordnance. "Bomb" is the wrong word to use for this new weapon. It is not a bomb. It is not an explosive. It is a poisonous thing that kills people by its deadly radioactive reaction, more than by the explosive force it develops.

The lethal possibilities of atomic warfare in the future are frightening. My own feeling was that in being the first to use it, we had adopted an ethical standard common to the barbarians of the Dark Ages. I was not taught to make war in that fashion, and wars cannot be won by destroying women and children. We were the first to have this weapon in our possession, and the first to use it. There is a practical certainty that potential enemies will have it in the future and that atomic bombs will sometime be used against us.

That is why, as a professional military man with a half century of service to his government, I come to the end of my war story with an apprehension about the future.

These new concepts of "total war" are basically distasteful to the soldier and sailor of my generation. Employment of the atomic bomb in war will take us back in cruelty toward noncombatants to the days of Genghis Khan.

It will be a form of pillage and rape of a society, done impersonally by one state against another, whereas in the Dark Ages it was a result of individual greed and vandalism. These new and terrible instruments of uncivilized warfare represent a modern type of barbarism not worthy of Christian man.

One of the professors associated with the Manhattan Project told me that he had hoped the bomb wouldn't work. I wish that he had been right.

Perhaps there is some hope that its capacity for death and terror among the defenseless may restrain nations from using the atom bomb against each other, just as in the last war such fears made them avoid employment of the new and deadlier poison gases developed since World War I.

However, I am forced to a reluctant conclusion that for the security of my own country which has been the guiding principle in my approach to all problems faced during my career, there is but one course open to us:

Until the United Nations, or some world organization, can guarantee—and have the power to enforce that guarantee—that the world will be spared the terrors of atomic warfare, the United States must have more and better atom bombs than any potential enemy.

6. ARTHUR H. COMPTON, SELECTIONS FROM HIS MEMOIRS.*

Many commentators have sought for hidden, less obvious reasons for our use of the bombs against Japan. They have not considered as adequate the view that their use was important in achieving a surrender without the necessity of a tremendously costly invasion.

One such suggestion is that the United States saw in atomic weapons an assurance that American arms would dominate the Japanese surrender and occupation. By those who so contend, Hiroshima is considered a sacrifice to the American desire to achieve a diplomatic victory over Russia in the "cold war" that had been already foreseen. Otherwise, they say, why all the hurry? ...

Even if this hypothesis were correct, it does not seem to me reprehensible. I see no reason to suppose that the loss of lives or the material damage would have been less if surrender had been forced by Russian armies attacking in Manchuria than by the bombing of military tar-

---

* From Chapter IV of Arthur H. Compton, *Atomic Quest, A Personal Narrative.* Oxford University Press, 1956. Reprinted by permission.

gets in the cities of Japan's homeland. One would expect rather that the Japanese would be more sensitive and would react more quickly to damage that they saw happening at home. Lives and property on the continent of Asia were of no less human worth than those in Japan. Nor would I see anything wrong in a desire by the Americans to have the credit for the victory go to themselves rather than to the Russians if in fact they could earn the victory. There are also those who argue that the Russians made haste to enter the war by 8 August in order that they might dominate the Japanese peace negotiations. Why not? The only moral point involved, as I see it, is whether lives were needlessly sacrificed in order to bring the war to a close under conditions conducive to a just peace. From what has been said above it is evident that something extraordinary was necessary. Even with both the atomic bombing and the Russian declaration of war it was nearly impossible for the Japanese government to achieve surrender. One can hardly believe that the Russian attack of itself would have given sufficient incentive. It seems that the atom bomb did give that incentive.

As a matter of fact, however, I can find no evidence that such political considerations actually played a part in the American decision to use the atomic bomb on Japan. I have made a special point of investigating this question. . . . This I have done chiefly by talking with persons who took part in the critical decisions.

In the discussions that I heard before the bomb was dropped, the role of Russia with relation to Japanese surrender was hardly mentioned and then only as to whether Russia would enter in time to help in saving American lives. My brother Karl, who was present throughout the sessions of the Interim Committee, confirmed to me that he could not recall the position of America as against Russia ever arising in connection with the Japanese war. I discussed the argument . . . also with General Marshall. That the bomb was used to gain political advantage he denied absolutely. He said the one and only reason that convinced him the bomb should be used was that by bringing the war quickly to a close the lives of many men would be saved.

It is true that in Churchill's account of the Potsdam proceedings he tells how he welcomed the possibility offered by the atomic bomb of defeating the Japanese without Russian help. But that is Britain speaking, not the United States.

Truman's statement to me was to the contrary. Not only did he tell

Stalin at once of the availability of a new type bomb which he hoped would be decisive, he was also repeatedly urging Stalin to enter the war as soon as possible. Everything I have been able to learn confirms the simple truth of the statement of W. Averell Harriman:

At Potsdam, more than five months after Yalta, the Joint Chiefs of Staff were still planning an invasion of the Japanese home islands and still considered Soviet participation in the Pacific war essential.

The date of using the atomic bombs was in fact determined solely by the technical considerations of their construction, testing, and preparation for delivery. They were used as soon as they could be made ready.

Our leaders were well aware that if victory could be reached in the Pacific war without revealing the possibility of the atomic bomb, it would be to our military advantage to avoid its use and keep it as a surprise weapon in case of war necessity at a later time.* This advice was not aimed at Russia in particular. I recall more than one occasion when General Groves stressed the fact that it is impossible to foretell what nation will be the enemy if future wars should develop. On this basis he argued that, if secrecy could be maintained, we should not expose our hand to any foreign nation as to the nature or availability of these new weapons. It was evident, however, that the availability of the atomic bomb could not be kept secret after the war. On the other

---

* Editor's Note: Earlier in this chapter, Arthur Compton describes General Marshall's opinion as expressed at a meeting of the "Interim Committee" on May 31, 1945: "General Marshall stated that from the point of view of the postwar safety of the nation he would have to argue against the use of the bomb in World War II, at least if its existence could be kept secret. Such use, he said, would show our hand. We would be in a stronger position with regard to future military action if we did not show the power we held.

"This led to a discussion about the possibility of maintaining secrecy about our development of atomic weapons. The members of the Scientific Panel were unanimous in the opinion that so many persons already knew of the wartime atomic studies that soon after the war it would be common knowledge that nuclear energy could be released and that it could not be long before an atomic explosion would somewhere be tried.

"This reply did not, however, answer fully General Marshall's objection to the use of the bomb. Even though the knowledge of the availability of atomic energy might become widespread, perhaps the details of the bomb itself would not be known outside of the United States and Britain. In any case, if the bomb were not used in the present war the compelling incentive for its development by other nations would be lacking.

"Though General Marshall was thus noting a real military objection to any demonstration of the bomb, he seemed to accept the view that its use was nevertheless important. This I verified in subsequent discussions. He was fully convinced at this time that the bomb should be used. This was primarily to bring the war quickly to a close and thereby to save lives."

hand, its actual use would provide the strongest possible stimulus toward the development of similar weapons by other powers.

The decision to use the bomb was thus not made to gain a postwar military advantage. We used it in spite of the recognition that we would thus impair our position relative to other nations.

7. HANSON W. BALDWIN, THE ATOMIC BOMB—THE PENALTY OF EXPEDIENCY.*

The utilization of the atomic bomb against a prostrate and defeated Japan in the closing days of the war exemplifies . . . the narrow, astigmatic concentration of our planners upon one goal, and one alone: victory.

Nowhere in all of Mr. Stimson's forceful and eloquent apologia for the leveling of Hiroshima and Nagasaki is there any evidence of an ulterior vision; indeed, the entire effort of his famous *Harper's* article, reprinted and rearranged in his book, *On Active Service,* is focused on proving that the bomb hastened the end of the war. But at what cost!

To accept the Stimson thesis that the atomic bomb should have been used as it was used, it is necessary first to accept the contention that the atomic bomb achieved or hastened victory, and second, and more important, that it helped to consolidate the peace or to further the political aims for which war was fought.

History can accept neither contention.

Let us examine the first. The atomic bomb was dropped in August. Long before that month started our forces were securely based in Okinawa, the Marianas and Iwo Jima; Germany had been defeated; our fleet had been cruising off the Japanese coast with impunity bombarding the shoreline; our submarines were operating in the Sea of Japan; even inter-island ferries had been attacked and sunk. Bombing, which started slowly in June, 1944, from China bases and from the Marianas in November, 1944, had been increased materially in 1945, and by August, 1945, more than 16,000 tons of bombs had ravaged Japanese cities. Food was short; mines and submarines and surface vessels and planes clamped an iron blockade around the main islands; raw materials were scarce. Blockade, bombing, and

---

* From Hanson W. Baldwin, *Great Mistakes of the War.* Published by Harper and Brothers. Copyright, 1949, 1950, by Hanson W. Baldwin. Reprinted by permission.

unsuccessful attempts at dispersion had reduced Japanese production capacity from 20 to 60 per cent. The enemy, in a military sense, was in a hopeless strategic position by the time the Potsdam demand for unconditional surrender was made on July 26.

Such, then, was the situation when we wiped out Hiroshima and Nagasaki.

Need we have done it? No one can, of course, be positive, but the answer is almost certainly negative.

The invasion of Japan, which Admiral Leahy had opposed as too wasteful of American blood, and in any case unnecessary, was scheduled (for the southern island of Kyushu) for Nov. 1, 1945, to be followed if necessary, in the spring of 1946, by a major landing on the main island of Honshu. We dropped the two atomic bombs in early August, almost two months before our first D-Day. . . . It followed the recommendations of Secretary Stimson and an "Interim Committee" of distinguished officials and scientists, who had found "no acceptable alternative to direct military use."

But the weakness of this statement is inherent, for none was tried and "military use" of the bomb was undertaken despite strong opposition to this course by numerous scientists and Japanese experts, including former Ambassador Joseph Grew. Not only was the Potsdam ultimatum merely a restatement of the politically impossible— unconditional surrender—but it could hardly be construed as a direct warning of the atomic bomb and was not taken as such by anyone who did not know the bomb had been created. A technical demonstration of the bomb's power may well have been unfeasible, but certainly a far more definite warning could have been given; and it is hard to believe that a target objective in Japan with but sparse population could not have been found. The truth is we did not try; we gave no specific warning. There were almost two months before our scheduled invasion of Kyushu, in which American ingenuity could have found ways to bring home to the Japanese the impossibility of their position and the horrors of the weapon being held over them; yet we rushed to use the bomb as soon as unconditional surrender was rejected. Had we devised some demonstration or given a more specific warning than the Potsdam ultimatum, and had the Japanese still persisted in continued resistance after some weeks of our psychological offensive, we should perhaps have been justified in the bomb's use; at least, our hands would have been more clean.

But, in fact, our only warning to a Japan already militarily defeated, and in a hopeless situation, was the Potsdam demand for unconditional surrender issued on July 26, when we knew Japanese surrender attempts had started. Yet when the Japanese surrender was negotiated about two weeks later, after the bomb was dropped, our unconditional surrender demand was made conditional and we agreed, as Stimson had originally proposed we should do, to continuation of the Emperor upon his imperial throne.

We were, therefore, twice guilty. We dropped the bomb at a time when Japan already was negotiating for an end of the war but before those negotiations could come to fruition. We demanded unconditional surrender, then dropped the bomb and accepted conditional surrender, a sequence which indicates pretty clearly that the Japanese would have surrendered, even if the bomb had not been dropped, had the Potsdam Declaration included our promise to permit the Emperor to remain on his imperial throne.

What we now know of the condition of Japan, and of the days preceding her final surrender on Aug. 15, verifies these conclusions. It is clear, in retrospect, (and was understood by some, notably Admiral Leahy, at the time) that Japan was militarily on her last legs. Yet our intelligence estimates greatly overstated her strength. . . .

It is therefore clear today—and was clear to many even as early as the spring of 1945—that the military defeat of Japan was certain; the atomic bomb was not needed.

But if the bomb did not procure victory, did it hasten it?

This question cannot be answered with equal precision, particularly since the full story of the Japanese surrender attempts has not been compiled. But a brief chronology of known events indicates that the atomic bomb may have shortened the war by a few days—not more.

The day before Christmas, 1944 (two months *before* the Yalta conference), U.S. intelligence authorities in Washington received a report from a confidential agent in Japan that a peace party was emerging and that the Koiso cabinet would soon be succeeded by a cabinet headed by Admiral Baron Suzuki who would initiate surrender proceedings.

The Koiso cabinet *was* succeeded by a new government headed by Suzuki in early April, 1945, but even prior to this significant change, the Japanese—in February, 1945—had approached the Russians with a request that they act as intermediary in arranging a peace with the Western powers. The Russian Ambassador, Malik, in Tokyo, was the channel of the approach. The Russians, however, set their price of mediation so high that the Japanese temporarily dropped the matter. The United States was not officially informed of this approach until after the end of the war. . . .

In April, 1945, as the United States was establishing a foothold on Okinawa, the Russians in effect denounced their neutrality agreement with Japan, and from then until July 12, the new cabinet was moving rapidly toward surrender attempts.

On July 12, fourteen days before we issued the Potsdam Proclamation, these attempts reached a clearly defined point. Prince Konoye was received by the Emperor on that day and ordered to Moscow as a peace plenipotentiary to "secure peace at any price." On July 13, Moscow was notified officially by the Japanese foreign office that the "Emperor was desirous of peace."

It was hoped that Moscow would inform the United States and Britain at the Potsdam conference of Japan's desire to discuss peace. But instead of an answer from the "Big Three," Ambassador Sato in Moscow was told by Molotov on August 8 of Russia's entry into the war against Japan, effective immediately. . . .

The first atomic bomb was dropped on Hiroshima on August 6; Russia entered the war on August 8; and the second atomic bomb was dropped on Nagasaki on August 9. . . .

In the words of Harry F. Kern, managing editor of *Newsweek,* who had made a special study, with the assistance of *Newsweek* correspondents, of the events surrounding the Japanese surrender:

"I think it's fair to say that the principal effect of the atom bomb on the Japanese surrender was to provide Suzuki with the immediate excuse for setting in motion the chain of events which resulted in the surrender. . . .

"However, I think it is also a reasonable surmise that the Russian declaration of war would have served the same purpose, and that the dropping of the bomb was therefore unnecessary. In no case was the dropping of the bomb the reason for the Japanese surrender, and I don't think we can say that it acted as anything more than a catalyst in advancing the plans of Suzuki and his supporters."

Or, as the Strategic Bombing Survey puts it, "it is the Survey's opinion that certainly prior to December 31, 1945, and in all probability prior to November 1, 1945, Japan would have surrendered even if the atomic bombs had not been dropped, even if Russia had not entered the war, and even if no invasion had been planned or contemplated."

This seems, in the light of history, a reasonable judgment, and, in view of our available intelligence estimates, one that we could have then made. It is quite possible that the atomic bombs shortened the war by a day, a week, or a month or two—not more.

But at what a price! For whether or not the atomic bomb hastened victory, it is quite clear it has not won the peace.

Some may point to the comparative tranquility of Japan under MacArthur in the postwar period as due in part to the terror of American arms created by the bomb. This is scarcely so; Japan's seeming tranquility is a surface one which has been furthered by a single occupation authority and the nature of the Japanese people. But I venture to estimate that those who suffered at Hiroshima and Nagasaki will never forget it, and that we sowed there a whirlwind of hate which we shall someday reap.

In estimating the effect of the use of the bomb upon the peace, we must remember, first, that we use the bomb for one purpose, and one only: not to secure a more equable peace, but to hasten victory. By using the bomb we have become identified, rightfully or wrongly, as inheritors of the mantle of Genghis Khan and all those of past history who have justified the use of utter ruthlessness in war.

It may well be argued, of course, that war—least of all modern war—knows no humanity, no rules, and no limitations, and that death by the atomic bomb is no worse than death by fire bombs or high explosives or gas or flame throwers. It is, of course, true that the atomic bomb is no worse qualitatively than other lethal weapons; it is merely quantitatively more powerful; other weapons cause death in fearful ways; the atomic bomb caused more death. We already had utilized fire raids, mass bombardment of cities, and flame throwers in the name of expediency and victory prior to August 6, even though many of our people had recoiled from such practices.

Even as late as June 1, 1945, Stimson "had sternly questioned his Air Forces leader, wanting to know whether the apparently indiscriminate bombings of Tokyo were absolutely necessary. Perhaps, as he [Stimson] later said, he was misled by the constant talk of 'precision bombing,' but he had believed that even air power could be limited in its use by the old concept of 'legitimate military targets.'

Now in the conflagration bombings by massed B-29's, he was permitting a kind of total war he had always hated, and in recommending the use of the atomic bomb he was implicitly confessing that there could be no significant limits to the horror of modern war."

If we accept this confession—that there can be no limits set to modern war—we must also accept the bitter inheritance of Genghis Khan and the mantles of all the other ruthless despoilers of the past.

In reality, we took up where these great conquerors left off long before we dropped the atomic bomb. Americans, in their own eyes, are a naively idealistic people, with none of the crass ruthlessness so often exhibited by other nations. Yet in the eyes of others our record is very far from clean, nor can objective history palliate it. Rarely have we been found on the side of restricting horror; too often we have failed to support the feeble hands of those who would limit war. We did not ratify the Hague convention of 1899, outlawing the use of dumdum (expanding) bullets in war. We never ratified the Geneva Protocol of 1925, outlawing the use of biological agents and gas in war. At the time the war in the Pacific ended, pressure for the use of gas against Japanese island positions had reached the open discussion stage, and rationalization was leading surely to justification, an expedient justification since we had air superiority and the means to deluge the enemy with gas, while he had no similar way to reply. We condemned the Japanese for their alleged use of biological agents against the Chinese, yet in July and August, 1945, a shipload of U.S. biological agents for use in destruction of the Japanese rice crop was en route to the Marianas. And even before the war, our fundamental theory of air war, like the Trenchard school of Britain, coincided, or stemmed from, the Douchet doctrine of destructiveness: the bombardment of enemy cities and peoples.

Yet surely these methods—particularly the extension of unrestricted warfare to enemy civilians—defeated any peace aims we might have had, and had little appreciable effect in hastening military victory. For in any totalitarian state, the leaders rather than the peoples must be convinced of defeat, and the indiscriminate use of mass or area weapons, like biological agents and the atomic bomb, strike at the people, not the rulers. We cannot succeed, therefore, by such methods, in drawing that fine line between ruler and ruled that ought to be drawn in every war; we cannot hasten military victory by slaughtering the led; such methods only serve to bind the led closer to their leaders. Moreover, unrestricted warfare can never lay the ground-work for a more stable peace. Its heritage may be the salt-sown fields of Carthage, or the rubble and ruin of a Berlin or Tokyo or Hiroshima; but neither economically nor pyschologically can unrestricted warfare—atomic warfare or biological warfare—lead anywhere save to eventual disaster.

During the last conflict we brought new horror to the meaning of war; the ruins of Germany and Japan, the flame-scarred tissues of the war-wounded attest our efficiency. And on August 6, 1945, that blinding flash above Hiroshima wrote a climax to an era of American expediency. On that date we joined the list of those who had introduced new and horrible weapons for the extermination of man; we joined the Germans who had first utilized gas, the Japanese with their biological agents, the Huns and the Mongols who had made destruction a fine art.

It is my contention that in the eyes of the world the atomic bomb has cost us dearly; we have lost morally; we no longer are the world's moral leader as in the days of the Wilsonian Fourteen Points. It is my contention that the unlimited destruction caused by our unlimited methods of waging war has caused us heavy economic losses in the forms of American tax subsidies to Germany and Japan. It is my contention that unrestricted warfare and unlimited aims cost us politically the winning of the peace.

But it is not only—and perhaps not chiefly—in public opinion or in the public pocketbook or even in public stability that we have suffered, but in our own souls. The American public is tending to accept the nefarious doctrine that the ends justify the means, the doctrine of exigency. . . .

The use of the atomic bomb, therefore, cost us dearly; we are now branded with the mark of the beast. Its use may have hastened victory—though by very little—but it has cost us in peace the pre-eminent moral position we once occupied. Japan's economic troubles are in some degree the result of unnecessary devastation. We have embarked upon Total War with a vengeance; we have done our best to make it far more total. If we do not soon reverse this trend, if we do not cast about for means to limit and control war, if we do not abandon the doctrine of expediency, of unconditional surrender, of total victory, we shall someday ourselves become the victims of our own theories and practices. . . .

8. GERTRUDE STEIN, REFLECTION ON THE ATOMIC BOMB.*

They asked me what I thought of the atomic bomb. I said I had not been able to take any interest in it.

I like to read detective and mystery stories, I never get enough of them but whenever one of them is or was about death rays and atomic bombs I never could read them. What is the use, if they are really as destructive as all that there is nothing left and if there is nothing there is nobody to be interested and nothing to be interested about. If they are not as destructive as all that then they are just a little more or less destructive than other things and that means that in spite of all destruction there are always lots left on this earth to be interested or to be willing and the thing that destroys is just one of the things that concerns the people inventing it or the people starting it off, but really nobody else can do anything about it so you have to just live along like always, so you see the atomic (bomb) is not at all interesting, not any more interesting than any other machine, and machines are only interesting in being invented or in what they do, so why be interested. I never could take any interest in the atomic bomb, I just couldn't any more than in everybody's secret weapon. That it has to be secret makes it dull and meaningless. Sure it will destroy a lot and kill a lot, but its the living that are interesting not the way of killing them, because if there were not a lot left living how could there be any interest in destruction. Alright, that is the way I feel about it. And really way down that is the way everybody feels about it. They think they are interested about the atomic bomb but they really are not not any more than I am. Really not. They may be a little scared, I am not so scared, there is so much to be scared of so what is the use of bothering to be scared, and if you are not scared the atomic bomb is not interesting.

Everybody gets so much information all day long that they lose their common sense. They listen so much that they forget to be natural. This is a nice story.

---

* From The *Yale Poetry Review*, December 1947. (This is the very last piece that Miss Stein wrote before her death in 1946. The Editors provisionally titled it "Reflection on The Atomic Bomb.") Reprinted by permission.

The Foreign Policy of England*

BY SIR WINSTON CHURCHILL

[1948]

HERE is the place to set forth the principles of British policy towards Europe which I had followed for many years and follow still. I cannot better express them than in the words which I used to the Conservative Members Committee on Foreign Affairs, who invited me to address them in private at the end of March, 1936.

For four hundred years the foreign policy of England has been to oppose the strongest, most aggressive, most dominating Power on the Continent, and particularly to prevent the Low Countries falling into the hands of such a Power. Viewed in the light of history, these four centuries of consistent purpose amid so many changes of names and facts, of circumstances and conditions, must rank as one of the most remarkable episodes which the records of any race, nation, state, or people can show. Moreover, on all occasions England took the more difficult course. Faced by Philip II of Spain, against Louis XIV under William III and Marlborough, against Napoleon, against William II of Germany, it would have been easy and must have been very tempting to join with the stronger and share the fruits of his conquest. However, we always took the harder course, joined with the less strong Powers, made a combination among them, and thus defeated and frustrated the Continental military tyrant whoever he was, whatever nation he led. Thus we preserved the liberties of Europe, protected the growth of its vivacious and varied society, and emerged after four terrible struggles with an ever-growing fame and widening Empire, and with the Low Countries safely protected in their independence. Here is the wonderful unconscious tradition of British foreign policy. All our thoughts rest in that tradition today. I know of nothing which has occurred to alter or weaken the justice, wisdom, valour, and prudence upon which our ancestors acted. I know of nothing that has happened to human nature which in the slightest degree alters the validity of their conclusions. I know of nothing in military, political, economic, or scientific fact which makes me feel that we might not, or cannot, march along the same road. I venture to put this very general

---

* From *The Gathering Storm*, copyright 1948 by Houghton Mifflin Co. Reprinted by permission.

proposition before you because it seems to me that if it is accepted, everything else becomes much more simple.

Observe that the policy of England takes no account of which nation it is that seeks the overlordship of Europe. The question is not whether it is Spain, or the French Monarchy, or the French Empire, or the German Empire, or the Hitler régime. It has nothing to do with rulers or nations; it is concerned solely with whoever is the strongest or the potentially dominating tyrant. Therefore, we should not be afraid of being accused of being pro-French or anti-German. If the circumstances were reversed, we could equally be pro-German and anti-French. It is a law of public policy which we are following, and not a mere expedient dictated by accidental circumstances, or likes and dislikes, or any other sentiment.

The question, therefore, arises which is today the Power in Europe which is the strongest, and which seeks in a dangerous and oppressive sense to dominate. Today, for this year, probably for part of 1937, the French Army is the strongest in Europe. But no one is afraid of France. Everyone knows that France wants to be let alone, and that with her it is only a case of self-preservation. Everyone knows that the French are peaceful and overhung by fear. They are at once brave, resolute, peace-loving, and weighed down by anxiety. They are a liberal nation with free parliamentary institutions.

Germany, on the other hand, fears no one. She is arming in a manner which has never been seen in German history. She is led by a handful of triumphant desperadoes. The money is running short, discontents are arising beneath these despotic rulers. Very soon they will have to choose, on the one hand, between economic and financial collapse or internal upheaval, and on the other, a war which could have no other object, and which, if successful, can have no other result, than a Germanised Europe under Nazi control. Therefore, it seems to me that all the old conditions present themselves again, and that our national salvation depends upon our gathering once again all the forces of Europe to contain, to restrain, and if necessary to frustrate, German domination. For, believe me, if any of those other Powers, Spain, Louis XIV, Napoleon, Kaiser Wilhelm II, had with our aid become the absolute masters of Europe, they could have despoiled us, reduced us to insignificance and penury on the morrow of their victory. We ought to set the life and endurance of the British Empire and the greatness of this island very high in our duty, and not be led astray by illusions about an ideal world, which only means that other and worse controls will step into our place, and that the future direction will belong to them.

It is at this stage that the spacious conception and extremely vital organisation of the League of Nations presents itself as a prime factor. The League of Nations is, in a practical sense, a British conception, and it harmonises perfectly with all our past methods and actions. Moreover, it harmonises with those broad ideas of right and wrong, and of peace based upon controlling the major aggressor, which we have always followed. We wish for the reign of law and freedom among nations and within nations, and it was for that, and nothing less than that, that those bygone architects of our repute, magnitude, and civilisation fought, and won. The dream of a reign of international law and of the settlement of disputes by patient discussion, but still in accordance with what is lawful and just, is very dear to the British people. You must not underrate the force which these ideals exert upon the modern British democracy. One does not know how these seeds are planted by the winds of the centuries in the hearts of the working people. They are there, and just as strong as their love of liberty. We should not neglect them, because they are the essence of the genius of this island. Therefore, we believe that in the fostering and fortifying of the League of Nations will be found the best means of defending our island security, as well as maintaining grand universal causes with which we have very often found our own interests in natural accord.

My three main propositions are: First, that we must oppose the would-be dominator or potential aggressor. Secondly, that Germany under its present Nazi régime and with its prodigious armaments, so swiftly developing, fills unmistakably that part. Thirdly, that the League of Nations rallies many countries, and unites our own people here at home in the most effective way to control the would-be aggressor. I venture most respectfully to submit these main themes to your consideration. Everything else will follow from them.

It is always more easy to discover and proclaim general principles than to apply them. First, we ought to count our effective association with France. That does not mean that we should develop a needlessly hostile mood against Germany. It is a part of our duty and our interest to keep the temperature low between these two countries. We shall not have any difficulty in this so far as France is concerned. Like us, they are a parliamentary democracy with tremendous inhibitions against war, and, like us, under considerable draw-backs in preparing their defence. Therefore, I say we ought to regard our defensive association with France as fundamental. Everything else must be viewed in proper subordination now that the times have become so sharp and perilous. Those who are possessed of a definite body of doctrine and of deeply rooted convictions upon it will be in a much better position to deal with the shifts and surprises of daily affairs than those who are merely taking short views, and indulging their natural impulses as they are evoked by what they read from day to day. The first thing is to decide where you want to go. For myself, I am for the armed League of all Nations, or as many as you can get, against the potential aggressor, with England and France as the core of it. Let us neglect nothing in our power to establish the great inter-national framework. If that should prove to be beyond our strength, or if it breaks down through the weakness or wrong-doing of others, then at least let us make sure that England and France, the two surviving free great countries of Europe, can together ride out any storm that may blow with good and reasonable hopes of once again coming safely into port.

If we add the United States to Britain and France; if we change the name of the potential aggressor; if we substitute the United Nations Organisation for the League of Nations, the Atlantic Ocean for the English Channel, and world for Europe, the argument is not necessarily without its application today.

Letter to Horace Greeley*

BY ABRAHAM LINCOLN

[1862]

Executive Mansion,
Washington, August 22, 1862

Hon. Horace Greeley:

Dear Sir.

I HAVE just read yours of the 19th. addressed to myself through the New-York Tribune. If there be in it any statements, or assumptions of fact, which I may know to be erroneous, I do not, now and here, controvert them. If there be in it any inferences which I may believe to be falsely drawn, I do not now and here, argue against them. If there be perceptible in it an impatient and dictatorial tone, I waive it in deference to an old friend, whose heart I have always supposed to be right.

As to the policy I "seem to be pursuing" as you say, I have not meant to leave any one in doubt.

I would save the Union. I would save it the shortest way under the Constitution. The sooner the national authority can be restored; the nearer the Union will be "the Union as it was." If there be those who would not save the Union unless they could at the same time save slavery, I do not agree with them. If there be those who would not save the Union unless they could at the same time destroy slavery, I do not agree with them. My paramount object in this struggle *is* to save the Union, and is *not* either to save or to destroy slavery. If I could save the Union without freeing *any* slave I would do it, and if I could save it by freeing *all* the slaves, I would do it; and if I could save it by freeing some and leaving others alone I would also do that. What I do about slavery, and the colored race, I do because I believe it helps to save the Union; and what I forbear, I forbear because I do *not* believe it would help to save the

---

* Lincoln wrote this public letter in answer to a communication entitled "The Prayer of Twenty Millions," addressed to Lincoln by Greeley, editor of the *New York Tribune.*

Union. I shall do *less* whenever I shall believe what I am doing hurts the cause, and I shall do *more* whenever I shall believe doing more will help the cause. I shall try to correct errors when shown to be errors; and I shall adopt new views so fast as they shall appear to be true views.

I have here stated my purpose according to my view of *official* duty; and I intend no modification of my oft-expressed *personal* wish that all men everywhere could be free.

Yours,
A. Lincoln

APPENDIX

The Charter
of the United Nations

[1945]

WE the peoples of the United Nations, determined to save succeeding generations from the scourge of war, which twice in our lifetime has brought untold sorrow to mankind, and

to reaffirm faith in fundamental human rights, in the dignity and worth of the human person, in the equal rights of men and women and of nations large and small, and

to establish conditions under which justice and respect for the obligations arising from treaties and other sources of international law can be maintained, and

to promote social progress and better standards of life in larger freedom,

and for these ends to practice tolerance and live together in peace with one another as good neighbors, and

to unite our strength to maintain international peace and security, and

to ensure, by the acceptance of principles and the institution of methods, that armed force shall not be used, save in the common interest, and

to employ international machinery for the promotion of the economic and social advancement of all peoples,

have resolved to combine our efforts to accomplish these aims.

Accordingly, our respective Governments, through representatives assembled in the city of San Francisco, who have exhibited their full powers found to be in good and due form, have agreed to the present Charter of the United Nations and do hereby establish an international organization to be known as the United Nations.

CHAPTER I: PURPOSES AND PRINCIPLES

ARTICLE 1

The Purposes of the United Nations are:

1. To maintain international peace and security, and to that end: to take effective collective measures for the prevention and removal of threats to the peace, and for the suppression of acts of aggression or other breaches of the peace, and to bring about by peaceful means, and in conformity with the principles of justice and international law, adjustment or settlement of international disputes or situations which might lead to a breach of the peace;

2. To develop friendly relations among nations based on respect for the principle of equal rights and self-determination of peoples, and to take other appropriate measures to strengthen universal peace;

3. To achieve international cooperation in solving international problems of an economic, social, cultural, or humanitarian character, and in promoting and encouraging respect for human rights and for fundamental freedoms for all without distinction as to race, sex, language or religion; and

4. To be a center for harmonizing the actions of nations in the attainment of these common ends.

ARTICLE 2

The Organization and its Members, in pursuit of the Purposes stated in Article 1, shall act in accordance with the following Principles.

1. The Organization is based on the principle of the sovereign equality of all its Members.

2. All Members, in order to ensure to all of them the rights and benefits resulting from membership, shall fulfill in good faith the obligations assumed by them in accordance with the present Charter.

3. All Members shall settle their international disputes by peaceful means in such a manner that international peace and security, and justice, are not endangered.

4. All Members shall refrain in their international relations from the threat or use of force against the territorial integrity or political independence of any state, or in any other manner inconsistent with the Purposes of the United Nations.

5. All Members shall give the United Nations every assistance in any action it takes in accordance with the present Charter, and shall refrain from giving assistance to any state against which the United Nations is taking preventive or enforcement action.

6. The Organization shall ensure that states which are not Members of the United Nations act in accordance with these Principles so far as may be necessary for the maintenance of international peace and security.

7. Nothing contained in the present Charter shall authorize the United Nations to intervene in matters which are essentially within the domestic jurisdiction of any state or shall require the Members to submit such matters to settlement under the present Charter; but this principle shall not prejudice the application of enforcement measures under Chapter VII.

CHAPTER II: MEMBERSHIP

ARTICLE 3

The original Members of the United Nations shall be the states which, having participated in the United Nations Conference on International Organization at San Francisco, or having previously signed the Declaration by United Nations of January 1, 1942, sign the present Charter and ratify it in accordance with Article 110.

ARTICLE 4

1. Membership in the United Nations is open to all other peace-loving states which accept the obligations contained in the present Charter, and, in the judgment of the Organization, are able and willing to carry out these obligations.

2. The admission of any such state to membership in the United Nations will be effected by a decision of the General Assembly upon the recommendation of the Security Council.

ARTICLE 5

A member of the United Nations against which preventive or enforcement action has been taken by the Security Council may be suspended from the exercise of the rights and privileges of membership by the General Assembly upon the recommendation of the Security Council. The exercise of these rights and privileges may be restored by the Security Council.

ARTICLE 6

A Member of the United Nations which has persistently violated the Principles contained in the present Charter may be expelled from the Organization by the General Assembly upon the recommendation of the Security Council.

CHAPTER III: ORGANS

ARTICLE 7

1. There are established as the principal organs of the United Nations: a General Assembly, a Security Council, an Economic and Social Council, a Trusteeship Council, an International Court of Justice, and a Secretariat.

2. Such subsidiary organs as may be found necessary may be established in accordance with the present Charter.

ARTICLE 8

The United Nations shall place no restrictions on the eligibility of men and women to participate in any capacity and under conditions of equality in its principal and subsidiary organs.

CHAPTER IV: THE GENERAL ASSEMBLY

COMPOSITION

ARTICLE 9

1. The General Assembly shall consist of all the Members of the United Nations.

2. Each member shall have not more than five representatives in the General Assembly.

FUNCTIONS AND POWERS

ARTICLE 10

The General Assembly may discuss any questions or any matters within the scope of the present Charter or relating to the powers and functions of any organs provided for in the present Charter, and, except as provided in Article 12, may make recommendations to the Members of the United Nations or to the Security Council or to both on any such questions or matters.

ARTICLE 11

1. The General Assembly may consider the general principles of cooperation in the maintenance of international peace and security, including the principles governing disarmament and the regulation of armaments, and may make recommendations with regard to such principles to the Members or to the Security Council or to both.

2. The General Assembly may discuss any questions relating to the maintenance of international peace and security brought before it by any Member of the United Nations, or by the Security Council, or by a state which is not a Member of the United Nations in accordance with Article 35, paragraph 2, and, except as provided in Article 12, may make recommendations with regard to any such questions to the state or states concerned or to the Security Council or to both. Any such question on which action is necessary shall be referred to the Security Council by the General Assembly either before or after discussion.

3. The General Assembly may call the attention of the Security Council to situations which are likely to endanger international peace and security.

4. The powers of the General Assembly set forth in this Article shall not limit the general scope of Article 10.

ARTICLE 12

1. While the Security Council is exercising in respect of any dispute or situation the functions assigned to it in the present Charter, the General Assembly shall not make any recommendations with regard to that dispute or situation unless the Security Council so requests.

2. The Secretary-General, with the consent of the Security Council, shall notify the General Assembly at each session of any matters relative to the maintenance of international peace and security which are being dealt with by the Security Council and shall similarly notify the General Assembly, or the Members of the United Nations if the General Assembly is not in session, immediately the Security Council ceases to deal with such matters.

ARTICLE 13

1. The General Assembly shall initiate studies and make recommendations for the purpose of:

a. promoting international cooperation in the political field and encouraging the progressive development of international law and its codification;

b. promoting international cooperation in the economic, social, cultural, educational, and health fields, and assisting in the realization of human rights and fundamental freedoms for all without distinction as to race, sex, language, or religion.

2. The further responsibilities, functions, and powers of the General Assembly with respect to matters mentioned in paragraph 1 (b) above are set forth in Chapters IX and X.

ARTICLE 14

Subject to the provisions of Article 12, the General Assembly may recommend measures for the peaceful adjustment of any situation, regardless of origin, which it deems likely to impair the general welfare or friendly relations among nations, including situations resulting from a violation of the provisions of the present Charter setting forth the Purposes and Principles of the United Nations.

ARTICLE 15

1. The General Assembly shall receive and consider annual and special reports from the Security Council; these reports shall include an account of the measures that the Security Council has decided upon or taken to maintain international peace and security.

2. The General Assembly shall receive and consider reports from the other organs of the United Nations.

ARTICLE 16

The General Assembly shall perform such functions with respect to the international trusteeship system as are assigned to it under Chapters XII and XIII, including the approval of the trusteeship agreements for areas not designated as strategic.

ARTICLE 17

1. The General Assembly shall consider and approve the budget of the Organization.

2. The expenses of the Organization shall be borne by the Members as apportioned by the General Assembly.

3. The General Assembly shall consider and approve any financial and budgetary arrangements with specialized agencies referred to in Article 57 and shall examine the administrative budgets of such specialized agencies with a view to making recommendations to the agencies concerned.

VOTING

ARTICLE 18

1. Each member of the General Assembly shall have one vote.

2. Decisions of the General Assembly on important questions shall be made by a two-thirds majority of the members present and voting. These questions shall include: recommendations with respect to the maintenance of international peace and security, the election of the non-permanent members of the Security Council, the election of the members of the Economic and Social Council, the election of members of the Trusteeship Council in accordance with paragraph 1 (c) of Article 86, the admission of new Members to the United Nations, the suspension of the rights and privileges of membership, the expulsion of Members, questions relating to the operation of the trusteeship system, and budgetary questions.

3. Decisions on other questions, including the determination of additional categories of questions to be decided by a two-thirds majority, shall be made by a majority of the members present and voting.

ARTICLE 19

A Member of the United Nations which is in arrears in the payment of its financial contributions to the Organization shall have no vote in the General Assembly if the amount of its arrears equals or exceeds the amount of the contributions due from it for the preceding two full years. The General Assembly may, nevertheless, permit such a Member to vote if it is satisfied that the failure to pay is due to conditions beyond the control of the Member.

PROCEDURE

ARTICLE 20

The General Assembly shall meet in regular annual sessions and in such special sessions as occasion may require. Special sessions shall be convoked by the Secretary-General at the request of the Security Council or of a majority of the Members of the United Nations.

ARTICLE 21

The General Assembly shall adopt its own rules of procedure. It shall elect its President for each session.

ARTICLE 22

The General Assembly may establish such subsidiary organs as it deems necessary for the performance of its functions.

CHAPTER V: THE SECURITY COUNCIL

COMPOSITION

ARTICLE 23

1. The Security Council shall consist of eleven Members of the United Nations. The Republic of China, France, the Union of Soviet Socialist Republics, the United Kingdom of Great Britain and Northern Ireland, and the United States of America shall be permanent members of the Security Council. The General Assembly shall elect six other Members of the United Nations to be non-permanent members of the Security Council, due regard being specially paid, in the first instance to the contribution of Members of the United Nations to the maintenance of international peace and security and to the other purposes of the Organization, and also to equitable geographical distribution.

2. The non-permanent members of the Security Council shall be elected for a term of two years. In the first election of the non-permanent members, however, three shall be chosen for a term of one year. A retiring member shall not be eligible for immediate re-election.

3. Each member of the Security Council shall have one representative.

FUNCTIONS AND POWERS

ARTICLE 24

1. In order to ensure prompt and effective action by the United Nations, its Members confer on the Security Council primary responsibility for the maintenance of international peace and security,

and agree that in carrying out its duties under this responsibility the Security Council acts on their behalf.

2. In discharging these duties the Security Council shall act in accordance with the Purposes and Principles of the United Nations. The specific powers granted to the Security Council for the discharge of these duties are laid down in Chapters VI, VII, VIII, and XII.

3. The Security Council shall submit annual and, when necessary, special reports to the General Assembly for its consideration.

ARTICLE 25

The Members of the United Nations agree to accept and carry out the decisions of the Security Council in accordance with the present Charter.

ARTICLE 26

In order to promote the establishment and maintenance of international peace and security with the least diversion for armaments of the world's human and economic resources, the Security Council shall be responsible for formulating, with the assistance of the Military Staff Committee referred to in Article 47, plans to be submitted to the Members of the United Nations for the establishment of a system for the regulation of armaments.

VOTING

ARTICLE 27

1. Each member of the Security Council shall have one vote.

2. Decisions of the Security Council on procedural matters shall be made by an affirmative vote of seven members.

3. Decisions of the Security Council on all other matters shall be made by an affirmative vote of seven members including the concurring votes of the permanent members; provided that, in decisions under Chapter VI, and under paragraph 3 of Article 52, a party to a dispute shall abstain from voting.

PROCEDURE

ARTICLE 28

1. The Security Council shall be so organized as to be able to function continuously. Each member of the Security Council shall

for this purpose be represented at all times at the seat of the Organization.

2. The Security Council shall hold periodic meetings at which each of its members may, if it so desires, be represented by a member of the government or by some other specially designated representative.

3. The Security Council may hold meetings at such places other than the seat of the Organization as in its judgment will best facilitate its work.

ARTICLE 29

The Security Council may establish such subsidiary organs as it deems necessary for the performance of its functions.

ARTICLE 30

The Security Council shall adopt its own rules of procedure, including the method of selecting its President.

ARTICLE 31

Any Member of the United Nations which is not a member of the Security Council may participate, without vote, in the discussion of any question brought before the Security Council whenever the latter considers that the interests of that Member are specially affected.

ARTICLE 32

Any Member of the United Nations which is not a member of the Security Council or any state which is not a Member of the United Nations, if it is a party to a dispute under consideration by the Security Council, shall be invited to participate, without vote, in the discussion relating to the dispute. The Security Council shall lay down such conditions as it deems just for the participation of a state which is not a Member of the United Nations.

CHAPTER VI: PACIFIC SETTLEMENT OF DISPUTES

ARTICLE 33

1. The parties to any dispute, the continuance of which is likely to endanger the maintenance of international peace and security, shall, first of all, seek a solution by negotiation, enquiry, mediation, conciliation, arbitration, judicial settlement, resort to regional agencies or arrangements, or other peaceful means of their own choice.

2. The Security Council shall, when it deems necessary, call upon the parties to settle their dispute by such means.

ARTICLE 34

The Security Council may investigate any dispute, or any situation which might lead to international friction or give rise to a dispute, in order to determine whether the continuance of the dispute or situation is likely to endanger the maintenance of international peace and security.

ARTICLE 35

1. Any Member of the United Nations may bring any dispute, or any situation of the nature referred to in Article 34, to the attention of the Security Council or of the General Assembly.

2. A state which is not a Member of the United Nations may bring to the attention of the Security Council or of the General Assembly any dispute to which it is a party if it accepts in advance, for the purposes of the dispute, the obligations of pacific settlement provided in the present Charter.

3. The proceedings of the General Assembly in respect of matters brought to its attention under this Article will be subject to the provisions of Articles 11 and 12.

ARTICLE 36

1. The Security Council may, at any stage of a dispute of the nature referred to in Article 33 or of a situation of like nature, recommend appropriate procedures or methods of adjustment.

2. The Security Council should take into consideration any procedures for the settlement of the dispute which have already been adopted by the parties.

3. In making recommendations under this Article the Security Council should also take into consideration that legal disputes should as a general rule be referred by the parties to the International Court of Justice in accordance with the provisions of the Statute of the Court.

ARTICLE 37

1. Should the parties to a dispute of the nature referred to in Article 33 fail to settle it by the means indicated in that Article, they shall refer it to the Security Council.

2. If the Security Council deems that the continuance of the dis-

pute is in fact likely to endanger the maintenance of international peace and security, it shall decide whether to take action under Article 36 or to recommend such terms of settlement as it may consider appropriate.

Article 38

Without prejudice to the provisions of Articles 33 to 37, the Security Council may, if all the parties to any dispute so request, make recommendations to the parties with a view to a pacific settlement of the dispute.

CHAPTER VII: ACTION WITH RESPECT TO THREATS TO THE PEACE, BREACHES OF THE PEACE, AND ACTS OF AGGRESSION

Article 39

The Security Council shall determine the existence of any threat to the peace, breach of the peace, or act of aggression and shall make recommendations, or decide what measures shall be taken in accordance with Articles 41 and 42, to maintain or restore international peace and security.

Article 40

In order to prevent an aggravation of the situation, the Security Council may, before making the recommendations or deciding upon the measures provided for in Article 39, call upon the parties concerned to comply with such provisional measures as it deems necessary or desirable. Such provisional measures shall be without prejudice to the rights, claims, or position of the parties concerned. The Security Council shall duly take account of failure to comply with such provisional measures.

Article 41

The Security Council may decide what measures not involving the use of armed force are to be employed to give effect to its decisions, and it may call upon the Members of the United Nations to apply such measures. These may include complete or partial interruption of economic relations and of rail, sea, air, postal, telegraphic, radio, and other means of communication, and the severance of diplomatic relations.

ARTICLE 42

Should the Security Council consider that measures provided for in Article 41 would be inadequate or have proved to be inadequate, it may take such action by air, sea, or land forces as may be necessary to maintain or restore international peace and security. Such action may include demonstrations, blockade, and other operations by air, sea, or land forces of Members of the United Nations.

ARTICLE 43

1. All Members of the United Nations, in order to contribute to the maintenance of international peace and security, undertake to make available to the Security Council, on its call and in accordance with a special agreement or agreements, armed forces, assistance, and facilities, including rights of passage, necessary for the purpose of maintaining international peace and security.

2. Such agreement or agreements shall govern the numbers and types of forces, their degree or readiness and general location, and the nature of the facilities and assistance to be provided.

3. The agreement or agreements shall be negotiated as soon as possible on the initiative of the Security Council. They shall be concluded between the Security Council and Members or between the Security Council and groups of Members and shall be subject to ratification by the signatory states in accordance with their respective constitutional processes.

ARTICLE 44

When the Security Council has decided to use force it shall, before calling upon a Member not represented on it to provide armed forces in fulfillment of the obligations assumed under Article 43, invite that Member, if the Member so desires, to participate in the decisions of the Security Council concerning the employment of contingents of that Member's armed forces.

ARTICLE 45

In order to enable the United Nations to take urgent military measures, Members shall hold immediately available national air-force contingents for combined international enforcement action. The strength and degree of readiness of these contingents and plans for their combined action shall be determined, within the limits laid down in the special agreement or agreements referred to in Article

43, by the Security Council with the assistance of the Military Staff Committee.

ARTICLE 46

Plans for the application of armed force shall be made by the Security Council with the assistance of the Military Staff Committee.

ARTICLE 47

1. There shall be established a Military Staff Committee to advise and assist the Security Council on all questions relating to the Security Council's military requirements for the maintenance of international peace and security, the employment and command of forces placed at its disposal, the regulation of armaments, and possible disarmament.

2. The Military Staff Committee shall consist of the Chiefs of Staff of the permanent members of the Security Council or their representatives. Any Member of the United Nations not permanently represented on the Committee shall be invited by the Committee to be associated with it when the efficient discharge of the Committee's responsibilities requires the participation of that Member in its work.

3. The Military Staff Committee shall be responsible under the Security Council for the strategic direction of any armed forces placed at the disposal of the Security Council. Questions relating to the command of such forces shall be worked out subsequently.

4. The Military Staff Committee, with the authorization of the Security Council and after consultation with appropriate regional agencies, may establish regional subcommittees.

ARTICLE 48

1. The action required to carry out the decisions of the Security Council for the maintenance of international peace and security shall be taken by all the Members of the United Nations or by some of them, as the Security Council may determine.

2. Such decisions shall be carried out by the Members of the United Nations directly and through their action in the appropriate international agencies of which they are members.

ARTICLE 49

The Members of the United Nations shall join in affording mutual assistance in carrying out the measures decided upon by the Security Council.

ARTICLE 50

If preventive or enforcement measures against any state are taken by the Security Council, any other state, whether a Member of the United Nations or not, which finds itself confronted with special economic problems arising from the carrying out of those measures shall have the right to consult the Security Council with regard to a solution of those problems.

ARTICLE 51

Nothing in the present Charter shall impair the inherent right of individual or collective self-defense if an armed attack occurs against a Member of the United Nations, until the Security Council has taken the measures necessary to maintain international peace and security. Measures taken by Members in the exercise of this right of self-defense shall be immediately reported to the Security Council and shall not in any way affect the authority and responsibility of the Security Council under the present Charter to take at any time such action as it deems necessary in order to maintain or restore international peace and security.

CHAPTER VIII: REGIONAL ARRANGEMENTS

ARTICLE 52

1. Nothing in the present Charter precludes the existence of regional arrangements or agencies for dealing with such matters relating to the maintenance of international peace and security as are appropriate for regional action, provided that such arrangements or agencies and their activities are consistent with the Purposes and Principles of the United Nations.

2. The Members of the United Nations entering into such arrangements or constituting such agencies shall make every effort to achieve pacific settlement of local disputes through such regional arrangements or by such regional agencies before referring them to the Security Council.

3. The Security Council shall encourage the development of pacific settlement of local disputes through such regional arrangements or by such regional agencies either on the initiative of the states concerned or by reference from the Security Council.

4. This Article in no way impairs the application of Articles 34 and 35.

Article 53

1. The Security Council shall, where appropriate, utilize such regional arrangements or agencies for enforcement action under its authority. But no enforcement action shall be taken under regional arrangements or by regional agencies without the authorization of the Security Council, with the exception of measures against any enemy state, as defined in paragraph 2 of this Article, provided for pursuant to Article 107 or in regional arrangements directed against renewal of aggressive policy on the part of any such state, until such times as the Organization may, on request of the Governments concerned, be charged with the responsibility for preventing further aggression by such a state.

2. The term enemy state as used in paragraph 1 of this Article applies to any state which during the Second World War has been an enemy of any signatory of the present Charter.

Article 54

The Security Council shall at all times be kept fully informed of activities undertaken or in contemplation under regional arrangements or by regional agencies for the maintenance of international peace and security.

CHAPTER IX: INTERNATIONAL ECONOMIC AND SOCIAL COOPERATION

Article 55

With a view to the creation of conditions of stability and well-being which are necessary for peaceful and friendly relations among nations based on respect for the principle of equal rights and self-determination of peoples, the United Nations shall promote:

a. higher standards of living, full employment, and conditions of economic and social progress and development;

b. solutions of international economic, social, health, and related problems; and international cultural and educational cooperation; and

c. universal respect for, and observance of, human rights and fundamental freedoms for all without distinction as to race, sex, language, or religion.

ARTICLE 56

All Members pledge themselves to take joint and separate action in cooperation with the Organization for the achievement of the purposes set forth in Article 55.

ARTICLE 57

1. The various specialized agencies, established by intergovernmental agreement and having wide international responsibilities, as defined in their basic instruments, in economic, social, cultural, educational, health, and related fields, shall be brought into relationship with the United Nations in accordance with the provisions of Article 63.

2. Such agencies thus brought into relationship with the United Nations are hereinafter referred to as specialized agencies.

ARTICLE 58

The Organization shall make recommendations for the coordination of the policies and activities of the specialized agencies.

ARTICLE 59

The Organization shall, where appropriate, initiate negotiations among the states concerned for the creation of any new specialized agencies required for the accomplishment of the purposes set forth in Article 55.

ARTICLE 60

Responsibility for the discharge of the functions of the Organization set forth in this Chapter shall be vested in the General Assembly and, under the authority of the General Assembly, in the Economic and Social Council, which shall have for this purpose the powers set forth in Chapter X.

CHAPTER X: THE ECONOMIC AND SOCIAL COUNCIL

COMPOSITION

ARTICLE 61

The Economic and Social Council shall consist of eighteen Members of the United Nations elected by the General Assembly.

2. Subject to the provisions of paragraph 3, six members of the Economic and Social Council shall be elected each year for a term of three years. A retiring member shall be eligible for immediate re-election.

3. At the first election, eighteen members of the Economic and Social Council shall be chosen. The term of office of six members so chosen shall expire at the end of one year, and of six other members at the end of two years, in accordance with arrangements made by the General Assembly.

4. Each member of the Economic and Social Council shall have one representative.

FUNCTIONS AND POWERS

ARTICLE 62

1. The Economic and Social Council may make or initiate studies and reports with respect to international economic, social, cultural, educational, health, and related matters and may make recommendations with respect to any such matters to the General Assembly, to the Members of the United Nations, and to the specialized agencies concerned.

2. It may make recommendations for the purpose of promoting respect for, and observance of, human rights and fundamental freedoms for all.

3. It may prepare draft conventions for submission to the General Assembly, with respect to matters falling within its competence.

4. It may call, in accordance with the rules prescribed by the United Nations, international conferences on matters falling within its competence.

ARTICLE 63

1. The Economic and Social Council may enter into agreements with any of the agencies referred to in Article 57, defining the terms on which the agency concerned shall be brought into relationship with the United Nations. Such agreements shall be subject to approval by the General Assembly.

2. It may coordinate the activities of the specialized agencies through consultation with and recommendations to such agencies and through recommendations to the General Assembly and to the Members of the United Nations.

ARTICLE 64

1. The Economic and Social Council may take appropriate steps to obtain regular reports from the specialized agencies. It may make arrangements with the Members of the United Nations and with the specialized agencies to obtain reports on the steps taken to give effect to its own recommendations and to recommendations on matters falling within its competence made by the General Assembly.

2. It may communicate its observations on these reports to the General Assembly.

ARTICLE 65

The Economic and Social Council may furnish information to the Security Council and shall assist the Security Council upon its request.

ARTICLE 66

1. The Economic and Social Council shall perform such functions as fall within its competence in connection with the carrying out of the recommendations of the General Assembly.

2. It may, with the approval of the General Assembly, perform services at the request of Members of the United Nations and at the request of specialized agencies.

3. It shall perform such other functions as are specified elsewhere in the present Charter or as may be assigned to it by the General Assembly.

VOTING

ARTICLE 67

1. Each member of the Economic and Social Council shall have one vote.

2. Decisions of the Economic and Social Council shall be made by a majority of the members present and voting.

PROCEDURE

ARTICLE 68

The Economic and Social Council shall set up commissions in economic and social fields and for the promotion of human rights, and such other commissions as may be required for the performance of its functions.

ARTICLE 69

The Economic and Social Council shall invite any Member of the United Nations to participate, without vote, in its deliberations on any matter of particular concern to that Member.

ARTICLE 70

The Economic and Social Council may make arrangements for representatives of the specialized agencies to participate, without vote, in its deliberations and in those of the commissions established by it, and for its representatives to participate in the deliberations of the specialized agencies.

ARTICLE 71

The Economic and Social Council may make suitable arrangements for consultation with non-governmental organizations which are concerned with matters within its competence. Such arrangements may be made with international organizations and, where appropriate, with national organizations after consultation with the Member of the United Nations concerned.

ARTICLE 72

1. The Economic and Social Council shall adopt its own rules of procedure, including the method of selecting its President.

2. The Economic and Social Council shall meet as required in accordance with its rules, which shall include provisions for the convening of meetings on the request of a majority of its members.

CHAPTER XI: DECLARATION REGARDING NON-SELF-GOVERNING TERRITORIES

ARTICLE 73

Members of the United Nations which have or assume responsibilities for the administration of territories whose peoples have not yet attained a full measure of self-government recognize the principle that the interests of the inhabitants of these territories are paramount, and accept as a sacred trust the obligation to promote to the utmost, within the system of international peace and security established by the present Charter, the well-being of the inhabitants of these territories, and, to this end:

a. to ensure, with due respect for the culture of the peoples concerned, their political, economic, social, and educational advancement, their just treatment, and their protection against abuses;

b. to develop self-government, to take due account of the political aspirations of the peoples, and to assist them in the progressive development of their free political institutions, according to the particular circumstances of each territory and its peoples and their varying stages of advancement;

c. to further international peace and security;

d. to promote constructive measures of development, to encourage research, and to cooperate with one another and, when and where appropriate, with specialized international bodies with a view to the practical achievement of the social, economic, and scientific purposes set forth in this Article; and

e. to transmit regularly to the Secretary-General for information purposes, subject to such limitation as security and constitutional considerations may require, statistical and other information of a technical nature relating to economic, social, and educational conditions in the territories for which they are respectively responsible other than those territories to which Chapters XII and XIII apply.

ARTICLE 74

Members of the United Nations also agree that their policy in respect of the territories to which this Chapter applies, no less than in respect of their metropolitan areas, must be based on the general principle of good-neighborliness, due account being taken of the interests and well-being of the rest of the world, in social, economic, and commercial matters.

CHAPTER XII: INTERNATIONAL TRUSTEESHIP SYSTEM

ARTICLE 75

The United Nations shall establish under its authority an international trusteeship system for the administration and supervision of such territories as may be placed thereunder by subsequent individual agreements. These territories are hereinafter referred to as trust territories.

ARTICLE 76

The basic objectives of the trusteeship system, in accordance with the Purposes of the United Nations laid down in Article 1 of the present Charter, shall be:

a. to further international peace and security;

b. to promote the political, economic, social, and educational advancement of the inhabitants of the trust territories, and their progressive development towards self-government or independence as may be appropriate to the particular circumstances of each territory and its peoples and the freely expressed wishes of the peoples concerned, and as may be provided by the terms of each trusteeship agreement;

c. to encourage respect for human rights and for fundamental freedoms for all without distinction as to race, sex, language, or religion, and to encourage recognition of the interdependence of the peoples of the world; and

d. to ensure equal treatment in social, economic, and commercial matters for all Members of the United Nations and their nationals, and also equal treatment for the latter in the administration of justice, without prejudice to the attainment of the foregoing objectives and subject to the provisions of Article 80.

ARTICLE 77

1. The trusteeship system shall apply to such territories in the following categories as may be placed thereunder by means of trusteeship agreements:

a. territories now held under mandate;

b. territories which may be detached from enemy states as a result of the Second World War; and

c. territories voluntarily placed under the system by states responsible for their administration.

2. It will be a matter for subsequent agreement as to which territories in the foregoing categories will be brought under the trusteeship system and upon what terms.

ARTICLE 78

The trusteeship system shall not apply to territories which have become Members of the United Nations, relationship among which shall be based on respect for the principle of sovereign equality.

ARTICLE 79

The terms of trusteeship for each territory to be placed under the trusteeship system, including any alteration or amendment, shall be agreed upon by the states directly concerned, including the mandatory power in the case of territories held under mandate by a Member of the United Nations, and shall be approved as provided for in Articles 83 and 85.

ARTICLE 80

1. Except as may be agreed upon in individual trusteeship agreements, made under Articles 77, 79, and 81, placing each territory under the trusteeship system, and until such agreements have been concluded, nothing in this Chapter shall be construed in or of itself to alter in any manner the rights whatsoever of any states or any peoples or the terms of existing international instruments to which Members of the United Nations may respectively be parties.

2. Paragraph 1 of this Article shall not be interpreted as giving grounds for delay or postponement of the negotiation and conclusion of agreements for placing mandated and other territories under the trusteeship system as provided for in Article 77.

ARTICLE 81

The trusteeship agreement shall in each case include the terms under which the trust territory will be administered and designate the authority which will exercise the administration of the trust territory. Such authority, hereinafter called the administering authority, may be one or more states or the Organization itself.

ARTICLE 82

There may be designated, in any trusteeship agreement, a strategic area or areas which may include part or all of the trust territory to which the agreement applies, without prejudice to any special agreement or agreements made under Article 43.

ARTICLE 83

1. All functions of the United Nations relating to strategic areas, including the approval of the terms of the trusteeship agreements and of their alteration or amendment, shall be exercised by the Security Council.

2. The basic objectives set forth in Article 76 shall be applicable to the people of each strategic area.

3. The Security Council shall, subject to the provisions of the trusteeship agreements and without prejudice to security considera-

tions, avail itself of the assistance of the Trusteeship Council to perform those functions of the United Nations under the trusteeship system relating to political, economic, social, and educational matters in the strategic areas.

ARTICLE 84

It shall be the duty of the administering authority to ensure that the trust territory shall play its part in the maintenance of international peace and security. To this end the administering authority may make use of volunteer forces, facilities, and assistance from the trust territory in carrying out the obligations towards the Security Council undertaken in this regard by the administering authority, as well as for local defense and the maintenance of law and order within the trust territory.

ARTICLE 85

1. The functions of the United Nations with regard to trusteeship agreements for all areas not designated as strategic, including the approval of the terms of the trusteeship agreements and of their alteration or amendment, shall be exercised by the General Assembly.

2. The Trusteeship Council, operating under the authority of the General Assembly, shall assist the General Assembly in carrying out these functions.

CHAPTER XIII: THE TRUSTEESHIP COUNCIL

COMPOSITION

ARTICLE 86

1. The Trusteeship Council shall consist of the following Members of the United Nations:

a. those Members administering trust territories;

b. such of those Members mentioned by name in Article 23 as are not administering trust territories; and

c. as many other Members elected for three-year terms by the General Assembly as may be necessary to ensure that the total number of members of the Trusteeship Council is equally divided between those Members of the United Nations which administer trust territories and those which do not.

2. Each member of the Trusteeship Council shall designate one specially qualified person to represent it therein.

FUNCTIONS AND POWERS

ARTICLE 87

The General Assembly and, under its authority, the Trusteeship Council, in carrying out their functions, may:

a. consider reports submitted by the administering authority;

b. accept petitions and examine them in consultation with the administering authority;

c. provide for periodic visits to the respective trust territories at times agreed upon with the administering authority; and

d. take these and other actions in conformity with the terms of the trusteeship agreements.

ARTICLE 88

The Trusteeship Council shall formulate a questionnaire on the political, economic, social, and educational advancement of the inhabitants of each trust territory, and the administering authority for each trust territory within the competence of the General Assembly shall make an annual report to the General Assembly upon the basis of such questionnaire.

VOTING

ARTICLE 89

1. Each member of the Trusteeship Council shall have one vote.

2. Decisions of the Trusteeship Council shall be made by a majority of the members present and voting.

PROCEDURE

ARTICLE 90

1. The Trusteeship Council shall adopt its own rules of procedure, including the method of selecting its President.

2. The Trusteeship Council shall meet as required in accordance with its rules, which shall include provision for the convening of meetings on the request of a majority of its members.

ARTICLE 91

The Trusteeship Council shall, when appropriate, avail itself of the assistance of the Economic and Social Council and of the specialized agencies in regard to matters with which they are respectively concerned.

CHAPTER XIV: THE INTERNATIONAL COURT OF JUSTICE

ARTICLE 92

The International Court of Justice shall be the principal judicial organ of the United Nations. It shall function in accordance with the annexed Statute, which is based upon the Statute of the Permanent Court of International Justice and forms an integral part of the present Charter.

ARTICLE 93

1. All Members of the United Nations are *ipso facto* parties to the Statute of the International Court of Justice.

2. A state which is not a Member of the United Nations may become a party to the Statute of the International Court of Justice on conditions to be determined in each case by the General Assembly upon the recommendation of the Security Council.

ARTICLE 94

1. Each Member of the United Nations undertakes to comply with the decision of the International Court of Justice in any case to which it is a party.

2. If any party to a case fails to perform the obligations incumbent upon it under a judgment rendered by the Court, the other party may have recourse to the Security Council, which may, if it deems necessary, make recommendations or decide upon measures to be taken to give effect to the judgment.

ARTICLE 95

Nothing in the present Charter shall prevent Members of the United Nations from entrusting the solution of their differences to other tribunals by virtue of agreements already in existence or which may be concluded in the future.

ARTICLE 96

1. The General Assembly or the Security Council may request the International Court of Justice to give an advisory opinion on any legal question.

2. Other organs of the United Nations and specialized agencies, which may at any time be so authorized by the General Assembly, may also request advisory opinions of the Court on legal questions arising within the scope of their activities.

CHAPTER XV: THE SECRETARIAT

ARTICLE 97

The Secretariat shall comprise a Secretary-General and such staff as the Organization may require. The Secretary-General shall be appointed by the General Assembly upon the recommendation of the Security Council. He shall be the chief administrative officer of the Organization.

ARTICLE 98

The Secretary-General shall act in that capacity in all meetings of the General Assembly, of the Security Council, of the Economic and Social Council, and of the Trusteeship Council, and shall perform such other functions as are entrusted to him by these organs. The Secretary-General shall make an annual report to the General Assembly on the work of the Organization.

ARTICLE 99

The Secretary-General may bring to the attention of the Security Council any matter which in his opinion may threaten the maintenance of international peace and security.

ARTICLE 100

1. In the performance of their duties the Secretary-General and the staffs shall not seek or receive instructions from any government or from any other authority external to the Organization. They shall refrain from any action which might reflect on their position as international officials responsible only to the Organization.

2. Each Member of the United Nations undertakes to respect the exclusively international character of the responsibilities of the

Secretary-General and the staff and not to seek to influence them in the discharge of their responsibilities.

ARTICLE 101

1. The staff shall be appointed by the Secretary-General under regulations established by the General Assembly.

2. Appropriate staffs shall be permanently assigned to the Economic and Social Council, the Trusteeship Council, and, as required, to other organs of the United Nations. These staffs shall form a part of the Secretariat.

3. The paramount consideration in the employment of the staff and in the determination of the conditions of service shall be the necessity of securing the highest standards of efficiency, competence, and integrity. Due regard shall be paid to the importance of recruiting the staff on as wide a geographical basis as possible.

CHAPTER XVI: MISCELLANEOUS PROVISIONS

ARTICLE 102

1. Every treaty and every international agreement entered into by any Member of the United Nations after the present Charter comes into force shall as soon as possible be registered with the Secretariat and published by it.

2. No party to any such treaty or international agreement which has not been registered in accordance with the provisions of paragraph 1 of this Article may invoke that treaty or agreement before any organ of the United Nations.

ARTICLE 103

In the event of a conflict between the obligations of the Members of the United Nations under the present Charter and their obligations under any other international agreement, their obligations under the present Charter shall prevail.

ARTICLE 104

The Organization shall enjoy in the territory of each of its Members such legal capacity as may be necessary for the exercise of its functions and the fulfillment of its purposes.

ARTICLE 105

1. The Organization shall enjoy in the territory of each of its Members such privileges and immunities as are necessary for the fulfillment of its purposes.

2. Representatives of the Members of the United Nations and officials of the Organization shall similarly enjoy such privileges and immunities as are necessary for the independent exercise of their functions in connection with the Organization.

3. The General Assembly may make recommendations with a view to determining the details of the application of paragraphs 1 and 2 of this Article or may propose conventions to the Members of the United Nations for this purpose.

CHAPTER XVII: TRANSITIONAL SECURITY ARRANGEMENTS

ARTICLE 106

Pending the coming into force of such special agreements referred to in Article 43 as in the opinion of the Security Council enable it to begin the exercise of its responsibilities under Article 42, the parties to the Four-Nation Declaration, signed at Moscow, October 30, 1943, and France, shall, in accordance with the provisions of paragraph 5 of that Declaration, consult with one another and as occasion requires with other Members of the United Nations with a view to such joint action on behalf of the Organization as may be necessary for the purpose of maintaining international peace and security.

ARTICLE 107

Nothing in the present Charter shall invalidate or preclude action, in relation to any state which during the Second World War has been an enemy of any signatory to the present Charter, taken or authorized as a result of that war by the Governments having responsibility for such action.

CHAPTER XVIII: AMENDMENTS

ARTICLE 108

Amendments to the present Charter shall come into force for all Members of the United Nations when they have been adopted by a vote of two-thirds of the members of the General Assembly and ratified in accordance with their respective constitutional processes by two-thirds of the Members of the United Nations, including all the permanent members of the Security Council.

ARTICLE 109

1. A General Conference of the Members of the United Nations for the purpose of reviewing the present Charter may be held at a date and place to be fixed by a two-thirds vote of the members of the General Assembly and by a vote of any seven members of the Security Council. Each Member of the United Nations shall have one vote in the conference.

2. Any alteration of the present Charter recommended by a two-thirds vote of the conference shall take effect when ratified in accordance with their respective constitutional processes by two-thirds of the Members of the United Nations including all the permanent members of the Security Council.

3. If such a conference has not been held before the tenth annual session of the General Assembly following the coming into force of the present Charter, the proposal to call such a conference shall be placed on the agenda of that session of the General Assembly, and the conference shall be held if so decided by a majority vote of the members of the General Assembly and by a vote of any seven members of the Security Council.

CHAPTER XIX: RATIFICATION AND SIGNATURE

ARTICLE 110

1. The present Charter shall be ratified by the signatory states in accordance with their respective constitutional processes.

2. The ratifications shall be deposited with the Government of the United States of America, which shall notify all the signatory states of each deposit as well as the Secretary-General of the Organization when he has been appointed.

3. The present Charter shall come into force upon the deposit of ratifications by the Republic of China, France, the Union of Soviet Socialist Republics, the United Kingdom of Great Britain and Northern Ireland, and the United States of America, and by a majority of the other signatory states. A protocol of the ratifications

deposited shall thereupon be drawn up by the Government of the United States of America which shall communicate copies thereof to all the signatory states.

4. The states signatory to the present Charter which ratify it after it has come into force will become original Members of the United Nations on the date of the deposit of their respective ratifications.

ARTICLE III

The present Charter, of which the Chinese, French, Russian, English, and Spanish texts are equally authentic, shall remain deposited in the archives of the Government of the United States of America. Duly certified copies thereof shall be transmitted by that Government to the Governments of the other signatory states.

In faith whereof the representatives of the Governments of the United Nations have signed the present Charter.

Done at the city of San Francisco the twenty-sixth day of June, one thousand nine hundred and forty-five.

Universal Declaration of Human Rights*

[1948]

PREAMBLE

Whereas recognition of the inherent dignity and of the equal and inalienable rights of all members of the human family is the foundation of freedom, justice and peace in the world,

Whereas disregard and contempt for human rights have resulted in barbarous acts which have outraged the conscience of mankind, and the advent of a world in which human beings shall enjoy freedom of speech and belief and freedom from fear and want has been proclaimed as the highest aspiration of the common people,

Whereas it is essential, if man is not to be compelled to have recourse, as a last resort, to rebellion against tyranny and oppression, that human rights should be protected by the rule of law,

Whereas it is essential to promote the development of friendly relations between nations,

Whereas the peoples of the United Nations have in the Charter reaffirmed their faith in fundamental human rights, in the dignity and worth of the human person and in the equal rights of men and women and have determined to promote social progress and better standards of life in larger freedom,

Whereas Member States have pledged themselves to achieve, in cooperation with the United Nations, the promotion of universal respect for and observance of human rights and fundamental freedoms,

Whereas a common understanding of these rights and freedoms is of the greatest importance for the full realisation of this pledge,

Now therefore

---

* On December 10, 1948, the General Assembly of the United Nations adopted and proclaimed the Universal Declaration of Human Rights, the full text of which appears in the following pages. Following this historic act the Assembly called upon all member countries to publicize the text of the Declaration and "to cause it to be disseminated, displayed, read and expounded principally in schools and other educational institutions, without distinction based on the political status of countries or territories."

THE GENERAL ASSEMBLY
proclaims

This Universal Declaration of Human Rights as a common standard of achievement for all peoples and all nations, to the end that every individual and every organ of society, keeping this Declaration constantly in mind, shall strive by teaching and education to promote respect for these rights and freedoms and by progressive measures, national and international, to secure their universal and effective recognition and observance, both among the peoples of Member States themselves and among the peoples of territories under their jurisdiction.

Article 1 All human beings are born free and equal in dignity and rights. They are endowed with reason and conscience and should act towards one another in a spirit of brotherhood.

Article 2 Everyone is entitled to all the rights and freedoms set forth in this Declaration, without distinction of any kind, such as race, colour, sex, language, religion, political or other opinion, national or social origin, property, birth or other status.

Furthermore, no distinction shall be made on the basis of the political, jurisdictional or international status of the country or territory to which a person belongs, whether it be independent, trust, non-self-governing or under any other limitation of sovereignty.

Article 3 Everyone has the right to life, liberty and security of person.

Article 4 No one shall be held in slavery or servitude; slavery and the slave trade shall be prohibited in all their forms.

Article 5 No one shall be subjected to torture or to cruel, inhuman or degrading treatment or punishment.

Article 6 Everyone has the right to recognition everywhere as a person before the law.

Article 7 All are equal before the law and are entitled without any discrimination to equal protection of the law. All are entitled to equal protection against any discrimination in violation of this Declaration and against any incitement to such discrimination.

Article 8 Everyone has the right to an effective remedy by the competent national tribunals for acts violating the fundamental rights granted him by the constitution or by law.

Article 9 No one shall be subjected to arbitrary arrest, detention or exile.

Article 10 Everyone is entitled in full equality to a fair and public hearing by an independent and impartial tribunal, in the determination of his rights and obligations and of any criminal charge against him.

Article 11 (1) Everyone charged with a penal offence has the right to be presumed innocent until proved guilty according to law in a public trial at which he has had all the guarantees necessary for his defence.

(2) No one shall be held guilty of any penal offence on account of any act or omission which did not constitute a penal offence, under national or international law, at the time when it was committed. Nor shall a heavier penalty be imposed than the one that was applicable at the time the penal offence was committed.

Article 12 No one shall be subjected to arbitrary interference with his privacy, family, home or correspondence, nor to attacks upon his honour and reputation. Everyone has the right to the protection of the law against such interference or attacks.

Article 13 (1) Everyone has the right to freedom of movement and residence within the borders of each state.

(2) Everyone has the right to leave any country, including his own, and to return to his country.

Article 14 (1) Everyone has the right to seek and to enjoy in other countries asylum from persecution.

(2) This right may not be invoked in the case of prosecutions genuinely arising from non-political crimes or from acts contrary to the purposes and principles of the United Nations.

Article 15 (1) Everyone has the right to a nationality.

(2) No one shall be arbitrarily deprived of his nationality nor denied the right to change his nationality.

Article 16 (1) Men and women of full age, without any limitation due to race, nationality or religion, have the right to marry and to found a family. They are entitled to equal rights as to marriage, during marriage and at its dissolution.

(2) Marriage shall be entered into only with the free and full consent of the intending spouses.

(3) The family is the natural and fundamental group unit of society and is entitled to protection by society and the State.

Article 17 (1) Everyone has the right to own property alone as well as in association with others.

(2) No one shall be arbitrarily deprived of his property.

Article 18 Everyone has the right to freedom of thought, conscience and religion; this right includes freedom to change his religion or belief, and freedom, either alone or in community with others and in public or private, to manifest his religion or belief in teaching, practice, worship and observance.

Article 19 Everyone has the right to freedom of opinion and expression; this right includes freedom to hold opinions without interference and to seek, receive and impart information and ideas through any media and regardless of frontiers.

Article 20 (1) Everyone has the right to freedom of peaceful assembly and association.

(2) No one may be compelled to belong to an association.

Article 21 (1) Everyone has the right to take part in the government of his country, directly or through freely chosen representatives.

(2) Everyone has the right of equal access to public service in his country.

(3) The will of the people shall be the basis of the authority of government; this will shall be expressed in periodic and genuine elections which shall be by universal and equal suffrage and shall be held by secret vote or by equivalent free voting procedures.

Article 22 Everyone, as a member of society, has the right to social security and is entitled to realisation, through national effort and international co-operation and in accordance with the organisation and resources of each State, of the economic, social and cultural rights indispensable for his dignity and the free development of his personality.

Article 23 (1) Everyone has the right to work, to free choice of employment, to just and favourable conditions of work and to protection against unemployment.

(2) Everyone, without any discrimination, has the right to equal pay for equal work.

(3) Everyone who works has the right to just and favourable remuneration insuring for himself and his family an existence worthy of human dignity, and supplemented, if necessary, by other means of social protection.

(4) Everyone has the right to form and to join trade unions for the protection of his interests.

Article 24 Everyone has the right to rest and leisure, including reasonable limitation of working hours and periodic holidays with pay.

Article 25 (1) Everyone has the right to a standard of living adequate for the health and well-being of himself and of his family, including food, clothing, housing and medical care and necessary social services, and the right to security in the event of unemployment, sickness, disability, widowhood, old age or other lack of livelihood in circumstances beyond his control.

(2) Motherhood and childhood are entitled to special care and assistance. All children, whether born in or out of wedlock, shall enjoy the same social protection.

Article 26 (1) Everyone has the right to education. Education shall be free, at least in the elementary and fundamental stages.

Elementary education shall be compulsory. Technical and professional education shall be made generally available and higher education shall be equally accessible to all on the basis of merit.

(2) Education shall be directed to the full development of the human personality and to the strengthening of respect for human rights and fundamental freedoms. It shall promote understanding, tolerance and friendship among all nations, racial or religious groups, and shall further the activities of the United Nations for the maintenance of peace.

(3) Parents have a prior right to choose the kind of education that shall be given to their children.

Article 27 (1) Everyone has the right freely to participate in the cultural life of the community, to enjoy the arts and to share in scientific advancement and its benefits.

(2) Everyone has the right to the protection of the moral and material interests resulting from any scientific, literary or artistic production of which he is the author.

Article 28 Everyone is entitled to a social and international order in which the rights and freedoms set forth in this Declaration can be fully realised.

Article 29 (1) Everyone has duties to the community in which alone the free and full development of his personality is possible.

(2) In the exercise of his rights and freedoms, everyone shall be subject only to such limitations as are determined by law solely for the purpose of securing due recognition and respect for the rights and freedoms of others and of meeting the just requirements of morality, public order and the general welfare in a democratic society.

(3) These rights and freedoms may in no case be exercised contrary to the purposes and principles of the United Nations.

Article 30 Nothing in this Declaration may be interpreted as implying for any State, group or person any right to engage in any activity or to perform any act aimed at the destruction of any of the rights and freedoms set forth herein.

Final Communiqué of the
Asian-African Conference
at Bandung
[1955]

The Asian-African Conference, convened upon the invitation of the Prime Ministers of Burma, Ceylon, India, Indonesia and Pakistan met in Bandung from the 18th to the 24th April, 1955. In addition to the sponsoring countries the following 24 countries participated in the conference:

1. Afghanistan
2. Cambodia
3. People's Republic of China
4. Egypt
5. Ethiopia
6. Gold Coast
7. Iran
8. Iraq
9. Japan
10. Jordan
11. Laos
12. Lebanon
13. Liberia
14. Libya
15. Nepal
16. Philippines
17. Saudi Arabia
18. Sudan
19. Syria
20. Thailand
21. Turkey
22. Democratic Republic of Vietnam
23. State of Vietnam
24. Yemen

The Asian-African Conference considered problems of common interest and concern to countries of Asia and Africa and discussed ways and means by which their people could achieve fuller economic, cultural and political cooperation.

A. Economic Cooperation

1. The Asian-African Conference recognized the urgency of promoting economic development in the Asian-African region. There was general desire for economic cooperation among the participating countries on the basis of mutual interest and respect for national sovereignty. The proposals with regard to economic cooperation within the participating countries do not preclude either the desirability or the need for cooperation with countries outside the region, including the investment of foreign capital. It was further recognized that the assistance being received by certain participating countries from out-

side the region, through international or under bilateral arrangements, had made a valuable contribution to the implementation of their development programmes.

2. The participating countries agreed to provide technical assistance to one another, to the maximum extent practicable, in the form of: experts, trainees, pilot projects and equipment for demonstration purposes; exchange of know-how and establishment of national, and where possible, regional training and research institutes for imparting technical knowledge and skills in cooperation with the existing international agencies.

3. The Asian-African Conference recommended: the early establishment of the Special United Nations Fund for Economic Development; the allocation by the International Bank for Reconstruction and Development of a greater part of its resources to Asian-African countries; the early establishment of the International Finance Corporation which should include in its activities the undertaking of equity investment, and encouragement to the promotion of joint ventures among Asian-African countries in so far as this will promote their common interest.

4. The Asian-African Conference recognized the vital need for stabilizing commodity trade in the region. The principle of enlarging the scope of multilateral trade and payments was accepted. However, it was recognized that some countries would have to take recourse to bilateral trade arrangements in view of their prevailing economic conditions.

5. The Asian-African Conference recommended that collective action be taken by participating countries for stabilizing the international prices of and demand for primary commodities through bilateral and multilateral arrangements, and that as far as practicable and desirable, they should adopt a unified approach on the subject in the United Nations Permanent Advisory Commission on International Commodity Trade and other international forums.

6. The Asian-African Conference further recommended that: Asian-African countries should diversify their export trade by processing their raw material, wherever economically feasible, before export; intraregional trade fairs should be promoted and encouragement given to the exchange of trade delegations and groups of businessmen; exchange of information and of samples should be encouraged with a view to promoting intraregional trade and normal facilities should be provided for transit trade of land-locked countries.

7. The Asian-African Conference attached considerable importance to shipping and expressed concern that shipping lines reviewed from time to time their freight rates, often to the detriment of participating countries. It recommended a study of this problem, and collective action thereafter, to induce the shipping lines to adopt a more reasonable attitude. It was suggested that a study of railway freight of transit trade may be made.

8. The Asian-African Conference agreed that encouragement should be given to the establishment of national and regional banks and insurance companies.

9. The Asian-African Conference felt that exchange of information on matters relating to oil, such as remittance of profits and taxation, might eventually lead to the formulation of common policies.

10. The Asian-African Conference emphasized the particular significance of the development of nuclear energy for peaceful purposes, for the Asian-African countries. The Conference welcomed the initiative of the Powers principally concerned in offering to make available information regarding the use of atomic energy for peaceful purposes; urged the speedy establishment of the International Atomic Energy Agency which should provide for adequate representation of the Asian-African countries on the executive authority of the Agency; and recommended to the Asian and African Governments to take full advantage of the training and other facilities in the peaceful uses of atomic energy offered by the countries sponsoring such programmes.

11. The Asian-African Conference agreed to the appointment of Liaison Officers in participating countries, to be nominated by their respective national Governments, for the exchange of information and ideas on matters of mutual interest. It recommended that fuller use should be made of the existing international organizations, and participating countries who were not members of such international organizations, but were eligible, should secure membership.

12. The Asian-African Conference recommended that there should be prior consultation of participating countries in international forums with a view, as far as possible, to furthering their mutual economic interest. It is, however, not intended to form a regional bloc.

B. *Cultural Cooperation*

1. The Asian-African Conference was convinced that among the most powerful means of promoting understanding among nations is the development of cultural cooperation. Asia and Africa have been

the cradle of great religions and civilizations which have enriched other cultures and civilizations while themselves being enriched in the process. Thus the cultures of Asia and Africa are based on spiritual and universal foundations. Unfortunately contacts among Asian and African countries were interrupted during the past centuries. The peoples of Asia and Africa are now animated by a keen and sincere desire to renew their old cultural contacts and develop new ones in the context of the modern world. All participating Governments at the Conference reiterated their determination to work for closer cultural cooperation.

2. The Asian-African Conference took note of the fact that the existence of colonialism in many parts of Asia and Africa in whatever form it may be not only prevents cultural cooperation but also suppresses the national cultures of the people. Some colonial powers have denied to their dependent peoples basic rights in the sphere of education and culture which hampers the development of their personality and also prevents cultural intercourse with other Asian and African peoples. This is particularly true in the case of Tunisia, Algeria and Morocco, where the basic right of the people to study their own language and culture has been suppressed. Similar discrimination has been practised against African and coloured people in some parts of the Continent of Africa. The Conference felt that these policies amount to a denial of the fundamental rights of man, impede cultural advancement in this region and also hamper cultural cooperation on the wider international plane. The Conference condemned such a denial of fundamental rights in the sphere of education and culture in some parts of Asia and Africa by this and other forms of cultural suppression.

In particular, the Conference condemned racialism as a means of cultural suppression.

3. It was not from any sense of exclusiveness or rivalry with other groups of nations and other civilisations and cultures that the Conference viewed the development of cultural cooperation among Asian and African countries. True to the age-old tradition of tolerance and universality, the Conference believed that Asian and African cultural cooperation should be developed in the larger context of world cooperation.

Side by side with the development of Asian-African cultural cooperation the countries of Asia and Africa desire to develop cultural contacts with others. This would enrich their own culture and would also help in the promotion of world peace and understanding.

4. There are many countries in Asia and Africa which have not yet been able to develop their educational, scientific and technical institutions. The Conference recommended that countries in Asia and Africa which are more fortunately placed in this respect should give facilities for the admission of students and trainees from such countries to their institutions. Such facilities should also be made available to the Asian and African people in Africa to whom opportunities for acquiring higher education are at present denied.

5. The Asian-African Conference felt that the promotion of cultural cooperation among countries of Asia and Africa should be directed towards:

(I) the acquisition of knowledge of each other's country,

(II) mutual cultural exchange, and

(III) exchange of information.

6. The Asian-African Conference was of opinion that at this stage the best results in cultural cooperation would be achieved by pursuing bilateral arrangements to implement its recommendations and by each country taking action on its own, wherever possible and feasible.

C. Human Rights and Self-determination

1. The Asian-African Conference declared its full support of the fundamental principles of Human Rights as set forth in the Charter of the United Nations and took note of the Universal Declaration of Human Rights as a common standard of achievement for all peoples and all nations.

The Conference declared its full support of the principles of self-determination of peoples and nations as set forth in the Charter of the United Nations and took note of the United Nations resolutions on the rights of peoples and nations to self-determination, which is a pre-requisite of the full enjoyment of all fundamental Human Rights.

2. The Asian-African Conference deplored the policies and practices of racial segregation and discrimination which form the basis of government and human relations in large regions of Africa and in other parts of the world. Such conduct is not only a gross violation of human rights, but also a denial of the fundamental values of civilisation and the dignity of man.

The Conference extended its warm sympathy and support for the

courageous stand taken by the victims of racial discrimination, especially by the peoples of African and Indian and Pakistani origin in
South Africa; applauded all those who sustain their cause, re-affirmed
the determination of Asian-African peoples to eradicate every trace
of racialism that might exist in their own countries; and pledged to use
its full moral influence to guard against the danger of falling victims to
the same evil in their struggle to eradicate it.

D. Problems of Dependent Peoples

1. The Asian-African Conference discussed the problems of dependent peoples and colonialism and the evils arising from the subjection
of peoples to alien subjugation, domination and exploitation.

The Conference is agreed:

(a) in declaring that colonialism in all its manifestations is an evil
    which should speedily be brought to an end;
(b) in affirming that the subjection of peoples to alien subjugation,
    domination and exploitation constitutes a denial of fundamental
    human rights, is contrary to the Charter of the United Nations
    and is an impediment to the promotion of world peace and co-
    operation;
(c) in declaring its support of the cause of freedom and independence
    for all such people, and
(d) in calling upon the powers concerned to grant freedom and inde-
    pendence to such peoples.

2. In view of the unsettled situation in North Africa and of the per-
sisting denial to the peoples of North Africa of their right to self-
determination, the Asian-African Conference declared its support of
the rights of the people of Algeria, Morocco and Tunisia to self-
determination and independence and urged the French Government
to bring about a peaceful settlement of the issue without delay.

E. Other Problems

1. In view of the existing tension in the Middle East, caused by
the situation in Palestine and of the danger of that tension to world
peace, the Asian-African Conference declared its support of the rights
of the Arab people of Palestine and called for the implementation of
the United Nations Resolutions on Palestine and the achievement
of the peaceful settlement of the Palestine question.

2. The Asian-African Conference, in the context of its expressed at-

titude on the abolition of colonialism, supported the position of Indonesia in the case of West Irian based on the relevant agreements between Indonesia and the Netherlands.

The Asian-African Conference urged the Netherlands Government to reopen negotiations as soon as possible, to implement their obligations under the above-mentioned agreements and expressed the earnest hope that the United Nations would assist the parties concerned in finding a peaceful solution to the dispute.

3. The Asian-African Conference supported the position of Yemen in the case of Aden and the Southern parts of Yemen known as the Protectorates and urged the parties concerned to arrive at a peaceful settlement of the dispute.

F. Promotion of World Peace and Cooperation

1. The Asian-African Conference, taking note of the fact that several States have still not been admitted to the United Nations, considered that for effective cooperation for world peace, membership in the United Nations should be universal, called on the Security Council to support the admission of all those States which are qualified for membership in terms of the Charter. In the opinion of the Asian-African Conference, the following among participating countries, viz.: Cambodia, Ceylon, Japan, Jordan, Libya, Nepal, a unified Vietnam were so qualified.

The Conference considered that the representation of the countries of the Asian-African region on the Security Council, in relation to the principle of equitable geographical distribution, was inadequate. It expressed the view that as regards the distribution of the non-permanent seats, the Asian-African countries which, under the arrangement arrived at in London in 1946, are precluded from being elected, should be enabled to serve on the Security Council, so that they might make a more effective contribution to the maintenance of international peace and security.

2. The Asian-African Conference having considered the dangerous situation of international tension existing and the risks confronting the whole human race from the outbreak of global war in which the destructive power of all types of armaments, including nuclear and thermo-nuclear weapons, would be employed, invited the attention of all nations to the terrible consequences that would follow if such a war were to break out.

The Conference considered that disarmament and the prohibition of the production, experimentation and use of nuclear and thermonuclear weapons of war are imperative to save mankind and civilization from the fear and prospect of wholesale destruction. It considered that the nations of Asia and Africa assembled here have a duty towards humanity and civilization to proclaim their support for disarmament and for the prohibition of these weapons and to appeal to nations principally concerned and to world opinion, to bring about such disarmament and prohibition.

The Conference considered that effective international control should be established and maintained to implement such disarmament and prohibition and that speedy and determined efforts should be made to this end.

Pending the total prohibition of the manufacture of nuclear and thermo-nuclear weapons, this Conference appealed to all the powers concerned to reach agreement to suspend experiments with such weapons.

The Conference declared that universal disarmament is an absolute necessity for the preservation of peace and requested the United Nations to continue its efforts and appealed to all concerned speedily to bring about the regulation, limitation, control and reduction of all armed forces and armament, including the prohibition of the production, experimentation and use of all weapons of mass destruction, and to establish effective international control to this end.

G. Declaration on the Promotion of World Peace and Cooperation

The Asian-African Conference gave anxious thought to the question of world peace and cooperation. It viewed with deep concern the present state of international tension with its danger of an atomic world war. The Problem of peace is correlative with the problem of international security. In this connection, all States should cooperate, especially through the United Nations, in bringing about the reduction of armaments and the elimination of nuclear weapons under effective international control. In this way, international peace can be promoted and nuclear energy may be used exclusively for peaceful purposes. This would help answer the needs particularly of Asia and Africa, for what they urgently require are social progress and better standards of life in larger freedom. Freedom and peace are interdependent. The right of self-determination must be enjoyed by all peoples, and freedom and independence must be granted, with the least possible delay, to those who are still dependent peoples. Indeed, all nations should have the right freely to choose their own political and economic systems and their own way of life, in conformity with the purposes and principles of the Charter of the United Nations.

Free from mistrust and fear, and with confidence and goodwill towards each other, nations should practise tolerance and live together in peace with one another as good neighbours and develop friendly cooperation on the basis of the following principles:

1. Respect for fundamental human rights and for the purposes and principles of the Charter of the United Nations.
2. Respect for the sovereignty and territorial integrity of all nations.
3. Recognition of the equality of all races and of the equality of all nations large and small.
4. Abstention from intervention or interference in the internal affairs of another country.
5. Respect for the right of each nation to defend itself singly or collectively, in conformity with the Charter of the United Nations.
6. (a) Abstention from the use of arrangements of collective defence to serve the particular interests of any of the big powers.
   (b) Abstention by any country from exerting pressures on other countries.
7. Refraining from acts or threats of aggression or the use of force against the territorial integrity or political independence of any country.
8. Settlement of all international disputes by peaceful means, such as negotiation, conciliation, arbitration or judicial settlement as well as other peaceful means of the parties' own choice, in conformity with the Charter of the United Nations.
9. Promotion of mutual interests and cooperation.
10. Respect for justice and international obligations.

The Asian-African Conference declared its conviction that friendly cooperation in accordance with these principles would effectively contribute to the maintenance and promotion of international peace and security, while cooperation in the economic, social and cultural fields would help bring about the common prosperity and well-being of all.

The Asian-African Conference recommended that the five sponsoring countries consider the convening of the next meeting of the Conference, in consultation with the participating countries.

The Constitution
of the United States

The Federal Constitution

AS AGREED UPON BY THE CONVENTION

SEPTEMBER 17, 1787

WE, THE PEOPLE OF THE UNITED STATES, in order to form a more perfect Union, establish Justice, insure domestic Tranquillity, provide for the common Defence, promote the general Welfare, and secure the Blessings of Liberty to ourselves and our posterity, do ordain and establish this CONSTITUTION for the United States of America.

ARTICLE I. SECTION 1. All legislative powers herein granted shall be vested in a Congress of the United States which shall consist of a Senate and House of Representatives.

SECTION 2. The House of Representatives shall be composed of members chosen every second year by the people of the several States, and the electors in each State shall have the qualifications requisite for electors of the most numerous branch of the State legislature.

No person shall be a representative who shall not have attained to the age of twenty-five years, and been seven years a citizen of the United States, and who shall not, when elected, be an inhabitant of that State in which he shall be chosen.

Representatives and direct taxes shall be apportioned among the several States which may be included within this Union, according to their respective numbers, which shall be determined by adding to the whole number of free persons, including those bound to service for a term of years, and excluding Indians not taxed, three fifths of all other persons. The actual enumeration shall be made within three years after the first meeting of the Congress of the United States, and within every subsequent term of ten years, in such manner as they shall by law direct. The number of representatives shall not exceed one for every thirty thousand but each State shall have at least one representative; and until such enumeration shall be made, the

State of New Hampshire shall be entitled to choose three, Massachusetts eight, Rhode Island and Providence Plantations one, Connecticut five, New York six, New Jersey four, Pennsylvania eight, Delaware one, Maryland six, Virginia ten, North Carolina five, South Carolina five, and Georgia three.

When vacancies happen in the representation from any State, the executive authority thereof shall issue writs of election to fill such vacancies.

The House of Representatives shall choose their Speaker and other officers; and shall have the sole power of impeachment.

SECTION 3.   The Senate of the United States shall be composed of two senators from each State, chosen by the legislature thereof, for six years; and each senator shall have one vote.

Immediately after they shall be assembled in consequence of the first election, they shall be divided as equally as may be into three classes. The seats of the senators of the first class shall be vacated at the expiration of the second year, the second class at the expiration of the fourth year and the third class at the expiration of the sixth year, so that one third may be chosen every second year; and if vacancies happen, by resignation or otherwise, during the recess of the legislature of any State, the Executive thereof may make temporary appointments until the next meeting of the legislature, which shall then fill such vacancies.

No person shall be a senator who shall not have attained to the age of thirty years, and been nine years a citizen of the United States, and who shall not, when elected, be an inhabitant of that State for which he shall be chosen.

The Vice-President of the United States shall be president of the Senate, but shall have no vote, unless they be equally divided.

The Senate shall choose their other officers, and also a president *pro tempore*, in the absence of the Vice-President, or when he shall exercise the office of President of the United States.

The Senate shall have the sole power to try all impeachments. When sitting for that purpose they shall be on oath or affirmation. When the President of the United States is tried, the Chief-Justice shall preside. And no person shall be convicted without the concurrence of two thirds of the members present.

Judgment in cases of impeachment shall not extend further than to removal from office, and disqualification to hold and enjoy any office of honor, trust, or profit under the United States; but the party convicted shall, nevertheless, be liable and subject to indictment, trial, judgment, and punishment, according to law.

SECTION 4. The times, places, and manner of holding elections for senators and representatives shall be prescribed in each State by the legislature thereof; but the Congress may at any time by law make or alter such regulations, except as to the places of choosing senators.

The Congress shall assemble at least once in every year, and such meeting shall be on the first Monday in December, unless they shall by law appoint a different day.

SECTION 5. Each house shall be the judge of the elections, returns, and qualifications of its own members; and a majority of each shall constitute a quorum to do business; but a smaller number may adjourn from day to day, and may be authorized to compel the attendance of absent members, in such manner, and under such penalties, as each house may provide. Each house may determine the rules of its proceedings, punish its members for disorderly behavior, and, with the concurrence of two thirds, expel a member.

Each house shall keep a journal of its proceedings, and from time to time publish the same excepting such parts as may in their judgment require secrecy; and the yeas and nays of the members of either house on any question, shall, at the desire of one fifth of those present, be entered on the journal.

Neither house, during the session of Congress, shall, without the consent of the other, adjourn for more than three days, nor to any other place than that in which the two houses shall be sitting.

SECTION 6. The senators and representatives shall receive a compensation for their services, to be ascertained by law, and paid out of the treasury of the United States. They shall, in all cases, except treason, felony, and breach of the peace, be privileged from arrest during their attendance at the session of their respective houses, and in going to and returning from the same; and for any speech or debate in either house, they shall not be questioned in any other place.

No senator or representative shall, during the time for which he was elected, be appointed to any civil office under the authority of the United States, which shall have been created, or the emoluments whereof shall have been increased, during such time; and no person holding any office under the United States, shall be a member of either house during his continuance in office.

SECTION 7. All bills for raising revenue shall originate in the

House of Representatives; but the Senate may propose or concur with amendments as on other bills.

Every bill which shall have passed the House of Representatives and the Senate shall, before it becomes a law, be presented to the President of the United States; if he approve, he shall sign it; but if not, he shall return it, with his objections, to that house in which it shall have originated, who shall enter the objections at large on their journal, and proceed to reconsider it. If after such reconsideration two thirds of that house shall agree to pass the bill, it shall be sent, together with the objections, to the other house, by which it shall likewise be reconsidered, and if approved by two thirds of that house, it shall become a law. But in all such cases the votes of both houses shall be determined by yeas and nays, and the names of the persons voting for and against the bill shall be entered on the journal of each house respectively. If any bill shall not be returned by the President within ten days (Sundays excepted) after it shall have been presented to him, the same shall be a law, in like manner as if he had signed it, unless the Congress by their adjournment prevent its return, in which case it shall not be a law.

Every order, resolution, or vote, to which the concurrence of the Senate and the House of Representatives may be necessary (except on a question of adjournment), shall be presented to the President of the United States; and before the same shall take effect, shall be approved by him, or, being disapproved by him, shall be repassed by two thirds of the Senate and House of Representatives, according to the rules and limitations prescribed in the case of a bill.

SECTION 8. The Congress shall have power—

To lay and collect taxes, duties, imposts, and excises; to pay the debts and provide for the common defence and general welfare of the United States: but all duties, imposts, and excises, shall be uniform throughout the United States;

To borrow money on the credit of the United States;

To regulate commerce with foreign nations, and among the several States, and with the Indian tribes;

To establish a uniform rule of naturalization, and uniform laws on the subject of bankruptcies throughout the United States;

To coin money, regulate the value thereof, and of foreign coin, and fix the standard of weights and measures;

To provide for the punishment of counterfeiting the securities and current coin of the United States;

To establish post-offices and post-roads;

To promote the progress of science and useful arts, by securing for limited times to authors and inventors the exclusive right to their respective writings and discoveries;

To constitute tribunals inferior to the Supreme Court;

To define and punish piracies and felonies committed on the high seas, and offences against the law of nations;

To declare war, grant letters of marque and reprisal, and make rules concerning captures on land and water;

To raise and support armies, but no appropriation of money to that use shall be for a longer term than two years;

To provide and maintain a navy;

To make rules for the government and regulation of the land and naval forces;

To provide for calling forth the militia to execute the laws of the Union, suppress insurrections, and repel invasions;

To provide for organizing, arming, and disciplining the militia, and for governing such parts of them as may be employed in the service of the United States, reserving to the States respectively, the appointment of the officers, and the authority of training the militia according to the discipline prescribed by Congress;

To exercise exclusive legislation in all cases whatsoever, over such district (not exceeding ten miles square) as may, by cession of particular States, and the acceptance of Congress, become the seat of the government of the United States, and to exercise like authority over all places purchased by the consent of the legislature of the State in which the same shall be, for the erection of forts, magazines, arsenals, dock-yards, and other needful buildings; And

To make all laws which shall be necessary and proper for carrying into execution the foregoing powers, and all other powers vested by this Constitution in the government of the United States, or in any department or officer thereof.

SECTION 9.   The migration or importation of such persons as any of the States now existing shall think proper to admit, shall not be prohibited by the Congress prior to the year one thousand eight hundred and eight, but a tax or duty may be imposed on such importation, not exceeding ten dollars for each person.

The privilege of the writ of *habeas corpus* shall not be suspended, unless when in cases of rebellion or invasion the public safety may require it.

No bill of attainder or *ex-post-facto* law shall be passed.

No capitation, or other direct, tax shall be laid, unless in proportion to the *census* or enumeration herein before directed to be taken.

No tax or duty shall be laid on articles exported from any State. No preference shall be given by any regulation of commerce or revenue to the ports of one State over those of another; nor shall vessels bound to, or from, one State, be obliged to enter, clear, or pay duties in another.

No money shall be drawn from the treasury, but in consequence of appropriations made by law; and a regular statement and account of the receipts and expenditures of all public money shall be published from time to time.

No title of nobility shall be granted by the United States: And no person holding any office of profit or trust under them, shall, without the consent of the Congress, accept of any present, emolument, office, or title, of any kind whatever, from any king, prince, or foreign state.

SECTION 10. No State shall enter into any treaty, alliance, or confederation; grant letters of marque and reprisal; coin money; emit bills of credit; make any thing but gold and silver coin a tender in payment of debts; pass any bill of attainder, *ex-post-facto* law, or law impairing the obligation of contracts; or grant any title of nobility.

No state shall, without the consent of the Congress, lay any imposts or duties on imports or exports, except what may be absolutely necessary for executing its inspection laws; and the net proceeds of all duties and imposts, laid by any State on imports or exports, shall be for the use of the treasury of the United States; and all such laws shall be subject to the revision and control of the Congress. No State shall, without the consent of Congress, lay any duties of tonnage, keep troops, or ships of war, in time of peace, enter into any agreement or compact with another state, or with a foreign power, or engage in war, unless actually invaded, or in such imminent danger as will not admit of delay.

ARTICLE II. SECTION 1. The executive power shall be vested in a President of the United States of America. He shall hold his office during the term of four years, and, together with the Vice-President, chosen for the same term, be elected as follows:

Each State shall appoint, in such manner as the legislature thereof may direct, a number of electors, equal to the whole number of senators and representatives to which the State may be entitled in the Congress: but no senator or representative, or person holding an office of trust or profit under the United States, shall be appointed an elector.

The electors shall meet in their respective States, and vote by ballot for two persons, of whom one at least shall not be an inhabitant of the same State with themselves. And they shall make a list of all the persons voted for, and of the number of votes for each; which list they shall sign and certify, and transmit sealed to the seat of the government of the United States, directed to the president of the Senate. The president of the Senate shall, in the presence of the Senate and House of Representatives, open all the certificates, and the votes shall then be counted. The person having the greatest number of votes shall be the President, if such number be a majority of the whole number of electors appointed; and if there be more than one who have such majority, and have an equal number of votes, then the House of Representatives shall immediately choose by ballot one of them for President; and if no person have a majority, then from the five highest on the list the said House shall in like manner choose the President. But in choosing the President, the votes shall be taken by States, the representation from each State having one vote; a quorum for this purpose shall consist of a member or members from two thirds of the States, and a majority of all the States shall be necessary to a choice. In every case, after the choice of the President, the person having the greatest number of votes of the electors shall be the Vice-President. But if there should remain two or more who have equal votes, the Senate shall choose from them by ballot the Vice-President.

The Congress may determine the time of choosing the electors, and the day on which they shall give their votes; which day shall be the same throughout the United States.

No person except a natural-born citizen, or a citizen of the United States, at the time of the adoption of this Constitution, shall be eligible to the office of President; neither shall any person be eligible to that office who shall not have attained to the age of thirty-five years, and been fourteen years a resident within the United States.

In case of removal of the President from office, or of his death, resignation, or inability to discharge the powers and duties of the said office, the same shall devolve on the Vice-President, and the

Congress may by law provide for the case of removal, death, resignation, or inability, both of the President and Vice-President, declaring what officer shall then act as President, and such officer shall act accordingly, until the disability be removed, or a President shall be elected.

The President shall, at stated times, receive for his services a compensation, which shall neither be increased nor diminished during the period for which he shall have been elected, and he shall not receive within that period any other emolument from the United States, or any of them.

Before he enter on the execution of his office, he shall take the following oath or affirmation:

"I do solemnly swear (or affirm) that I will faithfully execute the office of President of the United States, and will, to the best of my ability, preserve, protect, and defend the Constitution of the United States."

SECTION 2. The President shall be commander-in-chief of the army and navy of the United States; and of the militia of the several States, when called into the actual service of the United States; he may require the opinion, in writing, of the principal officer in each of the executive departments, upon any subject relating to the duties of their respective offices, and he shall have power to grant reprieves and pardons for offences against the United States, except in cases of impeachment.

He shall have power, by and with the advice and consent of the Senate, to make treaties, provided two thirds of the senators present concur; and he shall nominate, and, by and with the advice and consent of the Senate, shall appoint ambassadors, other public ministers and consuls, judges of the Supreme Court, and all other officers of the United States, whose appointments are not herein otherwise provided for, and which shall be established by law. But the Congress may by law vest the appointment of such inferior officers, as they think proper, in the President alone, in the courts of law, or in the heads of departments.

The President shall have power to fill up all vacancies that may happen during the recess of the Senate, by granting commissions which shall expire at the end of their next session.

SECTION 3. He shall from time to time give to the Congress information of the state of the Union, and recommend to their consideration such measures as he shall judge necessary and expedient; he may, on extraordinary occasions, convene both houses, or either of them, and in case of disagreement between them, with respect to the time of adjournment, he may adjourn them to such time as he shall think proper; he shall receive ambassadors and other public ministers; he shall take care that the laws be faithfully executed, and shall commission all the officers of the United States.

SECTION 4. The President, Vice-President, and all civil officers of the United States shall be removed from office on impeachment for, and conviction of, treason, bribery, or other high crimes and misdemeanors.

ARTICLE III. SECTION 1. The judicial power of the United States shall be vested in one Supreme Court, and in such inferior courts as the Congress may from time to time ordain and establish. The judges, both of the supreme and inferior courts, shall hold their offices during good behavior, and shall, at stated times, receive for their services a compensation, which shall not be diminished during their continuance in office.

SECTION 2. The judicial power shall extend to all cases in law and equity arising under this Constitution, the laws of the United States, and treaties made, or which shall be made, under their authority; to all cases affecting ambassadors, other public ministers and consuls; to all cases of admiralty and maritime jurisdiction; to controversies to which the United States shall be a party; to controversies between two or more States; between a State and citizen of another State; between citizens of different States; between citizens of the same State claiming lands under grants of different States; and between a State, or the citizens thereof, and foreign states, citizens, or subjects.

In all cases affecting ambassadors, other public ministers and consuls, and those in which a State shall be party, the Supreme Court shall have original jurisdiction. In all the other cases before mentioned, the Supreme Court shall have appellate jurisdiction, both as to law and fact, with such exceptions, and under such regulations, as the Congress shall make.

The trial of all crimes, except in cases of impeachment, shall be by jury; and such trial shall be held in the State where the said crimes shall have been committed; but when not committed within any State, the trial shall be at such place or places as the Congress may by law have directed.

SECTION 3. Treason against the United States shall consist only in levying war against them, or in adhering to their enemies, giving them aid and comfort. No person shall be convicted of treason unless on the testimony of two witnesses to the same overt act, or on confession in open court.

The Congress shall have power to declare the punishment of treason, but no attainder of treason shall work corruption of blood, or forfeiture, except during the life of the person attainted.

ARTICLE IV. SECTION 1. Full faith and credit shall be given in each State to the public acts, records, and judicial proceedings of every other State. And the Congress may by general laws prescribe the manner in which such acts, records, and proceedings shall be proved, and the effect thereof.

SECTION 2. The citizens of each State shall be entitled to all privileges and immunities of citizens in the several States.

A person charged in any State with treason, felony, or other crime, who shall flee from justice, and be found in another State, shall, on demand of the executive authority of the State from which he fled, be delivered up, to be removed to the State having jurisdiction of the crime.

No person held to service or labor in one State, under the laws thereof, escaping into another, shall, in consequence of any law or regulation therein, be discharged from such service or labor, but shall be delivered up on claim of the party to whom such service or labor may be due.

SECTION 3. New States may be admitted by the Congress into this Union; but no new State shall be formed or erected within the jurisdiction of any other State, nor any State be formed by the junction of two or more States, or parts of States, without the consent of the legislatures of the States concerned, as well as of the Congress.

The Congress shall have power to dispose of and make all needful rules and regulations respecting the territory or other property belonging to the United States; and nothing in this Constitution shall be so construed as to prejudice any claims of the United States, or of any particular State.

SECTION 4. The United States shall guarantee to every State in this Union a republican form of government, and shall protect each of them against invasion, and on application of the legislature, or of the Executive (when the legislature cannot be convened), against domestic violence.

ARTICLE V. The Congress, whenever two thirds of both houses shall deem it necessary, shall propose amendments to this Constitution, or, on the application of the legislatures of two thirds of the several States, shall call a convention for proposing amendments, which, in either case, shall be valid to all intents and purposes, as part of this Constitution, when ratified by the legislatures of three fourths of the several States, or by conventions in three fourths thereof, as the one or the other mode of ratification may be proposed by the Congress: Provided, that no amendment which may be made prior to the year one thousand eight hundred and eight, shall in any manner affect the first and fourth clauses in the ninth section of the first article; and that no State, without its consent, shall be deprived of its equal suffrage in the Senate.

ARTICLE VI. All debts contracted and engagements entered into, before the adoption of this Constitution, shall be as valid against the United States under this Constitution, as under the Confederation.

This Constitution, and the laws of the United States which shall be made in pursuance thereof; and all treaties made, or which shall be made, under the authority of the United States, shall be the supreme law of the land; and the judges in every State shall be bound thereby, any thing in the Constitution or laws of any State to the contrary notwithstanding.

The senators and representatives before mentioned, and the members of the several State legislatures, and all executive and judicial officers, both of the United States and of the several States, shall be bound by oath or affirmation to support this Constitution; but no religious test shall ever be required as a qualification to any office or public trust under the United States.

ARTICLE VII. The ratification of the conventions of nine States shall be sufficient for the establishment of this Constitution between the States so ratifying the same.

DONE in convention, by the unanimous consent of the States present, the seventeenth day of September, in the year of our Lord one thousand seven hundred and eighty-seven, and of the independence of the United States of America the twelfth. In witness whereof, we have hereunto subscribed our names.

GEORGE WASHINGTON, *President, Deputy from Virginia.*

New-Hampshire
John Langdon
Nicholas Gilman

Massachusetts:
Nathaniel Gorham
Rufus King

Connecticut:
William Samuel Johnson
Roger Sherman

New York:
Alexander Hamilton

New Jersey:
William Livingston
David Brearley
William Paterson
Jonathan Dayton

Pennsylvania:
Benjamin Franklin
Thomas Mifflin
Robert Morris
George Clymer
Thomas Fitzsimons
Jared Ingersoll
James Wilson
Gouverneur Morris

Delaware:
George Read
Gunning Bedford, *Junior*
John Dickinson
Richard Bassett
Jacob Broom

Maryland:
James M'Henry
Daniel Jenifer,
    of St. Thomas
Daniel Carroll

Virginia:
John Blair
James Madison, *Junior*

North Carolina:
William Blount
Richard Dobbs Spaight
Hugh Williamson

South Carolina:
John Rutledge
Charles Cotesworth
    Pinckney
Charles Pinckney
Pierce Butler

Georgia:
William Few
Abraham Baldwin

Attest. WILLIAM JACKSON, *Secretary*

AMENDMENTS TO THE CONSTITUTION*

ARTICLE THE FIRST. Congress shall make no law respecting the establishment of religion, or prohibiting the free exercise thereof; or abridging the freedom of speech, or of the press; or the right of the people peaceably to assemble, and to petition the government for a redress of grievances.

---

* The first *ten* amendments were proposed in Congress during its *first* session, and on the 15th of December, 1791, were ratified. The *eleventh* amendment was proposed during the *first* session of the *third* Congress, and was announced by the President of the United States in a message to it, of date January 8th, 1798, as having been ratified. The *twelfth* amendment originated with Hamilton, and was proposed during the *first* session of the *eighth* Congress, and was adopted in 1804.

ARTICLE THE SECOND. A well regulated militia being necessary to the security of a free State, the right of the people to keep and bear arms shall not be infringed.

ARTICLE THE THIRD. No soldier shall, in time of peace, be quartered in any house without the consent of the owner; nor in time of war, but in the manner prescribed by law.

ARTICLE THE FOURTH. The right of the people to be secure in their persons, houses, papers, and effects, against unreasonable searches and seizures, shall not be violated, and no warrants shall issue, but upon probable cause, supported by oath or affirmation, and particularly describing the place to be searched, and the persons or things to be seized.

ARTICLE THE FIFTH. No person shall be held to answer for a capital or otherwise infamous crime, unless on a presentment or indictment of a grand jury, except in cases arising in the land or naval forces, or in the militia when in actual service in time of war or public danger; nor shall any person be subject for the same offence to be twice put in jeopardy of life or limb; nor shall be compelled in any criminal case to be witness against himself; nor be deprived of life, liberty, or property, without due process of law; nor shall private property be taken for public use without just compensation.

ARTICLE THE SIXTH. In all criminal prosecutions the accused shall enjoy the right of a speedy and public trial, by an impartial jury of the State and district wherein the crime shall have been committed, which district shall have been previously ascertained by law, and to be informed of the nature and cause of the accusation; to be confronted with the witness against him; to have compulsory process for obtaining witnesses in his favor, and to have the assistance of counsel for his defence.

ARTICLE THE SEVENTH. In suits at common law, where the value in controversy shall exceed twenty dollars, the right of trial by jury shall be preserved; and no fact tried by a jury, shall be otherwise re-examined in any court of the United States than according to the rules of the common law.

ARTICLE THE EIGHTH. Excessive bail shall not be required, nor excessive fines imposed, nor cruel and unusual punishments inflicted.

ARTICLE THE NINTH. The enumeration in the Constitution of certain rights, shall not be construed to deny or disparage others retained by the people.

ARTICLE THE TENTH. The powers not delegated to the United States by the Constitution, nor prohibited by it to the States, are reserved to the States respectively, or to the people.

ARTICLE THE ELEVENTH. The judicial power of the United States shall not be construed to extend to any suit in law or equity, commenced or prosecuted against one of the United States by citizens of another State, or by citizens or subjects of any foreign State.

ARTICLE THE TWELFTH. The electors shall meet in their respective States, and vote by ballot for President and Vice-President, one of whom, at least shall not be an inhabitant of the same State with themselves; they shall name in their ballots the person voted for as President, and in distinct ballots the person voted for as Vice-President; and they shall make distinct lists of all persons voted for as President, and of all persons voted for as Vice-President, and of the number of votes for each, which lists they shall sign and certify, and transmit sealed to the seat of government of the United States, directed to the President of the Senate; the President of the Senate shall, in the presence of the Senate and the House of Representatives, open all the certificates, and the votes shall then be counted; the person having the greatest number of votes for President, shall be the President, if such number be a majority of the whole number of electors appointed; and if no person have such majority, then from the persons having the highest numbers, not exceeding three, on the list of those voted for as President, the House of Representatives shall choose immediately, by ballot, the President. But in choosing the President, the votes shall be taken by States, the representation from each State having one vote; a quorum for this purpose shall consist of a member or members from two thirds of the States, and a majority of all the States shall be necessary to a choice. And if the House of Representatives shall not choose a President whenever the right of choice shall devolve upon them, before the fourth day of March next following, then the Vice-President shall act as President as in the case of the death or other constitutional disability of the President.

The person having the greatest number of votes as Vice-President, shall be the Vice-President, if such number be a majority of the whole number of electors appointed; and if no person have a majority, then from the two highest numbers on the list, the Senate shall choose the Vice-President; a quorum for the purpose shall consist of two thirds of the whole number of senators, and a majority of the whole number shall be necessary to a choice.

But no person constitutionally ineligible to the office of President shall be eligible to that of Vice-President of the United States.

The following amendment was ratified by Alabama, December 2, 1865, which filled the requisite complement of ratifying States, and was certified by the Secretary of State to have become valid as a part of the Constitution of the United States, December 18, 1865.

ARTICLE THE THIRTEENTH. SECTION 1. Neither slavery nor involuntary servitude, except as a punishment for crime, whereof the party shall have been duly convicted, shall exist within the United States, or any place subject to their jurisdiction.

SECTION 2. Congress shall have power to enforce this article by appropriate legislation.

The following amendment was certified by the Secretary of State to have become valid as a part of the Constitution of the United States, July 28, 1868.

ARTICLE THE FOURTEENTH. SECTION 1. All persons born or naturalized in the United States, and subject to the jurisdiction thereof, are citizens of the United States and of the States wherein they reside. No State shall make or enforce any law which shall abridge the privileges or immunities of citizens of the United States; nor shall any State deprive any person of life, liberty, or property without due process of law; nor deny to any person within its jurisdiction the equal protection of the laws.

SECTION 2. Representatives shall be apportioned among the several States according to their respective numbers, counting the whole number of persons in each State, excluding Indians not taxed. But when the right to vote at any election for the choice of electors for President and Vice-President of the United States, representatives in Congress, the executive and judicial officers of a State, or the members of the legislature thereof, is denied to any of the male inhabitants of such State, being twenty-one years of age, and citizens of the United States, or in any way abridged, except for participation in rebellion or other crime, the basis of representation therein shall be reduced in the proportion which the number of such male citizens shall bear to the whole number of male citizens twenty-one years of age in such State.

Section 3. No person shall be a senator or representative in Congress, or elector of President and Vice-President, or hold any office, civil or military, under the United States, or under any State, who, having previously taken an oath as a member of Congress, or as an officer of the United States, or as a member of any State legislature, or as an executive or judicial officer of any State, to support the Constitution of the United States, shall have engaged in insurrection or rebellion against the same, or given aid or comfort to the enemies thereof. But Congress may, by a vote of two thirds of each house, remove such disability.

Section 4. The validity of the public debt of the United States, authorized by law, including debts incurred for payment of pensions and bounties for services in suppressing insurrection or rebellion, shall not be questioned. But neither the United States nor any State shall assume or pay any debt or obligation incurred in aid of insurrection or rebellion against the United States, or any claim for the loss or emancipation of any slave; but all such debts, obligations, and claims shall be held illegal and void.

Section 5. The Congress shall have power to enforce, by appropriate legislation, the provisions of this article.

The following amendment was proposed to the legislatures of the several States by the fortieth Congress, on the 27th of February, 1869, and was declared, in a proclamation of the Secretary of State, dated March 30, 1870, to have been ratified by the legislatures of twenty-nine of the thirty-seven States.

Article the Fifteenth. Section 1. The right of citizens of the United States to vote shall not be denied or abridged by the United States, or by any State, on account of race, color, or previous condition of servitude.

Section 2. Congress shall have power to enforce this article by appropriate legislation.

Article the Sixteenth. The Congress shall have the power to lay and collect taxes on incomes, from whatever source derived, without apportionment among the several States, and without regard to any census or enumeration.

Article the Seventeenth. Section 1. The Senate of the United States shall be composed of two Senators from each State, elected by the people thereof, for six years; and each Senator shall have one vote. The electors in each State shall have the qualifications requisite for electors of the most numerous branch of the State legislatures.

SECTION 2. When vacancies happen in the representation of any State in the Senate, the executive authority of each State shall issue writs of election to fill such vacancies; Provided, That the legislature of any State may empower the executive thereof to make temporary appointment until the people fill the vacancies by election as the legislature may direct.

SECTION 3. This amendment shall not be so construed as to affect the election or term of any Senator chosen before it becomes valid as part of the Constitution.

ARTICLE THE EIGHTEENTH. SECTION 1. After one year from the ratification* of this article, the manufacture, sale, or transportation of intoxicating liquors within, the importation thereof into, or the exportation thereof from the United States and all territory subject to the jurisdiction thereof, for beverage purposes, is hereby prohibited.

SECTION 2. The Congress and the several States shall have concurrent power to enforce this article by appropriate legislation.

SECTION 3. This article shall be inoperative unless it shall have been ratified as an amendment to the Constitution by the legislatures of the several States, as provided in the Constitution, within seven years from the date of the submission hereof to the States by the Congress.

ARTICLE THE NINETEENTH. SECTION 1. The rights of citizens of the United States to vote, shall not be denied or abridged by the United States or by any State on account of sex.

SECTION 2. Congress shall have power to enforce this article by appropriate legislation.

ARTICLE THE TWENTIETH. SECTION 1. The terms of the President and Vice-President shall end at noon on the twentieth day of January, and the terms of Senators and Representatives at noon on the third day of January, of the years in which such terms would have ended if this article had not been ratified; and the terms of their successors shall then begin.

SECTION 2. The Congress shall assemble at least once in every

---

* Jan. 16, 1919.

year, and such meeting shall begin at noon on the third day of January, unless they shall by law appoint a different day.

SECTION 3. If, at the time fixed for the beginning of the term of the President, the President elect shall have died, the Vice-President elect shall become President. If a President shall not have been chosen before the time fixed for the beginning of his term, or if the President elect shall have failed to qualify, then the Vice-President elect shall act as President until a President shall have qualified; and the Congress may by law provide for the case wherein neither a President elect nor a Vice-President elect shall have qualified, declaring who shall then act as President, or the manner in which one who is to act shall be selected, and such persons shall act accordingly until a President or Vice-President shall have qualified.

SECTION 4. The Congress may by law provide for the case of the death of any of the persons from whom the House of Representatives may choose a President whenever the right of choice shall have devolved upon them, and for the case of the death of any of the persons from whom the Senate may choose a Vice-President whenever the right of choice shall have devolved upon them.

SECTION 5. Sections 1 and 2 shall take effect on the fifteenth day of October following the ratification of this article.

SECTION 6. This article shall be inoperative unless it shall have been ratified as an amendment to the Constitution by the legislatures of three-fourths of the several States within seven years from the date of its submission.

ARTICLE THE TWENTY-FIRST. SECTION 1. The eighteenth article of amendment to the Constitution of the United States is hereby repealed.

SECTION 2. The transportation or importation into any State, Territory, or possession of the United States for delivery or use therein of intoxicating liquors, in violation of the laws thereof, is hereby prohibited.

SECTION 3. This article shall be inoperative unless it shall have been ratified as an amendment to the Constitution by conventions in the several States, as provided in the Constitution, within seven years from the date of the submission hereof to the States by the Congress.

ARTICLE THE TWENTY-SECOND. SECTION 1. No person shall be

elected to the office of the President more than twice. No person who has held the office of the President or acted as President for more than two years of a term to which some other person was elected President shall be elected to the office of the President more than once. But this article shall not apply to any person holding the office of President when this article was proposed by the Congress and shall not prevent any person who may be holding the office of President or acting as President during the term within which this article becomes operative from holding the office of President or acting as President during the remainder of such a term.

SECTION 2. This article shall be inoperative unless it shall be ratified as an amendment to the Constitution by the legislators of three-fourths of the several States within seven years from the date of its submission to the States by the Congress.

The Farewell Address

BY GEORGE WASHINGTON

[1796]

FRIENDS AND FELLOW-CITIZENS: The period for a new election of a citizen, to administer the executive government of the United States, being not far distant, and the time actually arrived when your thoughts must be employed in designating the person who is to be clothed with that important trust, it appears to me proper, especially as it may conduce to a more distinct expression of the public voice, that I should now apprise you of the resolution I have formed, to decline being considered among the number of those out of whom a choice is to be made.

I beg you, at the same time, to do me the justice to be assured that this resolution has not been taken without a strict regard to all the considerations appertaining to the relation which binds a dutiful citizen to his country; and that in withdrawing the tender of service which silence, in my situation, might imply, I am influenced by no diminution of zeal for your future interest, no deficiency of grateful respect for your past kindness, but am supported by a full conviction that the step is compatible with both.

The acceptance of, and continuance hitherto, in the office to which your suffrages have twice called me, have been a uniform sacrifice of inclination to the opinion of duty, and to a deference for what appeared to be your desire. I constantly hoped that it would have been much earlier in my power, consistently with motives which I was not at liberty to disregard, to return to that retirement from which I had been reluctantly drawn. The strength of my inclination to do this, previous to the last election, had even led to the preparation of an address, to declare it to you; but mature reflection on the then perplexed and critical posture of our affairs with foreign nations, and the unanimous advice of persons entitled to my confidence, impelled me to abandon the idea.

I rejoice that the state of your concerns, external as well as internal, no longer renders the pursuit of inclination incompatible with the sentiment of duty or propriety, and am persuaded, whatever partiality may be retained for my services, that in the present circumstances of our country, you will not disapprove of my determination to retire.

The impressions with which I first undertook the arduous trust were explained on the proper occasion. In the discharge of this trust I will only say, that I have with good intentions contributed towards the organization and administration of the government, the best exertions of which a very fallible judgment was capable. Not unconscious, in the outset, of the inferiority of my qualifications, experience, in my own eyes, perhaps still more in the eyes of others, has strengthened the motives to diffidence of myself; and every day the increasing weight of years admonishes me more and more that the shade of retirement is as necessary to me as it will be welcome. Satisfied that if any circumstances have given peculiar value to my services they were temporary, I have the consolation to believe, that while choice and prudence invite me to quit the political scene, patriotism does not forbid it.

In looking forward to the moment which is intended to terminate the career of my public life, my feelings do not permit me to suspend the deep acknowledgment of that debt of gratitude which I owe to my beloved country for the many honors it has conferred upon me; still more for the steadfast confidence with which it has supported me; and for the opportunities I have thence enjoyed of manifesting my inviolable attachment, by services, faithful and persevering, though in usefulness unequal to my zeal. If benefits have resulted to our country from these services, let it always be remembered to your praise, and as an instructive example in our annals, that under circumstances in which the passions, agitated in every direction, were liable to mislead, amidst appearances sometimes dubious, vicissitudes of fortune often discouraging, in situations in which not unfrequently want of success has countenanced the spirit of criticism, the constancy of your support was the essential prop of the efforts, and the guarantee of the plans by which they were effected. Profoundly penetrated with this idea, I shall carry it with me to my grave, as a strong incitement to unceasing wishes that heaven may continue to you the choicest tokens of its beneficence; that your union and brotherly affection may be perpetual; that the free constitution, which is the work of your hands, may be sacredly maintained; that its administration, in every department, may be stamped with wisdom and virtue; that, in fine, the happiness of the people of these States, under the auspices of liberty, may be made complete by so careful a preservation and so prudent a use of this blessing as will acquire to them the glory of recommending it to the applause, the affection, and adoption of every nation which is yet a stranger to it.

Here, perhaps, I ought to stop. But a solicitude for your welfare, which cannot end but with my life, and the apprehension of danger, natural to that solicitude, urge me, on an occasion like the present, to offer to your solemn contemplation, and to recommend to your frequent review, some sentiments, which are the result of much reflection, of no inconsiderable observation, and which appear to me all-important to the permanency of your felicity as a people. These will be offered to you with the more freedom, as you can only see in them the disinterested warnings of a parting friend, who can possibly have no personal motive to bias his counsel. Nor can I forget, as an encouragement to it, your indulgent reception of my sentiments on a former and not dissimilar occasion.

Interwoven as is the love of liberty with every ligament of your hearts, no recommendation of mine is necessary to fortify or confirm the attachment.

The unity of government which constitutes you one people is also now dear to you. It is justly so, for it is a main pillar in the edifice of your real independence, the support of your tranquillity at home, your peace abroad, of your safety, of your prosperity, of that very liberty which you so highly prize. But as it is easy to foresee, that from different causes and from different quarters, much pains will be taken, many artifices employed, to weaken in your minds the conviction of this truth; as this is the point in your political fortress against which the batteries of internal and external enemies will be most constantly and actively (though often covertly and insidiously) directed, it is of infinite moment that you should properly estimate the immense value of your national union, to your collective and individual happiness; that you should cherish a cordial, habitual, and immovable attachment to it; accustoming yourselves to think and speak of it as of the palladium of your political safety and prosperity, watching for its preservation with jealous anxiety; discountenancing whatever may suggest even a suspicion that it can in any event be abandoned; and indignantly frowning upon the first dawning of every attempt to alienate any portion of our country from the rest, or to enfeeble the sacred ties which now link together the various parts.

For this you have every inducement of sympathy and interest. Citizens, by birth or choice, of a common country, that country has a right to concentrate your affections. The name of American, which belongs to you in your national capacity, must always exalt the just pride of patriotism more than any appellation derived from local discriminations. With slight shades of difference, you have the same religion, manners, habits, and political principles. You have, in a common cause, fought and triumphed together; the independence and liberty you possess are the work of joint councils and joint efforts, of common dangers, sufferings, and successes.

But these considerations, however powerfully they address themselves to your sensibility, are greatly outweighed by those which apply more immediately to your interest. Here every portion of our country finds the most commanding motives for carefully guarding and preserving the union of the whole.

The North, in an unrestrained intercourse with the South, protected by the equal laws of a common government, finds, in the productions of the latter, great additional resources of maritime and commercial enterprise, and precious materials of manufacturing industry. The South, in the same intercourse, benefiting by the agency of the North, sees its agriculture grow and its commerce expand. Turning partly into its own channels the seamen of the North, it finds its particular navigation invigorated; and while it contributes, in different ways, to nourish and increase the general mass of the national navigation, it looks forward to the protection of a maritime strength, to which itself is unequally adapted. The East, in like intercourse with the West, already finds, and in the progressive improvement of interior communications, by land and water, will more and more find a valuable vent for the commodities which it brings from abroad or manufactures at home. The West derives from the East supplies requisite to its growth and comfort, and what is perhaps of still greater consequence, it must of necessity owe the secure enjoyment of indispensable outlets for its own productions to the weight, influence, and the future maritime strength of the Atlantic side of the Union, directed by an indissoluble community of interest as one nation. Any other tenure, by which the West can hold this essential advantage, whether derived from its own separate strength, or from an apostate and unnatural connection with any foreign power, must be intrinsically precarious.

While, then, every part of our country thus feels an immediate and particular interest in union, all the parts combined cannot fail to find, in the united mass of means and efforts, greater strength, greater resource, proportionably greater security, from external danger, a less frequent interruption of their peace by foreign nations; and what is of inestimable value, they must derive from union an exemption from those broils and wars between themselves which so frequently afflict neighboring countries, not tied together by the same government, which their own rivalships alone would be sufficient to produce, but which opposite foreign alliances, attachments, and intrigues, would stimulate and embitter. Hence, likewise, they will avoid the necessity of those overgrown military establishments, which, under any form of government, are inauspicious to liberty, and which are to be regarded as particularly hostile to republican liberty. In this sense it is that your union ought to be considered as a main prop of your liberty, and that the love of the one ought to endear to you the preservation of the other.

These considerations speak a persuasive language to every reflecting and virtuous mind, and exhibit the continuance of the union as a primary object of patriotic desire. Is there a doubt whether a common government can embrace so large a sphere? Let experience solve it. To listen to mere speculation, in such a case, were criminal. We are authorized to hope that a proper organization of the whole, with the auxiliary agency of governments for the respective subdivisions, will afford a happy issue to the experiment. 'Tis well worth a fair and full experiment. With such powerful and obvious motives to union, affecting all parts of our country, while experience shall not have demonstrated its impracticability, there will always be reason to distrust the patriotism of those who, in any quarter, may endeavor to weaken its bands.

In contemplating the causes which may disturb our union, it occurs, as a matter of serious concern, that any ground should have been furnished for characterizing parties by geographical discriminations—Northern and Southern, Atlantic and Western—whence designing men may endeavor to excite a belief that there is a real difference of local interests and views. One of the expedients of party to acquire influence within particular districts is to misrepresent the opinions and aims of other districts. You cannot shield yourselves too much against the jealousies and heart-burnings which spring from these misrepresentations; they tend to render alien to each other those who ought to be bound together by fraternal affection. The inhabitants of our western country have lately had a useful lesson on this head. They have seen, in the negotiation by the executive, and in the unanimous ratification by the Senate, of the treaty with Spain, and in the universal satisfaction of that event throughout the United States, a decisive proof how unfounded were the suspicions propagated among them of a policy in the general government and in the Atlantic States, unfriendly to their interests in regard to the Mississippi; they have been witnesses to the formation of two treaties—that with Great Britain and that with Spain—which secure to them everything they could desire, in respect to our foreign relations, towards confirming their prosperity. Will it not be their wisdom to rely, for the preservation of these advantages, on the union by which they were procured? Will they not henceforth be deaf to those advisers, if such there are, who would sever them from their brethren, and connect them with aliens?

To the efficacy and permanency of your union, a government for the whole is indispensable. No alliances, however strict, between the parts, can be an adequate substitute; they must inevitably experience the infractions and interruptions, which alliances, in all times, have experienced. Sensible of this momentous truth, you have improved upon your first essay by the adoption of a constitution of government better calculated than your former for an intimate union, and for the efficacious management of your common concerns. This government, the offspring of our own choice, uninfluenced and unawed, adopted upon full investigation and mature deliberation, completely free in its principles, in the distribution of its powers, uniting security with energy, and containing within itself a provision for its own amendment, has a just claim to your confidence and your support. Respect for its authority, compliance with its laws, acquiescence in its measures, are duties enjoined by the fundamental maxims of true liberty. The basis of our political system is the right of the people to make and to alter the constitutions of government. But the constitution, which at any time exists, until changed by an explicit and authentic act of the whole people, is sacredly obligatory upon all. The very idea of the power and the right of the people to establish a government presupposes the duty of every individual to obey the established government.

All obstructions to the execution of the laws, all combinations and associations, under whatever plausible character, with the real design to direct, control, counteract, or awe the regular deliberation and action of the constituted authorities, are destructive of this fundamental principle, and of fatal tendency. They serve to organize faction, to give it an artificial and extraordinary force, to put in the place of the delegated will of the nation, the will of a party, often a small, but artful and enterprising minority of the community; and according to the alternate triumphs of different parties, to make the public administration the mirror of the ill-concerted and incongruous projects of faction, rather than the organ of consistent and wholesome plans, digested by common councils, and modified by mutual interests.

However combinations or associations of the above description may now and then answer popular ends, they are likely, in the course of time and things, to become potent engines, by which cunning, ambitious, and unprincipled men will be enabled to subvert the power of the people, and to usurp for themselves the reins of government; destroying afterward the very engines which have lifted them to unjust dominion.

Toward the preservation of your government and the permanency of your present happy state, it is requisite, not only that you speedily discountenance irregular opposition to its acknowledged authority, but also that you resist with care the spirit of innovation upon its principles, however specious the pretexts. One method of assault may be to effect, in the forms of the constitution, alterations which will impair the energy of the system, and thus to undermine what cannot be directly overthrown. In all the changes to which you may be invited, remember that time and habit are at least as necessary to fix the true character of governments as of other human institutions; that experience is the surest standard by which to test the real tendency of the existing constitution of a country; that facility in changes, upon the credit of mere hypothesis and opinion, exposes to perpetual change, from the endless variety of hypothesis and opinion. And remember especially, that for the efficient management of your common interests, in a country so extensive as ours, a government of as much vigor as is consistent with the perfect security of liberty, is indispensable. Liberty itself will find in such a government, with powers properly distributed and adjusted, its surest guardian. It is, indeed, little else than a name, where the government is too feeble to withstand the enterprises of faction; to confine each member of society within the limits prescribed by the laws, and to maintain all in the secure and tranquil enjoyment of the rights of person and property.

I have already intimated to you the danger of parties in the State, with particular reference to the founding of them on geographical discrimination. Let me now take a more comprehensive view, and warn you, in the most solemn manner, against the baneful effects of the spirit of party, generally.

This spirit, unfortunately, is inseparable from our nature, having its root in the strongest passions of the human mind. It exists under different shapes, in all governments, more or less stifled, controlled, or repressed. But in those of the popular form, it is seen in its greatest rankness, and is truly their worst enemy.

The alternate domination of one faction over another, sharpened by the spirit of revenge, natural to party dissensions, which, in different ages and countries, has perpetrated the most horrid enormities, is itself a frightful despotism. But this leads, at length, to a more formal and permanent despotism. The disorders and miseries, which result, gradually incline the minds of men to seek security and repose in the absolute power of an individual; and sooner or later, the chief of some prevailing faction, more able or more fortunate than his competitors, turns this disposition to the purposes of his own elevation on the ruins of public liberty.

Without looking forward to an extremity of this kind, (which, nevertheless, ought not to be entirely out of sight,) the common and continual mischiefs of the spirit of party are sufficient to make it the interest and duty of a wise people to discourage and restrain it.

It serves always to distract the public councils, and enfeeble the public administration. It agitates the community with ill-founded jealousies and false alarms; kindles the animosity of one part against another; foments occasionally riot and insurrection. It opens the door to foreign influence and corruption, which find a facilitated access to the government itself, through the channels of party passion. Thus the policy and the will of one country are subjected to the policy and will of another.

There is an opinion, that parties, in free countries, are useful checks upon the administration of the government, and serve to keep alive the spirit of liberty. This, within certain limits, is probably true; and, in governments of a monarchical cast, patriotism may look with indulgence, if not with favor, upon the spirit of party. But in those of popular character, in governments purely elective, it is a spirit not to be encouraged. From their natural tendency, it is certain there will always be enough of that spirit for every salutary purpose. And there being constant danger of excess, the effort ought to be, by force of public opinion, to mitigate and assuage it. A fire not to be quenched, it demands a uniform vigilance to prevent its bursting into a flame, lest, instead of warming it, it should consume.

It is important, likewise, that the habits of thinking, in a free country, should inspire caution in those entrusted with its administration, to confine themselves within their respective constitutional spheres, avoiding, in the exercise of the powers of one department, to encroach upon another. The spirit of encroachment tends to consolidate the powers of all the departments in one, and thus to create, whatever the form of government, a real despotism. A just estimate of that love of power, and proneness to abuse it, which predominate in the human heart, is sufficient to satisfy us of the truth of this position. The necessity of reciprocal checks in the exercise of political power, by dividing and distributing it into different depositaries, and constituting each the guardian of the public weal against invasion by the other, has been evinced by experiments ancient and modern: some of them in our country, and under our own eyes. To preserve them must be as necessary as to constitute them. If, in the opinion of the people, the distribution or modification of the constitutional powers, be, in any particular, wrong, let it be corrected by an amendment in the way which the constitution designates. But let there be no change by usurpation; for though this, in one instance, may be the instrument of good, it is the customary weapon by which free governments are destroyed. The precedent must always greatly overbalance, in permanent evil, any partial or transient benefit which the use can at any time yield.

Of all the dispositions and habits, which lead to political prosperity, religion and morality are indispensable supports. In vain would that man claim the tribute of patriotism, who should labor to subvert these great pillars of human happiness, these firmest props of the destinies of men and citizens. The mere politician, equally with the pious man, ought to respect and to cherish them. A volume could not trace all their connection with private and public felicity. Let it simply be asked, where is the security for property, for reputation, for life, if the sense of religious obligation desert the oaths, which are the instruments of investigation in courts of justice? And let us with caution indulge the supposition that morality can be maintained without religion. Whatever may be conceded to the influence of refined education on minds of peculiar structure, reason and experience both forbid us to expect, that national morality can prevail in exclusion of religious principles.

It is substantially true, that virtue or morality is a necessary spring of popular government. The rule, indeed, extends with more or less force to every species of free government. Who, that is a sincere friend to it, can look with indifference upon attempts to shake the foundation of the fabric?

Promote, then, as an object of primary importance, institutions for the general diffusion of knowledge. In proportion as the structure of a government gives force to public opinion, it is essential that public opinion should be enlightened.

As a very important source of strength and security, cherish public credit. One method of preserving it is to use it as sparingly as possible; avoiding occasions of expense by cultivating peace, but remembering also that timely disbursements to prepare for danger frequently prevent much greater disbursements to repel it; avoiding likewise the accumulation of debt, not only by shunning occasions of expense, but by vigorous exertions in time of peace to discharge the debts which unavoidable wars may have occasioned, not ungenerously throwing upon posterity the burden which we ourselves ought to bear. The execution of these maxims belongs to your representatives, but it is necessary that public opinion should co-operate. To facilitate to them the performance of their duty, it is essential that you should practically bear in mind, that towards the payment of debts there must be revenue; that to have revenue there must be taxes; that no taxes can be devised which are not more or less inconvenient and unpleasant; that the intrinsic embarrassment, inseparable from the selection of the proper objects (which is always the choice of difficulties) ought to be a decisive motive for a candid construction of the conduct of the government in making it, and for a spirit of acquiescence in the measures for obtaining revenue which the public exigencies may at any time dictate.

Observe good faith and justice towards all nations; cultivate peace and harmony with all; religion and morality enjoin this conduct; and can it be that good policy does not equally enjoin it? It will be worthy of a free, enlightened, and, at no distant period, a great nation, to give to mankind the magnanimous and too novel example of a people always guided by an exalted justice and benevolence. Who can doubt that, in the course of time and things, the fruits of such a plan would richly repay any temporary advantages that might be lost by a steady adherence to it? Can it be, that Providence has not connected the permanent felicity of a nation with its virtue? The experiment, at least, is recommended by every sentiment which ennobles human nature. Alas! is it rendered impossible by its vices?

In the execution of such a plan, nothing is more essential than that permanent, inveterate antipathies against particular nations, and passionate attachments for others, should be excluded; and that in place of them, just and amicable feelings towards all should be cultivated. The nation, which indulges towards another an habitual hatred, or an habitual fondness, is in some degree a slave. It is a slave to its animosity or to its affection, either of which is sufficient to lead it astray from its duty and its interest. Antipathy in one nation against another, disposes each more readily to offer insult and injury, to lay hold of slight causes of umbrage, and to be haughty and intractable, when accidental or trifling occasions of dispute occur.

Hence frequent collisions, obstinate, envenomed, and bloody contests. The nation, prompted by ill-will and resentment, sometimes impels to war the government, contrary to the best calculations of policy. The government sometimes participates in the national propensity, and adopts through passion what reason would reject; at other times, it makes the animosity of the nation subservient to projects of hostility instigated by pride, ambition and other sinister and pernicious motives. The peace often, and sometimes, perhaps, the liberty of nations, has been the victim.

So, likewise, a passionate attachment of one nation for another produces a variety of evils. Sympathy for the favorite nation facilitating the illusion of an imaginary common interest in cases where no real common interest exists, and infusing into one the enmities of the other, betrays the former into a participation in the quarrels and wars of the latter, without adequate inducement or justification. It leads also to concessions to the favorite nation of privileges denied to others, which is apt doubly to injure the nation making the concessions; by unnecessarily parting with what ought to have been retained; and by exciting jealousy, ill-will, and a disposition to retaliate, in the parties from whom equal privileges are withheld; and it gives to ambitious, corrupted, or deluded citizens (who devote themselves to the favorite nation) facility to betray, or sacrifice the interests of their own country, without odium, sometimes even with popularity; gilding, with the appearances of a virtuous sense of obligation, a commendable deference for public opinion, or laudable zeal for public good, the base or foolish compliances of ambition, corruption, or infatuation.

As avenues to foreign influence, in innumerable ways, such attachments are particularly alarming to the truly enlightened and independent patriot. How many opportunities do they afford to tamper with domestic factions; to practise the arts of seduction; to mislead public opinion; to influence or awe the public councils! Such an attachment of a small or weak nation, toward a great and powerful one, dooms the former to be the satellite of the latter.

Against the insidious wiles of foreign influence (I conjure you to believe me, fellow-citizens), the jealousy of a free people ought to be constantly awake; since history and experience prove, that foreign influence is one of the most baneful foes of republican government. But that jealousy, to be useful, must be impartial; else it becomes the instrument of the very influence to be avoided, instead of a defence against it. Excessive partiality for one foreign nation, and excessive dislike of another, cause those whom they actuate, to see danger only on one side; and serve to veil and even second the arts of influence on the other. Real patriots, who may resist the intrigues of the favorite, are liable to become suspected and odious; while its tools and dupes usurp the applause and confidence of the people, to surrender their interests.

The great rule of conduct for us, in regard to foreign nations is, in extending our commercial relations, to have with them as little political connection as possible. So far as we have already formed engagements, let them be fulfilled with perfect good faith. Here let us stop.

Europe has a set of primary interests, which to us have none, or a very remote relation. Hence she must be engaged in frequent controversies, the causes of which are essentially foreign to our concerns. Hence, therefore, it must be unwise in us to implicate ourselves, by artificial ties, in the ordinary vicissitudes of her politics, or the ordinary combinations and collisions of her friendships and enmities.

Our detached and distant situation invites and enables us to pursue a different course. If we remain one people, under an efficient government, the period is not far off when we may defy material injury from external annoyance; when we may take such an attitude as will cause the neutrality we may at any time resolve upon, to be scrupulously respected; when belligerent nations, under the impossibility of making acquisitions upon us, will not lightly hazard the giving us provocation; when we may choose peace or war, as our interest, guided by justice, shall counsel.

Why forego the advantages of so peculiar a situation? Why quit our own, to stand upon foreign ground? Why, by interweaving our destiny with that of any part of Europe, entangle our peace and prosperity in the toils of European ambition, rivalship, interest, humor, or caprice?

'Tis our true policy to steer clear of permanent alliances with any portion of the foreign world; so far, I mean, as we are now at liberty to do it; for let me not be understood as capable of patronizing infidelity to existing engagements. I hold the maxim no less applicable to public than to private affairs, that honesty is always the best policy. I repeat it, therefore, let those engagements be observed in their genuine sense. But, in my opinion, it is unnecessary, and would be unwise, to extend them.

Taking care always to keep ourselves, by suitable establishments, in a respectable defensive posture, we may safely trust to temporary alliances for extraordinary emergencies.

Harmony, and a liberal intercourse with all nations, are recommended by policy, humanity, and interest. But even our commercial policy should hold an equal and impartial hand; neither seeking nor granting exclusive favors or preferences; consulting the natural course of things; diffusing and diversifying, by gentle means, the streams of commerce, but forcing nothing; establishing, with powers so disposed, in order to give trade a stable course, to define the rights of our merchants, and to enable the government to support them, conventional rules of intercourse, the best that present circumstances and mutual opinion will permit, but temporary, and liable to be, from time to time, abandoned or varied, as experience and circumstances shall dictate; constantly keeping in view, that it is folly in one nation to look for disinterested favors from another; that it must pay, with a portion of its independence, for whatever it may accept under that character; that, by such acceptance, it may place itself in the condition of having given equivalents for nominal favors, and yet of being reproached with ingratitude for not giving more. There can be no greater error than to expect to calculate upon real favors from nation to nation. It is an illusion, which experience must cure, which a just pride ought to discard.

In offering to you, my countrymen, these counsels of an old and affectionate friend, I dare not hope they will make the strong and lasting impression I could wish; that they will control the usual current of the passions, or prevent our nation from running the course which has hitherto marked the destiny of nations! But, if I may even flatter myself, that they may be productive of some partial benefit, some occasional good; that they may now and then recur to moderate the fury of party spirit; to warn against the mischiefs of foreign intrigues; to guard against the impostures of pretended patriotism; this hope will be a full recompense for the solicitude for your welfare, by which they have been dictated.

How far, in the discharge of my official duties, I have been guided by the principles which have been delineated, the public records and other evidences of my conduct must witness to you and to the world. To myself the assurance of my own conscience is, that I have at least believed myself to be guided by them.

In relation to the still subsisting war in Europe, my proclamation of April 22, 1793, is the index to my plan. Sanctioned by your approving voice, and by that of your representatives in both Houses of Congress, the spirit of that measure has continually governed me, uninfluenced by any attempts to deter or divert me from it.

After deliberate examination, with the aid of the best lights I could obtain, I was well satisfied that our country, under all the circumstances of the case, had a right to take, and was bound in duty and interest to take, a neutral position. Having taken it, I determined, as far as should depend upon me, to maintain it with moderation, perseverance, and firmness.

The considerations which respect the right to hold this conduct, it is not necessary, on this occasion, to detail. I will only observe, that, according to my understanding of the matter, that right, so far from being denied by any of the belligerent powers, has been virtually admitted by all.

The duty of holding a neutral conduct may be inferred, without anything more, from the obligation which justice and humanity impose on every nation, in cases in which it is free to act, to maintain inviolate the relations of peace and amity towards other nations.

The inducements of interest for observing that conduct will best be referred to your own reflection and experience. With me, a predominant motive has been to endeavor to gain time to our country to settle and mature its yet recent institutions, and to progress, without interruption, to that degree of strength and consistency which is necessary to give it, humanly speaking, the command of its own fortunes.

Though, in reviewing the incidents of my administration, I am unconscious of intentional error, I am, nevertheless, too sensible of my defects, not to think it probable that I may have committed many errors. Whatever they may be, I fervently beseech the Almighty to avert or mitigate the evils to which they may tend. I shall also carry with me the hope that my country will never cease to view them with indulgence and that after forty-five years of my life dedicated to its service, with an upright zeal, the faults of incompetent abilities will be consigned to oblivion, as myself must soon be to the mansions of rest.

Relying on its kindness in this, as in other things, and actuated by that fervent love towards it, which is so natural to a man who views in it the native soil of himself and his progenitors for several generations, I anticipate, with pleasing expectations, that retreat in which I promise myself to realize, without alloy, the sweet enjoyment of partaking, in the midst of my fellow-citizens, the benign influence of good laws under a free government—the ever favorite object of my heart, and the happy reward, as I trust, of our mutual cares, labors, and dangers.